Sixth Edition

The American
DEMOCRACY
ALTERNATE EDITION

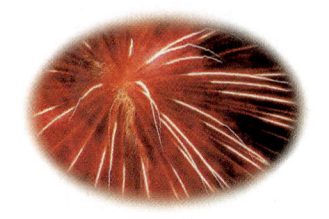

Thomas E. Patterson
Bradlee Professor of Government and the Press
John F. Kennedy School of Government
Harvard University

McGraw Hill

Boston   Burr Ridge, IL   Dubuque, IA   Madison, WI   New York   San Francisco   St. Louis
Bangkok   Bogotá   Caracas   Kuala Lumpur   Lisbon   London   Madrid   Mexico City
Milan   Montreal   New Delhi   Santiago   Seoul   Singapore   Sydney   Taipei   Toronto

McGraw-Hill Higher Education

A Division of The McGraw-Hill Companies

THE AMERICAN DEMOCRACY, SIXTH EDITION, ALTERNATE EDITION

Published by McGraw-Hill, a business unit of The McGraw-Hill Companies, Inc., 1221 Avenue of the Americas, New York, NY 10020. Copyright © 2003 by The McGraw-Hill Companies, Inc. All rights reserved. No part of this publication may be reproduced or distributed in any form or by any means, or stored in a database or retrieval system, without the prior written consent of The McGraw-Hill Companies, Inc., including, but not limited to, in any network or other electronic storage or transmission, or broadcast for distance learning.

Some ancillaries, including electronic and print components, may not be available to customers outside the United States.

This book is printed on acid-free paper.

1 2 3 4 5 6 7 8 9 0 VNH/VNH 0 9 8 7 6 5 4 3 2

ISBN 0-07-253140-1

Vice president and editor-in-chief: *Thalia Dorwick*
Publisher: *Lyn Uhl*
Sponsoring editor: *Monica Eckman*
Editorial coordinator: *Angelo W. Kao*
Marketing manager: *Katherine Bates*
Senior project manager: *Marilyn Rothenberger*
Production supervisor: *Enboge Chong*
Media technology producer: *Lance Gerhart*
Designer: *Michelle D. Whitaker*
Cover and interior designer: *Jamie O'Neal*
Cover image: © *Mark Wilson/Getty Images*
Spine and back cover images: © *Eyewire*
Senior photo research coordinator: *Nora Agbayani*
Photo Research: *Chris Hammond/PhotoFind, LLC*
Senior supplement producer: *David A. Welsh*
Compositor: *GAC-Indianapolis*
Typeface: *10/12 Palatino*
Printer: *Von Hoffmann Press, Inc.*

The credits section for this book begins on page C-1 and is considered an extension of the copyright page.

Library of Congress Cataloging-in-Publication Data

Patterson, Thomas E.
    The American democracy / Thomas E. Patterson.--Alternate ed.
      p. cm.
Includes bibliographical references and index.
    ISBN 0-07-253140-1 (softcover : alk. paper)
 1. United States--Politics and government. I. Title.
JK276 .P37 2003b
320.473--dc21

2002009393

www.mhhe.com

ABOUT
THE COVER

After the terrorist attacks of September 11, 2001, Americans showed their solidarity by flying the flag. On vehicles, homes, and lapels, 80 percent of Americans displayed the Stars and Stripes in the weeks that followed. It was a patriotic outpouring on a scale not seen since the attack on Pearl Harbor, sixty years earlier.

In seeking a cover photo for this edition of *The American Democracy*, my editors and I wanted an image that captured the spirit of Americans' response to the September 11 attacks. We also wanted an image that would solemnly mark the sacrifice of the nearly three thousand who were murdered on that tragic September day. Finally, we wanted an image that would embrace the whole of the American political experience, reflecting the nation's commitment to liberty, equality, and democracy. We looked through scores of photos to find the one that you see on the front cover. Photographed by Mark Wilson of Getty Images soon after the terrorist attacks, it pictures a young man holding a dipped flag on the steps of the Capitol as the sun is setting over the Washington monument and, beyond that, the Arlington National Cemetery.

We were not the only ones to find inspiration and solace in this particular photo. *Time* magazine featured it in a photo essay marking the national day of prayer and remembrance that President Bush announced shortly after the attacks. AOL displayed the photo on its website, coupling it with an audio of Julia Ward Howe's "The Battle Hymn of the Republic." One verse is a particularly fitting memorial to the darkness of September 11:

> I have seen Him in the watch-fires of a hundred circling camps;
> They have builded Him an altar in the evening dews and damps;
> I can read His righteous sentence by the dim and flaring lamps;
> His day is marching on.

ABOUT THE AUTHOR

Thomas E. Patterson is Benjamin Bradlee Professor of Government and the Press in the John F. Kennedy School of Government at Harvard University. He was previously Distinguished Professor of Political Science in the Maxwell School of Citizenship at Syracuse University. Raised in a small Minnesota town near the Iowa and South Dakota borders, he was educated at South Dakota State University and the University of Minnesota, where he received his Ph.D. in 1971.

He is the author of seven books and dozens of articles, which focus primarily on the media and elections. His most recent book, *The Vanishing Voter* (2002), describes and explains the long-term decline in Americans' electoral participation. An earlier book, *Out of Order* (1994), received national attention when President Clinton said every politician and journalist should be required to read it. Another of Patterson's books, *The Mass Media Election* (1980), received a *Choice* award as Outstanding Academic Book, 1980–1981. Patterson's first book, *The Unseeing Eye* (1976), was selected by the American Association for Public Opinion Research as one of the fifty most influential books of the past half century in the field of public opinion.

His research has been funded by major grants from the National Science Foundation, the Markle Foundation, the Smith-Richardson Foundation, the Ford Foundation, and the Pew Charitable Trusts.

To my children,
Alex and Leigh

CONTENTS IN BRIEF— ALTERNATE EDITION

Preface for the Instructor   xix
Preface for the Student: A Guided Tour   xxxi
Acknowledgments   xxxii

PART ONE
Foundations   2

1   American Political Culture: Seeking a More Perfect Union   4
2   Constitutional Democracy: Promoting Liberty and Self-Government   34
3   Federalism: Forging a Nation   66
4   Civil Liberties: Protecting Individual Rights   96
5   Equal Rights: Struggling Toward Fairness   130

PART TWO
Mass Politics   166

6   Public Opinion and Political Socialization: Shaping the People's Voice   168
7   Political Participation and Voting: Expressing the Popular Will   196
8   Political Parties, Candidates, and Campaigns: Defining the Voters' Choice   224
9   Interest Groups: Organizing for Influence   260
10 The News Media: Communicating Political Images   292

PART THREE
Governing Institutions   320

11 Congress: Balancing National Goals and Local Interests   322

Contents in Brief

12 The Presidency: Leading the Nation   360
13 The Federal Bureaucracy: Administering the Government   398
14 The Federal Judicial System: Applying the Law   430

PART FOUR
State and Local Governments   464

15 State and Local Politics: Maintaining Our Differences   466

Appendixes A-1
Glossary G-1
Notes N-1
Credits C-1
Index I-1

CONTENTS

Preface for the Instructor xix
Preface for the Student: A Guided Tour xxv
Acknowledgments xxxii

PART ONE
Foundations 2

1 American Political Culture: Seeking a More Perfect Union 4

Political Culture: The Core Principles of American Government 7

America's Core Values: Liberty, Equality, and Related Ideals 9
The Power of Ideals 12
The Limits of Ideals 13

Politics: The Process of Deciding on Society's Goals 18
Government, Power, Authority, and Policy 18
The Rules of the Game of Politics 21
Theories of Power 26

The Concept of a Political System and This Book's Organization 30

Summary 32
Key Terms 32
Suggested Readings 32
List of Websites 33

2 Constitutional Democracy: Promoting Liberty and Self-Government 34

Before the Constitution: The Colonial and Revolutionary Experiences 37
"The Rights of Englishmen" 37
The Declaration of Independence 39
The Articles of Confederation 41

Shays's Rebellion: A Nation Dissolving 42

Negotiating Toward a Constitution 43
The Great Compromise: A Two-Chamber Congress 44
The North-South Compromise: The Issue of Slavery 44
A Strategy for Ratification 45
The Ratification Debate 46
The Framers' Goals 48

Protecting Liberty: Limited Government 48
Grants and Denials of Power 49
Using Power to Offset Power 49
Separated Institutions Sharing Power: Checks and Balances 51
The Bill of Rights 53
Judicial Review 54

Providing for Self-Government 56
Democracy Versus Republic 56
Limited Popular Rule 57
Altering the Constitution: More Power to the People 59

Constitutional Democracy Today 63

Summary 64
Key Terms 65
Suggested Readings 65
List of Websites 65

3 Federalism: Forging a Nation 66

Federalism: National and State Sovereignty 68
The Argument for Federalism 70
The Powers of the Nation 72
The Powers of the States 73

Federalism in Historical Perspective 74
An Indestructible Union (1789–1865) 75
Dual Federalism and Laissez-Faire Capitalism (1865–1937) 78
Toward National Citizenship 83

Federalism Today 84
Interdependency and Intergovernmental Relations 85
Government Revenues and Intergovernmental Relations 87
A New Federalism: Devolution 90

The Public's Influence: Setting the Boundaries of Federal-State Power 93

Summary 94
Key Terms 95
Suggested Readings 95
List of Websites 95

4 Civil Liberties: Protecting Individual Rights 96

Freedom of Expression 99
The Early Period: The Uncertain Status of the Right of Free Expression 100
The Modern Period: Protecting Free Expression 101
Free Expression and State Governments 104
Libel and Slander 107
Obscenity 107

Freedom of Religion 110
The Establishment Clause 111
The Free-Exercise Clause 112

The Right of Privacy 114

Rights of Persons Accused of Crimes 117
Selective Incorporation of Procedural Rights 117
Limits on Defendants' Rights 121
Crime, Punishment, and Police Practices 123

The Courts and a Free Society 125

Summary 128
Key Terms 128
Suggested Readings 129
List of Websites 129

5 Equal Rights: Struggling Toward Fairness 130

The Struggle for Equality 132
African Americans 132
Women 135
Native Americans 141
Hispanic Americans 142
Asian Americans 145
Other Groups and Their Rights 146

Equality Under the Law 148
Equal Protection: The Fourteenth Amendment 148
Equal Access: The Civil Rights Acts of 1964 and 1968 150
Equal Ballots: The Voting Rights Act of 1965, as Amended 151

Equality of Result 153
Affirmative Action: Workplace Integration 154
School Integration: Busing 159

Persistent Discrimination: Superficial Differences, Deep Divisions 162

Summary 163
Key Terms 164
Suggested Readings 164
List of Websites 165

PART TWO
Mass Politics 166

6 Public Opinion and Political Socialization: Shaping the People's Voice 168

The Nature of Public Opinion 170
What Is Public Opinion? 170
How Informed Is Public Opinion? 172

The Measurement of Public Opinion 174
Public Opinion Polls 174
Problems with Polls 176

Political Socialization: How Americans Learn Their Politics 178
The Process of Political Socialization 178
The Agents of Political Socialization 179

Frames of Reference: How Americans Think Politically 182
Cultural Thinking: Common Ideas 183
Ideological Thinking: The Outlook for Some 183
Group Thinking: The Outlook of Many 185
Partisan Thinking: The Line That Divides 190

The Influence of Public Opinion on Policy 192

Summary 193
Key Terms 194
Suggested Readings 194
List of Websites 195

7 Political Participation and Voting: Expressing the Popular Will 196

Voter Participation 198
Factors in Voter Turnout: The United States in Comparative Perspective 199
Why Some Americans Vote and Others Do Not 205
The Impact of the Vote 209

Conventional Forms of Participation Other Than Voting 212
Campaign Activities 212
Community Activities 213
Lobbying Group Activities 214
Following Politics in the Media 214
Virtual Participation 216

Unconventional Activism: Social Movements and Protest Politics 217

Participation and the Potential for Influence 220

Summary 222
Key Terms 223
Suggested Readings 223
List of Websites 223

8 Political Parties, Candidates, and Campaigns: Defining the Voters' Choice 224

Party Competition and Majority Rule: The History of U.S. Parties 227
The First Parties 227
Andrew Jackson and Grassroots Parties 228
Republicans Versus Democrats: Realignments and the Enduring Party System 229
A New Realignment or a Dealignment? 231

Electoral and Party Systems 233
The Single-Member-District System of Election 234
Policies and Coalitions in the Two-Party System 234
Minor Parties 239

Party Organizations 242
The Weakening of Party Organizations 242
The Structure and Role of Party Organizations 243

The Candidate-Centered Campaign 250
Seeking Funds: The Money Chase 250
Creating Organizations: Hired Guns 252
Devising Strategy: Packaging the Candidate 253
Internet Politics: In the Web 255

Parties, Candidates, and the Public's Influence 256

Summary 258
Key Terms 258
Suggested Readings 259
List of Websites 259

9 Interest Groups: Organizing for Influence 260

The Interest-Group System 263
Economic Groups 264
Citizens' Groups 267
A Special Category of Interest Group: Governments 273

Inside Lobbying: Seeking Influence Through Official Contacts 273
Acquiring Access to Officials 274
Webs of Influence: Groups in the Policy Process 278

Outside Lobbying: Seeking Influence Through
    Public Pressure 280
   Constituency Advocacy: Grassroots Lobbying 281
   Electoral Action: Votes and PAC Money 281

The Group System: Indispensable but Biased 285
   The Contribution of Groups to Self-Government: Pluralism 285
   Flaws in Pluralism: Interest-Group Liberalism and Economic Bias 286
   A Madisonian Dilemma 288

Summary 289
Key Terms 290
Suggested Readings 290
List of Websites 291

10 The News Media: Communicating Political Images 292

The Development of the News Media: From Partisanship
    to Objective Journalism 295
   From a Partisan Press to an "Objective" One 295
   The Development of the Broadcast Media 298

Freedom and Conformity in the U.S. News Media 302
   Domination of News Production 304
   News Values and Imperatives 304
   "Megamedia": Mergers, Profits, and the News 305

The News Media as Link: Roles the Press Can and
    Cannot Perform 307
   The Signaler Role 308
   The Common-Carrier Role 308
   The Watchdog Role 311
   The Public Representative Role 313

Organizing the Public in the Media Age 317

Summary 318
Key Terms 318
Suggested Readings 318
List of Websites 319

PART THREE
Governing Institutions 320

11 Congress: Balancing National Goals and Local Interests 322

Congress as a Career: Election to Congress 324

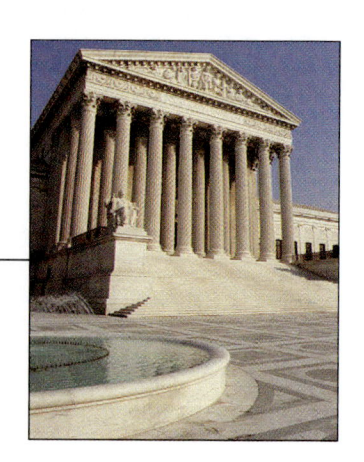

Contents

Using Incumbency to Stay in Congress 326
The Pitfalls of Incumbency 328
Safe Incumbency and Representation 331
Who Are the Winners in Congressional Elections? 332

Congressional Leadership 332
Party Leadership in Congress 334
Committee Chairs: The Seniority Principle 338
Oligarchy or Democracy: Which Principle Should Govern? 339

The Committee System 339
Committee Membership 340
Committee Jurisdiction 342

How a Bill Becomes a Law 342
Committee Hearings and Decisions 343
From Committee to the Floor 344
Leadership and Floor Action 345
Conference Committees and the President 346

Congress's Policymaking Role 346
The Lawmaking Function of Congress 347
The Representation Function of Congress 350
The Oversight Function of Congress 353

Congress: Too Much Pluralism? 356

Summary 357
Key Terms 358
Suggested Readings 358
List of Websites 359

12 The Presidency: Leading the Nation 360

Foundations of the Modern Presidency 363
Asserting a Claim to National Leadership 365
The Need for Presidential Leadership of an Activist Government 366

Choosing the President 369
Toward a More "Democratic" System of Presidential Election 369
The Campaign for Nomination 372
The Campaign for Election 374

Staffing the Presidency 379
Presidential Appointees 379
The Problem of Control 383

Factors in Presidential Leadership 384
The Force of Circumstance 385
The Stage of the President's Term 386
The Nature of the Issue: Foreign or Domestic 386
Relations with Congress 388
Nurturing Public Support 392

Summary 396

Key Terms 397
Suggested Readings 397
List of Websites 397

13 The Federal Bureaucracy: Administering the Government 398

Federal Administration: Form, Personnel, and Activities 401
The Federal Bureaucracy in Americans' Daily Lives 401
Types of Administrative Organizations 403
Federal Employment 406
The Federal Bureaucracy's Policy Responsibilities 407

Development of the Federal Bureaucracy: Politics and Administration 409
Small Government and the Patronage System 409
Growth in Government and the Merit System 410
Big Government and the Executive Leadership System 412

The Bureaucracy's Power Imperative 413
The Agency Point of View 414
Sources of Bureaucratic Power 415

Bureaucratic Accountability 418
Accountability Through the Presidency 419
Accountability Through Congress 421
Accountability Through the Courts 423
Accountability Within the Bureaucracy Itself 424

Reinventing Government 426

Summary 428
Key Terms 428
Suggested Readings 429
Lists of Websites 429

14 The Federal Judicial System: Applying the Law 430

The Federal Judicial System 432
The Supreme Court of the United States 433
Other Federal Courts 437
The State Courts 440

Federal Court Appointees 442
Selecting Supreme Court Justices and Federal Judges 442
Justices and Judges as Political Officials 444

The Nature of Judicial Decision Making 446
The Constraints of the Facts 447
The Constraints of the Law 447

Political Influences on Judicial Decisions 449
    Outside Influences on Court Decisions 450
    Inside Influences: The Justices' Own Political Beliefs 452

Judicial Power and Democratic Government 452
    The Debate over the Proper Role of the Judiciary 454
    The Judiciary's Proper Role: A Question of Competing Values 461

Summary 461
Key Terms 462
Suggested Readings 462
List of Websites 463

PART FOUR
State and Local Governments 464

15 State and Local Politics: Maintaining Our Differences 466

The Structure of State Governments 468
    The State Constitutions 469
    Branches of Government 471
    Citizens, Parties, and Elections 478

The Structure of Local Governments 479
    Types of Local Governments 481
    Local Elections and Participation 485

State and Local Finance 487
    Sources of Revenue 487
    The Ups and Downs of State and Local Finance 491

State and Local Policy 493
    Policy Priorities 493
    Public Policy Patterns 494
    The Politics of State and Local Policy 498

The Great Balancing Act: Localism in a Large Nation 501

Summary 503
Key Terms 503
Suggested Readings 503
List of Websites 504

Appendixes A-1
Glossary G-1
Notes N-1
Credits C-1
Index I-1

PREFACE for the Instructor

Anyone who writes an introductory American government text faces the challenge of describing and explaining a vast amount of scholarship. One way is to pile fact upon fact and list upon list. It's a common enough approach but it turns politics into a pretty dry subject. Politics doesn't have to be dry, and it certainly doesn't have to be dull. Politics has all the elements of drama and the added feature of affecting the everyday lives of real people.

The late twentieth century has been a period of extraordinary change in America, which has raised new challenges to the practice of government. New people in the millions from Asia and Latin America have joined the American community, bringing with them cultural traditions that have made our society richer and fuller but also more fragmented and contentious. Traditional institutions, from political parties to families, have weakened dramatically, straining the fabric of our politics but also creating the possibility of adaptive new arrangements. Minorities and women, long denied access to political and economic power, are seeking a fairer share, and sometimes getting it. America's workers and firms have built a highly productive economy but are now facing the risks and opportunities of the global marketplace. The cold war that dominated our attention in foreign policy for decades has been replaced by international terrorism and localized conflicts that raise troubling new issues of domestic and world insecurity, as the September 11, 2001, attacks on the World Trade Center and the Pentagon so tragically revealed.

Scholars are striving to keep pace with these changes. Never before has scholarship been so closely tied to the real world. If much of what political scientists study is arcane, we have increasingly tried to connect our work and our thinking to the everyday realities of politics. The result is a fuller understanding of how American government operates. I have tried in this book to convey this advancement in knowledge in an accurate and interesting way.

REACHING OUT TO THE STUDENT

This is a narrative-based text. It is the opposite of a text that piles list upon list and that divides its material into narrow compartments. A narrative text provides plenty of information, but it is always part of a larger discussion that is wrapped in "story" form.

Research indicates that the narrative style is a superior method for teaching students a "soft" science such as political science. They learn more readily because a narrative makes the subject more readable, more accessible, and more compelling. Studies also indicate that students can read attentively for a longer period of time when a text is narrative in form.

A narrative text weaves together theory, information, and examples in order to bring out key facts and ideas. The goal is to draw the students into the subject, give them a contextual understanding of major concepts and issues, and encourage them to think about the implications for themselves and society. To quicken this process, I begin each chapter by telling a story that addresses a basic issue. The chapter on civil liberties, for example, begins with the case of the Creighton family, whose home was raided in the middle of the night by gun-toting FBI agents who believed that the Creightons were harboring a relative who was suspected of bank robbery. The suspect was not found, and the Creightons, who were badly frightened by the intrusion, sued the FBI for wrongful search. Did the FBI have sufficient cause for a warrantless search? Or did the FBI violate the Creightons' constitutional rights? Where should society draw the line between its public safety needs and the rights of the individual? Such questions in the context of a real-life situation immediately plunge students into the chapter's subject and into the process of thinking about its importance.

This approach is part of a second pedagogical goal of this text: helping students to think critically. Critical thinking is, I believe, the most important skill that a student can acquire from a social science education. Students do not learn to think critically by engaging in rote memorization. They acquire the skill by reflecting on what they read, by resolving challenges to their customary ways of thinking, and by confronting difficult issues. To this end, I have attempted to structure the discussion in ways that ask students to think more deeply and systematically about politics. In the first chapter, for example, I discuss the inexact meanings, conflicting implications, and unfilled promise of Americans' most cherished ideals, including liberty and equality. The discussion includes the "Chinese Exclusion," a grotesque and not-well-known chapter in our history that should lead students to think what it means to be an American. And throughout the book, there are features designed to encourage students to think critically about important issues. For example, each chapter has a "Why Should I Care?" box that asks students to use the material in the chapter to resolve, at least in their own minds, difficult political issues. The "Why Should I Care?" box in the first chapter, for example, asks students to consider the meaning of the term of *personal security* in the context of the USA Patriot Act of 2001, which extends the government's power to conduct searches and detain suspects in the context of the war on terrorism. The basic question, of course, is how far the student would allow the government to depart from normal protections of individual rights in order to combat the terrorist threat.

Finally, I have attempted in this book to present American government through the analytical lens of political science but in a way that captures the vivid world of real-life politics. I regularly reminded myself while writing this book that only a tiny percentage of introductory students are interested in an academic political science career. Most of them take the course because it is required or because they enjoy politics. I have sought to write a book that will kindle political interest in the first type of student and deepen interest in the second type, while also giving them the systematic knowledge that a science of politics can provide. I had a model in mind for the kind of book that could achieve these goals. It was V. O. Key's absorbing *Politics, Parties, and Pressure Groups*, which I had read many years earlier as an undergraduate student. The late Professor Key was a masterful scholar who had a deep love of politics and who gently chided colleagues whose interest in political science was confined to the "science" part.

Few scholars can match Key's brilliance, but most political scientists share his fascination with politics. The result of their combined efforts is a body of knowledge about American government that is both precise and politically astute. This scholarship gives the text its unifying core. Political scientists have identified several major tendencies in the American political system that are a basis for a systematic understanding of how it operates, namely:

- Enduring ideals that are the basis of Americans' political identity and culture and that are a source of many of their beliefs, aspirations, and conflicts
- Extreme fragmentation of governing authority that is based on an elaborate system of checks and balances, which serves to protect against abuses of political power but also makes it difficult for political majorities to assert power when confronting an entrenched or intense political minority
- Many competing groups, which are a result of the nation's great size, population diversity, and economic complexity and which, separately, have considerable power over narrow areas of public policy
- Strong emphasis on individual rights, which is a consequence of the nation's political traditions and which results in substantial benefits to the individual and places substantial claims on the community
- Preference for the marketplace as a means of allocating resources, which has the effect of placing many economic issues beyond the reach of popular majorities

These tendencies are introduced in the first chapter and discussed frequently in subsequent chapters. If students forget many of the points made in this book, they may at least take away from the course a knowledge of the deep underpinnings of the American political system.

CHANGES FOR THIS EDITION

This test is *The Alternate Edition of the American Democracy*. It is designed for professors who prefer a text without policy chapters. (*The American Democracy*, 6th edition, is available for instructors who want the text with policy chapters. The ISBN for that version is 0-07-248121-8.

Both versions of the text have been shortened from the fifth edition. The reduction was achieved primarily by combining into one chapter the heretofore separate chapters on political parties and campaigns and by reducing the number of chapters on Congress and the presidency fron two each to one each. I also tightened the editing of other chapters, thereby reducing the number of words in those chapters without reducing their substantive content. These changes were made in response to instructors' observation that today's students are less accustomed to reading at length than their predecessors were.

A noteworthy change from previous editions is a heightened emphasis on liberty and equality as the two great principles of American democracy. The origins and nature of these ideals are discussed in the first chapter, which also points out the tension that can exist between them. Subsequent chapters have boxes entitled "Liberty and Equality" that ask students to grapple with issues related to these principles. New to this edition, these boxes help students to recognize just how thoroughly these ideals are embedded in American political practice and thought.

There is much that is new in the body of the text. The chapters have been thoroughly updated to include the latest scholarship and the most recent developments at home and abroad. The most substantial changes were occasioned by the war on terrorism, but there are many other changes as well, including the 2002 midterm elections. The role of the Internet in American politics continues to feature prominently in the text's instructional content. Each chapter includes one or more World Wide Web icons (identified by a globe within which "WWW" appears). Each icon indicates the availability of relevant supplementary material (self-quizzes, simulations, and graphics) on the text's website. The chapters also include "Historical Background" icons, which are new to this edition and identify key developments that helped shape the American political system.

I also emphasize developments that are a remembered part of students' lives. For most of them, Vietnam is ancient history, and the fall of the Berlin Wall is, at best, a distant memory. Students need to know about, and learn from, these events. But they sometimes learn more when asked to think deeply about events they believe they already thoroughly know.

To encourage students to engage today's issues, this text features a new box series entitled "Fighting Words." Each chapter includes a "Fighting Words" box that contains opposing opinions on a current controversy. Among the issues discussed in these boxes are Internet voting, the Kyoto accord on global warming, minority redistricting, school vouchers, and the electoral college.

These boxes and the other boxed features in the text are based on the same instructional philosophy that guided earlier editions. The boxes are not mere fillers or diversions. They are not meant to entertain in the way that some texts use titillating or trivial material to distract a student's attention. These boxes are part of a broad pedagogical strategy of heightening students' interest in politics. Once interest is generated, students naturally want to learn more about a subject and derive enjoyment through studying it.

In addition to the "Fighting Words," the "Liberty and Equality," and the "Why Should I Care?" boxes, each chapter has a "How the United States Compares" box and a "States in the Nation" box. The United States in many ways has the world's preeminent democracy, but it also has distinctive policies and practices. The American states, too, are quite different in their politics and policies, despite belonging to the same union. American students invariably gain a deeper understanding of their own communities when they recognize the ways in which their nation or state differs from others.

Finally, three types of boxes—each of them new to this edition—are sprinkled here and there throughout the book rather than appearing in each chapter. The "Citizenship" boxes are designed to encourage students to become involved in civic and political activities; the "Political Culture" boxes address issues of diversity within the context of the idea that Americans are "one people out of many"; and the "Global Perspective" boxes examine America's role in an increasingly interdependent world.

ANCILLARY PACKAGE

This text is accompanied by supplementary materials. Please contact your local McGraw-Hill representative or McGraw-Hill Customer Service (800-338-3987) for details concerning policies, prices, and availability, as some restrictions may apply.

For Instructors

Instructor's Manual/Test Bank by Willoughby Jarrell of Kennesaw State University   For each chapter, the instructor's manual includes the following: learning objectives, focus points and main points, a chapter summary, a list of major concepts, a lecture outline, alternative lecture objectives, class discussion topics, and a list of Internet resources. The test bank consists of approximately twenty to twenty-five multiple-choice questions, fifteen to twenty true-false questions, and five suggested essay topics per chapter, with answers given alongside the questions, and page references provided.

Test Bank CD-ROM This test bank in CD-ROM format draws on questions from the Instructor's Manual/Test Bank to assist professors in generating tests.

Instructor's Resource CD-ROM Tailored to the Table of Contents and format of the sixth edition, this CD integrates instructor's resources available in the Instructor's Manual/Test Bank with multimedia components, such as PowerPoint presentation, photographs, maps, and charts.

McGraw-Hill American Government Video Library This new series of ten-minute video lecture-launchers was produced for McGraw-Hill by Ralph Baker and Joseph Losco of Ball State University.

Video #1: Devolution within American Federalism: The Case of the Welfare System

0-07-303414-2

Video #2: Public Opinion and Participation: American Students Speak

0-07-229517-1

Video #3: Interest Groups

0-07-234442-3

Video #4: Women in Politics

0-07-242097-9

Video #5: Civil Liberties on the Internet

0-07-244205-0

Video #6: Affirmative Action and College Enrollment

0-07-244207-7

Video #7: The 2000 Campaign

0-07-250175-8

PageOut At www.mhhe.com/pageout, instructors can create their own websites. PageOut requires no prior knowledge of HTML; simply plug the course information into a template and click on one of sixteen designs. The process leaves instructors with a professionally designed website.

PRIMIS Online Instructors can use this textbook as a whole, or they can select specific chapters and customize this text to suit their specific classroom needs. The customized text can be created as a hardcopy or as an e-book. Also available in this format are custom chapters on **California Government** and **Texas Government.**

For Students and Instructors

This book's website includes all the materials included in the Study Guide as well as feedback for questions, crossword puzzles, interactive graphics, simulations, and more. There are also historical documents, audio speeches, a photo gallery, and videoclips from the newly developed McGraw-Hill American Government video library. Visit our website at www.mhhe.com/patterson6. For additional activities, simulations, web links, games, puzzles, and more, visit the Political Science Supersite at www.mhhe.com/socscience/polisci

PowerWeb for American Government A special product that offers daily news updates, weekly course updates, interactive activities, the best articles from the popular press, quizzing, instructor's manuals, student support study material and more.

For Students

Study Guide by Willoughby Jarrell of Kennesaw State University   Each chapter includes the following: learning objectives, focus and main points (to help direct students' attention to the most critical points), chapter summary, major concepts (listed and defined), annotated Internet resources, analytical thinking exercises, and test review questions—approximately ten true-false, fifteen multiple-choice, and five essay topics. The answers are provided at the end of each chapter.

Impeachment and Trial Supplement 0-107-235127-6 by Richard Semiatin of American University

YOUR SUGGESTIONS ARE INVITED

The American Democracy has now been in use in college classrooms for more than a decade. During that time, the text (including its concise version, *We the People*) has been adopted at more than five hundred colleges and universities. I am very grateful to all who have used it. I am particularly indebted to the many instructors and students over the years who have sent me suggestions or corrections. Professor Gary Teigen of Santa Ana College, for example, proposed an important change that has been made to Chapter 2 of this edition. You can contact me at the John F. Kennedy School of Government, Harvard University, Cambridge, MA 02138 or by e-mail: thomas_patterson@harvard.edu

Thomas E. Patterson

PREFACE for the Student: A Guided Tour

This book describes the American political system, which is one of the most interesting and intricate in the world. The discussion is comprehensive; there is a lot of information packed into the text. No student could possibly remember every tiny fact or observation that each chapter contains, but the main points of discussion are easily grasped if you make the effort.

The text has several features that will help you to understand the major points of discussion. Each chapter has, for example, an opening story that illustrates a central theme of the chapter. This story is followed by a brief summary of the chapter's main ideas.

The guided tour presented here describes the organization and special features of your text.

Thomas E. Patterson

Opening Illustration

A narration of a compelling event introduces the chapter's main ideas.

Robert and Sarisse Creighton and their three children were asleep when FBI agents and local police broke into their home in the middle of the night. Brandishing guns, the officers searched the house for a relative of the Creightons who was suspected of bank robbery. When asked to show a search warrant, the officers said, "You watch too much TV." The suspect was not there, and the officers left as abruptly as they had entered. The Creightons sued the FBI agent in charge, Russell Anderson, for violating their Fourth Amendment right against unlawful search.

The Creightons won a temporary victory when the Eighth U.S. Circuit Court of Appeals—noting that individuals are constitutionally protected against warrantless searches unless officers have good reason ("probable cause") for a search and unless they have good reason ("exigent circumstances") for conducting that search without a warrant—concluded that Anderson had been derelict in his duty. In the judgment of the appellate court, Anderson should have sought a warrant from a judge, who would have decided whether a search of the Creightons' home was justified.

The Supreme Court of the United States overturned the lower court's ruling. The Court's majority opinion said: "We have recognized that it is inevitable that law enforcement officials will in some cases reasonably but mistakenly conclude that probable cause is present, and we have indicated that in such cases those officials . . . should not be held personally liable." Justice John Paul Stevens and two other justices sharply dissented. Stevens accused the Court's majority of showing "remarkably little fidelity" to the Fourth Amendment.[2] Civil liberties groups claimed that the Court's decision gave police an open invitation to invade people's homes on the slightest pretext. However, the Court's decision was praised by law enforcement officials and conservatives, who contended that a ruling in the Creightons' favor would have made police hesitant to pursue suspects for fear of a lawsuit if a search failed to produce the person sought.

As this case illustrates, issues of individual rights are complex and political. No right is absolute. For example, the Fourth Amendment protects Americans not from *all* searches but from *unreasonable* searches. The public would be unsafe if law officials could never search for evidence of a crime or pursue a suspect into a home. Yet the public would also be unsafe if police could frisk people at will or invade their homes with impunity. The challenge to a civil society is to establish a level of police authority that balances the demands of public safety with those of individual freedom. The balance point, however, is always subject to dispute. Did FBI agent Anderson have sufficient cause for a warrantless search of the Creightons' home? Or was his evidence so weak that his forcible entry constituted an unreasonable search? Law enforcement officials and civil liberties groups had widely different opinions on these questions. Nor did the justices of the Supreme Court have a uniform view. Six of the justices sided with Anderson and three backed the Creightons' position.

This chapter examines issues of **civil liberties**: specific individual rights, such as freedom of speech and protection against self-incrimination, that are constitutionally

xxv

68 PART ONE Foundations

Patrick Henry was a leading figure in the American Revolution ("Give me liberty or give me death!"). He later opposed ratification of the Constitution on grounds that the national government should be a union of states and not also of people.

- *The power of government must be equal to its responsibilities.* The Constitution was needed because the nation's preceding system (under the Articles of Confederation) was too weak to accomplish its expected goals, particularly those of a strong defense and an integrated economy.
- *Federalism—the Constitution's division of governing authority between two levels, nation and states—was the result of political bargaining.* Federalism was not a theoretical principle, but a compromise made necessary in 1787 by the prior existence of the states.
- *Federalism is not a fixed principle for allocating power between the national and state governments, but a principle that has changed over the course of time in response to new political needs.* Federalism has passed through several distinct stages during the nation's history.
- *Contemporary federalism tilts toward national authority, reflecting the increased interdependence of American society.* However, there is a current trend toward reducing the scope of federal authority.

FEDERALISM: NATIONAL AND STATE SOVEREIGNTY

The delegates to the Philadelphia convention in 1787 included many of the nation's most prominent leaders, such as George Washington and Benjamin Franklin. Not all of America's top leaders were at the convention, however, and many of them were steadfastly opposed to a strong national government. When rumors circulated that the convention would propose a new form of government rather than an amended Articles of Confederation, Patrick Henry, an ardent supporter of state-centered government, said that he "smelt a rat." After the convention had adjourned, he realized that his fears were justified. "Who authorized them," he asked, "to speak the language of 'We, the People,' instead of 'We, the States'?"

Main Points

The chapter's three or four main ideas are summarized in the opening pages.

---

136 PART ONE Foundations

STATES IN THE NATION
Black and Latino Representation in State Legislatures

For a long period, minorities were barely visible in the state legislatures. The situation began to change after passage of the 1964 Civil Rights Act and the 1965 Voting Rights Act, but minorities are still underrepresented relative to their numbers in the population. Only 8 percent of state legislators in 2000 were black and a mere 3 percent were Hispanic. Alabama and Mississippi have the highest proportion (25 percent each) of African American state legislators. New Mexico has the highest number (37 percent) of Latino lawmakers. A few states, including Maine and North Dakota, have no legislator from either of these minority groups. Of course, these states have small minority populations while states such as Alabama, Mississippi, and New Mexico have much larger ones.

Percentage of black and Latino legislators
- 15% and higher
- 5 – 14.9%
- Less than 4.9%

Source: National Conference of State Legislatures, 2000.

"States in the Nation" Boxes

Each chapter has a box that compares the fifty states on some aspect of politics.

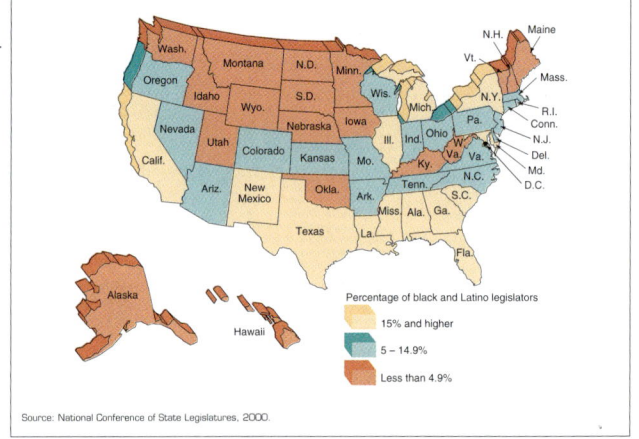

could not own and dispose of property without her husband's consent. Even the wife's body was not fully hers. A wife's adultery was ruled by the Supreme Court to be a violation of the husband's property rights![17]

The first women's rights convention in America was held in 1848 in Seneca Falls, New York, after Lucretia Mott and Elizabeth Cady Stanton had been barred from the main floor of an antislavery convention.[18] Thereafter, however, the struggle for women's rights became closely aligned with the abolitionist

xxvi

"Fighting Words" Boxes

Each chapter has a box that introduces a current controversy and includes opposing opinions on the issue.

"Historical Background" Icon

Identify key developments that helped shape American politics.

Figures and Tables

Each chapter has figures and tables that relate to points made in the discussion.

Major Concepts

The introduction of a major concept is signaled by **bold type** and accompanied by a concise definition. These concepts are also listed at the end of the chapter and are compiled in a glossary in the back of the text.

Sample Page Excerpts

110 — PART ONE — Foundations

Fighting Words

Should Sexually Explicit Material on the Internet Be Tightly Regulated?

In 1997, the Supreme Court struck down the Communications Decency Act on grounds that it was overly broad and would have the effect of reducing not only indecent content on the Internet but legitimate expression as well. The act made it a federal crime to transmit obscene material through the Internet to minors or to post such material in a way that made it accessible to them. The conflict between the congressional majority that enacted the legislation and the Supreme Court majority that invalidated it is part of society's continuing debate over how to regulate obscenity without infringing on First Amendment rights.

Yes: Opponents of the new law use harsh language like "censorship" to describe the Communications Decency Act . . . Those who cry censorship hide behind the First Amendment to make defense of those who would give pornography to children and engage children in sexual conversations. What a travesty . . . The Act makes it a crime to send indecent communications to children by means of a computer service or telecommunications device [and] to make indecent communications available to children on an open electronic bulletin board. . . . The heart and soul of the new law is its protections for children. It is not censorship. It is not prudishness. The new law does not prohibit consenting adults from engaging in constitutionally protected speech.
—Former U.S. Senator James Exon (D-Nebr.)

No: We are persuaded that the [act] lacks the precision that the First Amendment requires when a statute regulates the content of speech. In order to deny minors access to potentially harmful speech, the [act] effectively suppresses a large amount of speech that adults have a constitutional right to receive and to address to one another. . . . It is true that we have repeatedly recognized the governmental interest in protecting children from harmful materials. But that interest does not justify an unnecessarily broad suppression of speech addressed to adults. As we have explained, the Government may not "reduc[e] the adult population . . . to . . . only what is fit for children." . . . Knowledge that, for instance, one or more members of a 100-person chat group will be minor—and therefore that it would be a crime to send the group an indecent message—would surely burden communication among adults.
—*Reno v. ACLU* (1997)

web content. This test could become an imposing one. Because the Internet reaches into homes everywhere, content could be limited to what is found acceptable in more traditional communities rather than in communities where, in the Court's words, "avant garde culture is the norm."

FREEDOM OF RELIGION

Free religious expression is the precursor of free political expression, at least within the English tradition of limited government. England's Glorious, or Bloodless, Revolution of 1689 centered on the issue of religion and resulted in the Act of Toleration, which gave members of all Protestant sects the right to

---

206 — PART TWO — Mass Politics

Figure 7–2
The Perceived Effect of Electing a Republican or Democratic President, 2000. Most Americans believe that their lives and the country as a whole will not be greatly affected by whether the Republican or Democratic candidate wins the presidency.
Source: Used by permission of the Shorenstein Center Poll for the Vanishing Voter Project.

"How much difference will it make whether the Democrat or Republican candidate wins the presidency?"

To the lives of people like you?
- 31% Just some
- 18% Quite a bit
- 7% Great deal
- 4% Not sure
- 40% Little/none

To the future of the country as a whole?
- 35% Just some
- 21% Quite a bit
- 11% Great deal
- 5% Not sure
- 28% Little/none

Volunteers at a community event attempt to interest citizens in registering so that they can vote in the next election. Nearly all democracies have automatic voter registration. The United States does not, which makes voter registration efforts an important factor in election turnout.

Large differences in voter turnout are associated with citizens' sense of civic involvement, age, education, and economic class.

Feelings of Civic Duty, Apathy, and Alienation

civic duty The belief of an individual that civic and political participation is a responsibility of citizenship.

Regular voters are characterized by a strong sense of **civic duty**—that is, they regard participation in elections as one of the main responsibilities of citizenship. By election day in 1996, it was clear from the polls that Bill Clinton would handily defeat Bob Dole, yet regular voters were undeterred. Although they knew their votes would not sway the election, they voted anyway in order to fulfill their duty as citizens. This sense of duty is an attitude that is usually

xxvii

"How the United States Compares" Boxes

Each chapter has a box that compares the United States with other countries in regard to a major political feature.

HOW THE UNITED STATES COMPARES
Women's Equality: Representation in National Legislatures

Although conflict between groups is universal, the nature of the conflict is often particularized. Racial conflict in the United States cannot readily be compared with, say, religious conflict in Northern Ireland. The one form of inequality common to all nations is that of gender: nowhere are women equal to men in law or in fact. But there are large differences between countries. A study by the Population Crisis Committee ranked the United States third overall in women's equality, behind only Sweden and Finland. The rankings were based on five areas—jobs, education, social relations, marriage and family, and health; U.S. women had an 82.5 percent rating compared with men.

The inequality of women is also underscored by their underrepresentation in public office. There is no country in which women comprise as many as half the members of the national legislature. The Scandinavian countries rank highest in terms of the percentage of female lawmakers. Other northern European countries have lower levels, but the levels are higher than that of the United States. The accompanying figure indicates the approximate percentage of seats held by women in the largest chamber of each country's national legislature:

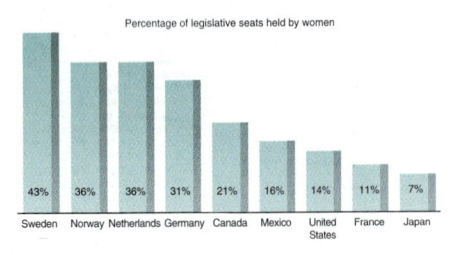

Percentage of legislative seats held by women

Sweden	Norway	Netherlands	Germany	Canada	Mexico	United States	France	Japan
43%	36%	36%	31%	21%	16%	14%	11%	7%

Source: Inter-Parliamentary Union, 2001.

Job-Related Issues: Family Leave, Comparable Worth, and Sexual Harassment

In recent decades, increasing numbers of women have sought employment outside the home. Government statistics indicate that three in five women worked outside the home in 1995 compared with only one in eight in 1950. Women have made gains in many traditionally male-dominated fields. For example, women now make up a third of the new lawyers who enter the job market each year. The change in women's status is also reflected in education statistics. In 1972 more white, black, and Hispanic men than women enrolled in coll[...] the reverse was true: more women than men of each group were e[...]

"Liberty and Equality" Boxes

Boxes in the margins ask you to critically analyze and integrate material presented in the chapter that relates to America's founding principles.

CHAPTER 3 Federalism: Forging a Nation

Protecting Liberty

Theorists such as Locke and Montesquieu had not proposed a division of power between national and local authorities as a further means of protecting liberty. Nevertheless, the Framers came to look upon federalism as part of the Constitution's system of checks and balances (see Chapter 2). Alexander Hamilton argued in *Federalist* No. 28 that the American people could shift their loyalties back and forth between the national and state governments in order to keep each under control. "If [the people's] rights are invaded by either," Hamilton wrote, "they can make use of the other as the instrument of redress."

Moderating the Power of Government

To the Anti-Federalists (opponents of the Constitution), the sacrifice of states' power to the nation was as unwise as it was unnecessary. They argued that a distant national government could never serve the people's interests as well as the states could. In support of their contention, the Anti-Federalists turned to Montesquieu, who had concluded that a small republic is more likely than a large one to respect and respond to the people it governs. When government encompasses a small area, he argued, its leaders are in closer touch with the people, have a better understanding of their needs, and a greater concern for their interests.

James Madison took issue with this argument. In *Federalist* No. 10, Madison contended that whether a government serves the common good is a function not of its size but of the range of interests that share political power. The problem with a smaller republic, Madison claimed, is that it is likely to have a dominant faction—whether it be large landholders, financiers, an impoverished majority, or some other group—that is strong enough to take full control of government, using this power to advance its selfish interests. A large republic is less likely to have such an all-powerful faction. If financiers are strong in one area of a large republic, they are likely to be weaker elsewhere, and the same will be true of other interests. By this reasoning, Madison concluded that political control in a large republic could not be won by a single interest but would require a joining of interests, each of which would be forced to limit its demands and to respect the interests of others. "Extend the sphere," said Madison, "and you take in a greater variety of parties and interests; you make it less probable that a majority of the whole will have a common motive to invade the rights of other citizens."

Strengthening the Union

The most telling argument in 1787 for a federal system, however, was that it would overcome the deficiencies of the Articles. The Articles had numerous flaws (including a very weak executive and a judiciary subservient to the state courts), and two of them were fatal: the government had neither the power to tax nor the power to regulate commerce.

Alexander Hamilton (1757–1804)

Alexander Hamilton was just thirty-two years old when he served as a delegate to the constitutional convention in Philadelphia. A strong nationalist, his *Federalist Papers* essays contributed to the ratification of the Constitution. George Washington appointed him to be the first secretary of the treasury, where he developed plans for the First Bank of the United States and for placing the federal government on a sound financial footing. He was fatally wounded in a duel with Aaron Burr, a political and personal foe.

Liberty & Equality

What's Your Opinion?

Large Versus Small Republics

During the debate over ratification of the Constitution, Americans argued over whether liberty and equality would be better protected by the states or by the nation. The Anti-Federalists argued that a small republic was closer to the people and therefore would do more to protect their rights. James Madison countered by saying that a large republic was preferable because it would have such a diversity of interests that compromise and tolerance among various groups would be required.

In your view, which side in this argument has the weight of American history behind it?

"Why Should I Care?" Boxes

Each chapter has a box that addresses a perennial issue affecting Americans' lives.

"Political Culture" Boxes

Some chapters have a box that examines diversity topics relating to the notion that Americans are "one people out of many."

Why Should I Care?

The USA Patriot Act of 2001: What Does Your Personal Security Mean?

The USA Patriot Act of 2001 was enacted less than two months after the September 11 terrorist attacks on the World Trade Center and the Pentagon. It was easily the most controversial domestic action taken by the U.S. government in the immediate aftermath of the bombings. The USA Patriot Act allows government, for example, to examine medical, financial, and educational records on the basis of a minimal standard of suspicion; to detain individuals for short periods without tangible evidence of wrongdoing; to deport noncitizens who have even minimal association with suspected terrorist groups; and to secretly search homes and offices in some instances.

According to its supporters, the legislative bill gave government tools with which to combat terrorism and thereby protect the lives of Americans. "We have the duty and the privilege to pass this historic legislation," said U.S. Representative James Sessenbrenner on the House floor. However, opponents argued that the bill included unwarranted incursions on individual rights. In expressing his intention to vote against the bill despite favoring many of its provisions, U.S. Senator Russ Feingold said that Congress fulfills its duty "only when it protects both the American people and the freedoms at the foundation of American society." Feingold argued that the bill gave law enforcement officials too much discretionary authority and could become a means of discriminating against Arabs and Muslims.

What's your view on the USA Patriot Act? Do you feel more or less secure because of it? How, primarily, do you define your security? Do you worry about becoming the victim of a terrorist attack? Or do you worry more about having your rights abused by officials engaged in the war on terrorism? Would you have the same opinion if, say, your religion or ethnicity was different than it is? How far are you willing to let government depart from normal protections of individual rights in order to combat the terrorist threat?

The legislation contains a sunset provision—after four years, the USA Patriot Act will expire unless Congress decides to extend it. Does this provision affect your opinion of the legislation? The Justice Department has promised not to abuse its new authority, saying that it will not target ethnic minorities or go on fishing expeditions into people's private lives. Does this verbal assurance affect your opinion of the legislation?

Capitalism is an alternative method for distributing economic costs and benefits. **Capitalism** holds that the government should interfere with the economy as little as possible. Free enterprise and self-reliance are the principles of capitalism. Firms are allowed to operate in a free and open marketplace, and individuals are expected to rely on their own initiative to establish their economic security. Firms decide what they will produce and the price they will charge for their goods and services while consumers decide on what they will buy at what price.

Like the rules of democracy and constitutionalism, the rules of capitalism are not neutral. If democracy responds to numbers and constitutionalism responds to individual rights, capitalism responds to wealth. Economic power is largely a function of accumulated wealth in the hands of either the individual or the firm. "Money talks" in a capitalist system, which means, among other things, that wealthier people will have by far the greater say in the distribution of costs and benefits through the economic system.

The United States does not have a purely capitalist system, because the government plays a role in regulating and stimulating the economy (see Chapter 15). The term *mixed economy* is used to define this hybrid form of economic system with its combination of socialist and capitalist elements. The United States

capitalism An economic system based on the idea that government should interfere with economic transactions as little as possible. Free enterprise and self-reliance are the collective and individual principles that underpin capitalism.

25

---

180   PART TWO   Mass Politics

Political Culture
One People Out of Many

National Pride

Americans are justifiably proud of their nation. It is the oldest continuous democracy in the world, an economic powerhouse, and a diverse yet peaceful society.

What Americans may not recognize, because it so much a part of everyday life in American, is the degree to which they are bombarded with messages and symbols of their nation's greatness. Political socialization in the United States is not the rigid program of indoctrination that some societies impose on their people. Nevertheless, Americans receive a thorough political education. Their country's values are impressed on them by every medium of communication: newspapers, daily conversations, television, movies, books. After the terrorist attacks of September 11, 2001, these tendencies reached new heights. The NBC television network outfitted its peacock logo with stars and stripes, and computer-generated flags festooned the other networks.

The words and symbols that regularly tell Americans of their country's greatness are important to its unity. Without a common ancestral heritage to bind them, Americans need other methods to instill and reinforce the idea that they are one people. As was discussed in Chapter 1, America's political ideals have this effect. So too do everyday reminders, such as the flying of the flag on homes and private buildings, a practice that is almost uniquely American. (Elsewhere, flags are rarely displayed except on public buildings.)

One indicator of Americans' political socialization is their high level of national pride. Harvard University's Pippa Norris (in Marion Sawer's edited volume, *The People's Choice*) constructed an index of national pride based on people's admiration for their country's political, economic, artistic, sporting, scientific, and other achievements. Americans ranked at the top, as shown by the following chart, which is based on Norris's index:

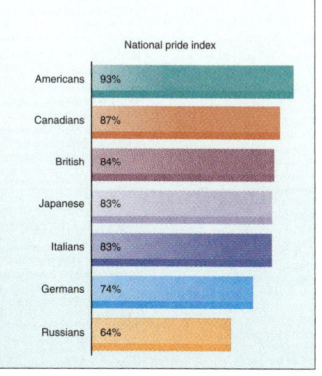

National pride index

Americans	93%
Canadians	87%
British	84%
Japanese	83%
Italians	83%
Germans	74%
Russians	64%

Families

The family is a powerful agent of socialization because children begin with no political attitudes of their own and are likely to accept uncritically those of their parents. The family has a near-monopoly on the attention of the young child, who also places great trust in what a parent says. By the time the child is a teenager and is not likely to listen to any advice a parent might offer, many of the

---

xxix

"Citizenship" Boxes

Some chapters have a box that provides advice and guidance for getting involved in civic and political activity.

Citizenship
Getting Involved, Making a Difference

Moral Action

In *Moral Man and Immoral Society*, Reinhold Niebuhr puzzled over how to reconcile morality and strategy when confronting official injustice. The citizen has a moral obligation to obey the law. But what if the law itself is immoral? Is it moral to disobey such a law, perhaps even through violent means? Niebuhr concluded that, although a strategy of violent opposition would be immoral, nonviolent resistance would not be. This tactic, he argued, involved a "harmonious joining" of the moral and strategic dimensions of political action. Refusal to obey an unjust law would be a moral act, as long as the refusal was nonviolent and the person was willing to accept the legal consequences.

Martin Luther King Jr. described himself as "transformed" by Niebuhr's argument, and he dedicated himself to a campaign of nonviolent resistance against laws that forcibly segregated the races. To prepare for the campaign, King went to India to study Gandhi's nonviolent tactics and then set up instructional workshops to teach others what he had learned. (One of these lessons focused on self-protection when being attacked by the police; the proper technique is to look the attacker in the eyes while using arms and legs to protect vital organs.) King also recruited a select group of young African-American men with physical strength and personal character to absorb a savage beating without fighting back. And as it happened, television images of brutal police attacks on passive demonstrators were instrumental in turning public opinion against the South's system of racial segregation.

The civil rights movement is an exceptional moment in the history of citizen action, but every activist should ask the same question that Niebuhr asked: What constitutes moral action? Political advocacy can be a severe test of moral character. It is tempting for the activist to slip into unethical practices—to fudge facts to strengthen an argument, to twist the meaning of an opponent's position, to appeal to people' irrational impulses. And the pressures to use these techniques mount when an opponent employs them.

Strategic action is not by itself immoral. Nor is there a moral dilemma when the activist operates within prescribed rules for political competition. Although many people are uncomfortable, for example, with the amount of money spent on modern campaigns for public office, there is nothing inherently immoral about campaign money that is raised in the manner prescribed by law. It becomes immoral only if its acceptance includes an implied promise of special influence. Nor is negative campaigning immoral in itself. It can become so if based on a strategy of lies and deceit, but campaign debate legitimately includes arguments about why an opponent should not be elected.

The line between moral and immoral action can be breached. Whatever the momentary gain, the loss is greater. The purpose of citizen action is to elevate public life. Immoral action saps the community's strength by corrupting the process through which collective decisions are made. Immoral action also corrupts those who engage in it by diminishing their sensitivity to the difference between right and wrong and between private ambition and public purpose.

The government has also acted to protect older Americans from discrimination. The Age Discrimination Act of 1975 and the Age Discrimination in Employment Act of 1967 prohibit discrimination against older workers in hiring for jobs in which age is not clearly a crucial factor in job performance. More recently, mandatory retirement ages for most jobs have been eliminated by law. Forced retirement for reasons of age is permissible only if justified by the nature of a particular job or the performance of a particular employee.

"Global Perspective"

These boxes appear in some chapters and examine America's role in an increasingly interdependent world.

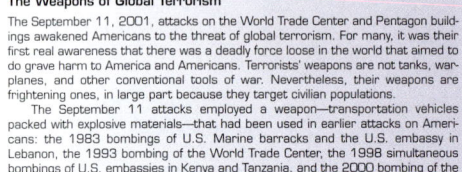

Americans in an Interdependent World

The Weapons of Global Terrorism

The September 11, 2001, attacks on the World Trade Center and Pentagon buildings awakened Americans to the threat of global terrorism. For many, it was their first real awareness that there was a deadly force loose in the world that aimed to do grave harm to America and Americans. Terrorists' weapons are not tanks, warplanes, and other conventional tools of war. Nevertheless, their weapons are frightening ones, in large part because they target civilian populations.

The September 11 attacks employed a weapon—transportation vehicles packed with explosive materials—that had been used in earlier attacks on Americans: the 1983 bombings of U.S. Marine barracks and the U.S. embassy in Lebanon, the 1993 bombing of the World Trade Center, the 1998 simultaneous bombings of U.S. embassies in Kenya and Tanzania, and the 2000 bombing of the U.S.S. Cole in Yemen. Such attacks are designed to kill large numbers of people and to spread fear and panic.

Assassination is a second terrorist weapon. The target is often an innocent civilian rather than a top government or military official, as in the case of *Wall Street Journal* reporter Daniel Pearl, who was murdered by Pakistani militants in 2002. Assassination is an old weapon of war, but it has taken on a new dimension with suicide bombers who blow themselves up in the process of killing and injuring those around them. Such attacks are designed to create fear and to inhibit people from traveling freely.

Weapons of mass destruction are also in the terrorist arsenal, but to date, they have not been used to great effect. Biological and chemical weapons have the potential to kill thousands, even millions, of people. Shortly after the September 11

---

world is not composed of equal sovereign states. Some are more powerful than others, and the strong sometimes bully the weak. Nevertheless, there is no international body that is recognized by all nations as the final (sovereign) authority on disputes between them.

As a result, the chief instruments of national security policy—diplomacy, military force, economic exchange, and intelligence gathering—differ from those of domestic policy.

The Policymaking Instruments

Diplomacy is the process of negotiation between countries. In most cases, nations prefer to settle their differences by talking rather than by fighting. Through negotiation, countries can usually reach agreement on common (mutual) problems. By definition, acts of diplomacy involve negotiations between two (*bilateral*) or more (*multilateral*) nations.

Military power is a second instrument of foreign policy, and it can be used *unilaterally*—that is, by a single nation acting alone. Most countries use military power as a defensive measure; they maintain forces, or enter into military alliances with other countries, in order to protect themselves from potential aggressors. Throughout the history of nations, however, there have always been a few

xxx

"Self Quiz" Icon
Identifies website where self-quiz and other support items can be found.

Summary
A short discussion, organized around the chapter's main points, summarizes each chapter's content.

Key Terms
A list of the chapter's major concepts facilitates review.

Suggested Readings
Annotated references encourage further pursuit of some of the best works of political science, both classic studies and recent research.

List of Websites
Annotated references to websites that provide information relevant to chapter's content.

---

222   PART TWO   Mass Politics

individuals still favored the plan. They would have been the principal beneficiaries of the Clinton plan, which called for universal health care insurance. On the other hand, most middle-income people and virtually all higher-income people already had health insurance, either through an individual policy or an employment-related group policy.

In sum, the pattern of individual political participation in the United States parallels the distribution of influence that prevails in the private sector. Those who have the most power through participation in the marketplace also have the most power through participation in the political arena. However, the issue of individual participation is only one piece of the larger puzzle of who rules America and for what purposes. Subsequent chapters will provide additional pieces.

Self-Quiz
www.mhhe.com/patterson6

SUMMARY

Political participation is involvement in activities designed to influence public policy and leadership. A main issue of democratic government is the question of who participates in politics and how fully they participate.

Voting is the most widespread form of active political participation among Americans. Yet voter turnout is significantly lower in the United States than in other democratic nations. The requirement that Americans must personally register in order to establish their eligibility to vote is one reason for lower turnout among Americans; other democracies place the burden of registration on government officials rather than on the individual citizen. The fact that the United States holds frequent elections also discourages some citizens from voting regularly. Finally, the major American political parties, unlike many of those in Europe, do not clearly represent the interests of opposing economic classes; thus the policy stakes in American elections are correspondingly lower. Some Americans do not vote because they think that policy will not change greatly regardless of which party gains power.

Prospective voting is one way the people can exert influence on policy through their participation. It is the most demanding approach to voting; voters must develop their own policy preferences and then educate themselves about the candidates' positions. Most voters are not well-enough informed about the issues to respond in this way. Retrospective voting demands less from voters: they need only decide whether the government has been performing well in terms of the goals and values they hold. The evidence suggests that the electorate is, in fact, reasonably sensitive to past governmental performance, particularly in the area of economic prosperity.

Only a minority of citizens engage in the more demanding forms of political activity, such as work on community affairs or on behalf of a candidate during a political campaign. The proportion of Americans who engage in these more demanding forms of activity exceeds the proportion of Europeans who do so. Nevertheless, only about one in every four Americans will take an active part in a political organization at some point in their lives. Most political activists are individuals of higher income and education; they have the skills and material resources to participate effectively and tend to take greater interest in politics. More than in any other Western democracy, political participation in the United States is related to economic status.

Social movements are broad efforts to achieve change by citizens who feel that government is not properly responsive to their interests. These efforts sometimes take place outside established channels; demonstrations, picket lines, and marches are common means of protest. Protesters are younger and more idealistic on average than are other citizens, but they are a very small proportion of the population. In addition, protest activities do not have much public support, despite the country's tradition of free expression.

Overall, Americans are only moderately involved in politics. They are concerned with political affairs but mostly immersed in their private pursuits, a reflection in part of this culture's emphasis on individualism. The lower level of participation among low-income citizens has particular significance in that it works to reduce their influence on public policy and leadership.

CHAPTER 7   Political Participation and Voting: Expressing the Popular Will   223

KEY TERMS

alienation
apathy
civic duty
political participation
prospective voting
registration
retrospective voting
social capital
social (political) movements
suffrage
voter turnout

SUGGESTED READINGS

Burns, Nancy, Kay Lehman Schlozman, and Sidney Verba. *The Private Roots of Public Action: Gender, Equality, and Public Action*. Cambridge, Mass.: Harvard University Press, 2001. An analysis of gender differences in political participation and their roots in patterns of everyday life.

Leighley, Jan. *Strength in Numbers: The Political Mobilization of Racial and Ethnic Minorities*. Princeton, N.J.: Princeton University Press, 2001. A study of the factors that motivate blacks and Hispanics to participate in politics.

Neuman, W. Russell, Marion R. Just, and Ann N. Crigler. *Common Knowledge: News and the Construction of Meaning*. Chicago: University of Chicago Press, 1992. An assessment of how citizens interpret and use the news they receive.

Patterson, Thomas E. *The Vanishing Voter*. New York: Knopf, 2002. A study of the decline in electoral participation and what might be done to reverse the trend.

Putnam, Robert. *Bowling Alone*. New York: Simon and Schuster, 2000. A provocative analysis of the trend in civic participation.

Rimmerman, Craig A. *The New Citizenship: Unconventional Politics, Activism, and Service*. Boulder, Colo.: Westview Press, 1997. An assessment of citizenship in the modern age.

Schudson, Michael. *The Good Citizen: A History of American Civic Life*. New York: Free Press, 1998. A thoughtful history of civic participation in America.

Verba, Sidney, Kay Schlozman, and Henry Brady. *Voice and Equality*. Cambridge, Mass.: Harvard University Press, 1995. A careful study of political attitudes and participation.

LIST OF WEBSITES

http://www.rockthevote.org/
Rock the Vote is an organization dedicated to helping young people realize and utilize their power to affect the civic and political life of their communities.

http://www.umich.edu/~nes/
The United States of Michigan's National Election Studies (NES) site provides survey data on voting, public opinion, and political participation.

http://www.vanishingvoter.org/
Harvard University's election study site provides data and analysis of public involvement in the 2000 presidential campaign.

http://www.vote-smart.org/
Project Vote Smart includes information on Republican and Democratic candidates and officials; also has the latest in election news.

xxxi

ACKNOWLEDGMENTS

Early in the writing of the first edition of *The American Democracy*, my editor and I concluded that it would be enormously helpful if a way could be found to bring into each chapter the judgment of those political scientists who teach the introductory course year in and year out. These instructors are most able to provide the required insight into improving the pedagogical value of an introductory text. This recognition led us to initiate what is still today the most thorough review process ever undertaken for an American government text. In addition to the chapter reviews of a select number of expert scholars, we sent each chapter to a dozen or so faculty members at U.S. colleges and universities of all types—public and private, large and small, four-year and two-year. These political scientists, 213 of them in all, had well over a thousand years of combined experience in the teaching of the introductory course, and they provided various constructive ideas. They will go unnamed here, but my debt to these scholars remains undiminished by time. Reviewers are the lifeblood of a text, and their contribution lasts far beyond the edition they help strengthen.

For the second, third, fourth, and fifth editions, we also sought suggestions from a large number of reviewers—130 in total. Their suggestions were detailed, lengthy, and extremely useful. It might be thought that the comprehensive nature of the first review process would have eliminated even the more minor defects. Nevertheless, these reviewers found some and, more than that, offered invaluable advice on the latest scholarship in their subfields within political science.

For this new edition, we again sought a wide range of advice. In fact, we asked reviewers for a more thorough assessment of the text than had been asked of previous reviewers. The reviewers for this edition concluded that an overall revision was not necessary. However, they offered a great many suggestions that have been adopted into this edition. I am grateful that they took so much time from their own work to improve mine. My thanks to:

Henry N. Carrier, *Brevard Community College*
Frank J. Coppa, *Union County College*
Ken Ellinger, *Dalton State College*
Robert T. Gillespie, *San Antonio College*
Anne Gordon, *Ohio University*
Eugene Goss, *Long Beach City College*
Lori Cox Han, *Austin College*
Paul Holder, *McLennan Community College*
Robert R. Klein, *Rutgers University*
Carol E. Meacham, *SUNY, Oneonta*
Steve Parker, *University of Nevada Las Vegas*
Renford R. Reese, *California State Polytechnic University, Pomona*
Glen W. Richardson Jr., *Kutztown University*
Kathleen Sedille, *Triton College*
Alson J. Slane, *Muhlenberg College*
Joseph Smith, *Grand Valley State University*

Finally, I want to acknowledge those at McGraw-Hill and Harvard University who contributed to the sixth edition. Monica Eckman, my editor, deserves a special thanks. Monica's enthusiasm for the text was a source of inspiration and a constant reminder of the importance of the revision process. Angela Kao, the editorial coordinator, provided assistance throughout the revision process. Marilyn Rothenberger also had a major impact. She carefully supervised the production of the sixth edition. Michelle Whitaker, Nora Agbayani, and Enboge Chong also worked hard to make this edition a reality. At Harvard, I had the constant and valuable support of my faculty assistant, Jamie Arterton. She flawlessly updated nearly all the tables and figures and provided the research materials that informed the text revisions.

Thomas E. Patterson

PART ONE

Foundations

The United States has the world's oldest constitution still in force. France has had fourteen constitutions during the same period in which the United States has had one. The British statesman William Gladstone in 1878 declared the U.S. Constitution to be "the most wonderful work ever struck off at a given time by the brain and purpose of man."

A reason why this remarkable system has endured is that the United States was founded on a set of common ideals that continue to serve as Americans' bond. Chapter 1 describes these ideals and their lasting influence on the nation's politics.

Chapters 2 and 3 examine how the writers of the Constitution resolved fundamental issues—liberty, self-government, and union. A central theme of these chapters is that basic constitutional issues are never fully settled. They are recurring sources of debate, and each generation is forced to find new answers.

Constitutional government is also a matter of individual rights, of a system in which people have basic freedoms that are constitutionally protected from infringement by government. Although these rights are rooted in principle, they are achieved through politics. Chapter 4 discusses how civil liberties—for example, free speech—are protected both from and through political action. Chapter 5 examines the degree to which Americans' rights are affected by characteristics such as gender and race.

CHAPTER OUTLINE

1. American Political Culture: Seeking a More Perfect Union 4
2. Constitutional Democracy: Promoting Liberty and Self-Government 34
3. Federalism: Forging a Nation 66
4. Civil Liberties: Protecting Individual Rights 96
5. Equal Rights: Struggling Toward Fairness 130

1

One hears people say that it is inherent in the habits and nature of democracies to change feelings and thoughts at every moment.... But I have never seen anything like that happening in the great democracy on the other side of the ocean. What struck me most in the United States was the difficulty experienced in getting an idea, once conceived, out of the head of the majority.

Alexis de Tocqueville[1]

American Political Culture:
Seeking a More Perfect Union

At 8:46 a.m. on September 11, 2001, an American Airlines passenger jet slammed into one of the twin towers of New York City's World Trade Center. Twenty minutes later, a second passenger jet rammed into the other tower. A third jet then plowed into the Pentagon building in Washington, D.C. Within two hours, the World Trade Center towers collapsed, killing all still inside, including police and firefighters who had rushed bravely into the buildings to help in the evacuation. Three thousand Americans were murdered that September morning, the highest death toll ever from an attack on American soil by a foreign adversary. The casualties would have been higher except for the bravery of passengers aboard United Airlines flight 93, who fought with its hijackers, causing the plane, which was aimed at Washington, D.C., to crash in a barren Pennsylvania field.

That evening, a somber George W. Bush addressed the nation. Urging Americans to stay calm and resolute, President Bush said: "America was targeted for an attack because we're the brightest beacon for freedom and opportunity in the world." Sprinkled throughout his speech were allusions to time-honored American ideals: liberty, justice, and the rule of law. "No one will keep that light from shining," said Bush.

The ideals that guided Bush's speech would have been familiar to any generation of Americans. The ideals that Bush used to console Americans on September 11, 2001, have been spoken when Americans have gone to war, declared peace, celebrated national holidays, launched major policy initiatives, and asserted new rights.[2] The ideals contained in Bush's speech were the same ones that had punctuated the speeches of George Washington and Abraham Lincoln, Susan B. Anthony and Franklin D. Roosevelt, Dr. Martin Luther King Jr. and Ronald Reagan.

The ideals were also there at the nation's beginning, when they were put into words in the Declaration of Independence and the Constitution. Of course, the practical meaning of these words has changed greatly during the nation's history. When the writers of the Constitution began the document with the words "We, the People," they did not have all Americans equally in mind. Black slaves, women, and men without property did not have the same rights as propertied white men.

Yet America's ideals have been remarkably enduring. Throughout their history Americans have embraced the same set of core values. They have quarreled over the meaning, practice, and fulfillment of these ideals, but they have never seriously questioned the principles themselves. As the historian Clinton Rossiter concluded, "There has been in a doctrinal sense, only one America."[3]

This book is about contemporary American politics, not U.S. history or culture. Yet American politics today cannot be understood apart from the nation's heritage. Government does not begin anew with each generation; it builds on the past. In the case of the United States, the most significant link between past and present lies in the nation's founding ideals. The Frenchman Alexis de Tocqueville was among the first to see that the main tendencies of American politics cannot be explained without taking into account the country's core beliefs. "Habits of the heart" was Tocqueville's description of Americans' ideals.[4]

Firefighters and other rescue workers stand at the site of the collapsed World Trade Center Towers, which were attacked earlier that day by terrorists who had hijacked commercial airliners. Nearly 3,000 Americans were murdered in the September 11, 2001 attacks.

This chapter briefly examines the principles that have helped shape American politics since the country's earliest years. The chapter also explains basic concepts, such as power and pluralism, that are important in the study of government and politics and describes the underlying rules of the American governing system, such as constitutionalism and capitalism. The main points made in this chapter are the following:

- *The American political culture centers on a set of core ideals—liberty, equality, self-government, individualism, diversity, and unity—that serve as the people's common bond.* These mythic principles have a substantial influence on what Americans will regard as reasonable and acceptable and on what they will try to achieve.

- *Politics is the process that determines whose values will prevail in society.* The play of politics in the United States takes place in the context of democratic procedures, constitutionalism, and capitalism and involves elements of majority, pluralist, bureaucratic, and elite rule.

- *Politics in the United States is characterized by a number of major patterns, including a highly fragmented governing system, a high degree of pluralism, an extraordinary emphasis on individual rights, and a pronounced separation of the political and economic spheres.*

POLITICAL CULTURE: THE CORE PRINCIPLES OF AMERICAN GOVERNMENT

The people of every nation have a few great ideals that characterize their political life, but as James Bryce observed, Americans are a special case.[5] Their ideals are the basis of their national identity. Other people take their identity from the common ancestry that led them gradually to gather under one flag. Thus, long before there was a France or a Japan, there were French and Japanese people, each a kinship group united through blood. Even today, it is kinship that links them. There is no way to become Japanese except to be born of Japanese parents. Not so for Americans. They are a multitude of peoples linked by a political tradition. The United States is a nation that was abruptly founded in 1776 on a set of principles that became its people's common bond.[6]

A strong bond of some kind was a necessity. Nationalities that warred constantly in Europe had to find a way to live together in the New World. Diversity became a watchword, and Americans' shared ideals contributed to a oneness, however uneasy, among nationalities that had never before trusted one another. Their effort to find common ground has been replayed many times during America's history. The United States is, and always has been, a nation of immigrants and of people struggling for a greater level of acceptance and unity. Today, the United States has a population of almost 300 million people, nearly all of whom can trace their ancestry to some other place (see Figure 1–1). Native Americans now make up about 1 percent of the population. They are outnumbered by Americans who have ancestral ties to Germany, Ireland, Africa, Poland, Mexico, or China, to name just a few of the places to which large numbers of Americans can trace their origins.

Yet Americans are also one people, brought together through allegiance to a set of commonly held ideals such as liberty and equality. These principles are habits of mind, a customary way of thinking about the world. They are part of what social scientists call **political culture,** a term that refers to the characteristic and deep-seated beliefs of a particular people about government and politics.[7] Not every American embraces the country's ideals with the same fervor or attributes to them the same meaning, but they are widely held.

America's core ideals are rooted in the European heritage of the first white settlers. They arrived during the Enlightenment period, when people were awakening to the idea of human progress. These settlers wanted freedom to practice religion and hoped for a greater measure of self-government. They did not, as some Americans assume, invent an entirely new way of life. Their beliefs were shaped by European thought and practice, which in turn had been molded by Greco-Roman and Judeo-Christian traditions. Many of the settlers were seeking a new beginning, but they did not shed their entire past while

political culture The characteristic and deep-seated beliefs of a particular people.

ALL COUNTRIES 65.8 million

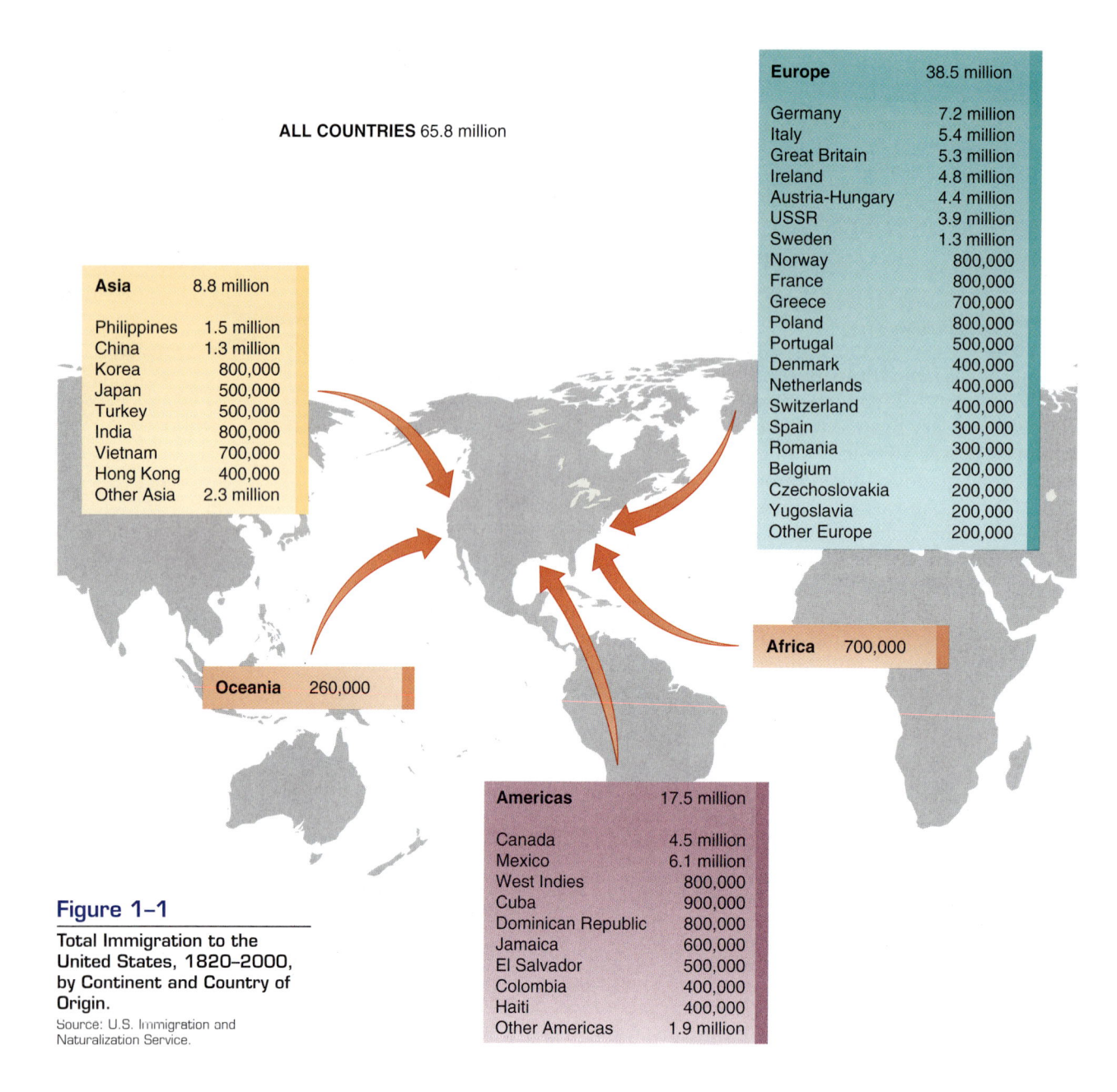

Europe	38.5 million
Germany	7.2 million
Italy	5.4 million
Great Britain	5.3 million
Ireland	4.8 million
Austria-Hungary	4.4 million
USSR	3.9 million
Sweden	1.3 million
Norway	800,000
France	800,000
Greece	700,000
Poland	800,000
Portugal	500,000
Denmark	400,000
Netherlands	400,000
Switzerland	400,000
Spain	300,000
Romania	300,000
Belgium	200,000
Czechoslovakia	200,000
Yugoslavia	200,000
Other Europe	200,000

Asia	8.8 million
Philippines	1.5 million
China	1.3 million
Korea	800,000
Japan	500,000
Turkey	500,000
India	800,000
Vietnam	700,000
Hong Kong	400,000
Other Asia	2.3 million

Africa	700,000

Oceania	260,000

Americas	17.5 million
Canada	4.5 million
Mexico	6.1 million
West Indies	800,000
Cuba	900,000
Dominican Republic	800,000
Jamaica	600,000
El Salvador	500,000
Colombia	400,000
Haiti	400,000
Other Americas	1.9 million

Figure 1–1

Total Immigration to the United States, 1820–2000, by Continent and Country of Origin.

Source: U.S. Immigration and Naturalization Service.

pursuing it. As the historian Paul Gagnon noted, "The first settlers did not sail into view out of a void, their minds as blank as the Atlantic Ocean. . . . Those who sailed west to America came in fact not to build a New World but to bring to life in a new setting what they had treasured most from the Old World."[8]

Colonial life enlarged their vision, which then found expression in the Declaration of Independence and the Constitution. Ideals became the defining feature of the American political experience. Later immigrants adopted them while also leaving a distinctive mark on the practice of these ideals. As each new generation of Americans has discovered, there is no fixed way to live out these

U.S. politics is remarkable for its historical continuity, which is celebrated here in a ceremony at the Capitol in Washington, D.C.

principles. In practice, these ideals have also meant different things to different people even within the same generation. Few observers would argue, however, with the proposition that *a defining characteristic of the American political system is its enduring and powerful set of political ideals.*

AMERICA'S CORE VALUES: LIBERTY, EQUALITY, AND RELATED IDEALS

An understanding of America's ideals begins with the recognition that the individual is paramount. The individual does not exist to glorify government. Government exists to enhance the individual. No clearer statement of this principle exists than the Declaration of Independence's reference to "unalienable rights"—freedoms that belong to each and every person and that cannot lawfully be denied by government.

Liberty is widely regarded as the most basic of American ideals. The United States, as historian Louis Hartz said, was "born free."[9] **Liberty** is the principle that individuals should be free to act and think as they choose, provided they do not infringe unreasonably on the freedom and well-being of others. The Declaration of Independence rings with the proclamation that people are entitled to "Life, Liberty and the Pursuit of Happiness." The preamble to the Constitution declares that the U.S. government is founded to secure "the Blessings of Liberty to ourselves and our Posterity." The Statue of Liberty stands in New York harbor as the symbol of the American nation, and the "Star-Spangled Banner" rings out with the words "land of the free."

At the time of the writing of the Constitution (1787), liberty was conceived as protection against unwarranted government interference in people's lives. Liberty was to be nurtured by restrictions on government. The First Amendment, for example, defines a set of actions that government is forbidden to take: "Congress shall make no law respecting the establishment of religion, or prohibiting the free exercise thereof; or abridging the freedom of speech, or of the press; or the right of the people to peaceably assemble, and to petition the Government for a redress of grievances."

Liberty The principle that individuals should be free to act and think as they choose, provided they do not infringe unreasonably on the rights and freedoms of others.

Thomas Jefferson
(1743–1826)

Thomas Jefferson was the principal author of the Declaration of Independence. It was Jefferson who coined the renowned words "Life, Liberty and the Pursuit of Happiness." A powerful advocate of personal freedom, he also wrote the state of Virginia's Bill of Rights. Elected to the presidency in 1800, his purchase of the Louisiana Territory from the French Emperor Napoleon in 1803 doubled the size of the United States. After retiring to his Monticello estate, Jefferson designed and founded the University of Virginia, which he proclaimed as his greatest achievement.

For a long period, America's vast wilderness and great distance from the Old World granted its people more liberty than perhaps even they could at first have imagined. Ordinary people had no reason to accept servitude when greater liberty was as close as the next area of unsettled wilderness. With time, however, this protection diminished and new threats to personal liberty emerged—for example, the periodic economic busts that rendered many families penniless or the discriminatory acts that denied African Americans access to public schools and accommodations. It became harder to think about liberty as simply the absence of government restraints. Gradually, Americans turned to government for help in attaining a fuller measure of their liberty. During the 1930s Great Depression, President Franklin D. Roosevelt spoke of "freedom from want" and persuaded Congress to enact employment and social security programs. During the 1960s, the Civil Rights Act and the Voting Rights Act were enacted to give black Americans the freedom to exercise their right to vote and the freedom to enter the restaurants, movie theaters, hotels, and other public accommodations that had been reserved for whites.

Equality is America's other towering ideal. **Equality** is the notion that all individuals are equal in their moral worth, are entitled to equal treatment under the law, and should have an equal political voice. America's first white settlers found in America a degree of equality that had been unthinkable in Europe. Its rigid aristocratic system based on land ownership was unenforceable in frontier America. Almost any settler who wanted to own land could do so. It was this natural sense of equality that Thomas Jefferson captured so forcefully in words in the Declaration of Independence: "We hold these truths to be self-evident, that all men are created equal."

Equality, however, has always been a less clearly defined concept than liberty. Even Jefferson professed not to know its exact meaning. A slave owner, Jefferson distinguished between free citizens, who were entitled to equal rights, and slaves, who were not. After slavery was abolished, Americans continued to argue over the meaning of equality, as they do today. Does it require the leveling of material condition, or of opportunities, or neither? What does it mean to say that Americans are equals? Despite differing opinions about such questions, the quest for and insistence on equality remains a distinctive feature of the American experience. Observers from Tocqueville to Bryce have seen fit to say that equality in America, as in no other country, is ingrained in people's thinking. Americans, said Bryce, reject "the very notion" that some people might be "better" than others merely because of birth or position.[10] And perhaps no ideal has so inspired Americans to political action as has their desire for fuller equality. The abolition movement, the suffrage movement, and the various civil rights movements are testimony to the depth and power of this ideal.

Of course, people differ in their natural endowments and their material resources, which means they are not equal in fact. Even today, poor people accused of crime do not have access to the same quality of legal assistance

equality The notion that all individuals are equal in their moral worth, in their treatment under the law, and in their political voice.

Fighting Words

Should English Be Made America's Official Language?

America's ideals are broad principles that include conflicting elements. The principle of diversity extols Americans' differences. The principle of unity proclaims that Americans are one people and one nation. These principles have clashed whenever newly arrived immigrants have been at issue. Should immigrants be allowed to maintain their distinctive characteristics? Or should their assimilation be accelerated? Which principle should govern—unity or diversity? The issue has emerged recently with the arrival of record numbers of Hispanic and Asian immigrants. A point of contention has been whether these new immigrants should be required to use English as the first language in school and in the conduct of government-related business.

Yes: We are one nation even though each of us may have ancestors who fought against each other in generations past. This has been made possible by our . . . common language. . . . The English language was both the language of opportunity and the language of unity. . . . Government multilingualism is divisive. . . . Michigan offers its driver test in 20 languages. There are 100 languages spoken in the Chicago school system. . . . Preserving national unity through making English this Nation's official language is . . . a critical issue. Look around the world. . . . Linguistic divisions swiftly lead to other divisions. . . . I submit that the time has indeed come for the English Language Amendment and I urge its adoption.
—U.S. Representative John Doolittle (R-Calif.)

No: Whereas, several bills have been introduced in the U.S. Congress to make English the official language of the United States; and whereas, the issue often has a divisive effect on the public and does not meet with the inclusive spirit and vision of a democratic and diverse society; and whereas, the passage and implementation of such legislation could restrict the program options that local school systems have for limited English proficient children; therefore, let it be resolved that the Council of the Great City Schools opposes federal legislation that mandates that English is the official U.S. language; and . . . opposes such legislation that may appear in state legislatures and on state ballots.
—Council of the Great City Schools

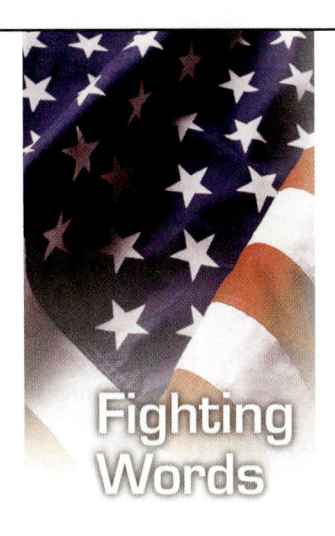

---

available to rich people. In principle, however, Americans are equals, as expressed, for example, in the phrase "one person, one vote" or in the phrase "equal justice under the law." These are not empty words. For example, although the poor have less access to legal assistance, no American citizen can be tried for a felony offense without the opportunity for legal counsel, at government expense if necessary.

Although liberty and equality are the preeminent American political ideals, other principles flow from them. **Popular consent** is the principle that the people are the ultimate source of governing authority. How could Americans have liberty and equality, much less hope to maintain it, without the consent of the governed and without mechanisms, such as elections, for granting or

popular consent The principle that the people are the ultimate source of governing authority.

withholding that consent? "Governments," the Declaration of Independence proclaims, "deriv[e] their just powers from the consent of the governed." In his Gettysburg Address, Lincoln extolled a government "of the people, by the people, for the people."

Individualism is a commitment to personal initiative, self-sufficiency, and material accumulation. It is related to the idea of liberty, which makes the individual the foundation of society, and is buttressed by the idea of equality, which holds that everyone should be given a fair chance to succeed. Individualism stems from the belief that people, if free to pursue their own path and if not unfairly burdened, can attain their fullest potential. Individualism has roots in the country's origins as a wilderness society. The early Americans developed a pride in their "rugged individualism" and from this experience grew the idea that people ought to try to make it on their own.

Unity and diversity are also part of what is sometimes called the American Creed—the set of core values that define the nation's political culture. **Unity** is the principle that Americans are one people and form an indivisible union. **Diversity** holds that individual and group differences should be respected and that these differences are themselves a source of strength. These two principles acknowledge at once both the differences and the oneness that are part of the American experience.

individualism The idea that people should take the initiative, be self-sufficient, and accumulate the material advantages necessary for their well-being.

unity The principle that Americans are one people and form an indivisible union.

diversity The principle that individual and group differences should be respected and are a source of national strength.

The Power of Ideals

America's ideals have had a strong impact on its politics. Ideals serve to define the boundaries of action. They do not determine exactly what people will do, but they have a marked influence on what people will regard as reasonable and desirable. If people believe, as Americans do, that politics exists to promote liberty and equality, they will attempt to realize these values through their political actions.

Why, for example, does the United States spend relatively less money on government programs for the poor and disadvantaged than do other fully industrialized democracies, including Germany, France, Switzerland, the Netherlands, Spain, Britain, Sweden, Italy, and Japan? Are Americans so much better off than these other people that they have less need for welfare programs? The answer is no. Of all these countries, the United States has in both relative and absolute terms the greatest number of hungry, homeless, and poor people. The reason the United States spends less on social welfare lies chiefly in the emphasis that American culture places on *individualism*. Americans have resisted giving government a larger social welfare role because of their deep-seated cultural belief that personal effort is the key to economic security (see Figure 1–2).

Of course, social welfare policy is not simply an issue of cultural differences. The welfare issue, like all other issues, is part of the rough and tumble of everyday politics everywhere. There are always powerful interests aligned on both sides of important issues. In the United States, the Republican party, business groups, antitax groups, and others have resisted the expansion of the government's social welfare role, while liberal Democrats, unions, minority groups, and others have from time to time argued for greater intervention. Nevertheless, Americans' belief in individualism, which has no exact equivalent in European society, has played a defining role in shaping U.S. welfare policy.

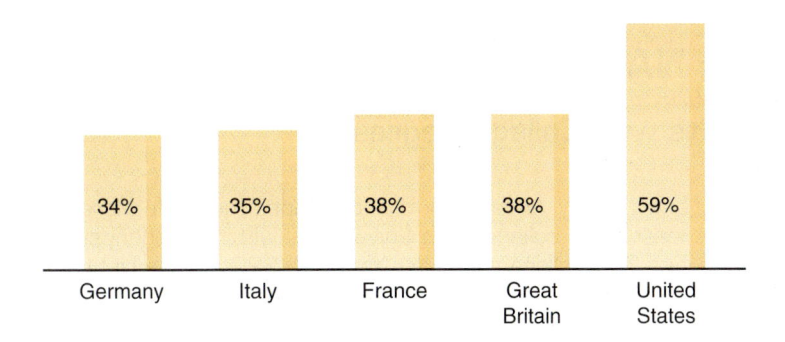

Figure 1–2

Opinions About the Source of Personal Success

Americans are more likely than Europeans to believe that personal effort is the key to success. Figures are the percentage of respondents who agreed with the statement "In the long run, hard work usually brings a better life."

Source: World Values Surveys, 1990–1997.

Germany	Italy	France	Great Britain	United States
34%	35%	38%	38%	59%

The distinctiveness of this cultural belief is evident in a Times-Mirror Center survey of opinions in Europe and the United States.[11] When asked whether it is the responsibility of the government "to take care of very poor people who can't take care of themselves," only 23 percent of Americans said they completely agreed. The Germans were the closest to the Americans in their response to this question, but more than twice as many of them, 50 percent, said they believed that the state should take care of the very poor. More than 60 percent of the British, French, and Italians held the same opinion. Americans do not necessarily have less sympathy for the poor; rather they place more emphasis on personal responsibility than Europeans do.[12]

The importance of individualism to American society is also evident in the emphasis on equal opportunity. If individuals are to be entrusted with their own welfare, they must be given a fair chance to succeed on their own. Nowhere is this philosophy more evident than in the country's elaborate system of higher education, which includes nearly three thousand two-year and four-year institutions. The system is designed to accommodate nearly every individual who wants to pursue a college education. More than a third of the nation's young people enter college, the world's highest rate. Western Europe has nothing comparable to the American system; fewer than one in five young people in these countries go to college. The difference is reflected in the number of citizens with college degrees (see "States in the Nation"). Even the American state that ranks lowest by this indicator—West Virginia with its 15.3 percent of adults who are college graduates—has a higher percentage of residents with a bachelor's degree than does the average European country.

Of course, the idea that success is within equal reach of all Americans who strive for it is far from accurate. Young people who grow up in abject poverty and without adequate guidance know all too well the limits on equality. In some inner-city areas, teenage boys are more likely to spend time in jail than to spend time at college.

The Limits of Ideals

Cultural beliefs originate in a country's political and social practices, but they are not perfect representatives of these practices. They are mythic ideas—symbolic positions taken by a people to justify and give meaning to their way of life.[13] Myths contain elements of truth, but they are far from the full truth.

STATES IN THE NATION

Percentage of Adults with College Degrees

Reflecting their culture beliefs of individualism and equality, Americans have developed the world's largest system of college education. Every state has at least eight colleges and universities within its boundaries and eleven states have more than 100. California with 322 colleges and New York with 320 are the highest ranking states by this measure. No European democracy has as many institutions of higher education as these two states. As a result of their cultural commitment to equal opportunity through education, many Americans have college degrees. On a state-by-state basis, the range is 15.3 percent in West Virginia to 34.6 percent in Colorado. The European average is less than 15 percent. American college graduates are concentrated in the urbanized and affluent states. Young people in these states can better afford the costs of college and are more likely to need a college degree for the work they seek.

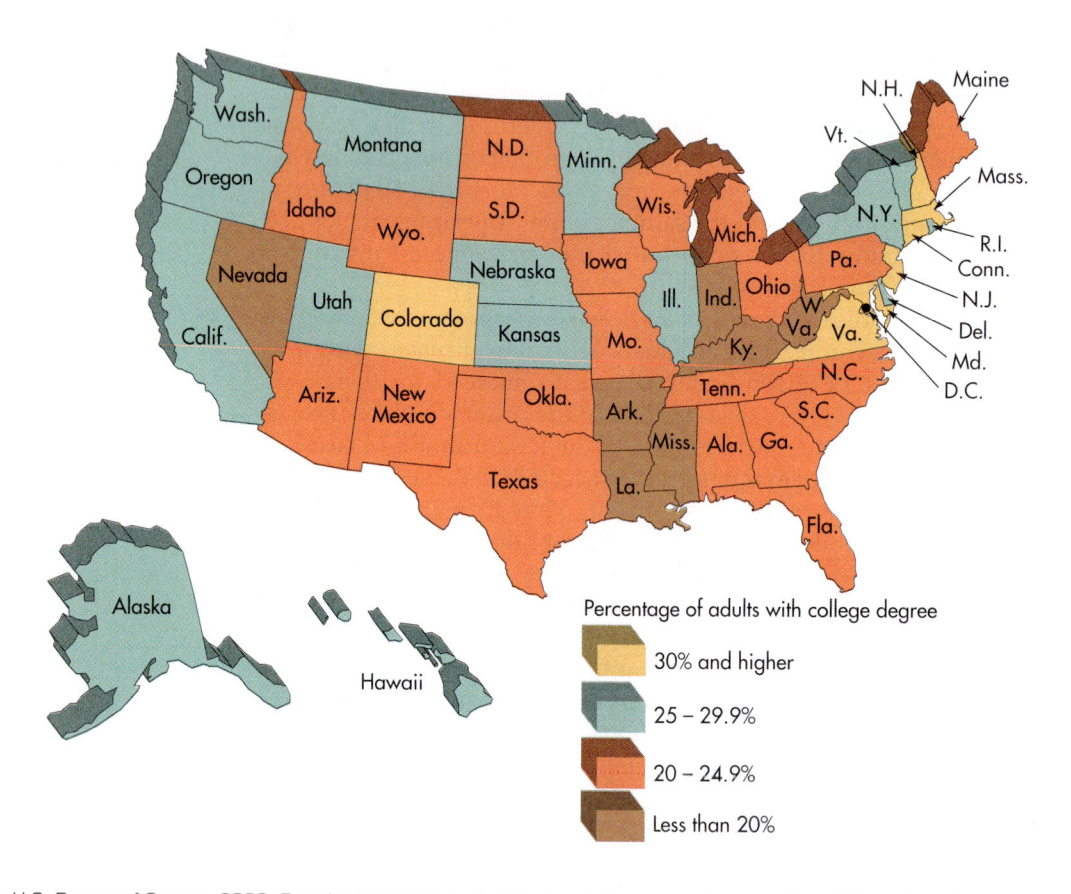

Percentage of adults with college degree
- 30% and higher
- 25 – 29.9%
- 20 – 24.9%
- Less than 20%

Source: U.S. Bureau of Census, 2000. Based on percentage of adults twenty-five years of age or older with a college degree.

High ideals do not come with a guarantee that a people will live up to them. The clearest proof of this failing in the American case is the human tragedy that began nearly four centuries ago and continues today. In 1619 the first black slaves were brought in chains to America. Slavery lasted 250 years. Slaves in the

The structure of U.S. society helps promote the American dream of success—for example, by encouraging young people to attend college.

field worked from dawn to dark (from "can see, 'til can't"), in both the heat of summer and the cold of winter. The Civil War changed the future of African Americans but did not ensure their equality. Slavery was followed by the Jim Crow era of legal segregation: black people in the South were forbidden by law to use the same schools, hospitals, restaurants, and restrooms as white people. For those who got uppish with their white superiors, there were beatings, firebombings, castrations, rapes, and worse—hundreds of African Americans were lynched by white vigilantes in the early 1900s. Today African Americans have equal rights under the law, but in fact they are far from equal. Compared with whites, blacks are twice as likely to live in poverty, twice as likely to be unable to find a job, and twice as likely to die in infancy.[14] There have always been at least two Americas, one for whites and one for blacks.

Despite the lofty claim that "all men are created equal," equality has never been an American birthright. In 1882 Congress suspended Chinese immigration on the assumption that the Chinese were an inferior people. Calvin Coolidge in 1923 asked Congress for a permanent ban on Chinese immigration, saying that people "who do not want to be partakers of the American spirit ought not to settle in America."[15] Not until 1965 was discrimination against the Chinese and other Asians effectively eliminated from U.S. immigration laws. The barriers to entry of Mexicans and Central and South Americans were also lowered at this time (Figure 1–3).

The claim that America is a gigantic melting pot has always been as much fable as fact. When Irish, Italian, and Eastern European immigrants reached this country's shores, they encountered nativist elements that scorned their ways of life and mocked their religions. In the 1800s, the Know Nothing Party sought to bar Catholics and Jews from settling in America. The Hispanic, Asian, and

Historical Background

www.mhhe.com/patterson6

Figure 1-3
The Changing Face of Immigration
Until 1965, immigration laws had favored European immigrants. The new laws favored Asians and Latin Americans.

Source: U.S. Immigration and Naturalization Service, 2002. Percentages are totals for each decade, e.g., the 2000 figures are for the 1991–2000 period.

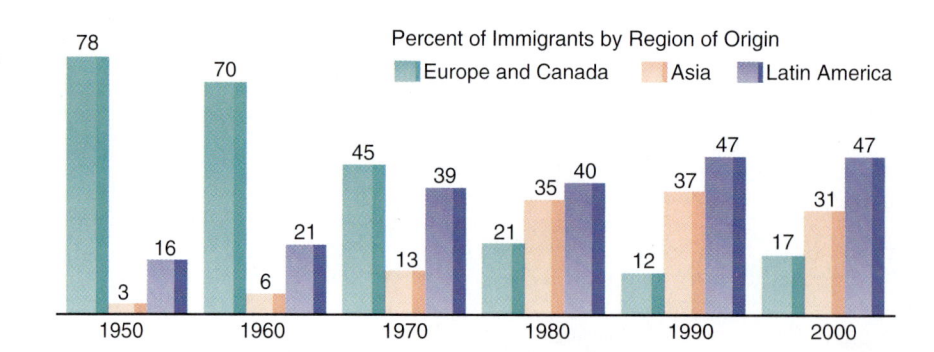

Percent of Immigrants by Region of Origin

Year	Europe and Canada	Asia	Latin America
1950	78	3	16
1960	70	6	21
1970	45	13	39
1980	21	35	40
1990	12	37	47
2000	17	31	47

Middle Eastern peoples who have come here more recently have also been made to feel less than fully welcome by many Americans whose ancestors settled here in earlier times. Recent polls, for example, indicate that sizable numbers of Americans would favor restricting immigration, particularly the influx of Spanish-speaking and Middle Eastern peoples. Support for restrictions rose even higher after the September 11, 2001, terrorist attacks. A Gallup poll in October indicated that seven times as many Americans favored a decrease in immigration as favored an increase.

Resistance to immigrant groups is not among the stories that Americans like to tell about themselves.[16] Such lapses of historical memory can be found among all peoples, but the tendency to recast history is perhaps exaggerated in the American case because Americans' beliefs are so idealistic (see Table 1–1). How could a nation that upholds the ideal of human equality have barred the Chinese, enslaved the blacks, betrayed the Indians, and subordinated women?

One reason America's ideals do not match reality is that they are general principles, not fixed rules of conduct. They derive from somewhat different experiences and philosophical traditions, and there are points at which they conflict. Equality and diversity, for instance, emphasize fairness and a full opportunity for all to partake of society's benefits, whereas liberty and individualism emphasize personal freedom and threats posed to it by political power. Conflict between these sets of beliefs is inevitable. Both are commendable, but the advancement of one set can come at some cost to the other. Take the issue of affirmative action. Proponents say that only through aggressive affirmative action programs will women and minorities receive the equal treatment in the job market to which they are entitled. Opponents say that aggressive affirmative action infringes unreasonably on the liberty of the employer and the initiative of the work force. Each side can say that it has America's ideals on its side, and no resort to logic can persuade either side that the opposing viewpoint should prevail.

Despite their inexact meanings, conflicting implications, and unfulfilled promise, the ideals of Americans have had a strong impact on the nation's politics. They still do. If racial, gender, ethnic, and other forms of intolerance constitute the sorriest chapter in the nation's history, the centuries-old struggle of Americans to create a more equal society is among the finest chapters. Few nations have battled so relentlessly against the insidious hatreds that stem from superficial human differences such as the color of one's skin. High ideals are more than mere abstractions. They are a source of human aspiration and, ultimately, of political and social change.

TABLE 1-1 Telling the American Story to Children
Americans' values and myths are reflected in their preferences in teaching children about the nation's history.

IN TEACHING THE AMERICAN STORY TO CHILDREN, HOW IMPORTANT IS THE FOLLOWING THEME?	ESSENTIAL/VERY IMPORTANT	SOMEWHAT IMPORTANT	SOMEWHAT UNIMPORTANT/ VERY UNIMPORTANT/ LEAVE IT OUT OF THE STORY
With hard work and perseverance, anyone can succeed in America.	83%	14%	4%
Our founders limited the power of government, so government would not intrude too much into the lives of its citizens.	74	19	8
America is the world's greatest melting pot in which people from different countries are united into one nation.	73	21	5
America's contribution is one of expanding freedom for more and more people.	71	22	6
Our nation betrayed its founding principles by cruel mistreatment of blacks and American Indians.	59	24	17
Our founders were part of a male-dominated culture that gave important roles to men while keeping women in the background.	38	28	35

Used by permission of the Survey of American Political Culture, James Davison Hunter and Carol Bowman, Directors, University of Virginia.

During the era of racial segregation in the South, this sign at the entrance to the Memphis public zoo meant that it was Tuesday—the only day that black people were allowed to go to the zoo. On the other six days of the week, the sign excluded black people from entering.

POLITICS: THE PROCESS OF DECIDING ON SOCIETY'S GOALS

Cultural ideals help shape what people expect from politics and how they conduct their politics. However, politics is more than the pursuit of shared ideals; it is also about getting one's own way. Commenting on the competitive nature of politics, Harold Lasswell described politics as the struggle over "who gets what, when, and how."[17]

Political conflict is rooted in two general conditions of society. One is *scarcity*. Society's resources are finite, but people's appetites are not. There is not enough wealth in even the richest of countries to satisfy everyone's desires. Conflict over the distribution of resources is the inevitable result. This conflict is evident, for example, in policy disputes over the financing of public schools. The quality of American schools varies widely. Affluent suburban districts have better schools and teachers than do poor inner-city districts, which reflects differences in each district's local tax base. In order to equalize quality, less affluent communities have pressed for the statewide funding of public schools, an approach that more affluent communities have resisted.

Differences in values are the other main source of political conflict. People see things in different ways. The right of abortion is freedom of choice to some and murder to others. People bring to politics a wide range of conflicting values—about abortion, about the environment, about the level of defense spending, about crime and punishment, about the poor, about the economy, about almost everything imaginable.

Politics in the United States is not the life-and-death struggle between opposing groups that typifies some countries, but there are many sources of contention. Perhaps no country has more competing interests than does the United States. Its settlement by people of many lands and religions, its enormous size and geographical diversity, and its economic complexity have made the United States a pluralistic nation. *This feature—competition for power among a great many interests of all kinds—is a major characteristic of American politics.*

It is a mistake to assume, however, that competition and conflict are the sum of politics. People must find agreeable ways of living together. Politics is not only a means of settling disputes, it is also a way of promoting collective interests. Politics is not solely about winners and losers, it is also about problem solving. Public safety and national defense are prime examples of people working together for an agreed-upon purpose. Public education is another. It reflects the older generation's willingness to tax itself for the benefit of the younger generation and ultimately for the benefit of society as a whole.

In sum, politics is a process that includes conflict *and* consensus, competition *and* cooperation. Accordingly, **politics** can be defined as simply the process through which a society makes its governing decisions.

politics The process through which a society makes its governing decisions.

Government, Power, Authority, and Policy

What is government? What is its purpose? It might be thought that the answer to these age-old questions is that government is a means by which people work together to solve their common problems. To be sure, government can serve the

Politics includes conflict and consensus. Women have had to struggle to be treated as equals in the workplace, but their efforts have been supported by public opinion and public policies.

collective good. But it can also serve the naked interests of a dominant faction, as in Stalin's Russia, Hitler's Germany, Saddam Hussein's Iraq, or Mullah Mohammed Omar's Afghanistan.

Government can be defined as the institutions, processes, and rules that are designed to facilitate control of a particular geographic area and its inhabitants.[18] There are only two things that all governments have in common. One is a capacity to raise revenues, usually in the form of taxation, to support governing activities. The other is coercion—the ability to compel inhabitants to abide by the government's rules. Without these capacities, a government would be unable to exercise control over the territory and the inhabitants it claims to rule.

Those individuals who decide issues are said to have **power,** a term that refers to the ability of persons or institutions to control policy decisions.[19] Power is a basic concept of politics. People who have sufficient power can impose taxes, permit or prohibit abortions, protect or take private property, provide or refuse welfare benefits, impose or relax trade barriers. With so much at stake, it is perhaps not surprising that power is widely sought and tightly guarded.

When power is exercised through the laws and institutions of government, the concept of authority applies. **Authority** can be defined as the recognized right of an individual, organization, or institution to make binding decisions. By this definition, government is not the only source of authority: parents have authority over their children; professors have authority over their students; firms have authority over their employees. However, government is a special case in that its authority is more encompassing in scope and more final in nature. Government's authority extends to all people in its geographical boundaries. It can be used to redefine the authority of the parent, the professor, or the firm. Government's authority is also the most coercive. It includes the power to arrest and imprison, even to punish by death those who violate its rules.

Government needs coercive power to ensure that its laws will be obeyed. Without this power, lawlessness would prevail, as it does in Colombia, where drug lords control large areas of the country. But government power itself can

government The institutions, processes, and rules that are specifically designed to facilitate control of a particular area and its inhabitants.

power The ability of persons or institutions to control policy.

authority The recognized right of an individual or institution to exercise power.

HOW THE UNITED STATES COMPARES

Americans as a Political People

By some standards, Americans are not a very political people. The United States ranks near the bottom, for example, in voter turnout. Barely half of Americans go to the polls in a presidential election, compared with 70 percent to 90 percent of adults in many democratic countries. In France, Italy, and Belgium, for example, turnout typically exceeds 80 percent.

In other ways, however, Americans are a highly political people. Americans have long believed in the exceptionalism of their political system. They have tended to believe that what works for them will also work for others and indeed that what works for Americans would be better for others than what they already have. In his book *World Politics and Personal Insecurity*, the political scientist Harold Lasswell wrote that "Americans who think about the problem of unifying the world tend to follow the precedent set in their own history." Presented after World War I with President Woodrow Wilson's plan for world peace based on American principles, the French premier Georges Clemenceau exclaimed, "This man Wilson with his Fourteen Points! The good Lord had only ten."

Given Americans' pride in their political system, it is not surprising that they attach great importance to political symbols. In Europe, national flags are not routinely displayed in public. In America, the flag is flown daily on government buildings and even on many private homes. The Pledge of Allegiance to the flag that is recited daily by American school children and the playing of the "Star-Spangled Banner" at public events have no equivalents in European nations. After the terrorist attacks on the World Trade Center and the Pentagon on September 11, 2001, American flags suddenly appeared on doors and vehicles throughout the country.

The distinctiveness of Americans' beliefs was evident in a five-nation Times Mirror survey that asked respondents whether they agreed with the statement, "I am very patriotic." As the accompanying graph shows, Americans ranked at the top; nearly 90 percent claimed to be highly patriotic. The disparity between the United States and Europe was particularly apparent among young adults. In Europe, young adults were substantially less likely to say they were patriotic than were older people. In the United States, the proportion of eighteen- to twenty-four-year-olds who said they were patriotic, 82 percent, was nearly as high as in other age groups.

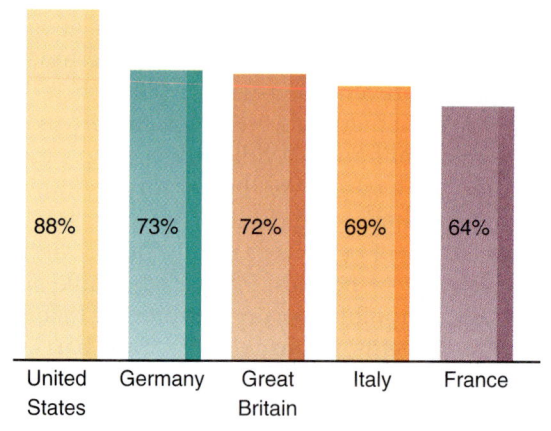

Percentage of people who say they are patriotic

United States	Germany	Great Britain	Italy	France
88%	73%	72%	69%	64%

be abused. In a perfect world, political power would be used in evenhanded ways for the benefit of all citizens. But the world is imperfect, and power can be used in selfish or cruel ways. "Power tends to corrupt, and absolute power tends to corrupt absolutely," was how Lord Acton described the problem.

Although no governing system can ensure that power will be applied fairly, the U.S. system strengthens this prospect through an elaborate set of *checks and balances*, including a division of authority among the executive, legislative, and judicial branches of government. Each branch acts as a check on the power of the others and balances their power by exercising power of its own. Many other democratic countries have no comparable fragmentation of power. *Extreme fragmentation of governing authority is a major characteristic of the American political system. This situation has profound implications for how politics is conducted, who wins out, and what policies result.*

Governments exercise authority through public policies. A **public policy** is a decision of government to pursue a course of action designed to produce an intended outcome. Policy can take the form of a particular program, such as Head Start, which provides disadvantaged preschool children with skills that will help them succeed once they start school. A policy can also be a set of actions that, taken together, are designed to achieve a particular objective. The war on terrorism that was launched in the aftermath of the September 11, 2001, attacks on the World Trade Center and the Pentagon, for example, was a policy that included military, intelligence, civil defense, and law enforcement activity. A policy can also be a decision not to take action, in which case the decision is meant to uphold the status quo. In any case, a public policy is a deliberate choice made by policymakers for the purpose of achieving a particular goal or set of goals.

public policy A decision of government to pursue a course of action designed to produce an intended outcome.

The Rules of the Game of Politics

The play of politics takes place according to rules that the participants accept. The rules establish the process by which power is exercised, define the legitimate uses of power, and establish the basis for allocating costs and benefits among the participants. In America, the rules of the game of politics include democracy, constitutionalism, and capitalism.

Democracy

Democracy is a set of rules designed to promote *self-government*. Democracy comes from the Greek words *demos,* which means "the people," and *kratis,* meaning "to rule." In simple terms, **democracy** is a form of government in which the people govern, either directly or through elected representatives (see Chapter 2).

democracy A form of government in which the people govern, either directly or through elected representatives.

Democratic government is based on the idea of the consent of the governed, which in practice has come to mean majority rule. The principle of majority rule, in turn, is based on the notion that the view of the many should prevail over the opinion of the few. Implicit in the notion is the possibility that today's minority may be tomorrow's majority, which means that issues and elections are rarely completely settled. The principle also represents a form of equality in that the vote of each citizen counts equally, a principle expressed by the phrase "one person, one vote." In practice, democracy in America works primarily through elections. There are other, more direct forms of democracy, such as the town meeting and the initiative, but the American system is mainly a representative one in which people's influence is based on their votes.

As Americans discovered during the 2000 campaign, even the one person, one vote principle is not inviolate. Al Gore received a half million more votes nationally than George W. Bush did but lost the election through the Electoral College. Each state has electoral votes equal in number to its representatives in

Democracy—the idea of a government of, for, and by the people—is an organizing principle of the American political system. In practice, democracy—and its accompanying feature, majoritarianism—is most clearly evident in elections when Americans through their votes choose their representatives.

Congress, and these votes are allocated to the candidate who wins its popular vote. The candidate with a majority of the electoral votes from all the states wins the presidency. Florida's electoral votes were decisive in the outcome of the 2000 election, and even in Florida, the one person, one vote principle did not hold completely. Thousands of Florida's ballots went uncounted because they could not be read by machine. After a failed effort to have them counted by hand, Gore conceded the election. Polls indicated that many Americans questioned the fairness of the election, but they accepted the outcome without violent protest. Bush's peaceful accession to the presidency is an indication of just how deeply Americans are committed to a system that operates by a set of rules rather than by force or dictate.

Constitutionalism

The concept of democracy implies that the will of the majority should prevail over the wishes of the minority. If taken to the extreme, however, this principle would allow a majority to ride roughshod over the minority. Such action could deprive the minority even of its liberty, a clearly unacceptable outcome. Individuals have rights and freedoms that cannot lawfully be denied by the majority.

Constitutionalism is a set of rules that restricts the lawful uses of power. In its original sense, constitutionalism in Western society referred to a government based on laws and constitutional powers.[20] **Constitutionalism** has since come

constitutionalism The idea that there are definable limits on the rightful power of a government over its citizens.

Free speech is a familiar aspect of constitutionalism. This anti–gun control rally took place in Austin, Texas.

to refer specifically to the idea that there are limits to the rightful power of government over citizens. In a constitutional system, officials govern according to law, and citizens have basic rights that government cannot take away or deny.[21] Free speech is an example. Government is prohibited by the First Amendment from interfering with the lawful exercise of free speech. No right is absolute, which means that some restrictions are allowed. No student, for example, has a First Amendment right to shout loudly and disrupt a classroom. Nevertheless, free speech is broadly protected by the courts. During the Vietnam War, thousands of demonstrations against U.S. policy took place without a single arrest and conviction for spoken words alone. There were instances where protesters were intimidated by police or jailed for destruction of property, but those who opposed the government's pursuit of the war had the opportunity to express their views freely without threat of being sent to prison. (Constitutionalism is discussed further in Chapters 2 through 5).

The constitutional tradition in the United States is at least as strong as the democratic tradition. In fact, *a defining characteristic of the American political system is its extraordinary emphasis on individual rights*. Issues that in other democracies would be resolved through elections and in legislative bodies are, in the United States, decided in courts of law as well. As Tocqueville noted, there is hardly a political issue in the United States that does not sooner or later become a judicial issue.[22] Abortion rights, nuclear power, busing, toxic waste disposal, and welfare services are among the scores of issues that in recent years have been played out in part as questions of rights to be settled through judicial action.

Aspects of the war on terrorism are sure to follow in this tradition. Opinion polls immediately after the September 11, 2001, bombings showed that most Americans were willing to grant government the authority to detain people who merely looked like they might be terrorists. Hundreds of people of Middle Eastern descent were in fact picked up and held for long periods by federal authorities. John Ashcroft, the attorney general of the United States, then asked Congress for explicit authority to detain noncitizens indefinitely based on mere suspicion of terrorism, a policy that would have reversed the long-standing legal principle that people in detention be brought before a judge on a specific charge within a relatively short period of time. Congress refused to grant this authority, but it did give law enforcement officials broad new powers of search and surveillance. Not all provisions of the USA Patriot Act of 2001 were controversial; for example, a provision that allowed for court-approved wiretaps of specific individuals as opposed to wiretaps of specific phone numbers was widely regarded as a necessary updating of wiretap policy. However, other provisions were opposed by civil liberties groups and by some members of Congress. Among these provisions were the authority to conduct secret searches as opposed to open searches, to conduct telephone and Internet surveillance with minimal judicial supervision as opposed to close supervision, and to conduct searches of medical, financial, and educational records without demonstrating probable cause that a crime had been committed. Some or all of these provisions are sure to be tested in the courts. (For a further discussion of the USA Patriot Act, see "Why Should I Care?")

Capitalism

Just as democracy and constitutionalism are systems of rules for allocating costs and benefits in American society, so too is capitalism. Societies have adopted alternative ways of organizing their economies. One way is *socialism*, which assigns government a large role in the ownership of the means of production, in regulating economic decisions, and in providing for the economic security of the individual. Under the form of socialism practiced in democratic countries, such as Sweden, the government does not attempt to manage the overall economy. Under *communism*, the government does take responsibility for overall management of the economy, including production quotas, supply points, and pricing.

Microsoft's Bill Gates speaks to an audience about his firm's international scope. Capitalism, the organizing principle of the American economic system, emphasizes marketplace competition and self-initiative. In recent years, this competition has centered on the challenges posed by new technologies and global markets.

Why Should I Care?

The USA Patriot Act of 2001: What Does Your Personal Security Mean?

The USA Patriot Act of 2001 was enacted less than two months after the September 11 terrorist attacks on the World Trade Center and the Pentagon. It was easily the most controversial domestic action taken by the U.S. government in the immediate aftermath of the bombings. The USA Patriot Act allows government, for example, to examine medical, financial, and educational records on the basis of a minimal standard of suspicion; to detain individuals for short periods without tangible evidence of wrongdoing; to deport noncitizens who have even minimal association with suspected terrorist groups; and to secretly search homes and offices in some instances.

According to its supporters, the legislative bill gave government tools with which to combat terrorism and thereby protect the lives of Americans. "We have the duty and the privilege to pass this historic legislation," said U.S. Representative James Sessenbrenner on the House floor. However, opponents argued that the bill included unwarranted incursions on individual rights. In expressing his intention to vote against the bill despite favoring many of its provisions, U.S. Senator Russ Feingold said that Congress fulfills its duty "only when it protects both the American people and the freedoms at the foundation of American society." Feingold argued that the bill gave law enforcement officials too much discretionary authority and could become a means of discriminating against Arabs and Muslims.

What's your view on the USA Patriot Act? Do you feel more or less secure because of it? How, primarily, do you define your security? Do you worry about becoming the victim of a terrorist attack? Or do you worry more about having your rights abused by officials engaged in the war on terrorism? Would you have the same opinion if, say, your religion or ethnicity was different than it is? How far are you willing to let government depart from normal protections of individual rights in order to combat the terrorist threat?

The legislation contains a sunset provision—after four years, the USA Patriot Act will expire unless Congress decides to extend it. Does this provision affect your opinion of the legislation? The Justice Department has promised not to abuse its new authority, saying that it will not target ethnic minorities or go on fishing expeditions into people's private lives. Does this verbal assurance affect your opinion of the legislation?

Capitalism is an alternative method for distributing economic costs and benefits. **Capitalism** holds that the government should interfere with the economy as little as possible. Free enterprise and self-reliance are the principles of capitalism. Firms are allowed to operate in a free and open marketplace, and individuals are expected to rely on their own initiative to establish their economic security. Firms decide what they will produce and the price they will charge for their goods and services while consumers decide on what they will buy at what price.

Like the rules of democracy and constitutionalism, the rules of capitalism are not neutral. If democracy responds to numbers and constitutionalism responds to individual rights, capitalism responds to wealth. Economic power is largely a function of accumulated wealth in the hands of either the individual or the firm. "Money talks" in a capitalist system, which means, among other things, that wealthier people will have by far the greater say in the distribution of costs and benefits through the economic system.

The United States does not have a purely capitalist system, because the government plays a role in regulating and stimulating the economy (see Chapter 15). The term *mixed economy* is used to define this hybrid form of economic system with its combination of socialist and capitalist elements. The United States

capitalism An economic system based on the idea that government should interfere with economic transactions as little as possible. Free enterprise and self-reliance are the collective and individual principles that underpin capitalism.

Figure 1–4
Average Amount of Taxes Paid by Citizens

Americans pay less in taxes than Europeans do.

Source: OECD, 2000. Percentages based on income taxes and employee contributions paid by average worker with two children.

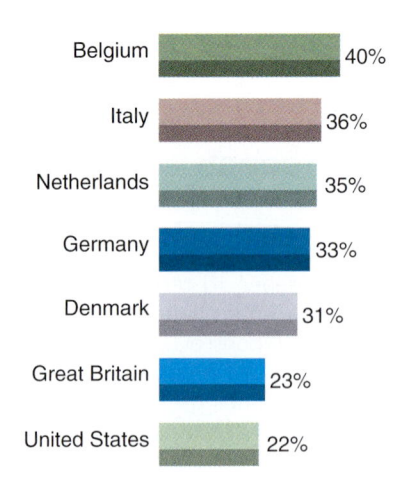

Country	Percentage
Belgium	40%
Italy	36%
Netherlands	35%
Germany	33%
Denmark	31%
Great Britain	23%
United States	22%

has more elements of the capitalist model and fewer elements of the socialist model than do the countries of Europe. Because of their strong tradition of individualism, Americans tend to restrict the scope of governmental action in the area of the economy. *A major characteristic of the American system is a relatively sharp distinction between what is political, and therefore to be decided in the public arena, and what is economic, and therefore to be settled in the private realm.*

For all practical purposes, this outlook places many kinds of choices, which in other countries are decided collectively, beyond the reach of political majorities in the United States. Although Americans complain that their taxes are too high, they are taxed at substantially lower rates than Europeans are (see Figure 1–4). This situation testifies to the extent to which Americans believe that wealth is more properly allocated through the economic marketplace than through government policy.

Theories of Power

The rules of the political game help decide who will exercise power and to what ends. The ultimate question about any political system is the issue of who governs. Is power widely shared and used for the benefit of the many? Or is power narrowly held and used to the advantage of the few? Although this entire book is in some respects an answer to these questions, it is useful here to consider what analysts have concluded about the American political system. Four broad theories predominate (see Table 1–2). None of them describes every aspect of American politics, but each has some validity.

Government by the People: Majoritarianism

majoritarianism The idea that the majority prevails not only in elections but also in determining policy.

A basic principle of democracy is the idea of majority rule. **Majoritarianism** is the notion that the majority prevails not only in the counting of votes but also in the determination of public policy.

Majorities do sometimes rule in America. Their power is perhaps most evident in those states that offer voters the opportunity to decide directly on policy initiatives, which then become law if they receive a majority vote. The majority's influence is also felt indirectly through the decisions of elected representatives.

TABLE 1-2 Theories of Power: Who Governs America?
There are four theories of power in America, each of which must be taken into account in any full explanation of the nation's policies.

THEORY	DESCRIPTION
Majoritarianism	Holds that numerical majorities determine issues of policy
Pluralism	Holds that policies are effectively decided through power wielded by special interests that dominate particular policy areas
Elitism	Holds that policy is controlled by a small number of well-positioned, highly influential individuals
Bureaucratic rule	Holds that policy is controlled by well-placed administrators within the government bureaucracy

When Congress in 1996 passed a welfare reform bill that included provisions requiring able-bodied welfare recipients to accept a job or job training after a two-year period or face a loss of their welfare benefits, it was acting in accord with the thinking of the majority of Americans who believe that employable individuals should be self-reliant. A more systematic assessment of the power of majorities is provided by Benjamin Page and Robert Shapiro's study of the relationship between majority opinions and more than three hundred policy issues in the period from 1935 to 1979. On major issues particularly, the researchers found that policy tended to change in the direction of change in majority opinion.[23]

Majorities do not always rule, however. In many policy areas, majority opinion is nonexistent or is ignored by policymakers. There are only a few issues at any moment that have the general public's attention and an even smaller number that it really cares about. Thus, majoritarianism cannot account for most of the policies of government. Other explanations are required.

Government by Groups: Pluralism

One of these explanations is provided by the theory of **pluralism,** which focuses on group activity and holds that many policies are effectively decided through power wielded by diverse (plural) interests.

Many policies are in fact more responsive to the interests of particular groups than to majority opinion. Agricultural subsidies, broadcast regulations, and corporate tax incentives are examples. In many cases, the general public has no real knowledge or opinion of issues that concern particular groups. For pluralists, the issue of whether interest-group politics serves the public good centers on whether it serves a diverse range of interests. Pluralists contend that it is misleading to view society only in terms of majorities that may or may not form around given issues. They see society as primarily a collection of separate interests. Farmers, broadcasters, and multinational corporations have different needs and desires and, according to the pluralist view, should have a disproportionate say in policies directly affecting them. Thus, as long as many groups have influence in their own area of interest, government is responding to the interests of most Americans. Pluralists such as Robert Dahl have argued that this is in fact the way the American political system operates most of the time.[24]

pluralism A theory of American politics that holds that society's interests are substantially represented through the activities of groups.

Political Culture
One People Out of Many

Hispanics: The New Largest "Minority"

Hispanic Americans were projected to surpass black Americans as the largest minority group early in the twenty-first century. Demographers were surprised when the 2000 census revealed that the change had already taken place. The census counted 33 million Hispanics compared with 31 million African Americans. The change came as some advocates were challenging the use of the term minority as a means of identifying a particular group of Americans; they contended that terms such as people of color were both more accurate and less stigmatizing. For the moment, however, minority remains an official designation for various government programs. America's five officially designated minorities are Hispanic Americans, African Americans, Asian Americans, Native Americans, and women (who, numerically, are a majority).

Although recent arrivals have helped make Hispanics the nation's largest minority group, Hispanics are one of the country's oldest ethnic groups. Some Hispanics are descendants of people who helped colonize the areas of California, Texas, Florida, New Mexico, and Arizona before those areas became part of the United States. The earliest Hispanics were here before the landing of the Mayflower.

As with all ethnic and racial groups, it is a mistake with Hispanics to use stereotypes that suggest its members have common backgrounds and characteristics. But Hispanics, like all other groups, have cultural tendencies that are somewhat distinctive. For example, the Hispanic culture is less individualistic and more community centered than is the northern European culture.

Hispanics are a growing political force in the American southwest. Like all groups that include a lot of new citizens, Hispanics have relatively low voting rates. But as they become further assimilated in American society, their turnout is expected to approach the national average, at which point they will hold the balance of political power in a number of states, including California.

Critics argue that pluralists wrongly assume that the public interest is somehow represented in a system that allows special interests, each in its own sphere, to set public policy (see Chapter 9). Any such outcome, they say, represents the triumph of minority rule over majority rule. Critics also say that many of society's interests are unable to compete effectively through group politics because of their lack of organization and money. They see a system biased in favor of a small number of powerful groups.

Government by a Few: Elitism

Elite theory offers in varying degrees a pessimistic view of the U.S. political system. **Elitism** holds that power in America is held by a small number of well-positioned, highly influential individuals. A leading proponent of elite theory was the sociologist C. Wright Mills, who argued that key policies are decided by an overlapping coalition of select leaders, including corporate executives, top military officers, and centrally placed public officials.[25] Other proponents of elite theory have defined the core group somewhat differently but their contention is the same: America is essentially run not by majorities or a plurality of groups but by a small number of well-placed and privileged individuals.

elitism The view that the United States is run essentially by a tiny elite (composed of wealthy or well-connected individuals) who control public policy through both direct and indirect means.

The Federal Reserve Board of Governors is a government body that through its interest-rate policies exerts a substantial influence on the American economy. The board meets in secrecy and is an example of the influence of political elites.

Proponents of elite theory differ, however, in the extent to which they believe elites control policy for their own purposes. Some theorists, including G. William Domhoff, hold the view that elites operate behind the scenes in order to manipulate government for selfish ends.[26] Other theorists argue that some elites, at least, seek to promote the general interest. Although elites always prefer stability to disruptive change, some pursue policies intended to benefit society as a whole. One such view holds that elites compete for power through the vote and that the electorate has at least some influence on the policy choices made by the winning side.[27]

It is clearly true that certain policies and governing processes are effectively controlled by a tiny circle of influential people. The nation's monetary policy, for example, is set by the decisions of the Federal Reserve Board ("The Fed"), which meets in secrecy and decides the interest rates that banks pay for the loans they receive from the Federal Reserve. These rates in turn affect the interest rates that banks charge their customers. The Fed is very responsive to the concerns of bankers. What is less clear is the Fed's responsiveness to the concerns of consumers.

Government by Administrators: Bureaucratic Rule

A fourth theory holds that power resides in large government bureaucracies in the hands of career administrators. The leading proponent of the theory of **bureaucratic rule** was the German sociologist Max Weber, who argued that all large organizations tend toward the bureaucratic form, with the effect that decision-making power devolves to administrators whose experience and knowledge of policy issues exceeds that of elected officials.[28] Another sociologist, Roberto Michels, propounded the "iron law of oligarchy," concluding that power inevitably gravitates toward experienced administrators at the top of large-scale organizations, even in the case of organizations that aim to be governed democratically.[29]

Bureaucratic politics raises the possibility of a large, permanent government run by unaccountable administrators. Elections come and go, but the

bureaucratic rule The tendency of large-scale organization to develop into the bureaucratic form, with the effect that administrators make key policy decisions.

Figure 1–5

The American Political System This book's chapters are organized within a political system's framework.

CONSTITUTIONAL FRAMEWORK

Includes provisions for limited government (e.g., checks and balances), representative government, civil liberties, and civil rights

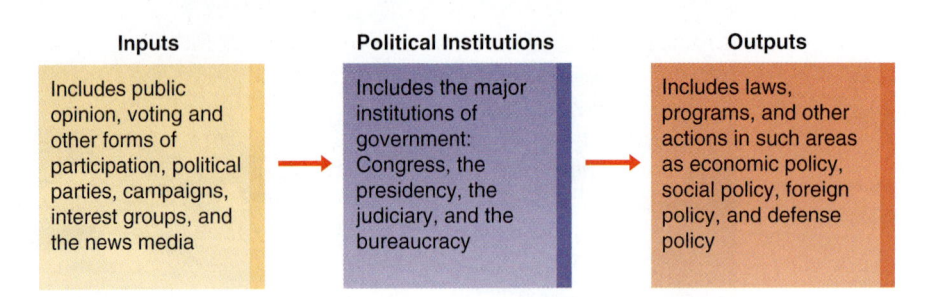

Inputs	Political Institutions	Outputs
Includes public opinion, voting and other forms of participation, political parties, campaigns, interest groups, and the news media	Includes the major institutions of government: Congress, the presidency, the judiciary, and the bureaucracy	Includes laws, programs, and other actions in such areas as economic policy, social policy, foreign policy, and defense policy

bureaucrats who staff executive agencies stay on and on. Government could not function without them, but in most cases, they are not instruments of the majority. Bureaucrats, in fact, make many key policy decisions in areas as diverse as the environment, health, and law enforcement (see Chapter 13).

Who Does Govern?

The perspective of this book is that each of these theories—majoritarianism, pluralism, elitism, and bureaucratization—must be taken into account in any full explanation of politics and power in America. Some policies are decided by majority influence, whereas others reflect the influence of special interests, administrators, and elites. The challenge is to distinguish the situations where each of these influence patterns predominates.

THE CONCEPT OF A POLITICAL SYSTEM AND THIS BOOK'S ORGANIZATION

As the foregoing discussion suggests, American government is based on a great many related parts. For this reason, it is useful to regard these components as constituting a **political system.** The parts are separate but they connect with one another, affecting how each performs. The political scientist David Easton, who was a pioneer in this conception of politics, said that it makes little sense to study political relations piecemeal when they are, in reality, "interrelated."[30]

political system The various components of American government. The parts are separate, but they connect with each other, affecting how each performs.

The complexity of government has kept political scientists from developing a fully explanatory model of the political system, but the concept of politics as a system is useful for instructional purposes. The concept emphasizes the actual workings of government rather than its institutional structures alone. To view politics as a system is to emphasize the connections between the parts and how change in one area affects the others. It is a dynamic conception in that the political system is constantly changing in response to new conditions and to the interplay of its various parts. And all these changes take place for a purpose. The political system is the mechanism through which society is governed.

The political-system approach characterizes this book, beginning with the organization of its chapters (see Figure 1–5). The political system operates against the backdrop of a constitutional framework that defines how power is to be obtained and exercised. This structure is the focus of the opening chapters, which examine how the Constitution defines, in theory and practice, the institutions of government and the rights of individuals. *Inputs* are another part of the political system; these are the demands that people and organizations place on government and the support they provide for institutions, leaders, and policies. These inputs are explored in chapters on public opinion, political participation, political parties, and election campaigns, interest groups, and the news media. The functioning of governing officials is then addressed in chapters on the nation's *political institutions:* Congress, the presidency, the federal bureaucracy, and the federal courts. Some of the discussion in these chapters is devoted simply to describing these institutions, but most of the discussion explores their relationships and how their actions are affected by inputs and the constitutional system in which they operate. Throughout the book, but particularly in the closing chapters, attention is given to the political system's *outputs:* policy decisions that are binding on society. These decisions, which are made by political institutions in respose to inputs, affect American life in many areas, including the economy, the environment, social welfare, education, foreign affairs, and national defense.

The chapters are collectively designed to convey a reliable body of knowledge that will enable the reader to think broadly and systematically about the nature of the American political system. To assist in this process, this chapter has identified five encompassing tendencies of American politics that will be examined more closely in later chapters. The United States has

- Enduring cultural ideals that are its people's common bond and a source of their political goals
- Extreme fragmentation of governing authority that is based on an elaborate system of checks and balances
- Many competing interests, which are the result of the nation's great size, population diversity, and economic complexity
- Strong emphasis on individual rights, which is a consequence of the nation's political traditions
- A relatively sharp separation of the political and economic spheres, which has the effect of placing many economic issues outside the reach of political majorities

Underlying this book's concern with the broad patterns of the American political system is a question that must be asked of any democracy: what is the relationship of the people to their government? The answer to this question is the foundation not only of a reasonable assessment of the state of American democracy but also of good citizenship. Responsible citizenship depends finally on an informed perspective, on a recognition of how difficult it is to govern effectively and yet how important it is to try. It cannot be said too often that the issue of governing is the most difficult issue facing any society. Nor can it be said too often that governing is a quest and a search, not a resolved issue. The Constitution's opening phrase, "We, the People," is a call to Americans to join that quest. E. E. Schattschneider said it clearly: "In the course of centuries, there has come a great deal of agreement about what democracy is, but nobody has a monopoly on it and the last word has not been spoken."[31]

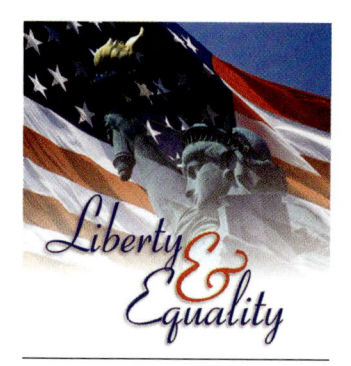

What's Your Opinion?

Scarcity and Cultural Values

In 1940, Senator Kenneth Wherry soberly exclaimed, "With God's help, we will lift Shanghai up and up, ever up, until it is just like Kansas City." Like many Americans before and since, Wherry assumed that our political values could thrive anywhere else in the world. In actuality, however, liberty and equality have tended to flourish only in societies where wealth is substantial and widely shared. In poor or stratified societies, people differ greatly in their rights and privileges, a condition that is often enforced by authoritarian government. Why do American values not flourish in poorer societies? Does scarcity make people selfish and fearful to the point where the few who have more feel a need to repress the many who have less? Could liberty and equality have taken deep root in the United States several centuries ago if not for the New World's natural abundance?

The U.S. government at times has pressured poorer countries that have repressive regimes to have greater respect for their people's rights. How would you rate the likely success of that strategy in comparison with one that focused on the economic development of such countries?

SUMMARY

The United States is a nation that was formed on a set of ideals. Liberty and equality are the foremost of these ideals, which also include the principles of popular consent, individualism, diversity, and unity. These ideals became Americans' common bond and today are the basis of their political culture. Although they are mythic, inexact, and conflicting, these ideals have had a powerful effect on what generation after generation of Americans has tried to achieve politically for themselves and others.

Self Quiz

Politics is the process by which it is determined whose values will prevail in society. The basis of politics is conflict over scarce resources and competing values. Those who have power win out in this conflict and are able to control governing authority and policy choices. In the United States, no one faction controls all power and policy. Majorities govern on some issues, while groups, elites, and bureaucrats each govern on other issues.

The play of politics in the United States takes place through rules of the game that include democracy, constitutionalism, and capitalism. Democracy is rule by the people, which in practice refers to a representative system of government in which the people rule through their elected officials. Constitutionalism refers to rules that limit the rightful power of government over citizens. Capitalism is an economic system based on a free market principle that allows the government only a limited role in determining how economic costs and benefits will be allocated.

KEY TERMS

authority
bureaucratic rule
capitalism
constitutionalism
democracy
diversity
elitism

equality
government
individualism
liberty
majoritarianism
pluralism
political culture

political system
politics
popular consent
power
public policy
unity

SUGGESTED READINGS

Dahl, Robert. *On Democracy*. New Haven, Conn.: Yale University Press, 1998. A handbook on democracy by a leading advocate of pluralism.

DeLaet, Debra L. *U.S. Immigration Policy in an Age of Rights*. Westport, Conn.: Praeger Publishers, 2000. Analysis of the impact of civil rights action on the changes in U.S. immigration policy in recent decades.

Domhoff, G. William. *Who Rules America? Power and Politics in the Year 2000*. Mountain View, Calif.: Mayfield Publishing, 1998. A critical assessment of American government by a leading proponent of elite theory.

Eck, Diana L. *A New Religious America*. San Francisco: HarperSanFrancisco, 2001. A look at how the 1965 change in immigration law has altered religion and other aspects of American life.

Lipset, Seymour Martin. *American Exceptionalism: A Double-Edged Sword*. New York: Norton, 1996. Argues that Americans' tendency to view society in idealized terms is a source of both alienation and progress.

McElroy, John Harmon. *American Beliefs: What Keeps a Big Country and a Diverse People United*. Chicago: I. R. Dee, 1999. An examination of the role of beliefs in Americans' political identity.

Schmidt, Ronald. *Language Policy and Identity Politics in the United States*. Philadelphia: Temple University Press, 2000. A critical assessment of language policy and its role in Americans' identity.

LIST OF WEBSITES

http://www.conginst.org
A site that provides up-to-date survey data on the American political culture.

http://www.loc.gov
The Library of Congress website; it provides access to over seventy million historical and contemporary U.S. documents.

http://www.stateline.org
A University of Richmond/Pew Charitable Trusts site dedicated to providing citizens with information on major policy issues.

http://www.tocqueville.org
Includes biographical and other references to Alexis de Tocqueville and his writings.

2

The people must be governed by a majority, with whom all power resides. But how is the sense of this majority to be obtained?

Fisher Ames (1788)[1]

Constitutional Democracy:
Promoting Liberty and Self-Government

On the night of June 17, 1972, a security guard at the Watergate apartment-office complex in Washington, D.C., noticed that the latch on a basement door had been taped open. He called the police, who apprehended five burglars inside the National Democratic Party headquarters. As it turned out, the men had links to Republican President Richard Nixon's Committee to Re-elect the President.

Nixon called the incident "bizarre" and falsely denied that anyone on his staff had had anything to do with the break-in. The Watergate break-in, however, was just one incident in an orchestrated campaign of "dirty tricks" designed to ensure Nixon's reelection. Funded by illegal contributions and conducted through the CIA, IRS, FBI, Secret Service, and Nixon's own operatives (called the White House "plumbers"), the dirty-tricks campaign extended to wiretaps, tax audits, and burglaries of Nixon's political opponents (the "enemies list"), who included journalists and anti-war activists in addition to Democrats. Nixon told his close advisors: "I want you all to stonewall it, let them [the Watergate burglars] plead the Fifth Amendment, cover up, or anything else."[2]

Although the Nixon White House managed for a time to hide the truth (in one ploy, the president's assistants asked the CIA to tell the FBI to stop the Watergate investigation on fictitious "national security" grounds), the facts of the dirty-tricks campaign gradually became known. In early 1974 the House Judiciary Committee began impeachment proceedings, helped along, ironically, by Nixon's own words. During Senate hearings, a White House assistant revealed that Nixon had tape-recorded all his telephone calls and personal conversations in the Oval Office. At first Nixon refused to release the tapes, but then made public what he claimed were "all the relevant" ones. The House Judiciary Committee demanded additional tapes, as did the special prosecutor who had been appointed to investigate criminal aspects of the Watergate affair. In late July the Supreme Court of the United States, which included four justices appointed by Nixon, unanimously ordered the president to supply sixty-four additional tapes. Two weeks later, on August 9, 1974, Richard Nixon, citing a loss of political support, resigned from office, the first president in U.S. history to do so.

Nixon's downfall was owed in no small measure to the handiwork, two centuries earlier, of the writers of the Constitution. They were well aware that power could never be entrusted to the goodwill of leaders. "If angels were to govern men," James Madison wrote in *Federalist* No. 51, "neither external nor internal controls on government would be necessary." Madison's point, of course, was that leaders are not angels and, as mere mortals, are subject to temptation and vice, including a lust for power—hence the Framers' insistence on constitutional checks on power, as when they gave Congress the authority to impeach and remove a president from office.

The writers of the U.S. Constitution were intent on protecting *liberty* and therefore sought to restrict the use of political power. Yet they also wanted a government that would allow the majority to rule. The first objective was **limited government:** a

The Senate Judiciary Committee holds hearings on allegations of illegal acts by President Richard Nixon. The congressional investigation led to Nixon's resignation.

limited government A government that is subject to strict limits on its lawful uses of powers, and hence on its ability to deprive people of their liberty.

self-government The principle that the people are the ultimate source and proper beneficiary of governing authority; in practice, a government based on majority rule.

government that is subject to strict limits on its lawful uses of power. The second objective was **self-government:** a government that is subject to the will of the people as expressed through the preferences of a majority. Self-government requires that the voters' preferences find their way into public policy in a substantial and timely way. However, limited government requires restraints on the majority as a way of protecting the rights and interests of the minority. These considerations resulted in a constitution that has provision for majority rule but also has built-in restrictions on the exercise of majority power.

This chapter describes how the principles of self-government and limited government are embodied in the Constitution and explains the tension between them. The chapter also indicates how these principles have been modified in practice in the course of American history. The main points of this chapter are the following:

- *America during the colonial period developed traditions of limited government and self-government.* These traditions were rooted in governing practices, philosophy, and cultural values.

- *The Constitution provides for limited government mainly by defining lawful powers and by dividing those powers among competing institutions.* The Constitution, with its Bill of Rights, also prohibits government from infringing on individual rights. Judicial review is an additional safeguard of limited government.

- *The Constitution in its original form provided for self-government mainly through indirect systems of popular election of representatives.* The Framers' theory of self-government was based on the notion that political power must be separated from immediate popular influences if sound policies are to result.

- *The idea of popular government—in which the majority's desires have a more direct and immediate impact on governing officials—has gained strength since the nation's beginning.* Originally, the House of Representatives was the only institution subject to direct vote of the people. This mechanism has been extended to other institutions and, through primary elections, even to the nomination of candidates for public office.

BEFORE THE CONSTITUTION: THE COLONIAL AND REVOLUTIONARY EXPERIENCES

Early Americans' admiration for limited government was based partly on their English heritage. Unlike other European nations of the eighteenth century, England did not have an absolute monarchy. British courts had developed a system of precedent known as "common law," which guaranteed trial by jury and due process of law as safeguards of life, liberty, and particularly property. These rights were defended by the courts and ordinarily respected by the king and Parliament.

This tradition of limited government was evident in the American colonies. In each colony there was a right to trial by jury. There was also freedom of expression, although of a narrow kind. Religious freedom, for example, was not granted by all the colonies. Nevertheless, religious oppression of the kind that was commonplace in Europe was rare. There was also a degree of self-government in all the colonies. Each had an elected assembly, and although the assemblies were usually controlled by wealthier interests, they acted as representative bodies and grew increasingly powerful as the number of settlers increased.

"The Rights of Englishmen"

The Revolutionary War was partly a rebellion against England's failure to respect its own tradition of limited government in the colonies. Many of the colonial charters had conferred upon Americans "the rights of Englishmen," but British kings and ministers showed progressively less respect for this guarantee as time went on. The period after the French and Indian War (1755–1763) was a turning point in the relationship between the colonists and Britain. Until then the colonists had viewed themselves as loyal subjects of the Crown, and although there had been occasional disputes, few voices argued for independence. In fact, colonists had fought alongside British soldiers to drive the French out of Canada and the Western territories.

At the end of the French and Indian War, however, Britain imposed burdensome taxes on the colonists. The war with France, which had also been waged in Europe, had created a severe financial crisis for the British government, which looked to the increasingly prosperous colonies for revenues. The colonies were not accustomed to paying taxes to the British. The practice was for Britain to raise its revenues from tariffs on imports and exports while the colonists kept any tax revenues they raised. But the British Parliament in 1765

Historical Background

Life in colonial America was hard and sometimes dangerous. Colonial men often carried guns when traveling alone or with their families.

levied a stamp tax on colonial newspapers and business documents, disrupting commerce and public communication. Because the colonists were not represented in the British Parliament that had imposed the tax, the colonial pamphleteer James Otis declared that the Stamp Act violated the fundamental rights of the colonists as "British subjects and men." "No taxation without representation" became a rallying cry for the colonists.

Although Parliament backed down and repealed the Stamp Act, it then passed the Townshend Act, which imposed taxes on all paper, glass, lead, and tea entering the colonies. When the colonists protested, King George III sent additional British troops to America and interfered with colonial legislatures. These actions served only to arouse the colonists further. England then tried to placate the Americans by repealing the Townshend duties except for a nominal tea tax, which Britain retained in order to display its authority. The colonists viewed the tea tax as a petty insult, and in the "Boston Tea Party" of December 1773, a small band of patriots disguised as Native Americans boarded an English ship in Boston Harbor and dumped its cargo of tea overboard.

In 1774, the colonists met in Philadelphia at the First Continental Congress to define their demands of the British Crown: they called for free assembly, an end to the British military occupation, their own councils for the imposition of taxes, and trial by local juries. (British authorities had resorted to shipping "troublemakers" back to London for trial.) King George III refused their petition, and in 1775, British troops and colonial minutemen clashed at Lexington and Concord. Eight colonists died on the Lexington green in what became known as "the shot heard 'round the world."

Within a year, sporadic acts of defiance had become a full-scale revolution. In a pamphlet called *Common Sense,* which sold 120,000 copies in its first three months, Thomas Paine claimed that all of Europe was rife with political oppression and that America was humanity's last hope of liberty. "Freedom has been hunted around the globe.... Receive the fugitive, and prepare in time an asylum for mankind."

Citizenship
Getting Involved, Making A Difference

Personal Commitment

Effective citizen action begins with a question: what goal do I care enough about to try to make it a reality?

The question is easy enough, but many people go through life without having asked and answered it. They are citizens in a constricted sense. They may vote. They may even donate money on occasion to a political cause. But they never get deeply enough involved in the life of the society to leave a lasting mark on it. The citizens who make a larger contribution to their community are those who commit themselves to action on a cause in which they believe. They are citizens in the fullest sense of the word.

These two types of citizenship were clearly evident when terrorists bombed the World Trade Center and the Pentagon on September 11, 2001. Some Americans rushed to help the victims. Many people donated blood. Others sent money and clothing to the victims' families. Thousands from around the country went to the site of the World Trade Center to see whether they could help in the rescue effort. Other Americans worked within their own communities to promote tolerance for those of Middle Eastern descent and the Muslim faith. Still others helped local schools and organizations develop plans to prepare for and respond to future terrorist acts. Yet the war on terrorism for most Americans was something to be seen on television rather than something to be acted on directly, despite the great concern many of them felt about the issue.

So it goes, issue after issue. Most people sit on the sidelines, forgoing the opportunity to contribute substantially to public life. Because the United States has a federal system of government and a strong tradition of local government and free association, there are literally endless opportunities for people to get actively involved in politics and public affairs. Citizens interested in working on political campaigns can join local, congressional, statewide, and presidential campaigns. Volunteers interested in community affairs can choose from all sorts of local organizations, from churches to schools to community groups. The Internet now offers countless national and international organizations in which to participate actively. For example, the international campaign to ban land mines, for which Jody Williams won the 1997 Nobel Peace Prize, began when she used the Internet from her home to organize the effort.

The difference that committed activists can make was never more in evidence than at the founding of the United States. Even though the Revolutionary War eventually enlisted a large number of participants, agitators such as Sam Adams in Boston and Patrick Henry in Virginia awakened other Americans to colonial injustices. Then, during the debate over ratification of the Constitution, the *Federalist* essays of Madison, Hamilton, and Jay helped sway opinion in favor of the proposed change in the nation's government.

Activists are the defining spirit of the community, whether that community consists of the people of the world, the citizens of a nation, the residents of a local community, or the students on a college campus. If you haven't been active to this point, what might you do now to get involved?

The Declaration of Independence

Although grievances against Britain were the immediate cause of the American Revolution, ideas about the proper form of government were also on the colonists' minds. A century earlier, the English philosopher John Locke (1632–1704) had written that government must be restrained in its powers if it is to serve the common good. In his *Two Treatises of Government* (1690), Locke

Drafting the Declaration of Independence, a painting by J. L. Ferris. Benjamin Franklin, John Adams, and Thomas Jefferson (standing) drafted the historic document. Jefferson was the principal author; he inserted the inspirational words about liberty, equality, and self-government. Jealous of the attention that Jefferson later received, Adams declared that there wasn't anything in Jefferson's words that others hadn't already said.

inalienable (natural) rights
Those rights that persons theoretically possessed in the state of nature, prior to the formation of governments. These rights, including those of life, liberty, and property, are considered inherent and, as such, are inalienable. Since government is established by people, government has the responsibility to preserve these rights.

advanced the liberal principle that people have **inalienable rights** (or **natural rights**), including those of life, liberty, and property. In Locke's view, such rights belonged to people in their natural state before governments were created. When people agreed to come together (or, in Locke's term, entered into a "social contract") in order to have the protection that only organized government could provide, their natural rights were neither taken from them by government nor surrendered by them to government. If the government protected their natural rights, they were obliged to obey it, but if the government failed to protect their rights, they could rightfully rebel against it.[3]

Locke's ideas inspired a generation of American leaders.[4] The notion that people had natural and inalienable rights was a central theme of Paine's *Common Sense,* as was his claim that oppression justified revolution. Thomas Jefferson declared that Locke "was one of the three greatest men that ever lived, without exception," and Jefferson paraphrased Locke's ideas in key passages of the Declaration of Independence:

> We hold these truths to be self-evident, that all men are created equal, that they are endowed by their Creator with certain unalienable rights, that among these are life, liberty and the pursuit of happiness.
>
> That to secure these rights, governments are instituted among men, deriving their just powers from the consent of the governed.
>
> That whenever any form of government becomes destructive of these ends, it is the right of the people to alter or to abolish it, and to institute a new government.

This is a portion of Thomas Jefferson's handwritten draft of the Declaration of Independence, a formal expression of America's governing ideals.

The Declaration was a call to revolution rather than a framework for a new form of government, but the ideas it contained—liberty, equality, individual rights, self-government, lawful powers—were to become the basis, eleven years later, for the Constitution of the United States. (The Declaration of Independence and the Constitution are reprinted in their entirety in the appendices of this book.)

The Articles of Confederation

The first government of the United States was based, not on the Constitution, but on the Articles of Confederation. The Articles were adopted during the Revolutionary War and created a very weak national government that was subordinate to the states. This arrangement stemmed from the colonial experience. The colonies had always been governed separately, and their people considered themselves Virginians, New Yorkers, or Pennsylvanians as much as they thought of themselves as Americans. They naturally preferred a government that was constitutionally derived from the states. Moreover, they were leery of a powerful central government. The American Revolution was sparked by grievances against the arbitrary policies of King George III, and Americans were in no mood to replace him with a strong national authority of their own making.

Under the Articles of Confederation, each state retained its "sovereignty, freedom and independence." There was a national Congress, but its members were appointed and paid by their respective state governments. Each of the thirteen states had one vote in Congress, and the agreement of nine states was required to pass legislation. Moreover, any state could block constitutional change: the Articles of Confederation could be amended only by unanimous approval of the states.

The American union held together during the Revolutionary War out of necessity: the states had either to cooperate or to surrender to the British. But once the war ended, the states felt free to go their separate ways. Several states sent representatives abroad to negotiate their own separate trade agreements with foreign nations. New Hampshire, with its eighteen-mile coastline, even established its own navy. In a melancholy letter to Thomas Jefferson, George Washington wondered whether the United States deserved to be called a nation.

Congress was expected to provide for the nation's defense and establish the basis for a general economy, but the Articles of Confederation did not give it the powers necessary to achieve these goals. The Articles prohibited Congress from interfering in the states' commerce policies, and the states were soon engaged in ruinous trade wars. The Articles also denied to Congress the power to tax, and consequently it had no money with which to build a navy and hire an army. Its plight was dramatically evident soon after the Revolutionary War when unpaid army units mutinied and marched on Congress, whose members fled in panic to another location.

Shays's Rebellion: A Nation Dissolving

By 1784, the nation was unraveling. Congress was so weak that its members often did not bother to attend its sessions.[5] Finally, in late 1786, a revolt in western Massachusetts prompted leading Americans to conclude that the country's government had to be changed. A ragtag army of two thousand farmers, armed with pitchforks, marched on county courthouses to prevent foreclosures on their land and cattle. Many of the farmers were veterans of the Revolutionary War; their leader, Daniel Shays, had been a captain in the Revolutionary army. They had been given assurances during the Revolution that their land, which lay fallow because they were away at war, would not be confiscated for reasons of unpaid debts and taxes. They had also been told that they would get the back pay owed to them for their military service (Congress had run out of money during the Revolution). Instead, no back pay was received, and heavy new taxes were placed on farms. Many farmers faced loss of their property and even jail because they could not pay their creditors.

Although many Americans, including Jefferson, sympathized with the farmers, Shays's Rebellion scared propertied interests, and they called on the governor of Massachusetts to put down the revolt. He asked Congress for help, but it had no army to send.[6] The governor finally raised enough money to hire a militia that put down the rebellion, but Shays's Rebellion made it clear that

Historical Background

County courthouses in Massachusetts in 1786 were the scenes of brawls between angry farmers and citizens who supported the state's attempts to foreclose on farmers' property because of unpaid debts. The violence of Shays's Rebellion convinced many political leaders that anarchy was spreading and that a more powerful national government was required to stop it.

Congress and the army were weak and that mob action was increasing. Fear that anarchy would overtake the country was widespread. At Virginia's urging, five states met at the Annapolis Convention in late 1786 to address the crisis. They did not reach agreement on a solution but urged Congress to authorize a constitutional convention of all the states that would be held the following spring in Philadelphia. Congress did authorize the convention but placed a restriction on it: the delegates were to meet for "the sole and express purpose of revising the Articles of Confederation."

NEGOTIATING TOWARD A CONSTITUTION

The delegates to the Philadelphia constitutional convention ignored the instructions of Congress. They drafted a plan for an entirely new form of government. Prominent delegates (among them George Washington, Benjamin Franklin, and James Madison) were determined from the outset to establish an American nation built on a strong central government.

The Great Compromise: A Two-Chamber Congress

Debate at the constitutional convention of 1787 began over a plan put forward by the Virginia delegation, which was dominated by strong nationalists. The **Virginia Plan** (also called the large-state plan) called for a two-chamber Congress that would have supreme authority in all areas "in which the separate states are incompetent," particularly defense and interstate trade. The Virginia Plan also provided that the states would have numerical representation in Congress in proportion to their populations or tax contributions. Either way, representatives of the small states would be greatly outnumbered. Small states such as Delaware and Rhode Island would be allowed only one representative in the lower chamber, while large states such as Massachusetts and Virginia would have more than a dozen.

Not surprisingly, the Virginia Plan was roundly condemned by delegates from the smaller states. They rallied around a counterproposal made by New Jersey's William Paterson. The **New Jersey Plan** (also called the small-state plan) called for a stronger national government with the power to tax and to regulate commerce among the states; in most other respects, however, the Articles would remain in effect. Congress would have a single chamber in which each state, large or small, would have a single vote.

The debate over the New Jersey and Virginia Plans dragged on for weeks before the delegates reached what is now known as the **Great Compromise.** It provided for a bicameral (two-chamber) Congress: the House of Representatives would be apportioned among the states on the basis of population and the Senate on the basis of an equal number of votes (two) for each state. The small states would never have agreed to join a union in which their vote was always weaker than that of large states,[7] a fact reflected in Article V of the Constitution: "No state, without its consent, shall be deprived of its equal suffrage in the Senate."

The North-South Compromise: The Issue of Slavery

The separate interests of the states were also the basis for a second major agreement: the **North-South Compromise** over economic issues. The South had a slave-based agricultural economy, and its delegates feared that the North, which had a stronger manufacturing sector, would gain a numerical majority in Congress and then proceed to enact unfair tax policies. If Congress levied high import tariffs on finished goods from foreign nations in order to protect domestic manufacturers and placed heavy export tariffs on agricultural goods, the burden of financing the new government would fall mainly on the South. Its delegates also worried that northern representatives in Congress might tax or even bar the importation of slaves.

After extended debate, a compromise was reached. Congress was to be prohibited by the Constitution from taxing exports but could tax imports. In addition, Congress would be prohibited from passing laws to end the slave trade until 1808. The South also gained a constitutional provision requiring each state to return runaway slaves to their state of origin. A final bargain was the infamous "Three-fifths Compromise": for purposes of both taxation and representation in Congress, five slaves were to be considered the equivalent of three white people; in effect, a slave was to be counted as three-fifths of a human being.

Virginia (large-state) Plan A constitutional proposal for a strong Congress with two chambers, both of which would be based on numerical representation, thus granting more power to the larger states.

New Jersey (small-state) Plan A constitutional proposal for a strengthened Congress but one in which each state would have a single vote, thus granting a small state the same legislative power as a large state.

Great Compromise The agreement at the constitutional convention to create a two-chamber Congress with the House apportioned by population and the Senate apportioned equally by state.

North-South Compromise The agreement over economic and slavery issues that enabled northern and southern states to settle differences that threatened to defeat the effort to draft a new constitution.

The Constitution was written in Philadelphia during the summer of 1787 in the East Room of the Old Pennsylvania State House, where the Declaration of Independence had been signed a decade earlier. George Washington presided over the Constitutional Convention, but in this role, he was expected to remain neutral during the debate and thus he played a less active part in shaping the Constitution than did some other delegates.

Although the Philadelphia convention has been criticized for the compromise over slavery, the southern states' dependence on slavery was a formidable obstacle to union. Northern states had no economic use for forced labor and had few slaves, whereas southern states had based their economies on large slave populations (see Figure 2–1). John Rutledge of South Carolina asked during the convention debate whether the North regarded southerners as "fools." Southern delegates declared that they would bolt the convention and form their own union rather than join one that prohibited slavery.

A Strategy for Ratification

The compromises over slavery and the structure of the Congress took up most of the four months that the convention was in session. Some of the other issues, such as the structure and powers of the federal judiciary, were the subject of surprisingly little debate.

There remained a final issue, however: would those Americans not at the convention share the delegates' opinion of the Constitution? The delegates realized that ratification was not a sure thing. Congress had not authorized a wholesale restructuring of the federal government and had created a barrier to any such plan. In authorizing the Philadelphia convention, Congress had stated that any proposed change in the Articles would have to be "agreed to in Congress" and then "confirmed by [all of] the states." The delegates recognized that if they followed this procedure, which required unanimity, the Constitution had no chance of ratification. Rhode Island had refused even to send a delegation to the convention. In a bold move, the delegates established their own ratifying process. They instructed Congress to submit the document directly to the states, where it would become law after being approved by at least nine states in special ratifying conventions of popularly elected delegates. It was a masterful strategy: there was little hope that all thirteen state legislatures would approve the Constitution, but nine states through conventions might be persuaded to ratify

Figure 2-1
African Americans as a Percentage of State Population, 1790.
At the writing of the Constitution, African Americans (most of whom were slaves) were concentrated in the southern states.
Source: U.S. Bureau of the Census.

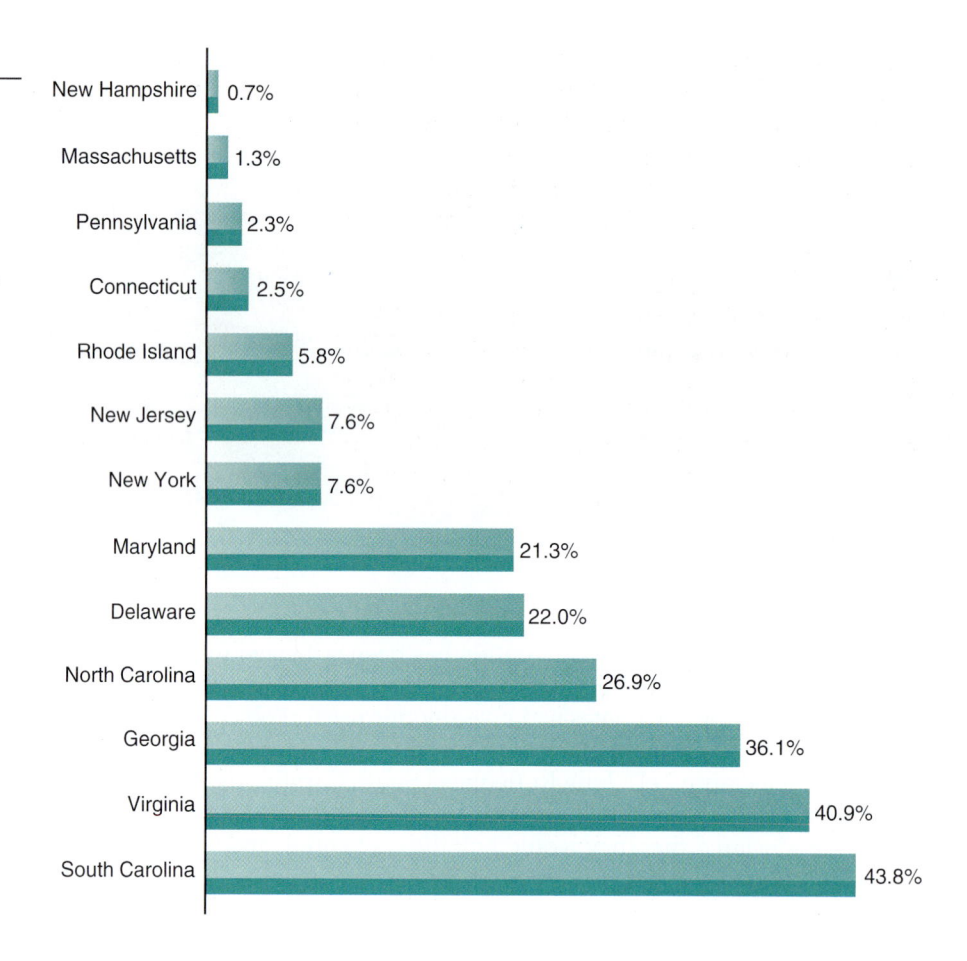

State	Percentage
New Hampshire	0.7%
Massachusetts	1.3%
Pennsylvania	2.3%
Connecticut	2.5%
Rhode Island	5.8%
New Jersey	7.6%
New York	7.6%
Maryland	21.3%
Delaware	22.0%
North Carolina	26.9%
Georgia	36.1%
Virginia	40.9%
South Carolina	43.8%

it. And indeed, North Carolina and Rhode Island were steadfastly opposed to the new union and did not ratify the Constitution until the eleven other states had ratified it and begun the process of establishing the new government.

The Ratification Debate

Anti-Federalists A term used to describe opponents of the Constitution during the debate over ratification.

The debate over ratification was a contentious one. The **Anti-Federalists** (as opponents of the Constitution were labeled) raised arguments that still echo in American politics. They claimed that the national government would be too powerful and would threaten the sovereignty of the separate states and the liberty of the people. Many Americans had an innate distrust of centralized power and worried that the people's liberty could be eclipsed as easily by a distant American government as it had been by the British king. The fact that the Constitution contained no bill of rights heightened this concern. Did its absence indicate that the central government would be free to define for itself what the people's rights would be?

The presidency was also a source of concern. No such office had existed under the Articles, and some worried that it would lead to the creation of an American monarchy. Even the motives of the men who wrote the Constitution came under attack. They were men of wealth and education and had acted in response to debtors' riots. Would the Constitution become a tool by which the wealthy ruled over those with little or no money? And who would bear the burden of additional taxation? For Americans struggling with local and state tax payments, the creation of yet another tax agency was hardly an attractive proposal.

Most Anti-Federalists acknowledged a need to strengthen national commerce and defense. What they opposed was the creation of a powerful national government as the mechanism. They favored a revision of the Articles of Confederation, which in their opinion could accomplish these goals without the risk of establishing a government that could threaten their liberties, their livelihoods, and their local interests.

The **Federalists** (as the Constitution's supporters called themselves) responded with a persuasive case of their own. Their strongest arguments were set forth by James Madison and Alexander Hamilton, who, along with John Jay, wrote a series of essays during the New York ratification debate. The essays were published in a New York City newspaper under the pen name Publius and were entitled "The Federalist." (The essays are collectively referred to as *The Federalist Papers* and are widely acknowledged as a brilliant political treatise.) Madison and Hamilton argued that the government of the Constitution would correct the defects of the Articles; it would have the power necessary to forge a secure and prosperous union. At the same time, because of restrictions on its powers, the new government would endanger neither the states nor personal liberty. In *Federalist* Nos. 47, 48, 49, 50, and 51, for example, Madison explained how the separation of national institutions was designed to both empower and restrict the federal government. (The Federalist and Anti-Federalist arguments are discussed further in Chapter 3.)

Whether the ratification debate changed many minds is unknown. Historical evidence indicates, however, that a majority of ordinary Americans opposed the Constitution's ratification. But their voice in the state ratifying conventions was smaller than that of wealthier interests, which, in the main, supported the change. The pro-ratification forces were also bolstered by the widespread assumption that George Washington would become the first president. He was far and away the most trusted and popular American leader. In the view of most historians, the fact that Washington had presided over the Philadelphia convention and the assumption that he would become the chief executive tipped the balance in favor of ratification.

Delaware was the first state to ratify the Constitution, and Connecticut, Georgia, and New Jersey followed, an indication that the Great Compromise had satisfied several of the small states. In the early summer of 1788, New Hampshire became the ninth state to ratify. The Constitution was law. But neither Virginia nor New York had ratified, and a stable union without these two major states was almost unthinkable. They were as large in area as many European countries and conceivably could survive as independent nations. They nearly did choose a separate course. In both states, the Constitution barely passed, and then only after the Federalists promised to support a bill of rights designed to protect individual freedoms from the power of the central government.

James Madison
(1751–1836)

James Madison is often called the "father of the Constitution" because he was instrumental in its writing and its ratification (through his *Federalist Papers* essays). He served as secretary of state during the Jefferson administration and was elected the fourth U.S. president in 1808. He helped lead the nation to victory over the British in the War of 1812 and, after leaving the presidency in 1817, spoke out often against the growing movement toward states' rights that led eventually to the Civil War.

Federalists A term used to describe proponents of the Constitution during the debate over ratification.

www.mhhe.com/patterson6

TABLE 2–1 Major Goals of the Framers of the Constitution

1. To establish a government strong enough to meet the nation's needs—an objective sought through substantial grants of power to the federal government in areas such as defense and commerce (see Chapter 3).
2. To establish a government that would not threaten the existence of the separate states—an objective sought through federalism (see Chapter 3) and through a Congress connected to the states through elections.
3. To establish a government that would not threaten liberty—an objective sought through an elaborate system of checks and balances.
4. To establish a government based on popular consent—an objective sought through provisions for the direct and indirect election of public officials.

Liberty & Equality

What's Your Opinion?

Constitutionalism

The Englishman James Bryce ranked America's written constitution as its greatest contribution to the practice of government. The Constitution offered the world a new model of government in which a written document defining the state's lawful powers was a higher authority than the actions of any political leader or institution.

The Framers' commitment to constitutionalism grew out of their recognition that although government must have coercive power in order to carry out the actions necessary to maintain a civil society, this same power can be used by unscrupulous leaders to strip others of liberty and equality.

Do you think these two considerations—the coercive power of government and the corruptibility of those in whom power is invested—lead almost inevitably to a belief in limited government and to the use of constitutional measures (such as checks and balances) as a means to control the uses of power? What historical examples, other than Watergate, can you think of that illustrate the significance of constitutional limitations on the exercise of power?

constitution The fundamental law that defines how a government will legitimately operate.

The Framers' Goals

A **constitution** is the fundamental law that defines how a government will legitimately operate: how its leaders will be chosen, the institutions through which these leaders will work, the procedures they must follow in making policy, and the powers they can lawfully exercise. The Constitution, which was written in Philadelphia in 1787, is exactly such a law. In theory, it is the highest law of the land: neither a popular majority nor a leader at the highest pinnacle of power stands above it. Its provisions define how power is to be acquired and can be used.

The Constitution reflected the Framers' vision of a proper government for the American people. Its provisions addressed four broad goals (see Table 2–1). One was the creation of a national government strong enough to meet the nation's needs, particularly in the areas of defense and commerce. Another goal was to preserve the states as governing entities. The states already existed and had the loyalty of their people. Accordingly, the Framers established a system of government (*federalism*) in which power is divided between the national government and the states. Federalism is discussed at length in Chapter 3, which will also explain how the Constitution laid the foundation for a strong national government.

The Framers' other goals were to establish a national government that was restricted in its lawful uses of power (limited government) and that gave the people a voice in their governance (self-government). These two goals and how they were written into the Constitution are the focus of the rest of this chapter.

PROTECTING LIBERTY: LIMITED GOVERNMENT

A challenge facing the Framers of the Constitution was how to control the coercive force of government. Government's unique characteristic is that it alone can legally arrest, imprison, and even kill people who break its rules.[8] Force is not the only basis of effective government, but government must be able to use force or lawless elements would take over society. The dilemma is that government itself can destroy civilized society by using its force to brutalize and intimidate its opponents. "It is a melancholy reflection," James Madison wrote to Thomas Jefferson shortly after the Constitution's ratification, "that liberty should be equally exposed to danger whether the government has too much or too little power."[9]

The men who wrote the Constitution sought to establish a government strong enough to enforce national interests, including defense and commerce among the states (see Chapter 3), but not so strong as to destroy liberty. Limited government was built into the Constitution through both grants and restrictions of political power.

Grants and Denials of Power

The Framers chose to limit the national government in part by confining its scope to constitutional **grants of power**. Congress's lawmaking powers are specifically listed in Article 1, section 8 of the Constitution. Seventeen in number, these listed powers include, for example, the powers to tax, to establish an army and navy, to declare war, to regulate commerce among the states, to create a national currency, and to borrow money. Authority *not* granted to the government by the Constitution is in theory denied to it. In a period where other governments had unrestricted powers, this limitation was remarkable.

grants of power The method of limiting the U.S. government by confining its scope of authority to those powers expressly granted in the Constitution.

The Framers also used **denials of power** as a means to limit government, prohibiting certain practices that European rulers had routinely used to intimidate political opponents. The French king, for example, could imprison a subject indefinitely without charge. The U.S. Constitution prohibits such action: individuals have the right to be brought before a court under a writ of habeas corpus for a judgment as to the legality of their confinement. The Constitution also forbids Congress and the states from passing *ex post facto* laws, under which citizens can be prosecuted for acts that were legal at the time they were committed.

denials of power A constitutional means of limiting government by listing those powers that government is expressly prohibited from using.

As a further denial of power, the Framers made the Constitution difficult to amend, thereby making it hard for those in power to increase their lawful authority by changing the Constitution. An amendment could be proposed only by a two-thirds majority in both chambers of Congress or by a national constitutional convention called by two-thirds of the state legislatures. Such a proposal would then become law only if ratified by three-fourths of state legislatures or state conventions. Congress has the power to decide whether state legislatures or state conventions will be used in the ratifying process. The Twenty-first Amendment is the only one where Congress specified state conventions as the ratifying mechanism; in all other cases, state legislatures have done the ratifying. (The Twenty-first Amendment repealed the Eighteenth Amendment, which had prohibited the manufacture, sale, and transportation of alcoholic beverages. Congress concluded that repeal was better addressed and more likely to occur in state conventions than in state legislatures.) The national constitutional convention as a means of proposing amendments has never been used. All amendments have originated with Congress.

Using Power to Offset Power

Although the Framers believed that grants and denials of power could act as controls on government, they had no illusion that written words alone would restrain power. As a consequence, they sought to check power with power. The idea was to divide the authority of government so that no single institution could exercise great power without the agreement of other institutions.[10]

This 1790s colored engraving by William Birch depicts a Philadelphia street scene. Philadelphia's role in the birth of the American nation is rivaled only by Boston's contribution.

separation of powers The division of the powers of government among separate institutions or branches.

The idea that a **separation of powers** was necessary to the preservation of liberty had been proposed decades earlier by the French theorist Montesquieu. His argument was widely accepted in America, and when the states drafted new constitutions after the start of the Revolutionary War, they built their governments around the concept of a separation of powers. Pennsylvania was an exception, and its experience only seemed to prove the necessity of separated powers. Unrestrained by an independent judiciary or executive, Pennsylvania's all-powerful legislature systematically deprived minority groups of their basic rights and freedoms: Quakers were disenfranchised for their religious beliefs, conscientious objectors to the Revolutionary War were prosecuted, and the right of trial by jury was eliminated.

In *Federalist* No. 10, Madison asked why governments often act according to the interests of overbearing majorities rather than according to principles of justice. Why, he asked, has liberty suffered so mightily at the hands of majorities? He attributed the cause to "the mischiefs of faction." People, he argued, are divided into opposing religious, geographical, ethnic, economic, and other factions. These divisions are natural and desirable in that free people have a right to their personal opinions and interests. Yet factions can themselves be a source of oppressive government. If a faction gains full power, it will use government to advance itself at the expense of all others. (*Federalist* No. 10 is widely regarded as the finest political essay ever written by an American. It is reprinted at the back of this book.)

Out of this concern came the Framers' special contribution to the doctrine of the separation of powers. They did not believe that it would be enough, as Montesquieu had suggested, to divide the government's authority strictly along institutional lines, granting all legislative power to the legislature, all judicial power to the courts, and all executive power to the presidency. This *total* separation would make it too easy for a single faction to exploit a particular kind of political power. A faction that controlled the legislature, for example, could enact laws ruinous to other interests. A better system of divided government would be one in which political power could be applied forcibly only when institutions agreed on its use. This system would require separated but *overlapping* powers. Since no one faction could easily gain control over all institutions, factions would have to work together, a process that would require each to moderate its demands and thus would serve many interests rather than one or a few.[11]

Separated Institutions Sharing Power: Checks and Balances

The Framers' concept of divided powers has been described by political scientist Richard Neustadt as the principle of **separated institutions sharing power**.[12] The separate branches are interlocked in such a way that an elaborate system of **checks and balances** is created (see Figure 2–2). No institution can act decisively without the support or acquiescence of the other institutions. Legislative, executive, and judicial powers in the American system are divided in such a way that they overlap; each of the three branches of government checks the others' powers and balances those powers with powers of its own. As natural as this system now might seem to Americans, most democracies are of the parliamentary type, where executive and legislative power are combined in a single institution rather than vested in separate ones. In a parliamentary system, the majority in the legislature selects the prime minister, who then serves as both the legislature leader and the chief executive (see "How the United States Compares.")

Shared Legislative Powers

Under the Constitution, Congress has legislative authority, but that power is partly shared with the other branches and thus checked by them. The president can veto acts of Congress, recommend legislation, and call special sessions of Congress. The president also has the power to execute—and thereby to interpret—the laws made by Congress.

The Supreme Court has the power to interpret acts of Congress that are disputed in legal cases. The Court also has the power of judicial review; it can declare laws of Congress void when it finds that they are not in accord with the Constitution.

Within Congress, there is a further check on legislative power: for legislation to be passed, a majority in each house of Congress is required. Thus the Senate and the House of Representatives can block each other from acting.

Shared Executive Powers

Executive power is vested in the president but is constrained by legislative and judicial checks. The president's power to make treaties and appoint high-ranking officials, for example, is subject to Senate approval. Congress also has the power to impeach and remove the president from office. In practical terms,

separated institutions sharing power The principle that, as a way to limit government, its powers should be divided among separate branches, each of which also shares in the power of the others as a means of checking and balancing them. The result is that no one branch can exercise power decisively without the support or acquiescence of the others.

checks and balances The elaborate system of divided spheres of authority provided by the U.S. Constitution as a means of controlling the power of government. The separation of powers among the branches of the national government, federalism, and the different methods of selecting national officers are all part of this system.

The Supreme Court—Judiciary Branch

The Supreme Court over the President: May declare executive action unlawful because it is not authorized by legislation; (by tradition) may declare presidential action unconstitutional.

The President—Executive Branch

The President over the Supreme Court: Nominates federal judges; may pardon those convicted in court; executes court decisions and thereby affects their implementation.

The Supreme Court over Congress: Has power to interpret legal disputes arising under acts of Congress and (by tradition) may declare acts of Congress unconstitutional.

The Congress—Legislative Branch

Congress over the President: May impeach and remove president; may override presidential veto; may investigate presidential action; must approve treaties and executive appointments; enacts the budget and laws within which presidential action occurs.

Congress over the Supreme Court: Decides the size of the federal court system, the number of Supreme Court justices, and the appellate jurisdiction of the Supreme Court; may impeach and remove federal judges; may rewrite legislation that courts have interpreted and may initiate constitutional amendments; confirms judicial nominees.

The President over Congress: May veto acts of Congress, recommend legislation, and call Congress into special session; executes, and thereby interprets, laws enacted by Congress.

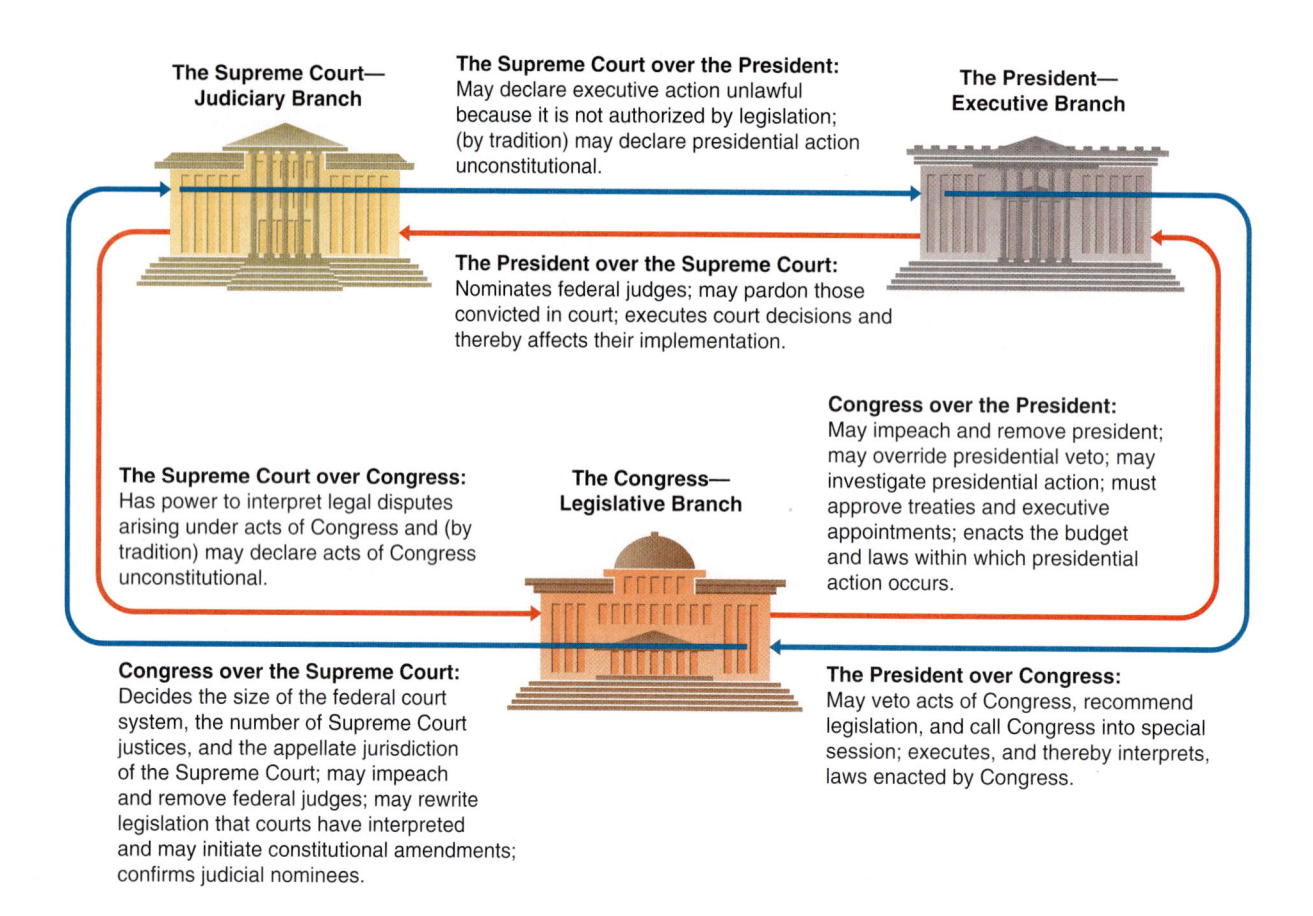

Figure 2–2

The System of Checks and Balances

This elaborate system of divided spheres of authority was provided by the U.S. Constitution as a means of controlling the power of government. The separation of powers among the branches of the national government, federalism, and the different methods of selecting national officers are all part of this system.

Congress's greatest checks on executive action are its lawmaking and appropriations powers. The executive branch cannot act without laws that authorize its activities or without the money that pays for these programs.

The judiciary's major check on the presidency is its power to declare an action unlawful because it is not authorized by the legislation that the executive claims to be implementing.

Shared Judicial Powers

Judicial power rests with the Supreme Court and with lower federal courts, which are subject to checks by the other branches of the federal government. Congress is empowered to establish the size of the federal court system, to restrict the Supreme Court's appellate jurisdiction in some circumstances, and to impeach and remove federal judges from office. More important, Congress can rewrite legislation that the courts have misinterpreted and can initiate amendments when it disagrees with the courts' rulings on constitutional issues.

The president has the power to appoint federal judges with the consent of the Senate and to pardon persons convicted in the courts. The president is also responsible for executing court decisions, a function that provides opportunities to influence the way rulings are implemented.

HOW THE UNITED STATES COMPARES

Checks and Balances

All democracies place constitutional limits on the power of government. The concept of rule by law, for example, is characteristic of democratic governments but not of authoritarian regimes. Democracies differ, however, in the extent to which political power is restrained through constitutional mechanisms. The United States is an extreme case in that its government rests on an elaborate system of constitutional checks and balances. The system employs a separation of powers among the executive, legislative, and judicial branches. It also includes judicial review, the power of the courts to invalidate actions of the legislature or executive. These constitutional restrictions on power are not part of the governing structure of all democracies.

Most democracies, for example, have parliamentary systems, which invest both executive and legislative leadership in the office of prime minister. Britain is an example of this type of system. Parliament under the leadership of the prime minister is the supreme authority in Britain. Its laws are not even subject to override by Britain's high court, which has no power to review the constitutionality of parliamentary acts.

COUNTRY	SEPARATION OF EXECUTIVE AND LEGISLATIVE POWERS?	JUDICIAL REVIEW?
Belgium	No	Yes
Canada	No	Yes
France	Yes	No
Germany	No	Yes
Great Britain	No	No
Italy	No	Yes
Japan	No	Yes
Mexico	Yes	Yes
United States	Yes	Yes

The Bill of Rights

Although the delegates to the Philadelphia convention discussed the possibility of placing a list of individual rights (such as freedom of speech and the right to a fair trial) in the Constitution, they ultimately decided that such a list was unnecessary because of the doctrine of expressed powers: government could not lawfully assume powers, such as the abridgment of human rights, that were not authorized by the Constitution. Moreover, the delegates concluded that a bill of rights was undesirable because government might feel free to disregard any right that was inadvertently left off the list or that emerged at some future time. These considerations did not allay the fears of leading Americans who believed that no possible safeguard of liberty should be omitted. "A bill of rights," Jefferson argued, "is what the people are entitled to against every government on earth, general or particular, and what no just government should refuse or rest on inference." Jefferson had included a bill of rights in the constitution he wrote for Virginia at the outbreak of the Revolutionary War, and all but four states had followed Virginia's example.

Opposition to the absence of a bill of rights led to its addition to the Constitution. Madison himself introduced a series of amendments during the First Congress, ten of which were soon ratified by the states. These amendments, traditionally called the **Bill of Rights,** include such rights as freedom of speech and religion and due process protections (such as jury trial and legal counsel) for persons accused of crimes. (These rights, termed *civil liberties,* are discussed at length in Chapter 4.)

Bill of Rights The first ten amendments to the Constitution. They include such rights as freedom of speech.

Why Should I Care?

The Bill of Rights: Why It Is Important to Your Liberty

The Bill of Rights was added to the Constitution despite the Framers' belief that it was unnecessary. In their view, the Constitution denied to the federal government any power not granted to it. From this perspective, there was no need, for example, for a guarantee of religious freedom because government was not authorized to deny people the right to worship as they pleased. The Framers feared, moreover, that any listing of rights would become a means of denying people rights that were not listed.

Other Americans in 1787 were not persuaded by this argument and said they would support ratification only if a bill of rights was added. To gain their backing, proponents of ratification promised that a bill of rights would be acted on in the first session of Congress. The first ten amendments to the Constitution—commonly called the Bill of Rights—was the result.

Can you think of any additional rights that you might have today if the Framers' position had prevailed? The Supreme Court has held, for example, that Americans are entitled to an "adequate" public school education but not an "equal" one because the Constitution does not list education as a basic individual right. If there were no Bill of Rights, do you think the courts would have concluded that all children have a right to an "equal" education?

Most constitutional scholars believe that, on balance, the Bill of Rights has enhanced personal liberty. It had the effect of transforming abstract rights (for example, "the right to life, liberty, and the pursuit of happiness") into concrete legal rights, thus giving people a basis for judicial action should their legal rights be abridged or denied. If you speak your mind publicly or are charged with a criminal offense, for example, you have a specific constitutional provision from which to claim your right. The Fifth Amendment, for example, gives you a right to counsel if accused of a crime. Of course, authorities sometimes ignore restrictions in the Bill of Rights and often get away with it. Nevertheless, the fact that the Bill of Rights contains specific guarantees increases the likelihood that authorities will respect them. By refusing to allow a suspect to talk with an attorney, for example, authorities run the risk of having a judge dismiss the case because of a constitutional violation.

The Bill of Rights also protects you by narrowing legislative options. In the aftermath of the September 11, 2001, attacks on the World Trade Center and Pentagon, for example, Congress debated various means of combating terrorism. Some of the proposals (for example, unrestricted surveillance of people's e-mail messages) were rejected in part because of a recognition that any such law would likely be struck down by the courts as unconstitutional.

The Bill of Rights is a precise expression of the concept of limited government. In consenting to be governed, the people agree to accept the authority of government in certain areas but not in others; the people's constitutional rights cannot lawfully be denied by governing officials.

Judicial Review

The writers of the Constitution both empowered and limited government. But who was to decide whether the government was operating within its constitutional powers? The Framers did not specifically entrust this power to a particular branch of government, although they did grant the Supreme Court the authority to decide on "all cases arising under this Constitution."

Limits on Government in the U.S. Constitution

Grants of power: powers granted to the national government by the constitution; powers not granted it are denied it unless they are necessary and proper to the carrying out of granted powers.

Separated institutions sharing power: the division of the national government's power among three branches, each of which is to act as a check on the powers of the other two.

Federalism: the division of political authority between the national government and the states, enabling the people to appeal to one authority if their rights and interests are not respected by the other authority.

Denials of power: powers expressly denied to the national and state governments by the Constitution.

Bill of Rights: the first ten amendments to the Constitution, which specify rights of citizens that the national government must respect.

Judicial review: the power of the courts to declare governmental action null and void when it is found to violate the Constitution.

Elections: the power of the voters to remove officials from office.

Most delegates to the Philadelphia convention apparently assumed that the Supreme Court would have the power to decide whether a governmental institution has acted within its constitutional powers and, if not, to nullify its action. There was precedent for this form of judicial authority in several states, and a form of it had existed during the colonial period. It is also noteworthy that the power of the courts to declare laws null and void was discussed and endorsed at the ratifying conventions of at least eight of the thirteen states.[13] Still, because the Constitution did not explicitly grant the judiciary this authority, it was a principle that had to be established in practice.

The opportunity arose with an incident that occurred after the election of 1800, in which John Adams lost his bid for a second presidential term after a bitter campaign against Jefferson. Between November 1800, when Jefferson was elected, and March 1801, when he was inaugurated, the Federalist-controlled Congress created fifty-nine additional lower-court judgeships, enabling Adams to appoint loyal Federalists to those positions before he left office. However, Adams's term expired before the secretary of state could deliver the judicial commissions to all the appointees. Without this formal authorization, an appointee could not take office. Knowing this, Jefferson told his secretary of state, James Madison, not to deliver them. William Marbury was one of those who did not receive his commission, and he asked the Supreme Court to issue a writ of mandamus (a court order that directs an official to take a specific action) requiring Madison to deliver it.

Marbury v. *Madison* (1803) became the foundation for judicial review by the federal courts. Chief Justice John Marshall wrote the *Marbury* opinion, which declared that Marbury had a legal right to his commission. The opinion also said, however, that the Supreme Court could not issue him a writ of mandamus because it lacked the constitutional authority to do so. Congress had granted the Court the power to issue such writs in an ordinary act of legislation—the Judiciary Act of 1789. Marshall pointed out that the Constitution prohibits any expansion of the Supreme Court's authority except through an amendment to the

Historical Background

> **John Marshall**
> (1755–1835)
>
> John Marshall forcefully expressed his nationalist views in important Supreme Court decisions during his thirty-four years as chief justice. A cousin of Thomas Jefferson, they were political opponents. Marshall was an ardent nationalist whereas Jefferson held that national power should not unduly intrude on the states. Marshall served for a time as John Adams's secretary of state before his appointment by Adams to the post of chief justice.

judicial review The power of courts to decide whether a governmental institution has acted within its constitutional powers and, if not, to declare its action null and void.

tyranny of the majority The potential of a majority to monopolize power for its own gain and to the detriment of minority rights and interests.

Constitution. That being the case, Marshall stated, the portion of the Judiciary Act that provided the authorization was constitutionally invalid.[14]

Marshall's decision was ingenious since it asserted the power of judicial review without creating the possibility of its rejection by either the executive or the legislative branch. In declaring that Marbury had a right to his commission, the Court in effect said that President Jefferson had failed in his constitutional duty to execute the laws faithfully. But since it did not order Jefferson to deliver the commission, he had no opportunity to refuse to comply with the Court's judgment. At the same time, the Court admonished Congress for passing legislation that exceeded its constitutional authority. And in the process of invalidating an act of Congress on constitutional grounds, the Court asserted its power of **judicial review**—that is, the power of the judiciary to decide whether a government official or institution has acted within the limits of the Constitution and, if not, to declare its action null and void.

PROVIDING FOR SELF-GOVERNMENT

"We the People" is the opening phase of the Constitution. It expresses the idea that, in the United States, the people will have the power to govern themselves. In a sense, there is no contradiction between this idea and the Constitution's provisions for limited government, since individual *liberty* is part of the process of *self-government.* If people cannot express themselves freely, they cannot be self-governing. In another sense, however, the contradiction is clear: restrictions on the power of the majority are a denial of its right to govern society as it chooses.

The Framers believed that the people deserved and required a voice in their government, but they also feared popular government. They worried that the people would become inflamed by a passionate issue or fiery demagogue and act without due regard for the interests of the minority. To the Framers, the great risk of popular government was **tyranny of the majority:** the people acting as an irrational mob that tramples on the rights of others. Their fear was not without foundation. The history of democracies was filled with popular excesses, and there were even examples from the nation's brief history. In 1786, for example, debtors had gained control of Rhode Island's legislature and made paper money a legal means of paying debts, even though existing contracts called for payment in gold. Creditors were then hunted down and held captive in public places so that debtors could come and pay them in full with worthless paper money. A Boston newspaper wrote that Rhode Island should be renamed *Rogue* Island.

Democracy Versus Republic

No form of self-government could eliminate completely the threat to liberty of majority tyranny, but the Framers believed that the danger would be greatly diminished by properly structured institutions.[15] Madison summarized the

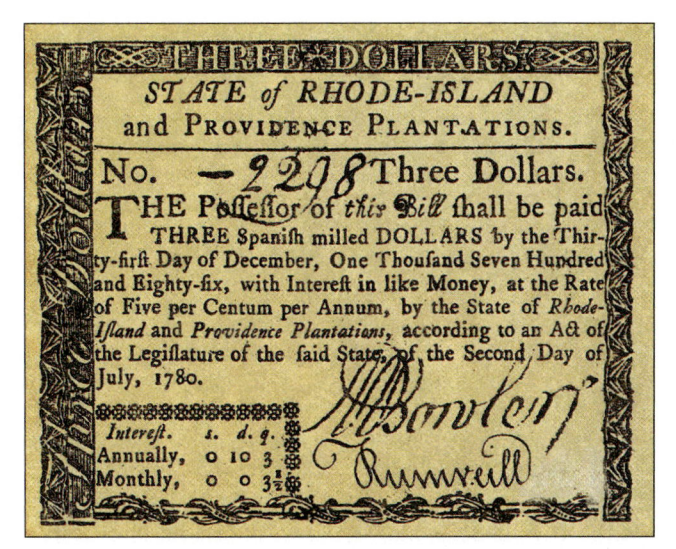

Rhode Island was nicknamed "Rogue Island" for its disregard of property rights. Shown here is the Rhode Island three dollar banknote, which came to be worth no more than the paper on which it was written and yet was used to pay off gold debts.

Framers' intent when he said in *Federalist* No. 10 that the Constitution was "a republican remedy" for the excesses historically associated with "democratic" rule. Today the terms **democracy, republic,** and **representative democracy** are often used interchangeably to refer to a system of government in which ultimate political power rests with the majority through its capacity to choose representatives in free and open elections. To the writers of the Constitution, however, *democracy* and *republic* had different meanings. When the Framers complained about the risks of democracy, they were referring to a government subject to immediate popular influence, either because the public participated directly in policy decisions (pure or direct democracy, as in Ancient Greece or New England town meetings) or because lawmakers acted out of fear of the public (mobocracy). In their use of the term *republic,* the Framers were referring to *representative democracy* in which elected officials met in representative institutions.

The Framers' concept of a proper system of representation was similar to an idea put forth by the English theorist Edmund Burke (1729–1797). In his *Letter to the Sheriffs of Bristol,* Burke argued that representatives should act as public **trustees:** they are obliged to promote the interest of those who elected them, but the nature of this interest is for the representatives, not the voters, to decide. Burke was concerned about the ease with which society could degenerate into selfishness, and he thought it imperative for representatives not to surrender their judgment to popular whim.

Limited Popular Rule

The Constitution provided that all power would be exercised through representative institutions. There was no provision for any form of direct popular participation in the making of policy decisions. In view of the fact that the United States was much too large to be governed directly by the people in popular assemblies, a representative system was necessary. Moreover, the separation of

democracy A form of government in which the people rule, either directly or through elected representatives.

republic Historically, the form of government in which representative officials met to decide on policy issues. These representatives were expected to serve the public interest but were not subject to the people's immediate control. Today, the term *republic* is used interchangeably with *democracy.*

representative democracy A system in which the people participate in the decision-making process of government not directly but indirectly, through the election of officials to represent their interests.

trustees Elected representatives whose obligation is to act in accordance with their own consciences as to what policies are in the best interests of the public.

TABLE 2-2 **Methods of Choosing National Leaders** Fearing the concentration of political power, the Framers devised alternative methods of selection and terms of service for national officials.

OFFICE	METHOD OF SELECTION	TERM OF SERVICE
President	Electoral College	4 years
U.S. senator	State legislature	6 years (one-third of senators' terms expire every 2 years)
U.S. representative	Popular election	2 years
Federal judge	Nominated by president, approved by Senate	Indefinite (subject to "good behavior")

powers meant that the majority's will, again by necessity, would be filtered through an institutional structure. The Framers went beyond what was necessary, however, and placed officials at a considerable distance from the people they represented (see Table 2–2).

The House of Representatives was the only institution that would be based on direct popular election—its members would be elected for two-year terms of office through vote of the people. Frequent and direct election of House members was intended to make government sensitive to the concerns of popular majorities.

U.S. senators would be appointed by the legislatures of the states they represented. Because state legislators were popularly elected, the people would be choosing their senators indirectly. Every two years, a third of the senators would be appointed to six-year terms. The Senate was expected to check and balance the House, which, by virtue of the more frequent and direct election of its members, would presumably be more responsive to popular opinion.

Presidential selection was an issue of considerable debate at the Philadelphia convention. Direct election of the president was twice proposed and twice rejected because it linked executive power directly to popular majorities. The Framers finally chose to have the president selected by the votes of electors (the so-called **Electoral College**). Each state would have as many **electoral votes** as it had members in Congress and could select its electors by any method it chose. The president would serve four years and be eligible for reelection.

The Framers decided that federal judges and justices would be appointed rather than elected. They would be nominated by the president and confirmed through approval by the Senate. Once confirmed, they would "hold their offices during good behavior." In effect, they would be allowed to hold office for life unless they committed a crime. Rather than a representative institution, the judiciary was a "guardian" institution that would uphold the rule of law and serve as a check on the elected branches of government.[17]

These differing methods of selecting national officeholders would not prevent a determined majority from achieving unbridled power, but control could not be attained easily or quickly. Unlike the House of Representatives, institutions such as the Senate, presidency, and judiciary would not yield to an impassioned majority in a single election. The delay would reduce the probability that government would degenerate into mob rule driven by momentary whims.

Electoral College An unofficial term that refers to the electors who cast the states' electoral votes.

electoral votes The method of voting that is used to choose the U.S. president. Each state has the same number of electoral votes as it has members in Congress (House and Senate combined). By tradition, electoral voting is tied to a state's popular voting. The candidate with the most popular votes in a state (or, in a few states, the most votes in a congressional district) receives its electoral votes.

How the National Political System was Made More Responsive to Popular Majorities

Earlier Situation	Subsequent Development
Separation of powers, as a means of dividing authority and blunting passionate majorities.	Political parties, as a means of uniting authorities and linking them with popular majorities.
Indirect election of all national officials except House members, as a means of buffering officials from popular influence.	Direct election of U.S. senators and popular voting for president (linked to electoral votes), as a means of increasing popular control of officials.
Nomination of candidates for public office through political party organizations.	Primary elections, as a means of selecting party nominees.

Altering the Constitution: More Power to the People

The Constitution's provisions for limited government have stood the test of time: in its structure and formal powers, the national government today has nearly the same features as the government established in 1789. This is not true, however, of the provisions for self-government: several of the original provisions have been amended. In no other constitutional area have Americans shown a greater willingness to devise new arrangements.

A desire for change was evident nearly as soon as the Constitution was unveiled. The Framers' conception of self-government was at odds with what the average American in 1787 believed was appropriate. It certainly was at odds with the spirit and letter of the state constitutions. Every state but South Carolina held annual legislative elections, and several states also chose their governors through annual election. And it was not long after ratification of the Constitution that Americans sought a stronger voice in their own governing.

Jeffersonian Democracy: A Revolution of the Spirit

Thomas Jefferson, who otherwise admired the Constitution, was among the prominent Americans who questioned its provisions for self-government. And it was Jefferson who may have spared the nation a bloody conflict over the issue of popular sovereignty. Under John Adams, the second president, the national government increasingly favored the nation's wealthy interests. Adams publicly suggested that the Constitution was designed for a governing elite, while Alexander Hamilton urged him to use force if necessary to suppress popular dissent.[18] Jefferson asked whether Adams, with the aid of a strong army, planned soon to deprive ordinary Americans of their liberty. Jefferson challenged Adams in the next presidential election and, upon defeating him, hailed the victory as the "Revolution of 1800."

Although Jefferson was a champion of the common people, he had no clear vision of how a popular government might work in practice. He believed that congressional majorities were the proper expression of popular majorities and

Historical Background

Pictured here is the Old Senate Chamber, where the U. S. Senate met until 1859, when a new and larger chamber was constructed. The Old Senate Chamber was the scene of heated debates over slavery. Daniel Webster, Henry Clay, and John C. Calhoun gained national reputations here. After the Senate vacated the chamber, it was occupied by the U.S. Supreme Court until 1935, when the Court's own building across the street from the Capitol was completed. Not until 1914 were U.S. senators chosen by direct vote of the people.

accordingly was reluctant to use his presidency as the instrument of the people.[19] Jefferson also had no illusions about a largely illiterate population's readiness for a significant governing role and feared the ruinous consequences of inciting the masses to contest the moneyed class. But Jefferson did found the nation's first political party (it was the forerunner of today's Democratic Party), which served to link like-minded leaders and thus act as a bridge across divided institutions of power. By and large, however, Jeffersonian democracy was a revolution of the spirit. Jefferson taught Americans to look upon the national government as belonging to all, not just to the privileged few.[20]

Jacksonian Democracy: Linking the People and the Presidency

Not until Andrew Jackson was elected in 1828 did the country have a powerful president who was willing and able to involve the public more fully in government. Jackson carried out the constitutional revolution that Jeffersonian democracy had foreshadowed.

Jackson recognized that the president was the only official who could legitimately claim to represent the people as a whole. Unlike the president, members of Congress were elected from separate states and districts rather than from the entire country. Yet the president's claim to popular leadership was diminished by the existence of the Electoral College. Jackson persuaded the states to choose their presidential electors on the basis of popular voting. Jackson's reform, which is still in effect today, basically places the selection of a president in the voters' hands. The winner of the popular vote in a state is awarded its electoral votes; hence the candidate who wins most of the popular votes in the states is also most likely to receive a majority of the electoral votes. Since Jackson's time, only three candidates—Rutherford B. Hayes in 1876, Benjamin Harrison in 1888, and George W. Bush in 2000—have won the presidency after losing the popular vote. (The Electoral College is discussed further in Chapter 12.)

The Progressives: Senate and Primary Elections

The Progressive era of the early 1900s brought another wave of democratic reforms. The Progressives rejected the Burkean idea of representatives as trustees; they embraced instead the idea of representatives as **delegates**—officeholders who are obligated to respond directly to the expressed opinions of the people whom they represent.

The Progressives succeeded primarily in changing the way that some state and local governments operate (see "States in the Nation"). Progressive reforms of these governments included nonpartisan local elections; recall elections, which enable citizens through petition to require a particular officeholder to submit to election before the expiration of his or her normal term of office; the initiative, which enables citizens through petition to place legislative measures on the ballot for enactment or rejection through popular voting; and the referendum, which permits legislative bodies to submit measures to the voters for enactment or rejection.

The Progressives also brought about two changes in the role of voters in national politics. One was the direct election of U.S. senators, who before the Seventeenth Amendment was ratified in 1913, had been chosen by state legislatures and were widely perceived as agents of big business (the Senate was nicknamed the "Millionaires' Club"). Senators who stood to lose their seats in a direct popular vote had blocked earlier attempts to amend the Senate election procedure. Eventually, however, the Senate was persuaded to support an amendment by pressure from the Progressives and by revelations that corporate bribes had influenced the selection of several senators. The second change was the **primary election,** which gives rank-and-file voters the opportunity to select party nominees. Nearly all states in the early 1900s adopted the primary election as a means of choosing nominees for at least some federal and state offices. Before this change, nominees were chosen by party leaders.

The Progressive era spawned attacks on the Framers. A prominent criticism was the historian Charles S. Beard's *Economic Interpretation of the Constitution.*[21] Arguing that the Constitution grew out of wealthy Americans' fears of the debtor rebellions, and noting that many of the Framers were themselves wealthy men, Beard claimed that the Constitution's elaborate systems of power and representation were devices for keeping power in the hands of the rich. Beard's thesis was challenged by other historians, and he later acknowledged that he had not taken the Framers' full array of motives into account. Their conception of separation of powers, for example, was a time-honored governing principle that had previously been incorporated in state constitutions. Although the Framers did not have great trust in popular rule, it would be a mistake to conclude they were foes of democracy. They were intent on balancing the demands of limited government with those of self-government and, in striking a balance, leaned toward the former, believing that the evil of unrestrained power was the greater danger to a civil society.

delegates Elected representatives whose obligation is to act in accordance with the expressed wishes of the people whom they represent.

primary election A form of election in which voters choose a party's nominees for public office. In most states, eligibility to vote in a primary election is limited to voters who are registered members of the party.

STATES IN THE NATION

Direct Democracy: The Initiative and Referendum

The Progressive movement's reforms included the initiative (which allows citizens through petition to place legislative measures on the ballot) and the referendum (which permits legislative bodies to submit proposals to the voters for approval or rejection). Not all states adopted these devices or have them today. Further, some states restrict their application (for example, limiting them to statutes or constitutional amendments, but not both) or grant their legislatures the power to modify or reject what citizens have done. The map identifies states that have the least restrictive forms of the initiative or referendum—that is, no substantial limit (aside from judicial review) on what state residents through their votes can directly decide. Existing initiative and referendum laws in most states were enacted in the early 1900s, which explains the pattern that can be seen on the map. In the Northeast, party machines saw the initiative and referendum as threats to their political control and blocked their enactment. In the South, political elites rejected the initiative and referendum out of fear that African Americans and poor whites could exercise power through these devices. By comparison, western states were more open politically and thus were more receptive to devices that would give power directly to the people.

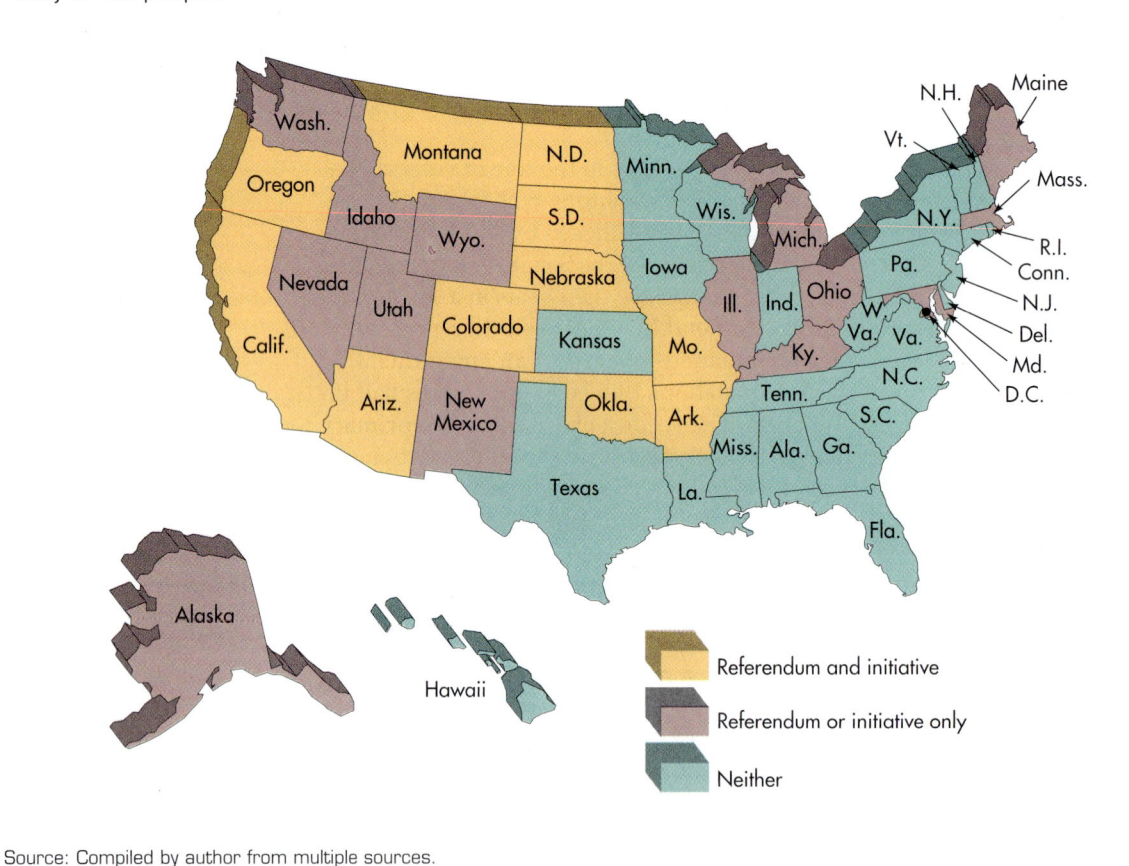

- Referendum and initiative
- Referendum or initiative only
- Neither

Source: Compiled by author from multiple sources.

Should Congress Be Subject to Term Limits?

What is the proper relationship between the electorate and its representatives? The question was a major focus of debate at the Philadelphia convention and is still heard today. An example is the term-limit movement, which has sought to restrict the number of years that an officeholder can remain in office. Term limits are intended to protect the public against politicians who would use the power of their office to stay in office indefinitely. Opponents say that term limits are unnecessary because voters have the power at the next election to decide whether an official should be removed from office. Although many states have adopted term limits for their legislatures, the courts have ruled that states do not have the power to restrict the terms of members of Congress. That action would have to originate with Congress. Several term-limit proposals have been introduced in Congress, but none has managed to gain the necessary support.

Yes: During the first 150 years of this country's history, term limits were unnecessary. Turnover in the U.S. House of Representatives was routinely over 50 percent. But in recent years, a rapacious desire for power has infiltrated our nation's legislature. Over the last decade we have experienced reelection rates averaging over 90 percent, creating a class of career politicians who have insulated themselves from the public will and grown less and less representative of the people. Like the Founding Fathers, the American people recognize the need for new blood in government. They have decided that it is time for their elected officials to return home at regular intervals. Term limits have seized the hearts and minds of millions of Americans frustrated with an unresponsive and arrogant government.
—*U.S. Term Limits organization*

No: The terms of Members of Congress are already limited. We face the voters every other year. We are given only a two-year term in the House. If the voters do not like what we are doing, they can easily kick us out. Elections are the best term limits ever invented. . . . Term limits are [also] unconstitutional. They were specifically considered by our Founding Fathers and specifically rejected, for a whole host of good reasons. . . . They would prohibit voters from voting for a candidate who might otherwise be their first choice. They would prohibit good people from running for office. [Also], very few Members of Congress would be able to develop experience and expertise about important matters on which they were expected to legislate. . . . Term limits solve a problem that does not exist. We should let the voters decide, and not just arbitrarily limit their choices.
—*Congressman John J. Duncan Jr. (R-Tenn.)*

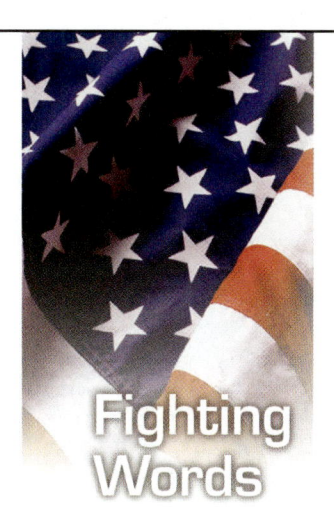

CONSTITUTIONAL DEMOCRACY TODAY

The type of government created in the United States in 1787 is today called a **constitutional democracy.** It is *democratic* in its provisions for majority influence through elections and *constitutional* in its requirement that power gained through elections be exercised in accordance with law and with due respect for individual rights.

constitutional democracy A government that is democratic in its provisions for majority influence through elections, and constitutional in its provisions for minority rights and rule by law.

By some standards, the American system of today is a model of *self-government*. The United States schedules the election of its larger legislative chamber (the House of Representatives) and its chief executive more frequently than any other democracy. In addition, it is the only country that relies extensively on primary elections instead of party organizations for the selection of party nominees. The principle of popular election to office, which the writers of the Constitution regarded as a prerequisite of popular sovereignty but to be used sparingly, has been extended further in the United States than anywhere else.

By other standards, however, the U.S. system is less democratic than many others. Popular majorities must work against the barriers to influence—the elaborate system of divided powers, staggered terms of office, and separate constituencies—that were devised by the Framers. In fact, the link between an electoral majority and a governing majority is far less direct in the American system than in nearly all other democratic systems. In the European parliamentary democracies, for example, legislative and executive power are not separated, are not subject to close check by the judiciary, and are acquired through the winning of a legislative majority in national elections. The Framers' vision was a different one, dominated by a concern with *liberty*, and therefore with controls on political power, a response to the experiences they brought with them to Philadelphia in the summer of 1787.

SUMMARY

The Constitution of the United States is a reflection of the colonial and revolutionary experiences of the early Americans. Freedom from abusive government was a reason for the colonies' revolt against British rule, but the English tradition also provided ideas about government, power, and freedom that were expressed in the Constitution and, earlier, in the Declaration of Independence.

The Constitution was designed in part to provide for a limited government in which political power would be confined to proper uses. The Framers wanted to ensure that the government they were creating would not itself be a threat to freedom. To this end, they confined the national government to expressly granted powers and also denied it certain specific powers. Other prohibitions on government were later added to the Constitution in the form of stated guarantees of individual liberties: the Bill of Rights. The most significant constitutional provision for limited government, however, was a separation of powers among the three branches. The powers given to each branch enable it to act as a check on the exercise of power by the others, an arrangement that, during the nation's history, has in fact served as a barrier to abuses of power.

The Constitution, however, made no mention of how the powers and limits of government were to be judged in practice. In its historic ruling in *Marbury* v. *Madison*, the Supreme Court assumed the authority to review the constitutionality of legislative and executive actions and to declare them unconstitutional and thus invalid.

The Framers of the Constitution respected the idea of self-government but distrusted popular majorities. They designed a government that they felt would temper popular opinion and slow its momentum, so that the public's "true interest" (which includes a regard for the rights and interests of the minority) would guide public policy. Different methods were established to select members of the House of Representatives and of the Senate, the president, and federal judges as a means of separating political power from momentary and unreflecting majorities.

Since the adoption of the Constitution, however, the public has gradually assumed more direct control of its representatives, particularly through measures affecting the way in which officeholders are chosen. Presidential voting (linked to the Electoral College), direct election of senators, and primary elections are among the devices aimed at strengthening the majority's influence. These developments are rooted in the idea, deeply held by ordinary Americans, that the people must have substantial direct control of their government if it is to serve their real interests.

KEY TERMS

Anti-Federalists
Bill of Rights
checks and balances
constitution
constitutional democracy
delegates
democracy
denials of power
Electoral College
electoral votes
Federalists
grants of power
Great Compromise
inalienable (natural) rights
judicial review
limited government
New Jersey (small-state) Plan
North-South Compromise
primary elections
representative democracy
republic
self-government
separated institutions sharing power
separation of powers
trustees
tyranny of the majority
Virginia (large-state) Plan

SUGGESTED READINGS

Beard, Charles S. *An Economic Interpretation of the Constitution.* New York: Macmillan, 1941. Argues that the Framers had selfish economic interests uppermost in mind when they wrote the Constitution.

Farrand, Max. *The Records of the Federal Convention of 1787.* New Haven, Conn.: Yale University Press, 1966. A four-volume work that includes all the important records of the Philadelphia convention.

Federalist Papers. Many editions, including a one-volume paperback version edited by Isaac Kramnick (New York: Penguin, 1987). A series of essays written by Alexander Hamilton, James Madison, and John Jay under the pseudonym Publius. The essays, published in a New York newspaper in 1787–88, explain the Constitution and support its ratification.

Hardin, Russell. *Liberalism, Constitutionalism, and Democracy.* New York: Oxford University Press, 1999. Analysis of the great ideas that underlie the Constitution.

Haskell, John. *Direct Democracy or Representative Government: Dispelling the Populist Myth.* Boulder, Colo.: Westview Press, 2001. Analysis of the two democratic philosophies that have affected American politics.

Sheldon, Garret Ward. *The Political Philosophy of James Madison.* Baltimore: Johns Hopkins University Press, 2000. A synthesis of James Madison's political philosophy in the context of the social and political history of his day.

Tocqueville, Alexis de. *Democracy in America,* vols. 1 and 2, ed. J. P. Mayer. New York: Doubleday/Anchor, 1969. A classic analysis (originally published 1835–1840) of American democracy by an insightful French observer.

LIST OF WEBSITES

http://www.nara.gov
The National Archives site; includes an in-depth look at the history of the Declaration of Independence.

http://odur.let.rug.nl/~usa/P/aj7/about/bio/jackxx.htm
A site that focuses on Andrew Jackson and his role in shaping U.S. politics.

http://www.yale.edu/lawweb/avalon/constpap.htm
Includes documents on the roots of the Constitution, the American Revolution, and the Constitutional Convention.

http://www.yale.edu/lawweb/avalon/presiden/jeffpap.htm
A site that includes the papers of Thomas Jefferson. His autobiography is among the available materials.

3

The question of the relation of the states to the federal government is the cardinal question of our Constitutional system. It cannot be settled by the opinion of one generation, because it is a question of growth, and each successive stage of our political and economic development gives it a new aspect, makes it a new question.

—Woodrow Wilson[1]

Federalism:
Forging a Nation

Senate Republican leader Trent Lott declared it a triumph for those who believe that the answers to America's problems are more likely to be found in Albany, Sacramento, and Jackson than in Washington. Senator Daniel Patrick Moynihan, an outspoken critic of the legislation, called it "the most brutal act of social policy since Reconstruction." He claimed that within a decade the legislation would push more than a million children into poverty.[2]

At issue was the nation's program of assistance for poor families and whether the program would be directed by the national government or the states. Since the 1930s, the program had been run out of Washington as an entitlement policy, which meant that every American family who met the eligibility criteria was entitled to assistance. For many liberal Democrats, it was the cornerstone of the idea that no needy American family, wherever it resided, would be denied help. Individual states had some leeway in deciding the amount of support a needy family would receive each month, but they had to participate in the program and contribute to its funding.

The new legislation ended this federal guarantee of cash assistance, replacing it with a system of cash grants to the states, which would assume responsibility for caring for welfare recipients and getting them into jobs. The legislation fulfilled the long-held desire of conservative Republicans to reduce welfare dependency and move welfare recipients into tax-paying jobs. It also met their goal of reducing the power of the federal government. Under the new program, states would have to support a needy family for five years but could deny benefits if, after two years, an able-bodied adult refused to accept a job or job training. And after five years, a state could unconditionally deny benefits to poor families.

The 1996 Welfare Reform Act is one of thousands of controversies during American history that have hinged on whether national or state authority should prevail. Americans possess what amounts to dual citizenship: they are citizens both of the United States and of the state where they reside. The American political system is a *federal system*, one in which constitutional authority is divided between a national government and state governments: each is assumed to derive its powers directly from the people and therefore to have sovereignty (final authority) over the policy responsibilities assigned to it. The federal system consists of nation *and* states, indivisible and yet separate.[3]

This chapter on American constitutionalism focuses on federalism. The nature of the relationship between the nation and the states was the most pressing issue when the Constitution was written in 1787, and this chapter describes how that issue helped shape the Constitution. The chapter's closing sections discuss how federalism has changed during the nation's history and conclude with a brief overview of contemporary federalism. The main points presented in the chapter are the following:

Patrick Henry was a leading figure in the American Revolution ("Give me liberty or give me death!"). He later opposed ratification of the Constitution on grounds that the national government should be a union of states and not also of people.

- *The power of government must be equal to its responsibilities.* The Constitution was needed because the nation's preceding system (under the Articles of Confederation) was too weak to accomplish its expected goals, particularly those of a strong defense and an integrated economy.

- *Federalism—the Constitution's division of governing authority between two levels, nation and states—was the result of political bargaining.* Federalism was not a theoretical principle, but a compromise made necessary in 1787 by the prior existence of the states.

- *Federalism is not a fixed principle for allocating power between the national and state governments, but a principle that has changed over the course of time in response to new political needs.* Federalism has passed through several distinct stages during the nation's history.

- *Contemporary federalism tilts toward national authority, reflecting the increased interdependence of American society.* However, there is a current trend toward reducing the scope of federal authority.

FEDERALISM: NATIONAL AND STATE SOVEREIGNTY

The delegates to the Philadelphia convention in 1787 included many of the nation's most prominent leaders, such as George Washington and Benjamin Franklin. Not all of America's top leaders were at the convention, however, and many of them were steadfastly opposed to a strong national government. When rumors circulated that the convention would propose a new form of government rather than an amended Articles of Confederation, Patrick Henry, an ardent supporter of state-centered government, said that he "smelt a rat." After the convention had adjourned, he realized that his fears were justified. "Who authorized them," he asked, "to speak the language of 'We, the People,' instead of 'We, the States'?"

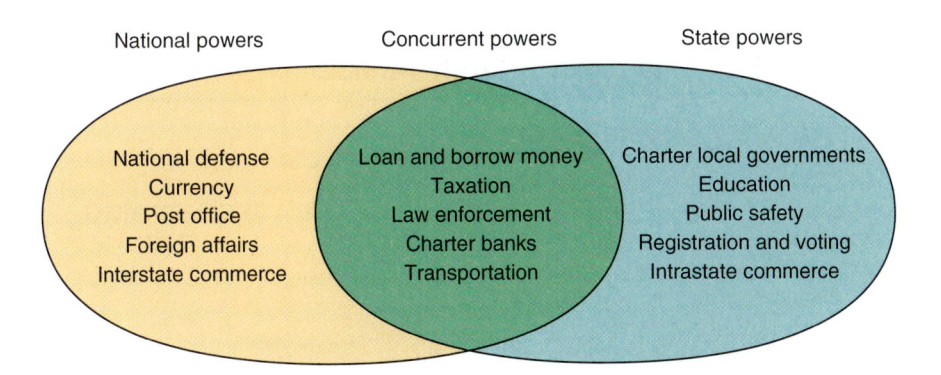

National powers	Concurrent powers	State powers
National defense Currency Post office Foreign affairs Interstate commerce	Loan and borrow money Taxation Law enforcement Charter banks Transportation	Charter local governments Education Public safety Registration and voting Intrastate commerce

Figure 3–1

Federalism as a Governing System: Examples of National, State, and Concurrent Powers
The American federal system divides sovereignty between a national government and the state governments. Each is constitutionally protected in its existence and authority, although their powers overlap somewhat even in areas granted to one level (for example, the federal government has a role in education policy).

The question—"people versus states?"—was dictated by the experience with the Articles of Confederation. The government of the Articles (see Chapter 2) was a union of states rather than also of people. The result was an inherently weak national government, since its strength rested entirely on the states' willingness to cooperate. If they refused to contribute to the collective effort, the national government had no sure way to make them comply. Georgia and North Carolina, for example, contributed no money at all to the national treasury between 1781 and 1786, and the national government could do nothing more than to implore them to pay a fair share of the costs of defense, diplomacy, and other national policies. The only realistic solution was a government based on the people. If ordered to pay taxes, individuals would either do so or face consequences—imprisonment or confiscation of property—that most of them would choose to avoid.

Although the need for a national government based directly on the people was therefore a goal of the writers of the Constitution, they also wanted to preserve the states as governing bodies. When Virginia's George Mason said he would never agree to a union that abolished the states, he was speaking for virtually all the delegates. The Philadelphia convention thereby devised a system of government that came to be known as **federalism.** Federalism is the division of **sovereignty,** or ultimate governing authority, between a national government and regional (that is, state) governments. Each directly governs the people and derives its powers from them.

American federalism is basically a system for dividing authority between sovereign national and state governments (see Figure 3–1). The system gives states the power to address local matters in separate ways, thus providing for a responsiveness to local values and differences. At the same time, federalism gives the national government the power to decide matters of broad national scope on a uniform basis. In practice, there is some overlap between state and national action, but there is also a division of responsibilities. The national government has primary responsibility for national defense and the currency, among other things, while the states have primary responsibilities for such policy areas as public education and police protection. The national and state governments also have some concurrent powers (that is, powers exercised over the same areas of policy); for example, each has the power to raise taxes and borrow money.

A federal system is different from a **confederacy,** which is the type of government established by the Articles. A confederacy is a union where the states alone are sovereign. The authority of the central government is derived from

federalism A governmental system in which authority is divided between two sovereign levels of government: national and regional.

sovereignty The ultimate authority to govern within a certain geographical area.

confederacy A governmental system in which sovereignty is vested entirely in subnational (state) governments.

HOW THE UNITED STATES COMPARES

Federal Versus Unitary Governments

Federalism involves the division of sovereignty between a national government and subnational (such as state) governments. It was invented in 1787 in order to maintain the preexisting American states while establishing an effective central government. Since then a number of other countries have established a *federal* government, but most countries have a *unitary* government, in which all sovereignty is vested in the national government. In some cases, countries have developed hybrid versions. Great Britain's government is formally unitary, but Parliament has granted some autonomy to regions. Mexico's system is formally federal, but in actuality nearly all power is concentrated in the national government.

COUNTRY	FORM OF GOVERNMENT
Canada	Federal
France	Unitary
Germany	Federal
Great Britain	Modified unitary
Italy	Modified unitary
Japan	Unitary
Mexico	Modified federal
United States	Federal
Sweden	Unitary

unitary system A governmental system in which the national government alone has sovereign (ultimate) authority.

the states, which can, at will, redefine the central government's authority. Federalism is also different from a **unitary system,** in which sovereignty is vested solely in the national government. In a unitary system, all regional and local governing units are subject to national authority. The people are citizens or subjects only of the national government, and the other governments derive their authority from the national government, which can, in theory at least, abolish them or redefine their authority.

In a federal system, because the national and state governments are both sovereign, each has powers that are not subject to the other's discretion. Moreover, each is protected constitutionally in its existence and from undue interference by the other in the conduct of its lawful affairs.

Federalism was invented in America in 1787. It was different not only from a confederate or unitary system but also from any form of government the world had known. The ancient Greek city-states and the medieval Hanseatic League were confederacies. The governments of Europe were unitary in form. The United States of America would be the first nation to be governed through a true federal system.

The Argument for Federalism

Unlike many other decisions made at the Philadelphia convention, federalism had no clear basis in political theory. Federalism was a practical necessity: there was a need for a stronger national government and yet the states existed and were intent on retaining their sovereignty.

Nevertheless, the Framers developed arguments for the superiority of this type of political system. Federalism, they said, would protect liberty, moderate the power of government, and provide the foundation for a strong and energetic national government.

Protecting Liberty

Theorists such as Locke and Montesquieu had not proposed a division of power between national and local authorities as a further means of protecting liberty. Nevertheless, the Framers came to look upon federalism as part of the Constitution's system of checks and balances (see Chapter 2). Alexander Hamilton argued in *Federalist* No. 28 that the American people could shift their loyalties back and forth between the national and state governments in order to keep each under control. "If [the people's] rights are invaded by either," Hamilton wrote, "they can make use of the other as the instrument of redress."

Alexander Hamilton
(1757–1804)

Alexander Hamilton was just thirty-two years old when he served as a delegate to the constitutional convention in Philadelphia. A strong nationalist, his *Federalist Papers* essays contributed to the ratification of the Constitution. George Washington appointed him to be the first secretary of the treasury, where he developed plans for the First Bank of the United States and for placing the federal government on a sound financial footing. He was fatally wounded in a duel with Aaron Burr, a political and personal foe.

Moderating the Power of Government

To the Anti-Federalists (opponents of the Constitution), the sacrifice of states' power to the nation was as unwise as it was unnecessary. They argued that a distant national government could never serve the people's interests as well as the states could. In support of their contention, the Anti-Federalists turned to Montesquieu, who had concluded that a small republic is more likely than a large one to respect and respond to the people it governs. When government encompasses a small area, he argued, its leaders are in closer touch with the people, have a better understanding of their needs, and a greater concern for their interests.

James Madison took issue with this argument. In *Federalist* No. 10, Madison contended that whether a government serves the common good is a function not of its size but of the range of interests that share political power. The problem with a smaller republic, Madison claimed, is that it is likely to have a dominant faction—whether it be large landholders, financiers, an impoverished majority, or some other group—that is strong enough to take full control of government, using this power to advance its selfish interests. A large republic is less likely to have such an all-powerful faction. If financiers are strong in one area of a large republic, they are likely to be weaker elsewhere, and the same will be true of other interests. By this reasoning, Madison concluded that political control in a large republic could not be won by a single interest but would require a joining of interests, each of which would be forced to limit its demands and to respect the interests of others. "Extend the sphere," said Madison, "and you take in a greater variety of parties and interests; you make it less probable that a majority of the whole will have a common motive to invade the rights of other citizens."

What's Your Opinion?

Large Versus Small Republics

During the debate over ratification of the Constitution, Americans argued over whether liberty and equality would be better protected by the states or by the nation. The Anti-Federalists argued that a small republic was closer to the people and therefore would do more to protect their rights. James Madison countered by saying that a large republic was preferable because it would have such a diversity of interests that compromise and tolerance among various groups would be required.

In your view, which side in this argument has the weight of American history behind it?

Strengthening the Union

The most telling argument in 1787 for a federal system, however, was that it would overcome the deficiencies of the Articles. The Articles had numerous flaws (including a very weak executive and a judiciary subservient to the state courts), and two of them were fatal: the government had neither the power to tax nor the power to regulate commerce.

It could take weeks to travel overland or by ship from the most distant points in the American states. The great size of America when compared with European countries was used as an argument by both those who favored a strong union and those who opposed it.

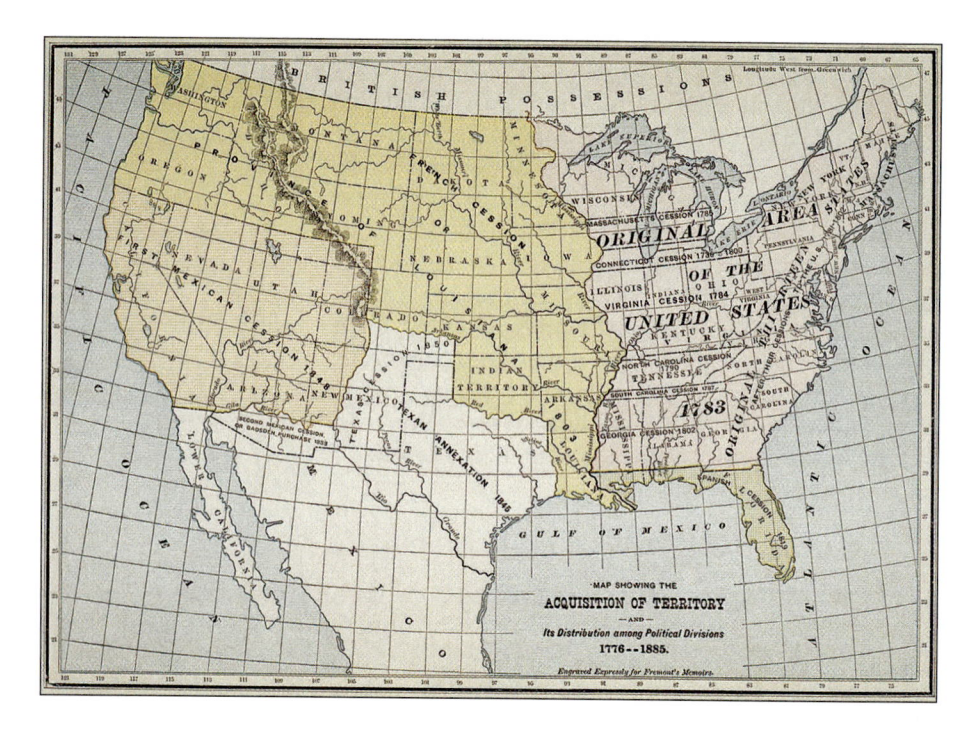

Historical Background

Under the Articles, Congress was given responsibility for national defense but was not granted the power to tax, and so it had to rely on the states for the money to maintain an army and navy. During the first six years under the Articles, Congress asked the states for $12 million but received only $3 million—not even enough to pay the interest on Revolutionary War debts. By 1786 the national government was so desperate for funds that it sold the navy's ships and had fewer than a thousand soldiers in uniform—this at a time when England had an army in Canada and Spain occupied Florida.

Congress was also expected to shape a national economy, yet it was powerless to do so because the Articles forbade interference with the states' commerce policies. States imposed trade barriers on each other. Connecticut placed a higher tariff on finished goods from Massachusetts than it did on the same goods shipped from England. New Jersey imposed a duty on foreign-made goods shipped from other states. New York responded by taxing goods from New Jersey shipped through New York ports.

The Articles of Confederation showed the fallacy of the adage "That government is best which governs least." The consequences of an overly weak authority were abundantly clear: public disorder, economic chaos, and inadequate defense.

The Powers of the Nation

The Philadelphia convention met to decide the powers of the national government. The delegates had not been sent to determine how state government should be structured. Accordingly, the U.S. Constitution focuses on the lawful authority of the national government, which is provided through *enumerated* and *implied powers*. Authority that is not in this way granted to the national government is left—or "reserved"—to the states. Thus the states have *reserved powers*.

Enumerated Powers

Article 1 of the Constitution grants to Congress seventeen **enumerated (expressed) powers.** These powers were intended by the Framers to be the basis for a government strong enough to forge a union that was secure in its defense and stable in its commerce. Congress's powers to regulate commerce among the states, to create a national currency, and to borrow money, for example, would provide a foundation for a sound national economy. Its power to tax, combined with its authority to declare war and establish an army and navy, would enable it to provide for the common defense. In addition, the Constitution prohibited the states from actions that would interfere with the national government's exercise of its lawful powers. Article 1, Section 10 forbids the states to make treaties with other nations, raise armies, wage war, print money, or make commercial agreements with other states without the approval of Congress.

The writers of the Constitution recognized that the lawful exercise of national authority would at times conflict with the actions of the states. In such instances, national law was intended to prevail. Article 6 of the Constitution grants this dominance in the so-called **supremacy clause,** which provides that "the laws of the United States . . . shall be the supreme law of the land."

enumerated (expressed) powers The seventeen powers granted to the national government under Article 1, Section 8 of the Constitution. These powers include taxation and the regulation of commerce as well as the authority to provide for the national defense.

supremacy clause Article 6 of the Constitution, which makes national law supreme over state law when the national government is acting within its constitutional limits.

Implied Powers

The Framers of the Constitution also recognized that an overly narrow definition of national authority would result in a government incapable of adapting to change. Under the Articles of Confederation, Congress was strictly limited to those powers expressly granted to it, inhibiting its ability to respond effectively to the country's changing needs after the Revolutionary War. Concerned that the enumerated powers by themselves might be too restrictive of national authority, the Framers added the **"necessary and proper" clause,** or, as it later came to be known, the **elastic clause.** Article 1, Section 8 gives Congress the power "to make all laws which shall be necessary and proper for carrying into execution the foregoing [enumerated] powers." This grant gave the national government **implied powers:** the authority to take action that is not expressly authorized by the Constitution but that supports actions that are so authorized.

"necessary and proper" clause (elastic clause) The authority granted Congress in Article 1, Section 8 of the Constitution "to make all laws which shall be necessary and proper" for the implementation of its enumerated powers.

implied powers The federal government's constitutional authority (through the "necessary and proper" clause) to take action that is not expressly authorized by the Constitution but that supports actions that are so authorized.

The Powers of the States

The Framers' preference for a sovereign national government was not shared in 1787 by all Americans. Although Anti-Federalists recognized a need to strengthen defense and interstate commerce, they feared the consequences of a strong central government. The interests of the people of New Hampshire were not identical to those of Georgians or Pennsylvanians, and the Anti-Federalists argued that only state-centered government would protect and preserve this *diversity.*

The Federalists responded by asserting that the national government would have no interest in submerging the states.[4] The national government would take responsibility for establishing a strong defense and for promoting a sound economy, while the states would retain nearly all other governing functions,

Why Should I Care?

Federalism: Who Governs Affects You

When Americans think about the question "who governs," they usually think in terms of whether the Republicans or the Democrats are in power. For much of America's history, however, the question evoked thoughts of federalism. Would the nation decide? Or would the states decide?

Even though Americans are governed more uniformly today than in the past, the issue of state or nation is still a critical one. Abortion is perhaps the preeminent example. The Supreme Court's *Roe v. Wade* (1973) decision made the choice of an abortion a constitutionally protected right in some circumstances. Before then, abortion was governed strictly by state laws, and most states banned it entirely. States still have some authority in the area (for example, they can impose a parental-consent requirement on minors in some circumstances), but they are prevented by federal law from outlawing it entirely.

Federal power has also lost out to state power in some policy areas. For example, two federal acts—the Age Discrimination Act and the Americans with Disabilities Act—have recently been judged not to apply to the actions of state governments. State governments have broad discretion in their treatment, for example, of elderly and disabled employees and job seekers.

The list of examples could be extended, but the point would be the same: how you are governed depends to a degree on who does the governing. Policy issues are not determined solely by whether the Republicans or the Democrats are in charge. They are affected also by whether the decisions are made in Washington or the state capital. For that reason, every American has a stake in how power is divided between the national and state governments.

---

including oversight of public morals, education, and safety. The national government, Madison said, would neither want these responsibilities nor have the competence to fulfill them.[5]

This argument did not persuade the Anti-Federalists that their fears of a powerful national government were unfounded. Even some of the Americans who were otherwise inclined to support the proposed constitution worried that it would lead to an overly powerful national government. The supremacy and "necessary and proper" clauses were particularly worrisome, because they provided a constitutional basis for future expansions of national authority. Such concerns led to demands for a constitutional amendment that would protect the states against encroachment by the national government. Ratified in 1791 as the Tenth Amendment to the Constitution, it reads: "The powers not delegated to the United States by the Constitution, nor prohibited by it to the States, are reserved to the States." The states' powers under the U.S. Constitution are thus called **reserved powers.**

reserved powers The powers granted to the states under the Tenth Amendment to the Constitution.

FEDERALISM IN HISTORICAL PERSPECTIVE

Since ratification of the Constitution two centuries ago, no aspect of it has provoked more frequent or bitter conflict than federalism. By establishing two levels of sovereign authority, the Constitution created competing centers of power and ambition, each of which was sure to claim disputed areas as belonging within its realm of authority.

Conflict between national and state authority was also ensured by the brevity of the Constitution. The Framers deliberately avoided detailed provisions, recognizing that brief phrases would give flexibility to the government they were creating. The document does not define what is meant by the "necessary and proper" clause, does not list any of the states' reserved powers, does not indicate whether the supremacy clause allows the states discretionary authority in areas where state and national responsibilities overlap, and does not indicate how *inter*state commerce (which the national government is empowered to regulate) differs from *intra*state commerce (which presumably is reserved for regulation by the states).

Not surprisingly, federalism has been a contentious and dynamic system, its development determined less by constitutional language than by the strength of contending interests and by the country's changing needs. Federalism can be viewed as having progressed through three historical eras, each of which has involved a different relationship between nation and states.

An Indestructible Union (1789–1865)

The issue during the first era, which lasted from the Constitution's beginnings in 1789 through the end of the Civil War in 1865, was the Union's survival. Given the state-centered history of America before the Constitution, it was inevitable that the states would dispute national policies that threatened their separate interests.

The Nationalist View: McCulloch v. Maryland

A first dispute over federalism arose when President George Washington's secretary of the treasury, Alexander Hamilton, persuaded Congress to establish the First Bank of the United States. Thomas Jefferson, Washington's secretary of state, opposed the bank on the grounds that its activities would benefit commercial interests and would harm small farmers, who in Jefferson's view were the backbone of the new nation. Jefferson claimed that the bank was unlawful because the Constitution did not explicitly authorize the creation of a national bank. Hamilton and his supporters claimed that because the federal government had constitutional authority to regulate currency, it had the "implied power" to establish a national bank.

Hamilton's view prevailed when Congress in 1791 established the First Bank of the United States, granting it a twenty-year charter. When the bank's charter expired in 1811, however, Congress did not renew it. Then in 1816, Congress established the Second Bank of the United States over the objections of state and local bankers. Responding to their complaints, several states, including Maryland, attempted to drive the Second Bank of the United States out of existence by levying taxes on its operations within their borders. Edwin McCulloch, who was head cashier of the Maryland branch of the U.S. Bank, refused to pay the Maryland tax, and the resulting dispute reached the Supreme Court.

John Marshall, the chief justice of the Supreme Court, was, like Hamilton, a strong nationalist, and in *McCulloch v. Maryland* (1819) the Court ruled decisively in favor of national authority. It was reasonable, Marshall concluded, to infer that a government with powers to tax, borrow money, and regulate

Historical Background

A first dispute over federalism was whether the Constitution allowed the creation of a Bank of the United States (shown here in an early nineteenth-century painting). The Constitution had a clause on the printing of currency but not on the establishment of a bank itself.

commerce could establish a bank in order to exercise those powers properly. Marshall's argument was a clear statement of *implied powers*—the idea that, through the "necessary and proper" clause, the national government's powers extend beyond a narrow reading of its enumerated powers.

Marshall also addressed the meaning of the Constitution's supremacy clause. The state of Maryland argued that it had the sovereign authority to tax the national bank even if the bank was a legal entity. The Supreme Court rejected Maryland's position, concluding that valid national law prevailed over conflicting state law. Because the national government had the power to create the bank, it could also protect the bank from actions by the states, such as taxation, that might destroy it.[6]

The *McCulloch* decision served as precedent for future assertions of national authority, including a second landmark decision by the Marshall Court. In *Gibbons v. Ogden* (1824), the Court ruled on the power of Congress to regulate commerce. The state of New York had granted a monopoly to Aaron Ogden to operate a ferry between New York and New Jersey. When Thomas Gibbons set up a competing ferry under a federal coastal licensing agreement, Ogden tried to prevent Gibbons from operating it. Marshall invalidated the New York monopoly, saying it intruded on Congress's power to regulate commerce among the states. Going further, Marshall ruled that Congress's power extended *into* a state when commerce between two or more states was at issue.[7]

Marshall's opinions asserted that legitimate uses of national power took precedence over state authority and that the "necessary and proper" clause and the commerce clause were broad grants of national power. As a nationalist, Marshall was providing the U.S. government the legal justification for expanding its power in ways that fostered the development of the nation as a nation rather than as a collection of states. This constitutional vision was of utmost significance. As Justice Oliver Wendell Holmes Jr. noted a century later, the Union could not have survived if each state had been allowed to determine for itself the extent to which national authority restricted its actions.[8]

The States'-Rights View: The Dred Scott Decision

Although John Marshall's rulings helped strengthen national authority, the issue of slavery posed a growing threat to the Union's survival. A resurgence of cotton farming in the early nineteenth century revived the South's flagging dependence on slaves and heightened white southerners' fears that Congress might move to abolish slavery. Southerners consequently did what others have done throughout American history: they devised a constitutional argument to fit their political needs. John C. Calhoun of South Carolina argued that the Constitution had created "a government of states . . . not a government of individuals."[9] This line of reasoning led Calhoun to his famed "doctrine of nullification," which declared that each state had the constitutional right to nullify a national law.

In 1832 South Carolina invoked this doctrine, declaring "null and void" a tariff law that favored northern interests. President Andrew Jackson retorted that South Carolina's action was "incompatible with the existence of the Union," a position that was strengthened when Congress authorized Jackson to use military force against South Carolina. The state backed down when Congress agreed to amend the tariff act slightly.

The clash foreshadowed a confrontation of far greater scope and consequence: the Civil War. War between the states would not break out for another thirty years, but in the interim, conflicts over states' rights intensified.[10] Westward expansion and immigration into the northern states were tilting power in Congress toward the free states, which increasingly signaled their determination to outlaw slavery in the United States at some future time. Attempts to find a compromise acceptable to both the North and the South were fruitless.

The Supreme Court's infamous *Dred Scott* decision exemplifies the conflict. Dred Scott, a slave, applied for his freedom when his master died, citing a federal law—the Missouri Compromise of 1820—that made slavery illegal in a free state or territory. Scott had lived in the North four years, but the Supreme Court in a 7-2 decision ruled that slaves were "property" and that persons of African descent were barred from citizenship and thereby could not sue for their freedom in federal courts. The Court also invalidated the Missouri Compromise, declaring that Congress had no authority to outlaw slavery in any part of the United States.[11]

The *Dred Scott* decision outraged many northerners and contributed to a sectional split in the majority Democratic party that enabled the Republican Abraham Lincoln to win the presidency in 1860 with only 40 percent of the popular vote. Lincoln had campaigned for the gradual, compensated abolition of slavery. By the time he assumed office, seven southern states had already seceded from the Union. In justifying his decision to wage civil war on these states, Lincoln said, "The Union is older than the states." In 1865 the superior strength of the Union army settled by force the question of whether national authority would be binding on the states.

John C. Calhoun
(1782–1850)

John C. Calhoun was a champion of states' rights and of slaveholding. He was Andrew Jackson's first vice president, but he resigned that post after Jackson came out strongly against Calhoun's doctrine of nullification. Calhoun then returned to the U.S. Senate to fight for his proposal. Later Calhoun secured passage of a gag rule that for a period prohibited the discussion of slavery in the Senate.

www.mhhe.com/patterson6

Southern delegates at the constitutional convention sought assurances that Congress would not bar the importation and sale of slaves and that their slave-based agricultural economy would be protected. The photo shows a Civil War–era building in Atlanta that was a site of slave auctions.

The American Civil War was the bloodiest conflict the world had yet known. Ten percent of fighting-age males died in the four-year war, and uncounted others were wounded. The death toll—618,000 (360,000 from the North, 258,000 from the South)—exceeded that of the American war dead in World War I, World War II, the Korean War, and the Vietnam War combined. And this death toll was in a nation with a population that was only one-ninth the size it is today.

Dual Federalism and Laissez-Faire Capitalism (1865–1937)

Although the Civil War preserved the Union, new challenges to federalism were surfacing. Constitutional doctrine held that certain policy areas, such as interstate commerce and defense, were the clear and exclusive province of national authority, whereas other policy areas, such as public health and intrastate commerce, belonged clearly and exclusively to the states. This doctrine, known as **dual federalism,** was based on the idea that a precise separation of national and state authority was both possible and desirable. "The power which one possesses," said the Supreme Court, "the other does not."[12]

American society, however, was in the midst of changes that raised questions about the suitability of dual federalism as a governing concept. The Industrial Revolution had given rise to large business firms, which were using

dual federalism A doctrine based on the idea that a precise separation of national power and state power is both possible and desirable.

their economic power to dominate markets and exploit workers. Government was the logical counterforce to this economic power. Which level of government—state or national—would regulate business?

There was also the issue of the former slaves. The white South had lost the war but was hardly of a mind to share power and opportunity with newly freed black people. Would the federal government be allowed to intervene in state affairs to ensure the fair treatment of African Americans?

Dual federalism became a barrier to an effective response to these issues. From the 1860s through the 1930s, the Supreme Court held firm to the idea that there was a sharp line between national and state authority and, in both areas, a high wall of separation between government and the economy. This era of federalism was characterized by state supremacy in racial policy and by business supremacy in commerce policy.

The Fourteenth Amendment and State Discretion

Ratified after the Civil War, the Fourteenth Amendment was intended to protect citizens (especially black Americans) from discriminatory actions by state governments.[13] A state was prohibited from depriving "any person of life, liberty, or property without due process of law," from denying "any person within its jurisdiction the equal protection of the laws," and from abridging "the privileges or immunities of citizens of the United States."

Supreme Court rulings during subsequent decades, however, helped to undermine the Fourteenth Amendment's promise. The Court held, for example, that the Fourteenth Amendment did not substantially limit the power of the states to regulate rights of person and property[14] and that the Fourteenth Amendment was not meant to prevent discrimination by private owners of hotels, restaurants, and other accommodations that catered to the general public.[15] Then, in *Plessy v. Ferguson* (1896), the Court issued its infamous "separate but equal" ruling. A black man, Adolph Plessy, had been convicted of violating a Louisiana law that required white and black citizens to ride in separate railroad cars. The Supreme Court upheld his conviction, concluding that state governments could require blacks to use separate railroad cars and other accommodations as long as those facilities were "equal" in quality to those reserved for use by whites. "If one race be inferior to the other socially," the Court concluded, "the Constitution of the United States cannot put them on the same plane." The lone dissenting justice in the case, John Marshall Harlan, had harsh words for his colleagues: "Our Constitution is color-blind and neither knows nor tolerates classes among citizens. . . . The thin disguise of 'equal' accommodations . . . will not mislead anyone nor atone for the wrong this day done."[16]

Historical Background

With its *Plessy* decision, the Court undercut the Fourteenth Amendment and allowed southern states to establish a thoroughly racist system of legalized segregation. Black children were forced into separate schools that seldom had libraries and usually had few teachers, most of whom had no formal training. Hospitals for blacks had few doctors and nurses and almost no medical supplies and equipment. Legal challenges to these discriminatory practices were generally unsuccessful. The *Plessy* ruling had become a justification for the separate and *unequal* treatment of black Americans. For the next seven decades, the states'-rights doctrine was often invoked by white southerners as a guise for the perpetuation of racism.

After the Civil War Reconstruction, the white majority in the South used the power of government to enforce a two-race society in which the public schools and other public facilities for blacks were vastly inferior to those for whites.

Judicial Protection of Business

Through its rulings after the Civil War, the Supreme Court also provided a constitutional basis for uncontrolled private power. The Supreme Court was dominated by adherents of the doctrine of laissez-faire capitalism (which holds that business should be "allowed to act" without interference), and they interpreted the Constitution in ways that frustrated government's attempts to regulate business activity. In 1886, for example, the Court decided that corporations were "persons" within the meaning of the Fourteenth Amendment, and thus their property rights were protected from substantial regulation by the states.[17] The irony was inescapable. A constitutional amendment that had been enacted to protect the newly freed slaves was ignored for this purpose but was used instead to protect fictitious persons—business corporations.

The Court also weakened the national government's regulatory power by narrowly interpreting its commerce power. The Constitution's **commerce clause** says that Congress shall have the power "to regulate commerce" among the states but does not spell out the economic activities included in the grant of power. When the federal government invoked the Sherman Antitrust Act (1890) in an attempt to break up a monopoly on the manufacture of sugar, the Supreme Court blocked the action, claiming that interstate commerce covered only the "transportation" of goods, not their "manufacture."[18] Manufacturing was deemed part of intrastate commerce and thus, according to the dual federalism doctrine, subject to state regulation only. However, because the Court had previously decided that the states' regulatory powers were restricted by the Fourteenth Amendment, the states were relatively powerless to control manufacturing activity.

Although the national government subsequently made some headway in business regulation, the Supreme Court remained an obstacle. An example is the case of *Hammer v. Dagenhart* (1918), which arose from a 1916 federal act that

commerce clause The clause of the Constitution (Article 1, Section 8) that empowers the federal government to regulate commerce among the states and with other nations.

Between 1865 and 1937, the Supreme Court's rulings severely restricted national power. Narrowly interpreting Congress's constitutional power to regulate commerce, the Court forbade Congress to regulate child labor and other aspects of manufacturing.

prohibited the interstate shipment of goods produced by child labor. The act was popular because factory owners were exploiting children, working them for long hours at low pay. Citing the Tenth Amendment, the Court invalidated the law, ruling that factory practices could be regulated only by the states.[19] However, in an earlier case, *Lochner v. New York* (1905), the Court had prevented a state from regulating labor practices, concluding that such action was a violation of firms' property rights.[20]

In effect, the Supreme Court had denied both Congress and the states the authority to decide economic issues. As the constitutional scholars Alfred Kelly, Winifred Harbison, and Herman Belz concluded, "No more complete perversion of the principles of effective federal government can be imagined."[21]

National Authority Prevails

Judicial supremacy in the economic sphere ended abruptly in 1937. For nearly a decade, the United States had been mired in the Great Depression, which President Franklin D. Roosevelt's New Deal was designed to alleviate. The Supreme Court, however, had ruled much of the New Deal's economic recovery legislation to be unconstitutional. A constitutional crisis of historic proportions seemed inevitable until the Court suddenly reversed its position. In the process, American federalism was fundamentally and forever changed.

The Great Depression revealed clearly that Americans had become a national community with national economic needs. By the 1930s, more than half the population lived in cities (only 20 percent did so in 1860), and more than ten million workers were employed by industry (only one million were so employed in 1860). Urban workers were typically dependent on landlords for their

Historical Background

During the Great Depression, shantytowns were erected in most cities by people who had lost heir jobs and homes. State and local governments could not cope with the enormous problems created by the Great Depression, so the federal government stepped in with its New Deal programs, greatly changing the nature of federal-state relations.

housing, on farmers and grocers for their food, and on corporations for their jobs. Farmers were more independent, but they too were increasingly a part of a larger economic network. Their income depended on market prices and shipping and equipment costs.[22]

This economic interdependence meant that no area of the economy was immune if things went wrong. When the depression hit in 1929, its effects could not be contained. A decline in spending was followed by a drop in production, a loss of jobs, unpaid rents and grocery bills, and a shrinking market for foodstuffs, which led to a further decline in spending, and so on, creating a relentless downward spiral. At the depths of the Great Depression, one-fourth of the nation's work force was unemployed.

The states by tradition had responsibility for welfare, but they were nearly penniless because of declining tax revenues and the growing ranks of poor people. The New Deal programs offered a way out of the crisis; for example, the National Industry Recovery Act (NIRA) of 1933 called for a massive public works program to create jobs and for coordinated action by major industries. However, the New Deal was opposed by economic conservatives (who accused Roosevelt of leading the nation down the road to communism) and by justices of the Supreme Court. In *Schechter v. United States* (1935), the Court invalidated the Recovery Act by a 5-4 vote, ruling that it usurped powers reserved to the states.[23]

Frustrated by the Court, Roosevelt in 1937 proposed his famed Court-packing plan. Roosevelt recommended that Congress enact legislation that would permit an additional justice to be appointed to the Court whenever a seated member passed the age of seventy. The number of justices would increase, and Roosevelt's appointees would presumably be more sympathetic to his programs. Roosevelt's scheme was resisted by Congress, but the controversy ended with "the switch in time that saved nine," when, for reasons that have never become fully clear, Justice Owen Roberts abandoned his opposition to Roosevelt's policies and thus gave the president a 5-4 majority on the Court.

Within months, the Court upheld the 1935 National Labor Relations Act, which gave employees the right to organize and bargain collectively.[24] In passing the act, Congress had argued that labor-management disputes disrupt the nation's economy and therefore could be regulated through the commerce clause. In upholding the act, the Supreme Court in effect granted Congress the authority to apply its commerce powers broadly.[25] During this same period, the Court also loosened its restrictions on Congress's use of its taxing and spending powers.[26] These decisions removed the constitutional barrier to increased federal authority, a change that the Court later acknowledged when it said that Congress's commerce power is "as broad as the needs of the nation."[27]

In effect, the Supreme Court had finally recognized the obvious: that an industrial economy is not confined by state boundaries and must be subject to some level of national regulation if it is to serve the nation's needs and interests. It was a principle that business itself also increasingly accepted. The nation's banking industry, for example, was saved in the 1930s from almost complete collapse by the creation of a federal regulatory agency, the Federal Deposit Insurance Corporation (FDIC). By insuring depositors' savings against loss, the FDIC gave depositors the confidence to keep their money in banks, enabling many banks to remain solvent despite the depression.

After the depression era and until recently, the Supreme Court gave Congress almost complete discretion in the enactment of policies affecting state governments and business firms. The extent of Congress's power was evident, for example, in the 1964 Civil Rights Act, which forbids racial discrimination by the private operators of hotels and restaurants on the grounds that they provide lodging and food to travelers engaged in interstate commerce.[28]

Toward National Citizenship

The fundamental change in the constitutional doctrine of federalism as applied to economic issues that took place in the 1930s is paralleled by similar changes in other areas. One area is civil rights. As will be discussed in Chapter 5, federal authority has compelled states and localities to eliminate government-sponsored discrimination and, in some cases, to create compensatory opportunities for minorities and women. In 1954, for example, the Supreme Court held that racial segregation in public schools was unconstitutional on grounds that it violated the Fourteenth Amendment.[29]

The idea that Americans are equal in their rights regardless of where they reside has also been applied in other areas. As Chapter 4 will discuss, states have been required to broaden individual rights of free expression and fair trial. An example is the Supreme Court's *Miranda* ruling, which requires police officers to inform crime suspects of their rights at the time of arrest.[30]

Of course, important differences remain in the rights and privileges of the residents of the separate states, as could be expected in a federal system. The death penalty, for example, is legal in some states but not others, and states differ greatly in terms of their services, such as the quality of their public schools. Nevertheless, national citizenship—the notion that Americans should be equal in their rights and opportunities regardless of the state in which they live—is a more encompassing idea today than in the past.

GLOBAL Perspective

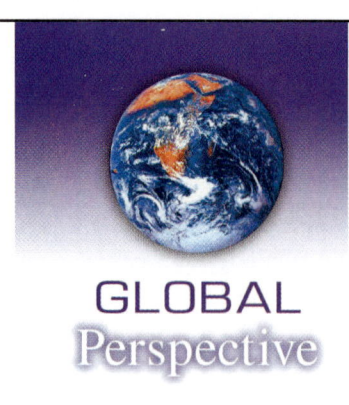

Americans in an Interdependent World

Citizens of the World, Too?

Americans have a form of dual citizenship. They are citizens of their nation and also of the state in which they reside. They are subject to the laws of both levels of government and enjoy the rights and privileges of each of them.

Are Americans also becoming citizens of the world in a meaningful sense? In *The End of the Nation State*, Kenichi Ohmae argues that global economic change is altering traditional patterns of governing and citizenship. Nations' economies are now less within their own control as a result of mushrooming growth in international trade. Giant multinational corporations make decisions about production, supply, and pricing that have little relationship to national boundaries and that generate pressure for global free trade and international standards. And of course the trend toward international rules is not confined to those rules associated with economic globalization. Since its formation after World War II, the United Nations has issued countless resolutions and directives aimed at the internal affairs of particular countries.

In effect, as the world has gotten smaller, nations have faced pressures to give up some of their authority to international bodies. An example is the World Trade Organization, which requires its members, including the United States, to follow open trade policies buttressed by regulations that are designed to promote fair trade among the members. When WTO nations have a dispute, it is reviewed and member states are expected to abide by the findings.

Compared with many nations, the United States has been somewhat reluctant to defer to collective agreements. During the past decade, for example, the United States has refused to sign the international treaty to ban land mines, has refused to sign the Kyoto accord to combat global warming, and has refused to back a permanent international war crimes tribunal. Nevertheless, more so than in the past, the United States, like other nations, has seen a need to give up some control over its national policies. In this respect, Americans are subject to the decisions of international bodies as well as those of their state and national governments.

FEDERALISM TODAY

Since the 1930s, the relation of the nation to the states has changed so fundamentally that dual federalism is no longer even a roughly accurate description of the American situation.[31]

An understanding of the nature of federalism today requires a recognition of two countervailing trends. The first is a long-term *expansion* of national authority that began in the 1930s and continued for the next half century. The national government now operates in many policy areas that were once almost exclusively within the control of states and localities. The national government does not dominate these policy areas, but it does have a significant role. Much of this influence stems from social welfare policies that were enacted in the 1960s as part of President Lyndon Johnson's Great Society program, which included initiatives in health care, public housing, nutrition, welfare, urban development, and other areas reserved previously to states and localities.

The second trend is more recent and involves a partial *contraction* of national authority. Known as "devolution," the recent trend involves "the passing down" of authority from the national government to the state and local levels. Devolution has reversed the decades-long increase in federal authority but only in some areas and then only to a modest degree.

Stated differently, the national government's policy authority has expanded greatly since the 1930s, even though that authority has been reduced somewhat in recent years. What follows is an explanation of the first of these trends: the expansion of federal authority since the New Deal era.

Interdependency and Intergovernmental Relations

Interdependency is a primary reason why national authority increased dramatically in the twentieth century. Modern systems of transportation, commerce, and communication transcend local and state boundaries. These systems are national, even international, in scope, which means that problems affecting Americans in one part of the country are likely also to affect Americans living elsewhere. This situation has required Washington to assume a larger policy role: national problems ordinarily require national solutions.

This situation has also encouraged national, state, and local policymakers to work together to solve policy problems. This collaborative effort has been described as **cooperative federalism**.[32] The difference between this system of federalism and the older dual federalism has been likened to the difference between a marble cake, whose levels flow together, and a layer cake, whose levels are separate.[33]

cooperative federalism The situation in which the national, state, and local levels work together to solve problems.

Cooperative federalism is based on shared policy responsibilities rather than sharply divided ones. An example is Medicaid, which provides health care for the poor. The Medicaid program is jointly funded by the national and state governments, operates within eligibility standards set by the national government, and gives states some latitude in determining the benefits that recipients receive. The Medicaid program is not an isolated example. Literally hundreds of policy programs today are run jointly by the national and state governments. In many cases, local governments are also involved. The characteristics of these programs are the following:

- Jointly funded by the national and state governments (and sometimes by local governments too)
- Jointly administered, with the states and localities providing most of the direct service to recipients and a national agency providing general administration
- Jointly determined, with both the state and national governments (and sometimes the local governments) having a say in eligibility and benefit levels, and with federal regulations, such as those prohibiting discrimination, giving an element of uniformity to the various state and local efforts

Cooperative federalism should not be interpreted to indicate that the states are now powerless and dependent. States have retained most of their traditional authority. In fact, the states have a larger influence than Washington does in

86   PART ONE   Foundations

Texas Attorney General John Cornyn speaks at a gathering of federal, state, and local law enforcement officials. Cooperative federalism brings together officials from all levels of government in joint efforts to solve common problems.

Figure 3-2

Federal and State/Local Government Employees, as Percentage of All Government Employees Who Work in Selected Policy Areas

Although federal authority has reached into areas traditionally dominated by the state governments, state and local governments still dominate many policy areas. One indicator is the high percentage of government employees in selected areas who work for state or local governments.

Source: U.S. Bureau of the Census, 2002.

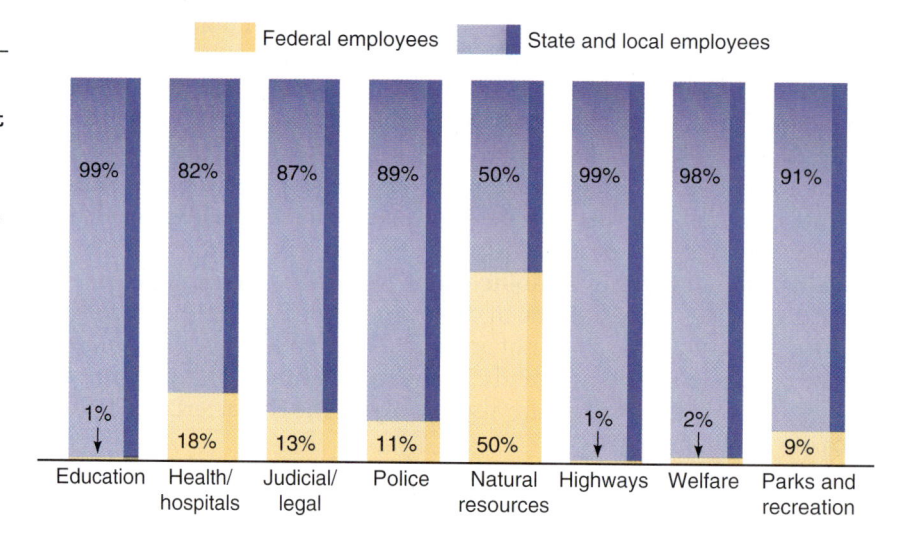

Federal employees | State and local employees

Policy Area	Federal	State/Local
Education	1%	99%
Health/hospitals	18%	82%
Judicial/legal	13%	87%
Police	11%	89%
Natural resources	50%	50%
Highways	1%	99%
Welfare	2%	98%
Parks and recreation	9%	91%

many policy areas (see Figure 3–2). Nearly 95 percent of the funding for public schools, for example, is provided by states and localities, which also set most of the education standards, from teachers' qualifications to course requirements to the length of the school day. Moreover, the policy areas dominated by the states—such as education, law enforcement, and transportation—tend to be those that have the greatest impact on people's daily lives. Finally, contrary to what many Americans might think, state and local governments have nearly six times as many employees as the federal government.

Nevertheless, the federal government's involvement in policy areas traditionally reserved for the states has increased its policy influence and has diminished state-to-state policy differences.³⁴ Before the enactment of the federal Medicaid program in 1965, for example, poor people in many states were not entitled to government-paid health care. Now most poor people are eligible regardless of where in the United States they live.

Government Revenues and Intergovernmental Relations

The interdependence of different sectors of modern American society is one of two factors that have propelled a larger federal role in domestic policy. The other is the federal government's superior taxing and borrowing capacity. States and localities are in an inherently competitive situation with regard to taxation. A state or locality cannot raise taxes very high without losing residents to a place where taxes are lower. Moreover, the federal government depends almost entirely on forms of taxation, such as personal and corporate income taxes, that automatically produce more revenue as the economy expands. State and local governments depend more heavily than does Washington on less flexible revenue sources, such as license fees and property taxes. The result is that the federal government raises more tax revenues than do all fifty states and the thousands of local governments combined (see Figure 3–3). Moreover, because it controls the American dollar, the federal government has a nearly unlimited ability to borrow money to cover its deficits.

Fiscal Federalism

The federal government's revenue-raising advantage has helped make money the basis for many of the relations between the national government and the states and localities. **Fiscal federalism** refers to the expenditure of federal funds on programs run in part through state and local governments.³⁵ The federal government provides some or all the money for a program through **grants-in-aid** (cash payments) to states and localities, which then administer the program.

The pattern of federal assistance to states and localities during the last four decades is shown in Figure 3–4. Federal grants-in-aid increased manyfold during this period. A sharp rise occurred in the late 1960s and early 1970s as a result of President Johnson's Great Society programs. Even at the height of the New Deal, federal aid had accounted for less than 10 percent of state and local spending. With Johnson's Great Society, however, the figure rose above 20 percent and has remained in that range ever since. In other words, roughly one in every five dollars spent by local and state governments in recent decades was raised not by them, but by the government in Washington (see "States in the Nation").

Cash grants to states and localities have extended Washington's influence over policy.³⁶ Through the funds it provides and the conditions it attaches to the use of those funds, Washington affects the policy choices of state and local governments. They can reject a grant-in-aid, but if they accept it, they must spend it in the specified ways. And since most grants require states to contribute matching funds, the federal programs in effect determine how states will use some of

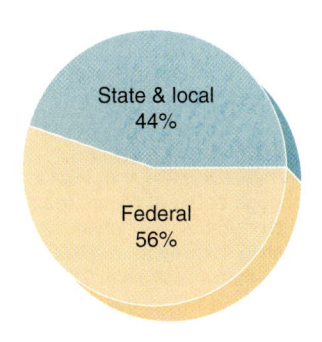

Figure 3–3
Federal, State, and Local Shares of Government Tax Revenue
The federal government raises more tax revenues than all state and local governments combined.
Source: U.S. Department of Commerce, 2002.

State & local 44%
Federal 56%

fiscal federalism A term that refers to the expenditure of federal funds on programs run in part through states and localities.

grants-in-aid Federal cash payments to states and localities for programs they administer.

Figure 3-4

Federal Grants to State and Local Governments

Federal aid to states and localities has increased dramatically since the 1950s, although some of the increase is attributable to inflation. One dollar in 1955 was worth the same as five dollars in 2000. In terms of 1955 dollars, federal grants totaled about $50 billion in 2000.

Source: U.S. Census Bureau.

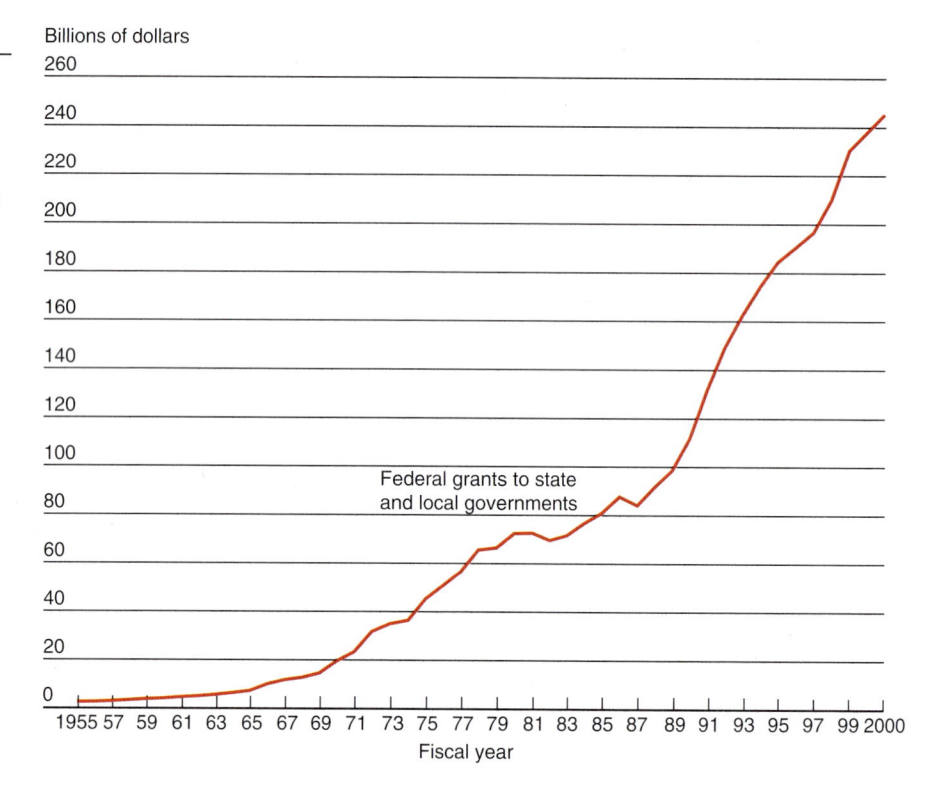

their own tax dollars. Federal grants have also pressured state and local officials to accept broad national goals, such as the elimination of racial and other forms of discrimination. A building constructed with the help of federal funds, for example, must be accessible to persons with disabilities.

Nevertheless, federal grants-in-aid also serve the policy interests of state and local officials. They have often complained that federal grants contain too many restrictions and infringe too much on their authority, but they have been eager to obtain the money, since it permits them to offer services they could not otherwise provide. An example is a 1994 federal grant program that has enabled local governments to put seventy-five thousand additional police officers on the streets.

Categorical and Block Grants

State and local governments receive two major types of assistance, categorical grants and block grants, which are differentiated by the extent to which Washington defines the conditions of their use.

Categorical grants are the more restrictive; they can be used only for a designated activity. An example is funds directed for use in school lunch programs. These funds can be used only in support of school lunches; they cannot be diverted for other school purposes, such as the purchase of textbooks or the hiring of teachers. **Block grants** are less restrictive. The federal government specifies the general area in which the funds must be used, but state and local

categorical grants Federal grants-in-aid to states and localities that can be used only for designated projects.

block grants Federal grants-in-aid that permit state and local officials to decide how the money will be spent within a general area such as education or health.

STATES IN THE NATION

Federal Grants-in-Aid as a Percentage of Total State Revenue

Federal assistance accounts for a significant share of state revenue, but the state-to-state variation is considerable. Louisiana is at one extreme: 34.6 percent of its total revenue comes from federal grants. Nevada is at the other extreme: only 14.5 percent of its revenue comes from federal assistance. Ironically, states in the South, where anti-Washington sentiment is relatively high, tend to get a larger percentage of their revenue through federal grants than most other states do. Many of the grant programs are designed to assist people with low incomes, and poverty is more widespread in the South than in other regions. Moreover, southern states have traditionally provided fewer government services, and federal grants therefore constitute a larger proportion of their state budgets.

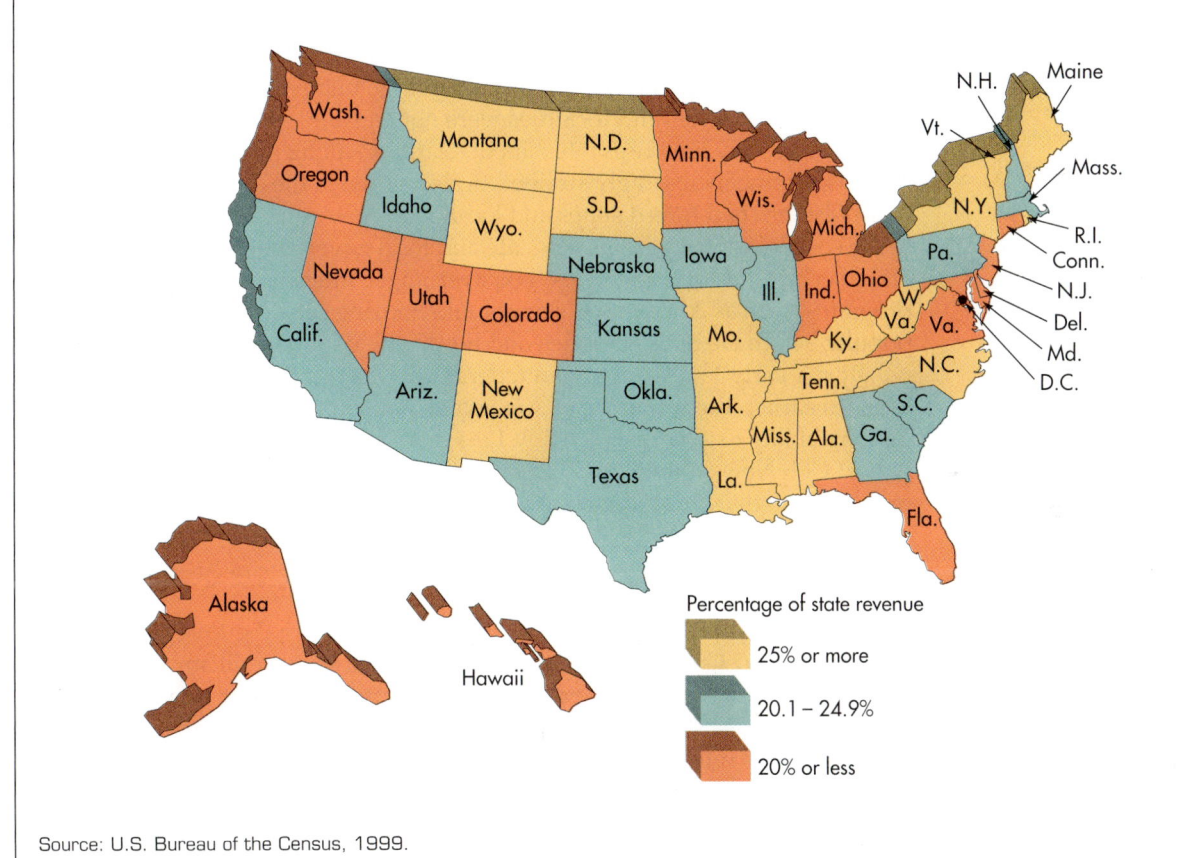

Percentage of state revenue:
- 25% or more
- 20.1 – 24.9%
- 20% or less

Source: U.S. Bureau of the Census, 1999.

---

officials select the specific projects. A block grant targeted for the health area, for example, might give state and local officials leeway in deciding whether to use the money on hospital construction, medical equipment, or some other health care activity.

State and local officials have naturally preferred federal money that comes with fewer strings attached, so they have favored block grants. On the other hand, members of Congress have at times preferred categorical grants, since this form of assistance gives them more control over how state and local officials will spend federal funds.[37] Recently, however, officials at all levels have looked to block grants as the key to a more workable form of federalism. This tendency is part of a larger trend—that of devolution.

A New Federalism: Devolution

devolution The passing down of authority from the national government to the state and local governments.

Devolution is the idea that American federalism will be improved by a shift in authority from the federal government to the state and local governments. Devolution is reshaping American federalism and is attributable to both practical and political developments.

Budgetary Pressures and Public Opinion

As a practical matter, the growth in federal assistance had slowed by the early 1980s. The federal government was facing huge budget deficits, and large new grants-in-aid to states and localities were not feasible.

As budgetary pressures intensified, relations among national, state, and local officials became increasingly strained. A slowdown in the annual increase in federal assistance had forced states and localities to pay an increasingly larger share of the costs of joint programs. As state and local governments raised taxes or cut other services to meet the costs, taxpayer anger intensified. Some of the grant programs, such as AFDC, food stamps, and housing subsidies, had not been very popular before the budget crunch and now came under even heavier criticism.

By the early 1990s, American federalism was positioned for a change. Two decades earlier, three-fourths of Americans had expressed confidence in Washington's ability to govern effectively. Less than half the public now held this view. A 1993 CBS News/New York Times survey indicated that 69 percent of Americans believed that "the federal government creates more problems than it solves."

The Republican Revolution

When the Republican party scored a decisive victory in the 1994 congressional elections, Newt Gingrich declared that "1960s-style federalism is dead." Republican lawmakers proposed to cut some programs, but even more, they sought to increase state and local control. They proposed to lump dozens of categorical grants into a few block grants, thus giving states and localities more control of how money would be spent.

That Republicans would lead the move to a more decentralized form of federalism was no surprise. Although both parties had initiated expansions of federal authority, Republicans had more often questioned the overall result. Republican presidents Richard Nixon, Ronald Reagan, and George Bush all advocated some version of a "new federalism" in which some areas of public policy for which the federal government had assumed responsibility would be returned to state and localities.[38]

Upon taking control of Congress in 1995, Republican lawmakers acted to reduce unfunded mandates, the federal programs that require action by states or localities but provide no or insufficient funds to pay for it. For example, states and localities are required by federal law to make their buildings accessible to

When the 1994 elections were over, Newt Gingrich declared that "1960s-style federalism is dead." As Speaker of the House of Representatives, Gingrich then helped enact major changes in federal-state relations.

the physically handicapped, but Washington pays only part of the cost of these accommodations. In the Unfunded Mandates Reform Act of 1995, Congress eliminated some of these mandates, although under threat of a presidential veto it exempted those that deal with civil rights and liberties. The GOP-controlled Congress also took action to lump additional categorical grants into block grants, thus giving states more control over how federal money would be spent.

The most significant legislative change came a year later, when the Republican Congress enacted the sweeping 1996 Welfare Reform Act. Its key element is the Temporary Assistance for Needy Families block grant (TANF), which ended the decades-old program that granted cash assistance to every poor family with children. TANF restricts a family's eligibility for federal assistance to five years, and after two years, a family head normally has to go to work or the benefits cease. Moreover, TANF gives states wide latitude in setting benefit levels, eligibility criteria, and other regulations affecting aid for poor families. Ironically, TANF actually increased the level of federal grant spending because Washington picked up a larger share of welfare costs. But states gained more control over how the funds would be spent. (TANF and other aspects of the 1996 welfare reform legislation are discussed further in later chapters.)

After passage of the 1996 Welfare Reform Act, congressional efforts to roll back federal authority declined sharply. Devolution had hardly rolled back a half century of Washington-centered federalism, nor had it blunted new federal assistance programs. Among the federal initiatives enacted recently are grants for classroom modernization and the hiring of additional teachers.

Although it is uncertain how far devolution will be extended, American federalism has clearly entered a new stage, where answers to the nation's domestic problems will be sought less in Washington than in the states and localities. Devolution has resulted in a modification of fiscal and cooperative federalism rather than their demise. The federal government will continue to be

> ### William H. Rehnquist
> (1924–)
>
> William H. Rehnquist graduated at the top of his Stanford Law School class and almost immediately got involved in politics, which led eventually to his appointment to the Supreme Court in 1971 as an associate justice. President Reagan appointed him chief justice when Warren Burger retired from that post in 1986. Rehnquist's major contribution to federalism has been a series of decisions that have limited Congress's authority to enact laws binding on the states.

a part of the answer to problems in policy areas once reserved almost exclusively to the states. Because of the complexity of modern policy issues and because of the interdependency of American society, the states will never regain the level of autonomy that they exercised in the early twentieth century. Through devolution, however, they have acquired a greater degree of discretionary authority in some policy areas.

Devolution, Judicial Style

In the five decades after the 1930s, the Supreme Court granted Congress broad discretion in the enactment of policies affecting state and local governments. In *Garcia v. San Antonio Authority* (1985), for example, the Court held that federal minimum wage standards apply even to employees of state and local governments.[39] States and localities are prohibited from paying their employees less than the federally mandated minimum wage.

In recent years, however, the Supreme Court has restricted congressional authority somewhat. Chief Justice William Rehnquist and some of the other Republican appointees on the Supreme Court believe that Congress in some instances has encroached on powers properly reserved through the Tenth Amendment to state governments. In *United States v. Lopez* (1995), for example, the Court struck down a federal law that prohibited the possession of guns within a thousand feet of a school. Congress had justified the law as an exercise of its commerce power, but the Court stated that the ban had "nothing to do with commerce, or any sort of economic activity."[40] Two years later, in *Printz v. United States* (1997), the Court struck down that part of the federal Handgun Violence Prevention Act (the so-called Brady bill) that required local law-enforcement officers to conduct background checks on prospective handgun buyers. The Court said the provision violated the "principle of separate state sovereignty," arguing that the federal government cannot "command" local officials "to administer or enforce a federal regulatory program."[41] In *Kimel v. Florida Board of Regents* (2000), the Supreme Court held that Congress did not have the authority to require state governments to comply with the federal law that bars discrimination against older workers. Age discrimination is not among the forms of discrimination expressly prohibited by the U.S. Constitution, and the Court declared that states have the power to decide for themselves the age-related policies that will apply to their employees.[42] In a 2002 case, *Board of Trustees of the University of Alabama v. Garrett*, the Court extended this ban to include people with disabilities, saying they cannot sue a state for violations of the American With Disabilities Act.[43]

Through these and other recent decisions, the Court has sought to expand states' immunity from federal authority. However, the Court has not repudiated the principle established in the 1930s that Congress's commerce and spending powers are broad and substantial. In *Reno v. Condon* (2000), for example, the Court ruled that the states have to comply with a federal law barring them from selling to private firms or groups their databases of personal information obtained from automobile license applicants. The majority opinion, which was

Should States Have Authority to Legalize Marijuana Use for Medical Purposes?

Federalism has been a source of uncounted disputes between states and the national government. One of the more unusual is the current controversy over the medical use of marijuana and whether states have authority to create exceptions to a federal ban on marijuana. California is among a small number of states that in recent years have enacted laws approving the use of marijuana to relieve pain and other symptoms of illness. These laws, however, contradict the federal Controlled Substances Act, which prohibits the manufacture, distribution, and use of various drugs, including marijuana. In 2001, the Supreme Court ruled in *United States v. Oakland Cannabis Buyers' Cooperative* that marijuana has no medical value, a judgment disputed by Lyn Nofziger, who served as an advisor to President Ronald Reagan.

Yes: When our grown daughter was undergoing chemotherapy for lymph cancer, she was sick and vomiting constantly as a result of her treatments. No legal drugs . . . helped her situation. As a result we finally turned to marijuana which, of course, we were forced to obtain illegally. With it, she kept her food down, was comfortable and even gained weight . . . A doctor should have every possible medication—including marijuana— in his armamentarium. If doctors can prescribe morphine and other addictive medicines, it makes no sense to deny marijuana to sick and dying patients.
—Lyn Nofziger, Republican consultant

No: The Controlled Substances Act prohibits the manufacture and distribution of various drugs, including marijuana. In this case, we must decide whether there is a medical necessity exception to these prohibitions. We hold that there is not. . . . The statue reflects a determination that marijuana has no medical benefits worthy of exception. . . . [Marijuana] has no clearly accepted medical use . . . has a high potential for abuse . . . and has a lack of accepted safety for use under medical supervision.
—Majority Opinion, U.S. Supreme Court

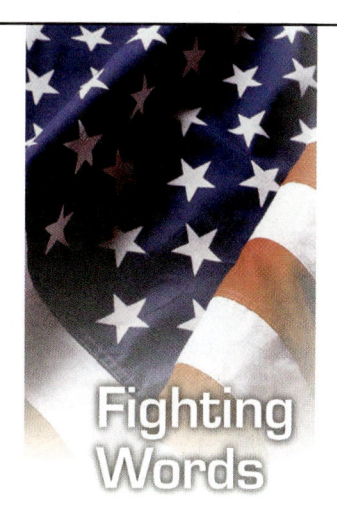

Fighting Words

---

written by Chief Justice Rehnquist, declared that the information in these databases is "an article of commerce" and thus is subject to regulation through Congress's commerce power. The Court noted that the law also applied to "private resellers" and was aimed at regulating "the owners of databases," which in this case included the states.[44]

THE PUBLIC'S INFLUENCE: SETTING THE BOUNDARIES OF FEDERAL-STATE POWER

The ebb and flow in Washington's power in the twentieth century coincided closely with public opinion. The American people have had a decisive voice in determining the relationship between the federal and state governments.

During the Great Depression, when it was clear that the states would be unable to help, Americans turned to Washington for relief. For people without jobs, the fine points of the Constitution were of little consequence. President Roosevelt's programs were a radical departure from the past but quickly gained widespread support.[45] The second great wave of federal social programs—President Lyndon Johnson's Great Society—was also driven by public demands. Income and education levels had risen dramatically after the Second World War, and Americans wanted more and better services from government. When the states were slow to respond, Americans pressured federal officials to act.[46] Public opinion is also behind the recent rollback in federal authority. The Republican takeover in 1995 was in large part a result of Americans' increased dissatisfaction with the performance of the federal government.[47]

The public's role in defining the boundaries between federal and state power would come as no surprise to the Framers of the Constitution. For them, federalism was a pragmatic issue, one to be decided by the nation's needs rather than by inflexible rules. And indeed, each succeeding generation of Americans has seen fit to devise a balance of federal and state power that would serve its interests. The historian Daniel Boorstin said the true genius of the American people is their pragmatism; their willingness to try new ways when the old ones stop working.[48] In few areas of governing has this ingenuity been more apparent than in Americans' approach to federalism.

Self-Quiz
www.mhhe.com/patterson6

SUMMARY

A foremost characteristic of the American political system is its division of authority between a national government and the states. The first U.S. government, established by the Articles of Confederation, was essentially a union of the states.

In establishing the basis for a stronger national government, the U.S. Constitution also made provision for safeguarding state interests. The result was the creation of a federal system in which sovereignty was vested in both national and state governments. The Constitution enumerates the general powers of the national government and grants it implied powers through the "necessary and proper" clause. Other powers are reserved to the states by the Tenth Amendment.

From 1789 to 1865, the nation's survival was at issue. The states found it convenient at times to argue that their sovereignty took precedence over national authority. In the end, it took the Civil War to cement the idea that the United States was a union of people, not of states. From 1865 to 1937, federalism reflected the doctrine that certain policy areas were the exclusive responsibility of the national government, whereas other policy areas belonged exclusively to the states. This constitutional position permitted the laissez-faire doctrine that big business was largely beyond governmental control. It also allowed the states in their public policies to discriminate against African Americans. Federalism in a form recognizable today began to emerge in the late 1930s.

In the areas of commerce, taxation, spending, civil rights, and civil liberties, among others, the federal government now has an important role, one that is the inevitable consequence of the increasing complexity of American society and the interdependence of its people. National, state, and local officials now work closely together to solve the country's problems, a situation that is described as cooperative federalism. Grants-in-aid from Washington to the states and localities have been the chief instrument of national influence. States and localities have received billions in federal assistance; in accepting that money, they have also accepted both federal restrictions on its use and the national policy priorities that underlie the granting of the money.

In recent years, the relationship between the nation and the states has again become a priority issue. Power is shifting downward to the states, and a new balance in the ever-evolving system of U.S. federalism is taking place. This change, like changes throughout U.S. history, has sprung from the demands of the American people.

KEY TERMS

block grants
categorical grants
commerce clause
confederacy
cooperative federalism
devolution
dual federalism
enumerated powers (expressed powers)
federalism
fiscal federalism
grants-in-aid
implied powers
"necessary and proper" clause (elastic clause)
reserved powers
sovereignty
supremacy clause
unitary system

SUGGESTED READINGS

Beer, Samuel H. *To Make a Nation: The Rediscovery of American Federalism.* Cambridge, Mass.: The Belknap Press of Harvard University Press, 1993. An innovative interpretive framework for understanding the impact of federalism and nationalism on the nation's development.

Conlan, Timothy. *From New Federalism to Devolution.* Washington, D.C.: Brookings Institution Press, 1998. A careful analysis of the changing nature of modern federalism.

Cornell, Saul. *The Other Founders: Anti-Federalism and the Dissenting Tradition in America.* Chapel Hill: University of North Carolina Press, 1999. An analysis of Anti-Federalist thought, its origins, and its legacy.

Elkins, Stanley, and Eric McKitrick. *The Age of Federalism: The Early American Republic, 1788–1800.* New York: Oxford University Press, 1993. An award-winning book on the earliest period of American federalism.

Ross, William G. *A Muted Fury: Populists, Progressives, and Labor Unions Confront the Courts, 1890–1937.* Princeton, N.J.: Princeton University Press, 1993. A valuable study of the political conflict surrounding the judiciary's laissez-faire doctrine in the 1890–1937 period.

Thompson, Tommy. *Power to the People: An American State at Work.* New York: HarperCollins, 1996. An argument for state-centered federalism by one of its leading practitioners, the former governor of Wisconsin.

Walker, David B. *The Rebirth of Federalism*, 2d ed. Chatham, N.J.: Chatham House Publishers, 2000. An optimistic assessment of the state of today's federalism.

LIST OF WEBSITES

http://lcweb2.loc.gov/ammem/amlaw/lawhome.html
A site containing congressional documents and debates from 1774 to 1873.

http://www.statesnews.org
The site of the Council of State Governments; includes current news from each of the states and basic information about their governments.

http://www.temple.edu/federalism
The site of the Center for the Study of Federalism, located at Temple University; it offers information and publications on the federal system of government.

http://www.yale.edu/lawweb/avalon/federal/fed.htm
A documentary record of the Federalist Papers, the Annapolis Convention, the Articles of Confederation, the Madison Debates, and the U.S. Constitution.

4

A bill of rights is what the people are entitled to against every government on earth, general or particular, and what no just government should refuse, or rest on inference.

—Thomas Jefferson[1]

Civil Liberties:
Protecting Individual Rights

Robert and Sarisse Creighton and their three children were asleep when FBI agents and local police broke into their home in the middle of the night. Brandishing guns, the officers searched the house for a relative of the Creightons who was suspected of bank robbery. When asked to show a search warrant, the officers said, "You watch too much TV." The suspect was not there, and the officers left as abruptly as they had entered. The Creightons sued the FBI agent in charge, Russell Anderson, for violating their Fourth Amendment right against unlawful search.

The Creightons won a temporary victory when the Eighth U.S. Circuit Court of Appeals—noting that individuals are constitutionally protected against warrantless searches unless officers have good reason ("probable cause") for a search and unless they have good reason ("exigent circumstances") for conducting that search without a warrant—concluded that Anderson had been derelict in his duty. In the judgment of the appellate court, Anderson should have sought a warrant from a judge, who would have decided whether a search of the Creightons' home was justified.

The Supreme Court of the United States overturned the lower court's ruling. The Court's majority opinion said: "We have recognized that it is inevitable that law enforcement officials will in some cases reasonably but mistakenly conclude that probable cause is present, and we have indicated that in such cases those officials . . . should not be held personally liable." Justice John Paul Stevens and two other justices sharply dissented. Stevens accused the Court's majority of showing "remarkably little fidelity" to the Fourth Amendment.[2] Civil liberties groups claimed that the Court's decision gave police an open invitation to invade people's homes on the slightest pretext. However, the Court's decision was praised by law enforcement officials and conservatives, who contended that a ruling in the Creightons' favor would have made police hesitant to pursue suspects for fear of a lawsuit if a search failed to produce the person sought.

As this case illustrates, issues of individual rights are complex and political. No right is absolute. For example, the Fourth Amendment protects Americans not from *all* searches but from *unreasonable* searches. The public would be unsafe if law officials could never search for evidence of a crime or pursue a suspect into a home. Yet the public would also be unsafe if police could frisk people at will or invade their homes with impunity. The challenge to a civil society is to establish a level of police authority that balances the demands of public safety with those of individual freedom. The balance point, however, is always subject to dispute. Did FBI agent Anderson have sufficient cause for a warrantless search of the Creightons' home? Or was his evidence so weak that his forcible entry constituted an unreasonable search? Law enforcement officials and civil liberties groups had widely different opinions on these questions. Nor did the justices of the Supreme Court have a uniform view. Six of the justices sided with Anderson and three backed the Creightons' position.

This chapter examines issues of **civil liberties:** specific individual rights, such as freedom of speech and protection against self-incrimination, that are constitutionally

civil liberties The fundamental individual rights of a free society, such as freedom of speech and the right to a jury trial, which in the United States are protected by the Bill of Rights.

Bill of Rights The first ten amendments to the Constitution, which set forth basic protections for individual rights to free expression, fair trial, and property.

protected against infringement by government. As seen in Chapter 2, the Constitution's failure to enumerate individual freedoms led to demands for the **Bill of Rights.** Enacted in 1791, these first ten amendments to the Constitution specify certain rights of life, liberty, and property that the national government is obliged to respect. A later amendment, the Fourteenth, became the basis for extending these protections of individual rights to actions by state and local governments.

Rights have full meaning only as protected in law. A constitutional guarantee of free speech, for example, is worth no more than the paper on which it is written if authorities can prevent people from speaking freely. Judicial action is important in defining what people's rights mean in practice and in setting and in enforcing limits on official action that may infringe on these rights. In some areas, the judiciary devises a specific test to determine whether government action is lawful. A test applied in the area of free speech, for example, is whether general rules (such as restrictions on the time and place of a public gathering) are applied fairly to all groups. Government officials do not meet this test if they apply one set of rules for groups that they like and a harsher set of rules for those they dislike.

Issues of individual rights have become increasingly complex and important. The writers of the Constitution could not possibly have foreseen the United States of the early twenty-first century, with its huge national government, enormous corporations, pervasive mass media, urban crowding, and vulnerability to terrorist acts. These developments are potential threats to individual liberty, and the judiciary in recent decades has seen fit to expand the rights to which individuals are entitled. However, these rights are constantly being balanced against competing individual rights and society's collective interests. The Bill of Rights operates in an untidy world where people's highest aspirations collide with their worst passions, and it is at this juncture that issues of civil liberties arise. Should an admitted murderer be entitled to recant a confession? Should the press be allowed to print military secrets whose publication might jeopardize national security? Should prayer be allowed in the public schools? Should extremist groups be allowed to publicize their messages of prejudice and hate? Such questions are among the subjects of this chapter, which focuses on the following major points:

- *Freedom of expression is the most basic of democratic rights, but like all rights, it is not unlimited.* Free expression recently has been strongly supported by the Supreme Court.

- *"Due process of law" refers to legal protections (primarily procedural safeguards) that are designed to ensure that individual rights are respected by government.*

- *During the last half century particularly, the civil liberties of individual Americans have been substantially broadened in law and given greater judicial*

Exercising their right of free expression, antiabortion protesters gather outside a government building.

protection from action by all levels of government. Of special significance has been the Supreme Court's use of the Fourteenth Amendment to protect these individual rights from action by state and local governments.

- *Individual rights are constantly being weighed against the demands of majorities and the collective needs of society.* All political institutions are involved in this process, as is public opinion, but the judiciary plays the central role in it and is the institution that is most partial to the protection of civil liberties.

FREEDOM OF EXPRESSION

Freedom of political expression is the most basic of democratic rights. Unless citizens can openly express their political opinions, they cannot properly influence their government or act to protect their other rights. As the Supreme Court concluded in 1984, "The freedom to speak one's mind is not only an aspect of individual liberty—and thus a good unto itself—but also is essential to the common quest for truth and the vitality of society as whole."[3]

It is for such reasons that the First Amendment provides the foundation for **freedom of expression**—the right of individual Americans to hold and communicate views of their choosing. For many reasons, such as a desire to conform to social pressure or a fear of harassment, Americans do not always choose to express themselves freely. Nevertheless, the First Amendment provides for freedom of expression by prohibiting laws that would abridge the freedoms of conscience, speech, press, assembly, and petition.

freedom of expression
Americans' freedom to communicate their views, the foundation of which is the First Amendment rights of freedom of conscience, speech, press, assembly, and petition.

Oliver Wendell Holmes Jr.
(1841–1935)

Oliver Wendell Holmes Jr. was nominated for the Supreme Court in 1901 by President Theodore Roosevelt and served for more than three decades. The son of a famous writer and physician, Holmes was a leading intellectual force on the Court. An advocate of judicial restraint, he nonetheless argued that the law had to keep pace with society. He helped lay the foundation for an interpretation of the First Amendment that limited government's ability to restrict free expression.

Freedom of expression, like other rights, is not absolute. It does not entitle individuals to say or do whatever they want, to whomever they want, whenever they want. Free expression can be denied, for example, if it endangers national security, wrongly damages the reputations of others, or deprives others of their basic freedoms. An individual's private thoughts are completely free, but words and actions may not be. The Supreme Court has ruled, for example, that abortion protesters can be arrested if they violate laws or court orders that bar them from protesting within a certain distance of abortion clinics or from physically interfering with a woman's attempt to enter a clinic.[4]

In recent decades, free expression has received broad protection from the courts. Today, under most circumstances, Americans can freely verbalize their political views without fear of governmental interference. In earlier times, however, Americans were less free to express their political views.

Historical Background

The Early Period: The Uncertain Status of the Right of Free Expression

The first legislative attempt by the U.S. government to restrict free expression was the Sedition Act of 1798, which made it a crime to print false or malicious newspaper stories about the president or other national officials. Thomas Jefferson called the Sedition Act an "alarming infraction" of the Constitution and, upon replacing John Adams as president in 1801, pardoned those who had been convicted under it. Because the Supreme Court did not review the sedition cases, however, the judiciary's position on free expression remained an open question. The Court also did not rule on free speech during the Civil War era, when the government severely restricted individual rights.

In 1919 the Court finally ruled on a case that challenged the national government's authority to restrict free expression. Two years earlier, Congress had passed the Espionage Act, which prohibited forms of dissent deemed to be harmful to the nation's effort in World War I. Nearly two thousand Americans were convicted for such activities as interfering with draft registration and distributing antiwar leaflets. The Supreme Court upheld one of these convictions in *Schenck v. United States* (1919), ruling unanimously that the Espionage Act of 1917 was constitutional. In the opinion written by Justice Oliver Wendell Holmes, the Court said that Congress could restrict speech that was "of such a nature as to create a clear and present danger" to the nation's security. In a famous passage, Holmes argued that not even the First Amendment would permit a person to falsely yell "fire" in a crowded theater and create a panic that could kill or injure innocent people.[5] Although the **clear-and-present-danger test** has been superseded by a more rigorous standard (the imminent lawless action test, discussed later in this chapter in the context of *Brandenburg v. Ohio*), it served to place a limit on the government's authority over free expression. Political speech that did *not* pose a clear and present danger could *not* be restricted.

clear-and-present-danger test A test devised by the Supreme Court in 1919 in order to define the limits of free speech in the context of national security. According to the test, government cannot abridge political expression unless it presents a clear and present danger to the nation's security.

Why Should I Care?

Civil Liberties and National Security

At the writing of the Constitution, Alexander Hamilton claimed that war is always a threat to civil liberties. The freedoms that people enjoy in peacetime are restricted in wartime. The current war on terrorism is an example. After September 11, 2001, for example, Congress gave the Central Intelligence Agency (CIA) authority to engage in certain types of clandestine domestic surveillance. The CIA may, for instance, read secret grand jury testimony without first seeking a judge's approval to do so.

When the CIA was created in 1947 as part of America's effort at containing the spread of communism, President Truman insisted that the CIA's surveillance activities be limited to foreign soil. Fascist and communist governments, said Truman, spy on their citizens. Democratic governments do not. Accordingly, the CIA was prohibited from conducting surveillance operations within the United States. Two decades later, Congress discovered that the CIA had violated its mandate. The CIA had tapped Americans' phones, opened their mail, and burglarized their homes and offices. Congress responded with new restrictions on and closer oversight of the CIA. This action, however, had the effect of limiting the coordination between the CIA and the FBI, which, according to some analysts, contributed to the failure of U.S. officials to uncover plans for the terrorist attacks on the World Trade Center and Pentagon on September 11, 2001. Although both agencies had information that indicated a major terrorist act was in the offing, they did not closely coordinate the intelligence reports they had gathered.

Nearly every analyst now agrees that domestic surveillance will have to increase if America is to be made safe from terrorism. Many analysts also believe that the CIA should be part of that effort, although they disagree on the extent of that authority. The CIA itself would like extensive powers. In 2002, for example, it requested authority to intercept e-mail messages routed to the United States from abroad without having to obtain a warrant from a judge.

Where do you stand on the issue of domestic surveillance? What trade-offs between personal freedom and physical security are you willing to make in the context of the war on terrorism? How far would you let the CIA go in conducting surveillance on American citizens? Would you make a distinction between American citizens and the noncitizens who live here, granting the CIA more leeway in the case of the latter group?

John Ashcroft, the attorney general of the United States, has said that people who oppose greatly expanded surveillance and detention as tools in the war on terrorism are, in effect, choosing to side with the terrorists. The *New York Times* columnist Anthony Lewis argues that, if the war on terrorism is waged at the expense of civil liberties, Americans will have lost sight of what they are fighting to protect. Which view comes closer to your own?

The Modern Period: Protecting Free Expression

Until the twentieth century, the tension between national security interests and free expression was not a pressing dilemma for the United States. The country's great size and ocean barriers provided protection from potential enemies, minimizing concerns of internal subversion. World War I, however, intruded on America's isolation, and World War II brought it to an abrupt end. Since then, Americans' rights of free expression have been defined largely in the context of national security concerns.

This tendency is clearly evident in recent government actions in the war on terrorism, including the USA Patriot Act of 2001 (see Chapter 1). The government's powers of surveillance and detention have been expanded, which has narrowed the legal protections provided to those people who are even remotely

Free Speech and Assembly

During the cold war that developed after World War II, many Americans perceived the Soviet Union as bent on destroying the United States through internal subversion and global expansion. In this period, the Supreme Court allowed government to put substantial limits on free expression. In 1951, for example, the Court upheld the convictions of eleven members of the U.S. Communist party who had been prosecuted under a law that made it illegal to advocate the forceful overthrow of the U.S. government.[6]

By the late 1950s, however, fear of internal communist subversion was subsiding, and the Supreme Court expanded the scope of permissible speech.[7] The Court implicitly embraced a legal doctrine first outlined by Justice Harlan Fiske Stone in 1938. Stone argued that First Amendment rights of free expression are the basis of Americans' liberty and ought to have a "preferred position" in the law. If government can control what people know and say, it can manipulate their opinions and thereby deprive them of the right to decide for themselves how they will be governed. Therefore, government should be broadly prohibited from restricting free expression.[8]

This philosophy has led the Supreme Court to rule that government officials must show that national security is directly and substantially imperiled before they can lawfully prohibit citizens from speaking out or assembling. For example, during the Vietnam era, despite the largest sustained protest movement in America's history, not a single individual was convicted solely for voicing objections to the government's war policy. (Some dissenters were found guilty on other grounds, such as inciting riots and assaulting the police.)

The Supreme Court's protection of **symbolic speech** has been less substantial than its protection of verbal speech. For example, the Court in 1968 upheld the conviction of a Vietnam protester who had burned his draft registration card. The Court said that government can prohibit action that threatens a legitimate public interest as long as the main purpose of the policy is not to restrict free expression. The Court concluded that the federal law prohibiting the destruction of draft cards was designed primarily to protect the military's need for soldiers, not to prevent people from criticizing government policy.[9]

The Supreme Court, however, has not granted the government broad power to restrict symbolic speech. In 1989, for example, the Court ruled that the burning of the American flag is a protected form of free expression. The ruling came in the case of Gregory Lee Johnson, a member of the Communist Youth Brigade. Johnson had set fire to a U.S. flag outside the hall in Dallas where the 1984 Republican National Convention was being held. The Supreme Court rejected the state of Texas's argument that flag burning is, in every instance, an imminent danger to public safety. A year later the Court struck down a new federal statute that made it a federal crime to burn or deface the flag.[10] "If there is a bedrock principle underlying the First Amendment," the Court ruled in the *Johnson* case, "it is that the Government may not prohibit the expression of an idea simply because society finds the idea itself offensive or disagreeable."[11]

Historical Background

symbolic speech Action (for example, the waving or burning of a flag) for the purpose of expressing a political opinion.

After the terrorist attacks on the World Trade Center and the Pentagon, the American flag suddenly appeared on offices, homes, and vehicles throughout the country. Kevin Sabia of Kent, Connecticut, chose to paint his house like a flag. Americans can also choose to burn the flag. In 1989, the Supreme Court declared flag burning to be a constitutionally protected right of free expression.

Government's authority to regulate activities that are related to free speech is also subject to certain limitations. In its landmark decision in *Buckley v. Valeo* (1976), for example, the Supreme Court held that Congress cannot restrict the amount of their own money that political candidates can spend on their own campaigns. Any such limit, the Court concluded, would infringe on candidates' freedom of speech. Legal limits on individual and group contributions to candidates, however, were upheld on grounds that such limitations were necessary to prevent the appearance and possibly the reality that officeholders would be unduly influenced by large donors.[12]

Press Freedom and Prior Restraint

Freedom of the press has also received strong judicial support in recent decades. In *New York Times Co. v. United States* (1971), the Court ruled that the *Times*'s publication of the "Pentagon papers" (secret government documents revealing official deception about the success of the Vietnam war policy) could not be blocked by the Department of Justice, which claimed that publication would hurt the war effort. The documents had been illegally obtained by antiwar activists, who had turned them over to the *Times* for publication. The Court ruled that "any system of prior restraints" on the press is unconstitutional unless the government can clearly justify the restriction.[13]

The unacceptability of **prior restraint**—government prohibition of speech or publication before the fact—is basic to the current doctrine of free expression. The Supreme Court has said that any attempt by government to prevent expression carries "a 'heavy presumption' against its constitutionality."[14] News organizations and individuals are legally responsible after the fact for what they report or say (for example, they can be sued by an individual whose reputation is wrongly damaged by their words), but generally government cannot stop them in advance from expressing their views. One exception is the reporting of military operations. During the Persian Gulf War, U.S. journalists on station in

prior restraint Government prohibition of speech or publication before the fact, which is presumed by the courts to be unconstitutional unless the justification for it is overwhelming.

Saudi Arabia had to work within limits placed on them by military authorities. In another exception to the doctrine of prior restraint, the courts have upheld the government's authority to ban uncensored publications by certain past and present government employees, such as CIA agents, who have taken part in classified national security activities.

On rare occasions, the government has asked the press to voluntarily withhold information. For example, when videotapes prepared by the terrorist leader Osama bin Laden found their way into the hands of U.S. news organizations several weeks after the bombings of September 11, 2001, the White House asked the television networks not to air them. Officials feared the tapes would serve the terrorists' propaganda goals and might contain coded messages that would trigger other terrorist acts. The networks agreed to screen and edit the tapes but did televise excerpts of bin Laden's statements.

Free Expression and State Governments

In 1790 Congress rejected a proposed amendment to the Constitution that would have applied the Bill of Rights to the states. Thus the freedoms guaranteed in the Bill of Rights were initially protected only from action by the national government, a constitutional arrangement that the Supreme Court upheld in *Barron v. Baltimore* (1833).[15] The effect was that the Bill of Rights had little practical meaning in the lives of ordinary Americans because state and local governments carry out most of the activities, such as law enforcement, where people's rights are at issue.

Not until the twentieth century did the Supreme Court begin to protect individual rights from infringement by state and local governments. The vehicle for this change was the **due process clause of the Fourteenth Amendment** to the Constitution.

due process clause (of the Fourteenth Amendment) The clause of the Constitution that has been used by the judiciary to apply the Bill of Rights to the actions of state governments.

The Fourteenth Amendment and Selective Incorporation

Ratified in 1868, the Fourteenth Amendment includes a clause that forbids a state from depriving any person of life, liberty, or property without due process of law (due process refers to the legal procedures that have been established as a means of protecting individuals' rights). Six decades later, the Supreme Court in *Gitlow v. New York* (1925) decided that the Fourteenth Amendment applied to state action in the area of freedom of expression. The Court upheld Benjamin Gitlow's conviction for violating a New York law that prohibited advocacy of the violent overthrow of the U.S. government, but warned that the states were not completely free to limit expression:

> For present purposes we may and do assume that freedom of speech and of the press—which are protected by the First Amendment from abridgement by Congress—are among the fundamental personal rights and "liberties" protected by the due process clause of the Fourteenth Amendment from impairment by the states.[16]

There is no indication that Congress, when it passed the Fourteenth Amendment after the Civil War, meant it to protect First Amendment rights from state action. The Supreme Court justified its new interpretation in the

TABLE 4–1 **Selective Incorporation of Rights of Free Expression** In the 1920s and 1930s, the Supreme Court selectively incorporated the free-expression provisions of the First Amendment into the Fourteenth Amendment so that these rights would be protected from infringement by the states.

SUPREME COURT CASE	YEAR	CONSTITUTIONAL RIGHT AT ISSUE
Gitlow v. New York	1925	Fourteenth Amendment protection of free expression
Fiske v. Kansas	1927	Free speech
Near v. Minnesota	1931	Free press
Hamilton v. Regents, U. of California	1934	Religious freedom
DeJonge v. Oregon	1937	Freedom of assembly and of petition

Gitlow case by reference to **selective incorporation**—the absorption of certain provisions of the Bill of Rights, particularly freedom of speech and press, into the Fourteenth Amendment so that these rights would be protected from infringement by the states. The Court reasoned that the Fourteenth Amendment's due process clause was largely meaningless if states could prohibit their residents from speaking freely.

The interpretation of the Fourteenth Amendment developed in the *Gitlow* case provided the Court with a legal basis for striking down state laws that infringed unreasonably on free expression. But the Supreme Court acts only in the context of specific cases; it does not have the authority to issue blanket rulings. Accordingly, further action by the Court could not occur until appropriate cases arose and reached the Court on appeal from lower courts. Within a dozen years (see Table 4–1), the Court had received four cases that enabled it to invalidate state laws that restricted expression in the areas of speech (*Fiske v. Kansas*), press (*Near v. Minnesota*), religion (*Hamilton v. Regents, University of California*), and assembly and petition (*DeJonge v. Oregon*).[17] The most famous of these rulings came in the *Near* case. Jay Near was the publisher of a Minneapolis weekly newspaper that regularly made scurrilous attacks on blacks, Jews, Catholics, and labor union leaders. His paper was closed down on authority of a state law that banned "malicious, scandalous, or defamatory" publications. Near appealed the shutdown, and the Supreme Court ruled in his favor, saying that the Minnesota law was "the essence of censorship."[18]

selective incorporation The absorption of certain provisions of the Bill of Rights (for example, freedom of speech) into the Fourteenth Amendment so that these rights are protected from infringement by the states.

Limiting the Authority of States to Restrict Expression

Since the 1930s, the Supreme Court has broadly protected freedom of expression from action by the states and by local governments, which derive their authority from the states. The Court has held that the states cannot restrict free expression except when such expression is almost certain to result in imminent lawlessness. A leading free speech case was *Brandenburg v. Ohio* (1969). The appellant was a Ku Klux Klan member who, in a speech delivered at a Klan rally, said that "revenge" might have to be taken if the national government "continues to

imminent lawless action test
A legal test that says government cannot lawfully suppress advocacy that promotes lawless action unless such advocacy is aimed at producing, and is likely to produce, imminent lawless action.

suppress the white Caucasian race." He was convicted of advocating force under an Ohio law prohibiting criminal syndicalism, but the Supreme Court reversed the conviction, saying the First Amendment prohibits a state from suppressing speech that advocates the unlawful use of force "except where such advocacy is directed to inciting or producing imminent lawless action, and is likely to produce such action."[19] This test—the likelihood of **imminent lawless action**—is a severe restriction on the government's power to restrict expression. It is rare when words alone immediately incite others to act lawlessly.

The Court has broadly held that hate speech cannot be silenced. This ruling came in a unanimous 1992 opinion that struck down a St. Paul, Minnesota, ordinance making it a crime to engage in speech likely to arouse "anger or alarm" on the basis of "race, color, creed, religion or gender." The Court said the First Amendment prohibits government from "silencing speech on the basis of its content."[20] This protection of violent *speech* does not, however, extend to violent *crimes*, such as assault, motivated by racial or other forms of prejudice. A Wisconsin law that provided for increased sentences for such crimes was challenged as a violation of the First Amendment. In a unanimous 1993 opinion, the Court said that the law was aimed at "conduct unprotected by the First Amendment" rather than the defendant's speech.[21]

In a key case involving freedom of assembly, the U.S. Supreme Court in 1977 upheld a lower-court ruling against local ordinances of Skokie, Illinois, which had been invoked to prevent a parade there by the American Nazi party.[22] Skokie had a large Jewish population, including many survivors of Nazi Germany's concentration camps. The Supreme Court held that the right of free expression takes precedence over the mere *possibility* that exercising the right may have undesirable consequences. Before government can lawfully prevent a speech or rally, it must offer persuasive evidence that an evil will almost certainly result from the event and must also demonstrate the lack of alternative ways (such as assigning police officers to control the crowd) to prevent the evil from happening.

The Supreme Court has recognized that freedom of speech and assembly may conflict with the routines of daily life. Accordingly, individuals do not have the right to hold a public rally in the middle of a busy intersection during rush hour, nor do they have the right to command immediate access to a public auditorium. The Court has held that public officials can regulate the time, place, and conditions of public assembly, provided that these regulations are reasonable and do not discriminate on the basis of the nature of these gatherings. In a 1992 case, the Court declared unconstitutional a local ordinance that imposed a fee of up to $1,000 to offset the costs of maintaining order at a public assembly; the more trouble expected, the higher the fee a group had to pay for permission to hold the assembly. The Court concluded that the First Amendment denies officials "unbridled discretion" in putting a price on speech "simply because it might offend a hostile mob."[23] Officials have an obligation to accommodate public gatherings and to treat *all* groups—including those that espouse unpopular views—in accordance with reasonable standards.

In general, the Supreme Court's position is that the First Amendment makes any government effort to regulate the *content* of a message highly suspect. In the flag-burning case, Texas was regulating the content of the message—contempt for the flag and the principles it represents. Texas could not have been regulating the act itself, for the Texas government's own method of disposing of worn-out flags is also to burn them. But a content-neutral regulation (no public rally can be held in the middle of a busy intersection at rush hour) is acceptable as long as it is reasonable and does not discriminate against certain groups or ideas.

Libel and Slander

The constitutional right of free expression is not a legal license to avoid responsibility for the consequences of what is said or written. If false information that greatly harms a person's reputation is published (**libel**) or spoken (**slander**), the injured party can sue for damages. The ease of winning such suits has obvious implications for free expression. Individuals and organizations are less likely to express themselves openly if they stand a good chance of subsequently losing a libel or slander suit.

Libel is the more compelling issue for the political process because it affects the news media's ability to criticize public officials. A leading decision in this area is *New York Times Co. v. Sullivan* (1964), in which the Court overruled an Alabama state court that had found the *Times* guilty of libel for printing an advertisement criticizing Alabama officials for physically assaulting black civil rights demonstrators. The Court ruled that libel of a public official requires proof of actual malice, which was defined as a knowing or reckless disregard for the truth.[24] It is *very* difficult to prove that a publication acted with reckless or deliberate disregard for the truth. In fact, no federal official has won a libel judgment against a news organization in the three decades since the *Sullivan* ruling. (The press has less protection against a libel judgment when its target is a private person rather than a public official. The courts regard the communication of information about private individuals as less basic to the democratic process than information about public officials, and therefore the press must take greater care in ascertaining the validity of claims about an ordinary citizen.)

The *Sullivan* decision notwithstanding, the greatest protection against a libel judgment is truthfulness. The Court has held that expressions of opinion deserve "full constitutional protection" against the charge of libel as long as they do not contain "a provably false factual connotation."[25]

libel Publication of material that falsely damages a person's reputation.

slander Spoken words that falsely damage a person's reputation.

Obscenity

In 1990 the director of a Cincinnati museum, Dennis Barrie, was charged with obscenity for holding an exhibit that included homoerotic art by the photographer Robert Mapplethorpe. Barrie was acquitted in a jury trial, but the incident provoked a controversy that extended to Congress. The exhibit was funded in part by a grant from the National Endowment for the Arts (NEA), and Congress enacted a law requiring the NEA to take "decency standards" into account in granting funds. Artists claimed that the law would have a chilling effect on artistic expression, but the Supreme Court in 1998 upheld Congress's authority to set limits on the uses of the funds it appropriates.[26]

Individuals do not have a constitutional right to demonstrate in any place at any time, but government is required to accommodate requests for marches and other displays of free expression.

Obscenity is a form of expression that is not protected by the First Amendment. However, the Supreme Court has found it difficult to define which publicly disseminated sexual materials are obscene and which are not. The Court has struggled to develop a standard that gives predictability to the law without endangering First Amendment rights.

The Court's first test was established in *Roth v. United States* (1957), when the Court defined obscenity as material that "taken as a whole" appealed to "prurient interest" and had no "redeeming social significance." The perspective was to be that of "the average person, applying contemporary community standards."[27] The test proved unworkable. Even the justices, when personally examining allegedly obscene material, would argue over whether it appealed to prurient interest and was without redeeming social value. In the end, they usually concluded that it had at least some social significance.

In *Miller v. California* (1973), the Court changed the test, saying that instead of having no redeeming social significance, the material had to have "serious literary, artistic, political, or scientific value." The Court also narrowed the "contemporary community standards" to the local level. The court said that what might offend residents of "Mississippi might be found tolerable in Las Vegas."[28] But this test proved too restrictive. The Court subsequently ruled that material cannot be judged obscene simply because the "average" local resident might object to it. "Community standards" were to be judged in the context of a "reasonable person"—someone whose outlook is broad enough to evaluate the

The Supreme Court in 1997 invalidated the Communications Decency Act, which had broadly outlawed indecent material on the Internet. The Court held that the law was so broad and so punitive that it would censor "a large amount of speech."

material on its overall merit rather than its most objectionable feature. The Court later also modified its content standard, saying that the material must be of a "particularly offensive type."[29] These efforts illustrate the difficulty of defining obscenity and, even more, of developing a legal standard that can be applied evenhandedly by courts when an obscenity case arises.

The Supreme Court has distinguished between obscene materials in public places and in the home. A unanimous ruling in 1969 held that what adults read and watch in the privacy of their homes cannot be made a crime.[30] The Court created an exception to this rule in 1990 by upholding an Ohio law making it a crime to possess pornographic photographs of children.[31] The Court reasoned that purchase and distribution contributed to the spread of the crime of using children in the production of child pornographic materials. Consistent with this reasoning, the Court in *Ashcroft v. Free Speech Coalition* (2002) held that pictures of adults, digitally altered to look like children, cannot be banned on that basis alone.

The shielding of children from the effects of sexually explicit material has also affected cable television policy. In 1996, the Supreme Court held that although cable operators are not required to scramble the signal of channels that provide adult programming, they must do so for individual subscribers who request that the signal be scrambled.[32]

The Internet is also a source of indecent material. To prevent this material from reaching children, Congress in 1996 passed the Communications Decency Act, which made it a federal crime to use the Internet to transmit obscene material to someone under eighteen years of age or to post material in a way that made it available to minors. In a key 1997 ruling, *Reno v. ACLU*, the Supreme Court declared the Decency Act to be unconstitutional. "We have repeatedly recognized the governmental interest in protecting children from harmful materials," the Court said. "But that interest does not justify an unnecessarily broad suppression of speech addressed to adults."[33] Congress responded with the Child Online Protection Act (COPA) of 1998, which defines indecency according to "contemporary community standards." In *Ashcroft v. ACLU* (2002), the Supreme Court in a narrow ruling upheld the community standards test for

Fighting Words

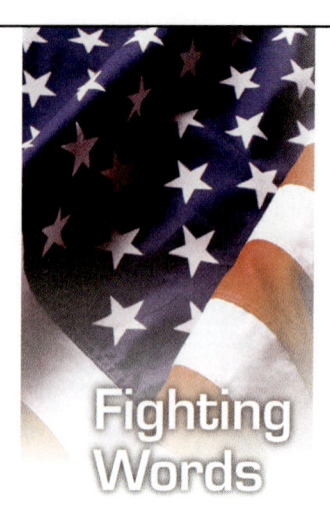

Should Sexually Explicit Material on the Internet Be Tightly Regulated?

In 1997, the Supreme Court struck down the Communications Decency Act on grounds that it was overly broad and would have the effect of reducing not only indecent content on the Internet but legitimate expression as well. The act made it a federal crime to transmit obscene material through the Internet to minors or to post such material in a way that made it accessible to them. The conflict between the congressional majority that enacted the legislation and the Supreme Court majority that invalidated it is part of society's continuing debate over how to regulate obscenity without infringing on First Amendment rights.

Yes: Opponents of the new law use harsh language like "censorship" to describe the Communications Decency Act . . . Those who cry censorship hide behind the First Amendment to make defense of those who would give pornography to children and engage children in sexual conversations. What a travesty . . . The Act makes it a crime to send indecent communications to children by means of a computer service or telecommunications device [and] to make indecent communications available to children on an open electronic bulletin board. . . . The heart and soul of the new law is its protections for children. It is not censorship. It is not prudishness. The new law does not prohibit consenting adults from engaging in constitutionally protected speech.
—Former U.S. Senator James Exon (D-Nebr.)

No: We are persuaded that the [act] lacks the precision that the First Amendment requires when a statute regulates the content of speech. In order to deny minors access to potentially harmful speech, the [act] effectively suppresses a large amount of speech that adults have a constitutional right to receive and to address to one another. . . . It is true that we have repeatedly recognized the governmental interest in protecting children from harmful materials. But that interest does not justify an unnecessarily broad suppression of speech addressed to adults. As we have explained, the Government may not "reduc[e] the adult population . . . to . . . only what is fit for children." . . . Knowledge that, for instance, one or more members of a 100-person chat group will be minor—and therefore that it would be a crime to send the group an indecent message—would surely burden communication among adults.
—Reno v. ACLU (1997)

---

web content. This test could become an imposing one. Because the Internet reaches into homes everywhere, content could be limited to what is found acceptable in more traditional communities rather than in communities where, in the Court's words, "avant garde culture is the norm."

FREEDOM OF RELIGION

Free religious expression is the precursor of free political expression, at least within the English tradition of limited government. England's Glorious, or Bloodless, Revolution of 1689 centered on the issue of religion and resulted in the Act of Toleration, which gave members of all Protestant sects the right to

The First Amendment's protection of free expression includes religious freedom, which has led the courts to hold that government cannot in most instances promote or interfere with religious practices.

worship freely and publicly. The English philosopher John Locke (1632–1704) extended this principle, arguing that legitimate government could not inhibit free expression, religious or otherwise. The First Amendment reflects this tradition, providing for freedom of religion along with freedom of speech, press, assembly, and petition.

In regard to religion, the First Amendment reads: "Congress shall make no law respecting an establishment of religion, or prohibiting the free exercise thereof." The prohibition on laws aimed at "establishment of religion" (the establishment clause) and its "free exercise" (the free-exercise clause) applies to states and localities through the Fourteenth Amendment.

The Establishment Clause

The **establishment clause** has been interpreted by the courts to mean that government may not favor one religion over another or support religion over no religion. (This position contrasts with that of a country such as England, where Anglicanism is the official, or "established," state religion, though no religion is prohibited.) The Supreme Court's interpretation of the establishment clause has been described as maintaining a "wall of separation" between church and state, which includes a prohibition on nondenominational support for religion.[34] The Court has taken a pragmatic approach, however, by permitting some establishment activities but disallowing others. The Court has permitted states to provide secular textbooks for use by church-affiliated schools,[35] for instance, but has forbidden states to pay part of the salaries of teachers in church-affiliated schools.[36] Such distinctions follow no strict logic but are based on judgments of whether government action involves "*excessive* entanglement with religion."[37] In allowing public funds to be used by religious schools for secular textbooks but not for teachers' salaries, the courts have indicated that, whereas it is relatively easy to ascertain whether the content of a particular textbook promotes religion, it would be much harder to determine whether a particular teacher was promoting religion in the classroom.[38]

In a key 2002 decision, however, the Supreme Court upheld an Ohio law that allows students in Cleveland's failing public schools to receive a tax-supported voucher to attend private or parochial school. The Court's majority

establishment clause The First Amendment provision that government may not favor one religion over another or favor religion over no religion, and that prohibits Congress from passing laws respecting the establishment of religion.

argued in *Zelman v. Simmons-Harris* that the program did not violate the establishment clause because students had a choice between secular and religious education. Four members of the Court dissented sharply with the majority's reasoning. Justice Stevens said the ruling had removed a "brick from the wall that was once designed to separate religion from government."[39]

Yet, the Court has held firm in its position, first announced in *Engel v. Vitale* (1962), that the establishment clause prohibits the reciting of prayers in public schools.[40] A year later the Court struck down Bible readings in public schools.[41] Religion is a strong force in American life, and the Supreme Court's school-prayer position has evoked strong opposition. An Alabama law attempted to circumvent the prayer ruling by permitting public schools to set aside one minute each day for silent prayer or meditation. In 1985, the Court declared the law unconstitutional, ruling that "government must pursue a course of complete neutrality toward religion."[42] The Court in 2000 reaffirmed the ban by extending it to include organized student-led prayer at public school football games.[43]

The Free-Exercise Clause

The First and Fourteenth Amendments also prohibit governmental interference with the free exercise of religion. The idea underlying the **free-exercise clause** is clear: Americans are free to hold any religious belief they choose.

Although people are free to believe what they want, they are not always free to act on their beliefs. The courts have allowed government interference in the exercise of religious beliefs when such interference is the secondary result of an overriding social goal. An example is the legal protection of children with life-threatening illnesses whose parents refuse to permit medical treatment on religious grounds. A court may order that such children be given medical assistance because the social good of saving their lives overrides their parents' free-exercise rights. And in 1986 the Supreme Court concluded that military regulations requiring standard headgear took precedence over an Orthodox Jewish serviceman's practice of wearing a yarmulke.[44] (Congress responded by enacting legislation that permits yarmulkes.)

In an important 1997 decision, the Court struck down the Religious Freedom Restoration Act, which was passed by a large congressional majority and with the backing of President Clinton. The law said that government at any level could not interfere with religious practices unless a "compelling reason," such as a danger to health or safety, was involved. In striking down the law, which had been challenged in a case where a city wanted to prevent a church from enlarging its building, the Court said that Congress lacked the authority through statute to redefine the meaning of the Constitution. The Court concluded that the law had placed more restrictions on government (for example, denying it the power to regulate construction when a church was at issue) than was required by the First Amendment's guarantee of religious freedom.[45]

In some circumstances, exceptions to certain laws have been permitted on free-exercise grounds. The Supreme Court ruled in 1972 that Wisconsin could not compel Amish parents to send their children to school beyond the eighth grade because this policy violates a centuries-old Amish religious practice of having children leave school and begin work at an early age.[46] In upholding free exercise in such cases, the Court may be said to have violated the establishment clause by granting preferred treatment to people who hold a particular religious

---

free-exercise clause A First Amendment provision that prohibits the government from interfering with the practice of religion or prohibiting the free exercise of religion.

Americans in an Interdependent World

Universal Human Rights

In his 2002 State of the Union Address, President George W. Bush declared that certain values are universal and that it was the responsibility of the United States to ensure their permanence and observance. Said Bush: "America will lead by defending liberty and justice because they are right and true and unchanging for all people everywhere. No nation owns these aspirations, and no nation is exempt from them. We have no intention of imposing our culture—but America will always stand firm for the nonnegotiable demands of human dignity: the rule of law, limits on the power of the state, respect for women, private property, free speech, equal justice, and religious tolerance."

Commentators praised Bush's statement but noted the apparent contradiction between his claim that these rights are "nonnegotiable" and his claim that the United States has no intention of "imposing our culture" on other nations. The rights listed by Bush coincide with American values. Other cultures take exception to some of these rights. Some cultures, for example, make sharp distinctions about the roles, rights, and privileges of men and women and have embedded these distinctions in law. Some cultures hold that there is only one true God and have embedded this belief in their constitutions. Some cultures as a matter of law believe that property, or at least much of it, should be held in common rather than privately owned.

Where would you draw the dividing line between what is properly "universal" and what is properly "cultural"? Even if you accept the notion of "universal" rights, how much latitude should nations have in balancing these rights against their cultural traditions?

What do you make of the fact that the world community itself has given some recognition to the notion of universal rights? In 1948, the United Nations General Assembly adopted the Universal Declaration of Human Rights. The Declaration recognizes that the "inherent dignity of all members of the human family is the foundation of freedom, justice and peace in the world." Among its list of rights are life and liberty, property ownership, freedom of expression, religious freedom, and freedom from abusive treatment by law enforcement and security officials.

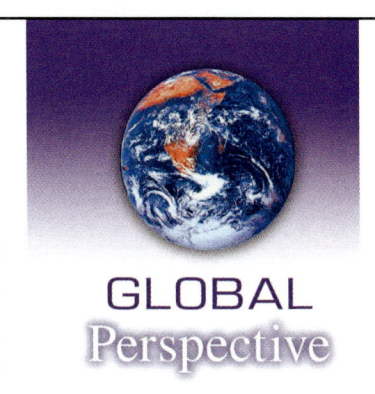

GLOBAL Perspective

---

belief. The Court has recognized the potential conflict between the free-exercise and establishment clauses and, as in other such situations, has tried to strike a reasonable balance between the competing claims.

When the free-exercise and establishment clauses cannot be balanced, the Supreme Court has been forced to make a choice. In 1987, the Court overturned a Louisiana law requiring that creationism (the Bible's account of how the world was created) be taught along with the theory of evolution in public school science courses. Creationism, the Court concluded, is a religious doctrine, not a scientific theory; thus its inclusion in public school curricula violates the establishment clause by promoting a religious belief.[47] Creationists viewed the Court's decision as a violation of their right to the free exercise of religion; they argued that their children were being forced to study a theory of evolution that contradicts the biblical account of human origins.

THE RIGHT OF PRIVACY

Until the 1960s, Americans' constitutional rights were confined largely to those enumerated in the Bill of Rights. This situation prevailed despite the Ninth Amendment, which reads: "The enumeration in the Constitution, of certain rights, shall not be construed to deny or disparage others retained by the people."

In 1965, however, the Supreme Court added to the list of individual rights, declaring that Americans have "a right of privacy." This judgment arose from the case of *Griswold v. Connecticut*, which challenged a state law prohibiting the use of birth control devices, even by married couples. The Supreme Court invalidated the statute, concluding that a state had no business interfering with a married couple's decision regarding contraception. The Court did not base its decision on the Ninth Amendment, but reasoned instead that the freedoms in the Bill of Rights imply an underlying right of privacy. Individuals have, said the Court, a "zone of [personal] privacy" that government cannot lawfully infringe upon.[48]

The right of privacy was the basis for the Supreme Court's ruling in *Roe v. Wade* (1973), which gave women full freedom to choose abortion during the first three months of pregnancy.[49] In overturning a Texas law prohibiting abortion except to save the life of the mother, the Supreme Court said that the right to privacy is "broad enough to encompass a woman's decision whether or not to terminate her pregnancy."

After *Roe*, antiabortion activists sought to reverse or weaken the Court's ruling. Attempts to pass a constitutional amendment that would ban abortions were unsuccessful, but abortion foes succeeded in a campaign to prohibit the use of government funds to pay for abortions for poor women. Then, in *Webster v. Reproductive Health Services* (1989), the Supreme Court upheld a Missouri law that prohibits abortions in public hospitals and by public employees.[50]

Abortion rights activists demonstrate outside the Supreme Court while the justices inside hear arguments on Pennsylvania's controversial abortion law. By a 5-4 vote, the Court narrowly reaffirmed the principle that a woman has the right to choose an abortion during the early months of pregnancy.

Figure 4–1
Americans' Opinions on Abortion

Since abortion was judged a constitutional right in 1973, Americans' opinions have not changed greatly.

Source: Gallup polls, various dates.

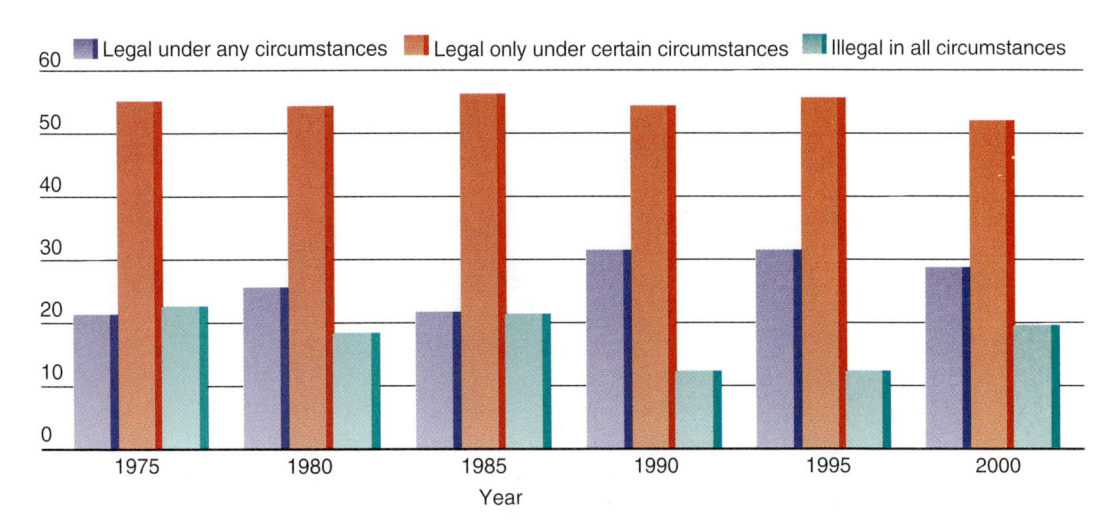

The *Webster* decision was followed in 1992 by a judgment in the Pennsylvania abortion case *Planned Parenthood v. Casey*. Pennsylvania's law placed a twenty-four-hour waiting period on women who sought an abortion, required doctors to counsel women on abortion and alternatives to abortion, required a minor to have a parent's consent or a judge's approval before having an abortion, and required a married woman to notify her husband before obtaining an abortion. Antiabortion advocates saw the Pennsylvania law as an opportunity for the Supreme Court to overturn the *Roe* precedent. However, in a decision that surprised many observers, the Court by a 5-4 margin reaffirmed the "essential holding" of *Roe v. Wade:* that a woman, because of the constitutional guarantee of privacy, has a right to abortion during the early months of pregnancy. The Court also ruled, however, that states can regulate abortion as long as they do not impose an "undue burden" on women seeking abortion. The Court concluded that the twenty-four-hour waiting period, physician counseling, and the informed-consent requirement for minors were not undue burdens and were therefore permissible. The spousal notification requirement, however, was judged to place a "substantial obstacle" in the path of women seeking abortion and was thereby declared unconstitutional.[51]

In a controversial 2000 ruling, *Stenberg v. Carhart*, the Supreme Court ruled that states may not ban partial-birth abortion (where the fetus's life is terminated during delivery) because it is the most appropriate medical procedure for protecting the life or health of the mother.[52] The ruling was applauded by pro-choice groups and condemned by pro-life groups.

Abortion will certainly be a leading controversy for years to come. The American public is divided on the issue (see Figure 4–1), and there are many deeply committed activists on both sides. As with other rights, the abortion issue is not only, or even primarily, fought out in the courts. Abortion opponents have waged demonstrations outside clinics in an effort to stop the practice. Some of these protests have erupted in violent acts toward women and staff who tried to enter the clinics. In 1994, Congress made it unlawful to block the entrance to abortion clinics or otherwise prevent people from entering.

Physician-assisted suicide has become a privacy-rights issue as medical advances have made it possible to keep terminally ill patients alive for long periods.

Although a right of privacy has been established in some areas of personal conduct, the Supreme Court has declined to extend it to other areas. In *Bowers v. Hardwick* (1986), for example, the Court upheld a Georgia law prohibiting sodomy, concluding that the right of privacy did not include homosexual acts among consenting adults.[53] States can choose to permit these acts, but they are not bound to do so by the Constitution of the United States.

The Court has also held that the right of privacy does not extend to the terminally ill who might want medical help in taking their own lives. This ruling came in response to New York and Washington state laws that ban physician-assisted suicide. The Court held that a state has a legitimate interest in protecting vulnerable people. Although the Court did not say so, it hinted in its ruling that a state might choose to permit physician-assisted suicide if there were proper safeguards in its use. But the Court was clear that "liberty" in the Fourteenth Amendment does not include a constitutional *right* to doctor-assisted suicide.[54]

Privacy questions are among the most contentious in American politics because of the moral and ethical issues they raise. Physician-assisted suicide, for example, is seen as a humane act by its proponents. What is the public benefit, they ask, in forcing the dying to accept prolonged and horrible suffering? A majority of Oregon voters in a statewide referendum concluded that there was no public benefit to this suffering and enacted the first state law that permits physician-assisted suicide. Opponents argue that society's interest in preserving life outweighs a patient's desire to die, that laws allowing doctors to assist a suicide would be abused, that doctors and relatives in some instances would persuade terminally ill patients to accept death against their will, and that depressed patients who ask to die will be granted their wish rather than be treated for their depression, after which they might choose to live. In 2002, the Justice Department announced its intention to try to shut down Oregon's program as a violation of the federal Controlled Substances Act, which prohibits certain uses of drugs.

RIGHTS OF PERSONS ACCUSED OF CRIMES

Due process refers to legal protections that have been established to preserve the rights of individuals. The most significant form of these protections is **procedural due process;** the term refers primarily to procedures that authorities must follow before a person can legitimately be punished for an offense.

The U.S. Constitution provides for several procedures designed to protect a person from wrongful arrest, conviction, and punishment. According to Article 1, Section 9, any person taken into police custody is entitled to seek a writ of habeas corpus, which requires law enforcement officials to bring him or her into court and state the legal reason for the detention. The Fifth and Fourteenth Amendments provide generally that no person can be deprived of life, liberty, or property without due process of law. And specific procedural protections for the accused are spelled out in the Fourth, Fifth, Sixth, and Eighth Amendments:

- *The Fourth Amendment* forbids the police to conduct searches and seizures unless they have probable cause to believe that a crime has been committed.
- *The Fifth Amendment* protects against double jeopardy (being prosecuted twice for the same offense); self-incrimination (being compelled to testify against oneself); indictment for a crime except through grand jury proceedings; and loss of life, liberty, and property without due process of law.
- *The Sixth Amendment* provides the right to have legal counsel, to confront witnesses, to receive a speedy trial, and to have a trial by jury in criminal proceedings.
- *The Eighth Amendment* protects against excessive bail or fines and prohibits the infliction of cruel and unusual punishment on those convicted of crimes.

These procedural protections have always been subject to interpretation. The Sixth Amendment, for example, provides the right to have legal counsel. But what if a person cannot afford a lawyer? For most of the nation's history, poor people had almost no choice but to act as their own attorneys. They had a right to counsel but could avail themselves of it only if they had the money to hire a lawyer. Today, if a person is accused of a serious crime and cannot afford a lawyer, the government must provide one. This change came about not through a constitutional amendment but through Supreme Court rulings that gave new meaning in practice to the Sixth Amendment.

Selective Incorporation of Procedural Rights

For most of the nation's history, the procedural protections in the Bill of Rights applied only to the actions of the national government. States in their criminal proceedings were not bound by them. There were limited exceptions, such as a 1932 Supreme Court ruling that a defendant charged in a state court with a crime carrying the death penalty had to be provided with an attorney.[55]

What's Your Opinion?

Procedural Due Process

"The history of liberty has largely been the history of the observance of procedural guarantees," said Justice Felix Frankfurter in *McNabb v. United States* (1943). No system of justice is foolproof. Even in the most honest systems, innocent people have been wrongly accused, convicted, and punished with imprisonment or death. But the scrupulous application of procedural safeguards, such as a defendant's right to legal counsel, greatly increases the likelihood that justice will prevail.

However, as recent police scandals in Dallas, Los Angeles, New York, and several other cities would indicate, constitutional guarantees are no assurance that people will be treated justly. Wrongful arrests and cooked-up evidence are not by any means the norm in U.S. law enforcement. But they occur with enough frequency to be a cause of concern to anyone committed to the principle of legal justice.

What do you think can be done to safeguard individuals' due process rights? Do you share the view of social theorists who say that when procedural due process is violated, the fault lies more with a public that is willing to tolerate abuses than with the few errant law enforcement officials who commit these abuses?

procedural due process The constitutional requirement that government must follow proper legal procedures before a person can be legitimately punished for an alleged offense.

www.mhhe.com/patterson6

The Court's general position, however, was that the states could decide for themselves what procedural rights their residents would have. A salient case was *Palko v. Connecticut* (1937). A Connecticut court had convicted Frank Palko of killing two policemen, and he was sentenced to life imprisonment. But Connecticut had a statute that permitted law enforcement authorities under certain conditions to appeal a sentence on the grounds that legal errors had been made at the trial. The authorities had wanted Palko to receive the death penalty, so they appealed the decision. Palko was tried again on the same charges and this time was sentenced to death. He appealed to the U.S. Supreme Court, claiming that Connecticut's second trial violated his right not to be tried twice for the same crime. The Fifth Amendment to the U.S. Constitution prohibits double jeopardy, and so do many state constitutions, but at the time Connecticut's did not. The Supreme Court refused to overturn Palko's second conviction, and he was executed.[56]

Justice Benjamin Cardozo wrote the Court's *Palko* opinion, which stated that the Fourteenth Amendment protects rights "fundamental" to liberty but not other rights provided in the Bill of Rights. Free expression is a "fundamental" right, since it is "the indispensable condition of nearly every other form of freedom." Some procedural due-process rights, such as protection against double jeopardy, are not in the same category, Cardozo claimed.

This view changed abruptly in the 1960s when the Supreme Court broadly required states to safeguard procedural rights. Changes in public education and communication made Americans more aware of their rights, and the civil rights movement dramatized the fact that rights were administered very unequally: the poor and minority group members had many fewer rights in practice than other Americans did. In response, the Supreme Court in the 1960s "incorporated" Bill of Rights protections for the accused in state courts by ruling that these protections are covered by the Fourteenth Amendment's guarantee of due process of law (see Table 4–2).

TABLE 4–2 **Selective Incorporation of Rights of the Accused** In the 1960s, the Supreme Court selectively incorporated the fair-trial provisions of the Fourth through Eighth Amendments into the Fourteenth Amendment so that these rights would be protected from infringement by the states.

SUPREME COURT CASE	YEAR	CONSTITUTIONAL RIGHT (AMENDMENT) AT ISSUE
Mapp v. Ohio	1961	Unreasonable search and seizure (Fourth)
Robinson v. California	1962	Cruel and unusual punishment (Eighth)
Gideon v. Wainwright	1963	Right to counsel (Sixth)
Malloy v. Hogan	1964	Self-incrimination (Fifth)
Pointer v. Texas	1965	Right to confront witnesses (Sixth)
Miranda v. Arizona	1966	Self-incrimination (Fifth)
Klopfer v. North Carolina	1967	Speedy trial (Sixth)
Duncan v. Louisiana	1968	Jury trial in criminal cases (Sixth)
Benton v. Maryland	1968	Double jeopardy (Fifth)

CHAPTER 4   Civil Liberties: Protecting Individual Rights

STATES IN THE NATION

The Death Penalty

Of the rights of the accused, none has proven more difficult to define in practice than the Eighth Amendment's prohibition against "cruel and unusual punishment." A 1972 Supreme Court decision (*Furman v. Georgia*) struck down the death penalty, ruling that its arbitrary application amounted to cruel and unusual punishment. States then revised their death penalty statutes to specify more precisely "the aggravating circumstances" that might justify a sentence of death, and the Supreme Court in *Gregg v. Georgia* (1976) upheld one such law. However, the odds that a convicted murderer will be sentenced to death vary dramatically from state to state and even within states because local prosecutors differ in how aggressively they pursue the death penalty in capital cases. Texas is far and away the leader in executions; roughly a third of all executions in the United States since 1976 have taken place in that state.

In a 2002 decision (*Askins v. Virginia*), the Supreme Court declared that the execution of the mentally retarded violates the Eight Amendment's "cruel and unusual" punishment clause because most states and nearly all countire ban such executions. In another 2002 decision (*Ring v. Arizona*), the Court held that the Sixth Amendment right to a jury trial prohibits judges (as opposed to juries) from deciding whether the death penalty will be imposed.

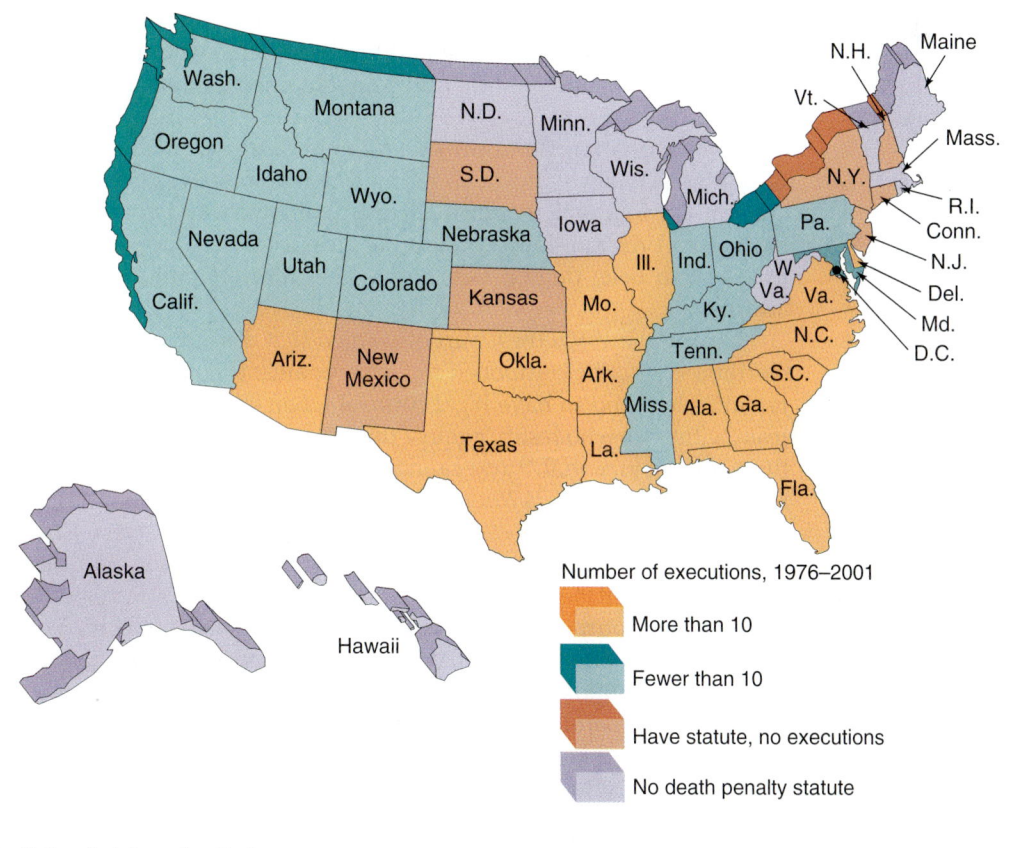

Number of executions, 1976–2001
- More than 10
- Fewer than 10
- Have statute, no executions
- No death penalty statute

Source: Death Penalty Information Center.

In recent decades the Supreme Court has restricted the scope of the "exclusionary rule." This rule excludes from use in court proceedings any evidence that is illegally obtained by law enforcement officials.

This selective incorporation process began with *Mapp v. Ohio* (1961). Dollree Mapp's home had been entered by Cleveland police, who, though they failed to find what they were looking for, happened to discover some pornographic material. Mapp's conviction for its possession was overturned by the Supreme Court on the grounds that she had been subjected to unreasonable search and seizure.[57] The Court ruled that illegally obtained evidence could not be used in state courts.

Two years later, the Court's decision in *Gideon v. Wainwright* (1963) required the states to furnish attorneys for poor defendants in all felony cases. Clarence Gideon, an indigent drifter, had been convicted and sentenced to prison in Florida for breaking into a poolroom. He successfully appealed on the grounds that he had been denied due process because he could not afford to pay an attorney.[58]

During the 1960s the Court also ruled that defendants in state criminal proceedings cannot be compelled to testify against themselves,[59] have the rights to remain silent and to have legal counsel when arrested,[60] have the right to confront witnesses who testify against them,[61] must be granted a speedy trial,[62] have the right to a jury trial,[63] and cannot be subjected to double jeopardy.[64] The most famous of these cases is *Miranda v. Arizona* (1966), as a result of which police are required to inform suspects of their rights at the time of arrest. Ernesto Miranda had confessed during police interrogation to kidnapping and raping a young woman. His confession led to his conviction, which he successfully appealed to the Supreme Court on the grounds that he had not been informed of his rights to remain silent and to have legal counsel present during interrogation. Using other evidence of Miranda's crime, the state of Arizona then retried and convicted him again. He was paroled from prison in 1972 and four years later was stabbed to death in a bar fight. Ironically, Miranda's assailant was read his "Miranda rights" when police arrested him. By now the wording has become familiar: "You have the right to remain silent. . . . Anything you say can and will be used against you in a court of law. . . . You have the right to an attorney."

In a 2000 case, *Dickerson v. United States*, the Supreme Court reaffirmed the *Miranda* decision, saying that because it had established "a constitutional rule," it was not subject to change by legislative action.[65]

Limits on Defendants' Rights

In the courtroom, the rights to counsel, to confront witnesses, and to remain silent are of paramount importance. Before that phase, the key protection is the Fourth Amendment's restriction on illegal search and seizure. This restriction holds that police must have suspicion of wrongdoing before they can search your person, your car, or your residence, although involvement in an offense can lead to a permissible search that uncovers wrongdoing of another kind. Without search and seizure protection, individuals could be subject to unrestricted police harassment and intimidation, which are characteristic of a totalitarian state, not a free society.

The Fourth Amendment, however, does not provide blanket protection against searches. In 1990, for example, the Supreme Court held that roadside checkpoints where police stop drivers to check them for signs of intoxication are legal as long as the action is systematic and not arbitrary (for example, stopping young drivers only would be unconstitutional). The Court justified its decision by saying roadblocks serve a public safety purpose.[66] However, the Court does not allow the same types of roadblocks to check for drugs in the car. In *Indianapolis v. Edmund* (2001), the Court held that narcotics roadblocks, because they serve a general law enforcement purpose rather than one specific to highway safety, violate the Fourth Amendment's requirement that police have suspicion of wrongdoing before they can search an individual's auto.[67]

The Court also ruled in 2001 (*Kyllo v. United States*) that police may not use a thermal imaging device in order to detect whether unusual heat sources are found in a home. The Court held that police cannot enter a home without a warrant based on suspicion of wrongdoing and that searches based on modern technology must meet the same standard.[68] In an earlier decision, the Court held that states may not exempt drug-related searches from the general requirement that, when entering a person's home with a search warrant, police must first knock and announce their presence.[69]

The Fourth Amendment protects people personally as well as in their homes and in their vehicles. The police cannot arbitrarily stop and search someone on the street or in other settings. In *Ferguson vs. Charleston* (2001), for example, the Court held that patients in public hospitals cannot be forced to take a test for illegal drugs if the purpose is to turn over to the police those patients who test positive. Such action, said the Court, constitutes an illegal search of the person.[70] Yet, the Court in *Board of Education of Independent School District No. 92 of Pottawatomie County v. Earls* (2002) held that random drug testing of high school students involved in extracurricular activities does not violate the ban on unreasonable searches.

In general, the Supreme Court in recent decades has reduced but not eliminated the protections afforded to the accused by *Mapp* and other 1960s rulings.

The Exclusionary Rule

This narrowing can be seen in the application of the **exclusionary rule,** which bars the use in trials of evidence obtained in violation of person's constitutional rights. The rule was formulated in a 1914 Supreme Court decision,[71] and its application was further expanded in federal cases. The *Mapp* decision extended the

exclusionary rule The legal principle that government is prohibited from using in trials evidence that was obtained by unconstitutional means (for example, illegal search and seizure).

exclusionary rule to state trial proceedings as well. Subsequent decisions of the Supreme Court broadened its application to the point where almost any type of illegally obtained evidence was considered inadmissible in a criminal trial.

In the 1980s, the Supreme Court reversed the trend by placing restrictions on the rule's application, concluding that illegally obtained evidence can be admitted in trials if the procedural errors are small, inadvertent, or ultimately inconsequential. In a key 1984 decision, for example, the Court ruled that illegally obtained evidence can be used against a defendant if the prosecution can prove that it would have discovered the evidence anyway.[72]

Recent Supreme Court decisions have further weakened the exclusionary rule. In the 1960s, the Court developed the principle that police had to have a solid basis ("probable cause") for believing that an individual was involved in a specific crime before they could stop a person and engage in search and seizure activity. This principle has been modified.

A key ruling is *Whren v. United States* (1996), which upheld the conviction of an individual who had been found with drugs in the front seat of his car. The police had no evidence (no "probable cause") to believe that drugs were in the car but they suspected the driver was involved in drug dealing and used a minor traffic infraction as a pretext to stop and check him. The Supreme Court accepted defense arguments that the police had no clear evidence for their suspicion, that the traffic infraction was not the real reason the individual was stopped, and that police usually do not stop a person for the infraction in question (turning a corner without signaling). But the Court concluded that the officers' motive was irrelevant, as long as an officer in some situations might reasonably stop a car for the infraction that occurred. Thus, the stop and search was deemed to meet the Fourth Amendment's reasonableness standard.[73]

The Court's objective has been to weaken the exclusionary rule without giving police unlimited discretion. In *U.S. v. Drayton et al.* (2002), for example, the Court upheld the conviction of two bus passengers who had been found with cocaine after voluntarily agreeing to a police search. They were not told of their right to refuse the search, and their attorneys argued the evidence was therefore inadmissible. The Supreme Court said police are not required by the Fourth Amendment "to advise bus passengers of their right . . . to refuse consent to searches" However, the Court also said police cannot tell passengers they must submit to a search and cannot threaten them into permitting one.[74]

Habeas Corpus Appeals

The Supreme Court has recently restricted habeas corpus appeals to federal courts by individuals who have been convicted of crimes in state courts. (Habeas corpus gives defendants access to federal courts in order to argue that their rights under the Constitution of the United States were violated when they were convicted in a state court.) A 1960s Supreme Court precedent had assured prisoners of the right to have their petitions heard in federal court unless they had "deliberately bypassed" the opportunity to make the appeal in state courts.[75]

This precedent was overturned in 1992 when the Court held that inmates can lose the right to a federal hearing even if a lawyer's mistake is the reason they failed to first present their appeal properly in state courts.[76] Another significant habeas corpus defeat for inmates occurred in 1993 when the Supreme

Court held that federal courts cannot overturn a state conviction on the basis of constitutional error unless the prisoner can demonstrate that the error contributed to the conviction.[77] Previously, the burden of proof was on the state: it had to prove that the error did not affect the case's outcome. Then, in *Felker v. Turpin* (1996), the Court upheld a recent federal law that severely restricts federal habeas corpus appeals by state prison inmates who have already filed one.[78]

Through these decisions, the Supreme Court has sought to prevent frivolous and multiple federal court appeals. State prisoners had used habeas corpus appeals to contest even small issues, and some—particularly those on death row—had filed appeal after appeal. An effect was to clog the federal courts and delay other cases. A majority of Supreme Court justices concluded that a more restrictive policy toward these appeals is required. They have held that it is fair to ask inmates to first pursue their options in state courts and then, except in unusual cases,[79] to confine themselves to a single federal appeal. Civil liberties groups have objected to the change, arguing that no procedure that would protect the innocent from wrongful punishment—particularly when the death penalty is at issue—is too big a burden to place on the courts.

However, no one claims that recent decisions mark a return to the lower procedural standards that prevailed before the 1960s. Many of the vital precedents set in that decade remain in effect, including the most important one of all: the principle that procedural protections guaranteed to the accused by the Bill of Rights must be observed by the states as well as by the federal government.

Crime, Punishment, and Police Practices

The theory and practice of procedural guarantees are often two quite different things, as Adrienne Cureton discovered on January 2, 1995. She is a plainclothes police officer who, with a uniformed partner, was called to the scene of a domestic dispute. When a struggle ensued, her partner radioed for help. When the officers arrived, Cureton and her partner had already handcuffed the homeowner. The officers barged in and mistook Cureton, an African American, for the other person involved in the dispute. They grabbed her by the collar, dragged her by the hair onto the porch, and clubbed her repeatedly with flashlights, despite her screams that she was a police officer.[80]

There is no reliable estimate of how often Americans' rights are violated in practice, but infringements of one sort or another are commonplace. Minorities and the poor are the more likely victims. Racial profiling (the assumption that certain groups are more likely to commit particular crimes) is a common police practice and results in the unequal treatment of minorities. A 1999 American Civil Liberties Union study found that although minority and white motorists were about equally likely to commit traffic infractions, 80 percent of the motorists stopped and searched by Maryland State Police on Interstate 95 were minorities and only 20 percent were white, despite the fact that white motorists constituted 75 percent of all drivers. A 1999 report by the New Jersey Attorney General's Office revealed a similar pattern in that state.

Profiling of a different kind came to the forefront after the terrorist attacks of September 11, 2001, when males of Middle Eastern descent were stopped and searched for reasons of appearance alone in airports and other places where further attacks were feared. Sixty-eight percent of Americans in one poll said they favored allowing police to stop and search people who might fit a terrorist profile.[81]

HOW THE UNITED STATES COMPARES

Law and Order

Individual rights are a cornerstone of the American governing system and receive strong protection from the courts. The government's ability to restrict free expression is severely limited, and the individual's right to a fair trial is protected through elaborate due process guarantees.

According to Amnesty International, a watchdog group that monitors human rights achievements and violations around the world, the United States has a good record in terms of its constitutional protection of civil liberties. A number of countries in Asia, Africa, eastern Europe, the Middle East, and Latin America are accused by Amnesty International of "appalling human rights catastrophes" that include the execution, torture, and rape of persons accused of crime or regarded as opponents of the government. Amnesty International does not rank the United States as high as the countries of northern Europe in terms of respect for human rights. Among other problems, Amnesty International faults police in the United States for "excessive force" in their treatment of prisoners and faults U.S. immigration officials for the forcible return of asylum seekers to their country of origin without granting them a hearing.

Although human rights groups admire America's elaborate procedural protections for those accused of crime, they are critical of its sentencing and incarceration policies. The United States is a world leader in the number of people it places behind bars and in the length of sentences for various categories of crime. Defenders of U.S. policy say that although overall crime rates are about the same here as elsewhere, there is more violent crime in America. Critics reply that although the murder rate is high in the United States, it is also true that more than half the people in prison were convicted of nonviolent offenses, such as drug use or a crime against property. Whatever the reasons, the United States is rivaled only by Russia in the proportion of its people who are in prisons.

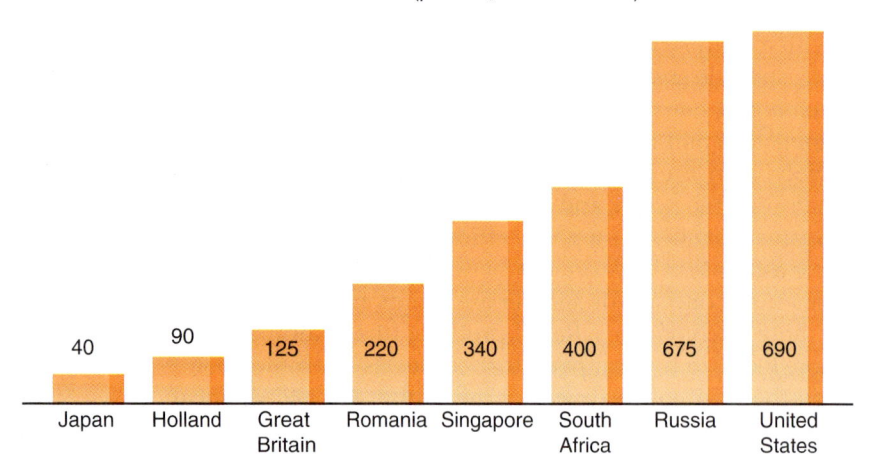

Incarceration rates (per 100,000 inhabitants)

Japan	40
Holland	90
Great Britain	125
Romania	220
Singapore	340
South Africa	400
Russia	675
United States	690

Source: The Sentencing Project, 2001 (U.S. and Russia); United Kingdom Home Office, 2001 (all others).

Another issue of justice in America is whether adherence to proper legal procedures produces reasonable outcomes. The Eighth Amendment prohibits "cruel and unusual punishment" for those convicted of crime, but judgments in this area are relatively subjective. Although the Supreme Court has ordered

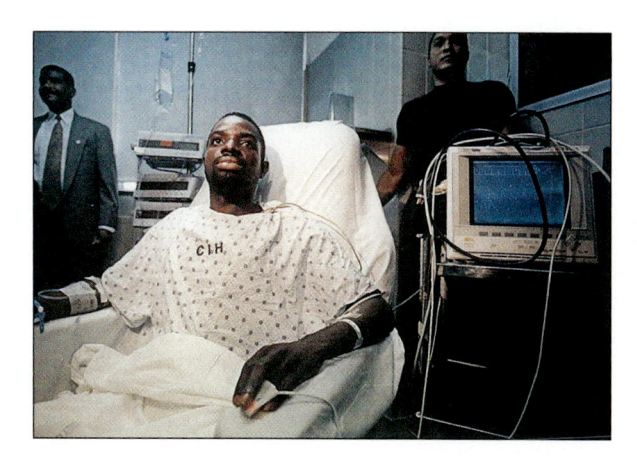

Abner Louima was sodomized with a wooden handle by a New York City police officer after having been taken into custody. Louima's case focused national attention on the issue of police brutality and dramatized the difference that can exist between the theory and reality of constitutional rights.

officials to relieve inmate overcrowding and to improve prison facilities in a few instances, it has concluded that inmates cannot sue over prison conditions unless prison officials show "deliberate indifference" to conditions.[82] The severity of a sentence can also be an Eighth Amendment issue. A divided Supreme Court in 1991 upheld a Michigan law that mandated life imprisonment without parole for a nonviolent first-offense conviction for possession of as little as 1.5 pounds of cocaine.[83] In general, the Court has shied away from Eighth Amendment decisions, preferring to leave those decisions to legislative bodies. In *Atkins v. Virginia* (2002), however, the Supreme Court outlawed the death penalty for the mentally retarded, saying it constitutes "cruel and unusual punishment." The Court noted that thirty states and nearly every country in the world prohibits such executions.[84]

In recent years, legislators in the United States have taken a tougher stance on crime. Congress and most states have mandated stiffer sentences, and the number of federal and state prisoners has more than doubled in the past decade. The United States has a larger proportion of its people behind bars than any country in the world (see "How the United States Compares").

THE COURTS AND A FREE SOCIETY

A free and democratic nation has a vital stake in maintaining individual freedoms. The United States was founded on the belief that individuals have an innate right to personal liberty—to speak their minds, to worship as they choose, to be free of police intimidation. The greatest threat to individual rights in a democratic society is a popular majority backed by elected leaders determined to carry out its will. Majorities have frequently preferred policies that would diminish the freedom of those who hold minority views, have unconventional lifestyles, or simply "look different" from the majority.

Americans are highly supportive of rights and freedoms expressed in abstract terms but are much less supportive—and in some cases antagonistic—when confronted with these same rights in concrete situations. For example, after the terrorist attacks of September 11, 2001, polls indicated that a third of Americans would favor putting Arab Americans under special surveillance, half said they would favor requiring Arab Americans to carry special identification

Figure 4–2

Opinions on Detaining People on Basis of Religion or Nationality as Part of War on Terrorism

Most Americans are willing to allow the government to detain and question people of certain religions and nationalities as part of the war on terrorism.

Source: Fox News/Opinion Dynamics Poll, November 28–29, 2001.

"As part of the war on terrorism, the federal government wants to question 5,000 Middle Eastern immigrants on the basis of their religion or nationality. Some local officials have refused to perform the questioning, suggesting the government needs to show more cause to question the visitors. Do you approve or disapprove of the government questioning these individuals?"

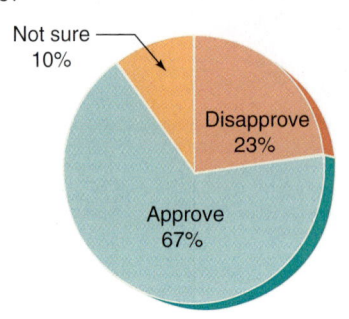

- Not sure 10%
- Disapprove 23%
- Approve 67%

cards, and a fourth said they would approve of special detention facilities for members of suspect groups.[85] Two-thirds said they would approve the detention of thousands of Middle Eastern immigrants for questioning (see Figure 4–2).

Greater support for individual rights exists among the political elite. Those who are most active politically, including officeholders and journalists, are more likely to express strong support for free expression and fair trial rights. They are also better positioned than the ordinary citizen to express their beliefs. However, they are not always willing to act. Often, the exercise of rights involves society's least savory characters—its murderers, rapists, drug dealers, and hate peddlers. Miscreants are hardly the type of person that engenders public support at any level.

The courts are not isolated from the public mood. They inevitably balance society's demand for safety and order against the rights of the individual. Nevertheless, the judicial branch can normally be expected to grant more consideration to the rights of the individual, however unpopular his or her views or actions, than will the general public or elected officials. How far the courts will go in protecting a person's rights depends on the facts of the case, the existing status of the law, prevailing social needs, and the personal views of the judges. Nevertheless, the courts regard the protection of individual rights as one of their most significant responsibilities, a perspective that is owed in no small measure to the Bill of Rights. It transformed the inalienable rights of life, liberty, and property into legal rights, thus putting them under judicial protection.[86]

Civil liberties are not blessings that government kindly bestows on the individual. Because of their constitutional nature, these rights are above government. In fact, it can be said that government exists to protect these rights. True, government does not always act lawfully; the temptations of power and the pressures of the majority can at times lead governmental institutions to usurp individual rights. The courts are not immune to these influences and have the added pressure of the obligation to seek an accommodation between the claims of individuals and the collective interests of society (which, of course, include respect for civil liberties). Although the courts have not always sided with individuals in their claims to rights, it is at least as noteworthy that they have not always sided with government in its claims against the individual.

CHAPTER 4   Civil Liberties: Protecting Individual Rights   127

In aftermath of the September 11, 2001, terrorist attacks, Arab Americans were subject to ethnic profiling at airports and other locations. Shown here is an Arab American protesting the practice of profiling.

Self-Quiz
www.mhhe.com/patterson6

Nevertheless, the judiciary alone cannot provide adequate protection for individual rights. A civil society rests also on enlightened representatives and a tolerant citizenry. If, for example, politicians and the public encourage police to infringe the rights of vaguely threatening minorities or nonconformists, the judiciary's protection of persons accused of crimes will not ensure justice. It may be said that the test of a truly civil society is not its treatment of popular ideas and of its best citizens but its willingness to tolerate ideas that the majority detests and to respect equally the rights of its least popular citizens.

SUMMARY

In their search for personal liberty, Americans added the Bill of Rights to the Constitution shortly after its ratification. These amendments guarantee certain political, procedural, and property rights against infringement by the national government. Freedom of expression is the most basic of democratic rights. People are not free unless they can freely express their views. Nevertheless, free expression may conflict with the nation's security needs during times of war and insurrection. The courts at times have allowed government to limit expression substantially for purposes of national security. In recent decades, however, the courts have protected a very wide range of free expression in the areas of speech, press, and religion.

The guarantees embodied in the Bill of Rights originally applied only to the national government. Under the principle of selective incorporation of these guarantees into the Fourteenth Amendment, the courts extended them to state governments, though the process was slow and uneven. In the 1920s and 1930s, First Amendment guarantees of freedom of expression were given protection from infringement by the states. The states continued to have wide discretion in criminal proceedings until the early 1960s, when most of the fair-trial rights in the Bill of Rights were given federal protection.

Due process of law refers to legal protections that have been established to preserve individual rights. The most significant form of these protections consists of procedures or methods (for example, the right of an accused person to have an attorney present during police interrogation) designed to ensure that an individual's rights are upheld. A major controversy in this area is the breadth of the exclusionary rule, which bars the use in trials of illegally obtained evidence. The right of privacy, particularly as it applies to the abortion issue, is also a source of controversy.

Civil liberties are not absolute but must be balanced against other considerations (such as national security or public safety) and against one another when different rights come into conflict. The judicial branch of government, particularly the Supreme Court, has taken on much of the responsibility for protecting and interpreting individual rights. The Court's positions have changed with time and conditions, but the Court has generally been more protective of and sensitive to civil liberties than have elected officials or popular majorities.

CHAPTER 4 — Civil Liberties: Protecting Individual Rights

KEY TERMS

- Bill of Rights
- civil liberties
- clear-and-present-danger test
- due process clause (of the Fourteenth Amendment)
- establishment clause
- exclusionary rule
- free-exercise clause
- freedom of expression
- imminent lawless action test
- libel
- prior restraint
- procedural due process
- selective incorporation
- slander
- symbolic speech

SUGGESTED READINGS

Abraham, Henry J. *Freedom and the Court.* New York: Oxford University Press, 1998. A comprehensive analysis of the Supreme Court's work on civil rights and civil liberties.

Epstein, Lee, and Thomas G. Walker. *Constitutional Law for a Changing America*, 2d ed. Washington, D.C.: Congressional Quarterly Press, 2000. An accessible introduction to U.S. constitutional law.

Hull, N. E. H., and Peter Charles Hoffer. *Roe v. Wade: The Abortion Rights Controversy in American History.* Lawrence: University Press of Kansas, 2001. A thorough assessment of both sides of the abortion conflict, beginning with the *Roe v. Wade* decision.

Lewis, Anthony. *Gideon's Trumpet.* New York: Random House, 1964. The riveting story of Clarence Gideon and the effects of his case on the right to legal counsel.

Nagel, Robert F. *Judicial Power and American Character.* New York: Oxford University Press, 1996. Concludes that the real protection for legal rights resides in political action rather than judicial decisions.

Perry, Michael J. *Religion in Politics: Constitutional and Moral Perspectives.* New York: Oxford University Press, 1997. A legal and philosophical analysis of the role of religion in politics.

Wirenius, John F. *First Amendment, First Principles.* New York: Holmes and Meier, 2000. Analysis of verbal acts and freedom of speech.

LIST OF WEBSITES

http://oyez.nwu.edu/
Includes information on Supreme Court rulings; particularly useful when studying nineteenth-century cases.

http://www.aclu.org/
The American Civil Liberties Union sites; it provides information on current civil liberties and civil rights issues, including information on recent and pending Supreme Court cases.

http://www.findlaw.com/casecode/supreme.html
An excellent source of information on Supreme Court and lower-court rulings.

http://www.mitretek.org/business_areas/justice/cjlinks/
A site dedicated to criminal justice questions with links to many additional sites that focus on particular issues.

5

I have a dream that one day this nation will rise up and live out the true meaning of its creed: "We hold these truths to be self-evident: that all men are created equal."

—Martin Luther King Jr.[1]

Equal Rights:
Struggling Toward Fairness

The producers of ABC television's *PrimeTime Live* put hidden cameras on two young men, equally well dressed and groomed, and then sent them on different routes to do the same things—search for an apartment, shop for a car, look at albums in a record store. The cameras recorded the reactions the two men received. One was greeted with smiles and was invited to buy, often at good prices. The other man was treated with suspicious looks, was sometimes made to wait, and was often asked to pay more. Why the difference? The explanation was simple: the young man who was routinely well received was white; the young man who was treated badly was an African American.

The Urban Institute had conducted a similar experiment a few months earlier. The experiment used pairs of specially trained white and black male college students who were the same in all respects—education, work experience, speech patterns, physical builds—except for their race. The students responded individually to nearly five hundred classified job advertisements in Chicago and Washington, D.C. The black applicants got fewer interviews, had shorter interviews, and were given fewer job offers than were the white applicants. An Urban Institute spokesperson said, "The level of reverse discrimination [favoring blacks over whites] that we found was limited, was certainly far lower than many might have been led to fear, and was swamped by the extent of discrimination against black job applicants."[2]

These two experiments suggest why some Americans are still struggling for equal rights. In theory, Americans are equal in their rights, but in reality, they are not now equal, nor have they ever been. African Americans, women, Hispanic Americans, the disabled, Jews, American Indians, Catholics, Asian Americans, homosexuals, and members of nearly every other minority group have been victims of discrimination in fact and in law. The nation's creed—"all men are created equal"—has encouraged minorities to believe that they deserve equal justice and has given weight to their claims for fair treatment. But full equality is far from being a universal condition of American life. Inequality is built into almost every aspect of our society. Here is but one example: African Americans with a correctable heart problem are only half as likely to receive the necessary surgery than are whites with the same problem.[3]

This chapter focuses on **equal rights,** or **civil rights**—terms that refer to the right of every person to equal protection under the laws and equal access to society's opportunities and public facilities. Chapter 4 explained that civil liberties refer to specific *individual* rights, such as freedom of speech, that are protected from infringement by government. Equal rights, or civil rights, have to do with whether individual members of differing *groups*—racial, sexual, and the like—are treated equally by government and, in some areas, by private parties. To oversimplify, civil liberties deal with issues of personal freedom, and civil rights deal with issues of equality.

Although the law refers to the rights of individuals first and to those of groups in a secondary and derivative way, this chapter concentrates on groups because the history of civil rights has been largely one of group claims to equality. The chapter emphasizes the following main points:

civil rights, or equal rights
The right of every person to equal protection under the laws and equal access to society's opportunities and public facilities.

- *Disadvantaged groups have had to struggle for equal rights.* African Americans, women, Native Americans, Hispanic Americans, Asian Americans, and others have all had to fight for their rights in order to come closer to equality with white males.

- *Americans have attained substantial equality under the law.* They have, in legal terms, equal protection of the laws, equal access to accommodations and housing, and an equal right to vote. Discrimination by law against persons because of race, sex, religion, and ethnicity is now almost nonexistent.

- *Legal equality for all Americans has not resulted in de facto equality.* African Americans, women, Hispanic Americans, and other traditionally disadvantaged groups have a disproportionately small share of America's opportunities and benefits. Existing inequalities, discriminatory practices, and political pressures are still major barriers to their full equality. Affirmative action and busing are policies designed to help the disadvantaged achieve full equality.

THE STRUGGLE FOR EQUALITY

Equality has always been the least fully developed of America's founding concepts. Not even Thomas Jefferson, who had a deep admiration for the "common man," believed that broad meaning could be given to the claim of the Declaration of Independence that "all men are created equal." To Jefferson, "equality" had a restricted, though significant, meaning: people are of equal moral worth and as such deserve equal treatment under the law.[4] Even then, Jefferson made a distinction between free men and slaves, who were not entitled to legal equality.

The history of America shows that disadvantaged groups have rarely achieved a greater measure of justice without a struggle.[5] Legal equality has rarely been bestowed by the more powerful upon the less powerful. Their gains have nearly always occurred through intense and sustained political movements, such as the civil rights movement of the 1960s, that have pressured established interests to relinquish or share their privileged status (see Chapter 7).

Disadvantaged groups have a shared history of political exclusion, struggles for empowerment, and policy triumphs, but they also have distinctive histories, as is evident by a brief look at the efforts of African Americans, women, Native Americans, Hispanic Americans, Asian Americans, and other groups to achieve a greater degree of equality.

African Americans

Of all America's problems, none has been as persistent as the white race's unwillingness to yield a fair share of society's benefits to members of the black race. The ancestors of most African Americans came to this country as slaves, after having been captured in Africa, shipped in chains across the Atlantic, and sold in open markets in Charleston and other seaports.

CHAPTER 5 Equal Rights: Struggling Toward Fairness

Two police dogs attack a black civil rights activist (*center left*) during the 1963 Birmingham demonstrations. Such images of hatred and violence shook many white Americans out of their complacency regarding race relations.

It took a civil war to bring slavery to an end, but the battle did not end institutionalized racism. When Reconstruction ended in 1877 with the withdrawal of federal troops from the South, whites in the region regained power and gradually reestablished racial segregation by enacting laws that prohibited black citizens from using the same public facilities as whites.[6] In *Plessy v. Ferguson* (1896), the Supreme Court endorsed these laws, ruling that "separate" facilities for the two races did not violate the Constitution as long as the facilities were "equal." "If one race be inferior to the other socially," the Court argued, "the Constitution of the United States cannot put them on the same plane."[7] The *Plessy* decision became a justification for the separate and *unequal* treatment of African Americans. Black children, for example, were forced into separate schools that rarely had libraries and had few teachers; they were given worn-out books that had been used previously in white schools.

Black leaders challenged these discriminatory state and local policies through legal action, but not until the late 1930s did the Supreme Court begin to respond favorably to their demands. The Court began modestly by ruling that where no public facilities existed for African Americans, they must be allowed to use those reserved for whites.[8]

The *Brown* Decision

Substantial judicial relief for African Americans was finally achieved in 1954 with *Brown v. Board of Education of Topeka*, arguably the most significant ruling in Supreme Court history. The case began when Linda Carol Brown, a black child in Topeka, Kansas, was denied admission to an all-white elementary school that she passed every day on her way to her all-black school, which was twelve blocks farther away. In its decision, the Court fully reversed its *Plessy* doctrine

Martin Luther King Jr.
(1929–1968)

Martin Luther King Jr. is the only American of the twentieth century to be honored with a national holiday. The civil rights leader was the pivotal figure in the movement to gain legal and political rights for black Americans. The son of a Baptist minister, King used rhetorical skills and nonviolent protest to sweep aside a century of governmental discrimination and to inspire other groups, including women and Hispanics, to assert their rights. Recipient of the Nobel Peace Prize in 1964 (the youngest person ever to receive that honor), King was assassinated in Memphis in 1968.

by declaring that racial segregation of public schools "generates [among black children] a feeling of inferiority as to their status in the community that may affect their hearts and minds in a way unlikely ever to be undone. . . . Separate educational facilities are inherently unequal."[9]

As a 1954 Gallup poll indicated, a sizable majority of southern whites opposed the *Brown* decision, and billboards were erected along southern roadways that called for the impeachment of Chief Justice Earl Warren. In the so-called Southern Manifesto, southern congressmen urged their state governments to "resist forced integration by any lawful means." In 1957, rioting broke out when Governor Orval Faubus called out the Arkansas National Guard to block the entry of black children to the Little Rock public schools. To restore order and carry out the desegregation of the Little Rock schools, President Dwight D. Eisenhower used his power as the nation's commander in chief to place the Arkansas National Guard under federal control. For their part, northern whites were neither strongly for nor strongly against school desegregation. A Gallup poll revealed that only a slim majority of whites outside the South agreed with the *Brown* decision.

The Black Civil Rights Movement

After *Brown*, the struggle of African Americans for their rights became a political movement. Perhaps no single event turned national public opinion so dramatically against segregation as a 1963 march led by Dr. Martin Luther King Jr. in Birmingham, Alabama. An advocate of nonviolent protest, King had been leading peaceful demonstrations and marches for nearly eight years before that fateful day in Birmingham.[10] As the nation watched in disbelief on television, police officers led by Birmingham's sheriff, Eugene "Bull" Connor, attacked King and his followers with dogs, cattle prods, and fire hoses.

The modern civil rights movement peaked with the triumphant March on Washington for Jobs and Freedom of August 2, 1963. Organized by Dr. King and other civil rights leaders, it attracted 250,000 marchers, one of the largest gatherings in the history of the nation's capital. "I have a dream," the Reverend King told the gathering, "that my four little children will one day live in a nation where they will not be judged by the color of their skin but by the content of their character."

A year later, after a months-long fight in Congress that was marked by every parliamentary obstacle that racial conservatives could muster, the Civil Rights Act of 1964 was enacted. The legislation provided African Americans and other minorities with equal access to public facilities and prohibited job discrimination. Even then, southern states resorted to legal maneuvering and other delaying tactics to blunt the new law's impact. The state of Virginia, for example, established a commission to pay the legal expenses of white citizens who were brought to court for violations of the federal act. Nevertheless, momentum was on the side of racial equality. The murder of two civil rights workers during

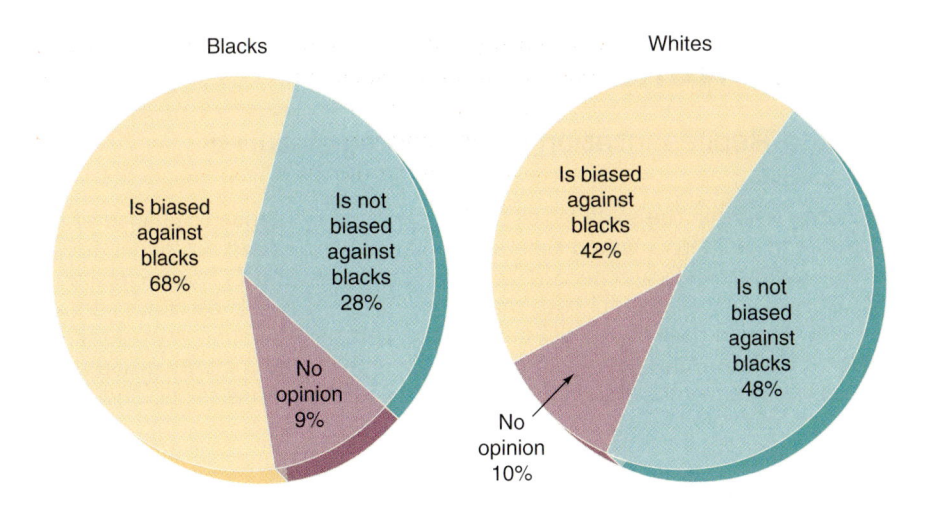

Figure 5–1

Opinions on Racial Bias in the Justice System
African Americans are much more likely than white Americans to believe that the courts are biased against black people.
Source: National Center for State Courts, 1999.

Blacks
- Is biased against blacks 68%
- Is not biased against blacks 28%
- No opinion 9%

Whites
- Is biased against blacks 42%
- Is not biased against blacks 48%
- No opinion 10%

a voter registration drive in Selma, Alabama, helped sustain the momentum.[11] President Lyndon Johnson, who had been a decisive force in the battle to pass the Civil Rights Act, called for new legislation that would end racial barriers to voting.[12] Congress's answer was the 1965 Voting Rights Act.

The Aftermath of the Civil Rights Movement

Although the most significant progress in history toward the legal equality of all Americans occurred during the 1960s, Dr. King's dream of a color-blind society has remained elusive.[13] Even the legal rights of African Americans do not, in practice, match the promise of the civil rights movement.[14] Studies have found, for example, that African Americans accused of crime are more likely to be convicted and to receive stiffer sentences than are white Americans on trial for comparable offenses. Federal statistics from the National Office of Drug Control Policy and the U.S. Sentencing Commission revealed that in 1997 black Americans accounted for more than 75 percent of crack cocaine convictions but only about 35 percent of crack cocaine users. It is hardly surprising that many African Americans believe that the nation has two standards of justice, an inferior one for blacks and a higher one for whites (see Figure 5–1).

One area where African Americans have made substantial progress since the 1960s is the winning of election to public office (see "States in the Nation"). Although the percentage of black elected officials is still far below the proportion of African Americans in the population, it has risen sharply over recent decades.[15] As of 2000, there were more than twenty black members of Congress and four hundred black mayors—including the mayors of some of this country's largest cities.

Women

The United States carried over from English common law a political disregard for women, forbidding them to vote, hold public office, and serve on juries.[16] Upon marriage, a woman essentially lost her identity as an individual and

STATES IN THE NATION

Black and Latino Representation in State Legislatures

For a long period, minorities were barely visible in the state legislatures. The situation began to change after passage of the 1964 Civil Rights Act and the 1965 Voting Rights Act, but minorities are still underrepresented relative to their numbers in the population. Only 8 percent of state legislators in 2000 were black and a mere 3 percent were Hispanic. Alabama and Mississippi have the highest proportion (25 percent each) of African American state legislators. New Mexico has the highest number (37 percent) of Latino lawmakers. A few states, including Maine and North Dakota, have no legislator from either of these minority groups. Of course, these states have small minority populations while states such as Alabama, Mississippi, and New Mexico have much larger ones.

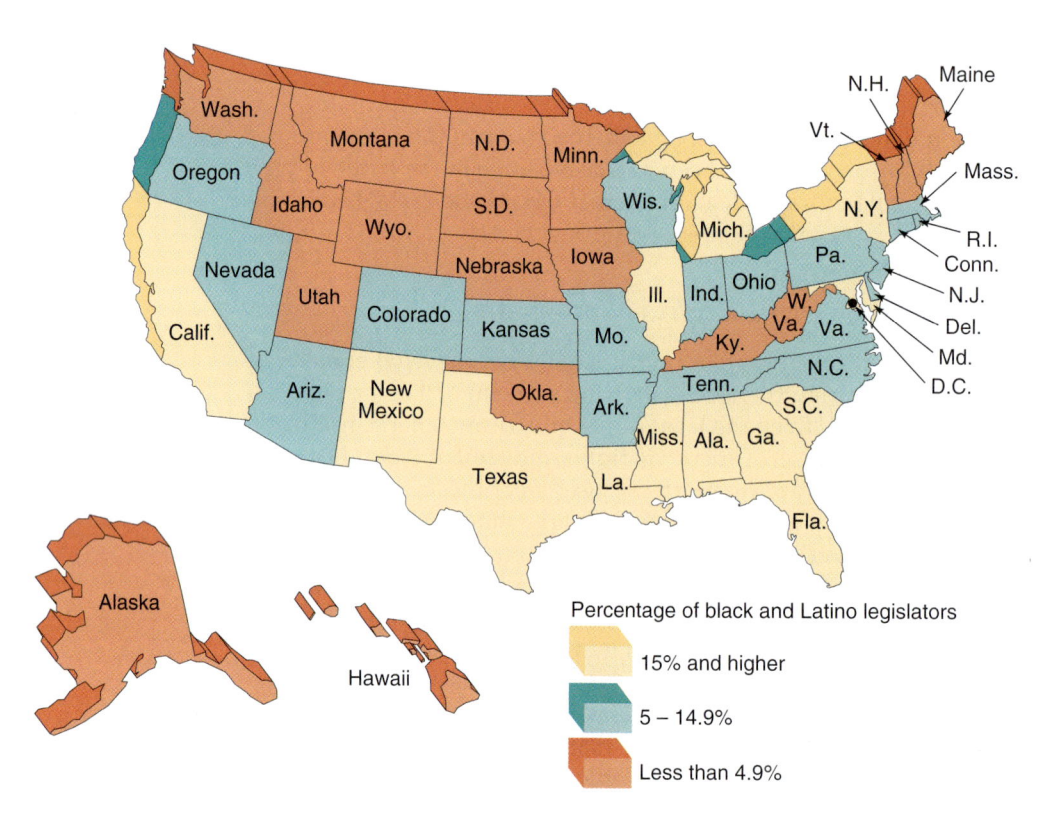

Percentage of black and Latino legislators
- 15% and higher
- 5 – 14.9%
- Less than 4.9%

Source: National Conference of State Legislatures, 2000.

could not own and dispose of property without her husband's consent. Even the wife's body was not fully hers. A wife's adultery was ruled by the Supreme Court to be a violation of the husband's property rights![17]

The first women's rights convention in America was held in 1848 in Seneca Falls, New York, after Lucretia Mott and Elizabeth Cady Stanton had been barred from the main floor of an antislavery convention.[18] Thereafter, however, the struggle for women's rights became closely aligned with the abolitionist movement, but the passage of the post–Civil War constitutional amendments proved to be a setback for the women's movement. The Fifteenth Amendment, for example, said that the right to vote could not be abridged on account of race or color, but said nothing about sex.[19] After decades of struggle, the Nineteenth Amendment was finally adopted in 1920, forbidding denial of the right to vote "by the United States or by any state on account of sex."

Women's Legal and Political Gains

Ratification of the Nineteenth Amendment encouraged leaders of the women's movement to propose in 1923 a constitutional amendment that would guarantee equal rights for women. Congress rejected that proposal and several subsequent ones. In 1973, however, Congress approved the Equal Rights Amendment (ERA) and submitted it to the states for ratification or rejection. The ERA failed by three states to get the three-fourths majority required for ratification.[20]

Although the ERA did not become part of the Constitution, it helped bring women's rights to the forefront at a time when developments in Congress and the courts were contributing significantly to the legal equality of the sexes.[21] Among the congressional initiatives that have helped women are the Equal Pay Act of 1963, which prohibits sex discrimination in salary and wages by some categories of employers; the Civil Rights Act of 1964, which prohibits sex discrimination in programs that receive federal funding; Title IX of the Education Amendment of 1972, which prohibits sex discrimination in education; the Equal Credit Act of 1974, as amended in 1976, which prohibits sex discrimination in the granting of financial credit; and the Civil Rights Act of 1991 and the Family Leave Act of 1993 (discussed later in this chapter).

Women have made clear gains in the area of appointive and elective offices.[22] In 1981, President Reagan appointed the first woman to serve on the Supreme Court, Sandra Day O'Connor. When the Democratic party in 1984 chose Geraldine Ferraro as its vice presidential nominee, it was the first time a woman ran on the national ticket of a major political party. The elections of California's Dianne Feinstein and Barbara Boxer in 1992 marked the first time that women occupied both U.S. Senate seats from a state.

Despite such signs of progress, women are still a long way from political equality with men.[23] Women occupy less than 15 percent of congressional seats and only 20 percent of statewide and city council offices (see "How the United States Compares").

Although women are underrepresented in political office, their vote is becoming increasingly powerful. Until the 1970s, there was almost no difference in the voting patterns of women and men. Today, there is a substantial **gender gap**: women and men differ substantially in their political attitudes and voting tendencies. Women are more supportive than men of government programs for the poor, minorities, children, and the elderly. They also have a greater tendency to cast their votes for Democratic candidates (see Figure 5–2). The gender gap is discussed further in Chapter 6.

Susan B. Anthony
(1820–1906)

Susan B. Anthony was a pioneer in the women's suffrage movement. She was twice arrested and fined in her adopted hometown of Rochester, New York, for organizing Election Day protests against laws denying women the vote. Anthony, who was also active in the temperance movement, served for a decade as president of the American Women Suffrage Association. She died before her dream of women's suffrage was fulfilled.

gender gap The tendency of women and men to differ in their political attitudes and voting preferences.

HOW THE UNITED STATES COMPARES

Women's Equality: Representation in National Legislatures

Although conflict between groups is universal, the nature of the conflict is often particularized. Racial conflict in the United States cannot readily be compared with, say, religious conflict in Northern Ireland. The one form of inequality common to all nations is that of gender: nowhere are women equal to men in law or in fact. But there are large differences between countries. A study by the Population Crisis Committee ranked the United States third overall in women's equality, behind only Sweden and Finland. The rankings were based on five areas—jobs, education, social relations, marriage and family, and health; U.S. women had an 82.5 percent rating compared with men.

The inequality of women is also underscored by their underrepresentation in public office. There is no country in which women comprise as many as half the members of the national legislature. The Scandinavian countries rank highest in terms of the percentage of female lawmakers. Other northern European countries have lower levels, but the levels are higher than that of the United States. The accompanying figure indicates the approximate percentage of seats held by women in the largest chamber of each country's national legislature:

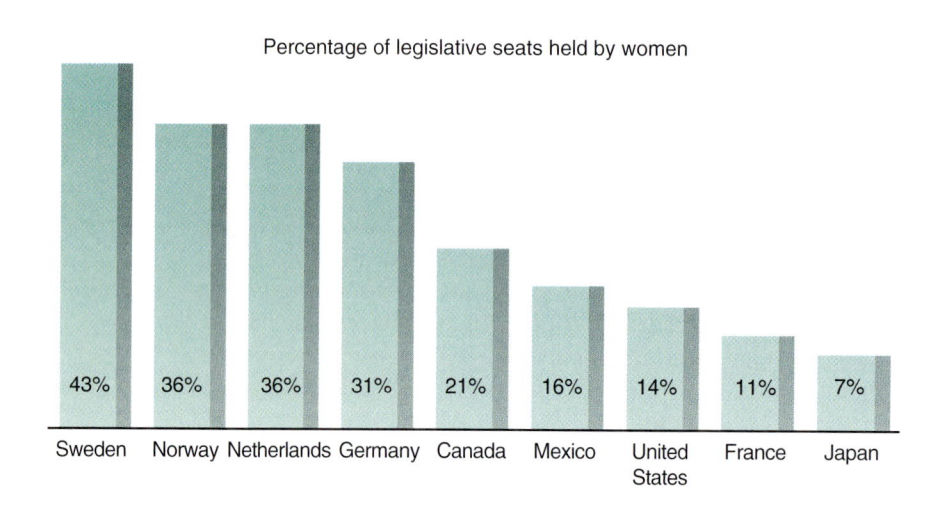

Percentage of legislative seats held by women

Sweden	Norway	Netherlands	Germany	Canada	Mexico	United States	France	Japan
43%	36%	36%	31%	21%	16%	14%	11%	7%

Source: Inter-Parliamentary Union, 2001.

Job-Related Issues: Family Leave, Comparable Worth, and Sexual Harassment

In recent decades, increasing numbers of women have sought employment outside the home. Government statistics indicate that three in five women worked outside the home in 1995 compared with only one in eight in 1950. Women have made gains in many traditionally male-dominated fields. For example, women now make up a third of the new lawyers who enter the job market each year. The change in women's status is also reflected in education statistics. In 1972, more white, black, and Hispanic men than women enrolled in college. By 1991, the reverse was true: more women than men of each group were enrolled.

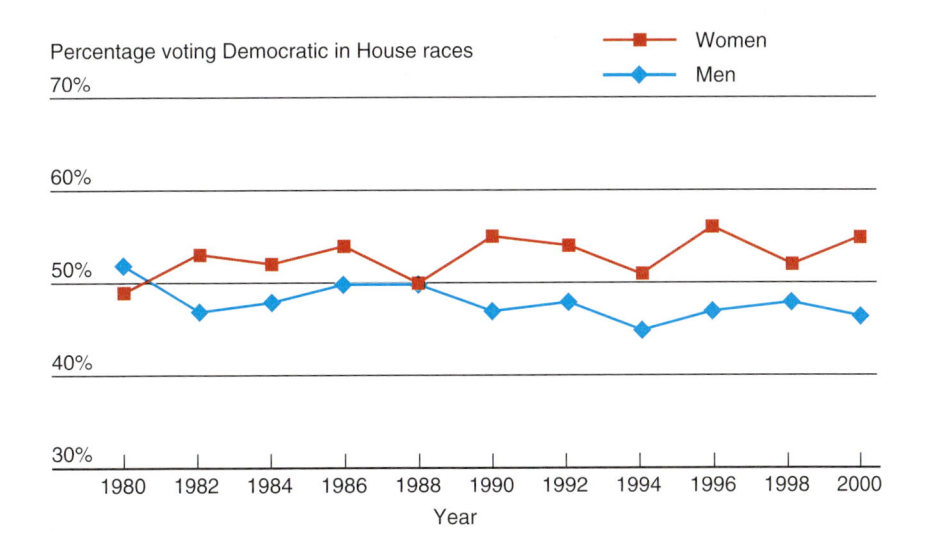

Figure 5–2

The Gender Gap in Congressional Voting
Women and men differ, on average, in their political behavior. For example, women are more likely than men to vote Democratic, as shown by the difference between the women's vote and the men's vote for Democratic candidates in recent U.S. House races.
Source: National Election Studies.

The majority of women with preschool children work outside the home, a situation that has created demands for government support of day care centers, parental leave, and other programs and services.

The increase in the number of women in the workplace has created demands for the expansion of programs such as day care centers and parental leave. In 1993, Congress passed the Family and Medical Leave Act, which provides up to twelve weeks of unpaid leave for employees, male or female, to care for a new baby or a seriously ill family member. Upon return from leave, employees must ordinarily be restored to their original or equivalent positions with equivalent pay, benefits, and other employment terms.

Figure 5–3

Median Annual Income of Full-Time Year-Round Male and Female Workers

Women's income has increased relative to men's income during the past quarter-century but is still substantially lower.

Source: U.S. Bureau of the Census, 2002.

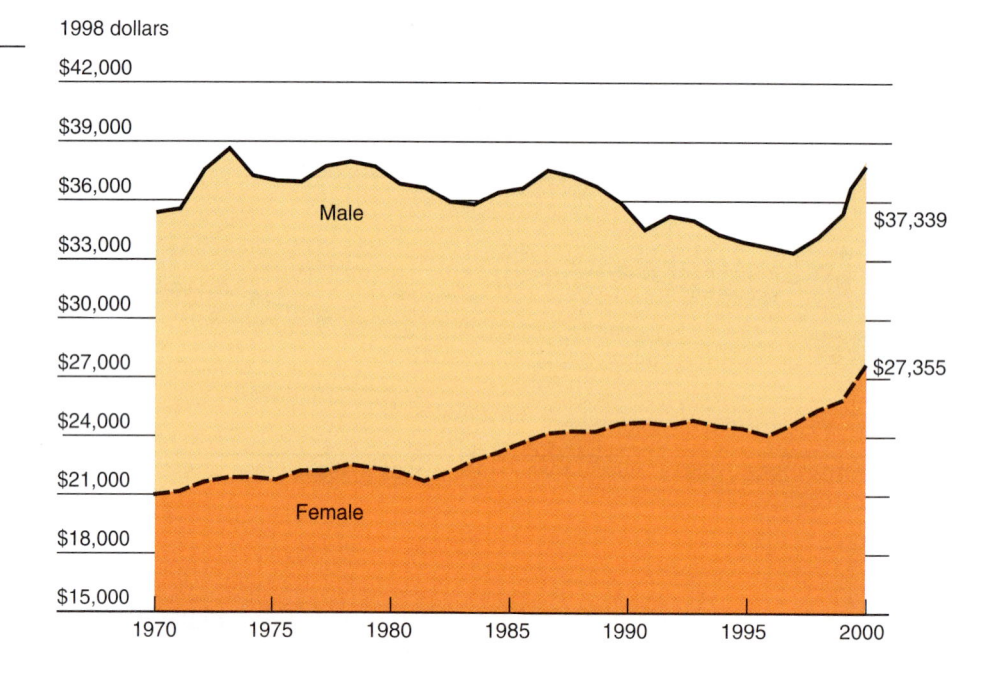

(Chart: 1998 dollars, 1970–2000. Male: $37,339; Female: $27,355.)

comparable worth The idea that women should get pay equal to men for work that is of similar difficulty and responsibility and that requires similar levels of education and training.

Nevertheless, women are less than equal to men when it comes to job opportunities and benefits. Women increasingly occupy managerial positions, but they are less likely than men to receive top promotions. The term *glass ceiling* refers to the invisible but nonetheless real barrier to advancement that talented women encounter after having reached the middle-management level.

Women also hold a disproportionate number of the low-wage jobs in society. Although the disparity is decreasing, the average pay for full-time women employees is only about three-fourths that of full-time men employees (see Figure 5–3). This situation has led to demands by women for equal pay for work that is of similar difficulty and responsibility and that requires similar levels of education and training—a concept called **comparable worth.** Advocates gained an early victory when the Supreme Court held in 1981 that female guards at a prison had to be paid the same as male guards even if their work assignments differed.[24] In general, however, proponents of comparable worth have had only limited success in persuading public and private employers to institute the policy.[25]

Workplace discrimination against women includes sexual harassment. Lewd comments and unwelcome advances are a part of everyday life for many working women, and the courts have taken an increasingly firm stand against companies that tolerate such behavior. In 1998, the Supreme Court ruled that a firm can be held liable for sexual misconduct by supervisors even if the firm was unaware of the misconduct and even if the employee did not suffer adverse job consequences. The Court also held, however, that a firm's liability is reduced when it has an aggressive program to guard against sexual harassment in the workplace.[26]

Members of the American Indian Movement stand watch in 1973 at Wounded Knee on the Oglala Sioux reservation in South Dakota. They had seized the hamlet in protest against federal policies toward Native Americans. The site of the armed protest was not a coincidence. In 1890, the U.S. cavalry massacred 146 Indians, including women and children, at this location.

Native Americans

When white settlers began arriving in America in large numbers during the seventeenth century, nearly ten million Native Americans were living in the territory that would become the United States. By 1900, the Native American population had plummeted to less than one million. Diseases brought by white settlers had taken a toll on the various Indian tribes, but so had wars and massacres. "The only good Indian is a dead Indian" is not simply a hackneyed expression from cowboy movies. It was part of a strategy of westward expansion, as settlers and U.S. troops alike mercilessly drove the eastern Indians from their ancestral lands to the Great Plains and then took those lands as well.

Today Native Americans number more than one million, about half of whom live on or close to reservations set aside for them by the federal government. Reservations are governed by treaties signed when they were established. State governments have no direct authority over federal reservations, and the federal government's authority is limited by the terms of a particular treaty. Although U.S. policy toward the reservations has changed over time, the current policy is to promote self-government and economic self-sufficiency.[27]

Native Americans are less than half as likely to attend college as other Americans, their life expectancy is more than ten years lower than the national average, and their infant mortality rate is more than three times higher than that of white Americans. In recent years, some Native American tribes have erected gaming casinos on reservation land. The casinos have brought jobs and income to the reservations but have also brought controversy—traditionalists argue that the casinos are destroying their tribal cultures.

The civil rights movement of the 1960s at first did not include Native Americans. Then, in the early 1970s, militant Native Americans occupied the Bureau of Indian Affairs in Washington, D.C., and later seized control of the village of

Wounded Knee on a Sioux reservation in southwestern South Dakota, exchanging gunfire with U.S. marshals. These episodes brought attention to the grievances of Native Americans and may have contributed to the passage in 1974 of legislation that granted Native Americans on reservations a greater measure of control over federal programs that affected them. Native Americans had already benefited from the legislative climate created by the civil rights movement of the 1960s. In 1968, Congress had enacted the Indian Bill of Rights, which gives Native Americans on reservations constitutional guarantees that are similar to those held by other Americans.

In recent years Native Americans have filed suit to reclaim lost ancestral lands and have won a few settlements. But they stand no realistic chance of getting back even those lands that had been granted them by federal treaty but were later sold off or simply taken forcibly by federal authorities. Native Americans were not even official citizens of the United States until an act of Congress in 1924. This status came too late to be of much help; their traditional way of life had already been seriously eroded.

Hispanic Americans

The fastest-growing minority in the United States is that of Hispanic Americans, that is, people of Spanish-speaking background. Hispanics are also one of the country's oldest ethnic groups. Some Hispanics are descendants of people who helped colonize the areas of California, Texas, Florida, New Mexico, and Arizona before they were taken over by the United States. But most Hispanics are recent immigrants or their descendants.

The 2000 census counted roughly 33 million Hispanics living in the United States, an increase of 40 percent over the 1990 census. Hispanics had surpassed African Americans as the nation's largest racial or ethnic minority group. They have emigrated to the United States primarily from Mexico and the Caribbean islands, mainly Cuba and Puerto Rico. About half of all Hispanics in the United States were born in Mexico or claim a Mexican ancestry. Hispanics are concentrated in their states of entry; thus Florida, New York, and New Jersey have large numbers of Caribbean Hispanics, while California, Texas, Arizona, and New Mexico have many immigrants from Mexico. More than half the population of Los Angeles is of Hispanic—mostly Mexican—descent.

The term *Hispanic* can be misleading if it is construed to mean a group of people who all think alike (see Table 5–1). Hispanics cover a wide political spectrum, from the conservative Republican-leaning Cuban Americans of southern Florida to the liberal Democratic-leaning Puerto Ricans of the Northeast. Hispanic Americans share a common language, Spanish, but they are not monolithic in their politics.[28]

Legal and Political Action

Hispanic Americans have benefited from laws and court rulings aimed primarily at protecting other groups. Thus, although the Civil Rights Act of 1964 was largely a response to the condition of black people, its provisions against discrimination apply broadly to other groups as well.

Nevertheless, Hispanics had their own civil rights movement. Its most publicized actions were the farm workers' strikes of the late 1960s and the 1970s that aimed at achieving basic labor rights for migrant workers. Migrants were working long hours for low pay, were living in shacks without electricity or plumbing, and were unwelcome in many local schools and in some local hospitals as well. Farm owners at first refused to bargain with the workers, but a well-organized national boycott of California grapes and lettuce forced that state to pass a law giving migrant workers the right to bargain collectively. The strikes were led in California by Cesar Chavez, who himself grew up in a Mexican-American migrant family. Chavez's tactics were copied in other states, particularly Texas, but the results were less successful.

Hispanics face some distinctive problems. The fact that many do not speak English led to a 1968 amendment to the 1964 Civil Rights Act that funds public school programs offering English instruction in the language of children for whom English is a second language. In addition, many Hispanics are illegal aliens and do not have the full rights of citizens. In *De Canas v. Bica* (1976), for example, the Supreme Court upheld a state law barring illegal aliens from employment.[29]

In 1986, Congress passed the landmark Immigration Reform and Control Act, commonly known as the Simpson-Mizzoli Act, which primarily affected Hispanics. The legislation offered citizenship to illegal aliens who could prove they had lived continuously in the United States for five years. Roughly two million Hispanics received their citizenship in this way. The act also mandated fines

Cesar Estrada Chavez
(1927–1993)

Cesar Chavez led the first successful farm workers' strike in U.S. history. Founder of the United Farm Workers of America, Chavez was called "one of the heroic figures of our time" by Robert F. Kennedy and is widely regarded as the most influential Latino leader in modern U.S. history. A migrant worker as a child, Chavez knew firsthand the deprivations suffered by farm laborers. Like Martin Luther King Jr., Chavez was an advocate of nonviolent protest, and he organized food boycotts that eventually caused agricultural firms to improve wages and working conditions for farm workers. In 1994, Chavez was posthumously awarded the Presidential Medal of Freedom, the highest civilian honor that an American can receive.

TABLE 5-1 **Hispanics' Party Identification, by National Origin** Hispanics share a common language and ancestry, but differ sharply in their political leanings.

PARTY IDENTIFICATION	PUERTO RICAN AMERICANS	MEXICAN AMERICANS	CUBAN AMERICANS
Democratic	64%	60%	19%
Independent	22	24	17
Republican	14	16	64
	100%	100%	100%

From *Latino National Political Survey*, reported in Rudolfo O. de la Garza, Angelo Falcon, F. Chris Garcia, and John A. Garcia, "Hispanic Americans in the Mainstream of U.S. Politics," *The Public Perspective*, July/August 1992, p. 19. © The Roper Center for Public Opinion Research, University of CT. Storrs, CT. Used by permission.

on employers who hired aliens without work permits; it was expected that the resulting lack of job opportunities would eliminate a main incentive for aliens to enter the country illegally.

The issue of illegal aliens was also addressed through California's controversial Proposition 187. Placed on the state's ballot in 1994 through a citizen petition, Proposition 187 received the votes of a majority of Californians even though a majority of the state's Mexican Americans voted against it. The initiative aimed to cut off public services to illegal immigrants, the great majority of whom are Mexicans. They would no longer receive state-funded food stamps, welfare, and medical care except in life-threatening circumstances, and they would no longer be eligible for public schooling at any level. Supporters of the initiative claimed it would save the state from bankruptcy (for example, 10 percent of California's primary and secondary school students are illegal aliens, and their education costs the state more than $1 billion annually).[30] To many of the state's Mexican Americans, the initiative was a thinly disguised attempt to keep additional people from Mexico out of the state. The implementation of Proposition 187 was delayed pending a court ruling on its constitutionality, and most of its key provisions were subsequently judged to be unconstitutional.

Growing Political Power

Hispanic Americans are an important political force in several states and communities, and their influence is likely to increase substantially in the future. Hispanics are projected to become the largest single population group in California in the current century. Their political involvement, like that of other immigrant groups, can be expected to increase as they become more deeply rooted in the society and economy. At present, about half of all Hispanic citizens are not registered to vote, and only about a third actually vote, which limits the group's

U.S. Congresswoman Loretta Sanchez (D-Calif.) represents a part of Orange County, California. Hispanic Americans are growing in political and cultural influence as their numbers increase in California, Arizona, New Mexico, Texas, and other states.

political power. Nevertheless, the sheer size of the Hispanic population in states such as Texas and California makes the group a potent political force, as was evident in the 2000 presidential campaign when both parties mounted a massive effort to woo Hispanic voters.

More than four thousand Hispanic Americans nationwide hold public office. Hispanics have been elected to statewide office in several states, including New Mexico and Arizona. About twenty Hispanic Americans currently serve in the House of Representatives.

Asian Americans

Chinese and Japanese laborers were the first Asians to come to the United States in large numbers. They were brought into western states during the late 1800s to work in mines and to build railroads. When the need for this labor declined, Congress in 1892 ordered a temporary halt to Chinese immigration. Over the next three decades, informal agreements kept all but a few Asians out of the country. In 1921, the United States ended its traditional policy of unlimited immigration and established immigration quotas based on country of origin. Western European countries were given large quotas and Asian countries tiny ones. About 150 Japanese a year were allowed to immigrate until 1930, when Congress excluded them entirely. Japan had protested a California law that prohibited persons of Japanese descent from buying property in the state. Rather than finesse what was called "the California problem," Congress bluntly told Japan that its people were not wanted in the United States.[31]

Discrimination against Asians did not ease substantially until 1965, when Congress enacted legislation that adjusted the immigration quotas to favor those who had previously been disadvantaged. This change in the law was a product of the 1960s civil rights movement, which sensitized national leaders to all forms of discrimination. About half a million people now emigrate to the United States each year, and a majority come from Asian and Latin American countries. Asian Americans numbered about twelve million in the 2000 census, or roughly 4 percent of the total U.S. population. Most Asian Americans live on the West Coast, particularly in California. China, Japan, Korea, India, Vietnam, and the Philippines are the ancestral home of most Asian Americans.

Asian Americans studying in a high school classroom. Many Asian American families emphasize academic achievement as a basis of personal advancement.

The rights of Asian Americans have been expanded primarily by court rulings and legislation, such as the Civil Rights Act of 1964, that were responses to the problems of other minorities. In a few instances, however, the rights of minorities have been defined by actions of Asian Americans. For example, in *Lau v. Nichols* (1974), a case involving Chinese Americans, the Supreme Court ruled that public schools with a large proportion of children for whom English is a second language must offer English instruction in the children's first language.[32]

In 1998, the second-language issue arose in the form of Proposition 227, a California ballot measure that called for a ban on bilingual education in the state's public schools. The measure received the support of a majority of voters despite opposition from teachers' groups and many within California's Hispanic and Asian communities. Children for whom English is a second language would have to take their courses in English after their first year in school. The constitutionality of Proposition 227 was challenged unsuccessfully in the courts, but some teachers do not abide by its provisions.

Asian Americans are an upwardly mobile group. The values of most Asian cultures include a commitment to hard work, which, in the American context, has included an emphasis on academic achievement. For example, Asians make up a disproportionate share of the students at California's leading public universities, which base admission primarily on high school grades and standardized test scores. However, Asian Americans are still underrepresented in certain areas of the workplace. According to U.S. government figures, Asian Americans account for about 5 percent of professionals and technicians, slightly more than their percentage of the total population. Yet they hold less than 2 percent of managerial jobs; past and present discrimination has kept them from obtaining their fair share of top business positions. They are also underrepresented politically. It was not until 1996, for example, that the first Asian American was elected governor of a state other than Hawaii.

Other Groups and Their Rights

Although civil rights efforts have been directed mainly at women and racial and ethnic minorities, other groups are also involved.

One such group is the roughly 40 million Americans who have a physical or mental disability that prevents them from performing a critical function, such as seeing, hearing, or walking. A goal of the disabled is equal access to society's opportunities, which was facilitated by the 1990 Americans with Disabilities Act. It grants the disabled the same employment and other protections enjoyed by other disadvantaged groups. In addition, the Education for All Handicapped Children Act of 1975 mandates that all children, however severe their disability, receive a free, appropriate education. Before the legislation, 4 million children with disabilities were getting either no education or an inappropriate one (as in the case of a blind child who is not taught Braille). The act requires that government actively take steps to ensure the education of such children. In a 1999 ruling, for example, the Supreme Court held that students who require special care at school are entitled to that care, provided that a physician is not needed to deliver it.[33] However, government and employers are not required to honor the disability claims of those with correctable impairments, such as nearsightedness or high blood pressure.[34]

Citizenship
Getting Involved, Making a Difference

Moral Action

In *Moral Man and Immoral Society,* Reinhold Niebuhr puzzled over how to reconcile morality and strategy when confronting official injustice. The citizen has a moral obligation to obey the law. But what if the law itself is immoral? Is it moral to disobey such a law, perhaps even through violent means? Niebuhr concluded that, although a strategy of violent opposition would be immoral, nonviolent resistance would not be. This tactic, he argued, involved a "harmonious joining" of the moral and strategic dimensions of political action. Refusal to obey an unjust law would be a moral act, as long as the refusal was nonviolent and the person was willing to accept the legal consequences.

Martin Luther King Jr. described himself as "transformed" by Niebuhr's argument, and he dedicated himself to a campaign of nonviolent resistance against laws that forcibly segregated the races. To prepare for the campaign, King went to India to study Gandhi's nonviolent tactics and then set up instructional workshops to teach others what he had learned. (One of these lessons focused on self-protection when being attacked by the police; the proper technique is to look the attacker in the eyes while using arms and legs to protect vital organs.) King also recruited a select group of young African-American men with physical strength and personal character to absorb a savage beating without fighting back. And as it happened, television images of brutal police attacks on passive demonstrators were instrumental in turning public opinion against the South's system of racial segregation.

The civil rights movement is an exceptional moment in the history of citizen action, but every activist should ask the same question that Niebuhr asked: What constitutes moral action? Political advocacy can be a severe test of moral character. It is tempting for the activist to slip into unethical practices—to fudge facts to strengthen an argument, to twist the meaning of an opponent's position, to appeal to people's irrational impulses. And the pressures to use these techniques mount when an opponent employs them.

Strategic action is not by itself immoral. Nor is there a moral dilemma when the activist operates within prescribed rules for political competition. Although many people are uncomfortable, for example, with the amount of money spent on modern campaigns for public office, there is nothing inherently immoral about campaign money that is raised in the manner prescribed by law. It becomes immoral only if its acceptance includes an implied promise of special influence. Nor is negative campaigning immoral in itself. It can become so if based on a strategy of lies and deceit, but campaign debate legitimately includes arguments about why an opponent should not be elected.

The line between moral and immoral action can be breached. Whatever the momentary gain, the loss is greater. The purpose of citizen action is to elevate public life. Immoral action saps the community's strength by corrupting the process through which collective decisions are made. Immoral action also corrupts those who engage in it by diminishing their sensitivity to the difference between right and wrong and between private ambition and public purpose.

The government has also acted to protect older Americans from discrimination. The Age Discrimination Act of 1975 and the Age Discrimination in Employment Act of 1967 prohibit discrimination against older workers in hiring for jobs in which age is not clearly a crucial factor in job performance. More recently, mandatory retirement ages for most jobs have been eliminated by law. Forced retirement for reasons of age is permissible only if justified by the nature of a particular job or the performance of a particular employee.

A group that until very recently had not received substantial legal protection is homosexuals. In *Bowers v. Hardwick* (1986), the Supreme Court upheld a state law banning sexual acts between consenting homosexual adults, ruling that the constitutional right of privacy does not extend to such acts.[35] Gay rights also were dealt a setback when the Supreme Court in 2000 ruled that the Boy Scouts, as a private organization that has a right to freedom of association, can ban gays because homosexuality is prohibited by the Scouts' creed.[36] Gays and lesbians are also prohibited from serving in the military but can be dismissed only if they engage in overt verbal or behavioral displays of homosexuality (the so-called don't ask, don't tell policy).

However, gays and lesbians gained a significant legal victory when the Supreme Court in *Romer v. Evans* (1996) struck down a Colorado constitutional amendment that nullified all existing and any new legal protections for homosexuals. In a 6-3 ruling, the Court said the Colorado law violated the Constitution's guarantee of equal protection because it subjects individuals to employment and other forms of discrimination simply because of their sexual preference. The Court concluded that the law had no reasonable purpose but was instead motivated by hostility toward homosexuals.[37]

Gay rights activists have petitioned state governments to recognize civil unions that would grant to same-sex couples the legal status and rights that married couples enjoy. So far, Vermont is the only state to do so. In contrast, numerous states have recently passed "defense of marriage acts" that explicitly deny civil union to gay and lesbian couples, which means that individuals in these relationships have no legal claim on their partner's health care benefits, property, and the like. The number of same-sex couples has increased dramatically, which means that the issue of civil union for gays and lesbians will remain a focus of policy action in coming years.

EQUALITY UNDER THE LAW

The catchphrase of nearly every group's claim to a more equal standing in American society has been "equality under the law." The importance that people attach to legal equality is understandable. Once secure in their legal rights, people are in a stronger position to seek equality in other arenas, such as the economic sector. Once encoded in law, a claim to equality can also force officials to take positive action on behalf of a disadvantaged group. Americans' claims to legal equality are contained in a great many laws, a few of which are particularly noteworthy.

Equal Protection: The Fourteenth Amendment

The Fourteenth Amendment, which was ratified in 1868, declares in part that no state shall "deny to any person within its jurisdiction the equal protection of the laws." Through this **equal protection clause,** the courts have protected such groups as African Americans and women from discrimination by state and local governments.

The Fourteenth Amendment's equal protection clause does not require government to treat all groups or classes of people the same way in all circumstances. In fact, laws routinely treat people unequally. By law, for example,

equal protection clause A clause of the Fourteenth Amendment that forbids any state to deny equal protection of the laws to any individual within its jurisdiction.

TABLE 5-2 Levels of Court Review for Laws That Treat Americans Differently

TEST	APPLIES TO	STANDARD USED
Strict scrutiny	Race, ethnicity	Suspect category—assumed unconstitutional in the absence of an overwhelming justification
Intermediate scrutiny	Gender	Almost suspect category—assumed unconstitutional unless the law serves a clearly compelling and justified purpose
Reasonable basis	Other categories (such as age and income)	Not suspect category—assumed constitutional unless no sound rationale for the law can be provided

twenty-one-year-olds can drink alcohol but twenty-year-olds cannot. The judiciary allows such inequalities because they are held to be "reasonably" related to a legitimate government interest. In applying this **reasonable basis test,** the courts give the benefit of doubt to government. It need only show that a particular law has a sound rationale. For example, the courts have held that the goal of reducing fatalities from alcohol-related accidents involving young drivers is a valid reason for imposing a twenty-one-year minimum age requirement for the purchase of alcohol. (The *Romer* decision discussed earlier is an example of a law that failed the reasonable basis test. The Supreme Court concluded that Colorado's law affecting gays had "no legitimate government purpose.")

The reasonable basis test does not apply, however, to racial or ethnic classifications, particularly when these categories serve to discriminate against minority group members (see Table 5–2). Any law that posits a racial or ethnic classification is subject to the **strict scrutiny test,** under which such a law is unconstitutional in the absence of an overwhelmingly convincing argument that it is necessary. The strict scrutiny test has virtually eliminated race and ethnicity as permissible classifications when the effect is to put members of a minority group at a disadvantage. The Supreme Court's position is that race and national origin are **suspect classifications**—that such classifications have invidious discrimination as their purpose and therefore any law containing such a classification is in all likelihood unconstitutional.

The strict scrutiny test emerged after the 1954 *Brown* ruling and became a basis for invalidating laws that discriminated against black people. As other groups, especially women, began to organize and press for their rights in the late 1960s and early 1970s, the Supreme Court gave early signs that it might expand the scope of suspect classifications to include gender. In the end, however, the Court announced in *Craig v. Boren* (1976) that sex classifications were permissible if they served "important governmental objectives" and were "substantially" related to the achievement of those objectives.[38] The Court thus placed sex distinctions in an intermediate (or almost suspect) category, to be scrutinized more closely than some other classifications (for example, income levels) but, unlike racial classifications, justifiable in some instances. In *Rostker*

reasonable basis test A test applied by courts to laws that treat individuals unequally. Such a law may be deemed constitutional if its purpose is held to be "reasonably" related to a legitimate government interest.

strict scrutiny test A test applied by courts to laws that attempt a racial or ethnic classification. In effect, the strict scrutiny test eliminates race or ethnicity as a legal classification when it places minority group members at a disadvantage.

suspect classifications Legal classifications, such as race and national origin, that have invidious discrimination as their purpose and are therefore unconstitutional.

Although women are excluded by law from having to register for the draft, they serve with distinction in the U.S. military.

v. Goldberg (1980), for example, the policy of male-only registration for the military draft was upheld on grounds that the exclusion of women from involuntary combat duty serves a legitimate and important purpose.[39]

The imprecise nature of the **intermediate scrutiny test** has led some scholars to question its validity as a legal principle. Nevertheless, when evaluating claims of sex discrimination, the judiciary applies a stricter level of scrutiny than is required by the reasonable basis test. Rather than give government broad leeway to treat men and women differently, the Supreme Court has recently invalidated most of the laws it has reviewed that contain sex classifications. A leading case is *United States v. Virginia* (1996), in which the Supreme Court determined that the male-only admissions policy at Virginia Military Institute (VMI), a 157-year-old state-supported college, was unconstitutional. The state had developed an alternative program for women at another college, but the Court concluded it was no substitute for the unique education and other opportunities that attendance at VMI could provide. (The VMI decision also had the effect of ending the all-male admissions policy of the Citadel, a state-supported military college in South Carolina.)[40]

intermediate scrutiny test A test applied by courts to laws that attempt a gender classification. In effect, the test eliminates gender as a legal classification unless it serves an important objective and is substantially related to the objective's achievement.

Equal Access: The Civil Rights Acts of 1964 and 1968

The Fourteenth Amendment applies only to action by government. It does not prohibit discrimination by private parties. As a result, for a long period in the nation's history, owners could legally bar black people from restaurants, hotels, and other accommodations, and employers could freely discriminate in their job practices. Since the 1960s private firms have had much less freedom to discriminate for reasons of race, sex, ethnicity, or religion.

Accommodations and Jobs

The Civil Rights Act of 1964 entitles all persons to equal access to restaurants, bars, theaters, hotels, gasoline stations, and similar establishments serving the general public. The legislation also bars discrimination in the hiring, promotion, and wages of employees of medium-sized and large firms. A few forms of job discrimination are still lawful under the Civil Rights Act of 1964. For example, an owner-operator of a small business can discriminate in hiring his or her coworkers, and a religious school can take the religion of a prospective teacher into account.

The Civil Rights Act of 1964 has nearly eliminated the most overt forms of discrimination in the area of public accommodations. Some restaurants and hotels may provide better service to white customers, but outright refusal to serve African Americans or other minority group members is rare. Such a refusal is a violation of the law and could easily be proved in many instances. It is harder to prove discrimination in job decisions; accordingly, the act has been less effective in rooting out employment discrimination—a subject that will be discussed in detail later in this chapter.

Housing

In 1968, Congress passed civil rights legislation designed to prohibit discrimination in housing. A building owner cannot refuse to sell or rent housing because of a person's race, religion, ethnicity, or sex. An exception is allowed for owners of small multifamily dwellings who reside on the premises.

Despite legal prohibitions on discrimination, housing in America remains highly segregated. Less than a third of all African Americans live in a neighborhood that is mostly white. One reason is that the annual income of most black families is substantially below that of most white families. Another reason is the practice of banks. At one time, they contributed to housing segregation by "redlining"—refusing to grant mortgage loans in certain neighborhoods. This practice drove down the selling prices of homes in these neighborhoods, which led to an influx of African Americans and an exodus of whites. Redlining is prohibited by the 1968 Civil Rights Act, but many of the segregated neighborhoods that it helped to create still exist.

Recent studies indicate that minority status is still a factor in the lending practices of some banks.[41] A 1998 report of the U.S. Conference of Mayors indicated that, among applicants with average or slightly higher incomes relative to their community, Hispanics and African Americans were twice as likely as whites to be denied a mortgage.[42]

Equal Ballots: The Voting Rights Act of 1965, as Amended

Free elections are perhaps the foremost symbol of American democracy, yet the right to vote has only recently become a reality for many Americans, particularly for African Americans.

The Nineteenth Amendment, which in 1920 gave women the right to vote, effectively ended resistance to women's suffrage; paradoxically, resistance to black suffrage was intensified by the Fifteenth Amendment, which in 1870 gave black persons the right to vote. Southern whites invented a series of devices, including whites-only primaries, poll taxes, and rigged literacy tests to keep African Americans from registering and voting.[43] For example, almost no votes were cast by African Americans between the years 1920 and 1946 in North Carolina.[44]

Liberty & Equality

What's Your Opinion?

Private Discrimination

The courts have ruled that private organizations are often within their rights in discriminating against individuals because of color, gender, creed, national origin, or other characteristics. The Fifth and Fourteenth Amendments only prohibit discrimination by government bodies.

Jews, Catholics, and blacks are among the groups that historically have been denied membership in private clubs and organizations. The most celebrated recent incident was the decision of the Boy Scouts of America (BSA) to revoke the membership of Scoutmaster James Dale. Dale is gay, and the BSA excludes homosexuals from membership. Dale's suit against the BSA went to the Supreme Court, which ruled in 2000 that the BSA, as a private organization, had the right to deny membership to homosexuals.

Issues of liberty and equality are at the forefront of such cases. Liberty is enhanced when private organizations are free to pick their members. But equality is diminished when people are denied opportunities because of their physical characteristics or lifestyles.

What's your opinion on the Dale-BSA dispute? What general limits, if any, would you impose on the discriminatory acts of private organizations?

Figure 5–4
Voter Turnout in Presidential Campaigns Among Black and White Americans, 1960–2000

Voter turnout among black Americans rose dramatically during the 1960s as legal obstacles to their voting were removed.

Source: U.S. Bureau of the Census.

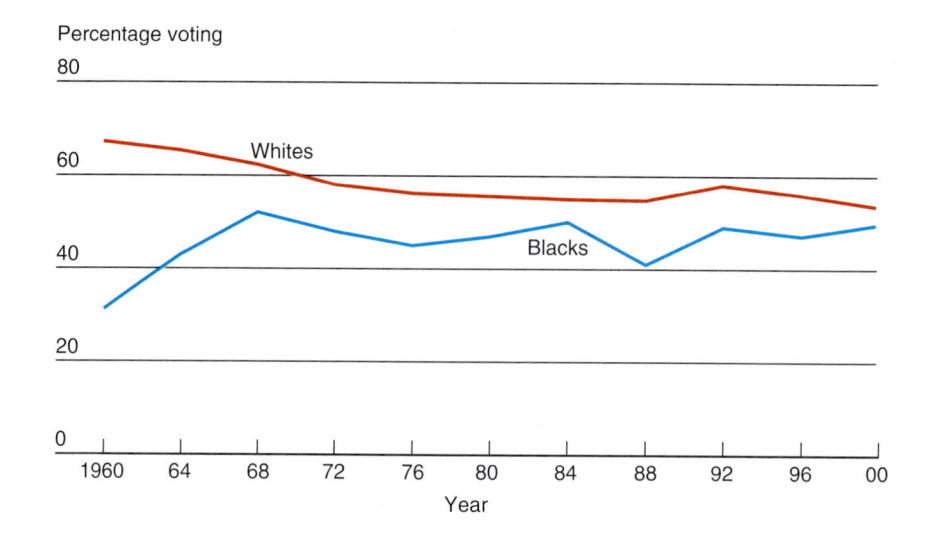

Barriers to black participation in elections began to crumble in the mid-1940s, when the Supreme Court declared that whites-only primary elections were unconstitutional.[45] Two decades later, through the Twenty-fourth Amendment, poll taxes were outlawed.

The major step toward equal voting rights for African Americans was passage of the Voting Rights Act of 1965, which forbids discrimination in voting and registration.[46] The legislation empowers federal agents to register voters and to oversee participation in elections. The Voting Rights Act, as interpreted by the courts, also eliminates literacy tests: local officials can no longer deny registration and voting for reasons of illiteracy. In fact, in communities where a language other than English is widely spoken, officials are now required by law to provide ballot materials in that language. If civil rights legislation has seldom had a significant and immediate impact on people's behavior, the Voting Rights Act is an exception. In the 1960 presidential election, voter turnout among African Americans was barely 30 percent nationwide. By 1968, three years after passage of the legislation, the turnout rate had jumped to more than 40 percent and was within 10 percentage points of the level for white Americans. In 1960, the gap was nearly 40 points (see Figure 5–4).

Congress renewed the Voting Rights Act in 1970, 1975, and 1982. The 1982 extension is noteworthy because it renewed the act for twenty years and requires states and localities to clear with federal officials any electoral change that has the effect, intended or not, of reducing the voting power of a minority group. When congressional district boundaries were redrawn after the 1990 census (see Chapter 11), the 1982 extension became the basis for the creation of districts that included a majority of Hispanic or African American voters. The result was the election of an unprecedented number of minority group members to Congress in 1992; Hispanic and African American representatives increased from 10 and 25 to 17 and 38, respectively.

However, the Supreme Court in 1996 ruled that the redistricting of four congressional districts in Texas and North Carolina was unconstitutional because race had been the "dominant" factor in their creation. The states were directed to redraw the districts. A year earlier, the Court had invalidated a

Georgia redistricting plan, holding that the state's Eleventh Congressional District violated the rights of white voters under the Fourteenth Amendment's equal protection clause. The Georgia district stretched from Savannah to Atlanta and had all sorts of twists and turns designed to exclude white residential areas. These rulings have not necessarily settled fully the issue of racial redistricting. The 1996 Texas and North Carolina cases were each decided by a 5-4 majority, and three of the justices in the majority indicated that there *might* be instances in which race, along with other factors, could be taken into account in redistricting decisions. But the Court's majority made it clear that race cannot be the *deciding* factor in redistricting arrangements.[47]

In a 2001 decision, *Easley v. Cromartie,* the Court granted states considerably more flexibility in drawing district lines. The Court held that, as long as a district's boundaries were based on partisan considerations, the fact that a large number of minority group members were concentrated in a district was not a violation of the equal protection clause. State legislatures routinely draw district boundaries in ways designed to increase the chances that the congressional seat will be won by a particular party. The Court has long held that this action is permissible. In *Easley v. Cromartie,* the Court said that, even though the North Carolina district in question contained a large proportion of black Americans, it was drawn with the goal of creating a safe Democratic seat and, as such, did not violate the Fourteenth Amendment.[48]

EQUALITY OF RESULT

America's disadvantaged groups have made significant progress toward equal rights, particularly during the past few decades. Through acts of Congress and rulings of the Supreme Court, most forms of government-sponsored discrimination—from racially segregated public schools to gender-based pension plans—have been banned.

However, civil rights problems involve deeply rooted conditions, habits, and prejudices and affect whole categories of people. For these reasons, a new civil rights policy rarely produces a sudden and dramatic change in society. Despite their greater equality in law, America's traditionally disadvantaged groups are still substantially unequal in their daily lives. Consider the issue of income disparity (see Figure 5–5). The average Asian American's income is about 90 percent of the average white person's income. But the average falls to 60 percent for African Americans and 55 percent for Hispanic Americans.

Such figures reflect **de facto discrimination,** which is discrimination that is a consequence of social, economic, and cultural biases and conditions. This type of discrimination is different from **de jure discrimination,** which is discrimination based on law, as in the case of segregation in southern public schools during the pre-*Brown* period. De facto discrimination is difficult to root out because it is embedded not in the law but in the very structure of society. **Equality of result** is the aim of policies intended to reduce or eliminate de facto discriminatory effects so that members of disadvantaged groups may obtain the same benefits as members of advantaged groups. Such policies are inherently more controversial because many Americans believe that government's responsibility extends no further than the removal of legal barriers to equality. This attitude

de facto discrimination Discrimination on the basis of race, sex, religion, ethnicity, and the like that results from social, economic, and cultural biases and conditions.

de jure discrimination Discrimination on the basis of race, sex, religion, ethnicity, and the like that results from a law.

equality of result The objective of policies intended to reduce or eliminate the effects of discrimination so that members of traditionally disadvantaged groups will have the same benefits of society as do members of advantaged groups.

Figure 5-5
U.S. per Capita Income, by Race and Ethnicity
The average income of white Americans is substantially higher than that of most other Americans.
Source: U.S. Bureau of the Census, 2002.

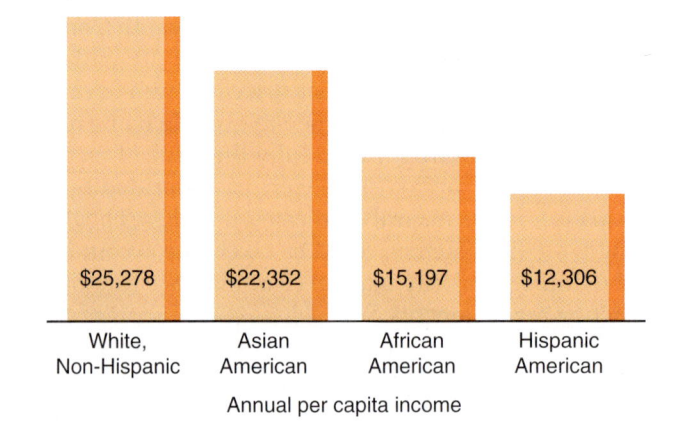

White, Non-Hispanic	Asian American	African American	Hispanic American
$25,278	$22,352	$15,197	$12,306

Annual per capita income

reflects the culture's emphasis on *individualism* and helps explain the lack of any large-scale government effort to reduce the economic and social gaps between Americans of varying racial and ethnic backgrounds. Nevertheless, a few policies—notably affirmative action and busing—have been implemented to achieve equality of result.

Affirmative Action: Workplace Integration

The difficulty of converting newly acquired legal rights into everyday realities is evident in the fact that, with passage of the 1964 Civil Rights Act, which prohibited discrimination in employment, women and minorities did not suddenly find it easier to obtain jobs for which they were qualified. Many employers maintained a deliberate though unwritten preference for white male employees, while other employers adhered to established employment procedures that continued to keep women and minorities at a disadvantage; membership in many union locals, for example, was handed down from father to son. Moreover, the Civil Rights Act did not compel employers to show that their hiring practices were not discriminatory. Instead, the burden of proof was on the woman or minority group member who had been denied a particular job. It was costly and often difficult to prove in court that one's sex or race was the reason that one had not been hired. In addition, a victory in court affected only the individual in question; such case-by-case settlements were no remedy for a situation in which established hiring practices kept millions of women and minorities from competing equally for job opportunities.

A broader remedy was obviously required, and the result was the emergence during the late 1960s of affirmative action programs. **Affirmative action** is a deliberate effort to provide full and equal opportunities in employment, education, and other areas for women, minorities, and individuals belonging to other traditionally disadvantaged groups. Affirmative action requires corporations, universities, and other organizations to establish programs designed to ensure that all applicants are treated fairly. Affirmative action also places the burden of proof on the providers of opportunities; to some extent, they must be able to demonstrate that any disproportionate granting of opportunities to white males is not the result of discriminatory practices.

affirmative action A term that refers to programs designed to ensure that women, minorities, and other traditionally disadvantaged groups have full and equal opportunities in employment, education, and other areas of life.

Since its inception in the 1960s, affirmative action policy has been a source of contentious debate but also a source of progress for women and minorities.

Opinions on Affirmative Action

Few issues in recent years have provoked more controversy than has affirmative action.[49] Although most Americans say they believe that minorities and women deserve a truly equal chance at jobs and other opportunities, they also say they worry that aggressive affirmative action programs will discriminate against more qualified males, an outcome that is called *reverse discrimination*.

Although opposition to affirmative action has increased in recent years, it is marked by ambivalence (see Figure 5–6). Americans oppose the making of hiring and admission decisions on the basis of race, yet a majority also indicates that diversity in the workplace and in college is a desirable goal and that special efforts to enable the historically disadvantaged to compete on more equal footing should be made. In a New York Times/CBS News poll, for example, a majority of whites said no to the question, "Do you believe that where there has been job discrimination against blacks in the past, preference in hiring or promotion should be given to blacks today?" But in the same poll, a majority of whites said yes to the question, "Do you believe there should be special educational programs to assist minorities in competing for college admissions?" These opinions are in line with traditional American attitudes (see Chapter 1). Americans generally endorse the idea of equal opportunity and thus tend to support programs that would give people a chance to compete for success. But they oppose policies that would give someone preferential treatment once the competition is underway.

"Which [position on affirmative action programs] comes closer to your own point of view?"

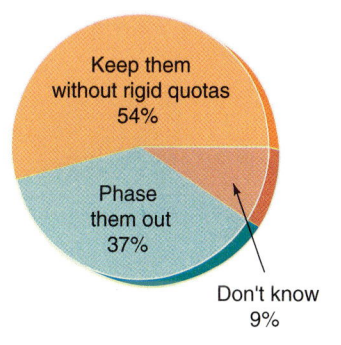

- Keep them without rigid quotas 54%
- Phase them out 37%
- Don't know 9%

Figure 5–6

Opinions on Affirmative Action
Americans' support for affirmative action has declined in recent years, but rather than eliminate the policy entirely, Americans prefer to retain it minus the quota or preference aspects.
Source: NBC News, Wall Street Journal Poll, March 2000.

Affirmative Action in the Law

Most issues that pit individuals against each other in a struggle over society's benefits eventually end up in the courts, and affirmative action is no exception (see Table 5–3). The policy was first tested before the Supreme Court in *University of California Regents v. Bakke* (1978). Alan Bakke, a white man, had twice been

TABLE 5-3 Key Decisions in the History of Affirmative Action Policy

YEAR	ACTION
1969	Nixon administration's Department of Labor initiates affirmative action policy
1978	Supreme Court in *Bakke* invalidates rigid quotas for medical school admissions but does not invalidate affirmative action
1980	Supreme Court in *Fullilove* upholds a quota system for minority-owned firms in granting of federal contracts
1980s	Supreme Court in a series of decisions narrows situations in which preferential treatment of minorities will be permitted
1991	In Civil Rights Act of 1991, Congress places burden of proof on business in situations where there is a pattern of white male dominance
1995	Supreme Court in *Adarand* eliminates fixed quotas in the granting of government contracts, which reversed the *Fullilove* (1980) precedent
1996	California voters enact Proposition 209, which bans public employment, education, and contracting programs based on race, ethnicity, or sex

denied admission to a University of California medical school, even though his admission test scores were higher than those of several minority group students who had been accepted. Bakke sued, claiming the school had a quota system for minorities that discriminated against white males. The Court ruled in Bakke's favor but did not invalidate affirmative action per se. The Court said only that rigid racial quotas were an impermissible form of affirmative action in determining medical school admissions.[50]

Bakke was followed by two rulings in favor of affirmative action programs, one of which—*Fullilove v. Klutnick* (1980)—upheld a quota system that required 10 percent of federal public works funds to be set aside for minority-owned firms.[51]

In the 1980s, the appointment of more conservative justices to the Supreme Court narrowed the scope of affirmative action policy. The Court held, for example, that preferential treatment of minorities could normally be justified only in cases where discrimination had been severe and that affirmative action could be applied only in a way that did not infringe on the rights of white employees to keep their jobs (thus restricting the use of race as a basis for determining which employees would be terminated in the case of job layoffs).[52]

Proponents of affirmative action succeeded, however, in shifting some of the burden of proof about discrimination from employees to employers. After the Supreme Court in the 1980s allowed business firms more latitude in defending their hiring practices,[53] Congress responded with the Civil Rights Act of 1991, which requires larger firms in some instances to prove why their overwhelmingly male or white work force is the result of business necessity (such as the nature of the work or the locally available labor pool) and not the result of systematic discrimination against women or minorities.

In a key 1995 decision, *Adarand v. Pena*, the Supreme Court sharply curtailed the federal government's affirmative action authority. The case arose when Adarand Constructors filed suit over a federal contract that was awarded

Should Affirmative Action Preferences End? The Case of One Florida

No civil rights policy has provoked more controversy in recent decades than affirmative action has. The application of quotas and preferences has contributed to a perception among some Americans that affirmative action discriminates against people who are white or male. Yet, as supporters of affirmative action have emphasized, the statistics indicate that the more typical victim of discrimination is a minority group member or a woman. In the past few years, opponents of affirmative action have gained ground. Minority preference systems in California and Texas, for example, have been terminated. In early 2000, Governor Jeb Bush announced that Florida would also halt its minority preference systems in college admissions and government contracts. His One Florida plan provoked a protest demonstration that was organized by civil rights leaders, including Jesse Jackson, Martin Luther King III, and the NAACP's Kweisi Mfume.

Yes: Today, I am announcing my One Florida initiative. . . . The old solutions have become increasingly controversial and divisive [and they] are no longer producing the kinds of results Floridians deserve. Preferences in higher education are being used to mask the failure of low performing schools in our K–12 system. . . . Likewise, preferences in contracting are failing to increase economic opportunities for minorities in a meaningful way, while discriminating against non-minorities who simply want a level field of competition.
—Governor Jeb Bush (R-Fla.)

No: [One Florida] is an affront to people of color and women who continue to suffer from discrimination when it comes to education, winning government contracts, and health care. . . . [This protest is about] people's dignity and humanity. We don't want to just expand the economic pie, we want to expand the number of pie eaters. . . . This is not about Florida alone, it's about the nation. The eyes of the nation are upon Florida. . . . The [protest] demonstration you see today did not just happen. You cannot continue to impose policy on [us] without any impact whatsoever.
—Kweisi Mfume, president, NAACP

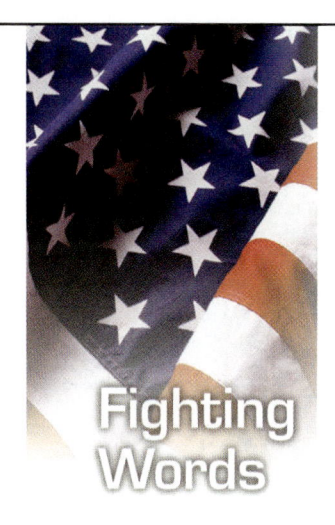

Fighting Words

to a Hispanic-owned company even though Adarand had submitted a lower bid. The Court in a 5-4 ruling said that the government had to prove that a preference program for minorities was a response to specific past acts of discrimination, not just discrimination in a historic sense. This decision reversed earlier precedents that allowed the federal government to give a preference to minority applicants. The Supreme Court held that set-aside contracts for minority applicants are unlawful unless, through costly and conclusive studies, the government can demonstrate past discrimination particular to a situation; and even then, it must devise a program "narrowly tailored" to the problem that is being remedied.[54] In other words, the government cannot issue general requirements (such as an automatic 10 percent set-aside of contracts for minority firms) as a means of remedying past discrimination.

Even supporters of affirmative action concluded that the *Adarand* decision likely marked the end of the era of extensive racial and gender preferences. By holding that affirmative action must be narrowly tailored and based on specific

Students at a California state university demonstrate against Proposition 209. The initiative proposed to end all racial, ethnic, and gender preferences in the awarding of university admissions, jobs, and government contracts in the state. The initiative passed by a 54 percent to 46 percent vote margin in 1996.

www.mhhe.com/patterson6

past acts of discrimination, the Court substantially restricted the authority of federal authorities to mandate broad affirmative action remedies. Earlier, the Court had restricted the authority of state and local governments to institute such requirements.

Another blow to affirmative action proponents was the California Civil Rights Initiative, which bans in California any public employment, education, or contracting program that is based on race, ethnicity, or sex. Known as Proposition 209, the initiative was placed on the 1996 ballot by citizen petition and approved 54 percent to 46 percent by California voters. The vote divided along racial, ethnic, and gender lines, with white males most strongly in favor and blacks and Hispanics most strongly opposed. The constitutionality of Proposition 209 was challenged by opponents, but the Supreme Court upheld it in 1997.

The Board of Regents of the University of California had earlier voted an end to affirmative action in university admissions, a policy that was also instituted at the University of Texas Law School and some other academic institutions. The effect was a dramatic decline in minority enrollment at these institutions. The entering classes at the Berkeley and Los Angeles campuses of the University of California in the fall of 1998, for example, had 50 percent fewer African Americans than the previous class. Hispanic enrollment also declined, although less dramatically.

Further restrictions on affirmative action are possible in the future, inasmuch as even some of its supporters believe that it is now heightening white resistance to other civil rights measures and that it is diminishing the accomplishments of women and minorities who would have gotten ahead even without the policy. It is unlikely, however, that affirmative action will be eliminated entirely. Statistical indicators show that women and minorities, as groups, are still at a substantial disadvantage to white males in terms of job hiring, pay, and promotion. In a few occupations, mostly in the professions, well-qualified women and minority group members are in high demand. In most settings, however, these people are at a substantial disadvantage, a situation that creates pressure on policymakers to maintain affirmative action in some form.

In 1998, the state of Texas devised an innovative response to the problem of equal opportunity. Recognizing the disparity in the quality of its public schools and other factors that result in lower average scores on standardized tests for minorities, the state established a policy that guarantees admission at the public university campus of his or her choice to any Texas high school student who graduates in the top 10 percent of the class. The 10 percent rule has met with little opposition from even the most outspoken critics of affirmative action, and those who favor affirmative action support this program "because it eliminates suspicion that students may have been admitted solely on the basis of race."[55]

School Integration: Busing

The 1954 *Brown* ruling mandated an end to *forced segregation* of public schools. Government would no longer be permitted to prevent minorities from enrolling in white schools. *Brown* did not, however, mandate school *integration*. Government was not required by *Brown* to take action to require white and minority children to attend school together, and *Brown* did little to change the face of America's schools. Ten years after *Brown*, less than 3 percent of black children were attending schools that were predominantly white. The proportion jumped to roughly 20 percent after passage of the 1964 Civil Rights Act, but the fact that black and white children lived in mostly separate neighborhoods meant that they would continue to attend separate schools. This situation set the stage for one of the few public policies that forced whites into close regular contact with blacks: the busing of children to achieve racial balance in schools.

The Swann *Decision and Its Aftermath*

In 1971, the Supreme Court took the controversial step of requiring the busing of children in some circumstances. Affirming a lower-court decision, the Supreme Court held in *Swann v. Charlotte-Mecklenburg County Board of Education* that the busing of children from one neighborhood to another was a permissible way for courts to compel the integration of public schools in which past years of official segregation had created residential patterns that had the effect of keeping the races in separate schools. Busing, the Court said, was allowed as a tool "in the interim period when remedial adjustments are being made to eliminate the dual school system."[56]

Few policies of recent times provoked so much controversy as the introduction of forced busing.[57] Surveys indicated that more than 80 percent of white Americans and a majority in Congress disapproved of forced busing. Angry demonstrations lasting weeks took place in Charlotte. When busing was ordered in Detroit and Boston, the protests turned violent. Unlike *Brown*, which affected mainly the South, *Swann* also applied to northern communities in which African Americans and whites lived apart as a result of economic and

Why Should I Care?

Equality: The American Birthright

In his acceptance speech at the 1996 Republican National Convention, Robert Dole said that any delegate who didn't believe in racial equality should leave through the nearest exit. If the country itself had exit doors, Dole's instructions would still make sense. Superficial differences in skin color, religion, gender, and the like should never be a basis for discriminatory words or actions.

Equality has always been America's most unrealized ideal. Since the introduction of slavery four hundred years ago, Americans have struggled to create a more equal society. Disadvantaged groups have had to fight to achieve a fuller measure of recognition and justice. It is not surprising that they would choose to make the fight. No people in human history have thought that second-class status is preferable to equal treatment. What is somewhat surprising, however, is the resistance of dominant groups to the more equal treatment of others. If the economic self-interest of the slaveowner somehow made slavery understandable, though no less abominable, what could possibly underlie discrimination today except blatant prejudice?

The negative aspects of inequality have long been part of the American experience. Less attention has been paid to the positive aspects of equality. In the absence of discrimination, people are more productive and more sociable in every phase of life. The economy, the society, and the polity all benefit from the more equal treatment of all citizens. There is wider affluence, less crime, and more civic trust. The effect can be compared to an upswing in the economic cycle. When the economy expands, employment and production expand, improving the position of everyone. So it is with a more equal society. Few are worse off, and society as a whole is better off.

The American experience has always been in part a grand experiment to see whether diverse peoples can live together in harmony and mutual respect. It is justifiably called an experiment because, in the history of the world, peaceful relations between different people within the same national boundaries have been difficult to achieve.

---

cultural differences as well as discriminatory real estate practices and local housing ordinances.

Despite the widespread protests, busing became a part of national policy. Each school day, tens of thousands of children were bused out of their neighborhoods to attend school with children of a different color. Busing's application was narrowed, however, by court-imposed restrictions on its use. The Supreme Court in 1974—perhaps in response to the protests over busing—held that it could be applied *across* school districts only in situations where it could be shown that school district boundaries were purposely drawn so as to segregate the races.[58] Because school districts in most states coincide with community boundaries, the effect of this position was to insulate most suburban schools from integration plans.

Does Busing Work?

Studies indicate that busing has contributed to more positive racial attitudes among children. Studies also show that the performance of black children on standardized tests improves when they attend white-majority schools and that the test performance of the white children is not adversely affected.[59]

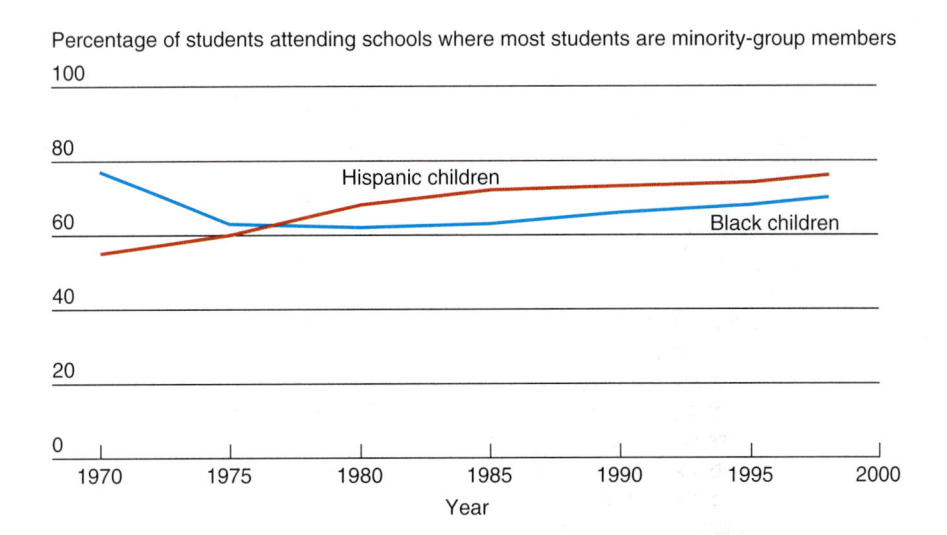

Figure 5-7

Segregation in Public Schools Has Been Increasing

In the past two decades, racial and ethnic segregation in America's public schools has increased. More than two-thirds of black and Hispanic children today attend a school in which most of the students are members of a minority group. An increase in the number of white non-Hispanic students attending private schools and a decrease in racial busing are factors in the trend.

Source: U.S. Department of Education, 1999.

However, busing has contributed to whites' departure from public schools, which, along with population and residential shifts, has made it increasingly difficult to achieve diversity in city schools. In Boston, for example, less than 20 percent of public school children today are white, compared with more than 50 percent when busing began there in 1974.

Busing also fragmented neighborhoods and forced children into long bus rides to and from school. Many black and white families alike were affected by what came to be called "busing fatigue." Parents asked, in effect, whether busing was worth the costs. That debate led the Prince George's County (Maryland) school board, which had a black majority, to abandon busing in 1998 and replace it with improved funding for neighborhood schools. Alvin Thornton, chair of the Prince George's County school board and a Howard University professor, argued that the change would increase "the sense of community" among the county's African Americans.[60]

Diversity and America's Schools

Prince George's County is among dozens of communities—including Seattle, Jacksonville, Minneapolis, Mobile, and Boston—that have dismantled their school busing programs in recent years. In 1999, the school district where busing policy began—Charlotte-Mecklenburg—joined the list. Federal judge Robert Potter ruled in an antibusing lawsuit that the school district could no longer take race into account in "assigning" children to its schools. Potter's decision followed a series of Supreme Court rulings in the 1990s that had held that busing was intended as a temporary, not permanent, solution to the problem of segregated schools;[61] that the performance of black students could not be the criterion for continuation of a busing program;[62] and that communities could devise alternative programs to replace their busing programs.[63]

The cutback in busing contributed to a decrease in school integration. Nationwide, integration peaked in the late 1980s and has declined steadily since then (see Figure 5-7). Only about a third of black children today attend a predominantly white school, which is about the same proportion as in 1970, before

Deacon John Hodge stands at the charred remains of Rising Star Baptist Church in Greensboro, Alabama. His church is one of more than two dozen predominantly black churches that were torched by arsonists in 1996 alone. The burnings are an ugly reminder that racism—"America's curse," in the words of the sociologist Gunner Myrdal—is still the nation's most conspicuous shortcoming.

busing was initiated. The proportion is even higher for Hispanic children—only about a fourth of them attend a predominantly white school.

Population and residential changes have also contributed to the decrease in school integration. The core cities of most U.S. metropolitan areas are increasingly populated by minorities. The movement of middle-class blacks and Hispanics to suburban communities has resulted in some degree of integration in their school districts, but the trend today is toward a more segregated educational system. The trend is unlikely to be reversed any time soon through public policy because *diversity*, unlike *equality*, has no explicit constitutional status. Government is compelled by the Constitution to treat people equally; it is not required to promote diversity. "Some say that diversity should be a compelling governmental purpose," says George Mason University professor David J. Armor, "but the Supreme Court says no."[64]

As busing recedes, the focus has shifted to parity in school financing. In comparison with predominantly white schools, those schools with mostly minority children have significantly larger classroom sizes, fewer certified teachers, and fewer resources, including library materials, computers, and science laboratories.[65] In Prince George's County and other communities that have dismantled busing programs, local and state governments have promised to increase the funding for predominantly minority schools.

PERSISTENT DISCRIMINATION: SUPERFICIAL DIFFERENCES, DEEP DIVISIONS

In 1944, the Swedish sociologist Gunnar Myrdal gained fame for his book *An American Dilemma*, whose title referred to deep-rooted racism in a country that proclaimed itself to be the epitome of an equal society.[66] Since then, legal obstacles to the mixing of the races have been nearly eliminated. Public opinion has also changed significantly in the past half century. In the early 1940s, a majority of white Americans believed that black children should not be allowed to go to school with white children; today less than 5 percent of white Americans express this belief. There are also visible signs of black progress. In the past two decades, increasing numbers of African Americans have attended college, received undergraduate degrees, obtained jobs as professional and managers, and moved into suburban neighborhoods.

Nevertheless, true equality for all Americans has remained elusive. The realities of everyday American life are still very different for its white and black citizens. For example, a black child born in the United States has more than twice the chance of dying before reaching his or her first birthday than a white child does. The difference in the infant mortality rates of whites and African Americans reflects differences in their nutrition, medical care, and education—in other words, differences in their access to the most basic resources of a modern society.

The history of equality in America is one of progress and of setbacks and, always, of new challenges. The latest is the treatment of Arab-Americans and Moslems in the aftermath of the terrorist attacks of September 11, 2001. Shortly afterward, a radio talk-show host suggested that all recent immigrants from the Middle East should be shipped back to their country of origin, a message eerily reminiscent of what some once said about black Americans and Asian Americans and, more recently, about Latin Americans. If the great majority of Americans have a lot more sense than was displayed by this particular talk-show host, they do not necessarily fully embrace the notion that the United States is "one people and one nation." They accept that idea in the abstract but often find it difficult to apply in everyday life. Equality is a difficult idea in practice because it requires people to shed preconceived and often deeply embedded notions about how other people think, behave, and feel. It is difficult for nearly everyone to get beyond superficial differences—whether they relate to skin color, national origin, religious preference, sex, or lifestyle—to the shared humanity that unites people of all backgrounds. Myrdal called discrimination "America's curse." He could have broadened the generalization. Discrimination is civilizations' curse, as evident in the scores of ethnic, national, and religious conflicts that have marked human history. But America is a special case because, as Lincoln said in his Gettysburg address, it was a nation founded "on the proposition that all men are created equal." No greater challenge faces America today, as has been true throughout its history, of living out the full meaning of its most imposing ideal.

Self-Quiz
www.mhhe.com/patterson6

SUMMARY

During the past few decades, the United States has undergone a revolution in the legal status of its traditionally disadvantaged groups, including African Americans, women, Native Americans, Hispanic Americans, and Asian Americans. Such groups are now provided equal protection under the law in areas such as education, employment, and voting. Discrimination by race, sex, and ethnicity has not been eliminated from American life but is no longer substantially backed by the force of law.

Traditionally disadvantaged Americans have achieved fuller equality primarily as a result of their struggle for greater rights. The Supreme Court has been an important instrument of change for minority groups. Its ruling in *Brown v. Board of Education* (1954), which declared racial segregation in public schools to be an unconstitutional violation of the Fourteenth Amendment's equal protection clause, was a major breakthrough in equal rights. Through its busing, affirmative action, and other rulings, the Court has also mandated the active promotion of integration and equal opportunities.

However, because civil rights policy involves large issues of social values and the distribution of society's resources, questions of civil rights are politically explosive. For this reason, legislatures and executives as well as the courts have been deeply involved in such issues, siding at times with established groups and sometimes backing the claims of underprivileged groups. Thus, Congress, with the support of President Lyndon Johnson, enacted the landmark Civil Rights Act of 1964; but Congress and recent presidents have been ambivalent about or hostile to busing for the purpose of integrating public schools.

In recent years, affirmative action programs—designed to achieve equality of result for African Americans, women, Hispanic Americans, and other disadvantaged groups—have become a civil rights battleground. Affirmative action has had the strong support of civil rights groups and has won the qualified endorsement of the Supreme Court but has been opposed by those who claim that it unfairly discriminates against white males. Busing is another issue that has provoked deep divisions within American society.

KEY TERMS

affirmative action
civil rights
comparable worth
de facto discrimination
de jure discrimination
equality of result
equal protection clause
equal rights
gender gap
intermediate scrutiny test
reasonable basis test
strict scrutiny test
suspect classifications

SUGGESTED READINGS

Armor, David. *Forced Justice: School Desegregation and the Law.* New York: Oxford University Press, 1995. An evaluation that concludes that the federal courts have overstretched their legal mandate by requiring school integration rather than simply school desegregation.

Bergmann, Barbara A. *In Defense of Affirmative Action.* New York: Basic Books, 1997. An economist's analysis of affirmative action that concludes that policy is necessary for women and broadly beneficial to society.

Howard, John R. *The Shifting Wind.* Albany: State University of New York Press, 1999. A review of the Supreme Court and civil rights from Reconstruction to the *Brown* decision.

McClain, Charles J. *In Search of Equality: The Chinese Struggle Against Discrimination in Nineteenth-Century America.* Berkeley: University of California Press, 1994. A careful study of how Chinese in nineteenth-century California used the legal system to fight racism and injustice.

Nagel, Joane. *American Indian Ethnic Renewal: Red Power and the Resurgence of Identity and Culture.* New York: Oxford University Press, 1996. Explores the meaning of activism for Native Americans' ethnic identification.

Reeves, Keith. *Voting Hopes or Fears? White Voters, Black Candidates, and Racial Politics in America.* New York: Oxford University Press, 1997. A critical assessment of race and politics in American society.

Skrentny, John David. *The Ironies of Affirmative Action: Politics, Culture, and Justice in America.* Chicago: University of Chicago Press, 1996. An empirical analysis of affirmative action and its impact.

Stavans, Ilan. *The Hispanic Condition: Reflections on Culture and Identity in America.* New York: HarperPerennial, 1996. An analysis of the behavioral and cultural differences and similarities among the major Hispanic groups.

LIST OF WEBSITES

http://www.airpi.org/
The website for the American Indian Policy Center, which was established by Native Americans in 1992; includes a political and legal history of Native Americans and examines current issues affecting them.

http://www.naacp.org
The website of the National Association for the Advancement of Colored People (NAACP); includes historical and current information on the struggle of African Americans for equal rights.

http://www.nclr.org
The website for the National Council of La Raza (NCLR), an organization dedicated to improving the lives of Hispanics; contains information on public policy, immigration, citizenship, and other subjects.

http://www.rci.rutgers.edu/~cawp
The website of the Center for the American Woman and Politics (CAWP) at Rutgers University's Eagleton Institute of Politics.

PART TWO

Mass Politics

"We are concerned about public affairs, but immersed in our private ones," Walter Lippmann wrote. Nevertheless, the integrity of the democratic process requires that citizens have significant opportunities to make their voices heard.

Citizens individually participate in public affairs. Their influence is greatest, however, when they join together in common purpose. This joining comes during elections and through intermediaries such as political parties, interest groups, and the media.

The chapters in this section explore these avenues of citizen politics. Chapter 6 examines the way Americans think politically and the effect of their opinions on government. Chapter 7 describes the nature and impact of citizen participation. Chapter 8 looks at parties, candidates, elections, and campaigns. Interest groups are the subject of Chapter 9, and the news media are addressed in Chapter 10.

All democracies depend on these instruments of popular influence, but the United States does so in relatively unique ways. For example, America's political parties are among the weakest in the world, while its interest groups and media are among the strongest. The consequences are significant. Political action enables Americans to make their voices heard, but the precise nature of this activity determines whose voices will be heard the loudest.

CHAPTER OUTLINE

- **6** Public Opinion and Political Socialization: Shaping the People's Voice 168
- **7** Political Participation and Voting: Expressing the Popular Will 196
- **8** Political Parties, Candidates, and Campaigns: Defining the Voter's Choice 224
- **9** Interest Groups: Organizing for Influence 260
- **10** The News Media: Communicating Political Images 292

6

To speak with precision of public opinion is a task not unlike coming to grips with the Holy Ghost.
—V. O. Key Jr.[1]

Public Opinion and Political Socialization:
Shaping the People's Voice

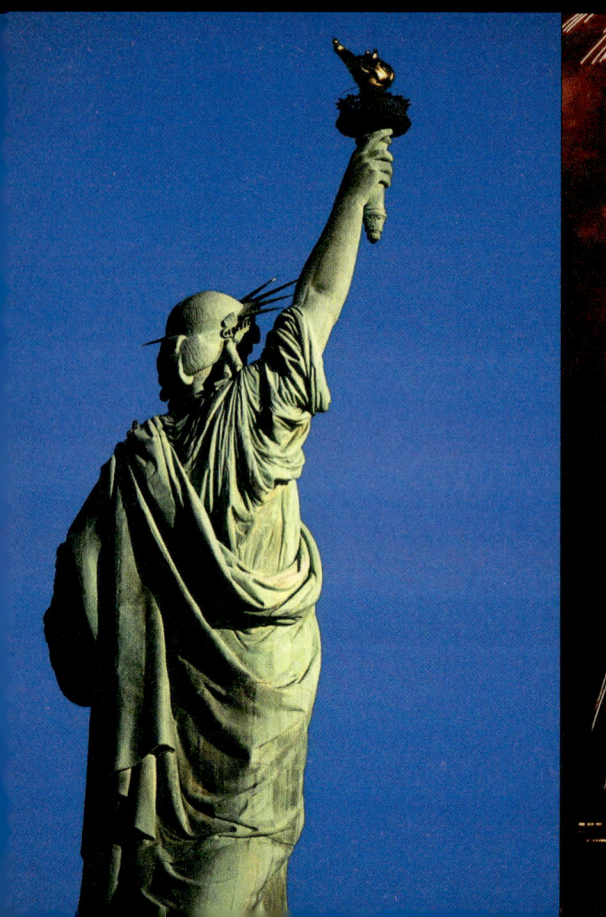

As information began to trickle in about the terrorists responsible for the attacks of September 11, 2001, on the World Trade Center and the Pentagon, most Americans were at a loss to add information of their own to their judgment about what had happened. What was the Al Qaeda network? Who was Osama bin Laden? Most Americans were unable even to say where Afghanistan was located or that the Taliban ruled it. Surveys taken after the attacks showed, however, that Americans were united in their support for retaliatory action. Asked in a Gallup poll shortly after the attack, nearly 90 percent said they favored a strong response.

The immediate aftermath of the terrorist attacks on American soil is a revealing example of the influence of public opinion on public policy. Public opinion on most policy issues is not deeply informed by facts. Moreover, public opinion is normally not a guide to a specific course of action. Bush was not forced by public opinion to launch a military assault on the Taliban regime in Afghanistan. However, public opinion did require that he take decisive action of some form and of some duration. The nature of that action was for Bush and his advisors to decide. When he announced that he had decided on a long-term "war on terrorism" through military, economic, intelligence-gathering, and diplomatic means, the public embraced that action as an appropriate response.

Public opinion has a central place in democratic societies because of the idea that democratic government springs from the will of the people. However, public opinion is not the well-formed phenomena that commentators sometimes suggest. Public opinion is seldom exact when it comes to questions of how to resolve society's problems. Political leaders typically have leeway in deciding a course of action. Rather than choosing to topple the regime in Afghanistan, for example, Bush could have chosen targeted attacks on terrorist groups around the globe as his initial course of action. He perhaps even had the option of a law enforcement response, relying on police efforts throughout the world to flush out and eliminate terrorist cells.

This chapter discusses public opinion and its influence on the U.S. political system. A major theme is that public opinion is a powerful and yet inexact force in American politics. The policies of the U.S. government cannot be understood apart from public opinion; at the same time, public opinion is not a precise determinant of public policy. This apparent paradox is explained by the fact that *self-government* in a large and complex country involves a division of labor between the public and its representatives. The public ordinarily affects only the general direction of its government. The main points made in this chapter are the following:

- *Public opinion consists of those views held by ordinary citizens that are openly expressed.* Public officials have many means of gauging public opinion but increasingly have relied on public opinion polls to make this determination.

- *The process by which individuals acquire their political opinions is called political socialization.* This process begins during childhood, when, through family and

In late 2001, the United States launched a massive air attack on the Taliban regime and its Al Qaeda ally in Afghanistan. In taking action, the Bush administration was responding to public opinion even though the air assault itself was a policy decided on in closed deliberations among President Bush and his advisors.

school, Americans acquire many of their basic political values and beliefs. Socialization continues into adulthood, during which peers, political institutions and leaders, and the news media are major influences.

- *Americans' political opinions are shaped by several frames of reference. Four of the most important are ideology, group attachments, partisanship, and political culture.* These frames of reference form the basis for political consensus and conflict among the general public.

- *Public opinion has an important influence on government but ordinarily does not directly determine what officials will do.* Public opinion works primarily to place limits on the choices made by officials.

THE NATURE OF PUBLIC OPINION

Public opinion is a relatively new concept in the history of political ideas. Not until democracy surfaced in the eighteenth century did the need arise to obtain some idea of what the people were thinking on political issues. If democracy is truly to be a government of and for the people, then the public's opinions must be a central concern.

What Is Public Opinion?

Today, *public opinion* is a widely used term. It is typically applied in ways that suggest that the people have a common set of concerns. In fact, however, it is not very meaningful to lump all citizens together as if they constituted a single coherent public.[2] There is, to be sure, an occasional issue of such power and breadth that it captures the attention of nearly all citizens. The large majority of

Public opinion includes contradictory elements. According to surveys, for example, most Americans say they want lower taxes but also say they want more public services. At a Boston rally, this demonstrator expresses anger with President Clinton's tax-increase legislation while also demanding that government provide free health care.

issues, however, attract the attention of some citizens but not most citizens. Agricultural conservation programs, for example, are of intense interest to some farmers, hunters, and environmentalists, but of little interest to other people. The tendency is so pervasive that opinion analysts have described America as a nation of *many* publics.[3]

There are many issues about which there is literally no majority opinion. On issues such as agricultural conservation programs, a form of *pluralist* democracy usually prevails. Government responds to the views of an intense minority. In other cases, *elitist* opinion prevails. On the question of U.S. relations with Finland, for example, there is little likelihood that ordinary citizens would know or care what the U.S. government does. In such instances, the policy opinions of an elite group of business and policy leaders ordinarily prevail. *Majority* opinion also can be decisive, but its influence is normally confined to a few broad issues that elicit widespread attention and concern, such as social security and employment. This situation may suggest a limited role for popular majorities, but such issues, although few in number, typically have the greatest impact on society as a whole.

Hence, any definition of the term *public opinion* cannot be based on the assumption that all citizens, or even a majority, are actively interested and have a preference about all aspects of political life. **Public opinion** can be defined as those opinions held by ordinary citizens that they are willing to express openly.[4] This expression need not be verbal. It could also take the form, for example, of a protest demonstration or a vote for one candidate rather than another. The crucial point is that a person's private thoughts on an issue become public opinion when expressed openly.

public opinion Those opinions held by ordinary citizens that they express openly.

Figure 6–1
Opinions on Taxing and Spending
People's opinions can be contradictory. Americans say, for example, that taxes are too high and yet also say, when asked about specific policy areas, that government is spending too little.
Used by permission of National Opinion Research Center, University of Chicago.

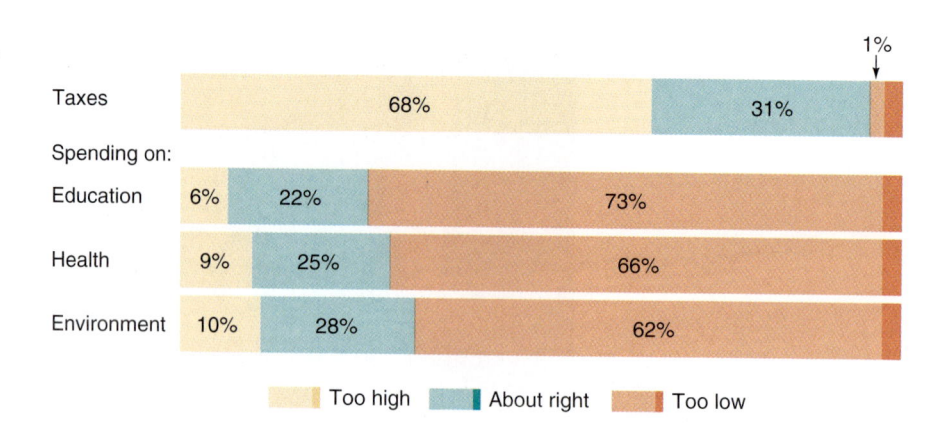

	Too high	About right	Too low	
Taxes	68%	31%		1%
Spending on: Education	6%	22%	73%	
Health	9%	25%	66%	
Environment	10%	28%	62%	

How Informed Is Public Opinion?

There are practical obstacles to government by public opinion in all instances. One obstacle is that people have differing opinions; in responding to one side of an issue, government is compelled to reject other preferences. Public opinion is also contradictory in many cases. Polls indicate, for example, that Americans would like better schools, health care, and other public services while they also favor a reduction in taxes (see Figure 6–1). A significant increase in the quantity and quality of social services cannot be accomplished without additional taxes. Which opinion of the people should govern—their desire for more services or their desire for lower taxes?

Another limitation on the role of public opinion is the public's relatively low level of political information. Some citizens pay close attention to politics, but most do not. Most citizens would "flunk" a current affairs test. In 1994, for example, a Times Mirror survey asked a cross-section of Americans five simple questions on people and events that were currently at the top of the news about international affairs. Only 6 percent of the respondents answered all five questions correctly, and 9 percent knew four answers. A total of 21 percent correctly answered only one question, and 37 percent could answer none of the questions. In other words, a majority of citizens knew little or nothing when asked relatively simple questions about world developments. (Citizens in several other countries were asked the same five questions; the results are summarized in "How the United States Compares.")

Although people with lower education levels are more likely to be uninformed, many college-educated people also lack basic information. A survey of Ivy League students found that a third could not identify the British prime minister, half could not name both U.S. senators from their state, and three-fourths could not identify Abraham Lincoln as the author of the phrase "a government of the people, by the people, and for the people."[5]

The public's lack of information is not as significant a factor as it might seem. Citizens do not necessarily have to be well informed about a situation to have a reasonable opinion about it. Opinions stem more from people's general beliefs, values, and policy orientations than from precise information about

HOW THE UNITED STATES COMPARES

Citizens' Awareness of Public Affairs

Americans' knowledge of public affairs is relatively low. Although most citizens say they follow the news regularly or often, they are not very attentive to what they see and hear. Even the simplest facts sometimes elude the average citizen's grasp. A Gallup poll found, for example, that a third of Americans were unable to name the vice president of the United States.

Low levels of public information are characteristic of most countries, but by some indicators Americans rank lower than do citizens of other western democracies. In a multicountry (including U.S.) survey conducted in 1994 by the Times Mirror Center for the People and the Press, Americans ranked next to last in terms of their ability to respond correctly to five questions about world leaders and events. Americans did their best on a question that asked them to name the president of Russia: 50 percent said Boris Yeltsin, but this total was far lower than the 94 percent of Germans who named Yeltsin. Americans had difficulty with the question that asked them to name the country that was threatening to withdraw from the nuclear nonproliferation treaty: only 22 percent correctly said Korea or North Korea compared with 45 percent of Germans. In light of America's leading role in the world, its citizens might be expected to be uniquely well informed about international affairs. However, they are less knowledgeable in this area than are Europeans, who live in closer proximity to other countries and who thus may be more attentive to world politics.

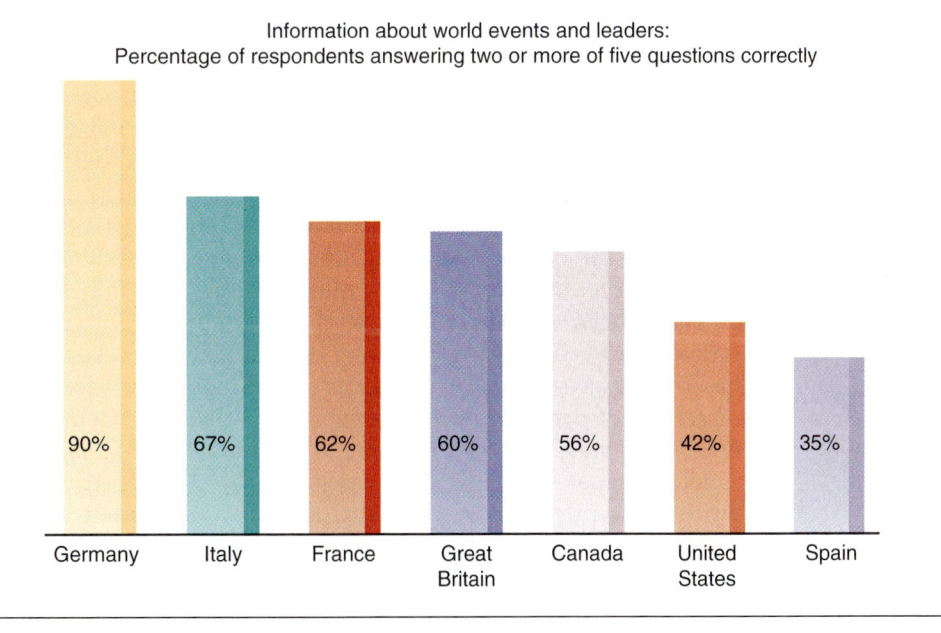

Information about world events and leaders:
Percentage of respondents answering two or more of five questions correctly

Germany	Italy	France	Great Britain	Canada	United States	Spain
90%	67%	62%	60%	56%	42%	35%

policy alternatives. Many people's opinions on the abortion issue, for example, derive from deep-seated religious beliefs. The fact that most individuals have only a foggy notion of Supreme Court rulings on the abortion issue does not make their opinions any less relevant. Similarly, people can have a considered view of how the United States should respond to foreign aggression without a detailed knowledge of the globe or top foreign leaders.

Nevertheless, the public's lack of information restricts the role it can play in policy disputes. Public opinion can direct government toward certain goals, but it rarely provides a detailed guide to the way these goals are to be accomplished. The choice of one course of action over another requires knowledge of the likely consequences of the various alternatives. The average citizen often lacks this knowledge.

THE MEASUREMENT OF PUBLIC OPINION

Woodrow Wilson once said he had spent nearly all his adult life in government and yet had never seen a "government." What Wilson was saying, in effect, was that government is a system of relationships. A government is not a building or a person; it is not tangible in the way that a car or a bottle of soda is. So it is with public opinion. No one has ever seen a "public opinion," and thus it cannot be measured directly. It must be assessed indirectly.

A time-honored method of interpreting public opinion is election returns. The vote is routinely interpreted by the press and politicians as an indicator of the public's mood—whether liberal or conservative, angry or satisfied, quiet or intense. When the Republicans piled up huge gains in the House and Senate in the 1994 congressional elections, pundits labeled it an angry backlash against government and the Democrats, who were in control of Congress and the presidency.

Letters to the editor in newspapers, e-mail messages to elected officials, and the size of crowds at mass demonstrations are other means of judging public opinion. Yet another device is the activity of lobbyists, who bring the concerns of their constituents to government's attention.

All these indicators of public opinion are important and deserve the attention of those in power. These indicators, however, have shortcomings as a guide to what is on the minds of the people. Elections offer the people only a yes-or-no choice between candidates, and different voters will make the same choice for quite different reasons. The winning candidate may claim that the public has based its choice on a particular issue or inclination, but election returns always mask a more complex reality. As for letter writers and demonstrators, they are not at all representative of the general population. Less than 1 percent of Americans participate each year in a mass demonstration, and fewer than 10 percent write to the president or a member of Congress. Studies have found that the views of letter writers and demonstrators are more intense and more extreme than those of other citizens.[6]

Public Opinion Polls

In an earlier day, such indicators as elections and letters to the editor were the only means by which public officials could gauge what the public was thinking. Today, they can also rely on polls or surveys, which provide a more systematic method of estimating public sentiment.

In a **public opinion poll,** a relatively few individuals—the **sample**—are interviewed in order to estimate the opinions of a whole **population,** such as the students of a college, the residents of a city, or the citizens of a country. If a

public opinion poll A device for measuring public opinion whereby a relatively small number of individuals (the sample) are interviewed for the purpose of estimating the opinions of a whole community (the population).

sample In a public opinion poll, the relatively small number of individuals who are interviewed for the purpose of estimating the opinions of an entire population.

population In a public opinion poll, the people (for example, the citizens of a nation) whose opinions are being estimated through interviews with a sample of these people.

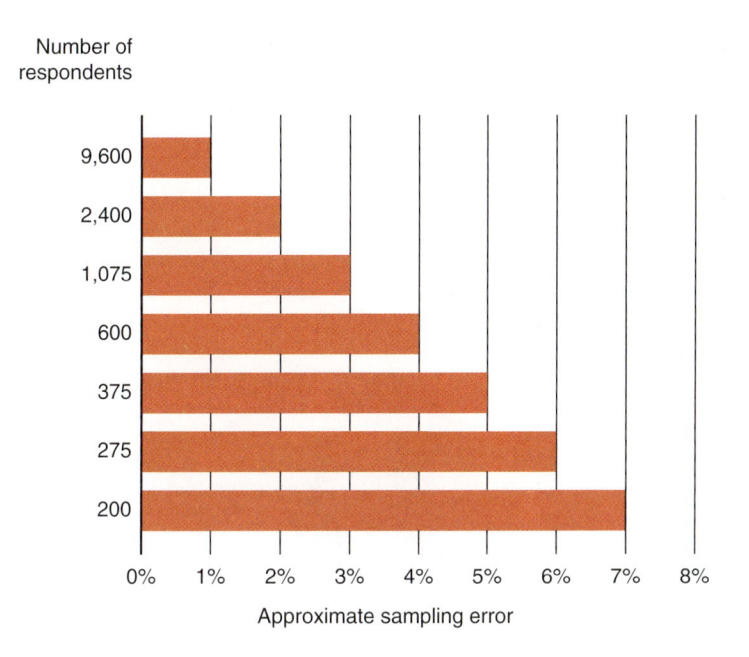

Figure 6-2

Relationship Between Sample Size and Sampling Error

The larger a poll's sample is, the smaller is the error in estimating the population from which the sample is taken. These figures are based on a 95 percent confidence level, which means that for a given sample size (e.g., 600), the chances are 19 in 20 (95 percent) that the sample will produce results that are within the sampling error (e.g., ±4 percent) of the results that would have been obtained if the whole population had been interviewed.

Number of respondents	Approximate sampling error
9,600	1%
2,400	2%
1,075	3%
600	4%
375	5%
275	6%
200	7%

sufficient number of individuals are chosen at random, their views will tend to be representative—that is, roughly the same as the views held by the population as a whole.

How is it possible to measure the thinking of a large population on the basis of a relatively small sample? How can interviews with, say, one thousand Americans provide a reliable estimate of what 250 million are thinking? The answer is found in the theory of probability. Opinion sampling is based on the mathematical laws of probability, which can be illustrated by the hypothetical example of a huge jar filled with a million marbles, half of them red and half of them blue. If a blindfolded person reaches into the jar, the likelihood of selecting a marble of a given color is fifty-fifty. And if one thousand marbles are chosen in this random way, it is likely that about half of them will be red and half will be blue. Opinion sampling works in the same way. If respondents are chosen at random from a population, their opinions will be approximately the same as those of the population as a whole.

The accuracy of a poll is usually expressed in terms of **sampling error,** which indicates the likelihood that the responses of the sample accurately represent the view of the population. As would be expected, the larger the size of the sample, the greater the likelihood that the sample's opinions will accurately reflect those of the population. Thus, the larger the sample is, the smaller the sampling error is (see Figure 6–2).

Many people assume that a poll of the United States, with its 250 million people, must have a much larger sample to achieve the same level of accuracy as, say, a poll of Massachusetts or Arizona. In fact, the mathematics of polling are such that sample size is the critical factor. Thus, a sample of one thousand people will have nearly the same level of accuracy whether the population is that of the nation, a state, or a large city.

sampling error A measure of the accuracy of a public opinion poll. The sampling error is mainly a function of sample size and is usually expressed in percentage terms.

President Harry Truman holds up the early edition *Chicago Tribune* with the headline "Dewey Defeats Truman." The *Tribune* was responding to analysts' predictions that Dewey would win the 1948 election.

A properly drawn sample of one thousand individuals has a sampling error of about plus or minus 3 percent, which is to say that the proportions of the various opinions expressed by the people in the sample are likely to be within 3 percent of those of the whole population. For example, if 55 percent of a sample of one thousand respondents say that they intend to vote for the Republican candidate for president, then the chances are high that 52 to 58 percent (55 percent plus or minus 3 percent) of the whole population plan to vote for the Republican.

The impressive record of the Gallup poll in predicting the outcomes of presidential elections indicates that the theoretical accuracy of polls can be matched in practice. For example, the Gallup poll predicted in 2000 that the vote would divide as follows: 47 percent for Bush, 45 percent for Gore, and 4 percent for Nader. The actual result was 48 percent, 48 percent, and 3 percent respectively. The Gallup organization has erred badly only once: it stopped polling several weeks before the 1948 election and missed a late trend that carried Harry Truman to victory over Thomas E. Dewey.

Problems with Polls

probability sample A sample for a poll in which each individual in the population has a known probability of being selected randomly for inclusion in the sample.

Mathematical estimations of poll accuracy require a **probability sample**—a sample in which each individual in the population has a known probability of being selected at random for inclusion. In practice, pollsters can only approximate this ideal. Because pollsters rarely have a list of all individuals in a population from which to draw a random sample, they usually base their sample on telephones or locations. Random-digit telephone sampling is the most commonly used technique. Pollsters use computers to pick random telephone numbers, which are then dialed by interviewers to reach respondents. Because the computer is as likely to pick one telephone number as any other and because 95 percent of U.S. homes have a telephone, a sample selected in this way is usually assumed to be representative of the population.

Fighting Words

Should Representatives Lead on the Basis of Opinion Polls?

A fundamental principle of democracy is that public opinion ought to be the foundation of government. However, the role that public opinion should play in specific policy decisions is, as it always has been, a subject of dispute. James Madison distinguished between the public's momentary passions and its enduring concerns, arguing that government is obliged to represent only the latter. In contrast, the Jacksonians and Progressives had a strong faith in the judgment of ordinary citizens and a distrust of entrenched elites. With the advent of the public opinion poll, it became possible to measure citizens' policy views more directly. Should policymakers follow the polls in making their decisions? Some analysts, including the pollster George Gallup, have held that leaders should act in close accord with the polls. Other analysts, including the sociologist Robert Nisbet, have argued that polls measure fleeting opinions about topical issues and that leaders in any event are obliged only to respond to the people's deep and enduring beliefs.

Yes: We are often told that the function of leadership is to lead. Not poll results, but that inner voice alone, should be heeded. . . . This is not the kind of leadership we want. In a democracy we demand that the views of the people be taken into account. This does not mean that leaders must follow the public's views slavishly; it does mean that they should have available an accurate appraisal of public opinion and take some account of it in reaching their decisions. . . . The task of the leader is to decide how best to achieve the goals set by the people.
—*George Gallup, founder of the Gallup poll*

No: [The idea] that opinion—of the kind that can be instantly ascertained by any poll or survey—must somehow govern, must therefore be incessantly studied, courted, flattered, and drawn upon in lieu of the judgment which true leadership alone is qualified to make . . . is worse than heresy. It is fatuous. For always present is the assumption . . . that there really is a genuine public opinion at any given moment on whatever issue may be ascendant on the national or the international scene.
—*Robert Nisbet, sociologist and social critic*

Some polls are not based on probability sampling. For example, news reporters sometimes conduct "people-in-the-street" interviews to obtain individual responses to political questions. Although a reporter may imply that the views of those interviewed are representative of the general public's view, there is a fallacy in this reasoning. The sample will be biased by where and when the reporter chooses to conduct the interviews. For example, interviews conducted on a downtown street at the noon hour will include a disproportionate number of business employees who are taking their lunch breaks. Housewives, teachers, and factory workers, not to mention farmers, are among the many groups that would be underrepresented in such a sample.

Polls can also be misleading if they include poorly worded questions or ask people about remote topics. For example, a Roper poll received national attention when it found that a third of Americans expressed doubt about whether the Holocaust had actually happened. However, the poll question was a double negative ("Does it seem possible or does it seem impossible to you that the Nazi extermination of the Jews never happened?"), and some analysts suggested that the survey respondents may have been confused by the wording of the question. In fact, they were. A follow-up poll that asked a straightforward question found that less than one in ten Americans said they doubted the Holocaust had occurred.

Despite these and other sources of error, the poll or survey is the most relied-upon method of measuring public opinion. More than one hundred organizations are in the business of conducting public opinion polls. Some, like the Gallup Organization, conduct polls that are then released to the news media by syndication. Most large news organizations also have their own in-house polls; one of the foremost of these is the CBS News/New York Times poll, which conducts about fifteen surveys annually for use in the *Times* and on CBS's newscasts. Finally, there are polling firms that specialize in conducting surveys for candidates and officeholders.

www.mhhe.com/patterson6

POLITICAL SOCIALIZATION: HOW AMERICANS LEARN THEIR POLITICS

Analysts have long been interested in the process by which public opinion is formed. The learning process by which people acquire their political opinions, beliefs, and values is called **political socialization.** Just as a language, a religion, or an athletic skill is acquired through a learning process, so too are people's political orientations. Political beliefs are not drawn from a hat; they are acquired. People are socialized to see the political world in certain ways. For most Americans, the socialization process starts in the family with exposure to the political loyalties and opinions of the parents. The schools later contribute to the process, as do the mass media, friends, and other influences. Political socialization is thus a lifelong process.

political socialization The learning process by which people acquire their political opinions, beliefs, and values.

The Process of Political Socialization

The process of political socialization in the United States has several major characteristics. First, although socialization continues throughout life, most people's political outlook is substantially influenced by their childhood learning. The **primacy tendency** refers to the fact that what is learned first is often lodged most firmly in one's mind.[7] Most people do not reflect deeply on how they acquired their political preferences. Basic ideas about race, gender, and political party, for example, are often formed uncritically in childhood, much in the way that belief in a particular religion, typically the religion of one's parents, is acquired.

A second characteristic of political socialization is that it is cumulative. The **structuring tendency** refers to the tendency of earlier learning to structure later learning.[8] This tendency is less a function of age itself than of an accumulated attachment to particular ideas or values. Of course, the fact that the United States is a diverse and mobile society makes a basic change in a person's political views possible, especially when previous and current experiences are at

primacy tendency The tendency for early learning to become deeply embedded in one's mind.

structuring tendency The tendency of earlier political learning to structure (influence) later learning.

Students in a North Carolina school reciting the Pledge of Allegiance. Such childhood socialization experiences can have a profound impact on an individual's basic political beliefs.

odds with one another. However, individuals have psychological defense mechanisms that protect their ingrained beliefs. When faced with situations that might challenge their original views, they can readily muster reasons for clinging to them because these views are deeply ingrained.

Dramatic political change is uncommon, and when it has occurred on a large scale, it has nearly always been preceded by an extraordinary event that has shaken people out of their complacency. In such instances, it is usually younger adults who are more responsive. Their beliefs are less firmly rooted in past experiences and are therefore more easily changed. The **age-cohort tendency** holds that a significant break in the pattern of political socialization is almost always concentrated among younger citizens. President Franklin Roosevelt's New Deal initiatives, which sought to alleviate the economic hardship of the Great Depression, resulted in a substantial increase in Democratic loyalists among first-time voters, but not among habitual ones.

age-cohort tendency The tendency for a significant break in the pattern of political socialization to occur among younger citizens, usually as the result of a major event or development that disrupts preexisting beliefs.

The Agents of Political Socialization

The socialization process takes place through a variety of influences, including family, schools, peers, mass media, and political leaders and events. It is helpful to consider briefly some ways in which these so-called **agents of socialization** affect the opinions that people have. Although these agents are discussed separately here, it should be kept in mind that, by and large, their influences overlap. Many of the same political values that people acquire at home and in school, for example, are emphasized regularly by the mass media and political leaders.

agents of socialization Those agents, such as the family and the media, that have a significant impact on citizens' political socialization.

Political Culture
One People Out of Many

National Pride

Americans are justifiably proud of their nation. It is the oldest continuous democracy in the world, an economic powerhouse, and a diverse yet peaceful society.

What Americans may not recognize, because it is so much a part of everyday life in America, is the degree to which they are bombarded with messages and symbols of their nation's greatness. Political socialization in the United States is not the rigid program of indoctrination that some societies impose on their people. Nevertheless, Americans receive a thorough political education. Their country's values are impressed on them by every medium of communication: newspapers, daily conversations, television, movies, books. After the terrorist attacks of September 11, 2001, these tendencies reached new heights. The NBC television network outfitted its peacock logo with stars and stripes, and computer-generated flags festooned the other networks.

The words and symbols that regularly tell Americans of their country's greatness are important to its unity. Without a common ancestral heritage to bind them, Americans need other methods to instill and reinforce the idea that they are one people. As was discussed in Chapter 1, America's political ideals have this effect. So too do everyday reminders, such as the flying of the flag on homes and private buildings, a practice that is almost uniquely American. (Elsewhere, flags are rarely displayed except on public buildings.)

One indicator of Americans' political socialization is their high level of national pride. Harvard University's Pippa Norris (in Marion Sawer's edited volume, *The People's Choice*) constructed an index of national pride based on people's admiration for their country's political, economic, artistic, sporting, scientific, and other achievements. Americans ranked at the top, as shown by the following chart, which is based on Norris's index:

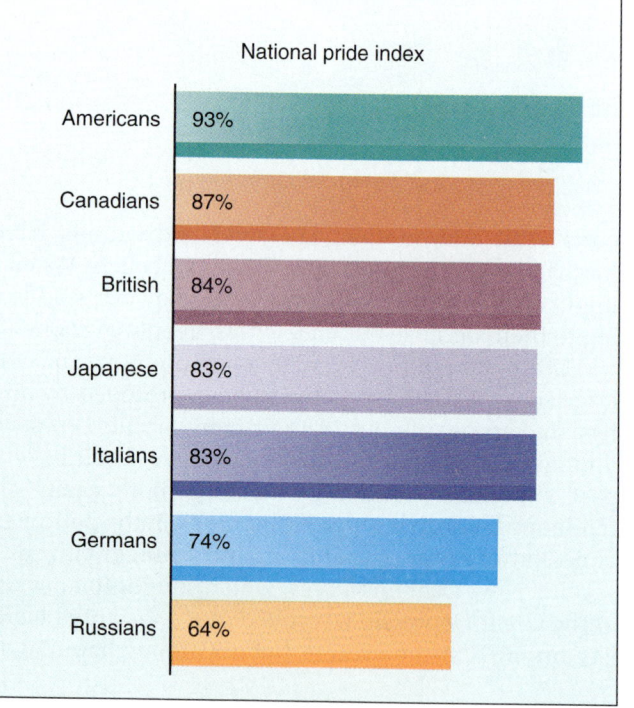

National pride index

Americans	93%
Canadians	87%
British	84%
Japanese	83%
Italians	83%
Germans	74%
Russians	64%

Families

The family is a powerful agent of socialization because children begin with no political attitudes of their own and are likely to accept uncritically those of their parents. The family has a near-monopoly on the attention of the young child, who also places great trust in what a parent says. By the time the child is a teenager and is not likely to listen to any advice a parent might offer, many of the beliefs and values that will stay with the child throughout life are already in place. Some of these orientations are overtly political. Many adults are Republicans or Democrats today largely because they accepted their parents' party loyalty. They now can give all sorts of reasons for preferring their party to the other. But the reasons come later in life; the loyalty comes first, during childhood. The family also contributes to basic orientations that, while not directly political, have political significance. For example, the American family tends to be more egalitarian than families in other nations, and American children often have a voice in family decisions. Such basic American values as equality, individualism, and personal freedom have their roots in patterns of family interaction.[9]

Schools

The school, like the family, has its major impact on children's basic political beliefs and values rather than on specific issues of policy. Teachers at the elementary level describe the exploits of national heroes such as George Washington, Abraham Lincoln, and Martin Luther King Jr. and extol the superiority of the country's economic and political systems.[10] Although students in the middle and high school grades receive a more nuanced version of American history, it tends to emphasize the nation's strengths and accomplishments—for example, its decisive role in the two world wars. U.S. schools are probably more instrumental in building support for the nation than are the schools in other democracies. The Pledge of Allegiance, which is recited daily in many U.S. schools, has no equivalent in European countries. Schools also contribute to Americans' sense of social equality. Most American children, regardless of family income, attend public schools and study a fairly standard curriculum. In many countries, even some in Europe, children are segregated by class in the schools they attend and, once in school, take courses that prepare some of them for manual labor and others for a university education.

Mass Media

The mass media are another powerful socializing agent. The themes and images that prevail in the media affect people's perceptions of their world. For example, exposure to crime and lawlessness on television can lead people to believe that society itself is more violent than it actually is (see Chapter 10) and may even provoke violence in some people. Similarly, people's perceptions of political leaders are affected to some extent by how these leaders are portrayed in the media. When leaders are repeatedly said to be manipulative and self-interested, for example, people tend to see them as manipulative and self-interested.[11]

Peers

Members of peer groups—friends, neighbors, and coworkers—tend to have similar political views. Belonging to a peer group usually reinforces what a person already believes. One reason is that most people trust the views of their friends and associates. Many individuals are also unwilling to deviate too far from what their peers think. In *Spiral of Silence,* Elisabeth Noelle-Neumann

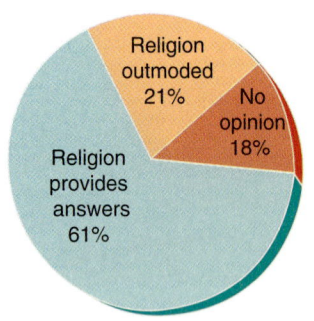

Figure 6–3

Opinions on Religion as an Answer to Today's Problems
Most Americans say that religion can answer all or most of today's problems; only a minority believe religion is old-fashioned and out of date.
Source: Gallup poll, December, 2001. Used with permission.

- Religion provides answers 61%
- Religion outmoded 21%
- No opinion 18%

contends that most individuals are conformist and are reluctant to speak out against prevailing opinions. The effect, she argues, is to make such opinions appear to be more widely held than they are, which can lead public officials to give them more attention than they may deserve.[12]

Political Institutions and Leaders

People look to political leaders and institutions, particularly the president and political parties, as guides to opinion. In the period immediately after the terrorist attacks on the World Trade Center and the Pentagon on September 11, 2001, most Americans were confused about who the enemy was and how the attack should be dealt with. That opinion changed dramatically ten days later after a televised speech by President Bush in which he identified the Al Qaeda and Taliban forces in Afghanistan as the immediate target of what would become a war on terrorism. In polls taken after the speech, about 90 percent of Americans said they agreed with Bush's plan of action.

Churches

Since the seventeenth-century Puritans, churches have played a substantial role in shaping Americans' social and political opinions. Most Americans say they believe in God, most attend church at least once in a while, and most adhere to a religion that teaches beliefs about the proper nature of society. Moreover, most Americans say that religion has answers to many of the problems facing today's society (see Figure 6–3). In all these respects, churches and religion are a more powerful force in the United States than in most other Western countries.

Scholars have not studied the impact of church attendance and religious instruction on political socialization as closely as they have studied other influences, such as the schools and the media, but churches are an important source of politically relevant attitudes, including society's obligations to children, the poor, and the unborn. (The impact of religion is discussed further in a later section of this chapter.)

FRAMES OF REFERENCE: HOW AMERICANS THINK POLITICALLY

What are the frames of reference that guide the political thinking of Americans? The question is important in at least two respects. First, the ways in which citizens think politically provide clues about the way in which public opinion is likely to affect government. The government in a democratic system is expected to act more often in accordance with public opinion than against it.

A second reason it is important to understand how the people think politically is that a shared frame of reference can bring citizens together in the pursuit of a common goal. The opinions of millions of Americans would mean almost nothing if each of these opinions were different from all the others. If enough people think the same way, however, they may be able to exert political power.

Religion is a powerful socializing force in American life. Churches, synagogues, mosques, and temples are places where Americans acquire values and beliefs that can affect their opinions about politics.

The subject of how Americans think politically fills entire books. Outlined here are four of the major frames of reference through which Americans evaluate political alternatives. The first tends to unite Americans; the other three give rise to differences of opinion among them.

Cultural Thinking: Common Ideas

As was indicated in Chapter 1, Americans are unusual in their commitment to a common set of ideals that define the nature of the American political experience. Such principles as individualism, equality, and self-government have always meant somewhat different things to different people but nonetheless are a source of opinion consensus. For example, government programs aimed at redistributing wealth from the rich to the poor are popular among Europeans but are less appealing to Americans, who have a deeper commitment to individualism.

There are limits, of course, to the degree to which Americans' basic beliefs shape their policy opinions. For nearly two centuries African Americans were inferior by law to white Americans, despite the American creed that "all men are created equal." Such inconsistencies speak to the all-too-human capacity to voice one idea and live another.

Nevertheless, Americans' political ideals are a powerful influence on public opinion. They affect the way in which disputes are argued and affect what people regard as reasonable and desirable. Americans' ideals serve to define the boundaries of acceptable political action and opinion (see Chapter 1).

Ideological Thinking: The Outlook for Some

Commentators on public opinion in the United States often use such ideological words as *liberal* and *conservative* in describing how ordinary citizens think about political issues. In the early 1980s, for example, analysts spoke of "a conservative tide" that was supposedly sweeping the country and displacing the liberal trend that had dominated American politics for most of the preceding fifty years.

ideology A consistent pattern of opinion on particular issues that stems from a core belief or set of beliefs.

Liberal and *conservative* are ideological terms. So too are such terms as *populist, progressive, libertarian, communist,* and *fascist.* An **ideology** is a consistent pattern of opinion on particular issues that stems from a core or basic belief. Communism, for example, is rooted in a belief in material equality, and a communist therefore would be expected to support wage and welfare policies designed to spread wealth more evenly across society.

Although ideological terms are often used to describe mass publics, they do not accurately describe how most people think about politics.[13] Nearly everyone has basic beliefs that affect their opinions, but most people do not apply them consistently across a wide range of issues. They may say, for example, that they favor free trade among nations but then oppose it in particular cases where it works to the disadvantage of U.S. firms or workers. Research indicates that no more than a third of Americans, and perhaps as few as a tenth, have a pattern of opinions on issues that is consistent enough to be described as a manifestation of a true ideology.[14] Further, most Americans are relatively pragmatic in their political judgments. Rather than applying an ideological framework, Americans tend to judge policies by whether they appear to be working or seem likely to work.

Nevertheless, analysts sometimes find it useful to measure the public's ideological tendencies. A standard method is to ask survey respondents whether they think of themselves as liberal, moderate, or conservative. The problem with this approach is that although people readily label themselves by these terms, many individuals are unable to say what the terms mean, or they provide inexact or inappropriate definitions. For this reason, pollsters have recently developed an alternative and less-direct method. They ask respondents two questions: "Do you support or oppose an activist role for government in determining the distribution of economic benefits in society?" and "Do you support or oppose activist government as a means of promoting a particular set of social values?" This method does not require that respondents know the meaning of ideological terms and yet provides a measure of people's general beliefs about government action in the broad areas of economic and social policy.

conservatives Those who emphasize the marketplace as the means of distributing economic benefits but look to government to uphold traditional social values.

liberals Those who favor activist government as an instrument of economic security and redistribution but reject the notion that government should favor a particular set of social values.

populists Those who favor activist government as a means of promoting both economic security and traditional values.

libertarians Those who oppose government as an instrument of traditional values and of economic security.

Responses to the two questions have been the basis for identifying four ideological types: conservatives, liberals, populists, and libertarians (see Figure 6–4). **Conservatives** are defined as individuals who oppose an activist role for government in providing economic benefits but look to government to uphold traditional social values. In contrast, **liberals** favor activist government as an instrument of economic redistribution but reject the notion that government should favor a particular set of social values. True liberals and conservatives could be expected to differ, for instance, on the issues of homosexual rights (a social values question) and government-guaranteed health care (an economic distribution question). Liberals would view homosexuality as a private issue and believe that government should ensure that everyone has access to adequate medical care. Conservatives would oppose government-mandated access to health care and favor government policies that actively discourage homosexual lifestyles. **Populists** are defined as individuals who share with conservatives a concern for traditional values but, like liberals, favor an active role for government in providing economic security. **Libertarians** are opposed to government intervention in both the economic and social spheres.

In sum, libertarians are the most committed to individual freedom, and populists are the most committed to government activism. Conservatives and liberals are committed to individual freedom in one area (the economic sphere

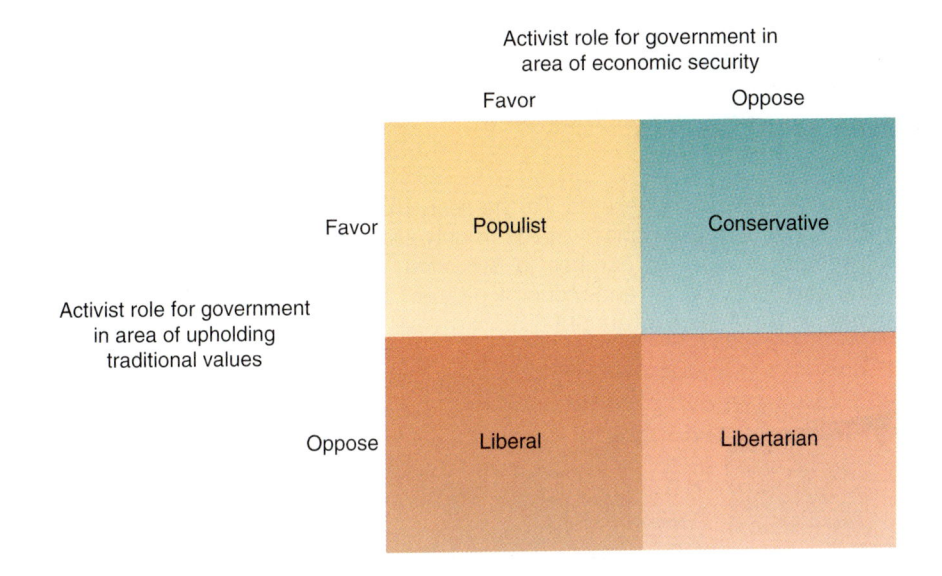

Figure 6–4

Types of Ideologies
Americans can be classified as liberals, conservatives, populists, or libertarians, depending on their attitudes toward the government's role in the areas of economic security and social values.

	Activist role for government in area of economic security	
	Favor	Oppose
Favor (traditional values)	Populist	Conservative
Oppose (traditional values)	Liberal	Libertarian

for conservatives, the social sphere for liberals) but to government activism in the other (the social sphere for conservatives, the economic sphere for liberals). Of these ideological types, conservatives are the largest group. A Gallup poll, for example, estimated that 31 percent of Americans are conservatives, 24 percent are libertarian, 17 percent are populist, and 13 percent are liberal.[15]

Group Thinking: The Outlook of Many

An early study of ideology by Philip Converse indicated that groups are a more important reference for Americans than is ideology; subsequent studies have confirmed his finding.[16] Many Americans see politics through the lens of a group to which they belong or with which they identify. These individuals nearly always pay closer attention to issues that affect the group's interests than to more remote issues. Farmers, for example, are more likely to follow agricultural issues than they are labor-management issues. A group outlook is a source of both consensus and conflict. Farmers generally approve of government price supports for commodities; this opinion unites farmers but pits them against other groups, including consumers.

Because of the country's great size, settlement by various immigrant groups, and economic pluralism, Americans are a very diverse people. Later chapters examine group tendencies more fully, but it is useful here to mention a few of the major group orientations: religion, class, region, race and ethnicity, gender, and age.

Religion

Religious differences have always been a source of solidarity within a group and a source of conflict with outsiders. At an earlier time, religion was a bitterly divisive force as newly immigrant Catholics and Jews encountered widespread hostility and discrimination from entrenched Protestant groups. Today, Catholics, Protestants, and Jews share similar opinions on most policy issues.

STATES IN THE NATION

Conservatives and Liberals

Nearly half of Americans describe themselves as moderates. Of the rest, the large majority are conservatives. According to a 2000 poll, liberals outnumber conservatives in only six states and the District of Columbia, although they are equal or nearly equal in number in six other states. The concentration of conservatives is especially high in the southern, plains, and mountain states where traditionalism and individualism are more widely embraced than in the coastal states of the northeast and west.

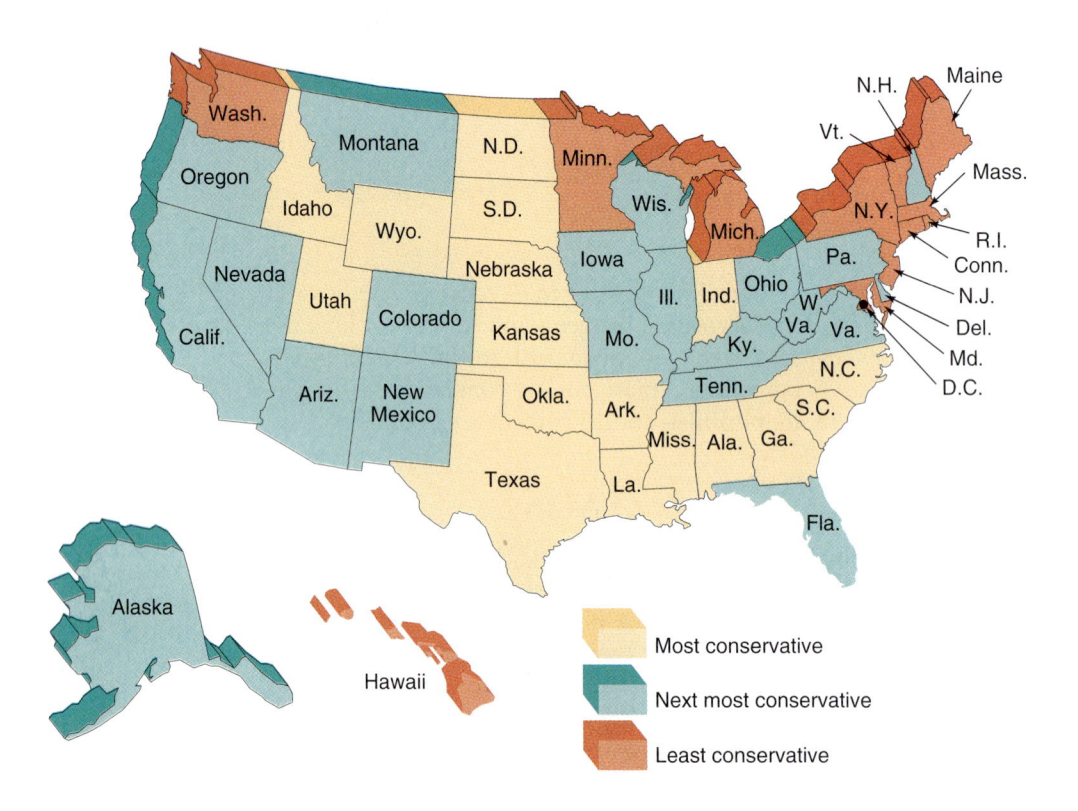

Source: CNN exit polls, 2000. Classification based on the difference in the proportions of self-identified conservatives and liberals in each state.

Nevertheless, some important religious differences remain, although the opposing sides are not always the same. Fundamentalist Protestants and Roman Catholics oppose legalized abortion more strongly than do other Protestants and Jews. In contrast, on some welfare issues, such as food programs for the poor, Catholics and Jews are more supportive than are Protestants, especially those of fundamentalist beliefs. Such differences have at least a partial basis in religious beliefs. A belief in self-reliance, for example, is part of the so-called Protestant ethic. Attitudes on abortion are tied to religious beliefs about whether human life begins at conception or at a later stage in the development of the fetus.

Economic class is related to Americans' opinions on a range of social and economic issues. Shown here is a work crew constructing formed wooden beams.

The most powerful religious force in contemporary American politics is the so-called religious right, which consists primarily of individuals who see themselves as born-again Christians and view the Bible as the infallible truth. Their views on such issues as homosexual rights, abortion, and school prayer differ significantly from those of the population as a whole. A Time/CNN survey found, for example, that born-again Christians are 37 percent more likely than other Americans to agree that "the Supreme Court and the Congress have gone too far in keeping religious and moral values like prayer out of our laws, schools, and many areas of our lives."

Class

Economic class has less influence on political opinion in the United States than in Europe, but it is nevertheless related to opinions on certain economic issues. For example, lower-income Americans are more supportive of social welfare programs, business regulation, and progressive taxation than are those in higher-income categories. An obstacle to class-based politics in the United States is that people with similar incomes, but differing occupations, do not share the same opinions. Support for collective bargaining, for example, is substantially higher among factory workers than among small farmers, service workers, and those in the skilled crafts. The interplay of class and opinion will be examined more closely in Chapter 9, which discusses interest groups.

Region

Region has declined as a basis of political opinions. The increased mobility of the U.S. population has resulted in the relocation of millions of Americans from the Northeast and Midwest to the South and West. Their beliefs on issues such as social welfare tend to be more liberal than those of people who are native to

Liberty & Equality

What's Your Opinion?

Americans' Ideologies

In the United States, the key dimensions of political conflict occur around the extent of government intervention in the economic marketplace and in the maintenance of traditional values. Government intervention in either sphere has implications for liberty—how much freedom should you have in deciding on your lifestyle and in your economic choices. Government intervention in the economic sphere can also affect equality: government has been the principal means of providing economic security for those vulnerable to market forces.

You can test your own ideology—and thus in a way your own conception of liberty and equality—by asking yourself the measurement questions used in Gallup surveys. Should government do more or do less in terms of leveling out the effects of the marketplace? Should government do more or do less in terms of promoting traditional social values? You are a libertarian if you favor less government action in both spheres. You are a populist if you favor more government action in both spheres. You are a conservative if you favor less intervention in the marketplace but more in the realm of social values. And you are a liberal if you favor more intervention in the marketplace and less in the realm of social values.

---

these regions. Nevertheless, regional differences are still evident in the areas of social welfare, civil rights, and national defense. Conservative opinions on these issues are more prevalent in the southern and mountain states than elsewhere (see "States in the Nation").

Race and Ethnicity

Race and ethnicity, as Chapter 5 pointed out, have a significant influence on opinions. Whites and African Americans, for example, differ on issues of integration: black people are more in favor of affirmative action, busing, and other measures designed to promote racial equality and integration. Racial and ethnic groups also differ on many pocketbook issues, largely as a result of the differences in their economic situations: African Americans are more supportive of social welfare programs and government-backed job and training programs. The crime issue is another area where opinion differences are pronounced and predictable: minorities are less trusting of police and the judicial system. An American Bar Association poll found, for example, that only one in four nonwhites believe that "law enforcement officials and police try to treat whites and minorities alike."

Gender

Although male-female differences of opinion are small on most issues, gender does affect opinion in some policy areas. Women are slightly more supportive than men, for example, of abortion rights and affirmative action. A 2000 Gallup poll found a 63 percent to 53 percent difference in support for affirmative action. The difference is even larger on some social welfare issues, such as poverty and education assistance.[17] A 2000 Washington Post/ABC News poll, for example, found that 72 percent of women compared with 57 percent of men favored increased spending for education. Some analysts suggest that such differences are accounted for in part by a tendency for women to think more in terms of the community as a whole and for men to think more in terms of self-reliance.

Women and men differ also in their opinions on the use of military force. In nearly every case, women are less supportive of military action than men are. When the buildup of U.S. forces was taking place in Vietnam, a 1965 Gallup poll indicated that 73 percent of men and 59 percent of women favored the escalation. The terrorist attacks on the World Trade Center and the Pentagon on September 11, 2001, produced an exception to the normal pattern. Men and women were almost equally likely (90 percent and 88 percent, respectively) to favor a military response. But they differed in expected ways when questioned about how the terrorist threat should be countered. Women were less likely than men to favor a long-term general war on terrorism (see Figure 6–5).

Differences such as these are a factor in the gender gap that was discussed in Chapter 5. Women and men do not differ greatly in their political views but there are persistent and predictable differences that lead them to respond somewhat differently to issues, events, and candidates. The politics of gender will be discussed further in Chapter 8.

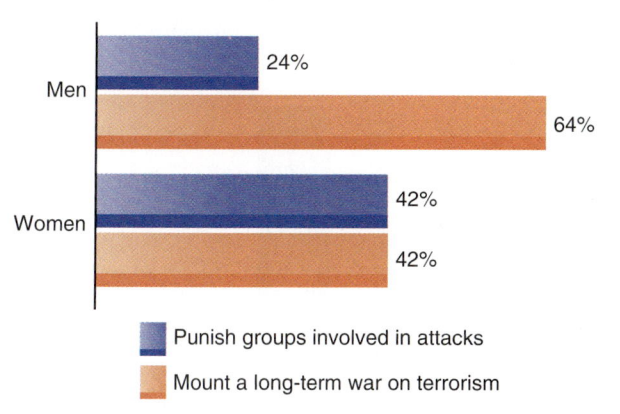

"Which [position] comes closer to your view about the actions the United States should take to deal with terrorism?"

	Punish groups involved in attacks	Mount a long-term war on terrorism
Men	24%	64%
Women	42%	42%

Figure 6-5

Gender and the Terrorist Threat

Compared with men, women are somewhat less inclined to see military force as the answer to conflict. This difference was evident shortly after the terrorist attacks of September 11, 2001, when women were more inclined than men to prefer a carefully targeted attack on terrorists as opposed to a long-term war on terrorism.

Source: Gallup poll, September 21–22, 2001.

Age

Another division of growing importance is the *age gap*. Young and old have always had somewhat divergent opinions as a consequence of differences in their ages and socialization experiences, but their disagreements are becoming greater. In her book *Young v. Old*, the political scientist Susan MacManus notes that the elderly tend to oppose increases in public school funding while supporting increases in social security and Medicare (government-assisted medical care for retirees). MacManus predicts that issues of age will increasingly dominate American politics and that the elderly have the political clout to prevail. They vote at a much higher rate than do young people, are better organized politically (through groups such as the powerful AARP), and are increasing in number as a result of lengthened life spans (the so-called graying of America). (The politics of age is also discussed in Chapters 8 and 9.)

Cross-Cutting Cleavages

Although group loyalties can have a powerful impact on people's opinions, their influence is diminished when identification with one group is offset by identification with other groups. In a pluralistic society such as the United States, groups tend to be "cross-cutting"—that is, each includes individuals from a range of other groups. Cross-cutting cleavages tend to produce moderate opinions. Faced with conflicting feelings arising out of identification with several groups, most people seek a balance between them when forming an opinion. However, in societies such as Northern Ireland where group loyalties are reinforcing rather than cross-cutting (Catholics tend to have much lower incomes, Protestants much higher ones), opinions are intensified by group identifications, and deep hatreds among the opposing camps can result. In America, Catholics and Protestants are not at each other's throats, largely because each group includes people of varying income, education, region, and so on. *Diversity* is a source of differences; it can also be a basis for harmony.

Percentage expressing agreement

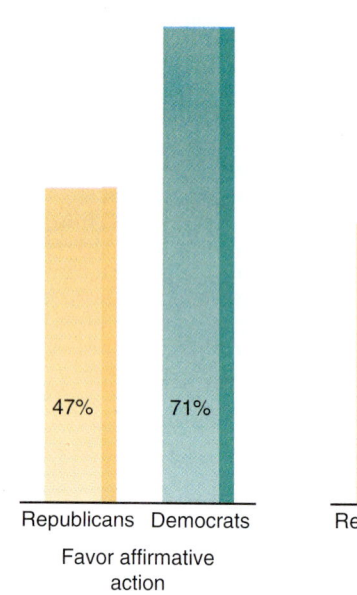

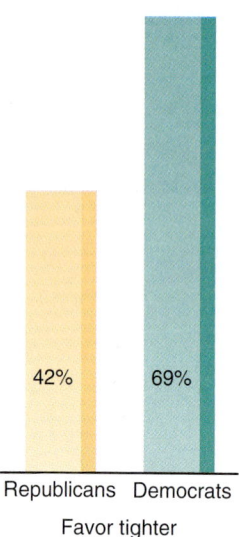

	Republicans	Democrats
Favor affirmative action	47%	71%
Favor tighter controls on gun ownership	42%	69%
Oppose school vouchers	40%	56%
Favor legal abortion under any circumstance	21%	36%

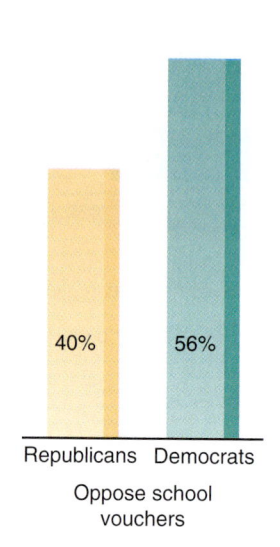

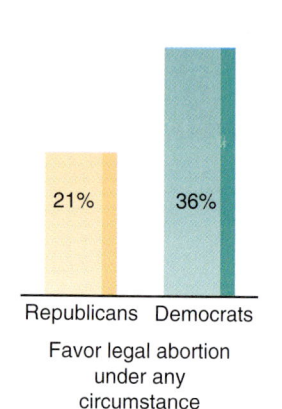

Figure 6–6

Partisanship and Issue Opinions

Republicans and Democrats differ significantly in their opinions on many policy issues. Source (in order of questions): Washington Post/ABC News, 2000; ABC News, 2002; Gallup, 2000; Gallup, 2000.

party identification The personal sense of loyalty that an individual may feel toward a particular political party.

Partisan Thinking: The Line That Divides

In the everyday play of politics, no source of opinion more clearly divides Americans than that of their partisanship. Figure 6–6 provides examples, but they indicate only a few of the differences. On nearly every major issue of economic, social, and foreign policy, Republicans and Democrats have views that are at least somewhat different. In many cases, such as spending programs for the poor, the differences are substantial.

Party identification refers to a person's ingrained sense of loyalty to a political party. Party identification is not formal membership in a party but instead an emotional attachment to a party—the feeling that "I am a Democrat" or "I am a Republican." Scholars and pollsters have typically measured party identification with a question of the following type: "Generally speaking, do you think of yourself as a Republican, a Democrat, an Independent, or what?" About 65 percent of adults call themselves Democrats or Republicans. Of the 35 percent who prefer the label "Independent," most say they lean slightly toward one party or the other.

Early studies of party identification concluded that partisan attitudes were highly stable and seldom changed over the course of adult life.[19] Subsequent studies have shown that party loyalties are more fluid than originally believed; they can be influenced by the issues and candidates of the moment.[20] Nevertheless, most adults do not switch their party loyalties easily, and a substantial proportion never waver from an initial commitment to a party, which can often be traced to childhood influences.

Once acquired, partisanship affects how people perceive and interpret events. For example, when the U.S. Supreme Court ruled against a manual recount of Florida votes, which decided the 2000 presidential election in George

George W. Bush accepting the acclaim of Republicans at the 2000 GOP National Convention. Partisanship is one of the strongest influences on the political opinions that Americans hold.

W. Bush's favor, the responses of Democrats, Independents, and Republicans differed sharply. A national poll indicated that 53 percent of Democrats and 25 percent of Independents but only 12 percent of Republicans had "less respect" for the Court because of its action.

For most people, partisanship is not simply a blind faith in the party of their choice. Some Republicans and Democrats know very little about their party's traditions, policies, or group commitments, and they unthinkingly embrace its candidates. However, party loyalties are not randomly distributed across the population but follow a pattern that would be predicted from the parties' traditions. The Democratic party, for example, has been the driving force behind social welfare and workers' rights polices, while the Republican party has been the spearhead for pro-business and tax reform policies. The fact that most union workers are Democrats and most businesspeople are Republicans is not mere coincidence. Their partisanship is rooted in their different life circumstances and the different policy traditions of the two parties.

Partisanship is obviously a strong force in American politics, but its influence is declining. In recent decades, the proportion of voters who identify with the Democratic or Republican party has declined and the proportion of Independents has increased. As a result, elections are more volatile than in the past. People are less likely to vote on the basis of a long-standing party loyalty and more likely to base their choice on the issues and candidates of the moment. This and other issues of partisanship are examined in depth at various points later in this book, particularly in Chapters 7, 8, 11, and 12.

Why Should I Care?

The World: The Importance of Informed Opinion

When Americans after September 11, 2001, began to hear about Afghanistan, the Taliban, Islam, and Al Qaeda, it was new information to most of them. Even though some of the information had been previously available through the news media, most Americans had not paid much attention to it.

Americans are generally uninformed about global affairs. The war on terrorism has increased their understanding of some parts of the world, but Americans typically have had less interest in what is occurring elsewhere than have comparably educated people in other countries. Analysts suggest that America's "ocean isolation" is a reason why its citizens are insular. Unlike Europeans, Americans are not surrounded by many other countries. But ocean isolation is not a complete explanation. Americans share a border with Canadians and Mexicans, for example, but know a lot less about Canada and Mexico than Canadians and Mexicans know about the United States.

International terrorism and the increasing globalization of the economy suggest that Americans should pay more attention to the larger world in which they live. Many Americans, for example, were mystified that their country had been targeted for the terrorist attacks. Their initial impulse was to say that the country had been attacked because it represents freedom. As Americans discovered, however, that explanation was incomplete. The terrorists had specific grievances with the United States, including its Middle Eastern policies. The terrorists' decision to target innocent civilians to express their discontent was cowardly and despicable, but as Americans came to understand during the months after the attacks, it was not rooted in envy.

Americans can no longer afford to be comfortable with their ocean isolation. An informed public is better positioned to participate in the making of policies that affect it. As the world shrinks, an expanded horizon is required. For good and ill, developments elsewhere increasingly affect Americans' lives. If Americans are to be in a position to help shape that world rather than being forced to respond to crises thrust on them by that world, they need to be more curious about it. You could start by paying attention to the international coverage in your local newspaper or on a news website.

THE INFLUENCE OF PUBLIC OPINION ON POLICY

Yet unanswered in the discussion is the central question about public opinion: What impact does it have on government?

The fundamental principle of democracy is that the people's view ought to prevail on public issues. This principle is difficult to put into practice. In any society of appreciable size, it is simply not possible for the people to directly formulate public policies and programs. However, democracy can be said to exist once officials take the public's views into account when making policy decisions and once the people have recourse to free and fair elections when they believe their opinions are being ignored.[21]

Some analysts argue that the public's views do not count for enough; the elites, it is claimed, are so entrenched and remote that they pay little attention to the preferences of ordinary citizens.[22] The most comprehensive study ever conducted of the relationship between public opinion and policy, however, concluded otherwise. In a study spanning fifty years of trends, Benjamin Page and Robert Shapiro found a substantial relationship between changes in public opinion and subsequent changes in public policy, particularly on highly visible issues. More often than not, policy changed in response to opinion rather than the reverse. In addition, the more important the issue, the more likely it was that policy adapted to changes in public opinion. Page and Shapiro concluded that U.S. officials are reasonably responsive to public opinion.[23]

Not all scholars have interpreted the evidence on public opinion and policy so favorably,[24] but there is little question that the public's views do have an impact. Public opinion is rarely powerful enough to force officials into a specific course of action, but public opinion does serve as a guiding force in public policy. There are many actions, for example, that officials dare *not* take for fear of public retribution. No politician who wants to stay in office is likely to say, for example, that social security for the elderly should be abolished. And there are many actions that politicians willingly take in order to appeal to the public.[25] In late 1999, for example, the GOP-controlled Congress passed a budget that included funding to hire thousands of new public school teachers. Congressional Republicans had opposed the measure, but education ranked near the top in polls of Americans' policy priorities and the 2000 election was just around the corner. Republicans, reluctant to hand the Democrats a potent campaign issue, enacted the funding measure.

Such examples, however, do not provide an answer to the question of whether government is *sufficiently* responsive to public opinion. This question, as was discussed earlier in the chapter, is a normative one, the answer to which rests on assumptions about the proper relationship between people's everyday opinions and what government does. The question is also complicated by the fact that politics includes a battle over the control of public opinion. People's views are neither fixed nor simply a product of personal circumstances. Public opinion is dynamic and can be changed, activated, and crystallized through political action.

In fact, one of the best indicators of the power of public opinion is the effort of political leaders to harness it in support of their goals. In American politics, popular demand for a policy is a powerful argument for that policy. For this reason and others, great effort is made to organize and represent public opinion through elections (Chapter 7), political parties (Chapter 8), interest groups (Chapter 9), the news media (Chapter 10), and political institutions (Chapters 11 to 14).

Self-Quiz
www.mhhe.com/patterson6

SUMMARY

Public opinion can be defined as those opinions held by ordinary citizens that they openly express. Public officials have many ways of assessing public opinion, such as the outcomes of elections, but have increasingly come to rely on public opinion polls. There are many possible sources of error in polls, and surveys sometimes present a misleading portrayal of the public's views. However, a properly conducted poll can provide an accurate indication of what the public is thinking and can dissuade political leaders from thinking that the views of the most vocal citizens (such as demonstrators and letter writers) are also the views of the broader public.

The process by which individuals acquire their political opinions is called political socialization. During childhood the family and schools are important sources of basic political attitudes, such as beliefs about the parties and the nature of the U.S. political and economic systems. Many of the basic orientations that Americans acquire during childhood remain with them in adulthood, but socialization is a continuing process. Major shifts in opinion during adulthood are usually the consequence of changing political conditions; for example, the Great Depression of the 1930s was the catalyst for wholesale changes in Americans' opinions on the government's economic role. There are also short-term fluctuations in opinion that result from new political issues, problems, and events. Individuals' opinions in these cases are affected by prior beliefs, peers, political leaders, and the news media. Events themselves are also a significant short-term influence on opinions.

The frames of reference that guide Americans' opinions include cultural beliefs, such as individualism, that result in a range of acceptable and unacceptable policy alternatives. Opinions can also stem from ideology, although most citizens do not have a strong and consistent ideological attachment. In addition, individuals develop opinions as a result of group orientations, notably religion, income, occupation, region, race, ethnicity, gender, or age. Partisanship is perhaps the major source of political opinions; Republicans and Democrats differ in their voting behavior and views on many policy issues. However, party loyalty has declined in importance in recent decades as a frame of reference for people's opinions.

Public opinion has a significant influence on government but seldom determines exactly what government will do in a particular instance. Public opinion serves to constrain the policy choices of officials. Some policy actions are beyond the range of possibility because the public will not accept change in existing policy or will not seriously consider policy that seems clearly at odds with basic American values. Evidence indicates that officials are reasonably attentive to public opinion on highly visible and controversial issues of public policy.

KEY TERMS

age-cohort tendency
agents of socialization
conservatives
ideology
liberals
libertarians
party identification
political socialization
population
populists
primacy tendency
probability sample
public opinion
public opinion poll
sample
sampling error
structuring tendency

SUGGESTED READINGS

Delli Carpini, Michael X., and Scott Keeter. *What Americans Know About Politics and Why It Matters.* New Haven, Conn.: Yale University Press, 1996. A synthesis of the American public's knowledge about politics.

Dunn, Charles W., and J. David Woodard. *The Conservative Tradition in America.* Lanham, Md.: Rowman & Littlefield, 1996. A study of the philosophical and political roots of conservatism from its origins to the present.

Jacobs, Lawrence, and Robert Shapiro. *Politicians Don't Pander.* Chicago: University of Chicago Press, 2000. An analysis that concludes politicians are not driven by polls.

MacManus, Susan A. *Young v. Old: Generational Combat in the Twenty-First Century.* Boulder, Colo.: Westview Press, 1996. A study of the emerging conflict in the political self-interest of younger and older Americans.

Noelle-Neumann, Elisabeth. *The Spiral of Silence,* 2d ed. Chicago: University of Chicago Press, 1993. An intriguing theory of how public opinion is formed and muted.

Sobel, Richard. *The Impact of Public Opinion on U.S. Foreign Policy Since Vietnam.* New York: Oxford University Press, 2001. A study of the relationship between public opinion and foreign policy.

Traugott, Michael W., and Paul J. Lavrakas. *The Voter's Guide to Election Polls,* 2d ed. Chatham, N.J.: Chatham House, 2000. A clear guide to survey methods and analysis with an emphasis on election polling.

Zaller, John R. *The Nature and Origins of Mass Opinion.* New York: Cambridge University Press, 1992. A superb analysis of the nature of public opinion.

LIST OF WEBSITES

http://www.gallup.com/
The website of the renowned Gallup Organization; includes the results of recent Gallup polls.

http://www.policy.com/
A nonpartisan site that provides a wealth of information about current public issues.

http://www.princeton.edu/~abelson/
The Princeton Survey Research Center's site offers results from surveys conducted by a variety of polling organizations.

http://www.publicagenda.org/
The nonpartisan Public Agenda's site; it provides opinions, analyses, and educational materials on current policy issues.

7

We are concerned in public affairs, but immersed in our private ones.
—Walter Lippmann[1]

Political Participation and Voting:
Expressing the Popular Will

At stake in the 2002 elections was control of the Congress. Which party would have the leading voice on legislation affecting education, health, welfare, and the environment? Which party would have the greater say in how America responded to the challenges and opportunities of the domestic and global economies? Which party would be entrusted with national security legislation? With so much at stake, it might be thought that Americans would have been eager to cast their ballots for the party of their choice. But in fact more than half of American adults did not vote in the 2002 elections. Despite a concerted get-out-the-vote campaign by the news media and public service groups, the number of people who did not vote was far greater than the number of votes the winning party received in the congressional races.

Voting is a form of **political participation**—a sharing in activities designed to influence public policy and leadership. Political participation involves other activities in addition to voting, such as joining political parties and interest groups, writing to elected officials, demonstrating for political causes, and giving money to political candidates.

Democratic societies are distinguished by their emphasis on citizen participation. The concept of self-government rests on the idea that ordinary people have a right, even an obligation, to involve themselves in the affairs of state. A political system that claims to represent the public's interest is not necessarily a truly democratic system; citizens must also be given meaningful opportunities to participate in the process. From this perspective, the extent of political participation—how much and by whom—is a measure of how fully democratic a society is.[2]

The question of participation also extends to the reasons people are politically involved or not involved. It is one thing if political participation is like attendance at a rock concert, which is mostly a matter of individual taste and proximity, and quite another if participation is like attendance at an elite prep school, which is mostly a matter of social privilege. A democratic political system implies that society will not place substantial barriers in the way of those who want to participate. This chapter points out that differences in the extent of political participation among Americans are explained by both individual and systemic factors, although the latter are more influential in the United States than in most other Western democracies. One result is that the participation rate in U.S. elections is less than that of other countries, particularly among citizens of lower income and less education. The major points made in this chapter are the following:

- *Voter turnout in U.S. elections is low in comparison with that of other democratic nations.* The reasons for this difference include the nature of U.S. election laws, particularly those pertaining to registration requirements and the scheduling of elections.

- *Most citizens do not participate actively in politics in ways other than voting.* Only a small proportion of Americans can be classified as political activists.

- *Most Americans make a sharp distinction between their personal lives and national life.* This attitude reduces their incentive to participate and contributes to a pattern of participation dominated by citizens with higher levels of income and education.

After a hard-fought, decades-long campaign, American women finally won the right to vote in 1920.

political participation A sharing in activities designed to influence public policy and leadership, such as voting, joining political parties and interest groups, writing to elected officials, demonstrating for political causes, and giving money to political candidates.

suffrage The right to vote.

Historical Background

VOTER PARTICIPATION

At the nation's founding, **suffrage**—the right to vote—was restricted to property-owning males. Tom Paine ridiculed this policy in *Common Sense*. Observing that a man whose only item of property was a jackass would lose his right to vote if the jackass died, Paine asked, "Now tell me, which was the voter, the man or the jackass?" It was not until 1840 that all states extended suffrage to propertyless white males, a change made possible by their continued demand for the vote and by the realization on the part of the wealthy that the nation's abundance and openness were natural protections against an assault on property rights by the voting poor.

Women did not secure the vote until 1920, with the ratification of the Nineteenth Amendment. In the 1870s, Susan B. Anthony tried to vote in her hometown of Rochester, New York, asserting that she had a right to do so as a U.S. citizen. The men who placed her under arrest charged her with "illegal voting" and insisted that her proper place was in the home. By 1920, men had run out of pretexts for keeping the vote from women. The best argument that the antisuffragists could muster was that women should not vote because they had no voting experience. Senator Wendell Phillips expressed the pro-suffrage view: "One of two things is true: either woman is like man—and if she is, then a ballot based on brains belongs to her as well as to him. Or she is different, and then man does not know how to vote for her as she herself does."[3]

African Americans had to wait nearly fifty years longer than women to be granted full suffrage. Blacks seemed to have won the right to vote with passage of the Fifteenth Amendment after the Civil War, but as was explained in Chapter 5, they were effectively disenfranchised in the South by a number of electoral tricks, including poll taxes, literacy tests, and whites-only primary elections. The poll tax was a fee of several dollars that had to be paid before one could register to vote. Since most blacks in the South were too poor to pay it, the poll tax barred them from voting. Not until the ratification of the Twenty-fourth

TABLE 7-1 **Opinions on Obligations of Citizens** Americans rank voting as one of the essential obligations of citizenship.

	ESSENTIAL OBLIGATION	VERY IMPORTANT OBLIGATION	SOMEWHAT IMPORTANT	PERSONAL PREFERENCE
Treating all people equally regardless of race or ethnic background	57%	33%	6%	4%
Voting in elections	53	29	9	9
Working to reduce inequality and injustice	41	42	12	6
Being civil to others with whom we may disagree	35	45	14	6
Keeping fully informed about the news and other public issues	30	42	19	10
Donating blood or organs to help with medical needs	20	37	18	26
Volunteering time to community service	16	42	26	16

Source: Used by permission of the 1996 Survey of American Political Culture, James Davison Hunter and Carol Bowman, Directors, University of Virginia.

Amendment in 1964 was the poll tax outlawed in federal elections. Supreme Court decisions and the Voting Rights Act of 1965 swept away other legal barriers to fuller participation by African Americans.

In 1971, the Twenty-sixth Amendment extended voting rights to include citizens eighteen years of age or older. Previously, nearly all states had restricted voting to those twenty-one years of age or older.

Today virtually any American—rich or poor, man or woman, black or white—who is determined to vote can legally and actually do so. Americans attach great importance to the power of their votes. They claim that voting is their greatest source of influence over political leadership and their strongest protection against an uncaring or corrupt government.[4] They also claim that voting is a basic act of citizenship (see Table 7-1). In view of this attitude and the historical struggle of various groups to gain voting rights, the surprising fact is that Americans are not active voters. Millions of them choose not to vote regularly, a tendency that sets them apart from citizens of most other Western democracies.

Factors in Voter Turnout: The United States in Comparative Perspective

Voter turnout is the proportion of persons of voting age who actually vote in a given election. Since the 1960s the turnout level in presidential elections has not reached 60 percent (see Figure 7-1). In the 1996 and 2000 elections, only about half of adults cast a vote for president.

Turnout is even lower in the midterm congressional elections that take place between presidential elections. Midterm election turnout has not reached 50 percent since 1920, nor made it past the 40 percent mark since 1970. After one midterm election, the cartoonist Rigby showed an election clerk eagerly asking a stray cat that had wandered into a polling place, "Are you registered?"[5]

voter turnout The proportion of persons of voting age who actually vote in a given election.

Figure 7–1

Voter Turnout in Presidential Elections, 1960–2000
Voter turnout has declined substantially since the 1960s.
Source: U.S. Bureau of the Census.

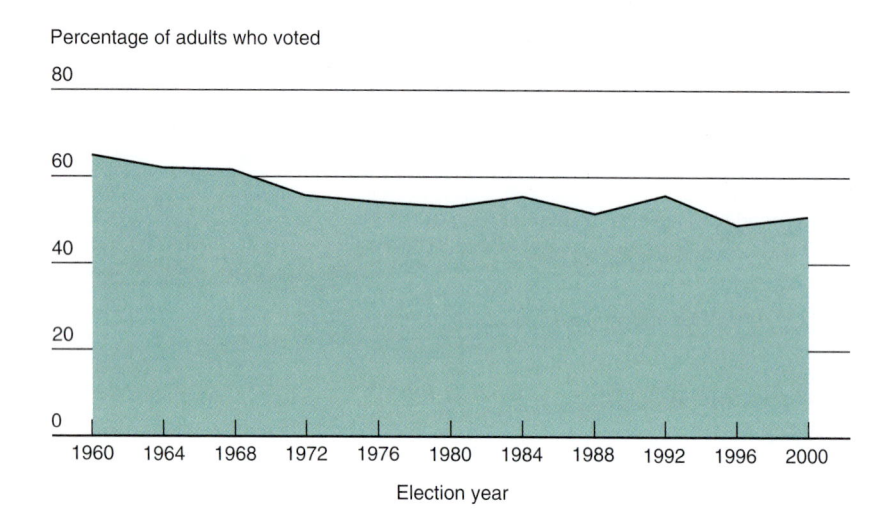

Nonvoting is far more prevalent in the United States than in nearly all other democracies (see "How the United States Compares"). In recent decades, turnout in major national elections has averaged less than 60 percent in the United States, compared with more than 90 percent in Belgium, more than 80 percent in France and Denmark, and more than 70 percent in Great Britain and Germany.[6] The disparity in turnout between the United States and other nations is not as great as these official voting rates indicate. Some nations calculate turnout solely on the basis of eligible adults, whereas the United States bases its figures on all adults, including noncitizens and other ineligible groups. Nevertheless, even when such statistical disparities are corrected, turnout in U.S. elections remains low in comparison with that of nearly every other Western democracy.

Voting does not require vast amounts of time. It takes most people longer to go to a video store and select a movie than it takes to go to the neighborhood polling place and cast a ballot. Thus, the explanation for the relatively low turnout rate of Americans must entail considerations other than the time it takes to vote. The major factors that depress turnout in U.S. elections in comparison with other democracies include registration requirements, the frequency of elections, and the lack of clear-cut differences between the political parties.

Registration Requirements

Before Americans are allowed to vote, they must be registered—that is, their names must appear on an official list of eligible voters. **Registration** began around 1900 as a way of preventing voters from casting more than one ballot during an election. Fraudulent voting had become a favorite tactic of political party machines in communities where the population was too large for residents to be personally known to poll watchers. However, the extra effort involved in registering placed an added burden on honest citizens. Because citizens could now vote only if they had registered beforehand, those people who forgot or otherwise failed to do so found themselves unable to participate on election day. Turnout in U.S. elections declined steadily after registration was instituted.[7]

registration The practice of placing citizens' names on an official list of voters before they are eligible to exercise their right to vote.

HOW THE UNITED STATES COMPARES

Voter Turnout

The United States ranks near the bottom among the world's democracies in the percentage of eligible citizens who participate in national elections. One reason for the low voter turnout is that individual Americans are responsible for registering to vote, whereas in most other democracies, voters are automatically registered by government officials. In addition, unlike some other democracies, the United States does not encourage voting by holding elections on the weekend or by imposing penalties, such as fines, on those who do not participate.

Another factor affecting the turnout rate in the United States is the absence of a major labor or socialist party, which would serve to bring lower-income citizens to the polls. In democracies where such parties exist, the turnout difference between upper- and lower-income groups is relatively small. In the United States, however, lower-income persons are much less likely to vote than higher-income persons are.

COUNTRY	APPROXIMATE VOTER TURNOUT	AUTOMATIC REGISTRATION?	SOCIAL DEMOCRAT, SOCIALIST, OR LABOR PARTY?	ELECTION DAY A HOLIDAY OR WEEKEND DAY?
Belgium	90%	Yes	Yes	Yes
Germany	85%	Yes	Yes	Yes
Denmark	85%	Yes	Yes	No
Italy	80%	Yes	Yes	Yes
Austria	80%	Yes	Yes	Yes
France	80%	No	Yes	Yes
Great Britain	60%	Yes	Yes	No
Canada	60%	Yes	No	No
Japan	60%	Yes	Yes	Yes
United States	50%	No	No	No

Source: Developed from multiple sources.

Although other democracies also require registration, they place this responsibility on government. In most European nations, public officials have the duty to enroll citizens on registration lists. The United States—in keeping with its *individualistic* culture—is one of the few democracies in which registration is the individual's responsibility.[8] In addition, registration laws have traditionally been established by the state governments, and some states make it relatively difficult for citizens to qualify. Registration periods and locations are usually not highly publicized, and many citizens simply do not know when or where to register.[9] Eligibility can also be a problem. In most states, a citizen must establish legal residency by living in the same place for a minimum period, usually thirty days, before becoming eligible to register.

Fighting Words

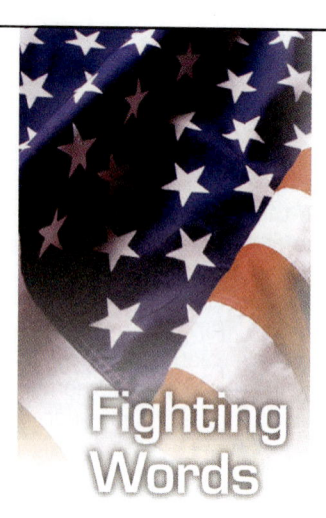

Should Voting through the Internet Be Allowed?

As nonvoting has increased and Internet use has spread, it was only a matter of time before voting through the Internet would be considered. In 2000, Arizona voters had the opportunity to vote online in the state's Democratic presidential primary. Several states are moving toward online voting for all elections, and the U.S. military has established a pilot online voting option for troops overseas. Advocates see online voting as the answer to the downward trend in voter turnout. Not everyone agrees that Internet voting is the solution. Opponents say that Internet voting would lead to a sharp increase in election fraud. They also note that Internet voting would disadvantage groups, primarily the poor and minorities, that have limited access to the Internet.

Yes: Voting is an important example of an information activity that could be improved with the help of the Internet. Where I live, we vote for judges, but I often don't know who deserves my ballot, since little information about their judicial records is available. I look forward to an Internet-based alternative. Instead of voting in person or mailing in an absentee ballot, I expect to be able to vote from my PC. While pondering the choices at my leisure, I'll be able to see what the candidates say about themselves, listen to speeches they've given, check their judicial records, read or watch news reports, survey their endorsements or the recommendations of nonpartisan groups, or even ask individuals I trust who they intend to vote for—all electronically. The result will be a better-informed vote, and probably greater participation.
—*Bill Gates, Chairman, Microsoft Corporation*

No: Statistics on Internet use raise concerns that Internet voting will only increase access for a limited population group. Although Internet use is rapidly expanding, the typical user is still an under-35 affluent male college graduate, and there is growing concern about the disparity of access for certain population groups. . . . For Internet voting to become a reality, it must be able to meet the same requirements that current public elections are required (though increasingly fail) to meet—guarantee of ballot secrecy, guarantee of ballot sanctity, and universal availability. . . . Only when the critical issues of security, access, and public confidence have been fully addressed should any U.S. jurisdiction open the Pandora's box that Internet voting could represent.
—*The Voting Integrity Project*

States with a tradition of lenient registration laws generally have a higher turnout than other states do. Idaho, Maine, Minnesota, New Hampshire, Wisconsin, and Wyoming, which are states that allow people to register at their polling place on election day, have high turnout rates. Those states that have erected the most barriers are in the South, where restrictive registration was originally intended to prevent black people from voting. These historical differences continue to be reflected in state voter turnout levels (see "States in the Nation").

In 1993, in an effort to increase registration levels nationwide, Congress enacted a voting registration law known as "motor voter." Its supporters predicted that the legislation, so named because it requires states to permit people

CHAPTER 7   Political Participation and Voting: Expressing the Popular Will

STATES IN THE NATION

State-by-State Voter Turnout in 2000 Presidential Election

Southern states have a tradition of more restrictive registration laws, and even today they tend to have lower rates of voter turnout. States with large recent immigrant populations, such as California and New York, also have lower turnout.

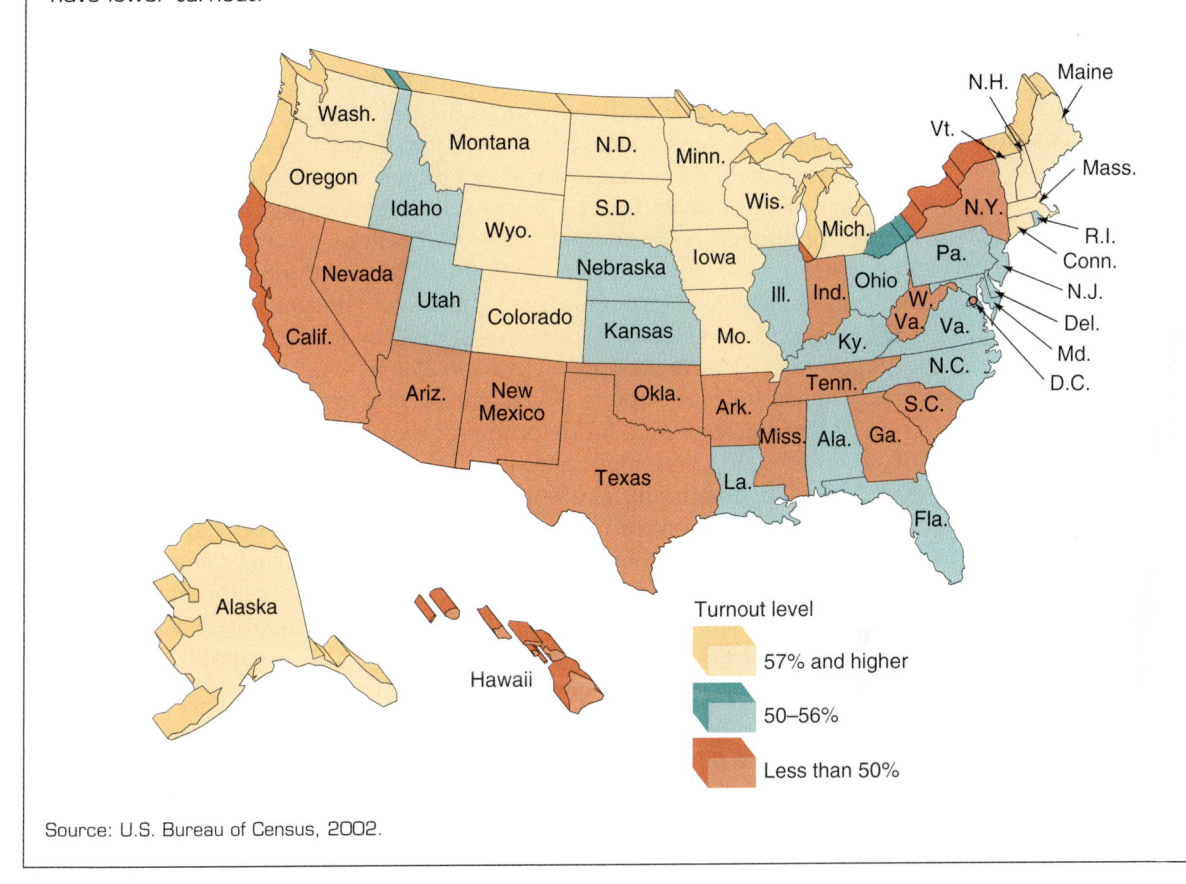

Turnout level:
- 57% and higher
- 50–56%
- Less than 50%

Source: U.S. Bureau of Census, 2002.

to register to vote when applying for a driver's license (it also requires states to provide registration through mail and at certain state welfare offices), would add as many as 50 million new voters to registration rolls by the end of the century. The prediction seemed optimistic, because state agencies cannot compel applicants to register. Congressional Republicans made their support of the legislation contingent on this nonmandatory provision. They had blocked the bill for several years, fearing that it would help the Democrats by adding mainly lower-income Americans to the registration rolls. For the same reason, Republican governors in several states, including California and South Carolina, delayed putting the law into effect. Partisan concerns have always played a role in shaping registration laws, but in this case they appear miscalculated. Registrations under the motor-voter law have been about evenly divided between the Republican and Democratic parties.

By the time of the 2000 presidential election, an estimated ten million additional people had been registered through the motor-voter law. Yet the increase did not result in a higher turnout rate; it actually declined between 1992 and 2000. Clearly, registration is only one of the factors underlying America's low turnout rate.

Ballots Cast but Not Counted

In the 2000 election, more than one hundred million votes were officially recorded as having been cast for president. However, more than two million other votes were cast but not counted. Some could not be read by a voting machine because the voter had not marked the ballot clearly or had placed a mark outside the designated space. Some were punch-card ballots that could not be read because the hole in the card was not punched through completely.

It has been estimated that 2 percent of all ballots cast in U.S. elections are spoiled for one reason or another. These votes rarely get attention because they do not affect an election's outcome. In the 2000 presidential election, however, they may have been decisive. George W. Bush won the presidency on the basis of a 537 vote victory in Florida, where tens of thousands of ballots went uncounted. His opponent, Al Gore, mounted a legal challenge to get the ballots counted, but it failed when the U.S. Supreme Court intervened to stop a hand recount on the grounds that the standards for determining a legal ballot were vague (see Chapter 14). The Florida vote highlighted a glaring weakness in the conduct of U.S. elections. Many communities are unable or unwilling to invest public funds in balloting systems that have a low error rate. Most of the inadequate machinery is found in minority areas. In Chicago, for example, the error rate is three times lower in white neighborhoods than in African-American neighborhoods, where older and less reliable balloting methods are used. By comparison, many Western European countries have uniform national standards for balloting and, apparently, a smaller percentage of uncounted ballots than does the United States.

Frequency of Elections

The United States holds more elections than any other nation. No other democracy has elections for the lower chamber of its national legislature (the equivalent of the U.S. House of Representatives) as often as every two years, and none schedules elections for chief executive as often as every four years.[10] In addition, elections of state and local officials in the United States are often scheduled separately from national races. Four-fifths of the states elect their governors in nonpresidential election years,[11] and 60 percent of U.S. cities hold elections of municipal officials in odd-numbered years.[12]

This staggered scheduling reflects in some cases a deliberate effort by state and local officials to insulate their election races from the possible effects of other campaigns. During Franklin D. Roosevelt's four terms as president, for example, Republicans in several states, including New York and Connecticut, backed constitutional amendments that required gubernatorial races to be held in nonpresidential years. The purpose was to prevent other Democratic candidates from riding into office on Roosevelt's coattails. Several Democratic-controlled legislatures took similar action in the 1950s, when the popular Republican Dwight D. Eisenhower was president.

Judge Robert Rosenberg of Broward County (Florida) Canvassing Board inspects an uncounted presidential ballot. Tens of thousands of such ballots were uncounted in Florida's decisive presidential vote contest.

The frequency of U.S. elections reduces turnout by increasing the effort required to participate in all of them.[13] Most European nations have less frequent elections, and the responsibility of voting is thus less burdensome. Many European nations also schedule their elections on Sundays or declare election day to be a national holiday, thus making it more convenient for working people to vote. In the United States, elections are traditionally held on Tuesdays, and most people must vote before or after work.

The contrast with European practice is especially marked in the case of primary elections. The United States is the only democratic nation in which party nominees are commonly chosen by voters through primary elections rather than by party leaders.[14] Consequently, Americans are asked to vote twice to fill a single office. Many voters skip the primaries, preferring to vote just once, in the general election.

Party Differences

A final explanation for low voter turnout in the United States has to do with voters' perception that there is not much difference between the major political parties (see Figure 7–2). More than half of Americans claim that it does not make a big difference whether the Republicans or the Democrats gain control of government.[15] This belief is not entirely unfounded. The two major American political parties do not normally differ greatly in their policies. Each party depends on citizens of all economic interests and social backgrounds for support; consequently, neither party can afford to take an extreme position that would alienate any sizable segment of the electorate. For example, both parties share a commitment to the private enterprise system and to social security for the elderly (see Chapter 8).

Parties in Europe tend to divide more sharply over economic policies. There the choice between a conservative party and a socialist party may mean a choice between private and government ownership of major industries. Studies indicate that turnout is higher in nations whose political parties represent clear-cut alternatives, particularly when religious or class divisions are involved. Conversely, turnout is lower when, as in the United States, a nation's parties compete for the loyalty of voters of all religions and classes.[16] European parties, particularly those on the left, are also more closely tied to other organizations, such as labor unions, which assist in the mobilization of the electorate.[17]

Why Some Americans Vote and Others Do Not

Even though turnout is lower in the United States than in other democracies, some Americans do vote in all or nearly all elections. But other Americans seldom or never vote. What accounts for such *individual* differences?

The factors that account for differences in public opinion (see Chapter 6) are not in all cases related to turnout differences. The turnout rates of men and women, for example, are similar.[18] Race was once a very significant predictor of turnout but has become less important. African Americans still have a lower turnout rate than do whites, but the difference, which is less than 10 percent in presidential elections, is much lower than the 40 percent difference that existed in 1960 (see Chapter 5).

Liberty & Equality

What's Your Opinion?

Voting: A Right?
On election day, officials unfailingly urge Americans "to get out and vote." Some of these officials are not to be taken seriously. On the whole, U.S. elections are conducted fairly and openly with the support of tens of thousands of public-minded officials and volunteer poll watchers. Lurking in the shadows, however, are official actions that serve to depress the vote. Registration closing date, early poll closings, and flawed voting machine are obstacles to fuller participation, just as in the past such actions as whites-only primaries and poll taxes were obstacles.

More so than in other Western democracies, voting in the United States has been subject to political manipulation. America's electoral history is replete with examples of public policies designed to deny or suppress the vote. Voting has been treated as a privilege rather than an inalienable right, something to be earned (or, in some cases, arbitrarily withheld) rather than something so intrinsic to citizenship that government makes every reasonable effort to promote its exercise.

What, in your opinion, explains the historical tendency? Do you think Americans' liberty and equality have been diminished by the tendency?

Figure 7-2

The Perceived Effect of Electing a Republican or Democratic President, 2000. Most Americans believe that their lives and the country as a whole will not be greatly affected by whether the Republican or Democratic candidate wins the presidency.

Source: Used by permission of the Shorenstein Center Poll for the Vanishing Voter Project.

"How much difference will it make whether the Democrat or Republican candidate wins the presidency?"

To the lives of people like you?
- 31% Just some
- 18% Quite a bit
- 7% Great deal
- 4% Not sure
- 40% Little/none

To the future of the country as a whole?
- 35% Just some
- 21% Quite a bit
- 11% Great deal
- 5% Not sure
- 28% Little/none

Volunteers at a community event attempt to interest citizens in registering so that they can vote in the next election. Nearly all democracies have automatic voter registration. The United States does not, which makes voter registration efforts an important factor in election turnout.

In contrast, age, education, and income do affect voter turnout, as do civic attitudes.

Feelings of Civic Duty, Apathy, and Alienation

civic duty The belief of an individual that civic and political participation is a responsibility of citizenship.

Regular voters are characterized by a strong sense of **civic duty**—that is, they regard participation in elections as one of the main responsibilities of citizenship. By election day in 1996, it was clear from the polls that Bill Clinton would handily defeat Bob Dole, yet regular voters were undeterred. Although they knew their votes would not sway the election, they voted anyway in order to fulfill their duty as citizens. This sense of duty is an attitude that is usually acquired as part of adolescent and childhood political socialization. When parents vote regularly and take an interest in politics, their children are likely to grow up viewing the vote as an important expression of their citizenship. Schools reinforce this belief by stressing the importance of the right to vote.

Many citizens do not have a strong sense of civic duty, and some of them display almost no interest in politics. **Apathy** is the term that describes a general lack of interest in or concern with politics. Just as some people would not attend the Super Bowl even if it were free and being played across the street, some people would not bother to vote even if a ballot were delivered to their door. As with civic duty, a sense of apathy is often the consequence of adolescent and childhood socialization. When parents disparage voting and other forms of political participation, their children are likely to hold a similar view when they reach voting age.

Alienation is the term that describes a sense of personal powerlessness that includes the notion that government does not care about the opinions of people like oneself.[19] Alienation diminishes people's interest in political participation.[20] It might be thought foolish for people to withdraw from politics when they believe government is inept and uncaring. Yet, for some individuals, the vote is as much an affirmation of citizenship as it is an opportunity to influence the direction of government. Most people know that their single vote is unlikely to affect the outcome of an election. When disgusted with government, they may choose simply to retreat from politics.

Voter turnout is associated with the level of trust in government, rising when it rises and falling when it falls.[21] For this reason, some analysts predict that voter turnout may increase somewhat in upcoming elections. After the September 11, 2001, terrorist attacks on the World Trade Center and the Pentagon, trust rose sharply as the government pursued its war on terrorism. A CBS News/New York Times poll in November found that 55 percent of Americans trusted government to do what is right most of the time. As recently as 1998, the level had stood at 26 percent. Trust had been very high in the early 1960s but fell during the Vietnam and Watergate periods. It remained low throughout most of the next three decades as economic setbacks, political scandals, and other developments undermined Americans' faith in their political leaders and institutions. Trust had begun to rebound in 1999 in response to the nation's booming economy but then jumped dramatically in late 2001.

apathy A feeling of personal noninterest or unconcern with politics.

alienation A feeling of personal powerlessness that includes the notion that government does not care about the opinions of people like oneself.

Age

When viewers tuned in MTV at various times in the 2000 presidential campaign, they might have thought at first that they had selected the wrong channel. Rather than a video of their favorite rock star, they saw the presidential candidates urging young people to vote.

The candidates had targeted the right audience for their get-out-the-vote message. Young adults are much less likely to vote than middle-aged citizens are. Even senior citizens, despite the infirmities of old age, have a far higher turnout rate than do voters under the age of thirty. Young people are less likely to have the political concern that can accompany such lifestyle characteristics as homeownership, a permanent career, and a family.[22] In fact, citizens under the age of thirty have a lower turnout rate than do all other demographic groups of comparable size.

Young adults have the lowest voter turnout rate of any major demographic group. Efforts to increase their participation include MTV's "Rock the Vote" campaign, which often features celebrity participants. Pictured here are (from left to right) humorist Bill Maher and singers Macy Gray and Moby.

Young voters have also contributed disproportionately to the decline in voter turnout in recent decades. Of the eligible eighteen- to twenty-four-year-olds, about half voted in 1972 compared with less than a third in 2000. On the other hand, turnout among those forty-five years of age and older declined only a few percentage points during this period.

Education

What does your college education mean? One thing it means is that you have a higher likelihood of becoming an active citizen. The difference is striking. Persons with a college education are about 40 percent more likely to vote than are persons with a grade school education. Researchers have concluded that education generates a greater interest in politics, a higher level of political information, a greater confidence that one can make a difference politically, and peer pressure to participate—all of which are related to the tendency to vote.[23]

Education, in fact, is the single best predictor of voter turnout. This fact led some analysts in the 1950s to conclude that increasing the overall level of education was the way to increase levels of turnout. Paradoxically, the overall education level of the American people has increased since then, but turnout has dropped. Political scientists have concluded that the positive effect of increased education levels has been more than offset by people's declining political interest and party loyalties.

Economic Class

Turnout is also strongly related to economic status, as measured by income level (see Figure 7–3). Americans at the bottom of the economic ladder are about half as likely to vote in presidential elections as are those at the top.[24] The difference is even larger in primaries and nonpresidential elections.[25]

In European democracies, economic status does not affect turnout to such a high degree. Europeans of lower income levels are encouraged to participate by class-based organizations and traditions—strong socialist parties, politically oriented trade unions, and class-based political ideologies.[26] The United States does not have, and never has had, a major socialist or labor party.[27] The Democratic

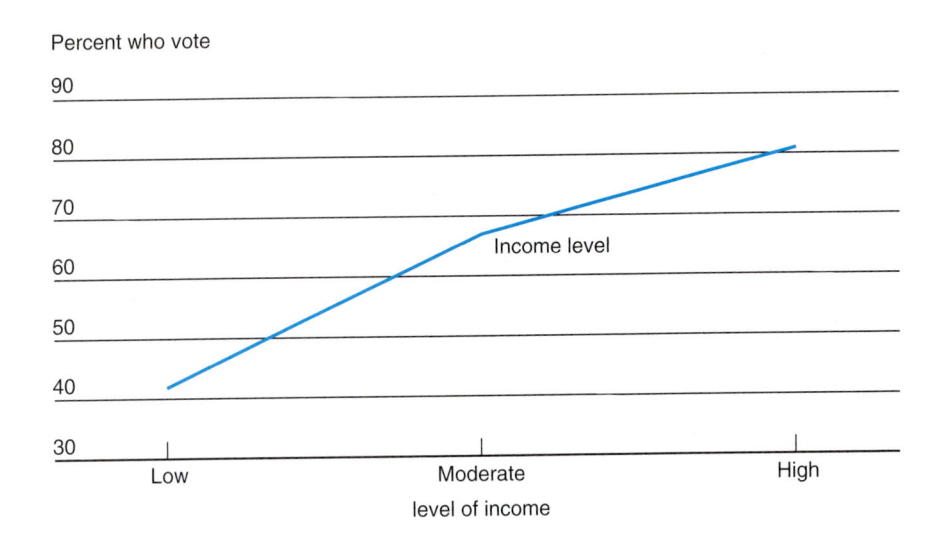

Figure 7-3

Voter Turnout and Level of Income
Americans of lower income are much less likely to vote.
Source: U.S. Bureau of the Census.

party by and large represents poorer Americans, but their interests tend to be subordinated to the party's concern for the American middle class, which, because of its size and voting regularity, is the key to victory in U.S. elections. In 2000, Americans in the bottom third by income were 30 percent more likely than those in the top third to say that the election's outcome would have no appreciable effect on their lives.[28]

The Impact of the Vote

Through their votes, the people choose the representatives who will govern in their name. But what is the relationship between the vote and the actions of government? What influence does the vote have on public policy? Fuller answers to these questions will be provided later (see Chapters 8, 11, and 12), but it is useful to consider at least a partial response at this point.

Elections do *not* ordinarily produce a popular mandate for the policies advocated by the winning candidate. A mandate requires voters to consciously choose between candidates on the basis of the promises they make during the campaign. A difficulty with this interpretation of election results is that voters are not usually well informed about candidates' policy positions. In U.S. House campaigns, less than half the voters can recall on their own the names of the two major-party nominees in their district, and even fewer can identify these candidates' positions on major issues.[29] In presidential races, the voters are better informed, but most of them cannot readily recall more than a few of the differences in the candidates' platforms.

Several influences combine to limit the voters' awareness of issues. The candidates do not always make their positions altogether clear, either because they fear that taking a firm stand will lose them votes or because they do not have specific policies in mind. Many candidates have dodged the abortion issue in recent years by expressing personal opposition to it while at the same time promising to uphold a woman's right to choose as long as the courts permit it.

Why Should I Care?

Voter Participation: Why It Matters

Some observers take comfort in low-turnout elections. They claim that the country is better off if less interested and less knowledgeable citizens stay home on election day. In a 1997 cover story in the *Atlantic Monthly*, Robert Kaplan wrote: "The last thing America needs is more voters—particularly badly educated and alienated ones—with a passion for politics." The gist of this age-old argument is that low turnout protects society from erratic or even dangerous shifts in power. However, America's voters have not acted whimsically. Except for an interlude in the 1780s, when the Articles of Confederation governed the United States, erratic voting has not been a persistent source of political instability.

On the other hand, a low participation rate is a problem. As the electorate has shrunk, it has become increasingly less representative of the public as a whole in its opinions. Polls indicate that even the outcomes of several recent elections would have changed if turnout had been substantially higher. And even if greater voter turnout would not have altered the outcomes, campaign platforms have always been tailored to those who do vote. As the political scientists Steve Rosenstone and Mark Hanson note in *Mobilization, Participation, and Democracy in America* (1993): "The idle go unheard: They do not speak up, define the agenda, frame the issues, or affect the choices leaders make."

Voting can strengthen democracy in other ways, too. When people vote, they are more attentive to politics and are better informed about issues affecting them. As the philosopher John Stuart Mill theorized a century ago, voting also deepens community involvement. Studies indicate that voters participate more frequently in community affairs and are more likely to work with others on community projects. Of course, these associations say more about the type of person who votes than about the effect of voting. But recent evidence, as Harvard University's Robert Putnam notes in *Bowling Alone* (2000), "suggests that voting itself encourages volunteering and other forms of good citizenship."

Voting among young adults in particular has fallen off dramatically. When eighteen- to twenty-one-year-old citizens gained eligibility to vote in the 1972 election, nearly 50 percent of them voted. In 2000, only about 30 percent did so. Unless the turnout trend among young voters is reversed, the overall turnout rate will continue to fall, because the oldest generation, those who grew up during the Depression and World War II, participate at very high rates. Some analysts believe that the terrorist attacks on the World Trade Center and the Pentagon in 2001 will have the effect of renewing interest in politics and thereby in voting. The future of voting participation in America could well rest on whether that prediction is accurate.

Changes in registration laws have made it easier for students to vote if they choose to do so. Voting is not a time-consuming task, and the benefits to the individual and society are considerable. Have you registered yet?

Additionally, the news media have increasingly focused their election coverage not on issues but on the strategic aspects of the candidates' pursuit of office. By covering campaigns as if they were a strategic game, the media deemphasize substantive issues of policy, thereby making it more difficult for the voters to discover where the candidates stand.

Finally, voters can hardly be aware of issues if they are personally inattentive to politics. Most citizens do not follow campaigns closely and do not necessarily gain knowledge of even highly publicized issues.[30] In 2000, only about half of adults could identify Bush's and Gore's positions even on the candidates' top issues—tax cuts and prescription drugs for the elderly, respectively.[31]

Voters have turned out in relatively low numbers in recent U.S. elections. Some analysts think the terrorist attacks on New York and Washington, D.C., in 2001 could reverse the trend.

There are, to be sure, some voters who are highly informed on the issues and cast their ballots on this basis. **Prospective voting** is a term used to describe this forward-looking type of voting. Prospective voting occurs when voters know the issue positions of the candidates and choose the candidate whose promises best match their own issue preferences.

A more prevalent form of voting is **retrospective voting,** which is the situation in which voters support the incumbent party or candidate when they are pleased with the performance and reverse their position when they are displeased. Bill Clinton's victories in 1992 and 1996 illustrate the importance that voters attach to past governmental performance. The U.S. economy in 1992 was in its longest recession since World War II, and the situation soured voters on the incumbent president George Bush. Three-fourths of the American public expressed dissatisfaction with his handling of the economy, and their dissatisfaction translated into Bush's defeat. He lost by a substantial margin to Clinton, who, despite people's reservations about his personal character, represented the prospect of change. According to the National Election Studies survey, about 80 percent of the voters who supported Bush in 1988 but who deserted him in 1992 believed that the economy was the nation's most important problem.

By 1996, the nation's economy had recovered. Economic growth was strong, jobs were plentiful, and consumer confidence was high. Clinton's opponent, Bob Dole, tried to persuade voters that Clinton's personal character was reason enough to deny him a second term. But voters were satisfied with Clinton's handling of the economy and returned him to office.

As in these cases, economic conditions are usually the key factor in the electorate's retrospective judgments. When voters' confidence in the in-party's handling of the economy has been high, its nominee has usually won the presidential election. Conversely, its nominee has usually lost when the voters are dissatisfied with the economy.[32] Congressional elections are affected to a lesser extent by national conditions because these races often hinge on local issues and incumbents' superior funding and name recognition (see Chapter 11).

prospective voting A form of electoral judgment in which voters choose the candidate whose policy promises most closely match their own preferences.

retrospective voting A form of electoral judgment in which voters support the incumbent candidate or party when its policies are judged to have succeeded and oppose the incumbent candidate or party when its policies are judged to have failed.

Retrospective voting is a somewhat weaker form of public control than prospective voting, because it occurs after the fact: government has already acted, and nothing can change what has taken place. Nevertheless, retrospective voting can be an effective form of popular control over policy because it forces public officials to anticipate the voters' likely response in the next election. The fear that they might be voted out of office by an electorate upset with their policies is a powerful constraint on elected representatives.[33]

CONVENTIONAL FORMS OF PARTICIPATION OTHER THAN VOTING

In one sense, voting is an unrivaled form of citizen participation. Free and open elections are the defining characteristic of democratic government, so voting is regarded as the most basic duty of citizens.[34] Voting is also the only form of citizen participation engaged in by a majority of adults in every democratic country.[35]

In another sense, however, voting is a restricted form of participation. Citizens have the opportunity to vote only at a particular time and place, and only on those predetermined items listed on a ballot. Voting takes up less than an hour a year for most citizens, and there is no guarantee that candidates will be able to keep the promises they made to the voters during the campaign. Other forms of participation offer a greater opportunity for personal influence or involvement. These may be divided into campaign activities, community activities, lobbying group activities, attentiveness to the news, and virtual participation.

Campaign Activities

A citizen may engage in such campaign-related activities as working for a candidate or a party, attending election rallies or meetings, contributing money, and wearing a candidate's campaign button. The more demanding of these activities, such as doing volunteer work for a candidate or a party, require a lot more time and effort than voting does. These activities are also less imbued with notions of civic duty than is voting.[36] Not surprisingly, the proportion of citizens who engage in these activities is relatively small. For example, less than one in twenty adult Americans say they worked for a party or a candidate within the past year. Most of these citizens are strong partisans with a keen interest in politics.

Nevertheless, campaign participation is higher in the United States than in Europe. A five-country comparative study found that Americans ranked ahead of citizens of Germany, Austria, the Netherlands, and Great Britain in such activities as volunteering to work for a party or a candidate during an election campaign.[37] One reason Americans, even though they vote at a lower rate than Europeans do, are more likely than Europeans to work in a campaign is that they have more opportunities to do so.[38] Elections take place more often in the United States, and citizens can become involved in an election campaign by volunteering to work for either a party or a candidate (see Chapter 8). In Europe, campaigns are organized through the parties, and participation opportunities for those who are not party members are restricted. Moreover, the United States is a federal system, which results in campaigns for national, state, and local

Youthful volunteers work to fix up a children's playground. Americans are more likely than citizens of other democracies to take part in voluntary community activities.

offices. A citizen who wishes to participate is almost certain to find an opportunity at one level of office or another. Most of the governments of Europe are unitary in form (see Chapter 2), which means that there are fewer elective offices and thus fewer campaigns in which to participate.

Community Activities

Many Americans participate in public affairs not through campaigns and political parties, but through local organizations such as parent-teacher associations, neighborhood groups, business clubs, church-affiliated groups, and hospital auxiliaries. Apart from their other purposes, these organizations also serve as a means to influence the public life of the community.

The actual number of citizens who participate actively in a community group is difficult to estimate, but the number is surely in the tens of millions. The United States has a tradition of community participation that goes back to colonial days. Moreover, compared with local communities in Europe, those in the United States have more authority over policy issues, which is an added incentive to participation. Because of increased mobility and other factors, Americans may be less tied to their local communities than in the past and therefore less involved in community action. Nevertheless, half of Americans claim that they volunteer time to groups and community causes, compared with 20 percent or less in most European countries. When it comes to donating money to a group, Americans also have an edge on Europeans (see Figure 7–4).

In a widely publicized book entitled *Bowling Alone*, Harvard's Robert Putnam claims that America is undergoing a decline in its **social capital** (the sum of the face-to-face civic interactions among citizens in a society).[39] Putnam argues that there has been a continuing erosion of civic engagement. The relationships fostered by this participation are the foundation of democratic life. They bring citizens together, broaden and deepen people's understanding of other points of view, and provide the skills that foster continued participation in public affairs. Putnam attributes the decline to television and other factors that are drawing people inward and away from participation in civic and political groups. Not all

social capital The sum of face-to-face interactions among citizens in a society.

Figure 7–4
Conventional Participation in Three Countries

Americans are more actively involved in volunteering time and donating money to groups and community causes than are the French or Germans.

Source: From Helmut I. Anheier, Lester M. Salamon, and Edith Archambault, "Participating Citizens; U.S.–Europe Comparisons in Volunteer Action," *The Public Perspective*, March/April 1994. © The Roper Center for Public Opinion Research, University of CT, Storrs, CT. Used by permission.

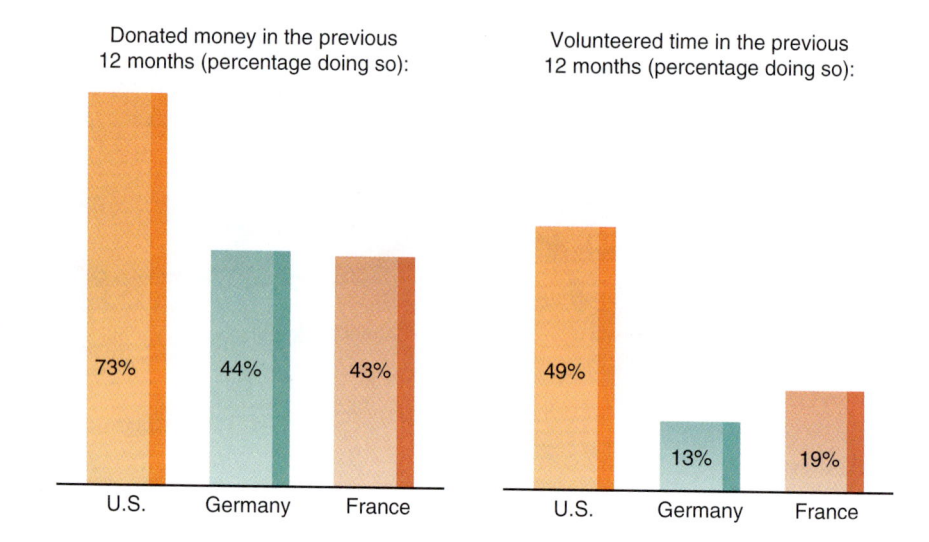

Donated money in the previous 12 months (percentage doing so):
- U.S.: 73%
- Germany: 44%
- France: 43%

Volunteered time in the previous 12 months (percentage doing so):
- U.S.: 49%
- Germany: 13%
- France: 19%

scholars accept Putnam's interpretation of trends in civic participation (some indicators point toward a rise in certain types of participation),[40] but no one challenges his assumption about the importance of high levels of civic participation. And no democratic theorist has suggested that there can be "too much" community involvement.

Lobbying Group Activities

Increasingly, Americans are also involved in public affairs through membership in lobbying groups. This form of participation seldom consists of more than the contribution of annual dues that enable a national organization to pressure government officials or otherwise attempt to influence public policy. Examples of these groups are the National Organization for Women, Common Cause, the Christian Moral Government Fund, the American Civil Liberties Union, and the National Conservative Political Action Committee. Chapter 9 discusses lobbying groups more fully.

Following Politics in the Media

Campaign work and community participation are active forms of political involvement. There is also a passive form of participation: following politics by reading newspapers and newsmagazines and by listening to news reports on television and radio. It can safely be said that no act of political participation takes up more of people's time than does news consumption. The news is important to citizen participation: if people are to participate effectively and intelligently in politics, they must be aware of what is taking place in their communities, in their nation, and in the world.

News about politics is within easy reach of nearly all Americans. More than 95 percent of U.S. homes have a television set, and about 50 percent of Americans receive a daily newspaper. However, the regular audience for news is much smaller than these figures suggest. The mere fact of having a television or

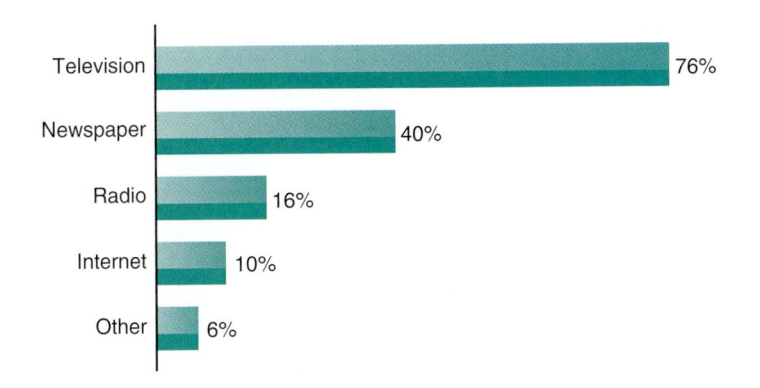

Figure 7-5

Americans' Major News Sources

When Americans are asked where they get most of their news, they mention television most often.

Television 76%
Newspaper 40%
Radio 16%
Internet 10%
Other 6%

Source: Pew Research Center for the People and the Press, February 2001. Totals more than 100 percent because of multiple responses.

getting a daily paper does not mean that a person pays close attention to the news these media provide. If the regular audience for politics is defined as those who read a newspaper's political sections or watch television newscasts on a regular basis, then about a third of Americans can be classified as closely attentive to the news. Another third follows the news intermittently, catching an occasional newscast or scanning a paper's news sections somewhat often. The final third pays no appreciable attention to the news either on television or in a newspaper.

Television is the medium through which most Americans get most of their news (see Figure 7–5). In recent decades, citizens who say television is their main source of news have substantially outnumbered those who rely mainly on a newspaper. Radio and magazines account for even smaller proportions. The figures are somewhat misleading in that people are asked where they get "most" of their news, not how much news they actually get. Some of the people who say they get "most" of their news from television do not watch the news a lot. They do not read a newspaper at all, so that even a little exposure to television news makes it their leading news source.

The news audience has shrunk considerably in size in recent years. Newspapers have lost audience to television newscasts, which in turn have lost audience to television entertainment programs. Before cable television was widely available, many television viewers had no alternative to a newscast during the dinner hour. With cable, viewers always have a wide variety of choices, and many viewers, as many as 40 percent by some estimates, choose to ignore the news unless a sensational event occurs, such as the terrorist attacks on the World Trade Center and Pentagon on September 11, 2001.

The audience for major televised political events has also fallen off. Although they are still a major attraction, even the October presidential debates get less attention than before (see Figure 7–6). The four Kennedy-Nixon debates in 1960 each attracted roughly 60 percent of all households with television sets. When debates resumed with Carter and Ford in 1976, viewers again flocked to their TVs, as they also did for the single Reagan-Carter face-off in 1980. Since then, however, except for the Clinton-Bush-Perot encounters in 1992, debate audiences have been declining. Only 46 percent of the country's television households watched the two Reagan-Mondale debates in 1984. Barely more than 36 percent saw the Bush-Dukakis debates in 1988. The Clinton-Dole debates in

Figure 7-6
Debate Audiences Have Steadily Declined

The audience for the October presidential debates has fallen by half since the 1970s.

Source: Adapted from Thomas E. Patterson, *The Vanishing Voter* (New York: Knopf, 2002), ch. 1.

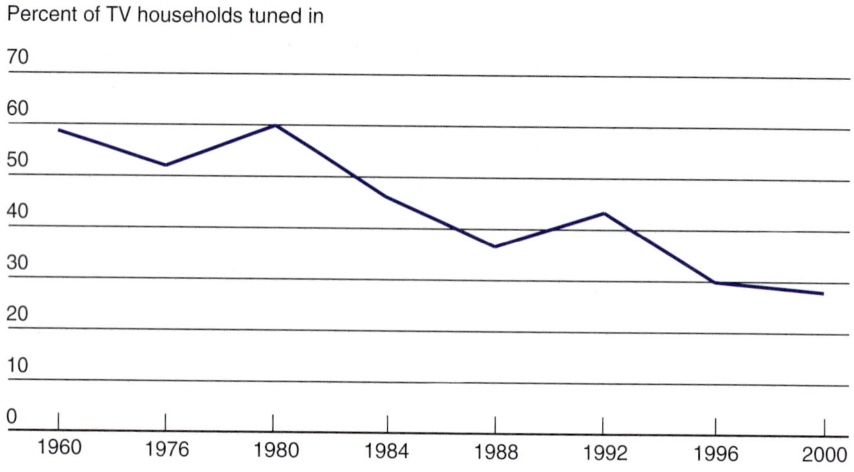

1996 averaged a mere 29 percent. The debate audiences in 2000 were widely expected to exceed that level. The Bush-Gore contest was much tighter than the Clinton-Dole race, and large numbers of voters had not yet settled on a candidate. Yet the audience rating for the first Bush-Gore debate was no higher than for the first Clinton-Dole debate. The third debate had a 26 percent rating—the lowest ever. The 2000 debates drew on average about 45 million viewers—25 percent fewer viewers than in 1960, a time when the United States had one hundred million fewer people.[41]

Young Americans in particular are ignoring politics. Americans under thirty years of age know less and care less about politics and pay less attention to newspapers than did each previous generation of the last half-century. Young people today are inclined toward television use generally but do not pay much attention to television news. Many of them apparently cannot be bothered with news in any form.[42]

Virtual Participation

The prospect of an entire generation of politically inattentive citizens is a disturbing one to many observers. Yet there is a glimmer of hope—the Internet. It is used more heavily by younger people and is packed with political information and participation possibilities.

Nevertheless, it is unclear whether the Internet will actually serve as an entry into the world of politics for large numbers of citizens. Most people use it primarily for entertainment, school assignments, shopping, and personal and business communication. On the other hand, there are thousands of chat rooms where politics and public affairs are discussed. In addition, nearly every major interest group has its own website, and many groups have developed a capacity to inform and activate their membership through e-mail. Finally, candidates for public office have developed websites to promote their campaigns; in the 2000 presidential election, the candidates used their sites to raise funds and enlist campaign volunteers.

A UCLA student works on the computer in her room. The Internet has vast but as yet unrealized potential as an instrument of mass political participation.

Reliable data are not available on the full extent of political participation through the Internet, but according to a recent survey, 7 percent of Americans claimed they get most of their news of public affairs from the Internet. The full impact of this new medium on citizen participation, however, is not likely to be known until its technological capacity is fully developed and today's computer-literate generation reaches adulthood.

UNCONVENTIONAL ACTIVISM: SOCIAL MOVEMENTS AND PROTEST POLITICS

Before mass elections became prevalent, the public often resorted to revolts and disorders as a way of expressing dissatisfaction with government. Tax and food riots were common forms of popular protest. The advent of elections allowed the masses to communicate their views in an institutionalized and less disruptive way. Elections are double-edged, however. Although they are commonly viewed as a means by which the people control the government, *elections are also a means by which the government controls the people.*[43] Because they have been freely chosen by the people to rule, representatives can claim that their policies reflect the popular will. It is difficult for people to claim they are justified in rioting against government policy that has been enacted by representatives they themselves placed in office.

Voting in elections is also limited to the options listed on the ballot. America's voters effectively have only two choices: they can back the Democratic or Republican party. No other party has much chance of victory, and any citizen who is dissatisfied with the major parties realistically has no way to express a policy preference through the ballot.

Social movements are an alternative form of influence. **Social movements,** or **political movements** as they are sometimes called, refer to broad efforts to achieve change by citizens who feel that government is not properly responsive

social (political) movements Active and sustained efforts to achieve social and political change by groups of people who feel that government has not been properly responsive to their concerns.

The high point of the civil rights movement was Dr. Martin Luther King's "I Have a Dream" address on the capitol mall in Washington, D.C., on August 28, 1963. A quarter of a million people, the largest gathering to that date on the mall, turned out for the rally.

to their interests.[44] Their efforts are sometimes channeled through traditional forms of participation, such as political lobbying, but citizens can also take to the streets in protest against government. Perhaps the most dramatic recent example occurred in late 1999 when a host of activists—trade unionists, environmentalists, and others—engaged police in what became known as the "Battle in

Political Culture

One People Out of Many

Exercise of the Vote

After decades of struggle, women gained the right to vote in 1920. Nevertheless, many women did not take advantage of it. Turnout had been 62 percent in 1916. It dropped to 49 percent in 1920 as less than 40 percent of women voted. Even as late as 1960, women voted at a rate that was nearly 10 percentage points below that of men.

The history of the exercise of women's right to vote is similar to that of other newly enfranchised groups. As groups and individuals have gained the right to vote through changes in suffrage laws or through citizenship, they have been slow to exercise that right. Hispanics who have become citizens in recent decades are about a third less likely than other citizens to vote on election day.

It might be thought that individuals who have just gained the right to vote would be the ones most eager to exercise it. However, like other aspects of social and cultural assimilation, a voting habit takes root slowly. Education and income are a reason; newly enfranchised groups usually rank below more established groups in these areas. The tendency also owes to the fact that the newly enfranchised are not accustomed to or necessarily comfortable with their newly granted right to vote. "It was not to be expected that the adult women who suddenly find themselves in possession of the franchise should be as conscientious in its exercise as men who from childhood had been encouraged to think politically," wrote Arthur M. Schlesinger and Erik McKinley Eriksson in a 1924 *New Republic* article.

Fifty years passed before the voting rate of women reached that of men. Only recently has the voting rate of black Americans reached a level that is close to the turnout rate among white Americans. The rate for Hispanics, although rising, is still far below the national average. The history of the franchise for immigrants from Ireland, Italy, and other countries is similar. Voting is not something that blossoms overnight. The merging of peoples and cultures—the creation of one out of many—is a slow and fitful process, even when it comes to voter turnout on election day.

Seattle." The World Trade Organization (WTO) was meeting in Seattle to discuss global economic issues, and the activists were protesting the weak environmental and labor provisions that had marked earlier trade agreements. Their actions disrupted the WTO's meeting and earned a promise that, somehow, their views would be incorporated in future WTO deliberations.[45]

Social movements do not always succeed, but they sometimes enable otherwise politically weak persons to force government to respond to their desires. For example, the timing and scope of the landmark 1964 Civil Rights Act and 1965 Voting Rights Act can be explained only as a response by Congress to the pressure created by the civil rights movement. Another effective social movement in the 1960s was the farm workers' movement, whose protests led to improved working and living conditions for migrant workers.

Protest movements seldom have broad public support. In May 1970, unarmed students at Kent State University and Jackson State University were shot to death by national guardsmen while protesting the Vietnam War. Opinion polls indicated a majority of Americans blamed the students and not the guardsmen for the tragedy. Most citizens apparently believe the proper way to express disagreement over public policy is through voting and not through protesting.

Protest politics in America goes back to the Boston Tea Party and earlier, but it has taken on new forms in recent years. Protest was traditionally a desperate act that began, often spontaneously, when a group had lost hope that it could succeed through more conventional methods. Today, however, protest is usually a calculated act—a means of bringing added attention and impetus to a cause.[46] These tactical protests often involve a great deal of planning, including, in some instances, the busing of thousands of people to Washington for a rally staged for television. Civil rights, environmental, agricultural, and pro- and antiabortion groups are among those that have staged tactical protests in Washington within the past few years.

Citizens who participate in social movements tend to be younger than nonparticipants, which is a reversal of the situation with voting. In fact, age is the best predictor of protest activity.[47] Participants in social movements also tend to emphasize nonmaterial values more than do nonparticipants. Social movements often develop in response to real or perceived injustices and thus attract idealists.[48]

PARTICIPATION AND THE POTENTIAL FOR INFLUENCE

Although Americans claim that political participation is important, most of them do not practice what they preach. Most citizens take little interest in participation except to vote, and a significant minority cannot even be persuaded that voting is worth their while. However, Americans are not completely apathetic: many millions of them give their time, effort, and money to political causes, and roughly a hundred million go to the polls in presidential elections.

Yet sustained political activism does not engage a large proportion of the public. Moreover, many of those who do participate are drawn to politics by a habitual sense of civic duty rather than by an intense concern with current issues. The emphasis that American culture places on *individualism* tends to discourage a sense of urgency about political participation. "In the United States, the country of individualism *par excellence*," William Watts and Lloyd Free write, "there is a sharp distinction in people's minds between their own personal lives and national life."[49] Although wars and severe recessions can lead the American public to turn to government, most people under most conditions expect to solve their own problems. This is not to say that Americans have a disdain for collective action. In their communities particularly, citizens frequently take part in collective efforts to support a local hospital, improve the neighborhood, and the like. But most Americans tend not to see their material well-being as greatly dependent on involvement in politics of the traditional kind.[50]

This tendency contributes to a class bias in American politics. For one thing, it helps maintain a relatively sharp distinction between that which is properly public (political) and that which is properly private (economic). The private component, which includes most economic relationships, is largely beyond the realm of political debate and action. Americans, said political scientist Robert Lane, have a preference for market justice rather than political justice.[51] They prefer to see benefits distributed primarily through the economic marketplace rather than through the policies of government. The nation's health care system

Police and protesters face off in 1999 at the World Trade Organization (WTO) meeting in Seattle. Although protest movements are an American tradition, they rarely receive strong public support.

is an example. Unlike the systems of Europe, which provide government-paid coverage for everyone, access to medical care in the United States is to some degree based on a person's ability to pay for it. There are nearly forty million Americans who do not have access to adequate health care because they cannot afford health insurance.

America's individualistic culture also contributes to a class bias by its effect on the participation level of lower-income groups. Citizens of lower economic status are substantially less involved politically. Citizens of higher economic status are more likely to have the financial resources and communication skills that encourage participation and make it personally rewarding. Among citizens who are most active in politics, three times as many have incomes in the top third as in the bottom third.[52] This difference is much greater than in other Western democracies, where the government assists poorer citizens in participating by assuming the burden of registering voters and by fostering class-based political organizations. By comparison, the poor in the United States must arrange their own registration and must choose between two political parties that are attuned primarily to middle-class interests.

The relatively low participation rate of the poor tends to reduce the influence of their opinions on public policy. Studies indicate that representatives are more responsive to the demands of participants than to those of nonparticipants,[53] although it must be kept in mind that participants do not always promote only their own interests. It would be a mistake, however, to conclude that large numbers of people regularly support policies that would mainly benefit others. For example, a turning point in the defeat of President Bill Clinton's health care reform proposal came when middle-class Americans decided that it might increase the cost and reduce the quality of their own medical care. According to Time/CNN polls, support for the Clinton plan dropped from 57 percent to 37 percent between September 1993 and July 1994. Although this decline reflected a loss of support among all groups, the drop was particularly acute among middle-income and higher-income groups. A majority of lower-income

Self-Quiz
www.mhhe.com/patterson6

SUMMARY

Political participation is involvement in activities designed to influence public policy and leadership. A main issue of democratic government is the question of who participates in politics and how fully they participate.

Voting is the most widespread form of active political participation among Americans. Yet voter turnout is significantly lower in the United States than in other democratic nations. The requirement that Americans must personally register in order to establish their eligibility to vote is one reason for lower turnout among Americans; other democracies place the burden of registration on government officials rather than on the individual citizen. The fact that the United States holds frequent elections also discourages some citizens from voting regularly. Finally, the major American political parties, unlike many of those in Europe, do not clearly represent the interests of opposing economic classes; thus the policy stakes in American elections are correspondingly lower. Some Americans do not vote because they think that policy will not change greatly regardless of which party gains power.

Prospective voting is one way the people can exert influence on policy through their participation. It is the most demanding approach to voting: voters must develop their own policy preferences and then educate themselves about the candidates' positions. Most voters are not well-enough informed about the issues to respond in this way. Retrospective voting demands less from voters: they need only decide whether the government has been performing well in terms of the goals and values they hold. The evidence suggests that the electorate is, in fact, reasonably sensitive to past governmental performance, particularly in relation to economic prosperity.

Only a minority of citizens engage in the more demanding forms of political activity, such as work on community affairs or on behalf of a candidate during a political campaign. The proportion of Americans who engage in these more demanding forms of activity exceeds the proportion of Europeans who do so. Nevertheless, only about one in every four Americans will take an active part in a political organization at some point in their lives. Most political activists are individuals of higher income and education; they have the skills and material resources to participate effectively and tend to take greater interest in politics. More than in any other Western democracy, political participation in the United States is related to economic status.

Social movements are broad efforts to achieve change by citizens who feel that government is not properly responsive to their interests. These efforts sometimes take place outside established channels; demonstrations, picket lines, and marches are common means of protest. Protesters are younger and more idealistic on average than are other citizens, but they are a very small proportion of the population. In addition, protest activities do not have much public support, despite the country's tradition of free expression.

Overall, Americans are only moderately involved in politics. They are concerned with political affairs but mostly immersed in their private pursuits, a reflection in part of this culture's emphasis on individualism. The lower level of participation among low-income citizens has particular significance in that it works to reduce their influence on public policy and leadership.

KEY TERMS

- alienation
- apathy
- civic duty
- political participation
- prospective voting
- registration
- retrospective voting
- social capital
- social (political) movements
- suffrage
- voter turnout

SUGGESTED READINGS

Burns, Nancy, Kay Lehman Schlozman, and Sidney Verba. *The Private Roots of Public Action: Gender, Equality, and Public Action.* Cambridge, Mass.: Harvard University Press, 2001. An analysis of gender differences in political participation and their roots in patterns of everyday life.

Leighley, Jan. *Strength in Numbers: The Political Mobilization of Racial and Ethnic Minorities.* Princeton, N.J.: Princeton University Press, 2001. A study of the factors that motivate blacks and Hispanics to participate in politics.

Neuman, W. Russell, Marion R. Just, and Ann N. Crigler. *Common Knowledge: News and the Construction of Meaning.* Chicago: University of Chicago Press, 1992. An assessment of how citizens interpret and use the news they receive.

Patterson, Thomas E. *The Vanishing Voter.* New York: Knopf, 2002. A study of the decline in electoral participation and what might be done to reverse the trend.

Putnam, Robert. *Bowling Alone.* New York: Simon and Schuster, 2000. A provocative analysis of the trend in civic participation.

Rimmerman, Craig A. *The New Citizenship: Unconventional Politics, Activism, and Service.* Boulder, Colo.: Westview Press, 1997. An assessment of citizenship in the modern age.

Schudson, Michael. *The Good Citizen: A History of American Civic Life.* New York: Free Press, 1998. A thoughtful history of civic participation in America.

Verba, Sidney, Kay Schlozman, and Henry Brady. *Voice and Equality.* Cambridge, Mass.: Harvard University Press, 1995. A careful study of political attitudes and participation.

LIST OF WEBSITES

http://www.rockthevote.org/
Rock the Vote is an organization dedicated to helping young people realize and utilize their power to affect the civic and political life of their communities.

http://www.umich.edu/~nes/
The University of Michigan's National Election Studies (NES) site provides survey data on voting, public opinion, and political participation.

http://www.vanishingvoter.org/
Harvard University's election study site provides data and analysis of public involvement in the 2000 presidential campaign.

http://www.vote-smart.org/
Project Vote Smart includes information on Republican and Democratic candidates and officials; also has the latest in election news.

8

Political parties created democracy and . . . modern democracy is unthinkable save in terms of the parties.
—E. E. Schattschneider[1]

Political Parties, Candidates, and Campaigns:
Defining the Voter's Choice

On opposite coasts and two weeks apart, the two parties faced off, each offering its own plan for a better America.

The Republicans met first, in Philadelphia. Their 2000 platform included a steep cut in personal income taxes, a limit on abortions, parental choice of schools, business deregulation, a partial privatization of the social security system, and a delegation of authority to state and local governments. The Republicans chose Texas governor George W. Bush, the son of former President George Bush, as their presidential nominee. Wyoming's Dick Cheney was selected as his running mate.

The Democrats met in Los Angeles, the same city where thirty-two years earlier Robert F. Kennedy had been assassinated at the end of a bitter Democratic nominating campaign that had nearly torn the party apart over the issue of the Vietnam War. This time, however, the Democrats were a united party. The Democrats chose Vice President Al Gore, a native of Tennessee, as their presidential nominee. His running mate was Senator Joseph Lieberman of Connecticut, the first Jewish American to be named to the national ticket of a major U.S. party. The Democrats' lengthy platform included tax benefits for low- and middle-income families, restrictions on handguns, protection of social security, reproductive freedom for women, and pledges to strengthen the nation's environmental, educational, and health systems.

The political parties, as their nominees and platforms illustrate, are in the business of offering the voting public a choice. Each party seeks to define itself in a way that will attract majority support.

Competition between political parties is the foundation of the public's influence through elections. The party is the one institution that develops broad policy and leadership choices and then presents them to the voting public to accept or reject. This process is what gives the citizens an opportunity, through elections, to influence how they will be governed. "It is the competition of political organizations that provides the people with an opportunity to make a choice," the political scientist E. E. Schattschneider once wrote. "Without this opportunity popular sovereignty amounts to nothing."[2]

A **political party** is an ongoing coalition of interests joined together in an effort to get its candidates for public office elected under a common label.[3] As such, a party is actually three election parties in one. There is, first, the *party in the electorate,* which consists of the voters who identify with it and support its candidates. This component of the party was discussed in Chapter 6 and is also addressed briefly in this chapter. The main subjects of this chapter, however, are the other two components: the *party as organization,* staffed and led by party activists, and the *party as candidates,* which consists of those individuals who run for public office under its label.[4]

A theme of this chapter is that party organizations are alive and well in America but are also secondary to candidates as the driving force in contemporary campaigns. **Party-centered politics** is an important dimension of U.S. elections, but much of what goes on in the campaign is better described by the term **candidate-centered politics.**

Democratic nominee Al Gore is surrounded by party faithful during the 2000 presidential campaign. Political parties have responsibility for selecting nominees and submitting them to the voters for acceptance or rejection. Competition between the parties gives the voters an opportunity to influence the direction of government.

political party An ongoing coalition of interests joined together to try to get their candidates for public office elected under a common label.

party-centered politics Election campaigns and other political processes in which political parties, not individual candidates, hold most of the initiative and influence.

candidate-centered politics Election campaigns and other political processes in which candidates, not political parties, have most of the initiative and influence.

For the most part, candidates for the presidency and Congress raise their own funds, form their own campaign organizations, and choose for themselves the issues on which they will run. Parties still play an important, indeed an indispensable, role in these elections, but their campaign role is secondary to that of the candidates.

This chapter explains this development and also explores the history of U.S. parties, the patterns of party politics, and the conduct of modern campaigns. The following points are emphasized in this chapter:

- *Political competition in the United States has centered on two parties, a pattern that is explained by the nature of America's electoral system, political institutions, and political culture.* Minor parties exist in the United States but have been unable to compete successfully for governing power.

- *To win an electoral majority, candidates of the two major parties must appeal to a diverse set of interests; this necessity normally leads them to advocate moderate and somewhat overlapping policies.* Only during periods of stress are America's parties likely to present the electorate with starkly different choices.

- *U.S. party organizations are decentralized and fragmented.* The national organization is a loose collection of state organizations, which in turn are loose associations of autonomous local organizations. This feature of U.S. parties can be traced to federalism and the nation's diversity, which have made it difficult for the parties to act as instruments of national power.

- *The ability of America's party organizations to control nominations and election to office is weak, which in turn enhances the candidates' role.*
- *Candidate-centered campaigns are based on the media and utilize the skills of professional consultants.* Money, strategy, and televised advertising are key components of today's presidential and congressional campaigns.

PARTY COMPETITION AND MAJORITY RULE: THE HISTORY OF U.S. PARTIES

Political parties give direction and strength to the people's votes. Through their numbers, citizens have the potential for great influence, but that potential cannot be realized unless they have the capacity to act together. Parties give them that capacity. When Americans go to the polls, they have a choice between the Republican and Democratic parties. This **party competition** narrows their options to two and in the process enables people with different opinions to render a common judgment. In electing a party, the voters choose its candidates, its philosophy, and its policies over those of the opposing party.

The history of democratic government is virtually synonymous with the history of parties. When the countries of eastern Europe gained their freedom a few years ago, one of their first steps toward democracy was the legalization of parties. When the United States was founded two centuries ago, the formation of parties was also a first step toward the erection of its democracy. The reason is simple: it is the competition between parties that gives popular majorities a chance to determine how they will be governed.[5]

party competition A process in which conflict over society's goals is transformed by political parties into electoral competition in which the winner gains the power to govern.

The First Parties

America's early leaders mistrusted parties. George Washington in his farewell address warned the nation of the "baneful effects" of parties, and James Madison likened parties to special interests. However, Madison's initial misgivings about parties gradually gave way to a grudging admiration; he recognized that they provided a way for like-minded people to jointly promote their vision of how the new nation should be governed.

America's parties originated in the rivalry within George Washington's administration between Thomas Jefferson, a supporter of states' rights and small landholders, and Alexander Hamilton, who promoted a strong national government and commercial interests (see Figure 8–1). When Hamilton's ideas prevailed in Congress, Jefferson and his followers formed a political party, the Republicans. By adopting this label, which was associated with popular government, the Jeffersonians sought to portray themselves as the rightful heirs to the American Revolution's legacy of self-government and political equality.

Hamilton responded by organizing his supporters into a formal party—the Federalists—and in the process created America's first competitive party system.

Historical Background

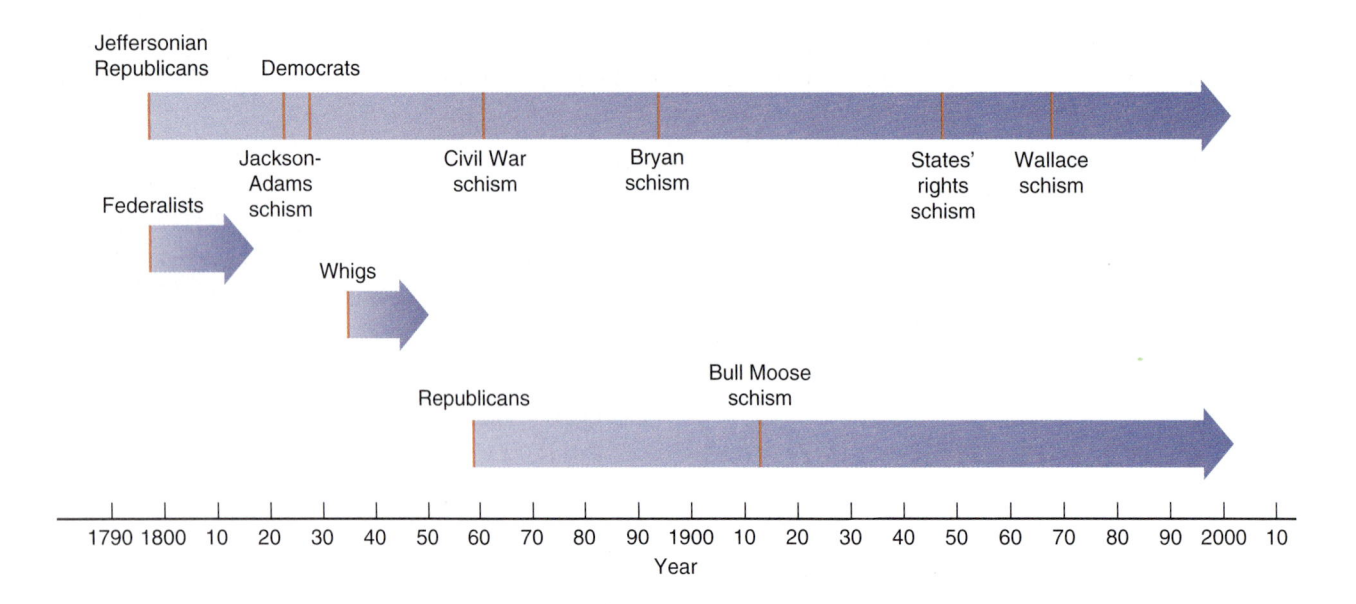

Figure 8–1
A Graphic History of America's Major Parties
The U.S. party system has been remarkable for its continuity. Competition between two major parties has been a persistent feature of the system.

The Federalists took their name from the faction that had supported ratification of the Constitution, thereby implying that they were the Constitution's true defenders. However, the Federalists' preoccupation with commercial and wealthy interests fueled Jefferson's claim that the Federalists were bent on establishing a government for the rich and wellborn. After Adams's defeat by Jefferson in the election of 1800, the Federalists and their philosophy never again held sway.

During the so-called Era of Good Feeling, when James Monroe ran unopposed in 1820 for a second presidential term, it appeared as if the nation might exist without parties. Yet by the end of Monroe's second term, policy differences had split the Republicans. The dominant faction, led by Andrew Jackson, retained Jefferson's commitment to the interests of ordinary people. This faction called itself Democratic Republicans, later shortened to Democrats. Thus, the Republican party of Jefferson is the forerunner of today's Democratic party rather than today's Republican party.

Andrew Jackson and Grassroots Parties

For all its shortcomings, competition between parties is the only system that can regularly mobilize collective influence on behalf of the many who are individually powerless against those few who have extraordinary wealth and prestige.[6]

This realization led Jackson during the 1820s to develop a **grassroots party**. Whereas Jefferson's party had been well organized only at the leadership level, Jackson sought a party that was built from the bottom up. Jackson's Democratic party consisted of committees and clubs at the national, state, and local levels, with membership open to all eligible voters. These organizational activities, along with more liberal suffrage laws, contributed to a nearly fourfold rise in voter turnout during the 1830s.[7] At the peak of Jacksonian democracy, Alexis de Tocqueville wrote, "The People reign in the American political world as the

grassroots party A political party organized at the level of the voters and dependent on their support for its strength.

Deity does in the universe."[8] Although Tocqueville exaggerated the people's true power, he caught the spirit of popular government that was behind the development of grassroots parties under Andrew Jackson.

In this period, a new opposition party, the Whigs, emerged to challenge the Democrats. The Whigs formed a residual party of sorts. Its followers were united not by a coherent philosophy of their own but by their opposition for one reason or another to the philosophy and policies of the Jacksonian Democrats.

Competition between the Whigs and the Democrats was relatively short-lived. During the 1850s the slavery issue began to tear both parties apart. The Whig party began to disappear, and a northern-based new party, the Republicans, arose as the main challenger to the Democrats. In 1860, the Democratic party's northern faction nominated for president Stephen A. Douglas, who held that the question of whether a new territory permitted slavery was for a majority of its voters to decide, while the southern faction nominated John C. Breckinridge, who called for the legalization of slavery in all territories. The Democratic vote in the fall election was split sharply along regional lines between these two candidates—with the result that the Republican nominee, Abraham Lincoln, was able to win the presidency with only 40 percent of the popular vote. However, the U.S. party system essentially collapsed in 1860, for the only time in the nation's history.[9] The issues of slavery and union were too powerful to be settled peaceably through political compromise and competition between political parties.

> ## Andrew Jackson
> (1767–1845)
>
> Andrew Jackson rose to national fame when, as a major general, he defeated the British at the Battle of New Orleans during the War of 1812. A Tennessee native, he won the presidency in 1828 after having lost in 1824 despite having received the most popular votes. He instituted political changes including grassroots parties that were designed to strengthen popular rule. The term "Jacksonian Democracy" became synonymous with his belief that ordinary people were capable of governing themselves.

Republicans Versus Democrats: Realignments and the Enduring Party System

After the Civil War, the nation settled into the pattern of competition between the Republican and Democratic parties that has prevailed ever since. The durability of these two parties is due not to their ideological consistency but to their remarkable ability to adapt during periods of crisis. By abandoning at these crucial times their old ways of doing things, the Republican and Democratic parties have essentially remade themselves—with new bases of support, new policies, and new public philosophies.

These periods of great political change are known as *realignments*. A **party realignment** involves four basic elements:

1. The disruption of the existing political order because of the emergence of one or more unusually powerful and divisive issues
2. An election contest in which the voters shift their support strongly in favor of one party
3. A major change in policy through the action of the stronger party
4. An enduring change in the party coalitions, which works to the lasting advantage of the dominant party

party realignment An election or set of elections in which the electorate responds strongly to an extraordinarily powerful issue that has disrupted the established political order. A realignment has a lasting impact on public policy, popular support for the parties, and the composition of the party coalitions.

> **Abraham Lincoln**
> *(1809–1865)*
>
> Abraham Lincoln (1809–1865) was a member of Congress from Illinois before his election to the presidency in 1860. Homely and gangly, Lincoln is regarded by many as America's greatest president for his principled leadership during the Civil War. His greatest legacy is the preservation of the American Union. The Emancipation Proclamation and the Gettysburg Address are two of his other legacies. He was assassinated at Ford's Theater in the nation's capital shortly after the start of his second term as president.

Realignments are rare. They do not occur simply because one party wrests control of government from the other. They involve deep and lasting changes in the party system that affect not just the most recent election but later ones as well. By this standard, there have been three clear-cut realignments since the 1850s.

The Civil War realignment, for example, brought about a thorough change in the party system. The Republicans replaced the Democrats as the nation's majority party. The Republicans were the dominant party in the larger and more populous North; the Democratic party was left with a stronghold in what became known as "the Solid South." During the next three decades, the Republicans held the presidency except for Grover Cleveland's two terms of office and had a majority in Congress for all but four of those years.

The 1896 election resulted in a further realignment of the Republican-Democratic party system. Three years earlier, an economic panic following a bank collapse had resulted in a severe depression. The Democrat Cleveland was president when the crash happened, and people blamed him and his party. When the Democrats then nominated William Jennings Bryan in 1896 on a cheap-credit platform (unlimited coinage of silver) that frightened many voters into believing that inflation would destroy their savings and the economy, the Republicans made additional gains in the Northeast and Midwest, solidifying their position as the nation's dominant party. During the four decades between the 1890s realignment and the next one in the 1930s, the Republicans held the presidency except for Woodrow Wilson's two terms and had a majority in Congress for all but six years.

The Great Depression of the 1930s triggered a thoroughgoing realignment of the American party system. The Republican Herbert Hoover was president when the stock market crashed in 1929, and many Americans blamed Hoover, his party, and its business allies for the economic catastrophe that followed. The Democrats became the country's majority party, and their political and policy agenda favored a significant social and economic role for the national government. Franklin D. Roosevelt's presidency was characterized by unprecedented policy initiatives in the areas of business regulation and social welfare (see Chapter 3). His election in 1932 began a thirty-six-year period of Democratic presidencies that was interrupted only by Dwight D. Eisenhower's two terms in the 1950s. In this period, the Democrats also dominated Congress, losing control only in 1947–1948 and 1953–1954.

The reason realignments have such a substantial effect on future elections is that they affect voters' *party identification* (see Chapter 6). Young voters in particular are likely to identify with the newly ascendant party, and they tend to maintain that identity, giving the party a solid base of support for years to come. In the 1930s, for example, the Democratic party's image as the party of the common people, jobs, and social security was vastly more appealing to young voters than the Republican party's image as the party of business and wealthy

The new order begins: Franklin D. Roosevelt rides to his inauguration with outgoing president Herbert Hoover after the realigning election of 1932.

interests. First-time voters in the 1930s came to identify by a two-to-one margin with the Democratic party, which established it as the nation's majority party and enabled it to dominate national politics for the next three decades.[10]

A New Realignment or a Dealignment?

A party realignment inevitably loses strength over time, because the issues that gave rise to it cannot remain dominant indefinitely. By the late 1960s, when the Democratic party was divided over the Vietnam War and civil rights, it was apparent that the era of New Deal politics was over.[11]

A realignment affecting part of the nation was soon evident. The South, which had been solidly Democratic at all levels, was becoming staunchly Republican in presidential elections and increasingly competitive at the state and local levels. As the Democratic party became increasingly identified as the party of civil rights and social change, it had less and less appeal to conservative white southerners.[12]

Yet Republican inroads were otherwise less dramatic or temporary. After 1968, the Republicans held the presidency for more years than the Democrats, and in 1994, they won a landslide midterm election victory that gave the GOP control of both houses of Congress for the first time in four elections. But at no time has the GOP been able to dominate presidential and congressional elections time after time the way that Democrats did during the height of the New Deal era. Nor has the GOP succeeded in gaining a decisive edge in terms of party identification. The proportion of Americans who call themselves Democrats has typically equaled or exceeded that of those who say they are Republicans. A

Figure 8-2

Partisan Identification

Party loyalties weakened in the late 1960s, and the proportion of independents increased.

Source: National Election Studies, 1952–1992; various surveys, 1993–2000.

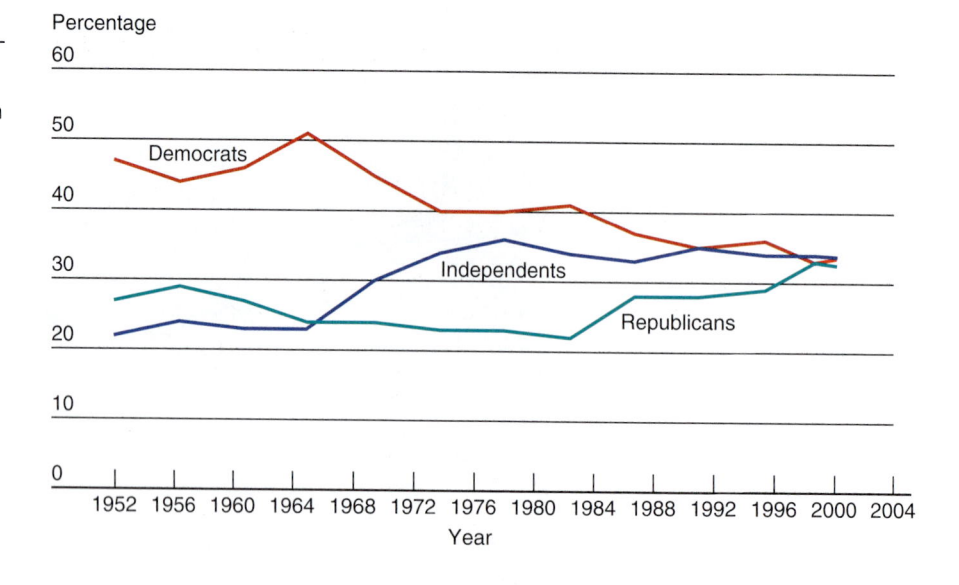

dealignment A situation in which voters' partisan loyalties have been substantially and permanently weakened.

split-ticket voting The pattern of voting in which the individual voter in a given election casts a ballot for one or more candidates of each major party.

straight-ticket voting The pattern of voting in which the individual voter in a given election supports only candidates of one party.

lasting realignment favorable to the Republican party could be taking place, but if so, it is unlike past ones—slower, more fitful, and less encompassing. And if such a realignment is taking place, it will be evident only after Republicans enjoy a period of sustained dominance.

An alternative explanation for what has been happening in American elections is put forth by advocates of the dealignment thesis. They suggest that the U.S. electoral system, rather than undergoing a realignment favorable to one party, has been in the process of **dealignment,** a partial but enduring movement of voters away from partisan loyalties.[13] The process is characterized by an electorate that wavers in its support of the parties.

Parties, in fact, have a weaker hold on the voters than in the past. As was noted in Chapter 6, the number of voters who describe themselves as Independents has increased significantly in recent decades (Figure 8–2). Moreover, people who today identify with a party are more likely to say it is only a weak attachment. These changes are reflected in increased **split-ticket voting**, where the voter selects candidates of both parties for different offices when casting a ballot. A few decades ago, the large majority of voters engaged in **straight-ticket voting,** supporting candidates of one party only.

The decline of partisanship began during the 1960s and 1970s when divisive issues arose and disrupted existing loyalties. The civil rights issue, for example, was unsettling not only to many southern Democrats but also to some white northern Democrats, particularly blue-collar workers from newer immigrant groups who felt that African Americans were making progress at their expense.[14] Vietnam, abortion, social welfare, and a host of other issues also divided followers of each party. Americans' trust in their elected representatives declined, as did their faith in parties.

Party loyalties have been weak ever since, and some analysts see little likelihood of a dramatic reversal. For one thing, voters of today are better educated and more likely to believe they can judge the candidates for themselves on the basis of what they hear through the media rather than on the basis of party

HOW THE UNITED STATES COMPARES

Party Systems

For nearly 160 years, electoral competition in the United States has centered on the Republican and Democratic parties. By comparison, most democracies have a multiparty system, in which three or more parties receive substantial support from voters. The difference is significant. In a two-party system, the parties tend to have overlapping coalitions and programs, because each party must appeal to the middle-of-the-road voters who provide the margin of victory. In multiparty systems, particularly those with four or more strong parties, the parties tend to separate themselves, as each tries to secure the enduring loyalty of voters who have a particular viewpoint.

Whether a country has a two-party or a multiparty system depends on several factors, but particularly the nature of its electoral system. The United States has a single-member plurality district system in which only the top vote getter in a district gets elected. This system is biased against smaller parties; even if they have some support in a great many races, they win nothing unless one of their candidates places first in an electoral district. By comparison, proportional representation systems enable smaller parties to compete; each party acquires legislative seats in proportion to its share of the total vote. All the countries in the chart that have four or more parties also have a proportional representation system of election.

NUMBER OF COMPETITIVE PARTIES

TWO	THREE	FOUR OR MORE
United States	Canada (at times)	Belgium
	Great Britain	Denmark
		France
		Germany
		Italy
		Netherlands
		Sweden

---

labels. Moreover, people today are protected by programs like social security and Medicare from the economic hardships that in the past fueled party realignments. Finally, Americans today want higher incomes and lower taxes, but they also want a cleaner environment, services for the elderly, and better schools. As a result, they are less likely to be drawn fully to either the Republican argument for a less active government or the Democratic argument for a more active one.[15]

If advocates of the dealignment thesis are correct, neither party will enjoy the prolonged success of the type the Democratic party had from the 1930s on. The predicted scenario is one of shifting support, with the Republicans prevailing at some times and the Democrats doing so at other times.

ELECTORAL AND PARTY SYSTEMS

The United States traditionally has had a **two-party system:** Federalists versus Jeffersonian Republicans, Whigs versus Democrats, and Republicans versus Democrats. These have not been the only American parties, but they have been the only ones with a realistic chance of acquiring political control. A two-party system, however, is the exception rather than the rule (see "How the United States

two-party system A system in which only two political parties have a real chance of acquiring control of the government.

Compares"). Most democracies have a **multiparty system,** in which three or more parties have the capacity to gain control of government, separately or in coalition. Why the difference? Why three or more major parties in most democracies but only two in the United States?

The Single-Member-District System of Election

A chief reason for the persistence of America's two-party system is the fact that the nation chooses its officials through plurality voting in **single-member districts.**[16] Each constituency elects a single candidate to a particular office, such as U.S. senator or representative; only the party that gets the most votes (a plurality) in a district wins the office. This system discourages minor parties. Assume, for example, that a minor party received exactly 20 percent of the vote in each of the nation's 435 congressional races. Even though one in five voters nationwide backed the minor party, it would not win any seats in Congress because none of its candidates had placed first in any of the 435 single-member-district races. The winning candidate in each case would be the major-party candidate who received the larger proportion of the remaining 80 percent of the vote.

By comparison, most European democracies use some form of **proportional representation,** in which seats in the legislature are allocated according to a party's share of the popular vote. This type of electoral system provides smaller parties an incentive to organize and compete for power. In the 1998 German elections, the Green party won slightly more than 5 percent of the national vote and received a proportionate number of the seats in the Bundestag, the German parliament. If the Greens had been competing under American electoral rules, they would not have won any seats and would have had no chance of exercising a share of legislative power. In Germany, the Greens even gained a share of executive power. The Social Democratic party won the most legislative seats in the 1998 German election but failed to gain an outright majority. The Social Democrats formed a coalition with the Green party, which received cabinet posts in return for its backing of a Social Democrat–led government.

Policies and Coalitions in the Two-Party System

The overriding goal of a major American party is to gain power by getting its candidates elected to office. Because there are only two major parties, however, the Republicans or Democrats can win consistently only by attracting majority support. In Europe's multiparty systems, a party can hope for a share of power if it has the firm backing of a minority faction. Not so in the United States. If either party confines its support to a narrow segment of society, it forfeits its chance of gaining control of government.

Seeking the Center, Usually

This situation encourages both parties to stay near the center of the political spectrum and to avoid the minority position on deeply divisive issues. American parties, Clinton Rossiter said, are "creatures of compromise."[17] The two parties

---

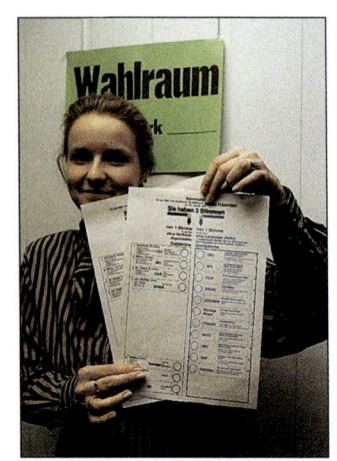

Germany's electoral system allocates legislative seats on the basis both of single-district voting and of the overall proportion of votes a party receives. This system requires that the German voter cast two ballots in legislative races: one to choose among the candidates in the particular district and one to choose among the parties. Shown here is a ballot from a German election. The left column lists the candidates for the legislative seat in a district, and the right column lists the parties. (Note the relatively large number of parties on the ballot.)

multiparty system A system in which three or more political parties have the capacity to gain control of government separately or in coalition.

single-member districts The form of representation in which only the candidate who gets the most votes in a district wins office.

proportional representation A form of representation in which seats in the legislature are allocated proportionally according to each political party's share of the popular vote. This system enables smaller parties to compete successfully for seats.

Republican presidential nominee George W. Bush reaches out to shake a voter's hand during the early months of the 2000 campaign. Bush sought to reverse Republican losses in recent elections by positioning the GOP closer to the political center.

typically try to develop stands that have broad appeal, or at least will not alienate significant blocs of voters. Any time a party makes a pronounced shift toward either extreme, the middle is left open for the opposing party. Barry Goldwater, the Republican presidential nominee in 1964, proposed the elimination of mandatory social security and said he might consider the tactical use of small nuclear weapons in such wars as the Vietnam conflict—extreme positions that cost him many votes. Eight years later, the Democrat nominee, George McGovern, took positions on Vietnam and income security that alarmed many voters and, like Goldwater, got buried in one of the greatest landslides in presidential history.

It is impossible to understand the dynamics of the U.S. party system without a recognition that the true balance of power in American elections rests with America's pragmatic and moderate voters rather than those who hold more extreme views. When congressional Republicans mistook their 1994 election victory as a mandate to trim assistance programs for the elderly, the poor, and children, they alienated many of the moderate voters who had contributed to their 1994 victory. These voters wanted "less" government but not a government that neglected society's most vulnerable citizens. After weak showings in the 1996 and 1998 elections, congressional Republicans shifted course. They unseated Speaker Newt Gingrich, replacing him with a more pragmatic conservative, Dennis Hastert. "We still need to prove that we can be conservative without being mean," was how one Republican member of Congress described the change in strategy.[18] The change in Republican outlook was also apparent in GOP presidential candidate George W. Bush's 2000 campaign slogan: "compassionate conservatism." These adjustments reflect a basic truth about U.S. politics: party ideology is acceptable as long as it is tinged with moderation.

Nonetheless, the Republican and Democratic parties do offer somewhat different alternatives and, at times, a clear choice. When Roosevelt was elected president in 1932, Johnson in 1964, and Reagan in 1980, the parties were relatively far apart in their priorities and programs. Roosevelt's New Deal, for example, was an extreme alternative within the American political tradition and caused a decisive split along party lines. A lesson of these periods is that the center of the American political spectrum can be moved. Candidates risk a crushing defeat by straying too far from established ideas during normal times, but they may do so with some chance of victory during turbulent times.

Another lesson of such periods is that public opinion is the critical element in partisan change. Critics who say that the Democratic and Republican parties fail to offer the voters a real choice ignore the parties' tendency to tailor their appeals to majority opinion.[19] When the public's mood shifts, the parties usually also shift. The Republicans' Contract with America in 1994, for example, was a response to public discontent with the federal government's taxing and spending policies. When the Republicans won in 1994, many Democratic officeholders also embraced cutbacks in federal power, thus shifting the entire party system toward the right. If GOP leaders misjudged just how far right the public was willing to go, they nonetheless redirected the nation's politics. President Clinton, a Democrat, summed up the change in his 1996 State of the Union address when he said: "The era of big government is over."

Party Coalitions

The groups and interests that support a party are collectively referred to as the **party coalition.** In multiparty systems, each party is supported by a relatively narrow range of interests. European parties tend to divide along class lines, with the center and right parties drawing most of their votes from the middle and upper classes and the left parties drawing theirs from the working class. By comparison, America's two-party system requires each party to accommodate a wide range of interests in order to gain the voting plurality necessary to win elections.[20] The Republican and Democratic coalitions are therefore very broad. Each includes a substantial proportion of voters of nearly every ethnic, religious, regional, and economic grouping. There are only a few sizable groups that are tightly aligned with a party. African Americans are the clearest example; they vote about 85 percent Democratic in national elections.

Although the Republican and Democratic coalitions overlap, they are hardly identical (see Figure 8–3). Each party likes to appear to be all things to all Americans, but in fact each builds its coalition through a process of both unification and division. If a party did not stand for something—if it never took sides—it would lose all support.

Since the 1930s, the major policy differences between the Republicans and the Democrats have involved the national government's role in solving social and economic problems. Each party has supported government action to promote economic security and social equality, but the Democrats have consistently favored a greater degree of governmental involvement. Virtually every major assistance program for the poor, elderly, and low-wage workers has been initiated by the Democrats. To some extent, the Democratic coalition draws support disproportionately from society's underdogs—blacks, union members, the poor, city dwellers, Hispanics, Jews, and other "minorities."[21] For a long period, the Democratic party was also the clear choice of the nation's elderly as a result of its support for old-age assistance programs and because the basic political

party coalition The groups and interests that support a political party.

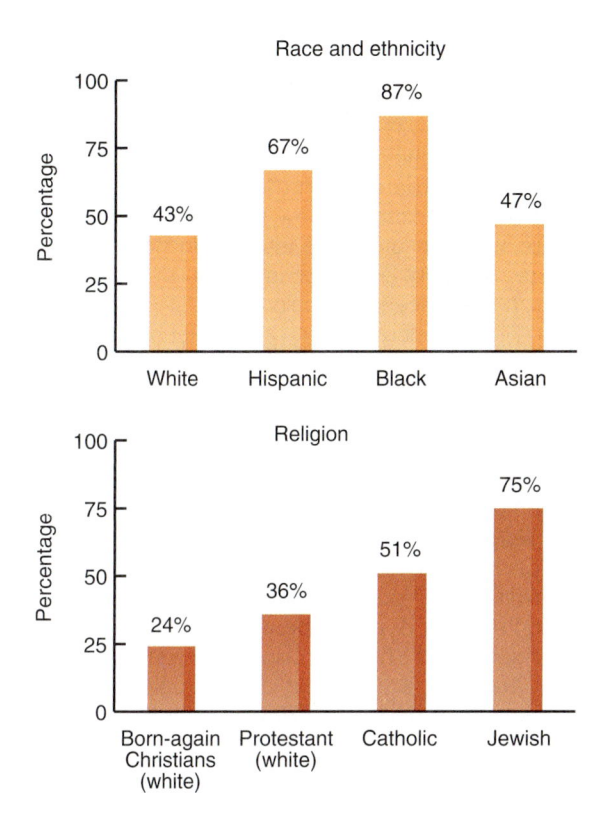

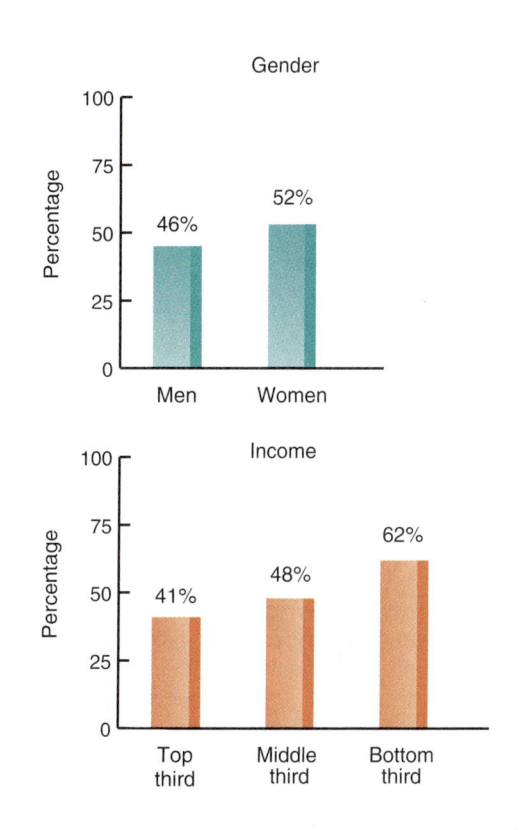

Figure 8-3

Race and ethnicity
- White: 43%
- Hispanic: 67%
- Black: 87%
- Asian: 47%

Gender
- Men: 46%
- Women: 52%

Religion
- Born-again Christians (white): 24%
- Protestant (white): 36%
- Catholic: 51%
- Jewish: 75%

Income
- Top third: 41%
- Middle third: 48%
- Bottom third: 62%

Figure 8–3

The Vote of Selected Demographic Groups in Recent Presidential Elections
Although the Democratic and Republican coalitions overlap substantially, there are important differences, as illustrated by the Democratic party's percentage of the two-party vote among some major demographic groups in recent elections.
Source: Compiled by author from NES and other surveys.

loyalties of the elderly were acquired during the New Deal era, a period favorable to the Democrats. Recently, however, elderly voters have split their vote nearly evenly between the parties.

The Democratic party's biggest gains recently have been with women, who traditionally had a voting pattern very similar to that of men. In recent elections, however, there has been a gender gap (see Chapter 6). Women have voted disproportionately for the Democratic party, apparently as a result of its positions on issues such as abortion rights, education spending, employment policies, and gun control.

The Republican coalition consists mainly of white middle-class Protestants. The GOP has historically been the party of tax cuts and business incentives. The GOP has also been more supportive of traditional values, as reflected, for example, in its support of school prayer and its opposition to abortion. Not surprisingly, the GOP has generally been the stronger party in the suburbs and other areas, such as the West and Midwest, where traditional values and a desire for lower taxes and less government regulation of economic activity are more pronounced.

The GOP has made big gains in recent decades among white fundamentalist Christians. They have been drawn to the GOP by its positions on abortion, school prayer, affirmative action, and other social issues. In recent presidential elections, the Republican nominee has garnered the votes of roughly 70 percent of fundamentalist Christians.

Why Should I Care?

Parties and Your Vote

In civics classes, students are often told to "vote for the person, not the party" or "vote on the issues, not the party." Commentators sometimes make the same pitch. On the whole, it's pretty bad advice.

To vote for the person is to assume that the individual officeholder wields singular power. But that's not true even in the case of the president. In choosing one presidential candidate over another, Americans are choosing more than the person who will sit behind the desk in the Oval Office. They are also selecting several hundred other executive officers, including the secretary of state, the attorney general of the United States, and the director of the Central Intelligence Agency. The president also nominates all federal judges and justices. The great majority of these individuals, including the judicial officers, will be of the same party as the president.

The election of a senator or a representative is also more than a decision about which individual will occupy a seat in Congress. Rarely does a single member of Congress have a decisive voice in legislation. Congress works through collective action. Power resides with the majority party in each chamber.

By the same token, a vote based on an issue is usually shortsighted. Once in office, a successful candidate will vote on scores of policy issues, not just the one or two issues that were the cornerstone of the election campaign. And what is the best predictor of how the successful candidate will vote on these issues? In nearly every case, the best predictor is the political party to which the officeholder belongs.

Party is also a more reliable voting cue than is an issue or candidate trait. Issues, for example, sometimes change with remarkable speed. An issue that dominated an election's debate can be overtaken by events and be a secondary issue by the time the winning candidates are sworn into office. On the other hand, partisanship tends to endure. Today's Democratic and Republican candidates and officeholders are not all that different in their policy leanings than their partisan counterparts of a decade or two ago. The policy inclinations of the Republican George W. Bush, for example, are not remarkably different from those of the Republican Ronald Reagan.

In recent decades, Americans have increasingly called themselves Independents rather than Democrats and Republicans. They pride themselves on "voting on the issue or the candidate rather than the party." Do you agree with that outlook? What argument would you make to support it?

The differences in the party coalitions were clearly evident in the 2000 presidential vote. Women, minorities, and lower-income Americans cast a majority of their votes for the Democratic nominee Al Gore, while men, whites, and higher-income Americans aligned primarily with the Republican nominee George W. Bush.

There is a self-limiting feature to the party coalitions. The larger a party becomes, the greater is the likelihood that conflict among the groups within it will occur. The New Deal, for example, brought black Americans into the Democratic coalition, where they coexisted with the white southern conservatives who had sided with the Democratic party since the Civil War. However, when the Democratic party in the 1950s and early 1960s began to respond to the civil rights issues of its black constituents, it alienated many white southerners, who then gravitated to the GOP. More recently, the growing number of fundamentalist Christians in the GOP has been a source of division within that party. Their strong views on issues such as abortion and school prayer are not shared by many traditional Republicans, which has enabled Democratic candidates in some races to attract support from these voters.

Minor Parties

Although the U.S. electoral system discourages the formation of third parties, the nation has always had minor parties—more than a thousand during the nation's history.[22] Most of them have been short-lived, and only a few have had a lasting impact. Only one minor party, the Republican party, has ever achieved majority status.

Minor parties in the United States have formed largely to advocate positions that their followers believe are not being adequately represented by either of the two major parties. When a minor party gains a large following, as has happened a few times in history, the major parties are inevitably transformed by its influence. They are forced to pay attention to the problems that are driving people to look outside the two-party system for leadership. A major party is always somewhat captive to its past, which is the source of many of its ideas and most of its followers. When conditions change, major parties are often slow to respond, and a minor party can capitalize on the emerging issues. In such a situation, one or both major parties typically awaken to the new issues, at which time the minor party usually begins to lose support. Nevertheless, the minor party will have served the purpose of making the major parties more responsive to the public's concerns.

Single-Issue Parties

Some minor parties form around a single issue of overriding concern to their supporters, such as the present-day Right-to-Life party, which was formed to oppose the legalization of abortion. Some single-issue parties have seen their policy goals enacted into law. The Prohibition party contributed to the ratification in 1919 of the Eighteenth Amendment, which prohibited the manufacture, sale, and transportation of alcoholic beverages (but was repealed in 1933). Single-issue parties usually disband when their issue is favorably resolved or fades in importance.[23]

Factional Parties

The Republican and Democratic parties are relatively adept at managing internal divisions. Although each party's support is diverse, the differences among its varying interests normally can be reconciled. However, there have been times when factional conflict within the major parties has led to the formation of minor parties.

The most successful of these factional parties at the polls was Theodore Roosevelt's Bull Moose party. In 1908 Roosevelt, after having served eight years as president, declined to seek a third term and handpicked William Howard Taft for the Republican nomination. When Taft as president showed neither Roosevelt's enthusiasm for a strong presidency nor his commitment to the goals of the Progressive movement, Roosevelt unsuccessfully challenged Taft for the 1912 Republican nomination. Roosevelt led a Progressive walkout to form the Bull Moose party (a reference to Roosevelt's claim that he was "as strong as a bull moose"). Roosevelt won 27 percent of the presidential vote to Taft's 25 percent, but the split within Republican ranks enabled the Democratic nominee, Woodrow Wilson, to win the presidency.

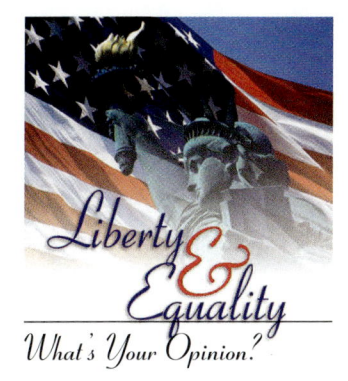

Liberty & Equality
What's Your Opinion?

Parties and Equality

Historically, parties have given weight to the voice of disadvantaged people. Their strength is in their numbers rather than in their wealth or status, and elections give them a chance to exercise that strength if they act together. It is no accident that the Jacksonians created the first American grassroots party in order to mobilize lower-class voters. The role of the political party in giving voice to the lower classes is even more evident in Europe, where labor and socialist parties emerged out of workers' movements.

As U.S. parties have weakened in recent decades, so has the political influence of Americans of lower income levels. The voting rate of citizens at the bottom of the income ladder is now about half that of those at the top. Party conflict in the first half of the twentieth century centered on the working class. It now inhabits the periphery of policy debates. The candidate-centered politics of today is mainly a politics of media and money and is primarily responsive to middle-class interests.

What do you make of this development? Is there a good alternative to the political party as an instrument for the aspirations of lower-income Americans? What might be done to increase the parties' responsiveness to their interests?

The States' Rights party in 1948 and George Wallace's American Independent party in 1968 are other examples of strong factional parties. These parties were formed by southern Democrats angered by northern Democrats' support of racial desegregation.

Deep divisions within a party give rise to factionalism and can lead eventually to a change in its coalition. The conflict over civil rights that began within the Democratic party during the Truman years continued for the next quarter-century, leading many southern whites to shift their party loyalty to the Republican party.

Ideological Parties

Other minor parties are characterized by their ideological commitment to a broad and radical philosophical position, such as redistribution of economic resources. Modern-day ideological parties include the Citizens party, the Socialist Workers party, and the Libertarian party, each of which operates on the fringe of American politics.

One of the strongest ideological parties in the nation's history was the Populist party. Its candidate in the 1892 presidential election, James B. Weaver, gained 8.5 percent of the national vote and won twenty-two electoral votes in six western states. The party began as an agrarian protest movement in response to an economic depression and the anger of small farmers over low commodity prices, tight credit, and the high rates charged by railroad monopolies to transport farm goods. The Populists' ideological platform called for government ownership of the railroads, a graduated income tax, low tariffs on imports, and elimination of the gold standard. The Populist party in 1896 endorsed the Democratic presidential nominee, William Jennings Bryan, and its support probably hurt the Democrats nationally. Large numbers of eastern Democrats abandoned their party's nominee in fear of the western Populists' radical ideas.[24]

The strongest minor party today is the Green party, an ideological party that holds liberal positions on the environment, labor, taxation, social welfare, and other issues. Its 2000 presidential nominee, consumer-rights advocate Ralph Nader, received 3 percent of the national vote. According to polls, Nader's support came primarily from voters who otherwise would have supported Democrat Al Gore, which tipped the election to the more conservative Republican nominee, George W. Bush. This outcome stirred a debate within Green party ranks. Some argued that the party should concentrate on local and state races, concluding that its participation in the 2000 presidential campaign served to elect the candidate whose policy goals were opposite its own. Others said that the Green party should continue to contest the presidential election so as to force the Democratic party toward more liberal policy positions.

Before the 2000 presidential election, the Reform party was America's strongest minor party. It originated in the 1992 independent candidacy of Ross Perot, who gained 19 percent of the presidential vote (second only to Roosevelt's 1912 percentage among candidates who were not major-party nominees). Perot's campaign was based on middle-class discontent with the major parties, was conducted almost entirely on television, and was funded by more than $60 million of his own money. Perot ran again in 1996 but as the nominee of the Reform party, which he had founded. This time, Perot accepted public funds for his campaign, which limited his spending to roughly $30 million (see

Jesse Ventura, who was chosen Minnesota's governor in 1998, is one of the few independent or third-party candidates to win a major elective office in the United States. Such candidates normally cannot surmount the built-in advantages possessed by major party nominees.

Chapter 12). He ran a media-based campaign that attracted 8 percent of the vote, which qualified the Reform party for public funding again in 2000. When Perot chose not to run in 2000, however, the Reform party nomination became a contest between its party regulars and supporters of conservative Pat Buchanan. Buchanan's nomination splintered the party, and he received less than 1 percent of the presidential vote. It appears doubtful that the Reform party will recover from its 2000 debacle, which included the defection of its most prominent officeholder, Jesse Ventura, a former professional wrestler who had been elected governor of Minnesota in 1998. Ventura renounced the Reform party and said he would campaign as an independent if he ran for reelection in 2002.

Are Conditions Ripe for a Strong Third Party?

The Perot and Nader candidacies are the first substantial third-party presidential candidacies in a quarter-century. Do they indicate that a strong third party will soon emerge in American politics?

The long history of the American party system would be enough to discourage almost anyone who is hoping that a strong third party will surface and remain strong for more than an election or two. The obstacles are substantial. As we have seen, the U.S. electoral system frustrates smaller parties by denying them anything but a symbolic victory in national politics. In addition, most Americans identify with either the Republican or the Democratic party, and the large majority of them regularly support their party's nominee. Finally, there is no powerful issue on the horizon that could serve as a rallying point for a strong third-party movement. Without such an issue, third parties, even if they do well in a single election (as Perot did in 1992), lack enduring appeal.

Nevertheless, Americans are increasingly dissatisfied with the way the two major parties are operating. According to a 2000 Harvard survey, about 30 percent of Americans believe that a third party is needed, even if they would not necessarily vote for its presidential candidate (see Figure 8–4). Americans are disgruntled by the partisan bickering that they think increasingly defines the relationship between Republican and Democratic officeholders. They also believe

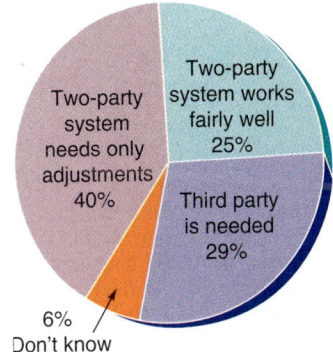

Figure 8–4
Americans' Opinions About the Need for a Strong Third Party
Most Americans say the two-party system works well or needs only some adjustments, but some believe that a strong third party is needed if the party system is to work effectively.
Source: Vanishing Voter Project National Survey, Joan Shorenstein Center on the Press, Politics, and Public Policy, Harvard University, 2000.

- Two-party system works fairly well 25%
- Third party is needed 29%
- Don't know 6%
- Two-party system needs only adjustments 40%

that money has come to play too large a role in Republican and Democratic politics and that candidates' campaign promises are too often broken once they take office.

PARTY ORGANIZATIONS

party organizations The party organizational units at national, state, and local levels; their influence has decreased over time because of many factors.

The Democratic and Republican parties have organizational units at the national, state, and local levels. These **party organizations** engage in a variety of activities, but their main purpose is the contesting of elections.

A century ago, party organizations were in control of nominations and elections. The party organizations still perform all the activities they formerly engaged in. They recruit candidates, raise money, develop policy positions, and canvass for votes. But they do not control these activities as completely as they once did.[25] For the most part, these activities are now dominated by the candidates themselves.[26]

The Weakening of Party Organizations

nomination The designation of a particular individual to run as a political party's candidate (its "nominee") in the general election.

Nomination refers to the selection of the individual who will run as the party's candidate in the general election. Until the early twentieth century, nominations were entirely the responsibility of party organizations. To be nominated, an individual had to be loyal to the party organization, a requirement that included a willingness to share with it the spoils of office: government jobs and contracts. The situation allowed party organizations to acquire campaign workers and funds, but also enabled unscrupulous party leaders to extort money from those seeking political favors. Reform-minded Progressives argued for *party democracy*, claiming that party organizations should operate according to the same principle that governs elections: power should rest with ordinary voters rather than with the party bosses (see Chapter 2).

primary election (direct primary) A form of election in which voters choose a party's nominees for public office. In most primaries, eligibility to vote is limited to voters who are registered members of the party.

The most serious assault of the Progressives on the part organizations was the introduction of the **primary election** (or **direct primary**) as a method of choosing nominees. In place of party-designated nominees, the primary system placed nomination in the hands of voters (see Chapters 2 and 12).

Primary elections take several forms. Most states conduct closed primaries, in which participation is limited to voters registered or declared at the polls as members of the party whose primary is being held. Other states use open primaries, a form that allows independents and voters of either party to vote in a party's primary, although voters are prohibited by law from participating in both parties' primaries simultaneously. A few states have a third form of primary, known as the blanket primary. These states provide a single primary ballot listing both the Republican and Democratic candidates by office. Each voter can cast only one vote per office, but can select a candidate of either party. Louisiana has a variation on this form in which all candidates are listed on the ballot but are not identified by party.

In most states, the winner of a primary election is the candidate who receives the largest number of votes, even if not a majority. In some border and southern states, however, there is a provision for a runoff primary if no candidate receives a majority of the vote (or, in North Carolina, 40 percent of the vote) in the regular primary. Slightly more than half the states have a sore-loser law that prevents a candidate who loses a primary from running as an independent or third-party candidate in the general election.

Primaries are the severest impediment imaginable to the strength of the party organizations. If primaries did not exist, candidates would have to work through party organizations in order to gain nomination, and they could be denied renomination if disloyal to the party's goals. Because of primaries, however, candidates have the option of seeking office on their own, and once elected (with or without the party's help), they can build an independent electoral base that effectively places them beyond the party's direct control.

Party organizations also lost influence over elections because of a decline in patronage. When a party won control of government a century ago, it also gained control of public jobs, which were doled out to loyal party workers. However, as government jobs in the early twentieth century shifted from patronage to the merit system (see Chapter 13), the party organizations lost control of many of these positions. Today, because of the expanded size of government, thousands of patronage jobs still exist. These government employees help staff the party organizations (along with volunteers), but most of them are more indebted to an individual politician than to a party organization. The people who work for members of Congress, for example, are all patronage employees, but they owe their jobs and their loyalty to their senator or representative, not their party.

In the process of taking control of nominations, candidates have also acquired control of most campaign money. At the turn of the century, when party machines were at their peak, most campaign funds passed through the hands of party leaders. Today, most of the money spent on congressional and presidential campaigns goes to the candidates without first passing through the parties.

In Europe, where there are no primary elections, the situation is very different. Parties control their nominations, and because of this, they also control campaign money and workers. Popular leaders in Europe are given fairly wide latitude by their party, but it is the parties, not the candidates, who are at the center of elections. A party's candidates are expected to campaign on the national platform and, if elected as a governing majority, to support its planks, which are formulated in conjunction with organizational leaders. A candidate who repudiates the party's platform is likely to be denied renomination in the next election.

The Structure and Role of Party Organizations

Although the influence of party organizations has declined, parties are not about to die out. Political leaders and activists need stable organizations through which they can work together, and the parties serve that purpose. Moreover, certain activities, such as voter registration drives and get-out-the-vote efforts on election day, benefit all of a party's candidates and are therefore more efficiently conducted through the party organization. Indeed, parties have staged a comeback of sorts.[27] National and state party organizations in particular have developed the capacity to assist candidates with fund-raising, polling, research, and media production, which are essential ingredients of a successful modern campaign.

Structurally, U.S. parties are loose associations of national, state, and local organizations (see Figure 8–5). The national party organizations cannot dictate the decisions of the state organizations, which in turn do not control the activities of

Figure 8–5

Formal Organization of the Political Party
U.S. parties are loosely structured alliances of national, state, and local organizations; most local parties are not as well organized as the formal chart implies.

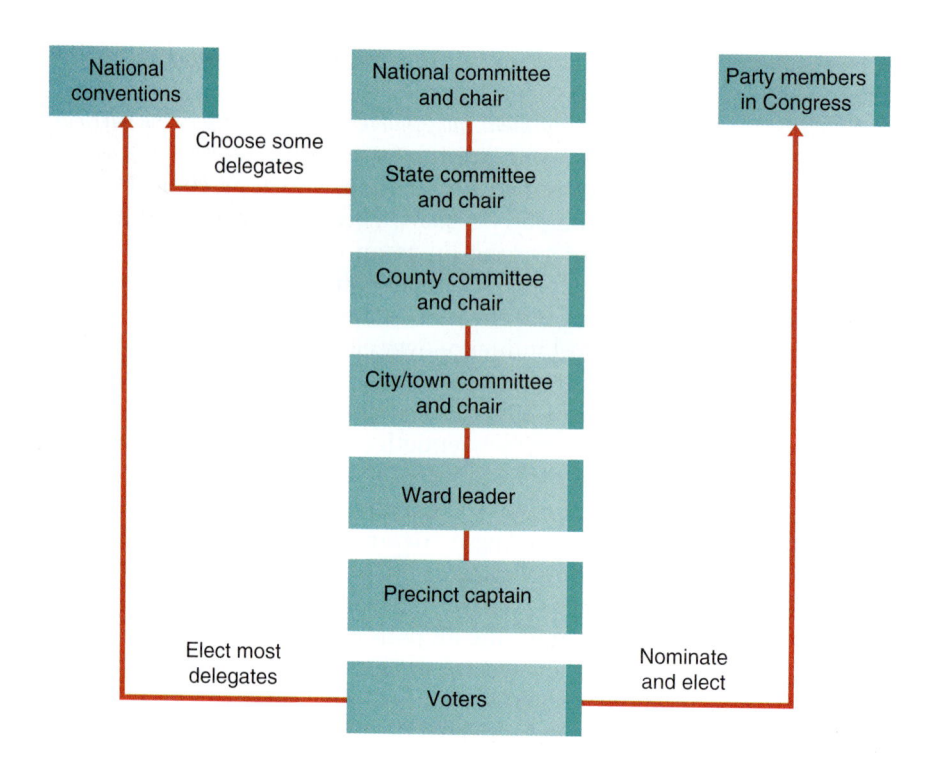

local organizations. However, there is communication between the levels because they all have a common interest in strengthening the party's position.[28]

Local Party Organizations

In a sense, U.S. parties are organized from the bottom up, not the top down. There are about five hundred thousand elective offices in the United States, of which fewer than five hundred are contested statewide and only two—the presidency and vice presidency—are contested nationally. All the rest are local offices; not surprisingly, at least 95 percent of party activists work within local organizations.

It is difficult to generalize about local parties because they vary greatly in their structure and activities. Today only a few local parties, including the Democratic organizations in Albany, Philadelphia, and Chicago, bear even a faint resemblance to the fabled old-time party machines that, in return for jobs and even welfare services, were able to control the vote on election day. Nevertheless, local parties tend to be strongest in urban areas and in the Northeast and Midwest, where parties traditionally have been more highly organized. In any case, local parties tend to specialize in elections that coincide with local electoral boundaries. Campaigns for mayor, city council, state legislature, county offices, and the like motivate most local parties to a greater degree than do congressional, statewide, and national contests.

In most urban areas, the party organizations today do not have enough workers to staff even a majority of local precincts (voting districts) on an ongoing basis. However, they do become more active during campaigns, when they open campaign headquarters, conduct registration drives, send mailings or de-

Chicago mayor Richard Daley speaks at a campaign event. He is the son of the legendary Chicago mayor of the same name, who headed the last of the big-city party machines. The earlier Mayor Daley "ruled" Chicago during a twenty-year, six-term reign that ended in the 1970s.

liver leaflets to voters, and help get out the vote. These activities are not trivial. Most local campaigns are not well funded, and the party's backing of a candidate can make the difference.

In most suburbs and towns, the party's role is less substantial. The parties exist organizationally but typically have little money and few workers; hence they cannot operate effectively as electoral organizations. The individual candidates must carry nearly the entire burden.

State Party Organizations

At the state level, each party is headed by a central committee made up of members of local party organizations and local and state officeholders. These state central committees do not meet regularly, and they provide only general policy guidance for the state organizations. Day-to-day operations and policy are directed by a chairperson, who is a full-time, paid employee of the state party. The central committee appoints the chairperson, but it often accepts the individual recommended by the party's leading politician, usually the governor or a U.S. senator.

In recent decades the state parties have expanded their budgets and staffs considerably and, therefore, have been able to play a more active electoral role.[29] In contrast, forty years ago about half of the state party organizations had no permanent staff at all. The increase in state party staff is largely due to improvements in communication technology, such as computer-assisted direct mail, which have made it easier for political organizations of all kinds, parties

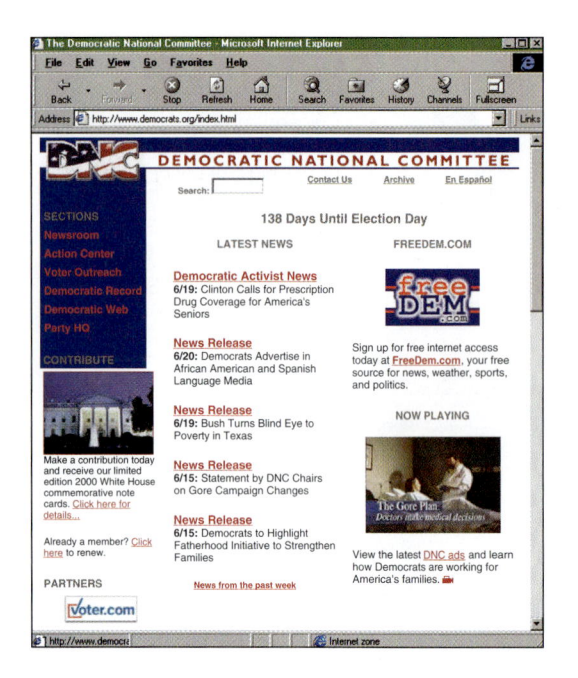

The home pages of the websites of the Democratic National Committee (DNC) and the Republican National Committee (RNC).

included, to raise funds. Having acquired the ability to pay for permanent staffs, state parties have used them to expand their activities, which range from polling to issues research to campaign management.

State party organizations concentrate on statewide races, including those for governor and U.S. senator,[30] and also focus on races for the state legislature. They play a smaller role in campaigns for national or local offices, and in most states, they do not endorse candidates in statewide primary contests.

National Party Organizations

The national party organizations are structured much like those at the state level: they have a national committee, a national party chairperson, and a support staff. The national headquarters for the Republican and Democratic parties are located in Washington, D.C. Although in theory the national parties are run by their committees, neither the Democratic National Committee (DNC) nor the Republican National Committee (RNC) has great power. The RNC (with more than 150 members) and the DNC (with more than 300 members) are too cumbersome to act as deliberative bodies. They meet only periodically, and their power is largely confined to setting organizational policy, such as determining the site of the party's presidential nominating convention and the rules governing the selection of convention delegates. They have no power to decide nominations or to determine candidates' policy positions.

The national party's day-to-day operations are directed by a national chairperson chosen by the national committee, although it defers to the president's choice when the party controls the White House. The national chairperson is supported by a permanent staff that concentrates on providing assistance in presidential and congressional campaigns.

This focus began in the 1970s when Republican leaders decided that a revamped national party organization could play a contributing role in to-

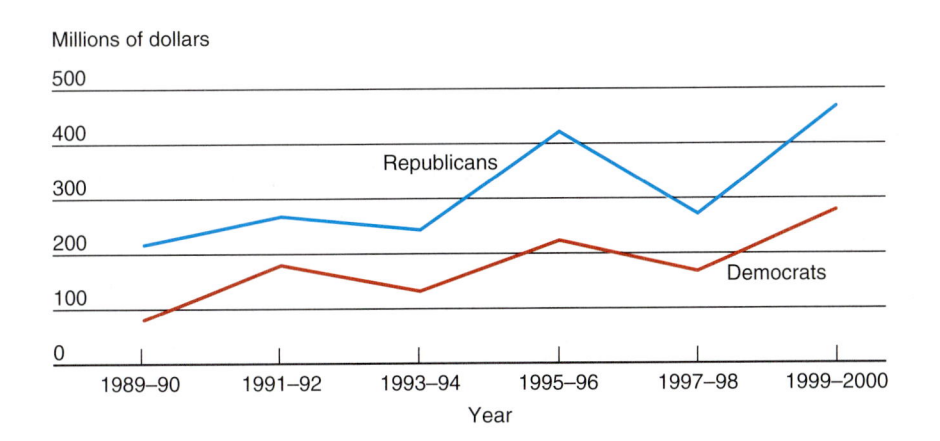

Figure 8-6

National Party Fund-raising, 1989–2000

Over the years, the Republican party has raised significantly more money than the Democratic party has. The figures include fund-raising by the DNC, RNC, DCCC, NRCC, DSCC, and NRSC. Soft-money (nonfederal) fund-raising is not included.

Source: Federal Elections Commission, 2002.

day's campaigns. The RNC developed campaign-management "colleges" and "seminars" for candidates and their staffs, compiled massive amounts of computer-based electoral data, sent field representatives to assist state and local party leaders in modernizing their operations, and established a media production division. The range of services the RNC provides is substantial. For example, the RNC tapes and catalogues C-SPAN's televised coverage of congressional debate and can instantly retrieve the statement of any speaker on any issue. Republican challengers use this material to create attack ads directed at Democratic incumbents, while Republican incumbents use it to show themselves acting forcefully on issues of concern to their constituents. The Republican model has also filtered down to the state Republican party committees, which, in varying degrees, provide the types of media, data research, and educational services that the national committee offers. In every recent election, Republicans have raised and spent substantially more money than the Democrats have (see Figure 8-6), reflecting the greater affluence of the GOP's constituents.

The DNC in the early 1980s followed the Republicans' example, but its later start and less affluent followers have kept the Democrats behind. Modern campaigns, as David Adamany notes, are based on "cash," and Democrats are relatively cash-poor.[31]

The Parties and Money

The parties' major role in campaigns is the raising and spending of money. The RNC and the DNC are major sources of campaign funds, as are the party campaign committees in the House and the Senate: the Democratic Congressional Campaign Committee (DCCC), the National Republican Congressional Committee (NRCC), the Democratic Senatorial Campaign Committee (DSCC), and the National Republican Senatorial Committee (NRSC).

These committees have more of a **service relationship** than a power relationship with their party's candidates. The party offers help to virtually any of its candidates who have a chance of victory. Without the ability to control the nominating process, the party has little choice but to embrace nearly all candidates who run under its banner. At a minimum, this approach increases the likelihood that the party will gain a congressional majority and thus acquire control of the committees and top leadership positions in the House and Senate

service relationship The situation where party organizations assist candidates for office but have no power to require them to support the party's main policy positions.

Fighting Words

Should Soft Money Have Been Banned?

No campaign finance issue of recent years received more attention than has soft money—unrestricted contributions to political parties. This loophole in the finance laws allowed millions of dollars—$500 million in the 1999–2000 election cycle alone—to slip into campaigns alongside restricted contributions. The issue of soft money was the subject of heated debate in Congress in 2002 in the aftermath of the Enron scandal, which included large soft money contributions by top corporate executives. The scandal helped opponents of soft money obtain the Senate and House votes necessary to restrict the practice. In the Senate, the leading proponent of a ban on soft money was John McCain, who for years had argued that it was corrupting the political process. A leading opponent was Mitch McConnell, who for years had argued that limits of almost any kind of campaign contributions were an intrusion on free expression.

Yes: The large amount of soft money given to both parties by various industries and the aggregate amount of tax breaks those industries received, I believe, . . . have impaired our integrity as political parties and as a legislative institution. . . . That is the problem I am trying to address with this legislation and no attack, no amount of head-in-the-sand pretense that soft money doesn't affect legislation will cause me to desist in my efforts. . . . If special interests did not believe their millions of dollars in donations buy them special consideration [they] wouldn't give us that money would they?
—U.S. Senator John McCain (R-Ariz.)

No: To limit "special interest" influence and overall spending, the government must limit all avenues of participation. Anything else is just a shell game. The reformers continue to grapple with a thorny catch-22: pass comprehensive reform or pass narrow, ineffective and arguably less blatantly unconstitutional reform. Of course, there is a third option: recognize the First Amendment as America's premier political reform and look upon all this issue advocacy . . . as [a] healthy indication of a vibrant democracy.
—U.S. Senator Mitch McConnell (R-Ky.)

(see Chapter 11). The party may also acquire some additional loyalty from officeholders as a result of the contributions it makes to their campaigns. But since the party is more or less willing to support any candidate whatever his or her policy positions, its money does not give it substantial control over how party members conduct themselves after they take office.

A party can legally give $10,000 directly to a House candidate and $37,500 to a Senate candidate. This funding, along with the money a candidate receives from individual contributors ($2,000 is the maximum per contributor) and interest groups ($5,000 is the maximum per group), is termed **hard money,** since it goes directly to the candidate and can be spent as he or she chooses.

Limits on party contributions were established when the campaign finance laws were reformed in the 1970s in response to the Watergate scandal. However, a loophole in the laws was exposed when a court ruling gave the parties a nearly unlimited opportunity to raise and spend campaign funds provided the funds were not channeled directly to a party's candidates. Although the law

hard money Campaign funds given directly to candidates to spend as they choose.

Figure 8-7

Soft and Hard Money, 1999–2000

By the 1999–2000 election cycle, soft money had come to rival hard money as a way of funding campaigns. The two major parties each raised nearly $250 million in soft money, which was almost half of all money raised by the Democratic Party and more than a third of the money raised by the GOP. In 2002, Congress enacted a ban on soft-money contributions.
Source: Federal Elections Commission, 2002.

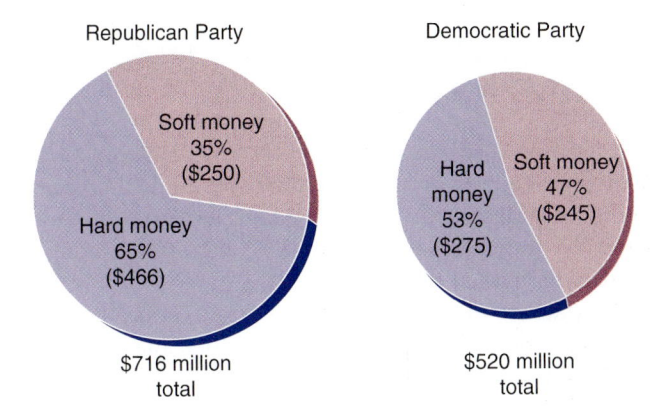

Republican Party
- Soft money 35% ($250)
- Hard money 65% ($466)
- $716 million total

Democratic Party
- Soft money 47% ($245)
- Hard money 53% ($275)
- $520 million total

limited how much an individual could give directly to a candidate for federal office, it did not restrict individual contributions to a political party. Thus, whereas a wealthy contributor could legally give a candidate only a limited amount, that same contributor could give an unlimited amount to the candidate's party. These contributions were **soft money** in the sense that a party could not hand it over directly to a candidate. But the party could use these contributions to support party activities such as voter registration and get-out-the-vote drives that could indirectly benefit its candidates. The party could also funnel soft money to state and local party organizations and, by concentrating it on organizations in areas with close races, could influence the outcome of those races. Finally, it could be used for generic party advertising—that is, ad campaigns based on the party and its message rather than on a particular candidate. In some cases, the line between the use of hard and soft money was hard to distinguish. In 1996, for example, the Democratic Party ran a $100 million ad campaign that did not directly urge voters to support Clinton but did include pictures of him and references to his accomplishments as president.

The significance of soft money was evident in the fund-raising figures from the 1999–2000 election cycle. The Democratic and Republican parties together received roughly $500 million in soft money contributions, compared with a combined $740 million in hard money contributions (see Figure 8–7). Soft money accounted for nearly half of all money taken in by the Democrats and more than a third of that received by the Republicans.

In his surprisingly strong bid for the 2000 Republican presidential nomination, John McCain urged a ban on soft money, which contributed to heightened interest within Congress in closing the loophole. In 2002, revelations that the bankrupt Enron Corporation had employed soft money contributions as part of its strategy to influence national energy policy and hide illegal business activity furthered the drive to end the practice. In the previous decade, Enron had contributed $4.4 million to Republican candidates and committees and $1.5 million to Democratic candidates and committees. Prodded by these revelations, Congress restricted soft money contributions, but few believe that the problem of money in politics can be solved once and for all. Every effort at campaign finance reform has encountered pitfalls, usually in the form of an unexpected loophole of one kind or another. Just as water always runs downhill, money always seems to find its way into election politics.

soft money Campaign contributions that are not subject to legal limits and are given to parties rather than directly to candidates.

THE CANDIDATE-CENTERED CAMPAIGN

Although competition between the Republican and Democratic parties provides the backdrop to today's campaigns, the campaigns themselves are largely controlled by the candidates, particularly in congressional, statewide, and presidential races. Each candidate has a personal organization, created especially for the campaign and disbanded once it is over.

Today's candidates tend to be self-starters. Some candidates still rise through the ranks of the party or are drafted because no other qualified persons are willing to run. But most candidates seek high office because they aspire to careers in politics. They are entrepreneurs who play what the political consultant Joe Napolitan called "the election game."[32] The game begins with money, lots of it.

Seeking Funds: The Money Chase

Campaigns for high office are expensive, and the costs keep rising. In 1980, about $250 million was spent on all Senate and House campaigns combined. The figure had jumped to $425 million by 1990 and topped $1 billion ($1,000 million) in 2000.

Because of the high cost of campaigns, candidates are forced to spend much of their time raising funds, which come primarily from individual contributors, interest groups (through PACs, discussed in Chapter 9), and political parties. The **money chase** is relentless.[33] It has been estimated that a U.S. senator must raise $10,000 a week on average throughout the entire six-year term in order to raise the $3 million or so that it takes to run a competitive Senate campaign in most states. A Senate campaign in a large state can cost several times that amount. In 2000, Representative Rick Lazio and First Lady Hillary Clinton raised nearly $70 million for the New York Senate race. House campaigns are

money chase A term used to describe the fact that U.S. campaigns are very expensive and that candidates must spend a great amount of time raising funds in order to compete successfully.

U.S. Senator Hillary Clinton is the only first lady to seek elective office. She moved to New York to compete in the state's Senate race in 2000. Clinton is shown here campaigning on the streets of New York City.

STATES IN THE NATION

Public Funding of State Elections

Public funding of federal elections is limited to the presidential campaign. The funds are given directly to presidential candidates who meet the qualifying criteria. About half the states also have public funding of election campaigns. Some of these states give the money to the political parties, which then allocate it to candidates or spend it on party activities, such as get-out-the-vote efforts. Other states give funds directly to candidates, although funding is often provided only to candidates for designated offices, such as governor. Many states use the same method of raising these funds that the federal government does: in filing their tax returns, residents can check a box indicating they are willing to have a few of their tax dollars spent on campaigns.

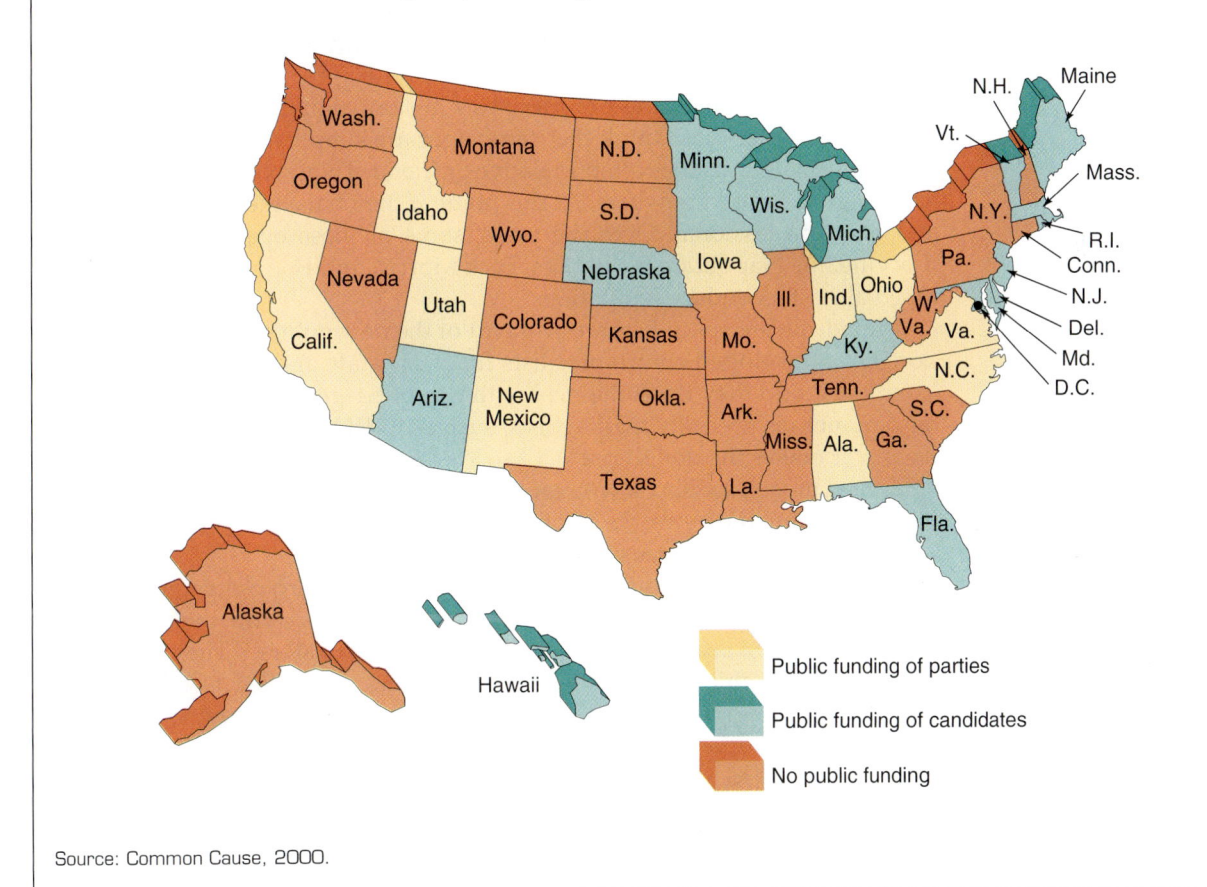

- Public funding of parties
- Public funding of candidates
- No public funding

Source: Common Cause, 2000.

---

less costly, but expenditures of $1 million or more are commonplace.[34] As for presidential elections, even the nominating race is expensive. It was generally thought that a candidate needs at least $20 million to have a realistic chance of gaining nomination, but even that figure may need revising. In 2000, Texas governor George W. Bush raised $75 million for his nominating campaign. (In presidential races, but not congressional ones, candidates are eligible to receive federal funds, a topic discussed in Chapter 12).

As might be expected, incumbents have a distinct advantage in fundraising. They have contributor lists from past campaigns and have acquired the public visibility and political clout that donors like. In recent House and Senate races, incumbents have outspent their challengers by more than 2 to 1.[35]

Creating Organization: Hired Guns

The "old politics" emphasized party rallies and door-to-door canvassing, which required organizations built around campaign volunteers. The "new politics" is based on the mass media and requires a much different kind of organizational structure. The key operatives are campaign consultants, pollsters, media producers, and fund-raising specialists. They are **hired guns** who charge hefty fees for their services. The "new king-makers" is the way the writer David Chagall characterized these pros.[36]

Some of the hired guns are specialists in campaign management. Inexperienced candidates often think that campaigns are simple to run and entrust the job to an amateur, who is often a relative or friend. They soon discover that their campaign is headed nowhere. At this point, if they have the money, they hire a seasoned professional. Over the years, some of these operatives, like James Carville, Joe Napolitan, Ed Rollins, Dick Morris, and Roger Ailes, have developed almost legendary reputations.

Fund-raising specialists are also part of the new politics. Direct mail operators have developed contributor lists for every state and nearly every type of candidacy, and they flood the mail with computer-generated letters. There are also numerous specialty mailing lists, such as EMILY's List (*early money is like yeast*, "it makes the dough rise"). EMILY's List was started in the 1980s to provide seed money for liberal women candidates. Effective fund-raisers also know how to tap into the networks of large contributors and interest groups who give to election campaigns (see Chapter 9).

Polling is another essential component of the modern campaign. Although candidates make use of the public polls conducted by Gallup, the news media, and other organizations, they also hire their own pollsters.[37] They also rely on focus groups, which are small groups of voters assembled to talk at length about the issues and candidates and, in some instances, to evaluate proposed themes and materials, such as televised political ads. Polls and focus groups enable candidates to identify messages that are likely to resonate with the voters. At one point in the 2000 presidential race, for example, George W. Bush shifted from the issue of taxes to issues of education and health care after polls indicated these issues were having a larger impact on undecided voters.

Media consultants are another staple of the modern campaign. These experts are adept at producing televised political advertising and creating the "photo-ops" and other staged events that attract news coverage. They also teach the candidates how to use the media properly. Inexperienced candidates soon discover that they cannot "just be themselves" when talking with journalists or participating in televised debates. They have to conform to the demands of the media, such as the preference of television journalists for sound bites: short, pithy statements that add zest and zing to a news story.[38]

hired guns A term that refers to the professional consultants who run campaigns for high office.

Citizenship

Getting Involved, Making a Difference

Political Strategy

"Political strategy" is a practice synonymous with modern campaigning, and it is a practice that is often scorned. The term seems to imply some form of manipulation. Nevertheless, strategy is an essential part of political action. Ideas don't suddenly turn into policies and programs. Candidates don't miraculously get elected to office. Strategic action is required to make these things happen.

And political strategy has always existed. It might be difficult today to acknowledge, for example, that the Constitution became law through strategic action. The Framers were men of vision, but they were also masterful politicians. They acted strategically from the moment of their arrival in Philadelphia. They closed the deliberations to outsiders and proceeded to ignore Congress's instructions that they were only to amend the Articles of Confederation. Proponents of the Virginia Plan rushed to get their proposal on the table, knowing that the order of discussion could well determine the outcome. When they were finished, the delegates stacked the dice in favor of the Constitution by declaring that it would become law when approved by nine states as opposed to the full thirteen that Congress had mandated.

The Framers used many of the strategic tools that today's political activists employ. They ran a media campaign. In scores of newspaper articles, Madison and Hamilton made the case for ratification. They were masters at framing their message. Their arguments were cast in the most favorable terms possible while a negative spin was placed on the Anti-Federalists' arguments. The Framers also shamelessly played on Americans' admiration of George Washington by saying he would become the nation's first president and would ensure the Constitution's success. And in the end, they used coercion to get North Carolina and Rhode Island to ratify; they said to these states that the others would not come to their defense if they were attacked by a foreign power.

The point is not that the Framers hoodwinked Americans. The Framers believed that the government of the Constitution was the best available option, and they made the strongest case possible for it. It was not, however, the only alternative available to Americans in 1787. The Anti-Federalists' idea of a state-centered union also had its backers. But the Anti-Federalists were not as well organized and were less effective in making their case, and the Framers' vision of a new government prevailed.

In sum, strategic thinking is a basic aspect of effective political action. Strategy is basically a plan for pursuing a particular goal. Strategy is not incompatible with the democratic process. Autocrats have no need for strategy; they rule by dictate. In a democracy, however, popular consent is the basis of government, and the strategy is part of the process of acquiring consent. Whether taking action on your campus or in your community, you should not hesitate to think strategically in the pursuit of your civic goals.

Devising Strategy: Packaging the Candidate

In the old days, candidates were nearly prepackaged. They were labeled as Democrats or Republicans, which was about all the guidance most voters wanted or needed. Party labels are still meaningful, but today's campaigns are also based on media images.

Often depicted as hollow deceptions, images are more typically rooted in factual arguments.[39] They are constructed by placing aspects of the candidate's partisanship, policy positions, record, and personality in the context of the

TABLE 8-1

Television Campaign Practices in Selected Democracies

In many democracies, free television time is provided to political parties, and candidates are not allowed to buy advertising time. The United States provides no free time to parties and allows candidates to purchase air time. Television debates are also a feature of many U.S. campaigns.

COUNTRY	PAID TV ADS ALLOWED?	UNRESTRICTED FREE TV TIME PROVIDED?	ARE TV DEBATES HELD?
Canada	Yes	Yes	Yes
France	No	Yes	Yes
Germany	Yes	Yes	Yes
Great Britain	No	Yes	No
Italy	No	Yes	Yes
Netherlands	No	No	Yes
United States	Yes	No	Yes

packaging A term of modern campaigning that refers to the process of recasting a candidate's record into an appealing image.

Simulation
www.mhhe.com/patterson6

air wars A term that refers to the fact that modern campaigns are often a battle of opposing televised advertising campaigns.

voters' "ideal" candidate, a process known as the **packaging** of a candidate.[40] The voters want a representative who is honest, able, straightforward, resolute, and responsive to their interests, but there are limits on the claims a candidate can reasonably make. It would be difficult, for example, for Democratic incumbents who have been long-time advocates of welfare spending to convincingly portray themselves as fiscal conservatives. Instead, they would base their images as responsive legislators on other issues, such as education and social security. In any case, officeseekers try to create a favorable portrayal of their candidacy that is also plausible. In a way, this type of packaging is as old as politics itself. Andrew Jackson's self-portrayal as "the champion of the people" is an image that any modern candidate could appreciate. What is new is the need to fit the image to the requirements of a media campaign. It must conform to a world of sound bites, thirty-second ads, and televised debates.

The battleground of the modern campaign is the mass media. Televised advertising in particular enables candidates to communicate directly, and on their own terms, with the voters.[41] Candidates spend heavily on the production and airing of televised ads, which account for more than half the expenditures in every presidential campaign and most congressional races. Indeed, televised ads are usually cited as the main reason for the high cost of U.S. campaigns. In most democracies, televised campaigning takes place through parties, which receive *free* air time to make their pitch. Many democracies even prohibit the purchase of televised advertising time by candidates (see Table 8-1).

Air wars is the term that the political scientist Darrell West applies to candidates' use of televised ads. Candidates increasingly play off each other's ads, seeking to gain the strategic advantage.[42] Modern production techniques enable well-funded candidates to get new ads on the air within a few hours' time, which allows them to rebut attacks and exploit fast-breaking developments. "Rapid-response" was the term used by the Clinton campaign in 1992 and 1996 for its capacity to counter Republican charges. For example, when Bush ads in the 1992 campaign accused Clinton of having raised taxes when governor of Arkansas, Clinton aired an immediate rebuttal based on his interpretation of his tax record.[43] Rapid-response has become a standard tactic in high-profile contests; both the Bush and the Gore campaigns employed the tactic in 2000.

The media campaign also takes place through news outlets, but coverage varies depending on the race and location. Many House candidates are nearly ignored by their local news media. The New York City media market, for example, includes more than a score of House districts in New York, New Jersey, Pennsylvania, and Connecticut, and candidates in these districts get little or no coverage from the New York media. The presidential campaign, in contrast, gets daily coverage from both national and local media. Between these extremes are Senate races and House races in less populated areas; they always get some news coverage and, if hotly contested, may get heavy coverage.

Candidates try to put a positive spin on their news coverage. They also try to campaign in ways that will lessen the negative spin they have come to expect from journalists. The news is mostly critical in tone, and a candidate's blunder or misstatement can result in a torrent of bad news.[44] As a result, candidates rely increasingly on scripted statements rather than spontaneous remarks when dealing with the press.

The media campaign also includes debates and talk-show appearances. Debates are particularly important because they often attract a large and attentive audience. But they are also risky encounters, since they give viewers a chance to directly compare the candidates. A weak or bumbled performance can seriously damage a candidate's chances in a close race. To reduce the risks, candidates often spend the day or two before a debate rehearsing their presentation.

Internet Politics: In the Web

New communication technology usually makes its way into campaign politics, and the Internet is no exception. Every presidential candidate in 2000 had a website. Each site was packed with information, but its main purposes were to generate public support, to raise money, and to attract and organize volunteers. Republican candidate John McCain raised more than $4 million for his campaign through Internet contributions.

Although television is still the principal mechanism of election politics, some observers believe that the Internet may eventually replace it, particularly in congressional races. E-mail is much cheaper than television advertising (or, for that matter, traditional mail) and can be more easily directed at supporters and swing voters. Because it is a targeted medium, the Internet may become the channel through which candidates attack each other with charges they feel are not adequately voiced through other channels. This tactic was used, for example, by Republican hopeful Steve Forbes in his unsuccessful effort to derail George W. Bush's 2000 nominating campaign. In one instance, the Forbes campaign e-mailed subscribers a copy of a newspaper column that

A campaign volunteer works the phone on behalf of George W. Bush's 2000 presidential campaign. Campaign volunteers are often more interested in a particular issue or candidate than a party.

mocked a Bush speech to teenagers that described "a drunken college escapade when he [Bush] stole a Christmas wreath." The message claimed that the "real lesson" in Bush's remarks was that "the criminal justice system works for rich, white men."[45]

PARTIES, CANDIDATES, AND THE PUBLIC'S INFLUENCE

Candidate-centered campaigns have some distinct advantages. First, they lend flexibility to and infuse new blood into electoral politics. When political conditions and issues change, self-directed candidates quickly adjust, bringing new ideas into the political arena. Strong party organizations are rigid by comparison. Until recently, for example, the British Labour party was controlled by old-line activists who refused to concede that changes in the British economy called for changes in the party's trade unionist and economic policies. The result was a series of humiliating defeats to the Conservative party that ended only after Tony Blair and other proponents of "New Labour" successfully rebuilt the party's image.

Second, candidate-centered campaigns encourage national officeholders to be responsive to local interests. In building personal followings among their state and district constituents, members of Congress respond to local needs. Nearly every significant domestic program enacted by Congress is adjusted to accommodate the interests of states and localities that would otherwise be hurt by the policy. Members of Congress are not obliged to support the legislative position of their party's majority, and they often extract favors for their constituents as the price of their support. Where strong national parties exist, national interests take precedence over local concerns. In both France and Britain, for example, the pleas of representatives of underdeveloped regions have often gone unheeded by their party's majority.

In other respects, however, candidate-centered campaigns have some real disadvantages. Often they degenerate into mere personality contests and are fertile ground for powerful special interest groups, which contribute much of the money that underwrites candidates' campaigns. Many groups give large sums of money to incumbents of both parties, which enables them to insulate themselves from an election's outcome. Whether the Republicans win or the Democrats win, they are assured of having friends in high places.

Candidate-centered campaigns also blur the connection between electing and governing by making it easier for officeholders to deny responsibility for government's actions. If national policy goes awry, an incumbent can always say that he or she is only one vote out of many and that the real problem resides with the president or with "others" in Congress.[46] By comparison, lawmakers in a party-centered system cannot easily evade responsibility for what the government has done. In such systems, public dissatisfaction with the performance of government often leads to the majority party's defeat in the next election.

The problem of accountability in the U.S. system is illustrated by surveys that have asked Americans about their confidence in Congress. Although most citizens do not have a high opinion of Congress as a whole, most citizens also say they have confidence in their own representative in Congress. This paradoxical attitude prevails in so many districts that the net result in most elections is a Congress whose membership is not greatly changed from the previous one (see Chapter 11). In the 2000 elections, despite a widespread view that Congress was bogged down in narrow-minded partisanship, less than 3 percent of incumbents seeking reelection were defeated.

Candidate-centered campaigns also make it difficult for voters to act in unison. Candidates of the same party in different constituencies stand for different things; these discrepancies deprive the national electorate of an opportunity to elect a lawmaking majority pledged to a common platform. Of course, U.S. elections produce lawmaking majorities, and it is safe to assume that most elected officials of a particular party share certain ideas even when they run and win on their own.[47] But this system is a far cry from one in which voters in all districts choose among candidates who are committed to sharply defined party platforms.

In sum, candidate-centered campaigns strengthen the relationship between the voters and their individual representative while at the same time weakening the relationship between the full electorate and their representative institutions. Whether this arrangement serves the public's interest is debatable. Most citizens are not even sure. A 2000 Harvard poll found that 68 percent of Americans agreed with the statement that today's politics "seem more like theater or entertainment than like something to be taken seriously." Nevertheless, it is clear that Americans do not want truly strong parties. Parties survived the shift to candidate-centered campaigns and will persist, but their heyday has passed. (Congressional and presidential campaigns are discussed further in Chapters 11 and 12, respectively.)

Self-Quiz
www.mhhe.com/patterson6

SUMMARY

Political parties serve to link the public with its elected leaders. In the United States, this linkage is provided by the two-party system; only the Republican and Democratic parties have any chance of winning control of government. The fact that the United States has only two major parties is explained by several factors: an electoral system—characterized by single-member districts—that makes it difficult for third parties to compete for power; each party's willingness to accept differing political views; and a political culture that stresses compromise and negotiation rather than ideological rigidity.

Because the United States has only two major parties, each of which seeks to gain majority support, their candidates normally tend to avoid controversial or extreme political positions. Candidates typically pursue moderate and somewhat overlapping policies. Nonetheless, Democratic and Republican candidates sometimes do offer sharply contrasting policy alternatives, particularly in times of political unrest.

America's parties are decentralized, fragmented organizations. The national party organization does not control the policies and activities of the state organizations, and they in turn do not control the local organizations. Traditionally the local organizations have controlled most of the party's work force because most elections are contested at the local level. Local parties, however, vary markedly in their vitality. Whatever their level, America's party organizations are relatively weak. They lack control over nominations and elections. Candidates can bypass the party organization and win nomination through primary elections. Individual candidates also control most of the organizational structure and money necessary to win elections. Recently the state and national party organizations have expanded their capacity to provide candidates with modern campaign services. Nevertheless, party organizations at all levels have few ways of controlling the candidates who run under their banners. They assist candidates with campaign technology, workers, and funds, but cannot compel candidates' loyalty to organizational goals.

American political campaigns, particularly those for higher-level office, are candidate centered. Most candidates are self-starters who become adept at "the election game." They spend much of their time raising campaign funds, and they build their personal organizations around hired guns: pollsters, media producers, and election consultants. Strategy and image making are key components of the modern campaign, as is televised political advertising, which accounts for roughly half of all spending in presidential and congressional races.

Because America's parties cannot control their candidates or coordinate their policies at all levels, they are unable to consistently present the voters with coherent, detailed platforms for governing. The national electorate as a whole is thus denied a clear choice among policy alternatives and has difficulty exerting a decisive and predictable influence through elections.

KEY TERMS

air wars
candidate-centered politics
dealignment
grassroots party
hard money
hired guns
money chase
multiparty system
nomination
packaging (of a candidate)
party-centered politics
party coalition
party competition
party organizations
party realignment
political party
primary election (direct primary)
proportional representation
service relationship
single-member districts
soft money
split-ticket voting
straight-ticket voting
two-party system

SUGGESTED READINGS

Aldrich, John H. *Why Parties? The Origin and Transformation of Political Parties in America*. Chicago: University of Chicago Press, 1995. An insightful analysis of what parties are and how they emerge and develop.

Flanigan, William H., and Nancy H. Zingale. *Political Behavior of the American Electorate*, 10th ed. Washington, D.C.: Congressional Quarterly Press, 2002. A study of Americans' electoral behavior.

King, Anthony. *Running Scared: The Victory of Campaigning over Governing in America*. New York: Free Press, 1997. An analysis of why America's leaders have succumbed to the pressure of the permanent campaign.

Lijphardt, Arend. *Electoral Systems and Party Systems: A Study of Twenty-Seven Democracies, 1945–1990*. New York: Oxford University Press, 1994. A comprehensive study of the relationship between electoral systems and party systems.

Patterson, Kelly D. *Political Parties and the Maintenance of Liberal Democracy*. New York: Columbia University Press, 1996. A systematic look at the effects of political parties on American government and politics.

Pomper, Gerald M. *The Election of 2000: Reports and Interpretations*. New York: Seven Bridges Press, 2001. An edited volume of assessments of the 2000 election by a team of thoughtful scholars and observers.

Rosenstone, Steven J., Roy L. Behr, and Edward H. Lazarus. *Third Parties in America,* 2d ed. Princeton, N.J.: Princeton University Press, 1996. An analysis of America's third parties and their impact on the two-party system.

West, Darrell M. *Air Wars: Television Advertising in Election Campaigns, 1952–1992,* 3rd ed. Washington, D.C.: Congressional Quarterly Press, 2001. A thorough study of the role of televised advertising in election campaigns.

LIST OF WEBSITES

http://www.democrats.org/
The Democratic National Committee's site; it provides information on the party's platform, candidates, officials, and organization.

http://www.greenparties.org
The Green party's website; it contains information on the party's philosophy and policy goals.

http://www.rnc.org/
Home page of the Republican National Committee; it offers information on Republican leaders, policy positions, and organizations.

http://www.jamescarvillesoffice.com
The website of James Carville, one of the nation's top campaign consultants and a frequent guest on talk-show programs.

> *The flaw in the pluralist heaven is that the heavenly chorus sings with a strong upper-class bias.*
> —E. E. Schattschneider[1]

9

Interest Groups:
Organizing for Influence

They launched their attack within hours of the announcement that congressional Republicans had included Medicare in their balanced-budget proposal. The GOP lawmakers planned a $1.1 trillion reduction in federal spending over seven years, including a $270 billion cut in health care for the elderly. Senior-citizen groups assailed the plan and quickly organized a mass demonstration outside the Capitol. The next step was an orchestrated campaign of thousands of angry calls, letters, telegrams, and faxes from retirees to their congressional representatives.

President Clinton sided with the seniors' lobby, promising to veto the Republican bill, which led to a showdown between Congress and the White House that forced a temporary shutdown of the federal government. In January 1996, after a six-week battle and with their poll ratings dropping almost daily, Republican lawmakers shelved their balanced-budget proposal.

The campaign against the Republicans' Medicare initiative suggests why interest groups are both admired and feared. On the one hand, groups have a legitimate right to express their views on public policy issues. It is entirely appropriate for senior citizens or any other group—whether farmers, consumers, business firms, or college students—to actively promote their interests through collective action. In fact, the *pluralist* theory of American politics (see Chapter 1) holds that society's interests are most effectively represented through the efforts of groups. An extreme statement of this view is Arthur F. Bentley's claim in 1908 that society is "nothing other than the complex of groups that compose it."[2] Although modern pluralists make far less sweeping claims, they do contend that the group process, on balance, is open to a great range of interests, nearly all of which benefit from organized activity in one significant way or another.

Yet groups can wield too much power. If a group gets its way at an unreasonable cost to the rest of society, the public interest is harmed. When the Republican budget package was prepared in Congress, polls indicated that most Americans wanted a balanced federal budget and were willing to bear a fair share of the costs. Did the senior-citizen lobby, in pursuit of its own narrow interest, derail a sound budgetary proposal? Or did the Republican package, which also included tax cuts for upper-income Americans, place on the elderly too much of the burden of a balanced budget?

Opinions on these questions differ widely, but there is no doubt that the special interest in some cases wrongly prevails over the general interest. Indeed, most observers are of the opinion that groups have achieved too much influence over public policy in recent decades. Some analysts describe the situation as the triumph of **single-issue politics:** separate groups organized around nearly every conceivable policy issue, with each group pressing its demands and influence to the utmost, at whatever cost to the broader society. The structure of the American political system provides fertile ground for group influence, particularly when a group seeks to protect government benefits it

single-issue politics The situation in which separate groups are organized around nearly every conceivable policy issue and press their demands and influence to the utmost.

interest group A set of individuals who are organized to promote a shared political interest.

already receives. The system's elaborate checks and balances make it relatively easy for a group, if it has support even within a single institution, to block efforts to cut its benefits. (This "Madisonian dilemma" will be explored more fully in the chapter's concluding section.)

An **interest group** can be defined as a set of individuals who are organized to promote a shared political interest. Also called a "faction" or "pressure group" or "special interest," an interest group is characterized by its formalized organization and by its pursuit of policy goals that stem from its members' shared interest. Thus, a bridge club or an amateur softball team is not an interest group because it does not seek to influence the political process. Organizations such as the Association of Wheat Growers, Common Cause, the National Organization for Women, the World Wildlife Fund, the National Rifle Association, and the Anti-Defamation League of B'nai B'rith are interest groups because, despite their differences, they all meet the definition's two criteria: each is an organized entity and each seeks to further its members' interests through political action.

Interest groups promote public policies, encourage the political participation of their members, support candidates for public office, and work to influence policymakers. Interest groups are thus similar to political parties in certain respects, but the two types of organizations differ in important ways. Major political parties address a broad range of issues so as to appeal to diverse blocs of voters. Parties exist to contest elections. They change their policy positions as the voters' preferences change; for the party, winning is almost everything. In comparison, interest groups focus on specific issues of immediate concern to their members; farm groups, for example, concentrate on agricultural policy. A group may involve itself in elections, but its purpose is to influence public policy.

This chapter examines the degree to which various interests in American society are represented by organized groups, the process by which interest groups exert influence, and the costs and benefits of group politics in regard to the public good. The main points made in the chapter are the following:

- *Although nearly all interests in American society are organized to some degree, those associated with economic activity, particularly business enterprises, are by far the most thoroughly organized.* Their advantage rests on their superior financial resources and on the fact that they offer potential members private goods (such as wages and jobs).

- *Groups that do not have economic activity as their primary function often have organizational problems.* They pursue public or collective goods (such as a safer environment) that are available even to individuals who are not group members, and so individuals may choose not to pay the costs of membership.

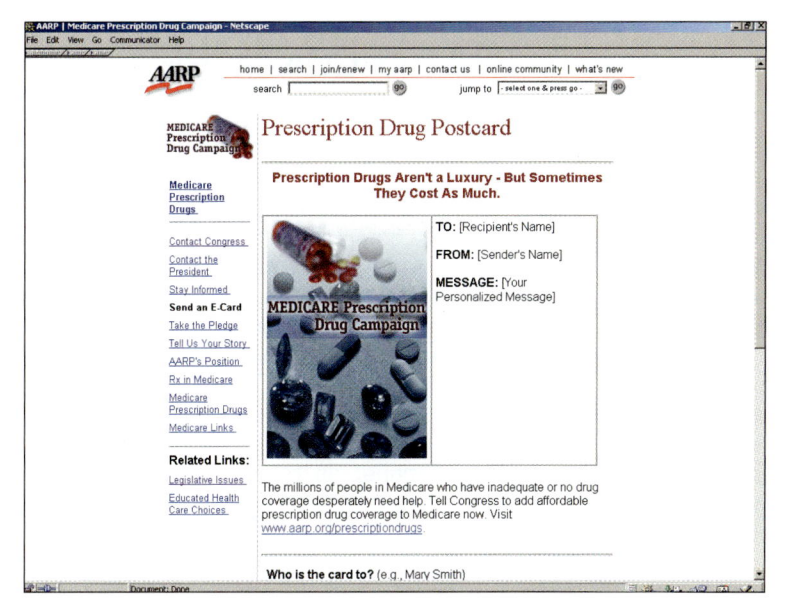

The American Association of Retired Persons (AARP) has roughly thirty million members and is the largest citizens' group. It regularly encourages its members to contact Congress on issues facing retirees, as in this electronic message on prescription drugs.

- *Lobbying and electioneering are the traditional means by which groups communicate with and influence political leaders.* Recent developments, including grassroots lobbying and PACs, have given added visibility to groups' activities.

- *The interest-group system overrepresents business interests and higher-income groups and fosters policies that serve a group's interest more than the public interest.* Thus, although groups are an essential part of the democratic process, they also distort that process.

THE INTEREST-GROUP SYSTEM

In the 1830s, the Frenchman Alexis de Tocqueville wrote that the "principle of association" was nowhere more evident than in America.[3] The country's tradition of free association has always made it easy for Americans to join together for political purposes, and their diverse interests have given them reason to seek influence through specialized groups. Few nations have as many separate economic, ethnic, religious, social, and geographic interests as the United States (see "How the United States Compares").

The extraordinary number of groups in the United States does not indicate, however, that the nation's various interests are equally well organized. Organizations develop when people with shared interests have the opportunity and the incentive to join together. Some individuals have the skills, money, contacts, or time to participate effectively in group politics, but others do not. Moreover, some groups are inherently more attractive to potential members than others are and thus find it easier to build large or devoted followings. Organizations also differ in their access to financial resources and thus differ also in their capacity for political action.

HOW THE UNITED STATES COMPARES

Groups: "A Nation of Joiners"

"A nation of joiners" is how the Frenchman Alexis de Tocqueville described the United States during his visit to this country in the 1830s.

Even today, Americans are more actively involved in groups and community causes than are Europeans. The American tradition of group activity is only one reason. Another is the structure of the U.S. political system. Because of federalism and the separation of powers, the American system offers numerous points at which groups can try to influence public policy. If unsuccessful with legislators, groups can turn to executives or the courts. If thwarted at the national level, groups can turn to state and local governments. By comparison, the governments of most other democratic nations are not organized in ways that facilitate group access and influence. France's unitary government, for example, concentrates power at the national level.

Such differences are reflected in citizens' participation rates. Americans are more likely to belong to groups than are the French, Italians, British, or Germans, as the accompanying figures from the World Values Survey indicate.

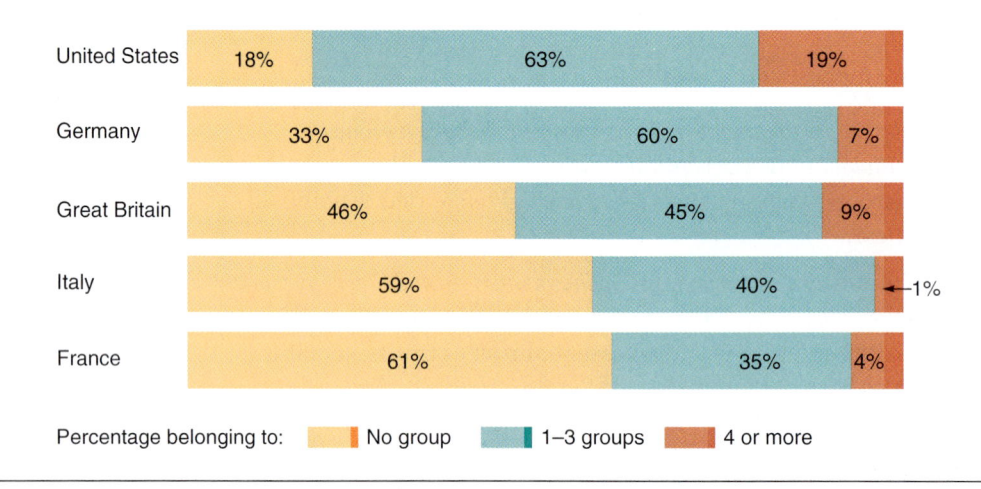

Country	No group	1–3 groups	4 or more
United States	18%	63%	19%
Germany	33%	60%	7%
Great Britain	46%	45%	9%
Italy	59%	40%	1%
France	61%	35%	4%

Percentage belonging to: No group | 1–3 groups | 4 or more

Therefore, a first consideration in regard to group politics in America is the issue of how thoroughly various interests are organized. Group politics is the politics of organization. Interests that are highly organized stand a good chance of having their views heard by policymakers. Poorly organized interests run the risk of being ignored.

Economic Groups

No interests are more fully or effectively organized than those that have economic activity as their primary purpose. An indication of their advantage is the fact that their Washington lobbyists outnumber those of other groups by more than two to one.

Economic groups include corporations, labor unions, farm groups, and professional associations. They exist primarily for economic purposes: to make profits, provide jobs, improve pay, or protect an occupation. For the sake of discussion, such organizations will be called **economic groups,** although it is important to recognize that their political goals can include policies that transcend the narrow economic interests of their members. Thus, the AFL-CIO concentrates on labor objectives, but it also takes positions on broader issues of foreign and domestic policy.

An Organizational Edge

One reason for the abundance of economic groups is their access to financial resources. Political activity does not come cheap. If a group is to make its views known, it normally must have a headquarters, an expert staff, and communication facilities. Economic groups can obtain the requisite money and expertise from their economic activities. Corporations have the greatest natural advantage. They do not have to charge membership dues or conduct fund-raisers to get money to support their lobbying. Their political money comes from the goods and services they produce and sell.

Some economic groups do depend on dues for their support, but they can offer prospective members a powerful incentive to join: **private (individual) goods,** which are the benefits that a group can grant directly to the individual member. For example, workers in the state of Michigan cannot hold automobile assembly jobs unless they belong to the United Auto Workers (UAW). The UAW has a **material incentive**—the economic lure of high wages—to attract potential members. Economic groups are highly organized in part because they serve the individual economic needs of potential members. The predominance of economic interests was predicted in *Federalist* No. 10, in which James Madison declared that property is "the most common and durable source of factions." Stated differently, nothing seems to matter quite so much to people as their pocketbooks and livelihoods.

Types of Economic Groups

Most economic groups are of four general types: business groups, labor groups, agricultural groups, and professional groups.

Business Groups. More than half of all groups formally registered to lobby Congress are business organizations. Nearly all large corporations and many smaller ones are politically active. They concentrate their activities on policies that touch directly on business interests, such as tax, tariff, and regulatory decisions.

Business firms are also represented through associations, such as the U.S. Chamber of Commerce, which represents nearly three million businesses of all sizes. Other business associations, such as the American Petroleum Institute, are confined to a single trade or industry. Because each trade association represents a single industry, it can promote the interests of member corporations even when these interests conflict with those of business generally. Thus, while the Chamber of Commerce promotes a global free trade policy, some trade associations seek protective tariffs because their member firms want barriers against foreign competition.

Business interests have the advantage of what the economist Mancur Olson calls "the size factor."[4] Although large groups can claim that government should pay more attention to them because they represent more people, small

economic groups Interest groups that are organized primarily for economic reasons, but that engage in political activity in order to seek favorable policies from government.

private (individual) goods Benefits that a group (most often an economic group) can grant directly and exclusively to individual members of the group.

material incentive An economic or other tangible benefit that is used to attract group members.

America's "Big Three" automakers—Chrysler, Ford, and General Motors—actively lobby government, sometimes working together to achieve policy goals that will promote their industry.

groups are usually more cohesive. Everyone is a consumer, but most consumers do not see any benefit in belonging to a consumer advocacy group. On the other hand, because business firms in a particular industry are few in number, they are likely to recognize the significance of working together. When the "Big Three" U.S. automakers—General Motors, Ford, and Chrysler—fought federally mandated safety and mileage-efficiency standards, the defection of any one of them would likely have meant defeat. But they stayed together and won concessions from the government. In the process, each automaker saved hundreds of millions of dollars in design and production costs on new autos. In one instance, the automakers gained a multiyear delay in the installation of air bags in all new cars. Their gain came at an unknown cost to consumers, whose newly purchased automobiles were less safe than they could have been.

Labor Groups. Since the 1930s, organized labor has been politically active on a large scale. Its goal has been to promote policies that benefit workers in general and union members in particular. Although some independent unions, such as the United Mine Workers, lobby actively, the dominant labor group is the AFL-CIO, which maintains its national headquarters in Washington, D.C. The AFL-CIO has more than thirteen million members in its ninety-seven affiliated unions, which include the International Brotherhood of Electrical Workers, the Sheet Metal Workers, the Communication Workers of America, and as of 1987, the giant International Brotherhood of Teamsters.

At one time, about a third of the U.S. work force was unionized, but today only about one-seventh of all workers belong to unions. Skilled and unskilled laborers have been the core of organized labor, and their numbers are decreasing while professionals, technicians, and service workers are increasing in number. Professionals have shown little interest in union organization, perhaps because they identify with management or see themselves as economically secure. Service workers and technicians are also more difficult for unions to organize than traditional laborers are because they work closely with managers and, often, in small offices.

Nevertheless, unions have made some inroads in recent decades in their efforts to organize service and public employees. Teachers, postal workers, police, firefighters, and social workers are among the public employee groups that

TABLE 9-1	The Largest Labor Unions, 1950 and 2000 The largest labor unions today represent service and public employees; fifty years ago, the largest unions represented skilled and unskilled workers.

1950	2000
1. United Auto Workers	1. National Education Association
2. United Steel Workers	2. International Brotherhood of Teamsters
3. International Brotherhood of Teamsters	3. United Food and Commercial Workers International
4. United Brotherhood of Carpenters & Joiners	4. American Federation of State, County, & Municipal Employees
5. International Association of Machinists	5. Service Employees International

Source: U.S. Department of Labor.

have become increasingly unionized. Today, the nation's largest unions are those that represent service and public employees rather than skilled and unskilled laborers (see Table 9–1).

Agricultural Groups. Farm organizations represent another large economic lobby. The American Farm Bureau Federation is the largest of the farm groups, with more than four million members. The National Farmers Union, the National Grange, and the National Farmers Organization are smaller farm lobbies. Agricultural groups do not always agree on policy issues. For instance, the Farm Bureau sides with agribusiness and owners of large farms, while the Farmers Union promotes the interests of smaller "family" farms.

There are also numerous specialty farm associations, including the Association of Wheat Growers, the American Soybean Association, and Associated Milk Producers. Each association acts as a separate lobby to try to obtain policies beneficial to its members' narrow agricultural interests.

Professional Groups. Most professions have lobbying associations. Perhaps the most powerful of these groups is the American Medical Association (AMA), which, with nearly three hundred thousand members, represents about half the nation's physicians. The AMA has consistently opposed any government policy that would limit physicians' autonomy. Other professional groups are the American Bar Association and the American Association of University Professors, each of which maintains a lobbying office in Washington.

Citizens' Groups

Although economic interests are the best organized groups, they do not have a monopoly on group activity. There are a great number and variety of other organized interests, which are referred to collectively as **citizens' groups** (or **noneconomic groups**). The members of groups in this category are

citizens' (noneconomic) groups Organized interests formed by individuals drawn together by opportunities to promote a cause in which they believe but that does not provide them significant individual economic benefits.

This 1873 lithograph illustrates the benefits of membership in the National Grange, an agricultural interest group.

purposive incentive An incentive to group participation based on the cause (purpose) that the group seeks to promote.

collective (public) goods Benefits that are offered by groups (usually citizens' groups) as an incentive for membership, but that are nondivisible (e.g., a clean environment) and therefore are available to nonmembers as well as members of the particular group.

free-rider problem The situation in which the benefits offered by a group to its members are also available to nonmembers. The incentive to join the group and to promote its cause is reduced because nonmembers (free riders) receive the benefits (e.g., a cleaner environment) without having to pay any of the group's costs.

drawn together not by the promise of direct economic gain but by **purposive incentives**—opportunities to promote a cause in which they believe.[5] Whether a group's goal is to protect the environment, reduce the threat of nuclear war, return prayer to the public schools, feed the poor at home or abroad, or whatever, there are citizens who are willing to participate simply because they believe the policy goal is a worthy cause.[6]

In comparison with economic groups, citizens' groups have a harder time acquiring the resources necessary for organization. These groups do not generate profits or fees as a result of economic activity. Moreover, the incentives they offer prospective members are not exclusive. Unlike the private or individual goods provided by many economic groups, most noneconomic groups offer **collective goods** (or **public goods**) as an incentive for membership. Collective goods are, by definition, benefits that must be shared; they cannot be allotted on an individual basis. The air people breathe and the national forests people visit are examples of collective goods. They are available to one and all, those who pay dues to a clean-air group or a wilderness group and those who do not.

The Free-Rider Problem

This characteristic of collective goods creates what is called the **free-rider problem**: individuals can receive the good even when they do not contribute to the group's effort. Take the case of an environmental group that successfully lobbies Congress for tougher air pollution laws. The collective good produced

Environmental activists protest against automobile and truck emissions, which are a leading cause of air pollution. Although environmental groups have been quite successful in attracting public support, they still confront the so-called free-rider problem—the fact that people will gain the benefit of a group's effort even if they do not contribute to it.

by the legislation—cleaner air—is available to group members and nonmembers alike. National Public Radio (NPR) is another example. Although NPR's programs are funded in part through listeners' donations, those who do not contribute can also listen to the programs. The noncontributors are free riders: they receive the benefit without paying any of the costs of providing it. About 90 percent of people who regularly listen to NPR do not contribute to their local station.

As the economist Mancur Olson notes, it is not rational, in a purely economic sense, for individuals to contribute to a citizens' group, because they can obtain the benefit without paying for it.[7] Moreover, the dues paid by any single member are too small to affect the group's success one way or another. Why pay dues to a clean-air group when any improvement in air quality from its lobbying efforts is available to everyone and when one's contribution is too small to make a real difference? Although many people do join such groups anyway, there is no doubt that the free-rider problem is a reason why citizens' groups are less highly organized than economic ones.

Citizens' groups try to surmount the free-rider problem by creating individual benefits, akin to those offered by economic groups, to make membership more attractive. Organizational newsletters and social activities are among the individual benefits that citizens' groups offer as a lure to membership. Computer-assisted direct mail has also helped citizens' groups attract members. Group organizers buy mailing lists and flood the mails with computer-typed "personal" letters asking recipients to pay a small annual membership fee. For some individuals, a fee of $25 to $50 annually represents no great sacrifice and offers the momentary satisfaction of supporting a cause in which they believe. Until the computer era, citizens' groups had great difficulty in identifying and contacting potential members, which is a reason why the number of such groups was so much smaller in the past than is true today. On the whole, however, the organizational advantages rest with economic groups. In nearly all respects, they have the upper hand on citizens' groups (see Table 9–2).

One area where citizens' groups have gained an edge is the Internet, which has made it easier for these groups to contact their members. Nearly every citizen group of any size has its own website, and many have developed the capacity to reach individual members with urgent and periodic messages. One of

Simulation
www.mhhe.com/patterson6

TABLE 9-2 Advantages and Disadvantages Held by Economic and Citizens' Groups Compared with economic groups, citizens' groups have fewer advantages and more disadvantages.

ECONOMIC GROUPS	CITIZENS' GROUPS
Advantages	*Advantages*
Economic activity provides the organization with the resources necessary for political action.	Members are likely to support leaders' political efforts because they joined the group in order to influence policy.
Individuals are encouraged to join the group because of economic benefits they individually receive (e.g., wages).	
Disadvantages	*Disadvantages*
Persons within the group may not support leaders' political efforts because they did not join the group for political reasons.	The group has to raise funds especially for its political activities.
	Potential members may choose not to join the group because they get collective benefits even if they do not join (the free-rider problem).

Jody Williams won the Nobel Peace Prize in 1997 for organizing a worldwide lobby of citizens' groups in a successful campaign to ban the use of land mines. The Internet was her primary means of organization.

the most successful citizen campaigns in history was conducted largely through the Internet. It was a global campaign aimed at the elimination of land mines, and its chief organizer, Jody Williams, received the Nobel Peace Prize in 1997 for her work. Through the Web, she linked together activists and groups throughout the world and, in the end, succeeded in getting one hundred countries to agree to an international treaty that bans the use of land mines and the destruction of those already in the ground.

Types of Citizens' Groups

Most citizens' groups are of three general types: public interest groups, single-issue groups, and ideological groups.

Public Interest Groups. Public interest groups are those that claim to represent the broad interests of society as a whole. Despite their label, public interest groups are not led by people elected by the public at large, and the issues they target are ones of their own choosing, not the public's. Just what constitutes the "public interest" is often a subject on which people disagree. And if disagreement exists, can either side truly claim to represent the "public interest"? Nevertheless, there is a basis for distinguishing the so-called public interest groups from economic groups: the latter seek direct material benefits for their members, while the former seek benefits that are less tangible and more broadly shared. For example, the National Association of Manufacturers, an economic group, seeks policies favorable to large corporations, while the League of Women Voters, a public interest group, seeks policies—such as simplified voter registration—that can benefit the public in general.

The League of Women Voters has existed for decades, but more than half of the currently active public interest groups were established after 1960. One of these organizations is Common Cause, which has more than two hundred thousand members. Their annual dues help support a seventy-person national staff of lobbyists, attorneys, and public relations experts. Common Cause, which describes itself as "a national citizens' lobby," concentrates on political reform in such areas as campaign finance. It has been a principal advocate of public funding of congressional campaigns. Its ongoing "People vs. PACs" campaign is aimed at reducing the influence of interest groups on elections.

Single-Issue Groups. A single-issue group is organized to influence policy in just one area. Notable current examples are the National Rifle Association and various right-to-life and pro-choice groups that have formed around the issue of abortion. The number of single-issue groups has risen sharply in the past two decades, and they now lobby on almost every conceivable issue, from nuclear arms to day care centers to drug abuse. Single-issue groups with a national membership are the most prominent, but many single-issue groups are organized at the local level.

Environmental groups are sometimes classified as public interest groups, but they may also be considered single-issue organizations in that most of them seek to influence public policy in a specific area, such as pollution reduction, wilderness preservation, or wildlife protection. The Sierra Club is one of the oldest of such groups. It was formed in the 1890s to promote the preservation of scenic areas. Also prominent are the National Audubon Society, the Wilderness Society, the Environmental Defense Fund, Greenpeace U.S.A., and the Izaak Walton League. Between 1960 and 1970, membership in environmental groups tripled in response to increased public concern about the quality of the environment.[8] Since then, membership in environmental groups has continued to grow.

Ideological Groups. Single-issue groups have a narrowly focused policy agenda. Other groups take a broader view, usually from the perspective of a general philosophical or moral stance. These groups have been labeled ideological

The Rev. Pat Robertson (standing at the microphones) founded the Christian Coalition, an ideological group. The Christian Coalition's website contains the phrase, "America's Leading Grassroots Organization Protecting Our Godly Heritage."

Citizenship
Getting Involved, Making a Difference

Groups and Social Capital

When the Frenchman Alexis de Tocqueville came to the United States in the 1830s, he marveled at the abundance of civic and political groups and concluded that they were the underlying strength of American democracy. Little has happened in the nearly two centuries since to change this conclusion. Recent research, in fact, confirms it. In his pioneering *Making Democracy Work* (1993), Harvard University's Robert Putnam found that the more abundant a society's voluntary associations are, the more likely it is that the society's institutions will act in the public interest. Putnam uses the term *civic community* to describe a society in which voluntary associations flourish.

Citizens *should* participate in voluntary groups. By doing so, they contribute to improvements in their community, whether it be a college campus, town, state, or the nation. Moreover, the relationships that develop among people as a result of civic participation enable individuals to better understand the opinions and values of others.

These benefits are substantial. Democratic theorists such as Rousseau, Jefferson, Mill, and Dewey argued that communities should be constructed in ways that encourage the individual to participate as fully as possible in civic affairs. The theorists' assumption was that citizens "invest" in a community when they are an integral part of it. The theorists also assumed that participation expands the individual's vision, giving him or her the capacity, in Rousseau's words, for "seeing things in general." Said differently, civic participation enables individuals to surmount a narrowly self-interested view of what is best for society.

Putnam argues that America has undergone a long-term decline in its *social capital* (the sum of its civic relationships). In *Bowling Alone* (2000), Putman presents evidence that indicates Americans are now less involved in community groups and other forms of social interaction. He attributes the change to television and other factors that produce social isolation. Not all scholars agree with Putnam's view of the trend (some indicators point toward a rise in certain types of group membership), but no one has challenged his assumption about the importance of maintaining high levels of civic participation. The relationships fostered by this participation are a foundation of democratic life. And no democratic theorist has suggested that there can be "too much" civic participation. The higher the level, the firmer the democratic base.

---

groups. An example is the Christian Moral Government Fund, which was organized to restore "Christian values" to American life and politics. Americans for Democratic Action (ADA) is another example of an ideological group. The ADA supports liberal positions on a wide range of social, economic, and foreign policy issues. Ideological groups on both the left and right have increased substantially in number since the 1960s.

Groups such as the National Organization for Women and the National Association for the Advancement of Colored People (NAACP) can also be generally classified as ideological groups. Although they represent a particular demographic group, they do so across a wide range of issues. The NAACP was formed in 1909 to promote the political interests of racial minorities, primarily through initiating lawsuits on their behalf.

A Special Category of Interest Group: Governments

While the vast majority of organized interests in the United States represent private concerns, a growing number of interest groups represent governments, both foreign and subnational.

The U.S. federal government makes policies that directly affect the economic development, political stability, and security of nations throughout the world. Arms sales, foreign aid, immigration, and import restrictions and other trade practices have a great impact on foreign nations. For this reason, most foreign nations supplement the political efforts made through their embassies with the services of paid lobbying agents in Washington. Although lobbying by foreign governments is subject to some restrictions, most governments have managed to circumvent these vague regulations. Roughly one thousand registered lobbyists represent foreign nations' interests in Washington.[9]

States, cities, and other governmental units within the United States also lobby heavily. Although most major cities across the United States and two-thirds of the states have at least one Washington lobbyist, cooperative lobbying is perhaps more important. The intergovernmental lobby includes such groups as the Council of State Governments, the National Governors Conference, the National Association of Counties, the National League of Cities, and the U.S. Conference of Mayors. These organizations represent the broad interests of cities and states while still allowing individual member cities and states to lobby for their particular interests.

The interests of subnational governments vary greatly. The problems of frostbelt states differ from those of sunbelt states; cities in the industrial Northeast face problems that are almost unknown in cities of the Southwest. These differences impose limits on the effectiveness of the intergovernmental lobby. Nonetheless, its presence in Washington has demonstrably influenced many major policy decisions that affect state and local governments.[10] In 2002, as Congress was preparing to renew and amend the Welfare Reform Act that went into effect five years earlier, the National Governors Conference lobbied heavily to ensure that the changes would reflect states' experiences with the program.

INSIDE LOBBYING: SEEKING INFLUENCE THROUGH OFFICIAL CONTACTS

Modern government provides a supportive environment for interest groups. First, modern government is involved in so many issues—business regulation, income maintenance, urban renewal, cancer research, and energy development, to name only a few—that hardly any interest in society could fail to benefit significantly from having influence over federal policies or programs.

Second, modern government is oriented toward action. Officials are inclined to look for policy solutions to problems rather than to let problems linger. For example, when forest fires raged out of control in western states in 2002 and destroyed property worth millions, Washington immediately granted assistance and funds to residents who had incurred losses and cleanup costs.

lobbying The process by which interest-group members or lobbyists attempt to influence public policy through contacts with public officials.

inside lobbying Direct communication between organized interests and policymakers, which is based on the assumed value of close ("inside") contacts with policymakers.

Groups seek support through **lobbying,** a term that refers broadly to efforts of groups to influence public policy through contact with public officials. The two main lobbying strategies may be labeled as "inside lobbying" and "outside lobbying."[11] Each strategy involves communication between public officials and group lobbyists, but the strategies differ as to what is communicated, who does the communicating, and who receives the communication. This section discusses **inside lobbying,** which is based on group efforts to develop and maintain close ("inside") contacts with policymakers. (Outside lobbying is described in the next section.)

Acquiring Access to Officials

Inside lobbying is designed to give a group direct access to officials in order to influence their decisions. Access is not the same as influence, which is the capacity to affect policy decisions. But access is a critical first step in the influence process.[12]

Lobbying once depended significantly on tangible inducements, sometimes including indirect or even outright bribes. This old form of lobbying survives, but modern lobbying generally involves more subtle and sophisticated methods than providing money or personal favors to officials. It focuses on supplying officials with information and indications of group strength that will persuade them to adopt the group's perspective.[13]

For the most part, inside lobbying is directed at policymakers who are inclined to support the group rather than those who have opposed it in the past. This tendency reflects both the difficulty of persuading opponents to change long-held views and the advantage of having trusted allies who will actively support the group's position in policy deliberations. Thus, union lobbyists work mainly with pro-labor officials, just as corporate lobbyists work mainly with policymakers who support business interests.

Money is the essential ingredient of inside lobbying efforts. The American Petroleum Institute, for example, with its abundant financial resources, can afford a downtown Washington office staffed by lobbyists, petroleum experts, and public relations specialists who help the oil companies maintain access to and influence with legislative and executive leaders.[14] Many groups spend $1 million or more annually on lobbying. Other groups survive with much less, but it is hard to run an effective lobbying effort on less than $100,000 a year. Given the costs of maintaining a Washington lobby, the domination by corporations and trade associations is understandable. They have the money to retain high-priced lobbyists, while many other interests do not.

The targets of inside lobbying are officials of all branches—legislative, executive, and judicial.

Lobbying Congress

The benefits of a close relationship with members of Congress are substantial. With support in Congress, a group can obtain the legislative help it needs to achieve its policy goals. By the same token, members of Congress also gain from working closely with lobbyists. The volume of legislation facing Congress is enormous, and members rely on trusted lobbyists to identify bills that deserve

Why Should I Care?

The Revolving Door: Officials and Lobbyists

As government has grown increasingly complex, people in Washington who know how the system works have become increasingly important actors. Not surprisingly, a revolving door has developed between positions in government and positions in lobbying groups. For example, Representative Bob Livingston, chair of the House Appropriations Committee, resigned from Congress in 1999 and soon thereafter started the Livingston Group, which lobbies Congress on behalf of business firms.

High-level officials and top lobbyists are familiar with the policy process and the issues within their sphere of responsibility. These skills are easily transferable from one type of job to the other.

The revolving door has obvious benefits. Policymakers need to be knowledgeable about public policy problems and need to have access to groups affected by these problems. The complexity of many issues today is such that it is impossible to make good policy decisions without detailed information about them. Moreover, because the U.S. governing system itself is complex—a result of its size and the division of powers—it is difficult for individuals to accomplish much of anything unless they know how to work the system.

Nevertheless, the revolving door between government and interest groups can result in abuses of power. Former lobbyists, when they take a government position, can do special favors for the groups they once represented. Former government officials, when they take a lobbying post, can use their contacts within government to obtain favorable treatment for the groups they now represent. To guard against unwarranted influence, there are some restrictions on those individuals who pass through the revolving door. The 1978 Ethics in Government Act, for example, prohibits former executive branch employees from lobbying their former agency for a year after leaving it and for two years on any matter that came within the employee's area of responsibility. There is, however, no such limit on former members of Congress. Moreover, they have the unique right to go directly onto the floor of the House or Senate to speak with current members. Former members usually represent groups with which they had close ties while they were in office.

The news media and public interest groups such as Congress Watch have taken on responsibility for guarding the revolving door. When they see a lobbyist-official relationship that has become too cozy, they try to bring it into public view. However, much of what transpires between lobbyists and officials takes place in private. What do you think should be done to ensure that the revolving door works to the public's benefit?

---

their attention and support. When Republican lawmakers took control of Congress in 1995, they invited corporate lobbyists to participate directly in drafting legislation affecting business. Congressional Democrats complained loudly, but Republicans said they were merely getting help from those who best understood business's needs and accused Democrats of having engaged in the same practice with organized labor when they were in power.

Lobbyists' effectiveness with members of Congress depends in part on their reputation for fair play. Congressional action normally requires compromise among competing interests. If a group is adamant about getting everything it wants—"my way or no way"—it is likely to end up with nothing. Lobbyists are also expected to play it straight. Said one congressman: "If any [lobbyist] gives me false or misleading information, that's it—I'll never see him again."[15] Arm-twisting is another unacceptable practice. During the debate over the North American Free Trade Agreement in 1993, the AFL-CIO threatened retaliation against congressional Democrats who supported the legislation. The backlash

Inside lobbying offers groups a chance to make their policy views known. Access to public officials is critical to the inside-lobbying strategy.

from these Democrats was so intense that the union backed down on its threat. The safe lobbying strategy is the aboveboard approach: provide information, rely on longtime allies among members of Congress, and push steadily but not too aggressively for legislative goals.

Lobbying Executive Agencies

As the scope of the federal government has expanded, lobbying of the executive branch has increased in importance. Bureaucrats make key administrative decisions and develop policy initiatives that the legislative branch later makes into law. By working closely with government agencies, groups can influence policy decisions at the implementation and initiation stages. In return, groups assist government agencies by providing information and lending support when their programs are reviewed by Congress and the president.

Nowhere is the link between groups and the bureaucracy more evident than in the regulatory agencies that oversee the nation's business sectors. For example, the Federal Communications Commission (FCC), which regulates the nation's broadcasters, uses information provided by broadcast organizations to decide many of the policies governing their activities. The FCC is sometimes cited as an example of agency capture. The capture theory suggests that regulatory agencies pass through a series of phases that constitute a life cycle. Early in an agency's existence, it regulates an industry on the public's behalf, but as the agency matures, its vigor declines until at best it protects the status quo and at worst it falls captive to the very industry it is supposed to regulate.[16] In the 1950s, the commercial networks successfully lobbied the FCC in a campaign against the establishment of a strong public sector television system. For example, public stations were assigned UHF frequencies while commercial stations held the more powerful VHF frequencies, which were also the only ones that most television sets of the 1950s were programmed to receive. Without access to a large audience, public television was in a weak position to request additional funding from Congress. Without more funds, it had to struggle to develop the type of programming that would attract a larger audience. The consequences of this vicious circle linger today. Compared with Europe, where public broadcasting was established early and on a solid footing, the U.S. system is very weak.

Research has shown that the capture theory describes only some agencies—and then only some of the time.[17] Agencies selectively cooperate with or oppose interest groups, depending on which strategy better suits agency purposes.[18] Agency officials are aware that they can lose support in Congress, which controls agency funding and program authorization, if they show too much favoritism toward an interest group.

Although instances of favoritism occur, the U.S. bureaucracy ranks high in comparison with other national bureaucracies in terms of its efficiency and honesty.[19] Its dealings with lobbying groups are important to effective administration, which includes an understanding of the impact of programs on affected interests. From the viewpoint of the interest group, the bureaucracy's need for information is a lobbying opportunity.

Lobbying the Courts

Court rulings in areas such as education and civil rights have made interest groups recognize that the judiciary too can help them reach their goals.[20] Interest groups have several judicial lobbying options, including efforts to influence the selection of federal judges. Right-to-life groups pressured the Reagan and Bush administrations to make opposition to abortion a prerequisite for nomination to the federal bench. The Clinton administration faced the opposite type of pressure from pro-choice groups on its judicial nominations.

Amicus curiae ("friend of the court") briefs are another method of judicial lobbying. An amicus brief is a written document in which a group brings its position on a particular case to a court's attention. For example, in the landmark affirmative action case *Regents of the University of California v. Bakke* (1978), fifty-eight amicus briefs representing the positions of more than one hundred organizations were filed with the Supreme Court at its invitation.

Groups typically try to influence public policy through the courts by filing lawsuits. For some organizations, such as the NAACP and the American Civil Liberties Union, legal action is the primary means of lobbying government. The NAACP, for example, has emphasized legal action since its founding in 1909 because it recognizes that minorities often lack influence with elected officials. The NAACP financed the 1954 *Brown* case, in which the Supreme Court declared that racial segregation of public schools is unconstitutional. Had the NAACP tried to achieve the same result by lobbying state legislators in the South, it almost certainly would have failed.

As interest groups increasingly resort to legal action, they often find themselves facing one another in court. Such environmental litigation groups as the Sierra Club Legal Defense Club, the Environmental Defense Fund, and the Natural Resources Defense Council have frequently sued oil, timber, and mining corporations.

Webs of Influence: Groups in the Policy Process

Lobbying efforts provide an incomplete picture of how groups obtain influence. To get a fuller picture, it is necessary to also consider two policy processes—iron triangles and issue networks—in which many groups are enmeshed.

Iron Triangles

iron triangle A small and informal but relatively stable group of well-positioned legislators, executives, and lobbyists who seek to promote policies beneficial to a particular interest.

An **iron triangle** consists of a small and informal but relatively stable set of bureaucrats, legislators, and lobbyists who seek to develop policies beneficial to a particular interest.[21] The three "corners" of one such triangle are the Department of Veterans Affairs (bureaucrats), the veterans' affairs committees of Congress (legislators), and veterans' groups such as the American Legion and the Veterans of Foreign Wars (lobbyists), which together determine many of the policies affecting veterans. Of course, the support of other players, including the president and a majority in Congress, is needed to enact new programs to benefit veterans. However, these other players often defer to the policy views voiced by the veterans' triangle, whose members have the most knowledge of the programs, problems, and policy needs of veterans.

A group in an iron triangle has an inside track to those legislators and bureaucrats who are in the strongest position to promote its cause. And because it can offer something of value to each of them in return, the relationship tends to be ironclad. The group provides lobbying support for the agency's funding and programs, and gives campaign contributions to its congressional allies. Agricultural groups, for example, contributed millions of dollars to congressional candidates in the 2002 campaign. Most of the money was given to incumbents, and of these contributions, most went to the campaigns of members of the House and Senate agriculture committees. Figure 9–1 summarizes the benefits that flow to each member of an iron triangle.

Issue Networks

issue network An informal and relatively open network of public officials and lobbyists who have a common interest in a given area and who are brought together by a proposed policy in that area. Unlike an iron triangle, an issue network disbands after the issue is resolved.

Iron triangles represent the pattern of influence only in certain policy areas and are less dominant now than in the past. A more common pattern of influence today is the **issue network,** which is an informal grouping of officials, lobbyists, and policy specialists (the "network") who are brought together temporarily by their shared interest in a particular policy problem (the "issue").

Issue networks are a result of the increasing complexity and interconnectedness of policy problems. The complexity of modern issues often makes it essential that a participant have specialized knowledge of the issue at hand in order to join in the debate. Thus, unlike iron triangles, where one's position is everything,

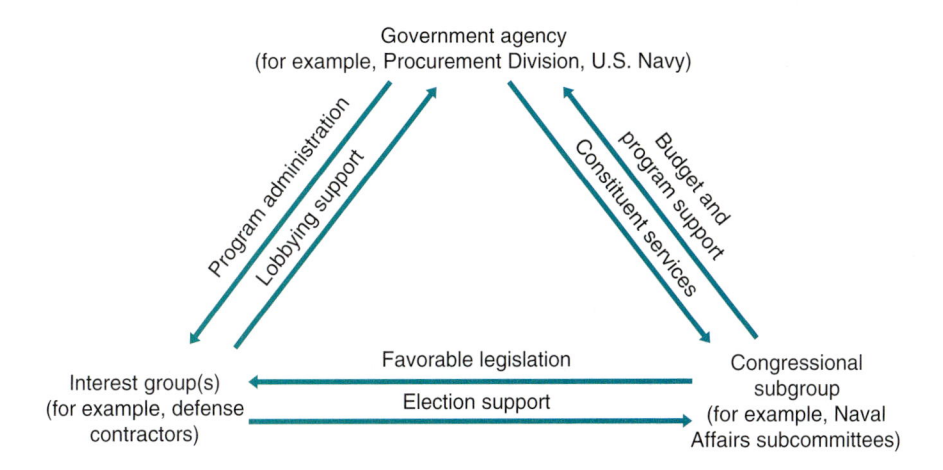

Figure 9-1
How an Iron Triangle Benefits Its Participants
An iron triangle works to the advantage of each of its participants—an interest group, a congressional subgroup, and a government agency.

Diagram:
- Government agency (for example, Procurement Division, U.S. Navy)
- Interest group(s) (for example, defense contractors)
- Congressional subgroup (for example, Naval Affairs subcommittees)
- Arrows: Program administration / Lobbying support (between agency and interest group); Budget and program support / Constituent services (between agency and congressional subgroup); Favorable legislation / Election support (between congressional subgroup and interest group)

an issue network is built around specialized interests and information. On any given issue, the participants might come from a variety of executive agencies, congressional committees, interest groups, and institutions such as universities or think tanks. And, unlike iron triangles, issue networks are less stable and less clearly defined. As the issue develops, new participants may join the debate and old ones drop out. Once the issue is resolved, the network disbands.[22]

An example of an issue network is the set of participants who would come together over the issue of whether a large tract of old forest should be opened to logging. A few decades ago, that issue would have been settled in an iron triangle consisting of the timber companies, the U.S. Forest Service, and some members of the House and Senate agriculture committees. But as forestlands have diminished and environmental concerns have grown, such issues can no longer be contained within the cozy confines of an iron triangle. Today, an issue network would form that included logging interests, the U.S. Forest Service, House and Senate agriculture committee members, research scientists, and representatives of environmental groups, the housing industry, and animal-rights groups. Unlike the old iron triangle, which was confined to like-minded interests, this issue network would include opposing interests (for example, the loggers and the environmentalists). And unlike an iron triangle, the issue network would dissolve once the issue was resolved; after it was settled, the various parties would go their separate ways.

Issue networks, then, differ substantially from iron triangles. In an iron triangle, it is a common interest that brings the participants together in a stable, long-lasting, and mutually beneficial relationship. In an issue network, it is an immediate issue that brings the participants together in a temporary network that is based on their ability to address the issue in a sophisticated way and where they play out their separate interests before disbanding once the issue is settled.

Iron triangles and issue networks, however, do have one thing in common. They are arenas in which organized interests operate. The interests of the general public may be taken into account in these webs of influence, but its direct role is ordinarily a small one.

The policy issues surrounding the technological revolution are extraordinarily complex, and issue networks tend to form when policy issues of this type arise.

TABLE 9–3 Tactics Used in Inside and Outside Lobbying Strategies
Inside and outside lobbying are based on different tactics.

INSIDE LOBBYING	OUTSIDE LOBBYING
Developing contacts with legislators and executives	Encouraging group members to write or phone their representatives in Congress
Providing information and policy proposals to key officials	Seeking favorable coverage by news media
Forming coalitions with other groups	Encouraging members to support particular candidates in elections
	Targeting group resources on key election races
	Making PAC contributions to candidates

OUTSIDE LOBBYING: SEEKING INFLUENCE THROUGH PUBLIC PRESSURE

outside lobbying A form of lobbying in which an interest group seeks to use public pressure as a means of influencing officials.

Although an interest group may rely solely on inside lobbying, this approach is not likely to be successful unless the group can demonstrate convincingly that its concerns reflect those of a vital constituency. Accordingly, groups make use of constituency connections when it is advantageous to do so. They engage in **outside lobbying,** which involves bringing public ("outside") pressure to bear on policymakers (see Table 9–3).[23]

The Houston headquarters of the now-bankrupt Enron Corporation. Until its collapse from illegal business practices, Enron was one of the nation's largest corporations and one of the most active lobbying groups in Washington.

Constituency Advocacy: Grassroots Lobbying

One form of outside pressure is **grassroots lobbying**—that is, pressure designed to convince government officials that a group's policy position has popular support.

No group illustrates grassroots lobbying better than the American Association of Retired Persons (AARP). With more than thirty million members and a staff of sixteen hundred employees, AARP has been a powerful lobby on retirement issues such as social security and Medicare. When major legislation affecting retirees is pending, AARP swings into action. AARP members generate more mail to Congress than any other group.[24]

As with other forms of lobbying, the precise impact of grassroots campaigns is usually difficult to assess. Some members of Congress downplay its influence, but all congressional offices monitor letters and phone calls from constituents as a way of tracking opinion in the member's state or district.

grassroots lobbying A form of lobbying designed to persuade officials that a group's policy position has strong constituent support.

Electoral Action: Votes and PAC Money

An "outside" strategy can also include election campaigns. "Reward your friends and punish your enemies" is a political adage that loosely describes how interest groups view elections. Organized groups work to elect their supporters and defeat their opponents. The possibility of electoral opposition from a powerful group can keep an officeholder from openly obstructing its goals. For example, opposition from the three-million-member National Rifle Association is a major reason the United States has lagged behind other Western societies in its handgun control laws, although polls show that most Americans favor such laws.

Figure 9-2

Growth in the Number of PACs, 1974-2000

The number of PACs began to increase sharply after campaign finance reforms were enacted in the early 1970s.

Source: Federal Elections Commission.

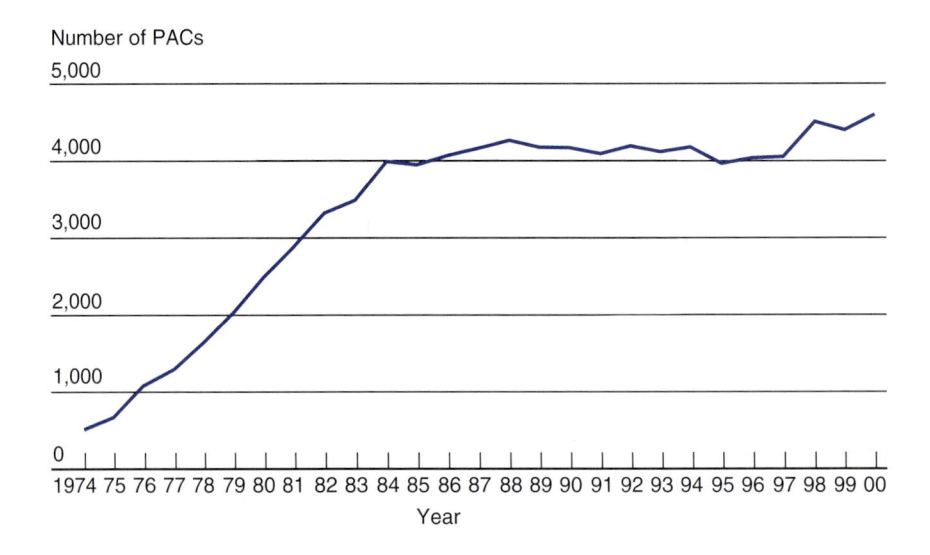

political action committee (PAC) The organization through which an interest group raises and distributes funds for election purposes. By law, the funds must be raised through voluntary contributions.

The principal way in which interest groups try to gain influence through elections is by contributing money to candidates' campaigns. As one lobbyist said, "Talking to politicians is fine, but with a little money they hear you better."[25] Money does not literally "buy" votes in Congress, but it does buy access. Members of Congress listen to the groups that fund their campaigns. Sometimes, they get into hot water because of it. When the Enron Corporation collapsed into bankruptcy in 2002, depleting the retirement accounts of its employees in the process, its deep connections in Washington quickly became known. In the previous decade, Enron and its top officials had contributed $6 million in campaign funds. Some members of Congress found themselves in the embarrassing position of holding investigative hearings on a company from which they had taken funds.

The vehicle for group contributions is the **political action committee (PAC)**. A group cannot give organizational funds (such as corporate profits or union dues) to candidates; but through its PAC, a group can raise money for election campaigns by soliciting voluntary contributions from members or employees. A PAC is legally limited in the amount it can contribute to the campaign of a candidate for federal office. The ceiling is $10,000 per candidate—$5,000 in the primary campaign and $5,000 in the general election campaign; there is no legal limit on the number of candidates a PAC can support. These financial limits do not apply to candidates for state and local office. Their campaigns are regulated by state laws, and many states allow PACs to make unlimited campaign contributions.

PACs mushroomed in the 1970s as a result of favorable changes in campaign finance laws (see Figure 9–2). There are now more than four thousand PACs, and PAC contributions account for roughly a third of total contributions to congressional campaigns. Because PAC money can be raised earlier and more quickly than money from individual contributors, PACs have become a critical factor in getting congressional campaigns off the ground. Their role is less sig-

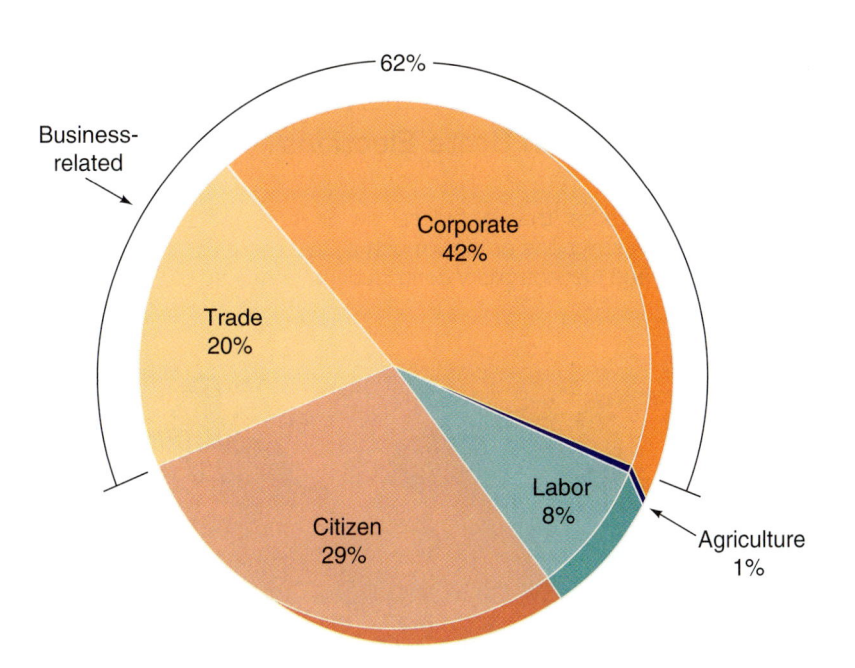

Figure 9–3
Percentage of PACs by Category
Most PACs represent business. Corporate and trade association PACs make up 62 percent of the total.
Source: Federal Election Commission figures, 2000.

Business-related: 62%
- Corporate 42%
- Trade 20%

Citizen 29%
Labor 8%
Agriculture 1%

nificant in presidential campaigns, which are larger in scale and publicly funded in part and therefore less dependent on PAC contributions.

PACs give most of their support to congressional incumbents. PACs typically contribute more than five times as much money to incumbents as to their challengers. PACs are well aware of the fact that incumbents are likely to win and thus to remain in a position to make policy. One PAC director, expressing a common view, said, "We always stick with the incumbent when we agree with them both."[26]

The tendency of PACs to back incumbents has to some extent blurred longstanding partisan divisions in campaign funding. Business interests are particularly pragmatic. Although they tend to favor Republican candidates, they are reluctant to anger Democratic incumbents. The result is that Democratic incumbents, particularly in House races, have received substantial support over the years from business-related PACs.[27] Other PACs, of course, are less pragmatic. The Christian Moral Government Fund, for example, backs only candidates who take conservative stands on issues such as school prayer and abortion.

More than 40 percent of all PACs are associated with corporations (see Figure 9–3). Examples include the Ford Motor Company Civic Action Fund, the Sun Oil Company Political Action Committee (Sunpac), and the Coca-Cola PAC. The next largest group of PACs consists of those linked to citizens' groups (that is, public interest, single-issue, and ideological groups), such as the liberal People for the American Way and the conservative NCPAC (National Conservative Political Action Committee). Ranking third are PACs tied to trade and professional associations, such as AMPAC (American Medical Association) and R-PAC (National Association of Realtors). Labor unions were once the major source of group contributions, but they now rank fourth.

STATES IN THE NATION

Limits on PAC Contributions in State Elections

Elections for state office are regulated by state law, rather than by federal law. States are free to set their own limits for nonfederal office. Some states place no restrictions on how much a PAC can give to a candidate. Of the states that limit contributions, only New York and Nevada allow contributions in excess of $10,000.

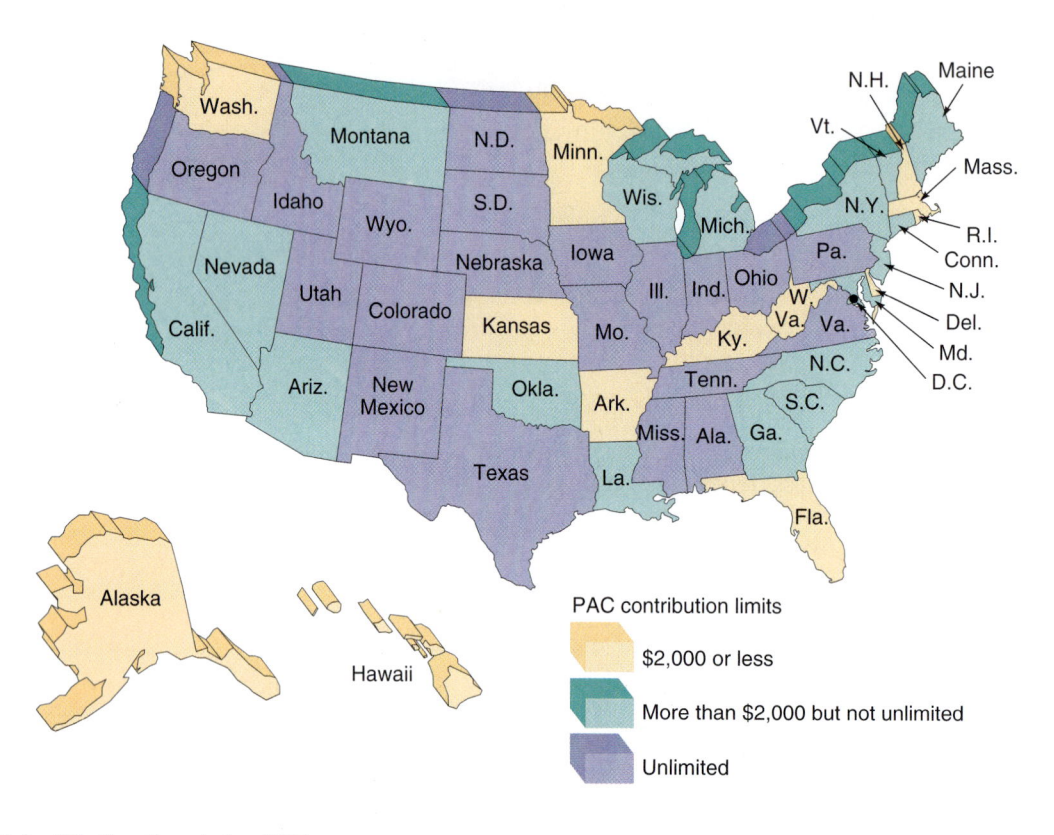

PAC contribution limits
- $2,000 or less
- More than $2,000 but not unlimited
- Unlimited

Source: Federal Elections Commission, 2001.

Advocates of PACs claim that groups have a right to be heard, which includes the right to express themselves with money. Advocates also say that a campaign finance system based on pooled contributions by individuals is superior to one in which candidates rely on a few wealthy donors.[28]

Critics argue, however, that PACs give interest groups altogether too much influence over public officials.[29] The opposition to PACs has increased in the last few years, as citizens have come to associate the influence of interest groups with favoritism and abuse in the enactment of policy. Although members of Congress deny that they are unduly influenced by PAC contributions, there has been a growing sentiment within Congress to place some restrictions on PACs. Agreement on the changes, however, has been difficult to achieve because of differences between Democrats and Republicans in the way they would reform the process and also because some incumbents are unwilling to support any change that would significantly alter the advantage they have under the present system.

THE GROUP SYSTEM: INDISPENSABLE BUT BIASED

As was noted in the introduction to this chapter, pluralist theory holds that organized groups provide for the representation of society's many and diverse interests. On one level, this claim is beyond dispute. Without groups to carry their message, most of society's interests would find it difficult to gain government's attention and support. Yet the issue of representation is also a question of whether all interests in society have a fair chance to succeed and whether some groups have undue influence, and here the pluralist argument is less compelling.

The Contribution of Groups to Self-Government: Pluralism

Group activity is an essential part of self-government. A major obstacle to popular sovereignty is the many difficulties that public officials encounter in trying to discover what the people want from government. To determine their wishes, lawmakers consult public opinion polls, meet with constituents, and assess the meaning of recent elections. Organized groups are an additional means of determining popular sentiment because they provide policymakers with a better picture of the policy concerns of various interests in society.[30] On any given issue, the policy positions that are likely to be expressed most clearly and intensely are those held by organized interests.

Moreover, government does not exist simply to serve majority interests. The fact that most people are not retirees or labor union members or farmers or college students or Hispanics does not mean that the special needs and concerns of such "minorities" are undeserving of attention. And what better instrument exists for promoting the interests of such "minorities" than organizations formed around them? Groups are not antithetical to the democratic process: they are basic to it.

Some pluralists even question whether such terms as *the common good* and *the collective interest* are very useful. If people disagree on society's goals and priorities, as they always do, how can it be said that people have a "common" or "collective" concern? As an alternative, pluralists contend that, because society has so many interests, the common good is ultimately best served by a process that enables a great many interests to gain favorable policies. Thus, if manufacturing interests prevail on one issue, environmentalists on another, farmers on a third, minorities on a fourth, and so on until many interests are served, the collective interest of society will have been promoted.[31]

Finally, interest groups often take up issues that are neglected by the party system. Party leaders typically shy from issues, such as affirmative action and abortion, on which the party's voters disagree. Such issues would get less notice if not for the groups that promote them. And when groups succeed in drawing

Fighting Words

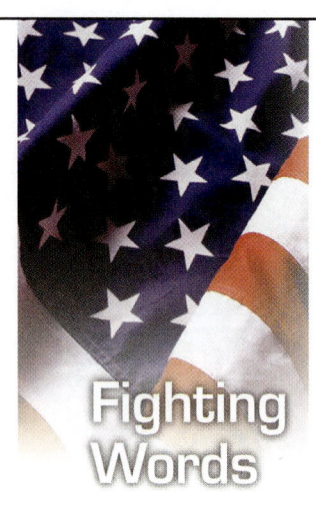

Have Interest Groups Hijacked the Initiative Process?

The initiative was pioneered by the Progressives of the early twentieth century, who saw it as a way to wrest power from the political bosses and corporate robber barons and place it in the hands of ordinary citizens. Twenty-four states allow the initiative, which requires the gathering of a sufficient number of citizens' signatures to place a legislative proposal (initiative) on the ballot. If a majority of voters approve it, the initiative becomes law, just as if it had been enacted by the legislature itself. In recent years, however, the initiative process has been used by interest groups to advance their policy agendas. They have the money to pay for the signature-gathering phase and to conduct a campaign for enactment of the initiative. To some observers, this tendency has corrupted the initiative process. Other observers claim that the initiative remains a bulwark of citizen-based politics.

Yes: [The initiative process is] now being driven very much by money. With their own political agendas, interest groups of all kinds have latched onto the device as a way of writing the law the way they would like it written without having to go through all the hoops of the normal governmental process. . . . I think it's particularly ironic that a device that was introduced into this country as a way of fighting special interest influence and the power of money now has been largely taken over by those same interest groups and by very wealthy millionaires who have the resources that it takes now to get an initiative on the ballot and to fight these campaigns to get them passed or defeated in the states.
—David S. Broder, author and journalist

No: The initiative and referendum process has been a critical tool to check the power of unresponsive and unaccountable government at the state and local level for 100 years. Through its use, women gained the right to vote, we can directly elect our U.S. Senators, we have direct primaries, term limits on 18 state legislatures, tax and spending limits, the eight-hour work day, environmental reforms and much, much more. In 1998 alone, the 100th anniversary of initiative and referendum, voters were heard on such issues as affirmative action, animal rights, term limits, tax limits, and medical marijuana, to name a few.
—The Initiative and Referendum Institute

---

attention to these issues, the parties are nearly compelled also to address them. In this sense, as the political scientist Jack Walker noted, the party and group systems "are complementary and together constitute a more responsive and adaptive system than either would be if they somehow operated on their own."[32]

Flaws in Pluralism: Interest-Group Liberalism and Economic Bias

Although pluralist theory offers some compelling arguments, it also has questionable aspects. In a direct attack on pluralism, Theodore Lowi argues that there is no concept of society's collective interest in a system that allows special

Sometimes the interests of a group clearly diverge from majority opinion, as when the National Association of Auto Dealers lobbied successfully against legislation that would have required automobile dealers to inform customers about any defects in used cars.

interests to determine for themselves which policy benefits they receive, regardless of how many interests are served.[33] When each group makes its own choice, the basis of decision in each case is not majority (collective) rule but minority (special-interest) rule.

It is seldom safe to assume that what a popular majority favors is what a special-interest group wants. Consider the case of the federal law that required auto dealers to list the known defects of used cars on window stickers. The law was repealed after an extensive lobbying campaign financed by contributions of more than $1 million by the National Association of Automobile Dealers to the reelection campaigns of members of Congress. Although an overwhelming majority of the general public would surely have favored retention of the law, the car dealers' view prevailed.

Lowi uses the term **interest-group liberalism** to describe the tendency of officials to support the policy demands of the interest group or groups that have a special stake in a policy. Interest-group liberalism constitutes a partial abdication by government of its authority over policy. In practical terms, it is the group as much as the government that decides policy. The adverse effects include an inefficient use of society's resources: groups get what they want, whether or not their priorities match those of society as a whole.

Another flaw in the pluralist argument resides in its claim that the group system is representative. Pluralists recognize that better-organized interests have more influence but argue that the group process is relatively open and that few interests are at a serious disadvantage. These claims contain an element of truth but are far from the complete truth.

As this chapter has pointed out, organization is a political resource that is distributed unequally across society. Economic interests, particularly corporations, are the most highly organized, and some analysts argue that group politics

interest-group liberalism The tendency of public officials to support the policy demands of self-interested groups (as opposed to judging policy demands according to whether they serve a larger conception of "the public interest").

works to the advantage of business.[34] This generalization is less valid today. In fact, many of the public interest groups formed in the past three decades were deliberately created to check and balance the influence of existing groups, particularly corporate lobbies.[35]

Big government has also brought the group political system into closer balance. Groups form not only to influence policy but also in response to policy. When new programs were created in the 1960s for the benefit of less advantaged interests in society, these interests mobilized to protect their newly acquired benefits. The National Welfare Rights Organization was formed during the 1960s after new welfare programs were established.[36] Many of the newer interest groups have had a significant impact in areas such as civil rights, the environment, social welfare programs for the elderly and the poor, public ethics, national security, and business regulation. Moreover, policy today is less often decided by the actions of one or a few groups. The group system is thus not closed and rigid; it is open to new interests and new patterns of influence.

Nevertheless, interests differ significantly in their level of organization. Well over half of all lobbying groups in Washington are still business-related. The interest-group system is biased toward America's economically oriented groups, particularly its corporations.

The group system is also slanted toward upper-middle-class interests. Studies indicate that individuals of higher socioeconomic status are disproportionately represented among group members and even more so among group leaders. These tendencies are predictable. Educated and affluent Americans have the skills and money to participate affectively in special-interest politics. Less advantaged Americans lack the money, information, contacts, and communication skills to participate even when they desire to do so. The poor, minorities, women, and the young are greatly underrepresented in the group politics system. A lack of organization does not ensure an interest's failure, just as the existence of organization does not guarantee success. However, organized interests are obviously in a better position to make their views known.

The business and class bias of the group system is especially significant because the most highly organized interests are, in a sense, those least in need of political clout. Corporations and affluent citizens already benefit from the distribution of society's material resources.

A Madisonian Dilemma

James Madison recognized the dilemma inherent in group activity. Although he worried that government would fall under the control of a dominant interest, whether of the majority or of the minority, he realized that a free society is obliged to permit the advocacy of self-interest. Unless people can promote the separate opinions that stem from differences in their talents, needs, values, and possessions, they do not have liberty.

Ironically, Madison's constitutional solution to the problem of factions has become part of the problem. The American system of checks and balances, with a separation of powers at its core, was designed primarily to prevent a majority faction from trampling on the interests of others. Indeed, throughout the nation's history, majorities have been frustrated in their efforts to gain full power by America's elaborate system of divided government.

Liberty & Equality

What's Your Opinion?

Interest Groups

Rarely is the tension between liberty and equality more evident than in the activities of interest groups. "Liberty is to faction what air is to fire," wrote James Madison in *Federalist* No. 10. Madison was lamenting the self-interested behavior of factions or, as they are called today, interest groups. Yet Madison recognized that the only way to suppress this behavior was to destroy the liberty that allows people to organize.

Interest groups tend to strengthen the already powerful and thus contribute to political inequality. As the political scientist E. E. Schattschneider said, the group system "sings with a strong upper-class bias."

Numerous efforts have been made to harness the power of groups without infringing on Americans' rights of free expression, assembly, and petition. Laws have been enacted that require lobbyists to register, report their lobbying expenditures, and identify the issues on which they are working. Other laws restrict group contributions to candidates for public office. Yet, nothing in the end seems to be all that effective in harnessing the self-interested actions of groups. Is there an answer to "Madison's dilemma"? Or are the excesses of group politics simply one of the costs of living in a free society?

Grassroots lobbying is based on pressure from constituents. These farmers traveled to Washington to protest the low prices they were getting for agricultural goods.

This same system, however, makes it relatively easy for minority factions—or, as they are called today, special-interest groups—to protect the government benefits they receive. Benefits are hard to eliminate because concerted action by the executive and both houses of Congress is usually required. If a group has strong support in even a single institution, it can usually fend off attempts to terminate its benefits. This support is ordinarily easy to acquire, because the group can provide resources—money or votes—in return. Jonathan Rauch uses the term *demosclerosis* to describe the debilitating effect on government: its resources are increasingly absorbed by entrenched interests and it consequently undergoes a progressive loss in its ability to respond to emerging needs. Like the arteriosclerosis that slowly deprives the human body of the oxygen-laden blood it needs to survive, demosclerosis slowly robs government of its capacity to respond.[37] Chapters 11 and 13 discuss further the issue of interest-group power.

Self-Quiz
www.mhhe.com/patterson6

SUMMARY

A political interest group is composed of a set of individuals organized to promote a shared political concern. Most interest groups owe their existence to factors other than politics. They form for economic reasons, such as the pursuit of profit, and maintain themselves by making profits (in the case of corporations) or by providing their members with private goods, such as jobs and wages. Such interest groups include corporations, trade associations, labor unions, farm organizations, and professional associations. Collectively, economic groups are by far the largest set of organized interests. The group system tends to favor interests that are already economically and socially advantaged.

Citizens' groups do not have the same organizational advantages as economic groups. They depend on voluntary contributions from potential members who may lack interest and resources or who recognize that they will get the collective good from a group's activity even if they do not participate (the free-rider problem). These citizens' groups include public interest, single-issue, and ideological groups. Their numbers have increased dramatically since the 1960s despite their organizational problems.

Organized interests seek influence largely by lobbying public officials and contributing to election campaigns. Using an inside strategy, lobbyists develop direct contacts with legislators, government bureaucrats, and members of the judiciary in order to persuade them to accept their group's perspective on policy. Groups also use an outside strategy, seeking to mobilize public support for their goals. This strategy relies in part on grassroots lobbying—encouraging group members and the public to communicate their policy views to officials. Outside lobbying also includes efforts to elect officeholders who will support group aims. Through political action committees (PACs), organized groups now provide nearly a third of all contributions received by congressional candidates.

The policies that emerge from the group system bring benefits to many of society's interests, and in some instances these benefits also serve the general interest. But when groups can essentially dictate policies, the common good is not served. The majority's interest is subordinated to group (minority) interests. In most instances, the minority consists of individuals who already have a substantial share of society's benefits.

KEY TERMS

citizens' (noneconomic) groups
collective (public) goods
economic groups
free-rider problem
grassroots lobbying
inside lobbying

interest group
interest-group liberalism
iron triangle
issue network
lobbying
material incentive

outside lobbying
political action committee (PAC)
private (individual) goods
purposive incentive
single-issue politics

SUGGESTED READINGS

Berry, Jeffrey M. *The New Liberalism: The Rising Power of Citizen Groups.* Washington, D.C.: Brookings Institution Press, 1999. An exploration of the influence that citizen groups exercise.

Browne, William P. *Cultivating Congress: Constituents, Issues, and Interests in Agriculture Policymaking.* Lawrence: University Press of Kansas, 1995. An analysis of the limits of "iron triangles" as a description of congressional policymaking.

Cigler, Allan J., and Burdett A. Loomis. *Interest Group Politics,* 5th ed. Washington, D.C.: Congressional Quarterly Press, 1998. A comprehensive analysis of interest group politics.

Gatz, Thomas L. *Improper Influence: Campaign Finance Law, Political Interest Groups, and the Problem of Equality.* Ann Arbor: University of Michigan Press, 1996. An analysis of how PACs have changed the process of representation through groups.

Grossman, Gene M. and Elhanan Helpman. *Interest Groups and Trade Policy.* Princeton, N.J.: Princeton University Press, 2002. An examination of the impact of groups' campaign and lobbying activities on trade policy.

Herrnson, Paul S., Ronald G. Shaiko, and Clyde Wilcox, eds. *The Interest Group Connection: Electioneering, Lobbying and Policymaking in Washington.* Chatham, N.J.: Chatham House Publishers, 1998. Essays and commentaries on groups and officials and the linkages between them.

Lowi, Theodore J. *The End of Liberalism,* 2d ed. New York: Norton, 1979. A thorough critique of interest groups' influence on American politics.

Olson, Mancur, Jr. *The Logic of Collective Action,* rev. ed. Cambridge, Mass.: Harvard University Press, 1971. A pioneering analysis of why some interests are more fully and easily organized than others.

LIST OF WEBSITES

http://www.fec/gov/
The Federal Election Commission site; it offers information on elections, voting, campaign finance, parties, and PACs. It also includes a citizens' guide to campaign contributions.

http://www/pirg.org
The Public Interest Research Group (PIRG) site. PIRG has chapters on many college campuses and the site provides state-by-state policy and other information.

http://www.sierraclub.org
The Sierra Club site; this organization, one of the oldest environmental protection interest groups, promotes conservation. Its website provides information on its activities.

http://www.townhall.com/
The website of the American Conservative Union (ACU); it includes policy and political information and has a lively chat room.

10

The press in America ... determines what people will think and talk about—an authority that in other nations is reserved for tyrants, priests, parties, and mandarins.
—Theodore H. White[1]

The News Media:
Communicating Political Images

Early on the morning of April 22, 2000, CNN interrupted its coverage to report a breaking story from Miami. Federal agents had just broken into the home where six-year-old Elian Gonzalez was staying and had taken him to a waiting plane that would fly him to Washington to be reunited with his father. Video pictures of the armed seizure followed almost immediately, and the story was soon playing on nearly every television news program in the country. As the day unfolded, viewers were to see Elian arriving in Washington while crowds of Cuban Americans gathered in Miami to protest the Justice Department's actions. For the next week, Elian's seizure and reactions to it filled the airwaves and front pages.

The seizure was the latest episode in a running news story that had begun months earlier when Elian was rescued at sea after his mother had drowned while trying to escape Cuba by boat. The young boy became the object of a political tug-of-war between Florida's Cuban American community and Cuba's Fidel Castro. Every move and countermove provoked a torrent of news coverage.

Not all developments receive such intensive news coverage. More new immigrants have arrived in the United States in the past two decades than during any comparable period in the nation's history. Their sheer number has strained the capacity of schools and other public organizations. In some communities, trailer houses have been converted into makeshift schoolrooms simply to get a roof over all students' heads. The impact of this great wave of immigration has been enormous and will affect the United States for years to come. Yet this development has only occasionally been mentioned in the news, let alone emblazoned in the headlines month after month.

Although the news has been compared to a mirror held up to society, it is actually a highly selective portrayal of reality. The **news** is mainly an account of overt, obtruding events, particularly those that are *timely* (new or unfolding developments rather than old or static ones), *dramatic* (striking developments rather than commonplace ones), and *compelling* (developments that arouse people's concerns and emotions as opposed to remote ones).[2] These characteristics of the news have a number of origins, not the least of which is that the news is a business. News organizations seek to make a profit, which leads them to prefer news stories that will attract and hold an audience. Thus, Elian Gonzalez became headline news the instant he was plucked from the sea, and he remained newsworthy while the political and legal process surrounding his status unfolded. The larger issue of the influx of immigrants into the United States during the past two decades is not considered particularly newsworthy, because it is a slow and steady process, dramatic only in its long-term implications. The columnist George Will notes that a development requires a defining event before it can become big news.[3] Without such an event, reporters have no peg on which to hang their stories.

News organizations and journalists, of either the print media (newspapers and magazines) or the broadcast media (radio and television), are referred to collectively as the **press** or the **news media.** The press is an increasingly important political actor. Its heightened influence is attributable in part to changes within the media. New

Federal agents seize Elian Gonzalez from the home of his Miami relatives. The Gonzalez story was one of the most heavily covered news events of recent years.

news The news media's version of reality, usually with an emphasis on timely, dramatic, and compelling events and developments.

press (news media) Those print and broadcast organizations that are in the news-reporting business.

technology, from television to cable to satellites, has dramatically increased the reach and speed of communication. In addition, the press has filled some of the void created by the decline in political parties and other political institutions.

Like political parties and interest groups, the press is a key link between the public and its leaders. In some ways, the press is better positioned than parties or groups to influence the public. On a daily basis, Americans connect to politics more through the news that is produced by the media than through the activities of parties or groups.

This chapter argues, however, that the news media are a very different kind of intermediary than either parties or interest groups and that problems arise when the press is asked to perform the same functions as these organizations. The chapter begins with a review of the media's historical development and the current trends in news reporting. It concludes with an analysis of the roles the press can and cannot perform adequately in the American political system. The main ideas represented in this chapter are the following:

- *The American press was initially tied to the nation's political party system (the partisan press) but gradually developed an independent position (the objective press).* In the process, the news shifted from a political orientation, which emphasizes political values and ideas, to a journalistic orientation, which stresses newsworthy information and evaluations.

- *Although the United States has thousands of separate news organizations, they present a common version of the news that reflects journalists' shared view of what the news is.* Freedom of the press in the United States does not result in a robust marketplace of ideas.

- *In fulfilling its responsibility to provide public information, the news media effectively perform three significant roles—those of signaler (the press brings relevant events and problems into public view), common carrier (the press serves as a channel through which political leaders can address the public), and watchdog (the press scrutinizes official behavior for evidence of deceitful, careless, or corrupt acts).* These roles are within the news media's capacity because they fit with the values, incentives, and accountability of the press.

- *The press cannot do the job of political institutions, even though it increasingly tries to do so.* The nature of journalism as it has evolved is incompatible with the characteristics required for the role of public representative.

THE DEVELOPMENT OF THE NEWS MEDIA: FROM PARTISANSHIP TO OBJECTIVE JOURNALISM

Democracy requires a free flow of information. Communication enables a free people to keep in touch with one another, with their leaders, and with important events. Recognizing the vital role of the press in the building of a democratic society, Thomas Jefferson wrote in 1787, "Were it left to me to decide whether we should have a government without newspapers, or newspapers without a government, I should not hesitate a moment to prefer the latter."[4]

America's early leaders were quick to see the advantages of promoting the establishment of newspapers. At Alexander Hamilton's urging, the *Gazette of the United States* was founded by John Fenno to promote the policies of George Washington's administration. Hamilton was secretary of the treasury and supported Fenno's paper by granting it the Treasury Department's printing contracts. Jefferson, who was secretary of state and Hamilton's adversary, complained that the newspaper's content was "pure Toryism." Jefferson persuaded Philip Freneau to start the *National Gazette* as the opposition Republican party's publication and supported it by granting Freneau authority to print State Department documents.

Early newspapers were printed on hand presses, a process that limited production and kept the cost of each copy beyond the reach of ordinary citizens—most of whom were illiterate anyway. Leading papers such as the *Gazette of the United States* had fewer than fifteen hundred subscribers and could not have survived without party support. Not surprisingly, the "news" they printed was a form of party propaganda.[5] In this era of the **partisan press,** publishers openly took sides on partisan issues. Their employees were expected to follow the party line. President James K. Polk once persuaded a leading publisher to fire an editor who was critical of Polk's policies.[6]

partisan press Newspapers and other communication media that openly support a political party and whose news in significant part follows the party line.

From a Partisan Press to an "Objective" One

Technological changes helped bring about the gradual decline of America's partisan press. After the invention of the telegraph in 1837, editors could receive timely information on developments in Washington and the state capital, and they had less reason to fill their pages with partisan arguments.[7] Another major

STATES IN THE NATION

In the News, or Out?

A few major media outlets dominate news production in the United States. The stories they carry tend to set the news agenda for other media. NBC News is one of these agenda setters. Not surprisingly, since it is based in New York City, NBC's coverage includes a disproportionate amount of coverage of New York. But what about other states? How much attention do they receive on the NBC nightly news? The fact is, coverage varies with events of the moment. The news highlights events that are colorful, sensational, or significant. A natural disaster can bring a state into the national media spotlight, but it may fade from view as soon as the crisis has passed. The map indicates the relative frequency with which the states were mentioned on the "NBC Nightly News with Tom Brokaw" during a recent one-year period.

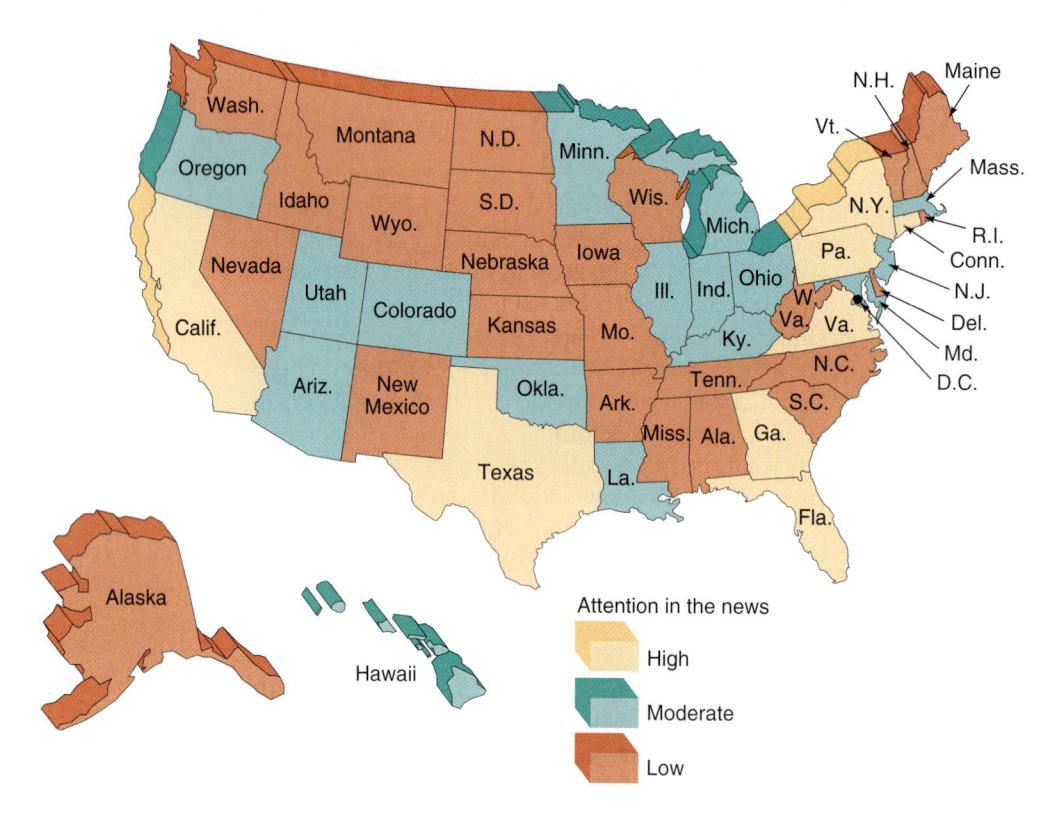

Attention in the news: High, Moderate, Low

Source: Data compiled by author from Nexis.

---

innovation was the rotary press (invented in 1815), a breakthrough that enabled commercially minded publishers to print their newspapers rapidly and cheaply and thus to increase their profit potential.[8] The *New York Sun* was the first paper to pass on the benefit of high-speed printing to subscribers by reducing the price of a daily copy from six cents to a penny. The *Sun*'s circulation rose to five thousand in four months and to ten thousand in less than a year.[9] Increased circulation and revenues gave newspapers independence from government and parties.

Yellow journalism was characterized by its sensationalism. William Randolph Hearst's *New York Journal* whipped up public support for a war in Cuba with Spain through inflammatory reporting on the sinking of the battleship *Maine* in Havana Harbor in 1898.

By the late nineteenth century, several American newspapers were printing a hundred thousand or more copies a day, and their large circulations enabled them to charge high prices for advertising. The period marked the height of newspapers' power and the low point in their sense of public responsibility.[10] A new style of reporting—"yellow journalism"—had emerged as a way of boosting circulation.[11] The "yellow" press—so called because some of these newspapers were printed on cheap yellow paper—emphasized "a shrieking, gaudy, sensation-loving, devil-may-care kind of journalism which lured the reader by any possible means."[12] A circulation battle between William Randolph Hearst's *New York Journal* and Joseph Pulitzer's *New York World* is believed to have contributed to the outbreak of the Spanish-American War through sensational (and largely inaccurate) reports on the cruelty of Spanish rule in Cuba. A young Frederic Remington (who later became a noted painter and sculptor), working as a news artist for Hearst, planned to return home because Cuba appeared calm and safe, but Hearst cabled back, "Please remain. You furnish the pictures and I'll furnish the war."[13]

The excesses of yellow journalism led some publishers to consider ways of reporting the news more responsibly. One step was to separate the newspaper's advertising department from its news department, thus reducing the influence of advertisers on news content. A second development was a new model of reporting called **objective journalism,** which was based on the reporting of "facts" rather than opinions and was "fair" in that it presented both sides of partisan debate.[14]

objective journalism A model of news reporting that is based on the communication of "facts" rather than opinions and that is "fair" in that it presents all sides of partisan debate.

A chief advocate of this new form of journalism was Adolph Ochs of *The New York Times*. Ochs bought the *Times* in 1896, when its circulation was 9,000; four years later, its readership had grown to 82,000. Ochs told his reporters that he "wanted as little partisanship as possible . . . as few judgments as possible."[15] The *Times*'s approach to reporting appealed particularly to educated readers, and by the early twentieth century it had acquired a reputation as the country's best newspaper. Objective reporting was also promoted through newly formed journalism schools. Among the first of these professional schools were those at Columbia University and the University of Missouri. The Columbia School of Journalism opened in 1912 with a $2 million grant from Pulitzer.

Objective journalism is still a component of news coverage. Although most newspapers have a partisan bias on their editorial pages, they tend to treat the Republican and Democratic parties equally on their news pages. Nevertheless, the influence of objective journalism is waning. Newspapers increasingly rely on an **interpretive style of reporting,** in which the journalist's job is to analyze, evaluate, and explain developments rather than merely report them. The older form of objective journalism (called **descriptive reporting,** because of its straightforward description of events) required that reporters stick to the "facts." The newer interpretive style allows them to speculate on what the facts mean. As explained later in the chapter, interpretive reporting has greatly increased journalists' ability to shape the news to fit their own views, including their skeptical opinion of politicians' motives and accomplishments.

interpretive reporting The style of reporting that aims to explain *why* something is taking place or has occurred.

descriptive reporting The style of reporting that aims to describe *what* is taking place or has occurred.

The Development of the Broadcast Media

Radio and Television: The Truly National Media

Until the early twentieth century, the print media were the only form of mass communication. Within a few decades, however, there were hundreds of radio stations throughout the nation. Broadcasting was the first truly *national* mass medium. Newspapers had local circulation bases, whereas radio could reach millions of Americans across the country simultaneously.

Television followed radio, and by the late 1950s more than 90 percent of American homes had a television set. The political potential of television was evident as early as 1952, when seventeen million homes tuned in to the national Republican and Democratic party conventions.[16] However, television newscasts of the 1950s were brief, lasting no more than fifteen minutes, and relied on news gathered by other organizations, particularly the Associated Press and other wire services. In the early 1960s, the three commercial networks—CBS, NBC, and ABC—expanded their evening newscasts to thirty minutes, and their audience ratings increased.[17] Simultaneously, they increased the size and funding of their news divisions, and television soon became the principal news medium of national politics.

Today, television provides a twenty-four-hour forum of political news and information. The advent of the Cable News Network (CNN) and C-SPAN in the late 1970s brought Americans round-the-clock communication. Television talk shows, such as *Larry King Live,* have broadened the range of choices available to politically interested viewers. A parallel development is the emergence of radio

Franklin D. Roosevelt was the first president to make effective use of the radio to communicate directly with the American people. He broadcast a series of fireside chats that reached millions of listeners across the country.

talk shows. Nearly a sixth of the American public claims to listen regularly to a politically oriented radio talk show, most of which have a conservative slant. The best known radio talk show host is Rush Limbaugh, who is known for his scathing attacks on Democratic politicians.

Even more so than their newspaper counterparts, television journalists rely on an interpretive style of reporting. The reason is that television journalists use a narrative or storytelling mode in order to appeal to an audience accustomed to entertainment programming. "Facts" alone do not tell a story; they have to be interpreted in a way that makes them into a story. Reuven Frank, a network executive and pioneer in television journalism, once told his correspondents: "Every news story should, without any sacrifice of probity or responsibility, display the attributes of fiction, of drama. It should have structure and conflict, problem and denouement, rising action and falling action, a beginning, a middle and an end."[18]

Government Licensing and Regulation of Broadcasters

At first the government did not carefully regulate broadcasting. The result was chaos. Nearby stations often used the same or adjacent radio frequencies, interfering with each other's transmissions. Finally, in 1934, Congress passed the Communications Act, which requires that broadcasters be licensed and meet certain performance standards. Congress established the Federal Communications Commission (FCC) to administer the act through regulations pertaining to such matters as signal strength, advertising rates and access, and political coverage.

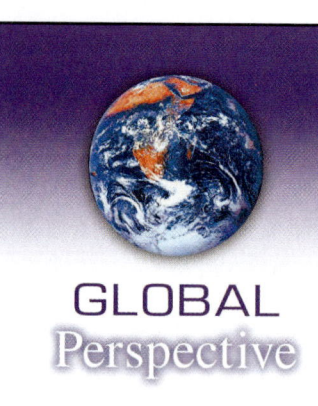

Americans in an Interdependent World

CNN and Foreign Policy

As the Palestinian suicide bombings continued and as Israel retaliated with tanks and helicopter gunships, President George W. Bush came under intense pressure to intervene. Although Bush had promised during the 2000 campaign that he would keep America from intervening in regional conflicts, he found it increasingly difficult to keep that promise as the Palestinian-Israeli struggle escalated. In early 2002, Bush gave in. He sent Secretary of State Colin Powell to the region to try to arrange a cease-fire as a first step in a peace process in which the United States would play an active role.

Was Bush's decision to renege on his campaign promise wholly a response to the deteriorating situation in the Middle East? Or was it partly forced on him by CNN's live, on-the-spot television coverage of the Middle East violence?

CNN has developed the capacity to provide live television coverage from almost anywhere in the world. The Israeli-Palestinian conflict was not the first time that television viewers had seen CNN's version of armed conflict. During the previous decade, Americans had been eyewitnesses to CNN's coverage of fighting in places such as the Persian Gulf, Bosnia, Kosovo, and Afghanistan. The Middle East conflict illustrated yet again that CNN had broken down the boundaries of space and time that once separated Americans from warfare in remote areas of the globe.

Some analysts believe that CNN's coverage has had a major influence on U.S. foreign policy. They point particularly to U.S. intervention in Somalia in the early 1990s. Civil war and famine in that country had created widespread malnutrition and resulted in thousands of deaths. CNN's pictures of long lines of starving refugees touched a responsive chord in the United States and other countries, and the United Nations sent a humanitarian mission to Somalia that included American soldiers. This intervention turned sour when warring Somali clans threatened the mission. An American military unit was ambushed and several dozen U.S. soldiers died. Television captured the haunting image of one of the dead soldiers being dragged by a mob through the streets of the Somali capital, and public opinion quickly shifted. Americans had supported the humanitarian mission, but they now wanted U.S. troops pulled out of Somalia as rapidly as possible. Within a short period, the troops were withdrawn.

Although the effect of global television on public policy can easily be exaggerated, it can sometimes force policymakers to act more hastily or in different ways than they might otherwise do. Some analysts see this effect as a positive development because it makes foreign policy more responsive to public opinion than it used to be. Most analysts, however, are critical of the development. They argue that television's pictures tend to reflect only the most incendiary aspects of a situation and thus serve to distort both the problem and the public's response to it.

Whatever its exact influence, CNN has become an important player in U.S. foreign policy. Analysts have a term for CNN's influence; it's called *the CNN effect*. Although CNN's audience is relatively small, it includes most of America's top foreign policy officials. (CNN is also watched closely by policymakers in other world capitals).

The principle of scarcity justifies the licensing and regulation of broadcast media. Because the number of available broadcasting frequencies is limited, those few individuals who are granted a broadcasting license are expected to serve the public interest in addition to their own. In principle, licensing is a means of controlling broadcasting. If a station fails to comply with federal broadcast regulations, the FCC can withdraw its license. However, the FCC seldom even threatens to revoke a license, for fear of being accused of restricting freedom of the press. A broadcast station can apply for renewal of its license by postcard and is virtually guaranteed FCC approval, which covers seven years for radio and five for television.

Because broadcast frequencies are a scarce resource, licensees are required by law to be somewhat evenhanded during election campaigns. Section 315 of the Communications Act imposes on broadcasters an "equal-time" restriction, which means that they cannot sell or give air time to a political candidate without granting equal opportunities to the other candidates running for the same office. (Election debates are an exception; broadcasters can televise them even if participation is limited to the Republican and Democratic nominees only.)

The Emergence of the Internet

Although the First Amendment protects each individual's right to press freedom, the right in practice has been reserved for a tiny few. The journalist A. J. Liebling wrote that freedom of the press belongs to those with the money to own one.[19] Even a modest-sized broadcast station or daily newspaper costs millions to buy; the largest media conglomerates are multibillion-dollar enterprises.

The Internet has weakened the traditional news media's control of the political information that Americans receive. Through the Internet, citizens and political leaders alike can communicate widely without having their messages filtered by the news media. Pictured here are the home pages of the U.S. House and Senate.

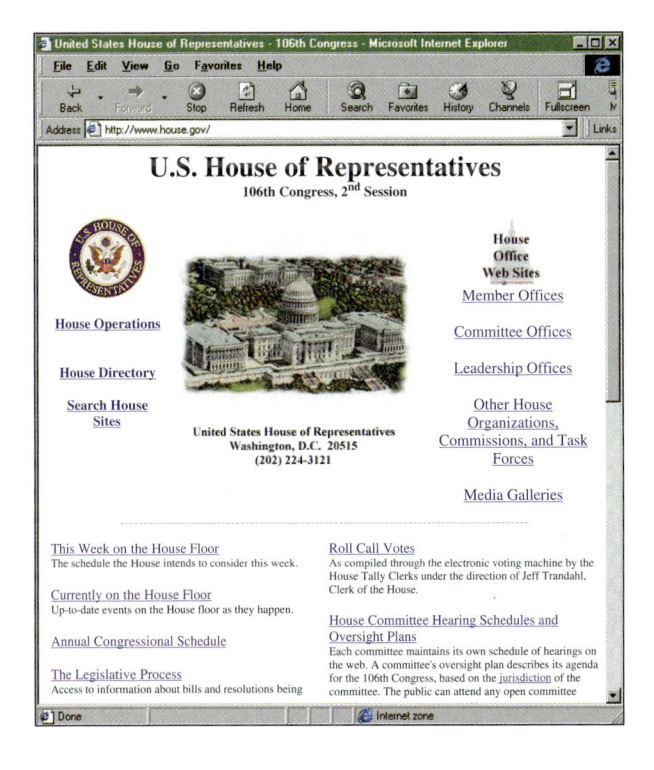

Access to the Internet is no substitute for ownership of a major news outlet, but it provides ordinary citizens at least the opportunity to exercise their free-press rights. By creating a website, the ordinary citizen can post information about public affairs, harangue officials, argue for public policies, and attempt to mobilize the support of others. There is no assurance of a wide audience, and in fact, most citizens have neither a personal website nor, if they do, a large following. But the Internet has reduced the barriers to citizen communication to a level not seen since the colonial days, when citizen-produced pamphlets were the major form of political expression.

The Internet has also provided political leaders and organizations a direct channel to the public. At all political levels, officeholders, parties, and interest groups now have websites that are used to inform and mobilize their followers. The Internet has reduced somewhat the traditional media's capacity to control the news agenda. Editors and reporters are "gatekeepers" who decide what will make the news and what will not. Although they still play this role, Internet communication has in some instances virtually forced "stories" upon them. The best known web outlet is likely the "Drudge Report," which was created by Matt Drudge and became a prime source of information for enterprising reporters. The Clinton-Lewinsky scandal, for example, surfaced in the "Drudge Report" four days before it appeared in the mainstream press.

FREEDOM AND CONFORMITY IN THE U.S. NEWS MEDIA

Some democracies impose significant legal restraints on the press. The news media in Britain are barred from reporting on anything that the government has labeled an "official secret," and the nation's tough libel laws inhibit the press from publishing unsubstantiated personal attacks.

In the United States, as pointed out in Chapter 4, the First Amendment gives the press substantial protection. The courts have consistently upheld the right of U.S. newspapers to report on politics as they choose. Broadcasters, as the equal-time restriction indicates, have less freedom under the law, but they are subject to much less government control than are broadcasters in Europe. In the case of both U.S. newspapers and broadcasters, the government cannot block publication of a news story unless it can convincingly demonstrate in court that the information would jeopardize national security. Although most Americans would permit censorship in time of armed conflict (see Figure 10–1), the courts have limited the government's ability to restrict press freedom even when the nation is at war. U.S. libel laws also strongly favor the press. A public figure who is attacked in a news story cannot collect libel damages unless he or she can demonstrate convincingly that the news organization was false in its accusations and knowingly or recklessly careless in its search for the truth.

Moreover, the U.S. government provides the news media with indirect economic support. Newspapers and magazines have a special postal rate that helps them keep their circulation costs low, and broadcasters pay only a few dollars annually in license fees for broadcasting rights that are worth hundreds of billions of dollars. Such policies have contributed to the development of a truly enormous news industry in the United States: 1,600 daily newspapers; 8,500

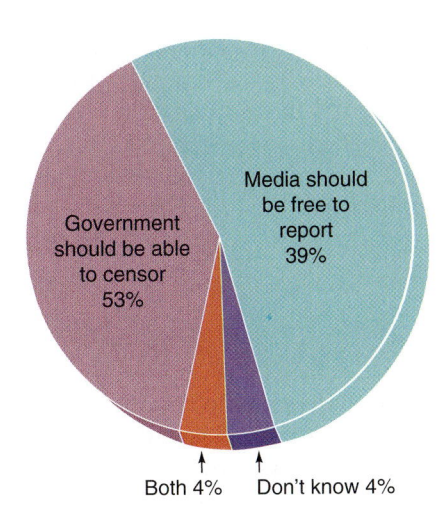

Figure 10–1

Opinions on Press Censorship in Time of War

When U.S. forces were attacking Afghanistan, more Americans said they would support government censorship than said they would give the press free rein in its reporting.

Source: Pew Research Center Survey, November 13–19, 2001.

- Government should be able to censor 53%
- Media should be free to report 39%
- Both 4%
- Don't know 4%

weeklies; 9,500 radio stations; 6 national television news networks; 850 local television stations; and 10,500 cable television systems.[20]

The audience reach of leading news organizations is substantial. Each weekday evening, more than twenty million Americans tune into a network newscast. *Time* and *Newsweek* magazines reach over three million readers each week. *U.S. News & World Report*'s weekly circulation exceeds two million copies. *The New York Times, The Wall Street Journal, USA Today,* and the *Los Angeles Times* have daily circulations exceeding one million readers. Another three dozen newspapers have circulations in excess of 250,000 readers. The average daily circulation of America's newspapers is roughly forty million; on Sunday, newspaper circulation jumps to sixty million.[21]

In view of the great number and the freedom of news organizations in the United States, it might be expected that Americans would have a lot of choice in the news they receive. However, the opposite is true. Each day, newspapers and broadcast stations from coast to coast tend to highlight the same national news stories and to interpret them in similar ways. Any number of terms—*pack journalism, groupthink, media concentration*—have been used to describe the fact that news reporting is fairly homogeneous.

The basic reason the news is pretty much the same everywhere is that America's reporters, unlike their counterparts in some European democracies, do not take sides in partisan disputes. They do sometimes differ on which facts, events, and issues are the most important, but these polite disagreements are a far cry from the disputes and diversity that characterized the nineteenth-century partisan press.

Of course, today's news organizations differ in the way they tell a given story. Broadcast news tends to be, in effect, headline news with pictures. A thirty-minute network news broadcast typically presents a dozen or so stories in the roughly twenty minutes allotted to news content (the other ten minutes being devoted to commercials). Newspapers have the space to present news developments in greater depth; some, like *The New York Times* (which labels itself "the newspaper of record"), provide substantial detail. The reporting styles of news organizations also vary. Although most of them present the news in an understated way, others tend toward sensationalism. For example, when Jeffrey Dahmer, a convicted murderer who had cannibalized his victims, was himself murdered in a Wisconsin prison in 1994, the *New York Post* gave its whole front page to the headline: "Death of a Monster." *The New York Times*, in contrast, gave the story a standard-size front-page headline, "Jeffrey Dahmer, Multiple Killer, Is Bludgeoned to Death in Prison." Such differences in approach, however, do not disguise the fact that most news organizations tell their audiences the same stories each day.

Domination of News Production

Another reason for the lack of diversity in national news reporting is that a few news organizations generate most of it. The quintessential case of concentrated news production is radio, with its "canned" network-provided news; almost no local radio station in the country produces its own national news reports.

The Associated Press (AP) is the major producer of news stories. It has three hundred full-time reporters stationed throughout the country and the world to gather news stories, which are relayed by satellite to subscribing newspapers and broadcast stations. More than 95 percent of the nation's dailies are serviced by AP, and some also subscribe to other wire services, such as Reuters and the New York Times.[22] Smaller dailies lack the resources to gather news outside their own localities and thus depend almost completely on wire service reports for their national and international coverage.[23] They may give these reports a local or partisan slant, but most of what they say is a rehash of wire service dispatches.

Television news production is similarly dominated by just a few organizations. The six major networks—ABC, CBS, NBC, PBS, Fox, and CNN—generate most of the news coverage of national and international politics. For news of the nation and the world, local stations depend on video transmissions fed to them by the networks.

News Values and Imperatives

Competitive pressures also lead the producers of news to report the same stories. No major news organization wants to miss an important story that others are reporting.[24]

The networks, wire services, and a few elite dailies, including *The New York Times, Washington Post, The Wall Street Journal, Los Angeles Times,* and *Chicago Tribune,* establish a national standard of story selection. Whenever one of them highlights an important story, the others jump on the bandwagon. The chief trendsetter among news-gathering organizations is *The New York Times*, which has been described as "the bulletin board" for other major newspapers, newsmagazines, and television networks.[25]

The imperatives of the fast pace of daily journalism also tend to make the news homogeneous.[26] Journalists have the task each day of filling a newspaper or broadcast with stories. Thus editors assign reporters to such beats as the White House and Congress, which can be relied on for a steady supply of news. On these beats the reporters of various news organizations see and hear the same things, exchange views on what is important, and not surprisingly, produce similar news stories.

What's Your Opinion?

Press Freedom

In the United States, government has little power to block the press from reporting information that could damage national security. The principle of "no prior restraint" holds that government cannot stop a publication or broadcast program unless it can convince a court that grave harm to the nation would result from release of the information. The U.S. press is also protected, as was explained in Chapter 4, by an imposing legal standard for libel. It is nearly impossible for a U.S official to win a libel suit against a newspaper, magazine, or broadcast organization even in situations where his or her reputation has been destroyed by false allegations.

By comparison, Britain's government has the power to prevent news organizations from reporting on national security issues. For example, there was a long period during which British journalists were prohibited from reporting stories on the Irish separatist issue that presented the conflict from the terrorists' viewpoint. British law also differs from American law when it comes to libel. Although libel judgments in Britain typically result in relatively small monetary awards, libel is much easier to prove in British courts than in American courts.

Which model of press freedom—the American or the British—do you prefer? What arguments would you make for and against each model?

U.S. journalists covering the war against the Taliban and Al Qaeda in Afghanistan. Most of the war correspondents were from the major networks, the wire services, and leading newspapers such as *The New York Times*. These news organizations supply most of the national and international news that Americans receive.

Finally, shared professional values guide journalists in their search for news.[27] Reporters are on the lookout for aspects of situations that lend themselves to interesting news stories—novel, colorful, and compelling developments.[28] Long practice at storytelling leads journalists to develop a common understanding of what the news is.[29] After the White House press corps has listened to a presidential speech, for example, nearly all the journalists in attendance are in agreement on what was most newsworthy about the speech, often only a single statement within it.

"Megamedia": Mergers, Profits, and the News

Over the past two decades and at an accelerating pace, media ownership has become increasingly concentrated. The trend reflects the high profitability of the media business and the economies of scale—the larger the media organization, the more it can leverage advertisers and achieve efficiencies in the production of news and entertainment. The net result has been the emergence of huge media conglomerates. Although *The New York Times* remains a family-controlled paper, nearly all other major news organizations have been absorbed into larger corporate entities. The ABC network and its news division, for example, are part of the Disney corporation, while CNN is part of Time Warner. The list could be extended but the point would be the same: U.S. news is largely in the hands of what the political scientist Dean Alger calls the "megamedia."[30]

One issue that surrounds this development is whether it is healthy to a democracy to have concentrated ownership of the means of public communication (see "Fighting Words"). Should so few entities control so much of what Americans see and hear through the mass media? Some observers say that the change is not all that significant because there is still competition between news organizations and because there is a degree of independence for news organizations within their corporate structures. Alger is not convinced: "It is . . . vital for democracy to have a truly diverse set of media sources present in the public

Fighting Words

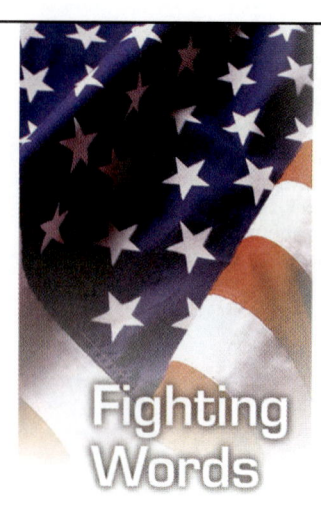

Do Media Mergers Serve the Public Interest? The Case of AOL and Time Warner

Giant corporations now control most of the nation's communication capacity. Most large newspapers and all three broadcast networks are embedded in media conglomerates. For example, the American Broadcasting Company (ABC) is owned by the entertainment giant Disney. The largest merger of all was announced in 2000 when AOL and Time Warner (owner of CNN, *Time* magazine, and dozens of other news outlets) agreed to merge. Are such concentrations of media power in the public interest? Advocates of these mergers claim that they foster the production and distribution of information on an unprecedented scale and with unparalleled benefit to society. Critics say that media concentration sacrifices diversity and the free flow of information to corporate profits. These differences are reflected in claims that were made when the AOL and Time Warner merger was announced.

Yes: This strategic combination with AOL accelerates the digital transformation of Time Warner by giving our creative and content businesses the widest possible canvas. The digital revolution has already begun to create unprecedented and instantaneous access to every form of media and to unleash immense possibilities for economic growth, human understanding, and creative expression. AOL Time Warner will lead this transformation. . . . The opportunities are limitless for everyone connected to AOL Time Warner—shareholders, consumers, advertisers, the creative and talented people who drive our success, and the global audiences we serve.
—Jerry Levin, CEO, Time Warner

No: Consumers do not want to be beholden to a giant media-Internet dictatorship, even if it promises to be a benevolent one. This is the sad result of [a] weak competition policy that has allowed enormous consolidations, which are likely to leave consumers with fewer choices, limited competition, and higher prices. . . . We want the FCC [Federal Communication Commission] to require open access, regardless of the promises made by the players. Long-term diversity of views, choices, service, and competitive prices require public responsibilities, not just wheeling and dealing among the parties.
—joint statement by Consumers Union, Consumer Federation of America, Media Access Project, and Center for Media Education

---

arena, a variety of alternative information and perspectives representing a real competition of approaches to news definitions and thoughts on the direction in which society should head. The continued advance of megamedia and their increasing domination of the prime mass media spell a profound constriction of that diversity and a severe diminution of the marketplace of ideas, and thus a danger to democracy."[31]

Another issue is the impact of media conglomerates on the quality of news content. As news organizations have become a part of larger corporations, they have increasingly had to adapt to the demands of the economic market. The news organization or division is only one part, and usually a relatively small part, of a very large corporation. A result has been a cutback in news-gathering capacity. ABC, CBS, and NBC News, for example, have closed many of their

The audience reach of the U.S. news media is truly substantial. More than twenty million Americans each evening watch a network newscast, and about half the adult population reads a daily paper. However, the news audience is shrinking, which has caused alarm among those in the news industry and those who believe that attention to news is critical to an informed citizenry.

overseas news bureaus. This cost-saving measure placed the networks in a weak position to report accurately on global terrorism in the immediate aftermath of the September 11, 2001, attacks on the World Trade Center and the Pentagon. The networks did not have seasoned reporters on station in Pakistan and Afghanistan when the attacks occurred.

News divisions have also been directed to compete more aggressively for audiences, because audience size determines advertising revenues. As a consequence, the news has become increasingly entertainment oriented. Critics say it is "infotainment" rather than real news. A study of network evening newscasts found that, over the past decade, the amount of news time devoted to government, politics, and public affairs has declined significantly while the amount given to lifestyle issues, celebrities, and human-interest subjects has risen sharply.[32]

THE NEWS MEDIA AS LINK: ROLES THE PRESS CAN AND CANNOT PERFORM

When the objective model of reporting came to dominate American news coverage, the relationship between the press and the public was fundamentally altered. The nineteenth-century partisan press gave its readers overt cues as to how to evaluate political issues and leaders. In the presidential election campaign of 1896, the *San Francisco Call* devoted 1,075 column-inches of photographs to the Republican ticket of McKinley-Hobart and only 11 inches to the Democrats, Bryan and Sewell.[33] Many European newspapers still function in this way, guiding their readers by applying partisan or ideological values to current events. The *Daily Telegraph*, for example, is an unofficial but fiercely loyal mouthpiece of Britain's Conservative party (see "How the United States Compares").

In contrast, U.S. news organizations do not routinely and consistently take sides in partisan conflict. Their main task is to report and analyze events. The media are thus very different from political parties and interest groups, the other major links between the public and its leaders. The media are driven by the search for interesting and revealing stories; parties and interest groups exist to articulate particular political opinions and values.

This distinction provides a basis for determining what roles the media can and cannot be expected to perform. The press is capable of fulfilling only those public responsibilities that are compatible with journalistic values: the signaler role, the common-carrier role, and the watchdog role. The media are less successful in their attempts to perform a fourth, politically oriented role: that of public representative.

The Signaler Role

As journalists see it, one of their responsibilities is to play the **signaler role,** alerting the public to important developments as soon as possible after they happen: a state visit to Washington by a foreign leader, a bill that has just been passed by Congress, a change in the nation's unemployment level, a demand by dairy farmers for higher milk prices, a terrorist bombing in a foreign capital.

The signaler role is one that the American media perform relatively well. The press is poised to converge on any fast-breaking major news event anywhere in the nation and nearly anywhere in the world. For instance, as the United States prepared to launch air strikes on Afghanistan in late 2001, hundreds of U.S. journalists descended on that region of the world. Their news stories kept Americans abreast of the progress of the war effort and the subsequent effort to create a post-Taliban government in Afghanistan.

The media are particularly well suited to signal developments from Washington. More than half of all reported national news emanates from the nation's capital, most of it from the White House and Congress. Altogether, more than ten thousand people in Washington work in the news business. The key players are the leading correspondents of the television networks and major newspapers, the heads of the Washington news bureaus, and a few top editors.[34]

The press, in its capacity as signaler, has the power to focus the public's attention. The term **agenda setting** has been used to describe the media's ability to influence what is on people's minds.[35] By covering the same events, problems, issues, and leaders—simply by giving them space or time in the news—the media place them on the public agenda.[36] The press, as Bernard Cohen notes, "may not be successful much of the time in telling people what to think, but it is stunningly successful in telling them what to think about."[37] This influence is most obvious in such situations as the war in Afghanistan, an event that drew widespread attention. For weeks on end, news of the fighting in Afghanistan was nearly inescapable.

The Common-Carrier Role

Journalists base many of their news stories on the words of public officials. The press thus plays what is labeled a **common-carrier role,** providing a channel through which political leaders can reach the public. The importance of this role

signaler role The accepted responsibility of the media to alert the public to important developments as soon as possible after they happen or are discovered.

agenda setting The power of the media through news coverage to focus the public's attention and concern on particular events, problems, issues, personalities, and so on.

common-carrier role The media's function as an open channel through which political leaders can communicate with the public.

HOW THE UNITED STATES COMPARES

Partisan Neutrality as a News Value

In the nineteenth century, the United States had a partisan press. Journalists were partisan actors, and news was a blend of reporting and advocacy. Facts and opinions were freely intermixed in news stories. This type of reporting gradually gave way to a model of journalism that emphasizes the "facts" and covers the two parties more or less equally. American journalists, through both print and television, seek impartiality in their daily news reporting. For example, a political scandal, whether it involves a Democrat or Republican, is a big story for any major U.S. news organization.

European news organizations are less committed to partisan neutrality. Many European newspapers are aligned with a party, and although they focus on events, their coverage has a partisan component. In Great Britain, for example, the *Daily Telegraph* often serves as a voice of the Conservative party, while the *Guardian* favors the liberal side. Broadcasters in most European countries are politically neutral by law and practice, but there are exceptions, as in the case of the French and Italian broadcasters.

The difference between the U.S. and European media is evident in a five-country survey that asked journalists whether they thought journalists should remain neutral in reporting on political parties. Compared with their counterparts in Great Britain, Germany, Sweden, and Italy, U.S. journalists were more likely to believe in partisan neutrality.

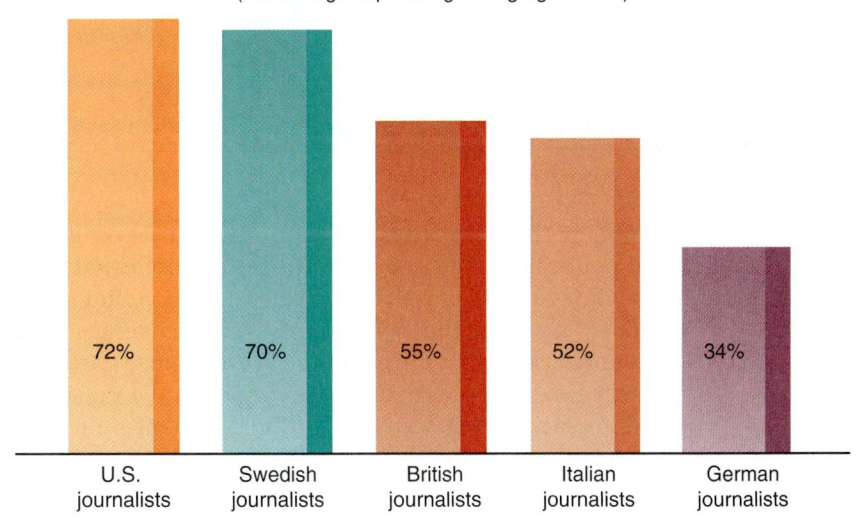

"Journalists should [not try] to influence the outcome of the conflict between political parties over the issues."
(Percentage expressing strong agreement)

U.S. journalists	Swedish journalists	British journalists	Italian journalists	German journalists
72%	70%	55%	52%	34%

Source: Thomas E. Patterson, Media and Democracy Project, in progress.

---

to officials and citizens alike is obvious. Citizens cannot very well support or oppose a leader's plans and actions if they do not know about them. And leaders need news coverage if they are to get the public's attention.

Not surprisingly, political leaders make a great effort to get coverage. They hold news conferences, issue press releases, and stage events in an effort to

Cable television brought with it twenty-four-hour news coverage. To fill that time, CNN has established more than thirty news bureaus, most of them overseas.

garner the media's attention.[38] Indeed, national news is mainly about the actions of political leaders and institutions, as is reflected in the hundreds of reporters who station themselves regularly at the Capitol and White House.

Officials try to get the most favorable news coverage they can. For example, the White House Press Office and the White House Office of Communications try to shape information in a way favorable to the president. Sometimes they succeed in placing their spin (that is, the president's interpretation) on the media's coverage of events.

However, the press today is less deferential to political leaders than in the past. Even though the president and Congress can expect coverage, the press increasingly places its own spin on these stories. Journalists, because of their increased celebrity status, their heightened skepticism of politicians since Vietnam and Watergate, and the greater latitude afforded them by the interpretive style of reporting, have become accustomed not only to covering what newsmakers say but also to having their own say. In 2002, as the Bush administration was trying to focus domestic coverage on its attempts to stimulate the economy, the press was concentrating on the Enron Corporation scandal and its links to the White House.

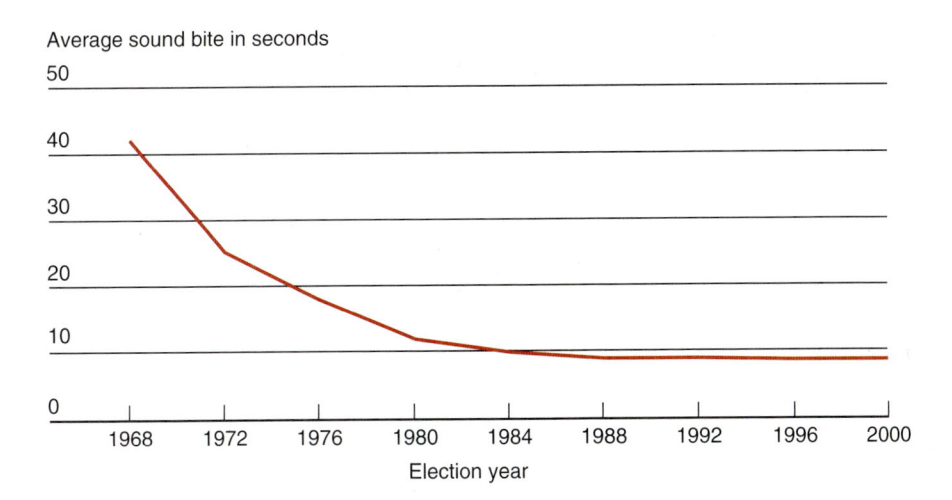

FIGURE 10–2

The Shrinking Sound Bite of Television Election Coverage

The average length of time that presidential candidates are shown speaking without interruption on television newscasts has declined sharply in recent elections.

Source: Adapted from Daniel C. Hallin, "Sound Bite News: Television Coverage of Elections 1968–1988," *Journal of Communication* 42 (Spring 1992): 6. The 1992–2000 data were provided by the Center for Media and Public Affairs.

In fact, the news today is as much journalist centered as it is newsmaker centered. For every minute that the presidential candidates spoke on the network newscasts during coverage of the 2000 campaign, for example, the journalists who were covering them talked for six minutes. It was once the case that a candidate's sound bite (the length of time within a television story that the candidate speaks without interruption) was about forty-five seconds in length on average.[39] In recent campaigns, the average sound bite has been less than ten seconds, which is barely enough time for the candidate to utter a full sentence (see Figure 10–2).

The Watchdog Role

Traditionally, the American press has accepted responsibility for protecting the public from deceitful, careless, incompetent, and corrupt officials.[40] In this **watchdog role,** the press stands ready to expose any official who violates accepted legal, ethical, and performance standards.

The most notable exercise of the watchdog role in recent decades took place during the Watergate scandal. Bob Woodward and Carl Bernstein of the *Washington Post* spent months uncovering evidence that high-ranking officials in the Nixon White House were lying about their role in the burglary of the Democratic National Committee's headquarters and in the subsequent cover-up. Virtually all the nation's media picked up on the *Post*'s revelations. Nixon was forced to resign, as was his attorney general, John Mitchell. The Watergate episode is a dramatic reminder that a vigilant press is one of society's best safeguards against abuses of political power.

There is an inherent tension between the watchdog role and the common-carrier role. The watchdog role demands that the journalist maintain a skeptical view of political leaders and keep them at a distance. The common-carrier role requires the journalist to maintain close ties with political leaders. In the period before Watergate, the common-carrier role was clearly the dominant orientation. It perhaps still is, but journalists have become increasingly critical of political leaders and institutions.

watchdog role The accepted responsibility of the media to protect the public from deceitful, careless, incompetent, and corrupt officials by standing ready to expose any official who violates accepted legal, ethical, or performance standards.

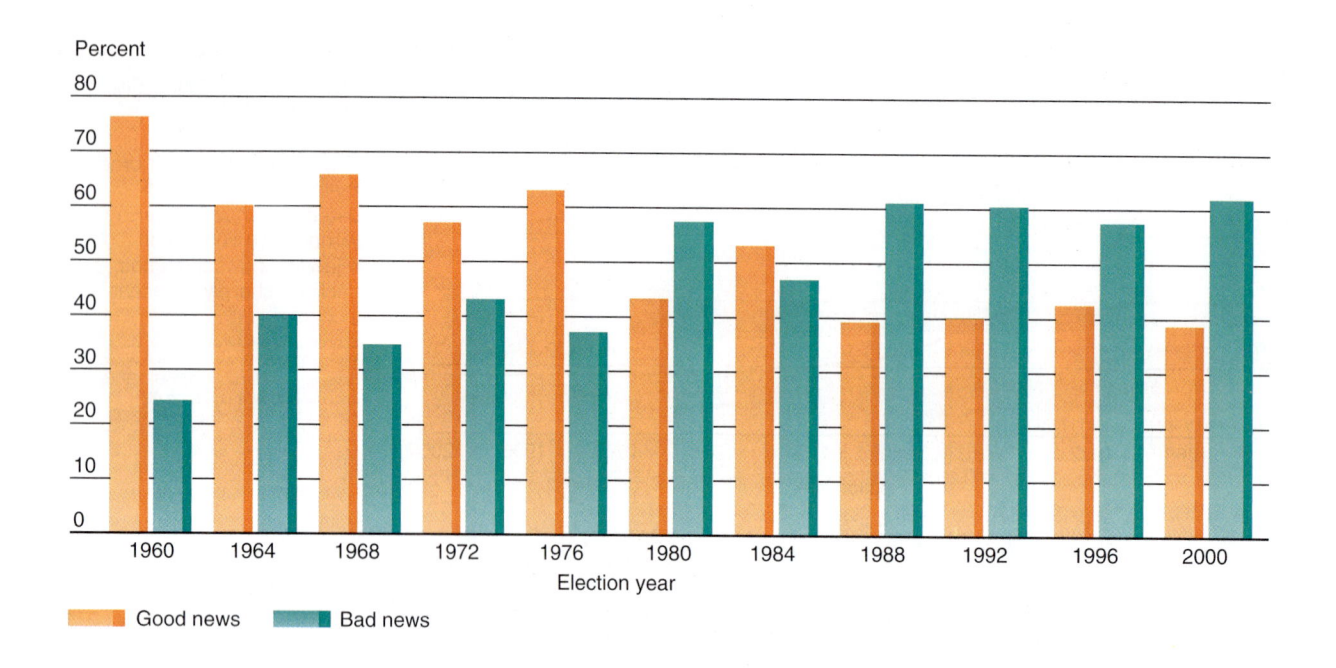

Figure 10-3

"Bad News" Coverage of Presidential Candidates Compared to "Good News" Coverage, 1960–2000

In the 1960s, candidates received largely favorable news coverage. Today, their coverage is mostly negative.

Source: Thomas E. Patterson, *Out of Order* (New York: Vintage, 1994), 20, for 1960–1992 coverage; Center for Media and Public Affairs, 1996, 2000.

Simulation
www.mhhe.com/patterson6

Some of this criticism revolves around scandals such as the Iran-Contra affair (President Reagan) and the Whitewater, Paula Jones, and Monica Lewinsky allegations (President Clinton). Most of the criticism, however, is leveled at the day-to-day conduct of politics. Journalists are intent on publicizing the missteps of political leaders. Given the enormous size of the U.S. government, there is plenty to criticize if journalists want to focus on it. The media's preference for "bad news" can be seen, for example, in the fact that negative coverage of presidential candidates has risen steadily in recent decades and now exceeds their positive coverage (see Figure 10–3).

"Bad news" characterizes the coverage of Democrats and Republicans alike. Although surveys indicate that most journalists lean toward the Democratic party in their personal beliefs, studies have found partisan bias to be a relatively small factor in political coverage.[41] Other influences, including the norm of objectivity, counterbalance the effect of partisanship on journalists' news decisions. On the other hand, journalists' skeptical view of politicians is not offset by other factors. There is no rule that limits negativity.[42] Coverage of the Democrat-controlled Congress of 1993–1994 by the national media was nearly 70 percent negative; when the Congress shifted to Republican hands in 1995–1996, its coverage too was nearly 70 percent negative in tone.[43] The fact is, the real bias of the press is not liberal as opposed to conservative, but a pronounced tendency to report what is wrong with politics and politicians rather than what is right.

Critics argue that the press has gone too far in its search for bad news, claiming that it now faults nearly everything that politicians say and do, thereby undermining the public trust on which effective leadership is built. Critics also complain that the press no longer has any respect for public officials' private lives—that everything from their bedroom behavior to decades-old "skeletons in the closet" are grist for news stories. Journalists claim that they are merely doing their job—that the public is better served by a highly skeptical

Allegations in 1998 of a sexual relationship between Monica Lewinsky and President Bill Clinton unleashed a media feeding frenzy that disrupted the White House's policy agenda.

and intrusive press than a compliant one. CNN correspondent Bob Franken said, "We historically are not supposed to be popular, and it's almost our role to be bearer of bad news."[44]

The public is ambivalent about the news media's skepticism. A 1997 Pew Research Center poll found that most Americans believe that press skepticism is a factor in keeping politicians from abusing public office. Yet the same poll also indicated that most Americans believe that the press gets in the way of efforts to solve society's problems. The press skepticism is thus seen as both an obstacle to effective governance and a form of protection against wayward politicians. Yet the press may actually be undermining its watchdog role by its zealous pursuit of scandal. When the public is deluged day after day with stories of wrongdoing in high places, its expectations of public officials decline and its confidence in the media's judgment diminishes. An effect is that the public may reject the media's outcries. Such was the public reaction to the news media's initial reporting of the Clinton-Lewinsky scandal. Even though the press intimated that the president would have to resign, the public reacted differently. The news coverage was so sensational, so lurid, and so rooted in hearsay that a majority of Americans concluded that it was unfair to Clinton and said that he should remain in office.

The Public Representative Role

Traditionally, the **public representative role**—that of spokesperson for and advocate of the public—has belonged to political leaders, political institutions, and political organizations. Today, however, many reporters believe they also have a mandate to represent the public. "[Our] chief duty," newscaster Roger Mudd claims, "is to put before the nation its unfinished business."[45]

public representative role A role whereby the media attempt to act as the public's representatives.

Although the press has to some degree always acted as a stand-in for the people, the desire of journalists to play the role of public advocate has increased significantly since the 1960s.[46] As journalists' status rose, they became more assertive, a tendency sharpened by the trend toward interpretive reporting. Vietnam and Watergate also contributed to the change; these events convinced many journalists that their judgments were superior to those of political leaders. James Reston of *The New York Times* said of Vietnam, "Maybe the historians will agree that the reporters and cameras were decisive in the end. They brought the issue of the war to the people, before the Congress and the courts, and forced the withdrawal of American power from Vietnam."[47]

The news media have also admirably represented the public during moments of crisis. The somber tone of CBS anchor Walter Cronkite's reporting of John F. Kennedy's assassination in 1963 helped Americans cope with the tragic loss of their president. On September 11, 2001, the media were again a reassuring presence in Americans' lives as they struggled to deal with the unthinkable murder of thousands of innocent people in the World Trade Center and the Pentagon. Nevertheless, there are at least two basic reasons for concluding that journalists are not nearly as well suited as political leaders to the role of public representative. First, the news media are not subject to the level of public accountability required of a public representative. Political institutions are made responsible to the public by a formal mechanism of accountability—elections. The vote gives officeholders a reason to act in the majority's interest, and it offers citizens an opportunity to boot from office anyone they feel has failed them. Thousands of elected officials have lost their jobs this way. The public has no comparable hold over the press. Journalists are neither chosen nor removable by the people. Irate citizens can stop watching a news program or buying a newspaper that angers them, but no major daily newspaper or television station has gone out of business as a result.

A second obstacle to journalists' attempts to play the role of public representative is that representation requires a point of view. Politics is essentially the mobilization of bias—that is, it involves the representation of particular values and interests. Political parties and interest groups, as explained in Chapters 8 and 9, exist to represent particular interests in society. But what political interests do the media represent? CBS News executive Richard Salant once said that his reporters covered stories "from nobody's point of view."[48] What he was saying, in effect, was that journalists do not consistently represent the political concerns of any segment of society. They respond to news opportunities, not to political interests. Above all, they prize good stories.

The O. J. Simpson murder-trial story is a prime example. The former football star's trial received more news coverage in 1994–95 than any public policy issue, foreign or domestic. Judged by the media's priorities, Simpson's fate was more important than health care, unemployment, Haiti, drug abuse, education, and every other national problem. The Clinton-Lewinsky-Starr saga is another example. In the first month, January 1998, the scandal filled a third of the news time on the network evening newscasts. It had to compete for time with the Winter Olympics, a papal visit to Cuba, the possibility of renewed war with Iraq, and the ravaging effects of the El Niño weather system.[49] Yet it received more coverage than all these developments combined. And it remained the top

Why Should I Care?

Informative News

For nearly four months in 2001, the Gary Condit story dominated America's news. It was not a distinction that was earned by Rep. Condit's stature (he was a backbench member of the House of Representatives) or by new developments (the known facts changed hardly at all during the story's run). The story's prominence owed to its ingredients—power, sex, and Condit's possible involvement in the disappearance of congressional intern Chandra Levy.

On September 11, 2001, the Condit story abruptly disappeared. The attacks on the World Trade Center and the Pentagon swept it out of the news, where it stayed for the most part.

Before September 11, however, international terrorism was not a leading news subject, even though there were public warnings of the danger it posed. Earlier that year, the U.S. Commission on National Security had predicted a "catastrophic attack" by international terrorists and had urged the creation of a homeland security agency. CIA director George Tenet had also sounded the alarm, saying in a Senate hearing that Osama bin Laden's "global network" was the "most immediate and serious" threat facing the nation. These warnings were almost completely ignored by the U.S. press. In the year preceding the World Trade Center and Pentagon attacks, for example, the Al Qaeda terrorist network was mentioned by name only once on the network evening newscasts.

The Condit and terrorism examples illustrate a frequent failing of U.S. news media in recent decades. In their pursuit of higher ratings, they have often been more interested in entertaining their audience than informing it. In the process, they have failed to fully meet their public service responsibility. The press has an obligation to provide its audience with a view of the world that does not lead people to think they are in the Land of Oz when in fact they are traveling through Kansas.

Of course, citizens themselves contribute to the problem by consuming titillating or trivial news. During the summer of 2001, the highest-rated television program was ABC correspondent Connie Chung's interview with Gary Condit. Unless citizens show a preference for serious news coverage, they are unlikely to get it on a regular basis.

Nevertheless, the press has an obligation to provide the public with informative news. As former NBC executive Rueven Frank said in a 1998 article in the *Columbia Journalism Review:* "This business of giving people what they want is a dope pusher's argument. News is something that people don't know they're interested in until they hear about it. The job of the journalist is to take what's important and make it interesting."

---

news story every month thereafter, even in periods when there were no new revelations or when more pressing issues arose, such as a financial crisis in Asia that threatened to weaken the U.S. economy. The Enron scandal is yet another example. In 2002, it was among the most heavily covered domestic stories, outranking even unemployment as a focus of news reporting.

Underlying the press's search for the dramatic story is the media's quest for profits. The bottom line, rather than the public interest, increasingly drives news coverage. Audience competition has intensified with the spread of cable television, and the news has become increasingly sensational. "All Monica All the Time" was how some critics described the press's coverage of the Lewinsky scandal. One network, MSNBC, chose to make the scandal nearly the sole focus of its programming, hoping that higher audience ratings and correspondingly higher advertising revenues would be the result.

Presidential politics is a favorite topic of the press. Here, Republican presidential nominee George W. Bush is surrounded by reporters during a 2000 campaign stop.

Even the media's terrorism coverage after September 11, 2001, gradually came to rest on commercial considerations. In the first months following the terrorist attacks on the World Trade Center and the Pentagon, the news media devoted huge amounts of news space and time to the attacks and to the nation's response. Americans heard things they had never been told before about Afghanistan, Pakistan, terrorism networks, and Islamic militants. Many daily newspapers added an extra section to accommodate the heavy coverage while television networks produced feature programs. However, once the U.S. military attack on Al Qaeda and Taliban forces in Afghanistan quieted down, the press began to revert to the pattern of its earlier coverage. A study by the Center for Responsible Journalism revealed that, six months after the terrorist attacks, network evening newscasts had nearly the same mix of stories that they had before the attacks occurred. International coverage was heavier than it had been in the earlier period, but the overall level of public affairs coverage was not. Meanwhile, news stories about celebrities, lifestyles, crime, and the like had returned to pre-attack levels, taking up nearly half of all news time. It was not as if the news media had exhausted the terrorism topic. The threat had not gone away, and it promised to take new and even more alarming forms, including attacks with biological, nuclear, and chemical agents. Americans had very little understanding of the nature of these threats or how they should respond if such attacks should occur. Yet, many of the nation's news organizations had returned to a type of news that was designed as much to entertain Americans as to inform them. Infotainment was not triumphant everywhere in the news system. Stalwart publications such as the *Washington Post* and *New York Times* continued to provide heavy coverage of the terrorism issue. But many other news organizations had gone back to their old formula: the presentation of titillating stories designed to capture audience attention.

The relentless search for attention-getting stories weakens the press's ability to provide citizens a clear understanding of what is broadly at issue in politics. It is a difficult job to formulate society's problems in a way that allows citizens to understand and act on them. The news media cannot do the job consistently well. The journalist Walter Lippmann put it plainly when he said:

> The press is no substitute for [political] institutions. It is like the beam of a searchlight that moves restlessly about, bringing one episode and then another out of darkness into vision. Men cannot do the work of the world by this light alone. They cannot govern society by episodes, incidents, and interruptions.[50]

ORGANIZING THE PUBLIC IN THE MEDIA AGE

Lippmann's point was not that news organizations are somehow inferior to political organizations but that each has a different role and responsibility in society. Democracy cannot operate effectively without a free press that acts effectively in its signaler, common-carrier, and watchdog roles. To keep in touch with one another and with the government, citizens must have access to timely and uncensored news about public affairs. In other words, the media must do their job well if democratic government is to succeed. However, the media cannot also be asked to do the job of political institutions. For reasons already noted, the task is beyond the media's capacity.

As previous chapters have emphasized, the problem of citizen influence is the problem of organizing the public so that people can act together effectively. The news media merely appear to solve this problem. The fact that millions of people each day receive the same news about their government does not mold them into an organized community. The news creates a pseudo-community: citizens feel they are part of a functioning whole until they try to act on their news awareness. The futility of media-centered democracy was dramatized in the movie *Network* when its central character, a television anchorman, became enraged at the nation's political leadership and urged his viewers to go to their windows and yell, "I'm mad as hell and I'm not going to take it anymore!" Citizens heeded his instructions, but the main effect was to raise the network's ratings. It was not clear what officials in Washington were expected to do about several million people leaning out their windows and shouting a vague slogan at the top of their lungs. The film vividly illustrated the fact that the news can raise public consciousness as a prelude to action, but the news itself cannot organize the public in any meaningful way. When public opinion on an issue is already formed, the media can serve as a channel for the expression of that opinion. But when society's choices are in their formative stage, the media are not ordinarily an adequate guide to the action that should be taken.[51]

Self-Quiz
www.mhhe.com/patterson6

SUMMARY

In the nation's first century, the press was allied closely with the political parties and helped the parties mobilize public opinion. Gradually the press freed itself from this relationship and developed a form of reporting, known as objective journalism, that emphasizes the fair and accurate reporting of newsworthy developments. The foundation of modern American news rests on the presentation and evaluation of significant events, not on the advocacy of partisan ideas. The nation's news organizations do not differ greatly in their reporting; broadcast stations and newspapers throughout the country emphasize many of the same events, issues, and personalities, following the lead of the major broadcast networks, a few elite newspapers, and the wire services.

The press performs four basic roles in a free society. In their signaler role, journalists communicate information to the public about events and problems that they consider important, relevant, and therefore newsworthy. The press also serves as a common carrier in that it provides political leaders with a channel for addressing the public. Third, the press acts as a public protector, or watchdog, by exposing deceitful, careless, or corrupt officials. The American media can and, to a significant degree, do perform these roles adequately.

The press is less well suited, however, to the other role it plays, that of public representative. This role requires a consistent political viewpoint and public accountability, neither of which the press possesses. The media cannot be substitutes for effective political institutions. The press's strength lies ultimately in its capacity to inform the public, not in its attempts to serve as the public's representative.

KEY TERMS

agenda setting
common-carrier role
descriptive reporting
interpretive reporting
news
objective journalism
partisan press
press (news media)
public representative role
signaler role
watchdog role

SUGGESTED READINGS

Bagdikian, Ben H. *The Media Monopoly,* 6th ed. Boston: Beacon Press, 2000. An examination of the growing power of the press, including tendencies toward monopolies of ownership and news production.

Cook, Timothy E. *Governing with the News: The News Media as a Political Institution.* Chicago: University of Chicago Press, 1997. An analysis of the press in its role as a political institution.

Downie, Leonard, Jr., and Robert G. Kaiser, *The News About the News: American Journalism in Peril.* New York: Knopf, 2002. A critical assessment of today's news media by two *Washington Post* journalists.

Kurtz, Howard. *Spin Cycle: Inside the Clinton Propaganda Machine.* New York: Free Press, 1998. A look at the Clinton White House's attempts to manage its news coverage.

Maltese, John Anthony. *Spin Control: The White House Office of Communications and the Management of Presidential News.* Chapel Hill: University of North Carolina Press, 1994. An assessment of how presidents attempt to manage news coverage.

Patterson, Thomas E. *Out of Order.* New York: Vintage Books, 1994. An analysis of how election news coverage has changed in recent decades.

Sabato, Larry J., Mark Stencel, and S. Robert Lichter. *Peep Show: Media and Politics in the Age of Scandal.* Lanham, Md.: Rowman & Littlefield, 2000. A penetrating critique of today's news.

Sparrow, Bartholomew H. *Uncertain Guardians.* Baltimore, Md.: Johns Hopkins University Press, 1999. A systematic assessment of the news media's political role and tendencies.

LIST OF WEBSITES

http://www.cmpa.com
The website for the Center for Media and Public Affairs (CMPA), a nonpartisan organization that analyzes news coverage on a continuing basis; its website provides analyses of news content that are useful for anyone interested in the media's political coverage.

http://www.drudgereport.com
The website through which Matt Drudge (The Drudge Report) has challenged the traditional media's control of the news.

http://www.fcc.gov
The Federal Communications Commission (FCC) website, which provides information on broadcasting regulation and current issues.

http://www.newslink.org/
Provides access to more than a thousand news organizations, including most U.S. daily newspapers.

PART THREE

Governing Institutions

American democracy is often described as government by the people. But direct democracy is a practical impossibility in a nation the size of the United States. Americans are governed largely through institutions.

A debate has long raged over the proper relationship between a people and their representatives. One view holds that representatives should follow the expressed opinions of the governed, for if they do not, they will promote their own narrow interests. Another view, first elaborated by the English theorist Edmund Burke, holds that representatives should exercise their best judgment in deciding policy; if they listen too closely to those who elected them, they will serve parochial interests rather than the general interests of society.

The governing system of the United States embodies both conceptions of representation. The presidency is a truly national office that, as Chapter 12 will describe, encourages its incumbent to take a national view of issues. On the other hand, Congress, as Chapter 11 will show, is both a national institution and a body that is subject to powerful local influences.

Americans are also governed through unelected bureaucrats and appointed judges. Their decisions, as Chapters 13 and 14 will describe, can in some instances be as far-reaching as those made by the people's elected representatives.

CHAPTER OUTLINE

11 Congress: Balancing National Goals and Local Interests 322

12 The Presidency: Leading the Nation 360

13 The Federal Bureaucracy: Administering the Government 398

14 The Federal Judicial System: Applying the Law 430

11

There are really two Congresses, not just one. Often these two Congresses are widely separated; the tightly knit, complex world of Capitol Hill is a long way from the world of [the member's district or state]—not only in miles, but in perspective and outlook as well.

Roger Davidson and Walter Oleszek[1]

Congress: Balancing National Goals and Local Interests

The Congressional action in 1998 on the $200 billion transportation bill revealed a lot about the institution. For the first time in a generation, the federal government had the luxury of a budget surplus. How would it be used? To cut taxes? To safeguard the future of the social security system? To provide a cushion against some future day when the economy turned sour and federal expenditures exceeded revenues?

As it happened, a first use of the surplus was to help fund the most expensive transportation bill in the nation's history. It was hard to argue that it was a bad use of the money. The nation's transportation infrastructure had been neglected for years, and there were plenty of bridges, roads, and mass transit systems in need of repair and expansion. Yet the $200 billion transportation bill was attractive to Congress in part because it provided public works projects and jobs for virtually every state and every congressional district in the nation. It was good policy, but it was also very good politics in an election year.

The story of the 1998 transportation bill illustrates the dual nature of Congress: it is both a lawmaking institution for the country and a representative assembly for states and districts.[2] Members of Congress have both an individual duty to serve the interests of their separate constituencies and a collective duty to protect the interests of the country as a whole. Attention to constituency interests is the common denominator of a national institution in which each member must please the voters back home in order to win reelection.[3]

This chapter examines Congress, beginning with congressional election and organization and concluding with congressional policymaking. The following points are emphasized in this chapter:

- *Congressional elections tend to have a strong local orientation and to favor incumbents.* Congressional office provides incumbents with substantial resources (free publicity, staff, and legislative influence) that give them (particularly House members) a major advantage in election campaigns. However, incumbency also has some liabilities that contribute to turnover in congressional membership.

- *Although party leaders in Congress provide collective leadership, the work of its Congress is done mainly through its committees and subcommittees, each of which has its separate leadership and policy jurisdiction.* The committee system of Congress allows a broad sharing of power and leadership, which serves the power and reelection needs of Congress's members but fragments the institution.

- *Congress lacks the direction and organization required for the development of comprehensive national policies, but it is well organized to handle policies of relatively narrow scope.* At times, Congress takes the lead on broad national issues, but ordinarily it does not do so.

- *Congress's policymaking role is based on three major functions: lawmaking, representation, and oversight.*

The U.S. Capitol in Washington, D.C., with the House wing in the foreground. The Senate meets in the wing at the right of the central rotunda (under the dome). The offices of the House and Senate party leaders—Speaker, vice president, majority and minority leaders and whips—are located in the Capitol. Other members of Congress have their offices in nearby buildings.

CONGRESS AS A CAREER: ELECTION TO CONGRESS

In the nation's first century, service in the Congress was not a career for most of its members. Before 1900 at least a third and sometimes as many as half the seats in Congress changed hands at each election. Most members left voluntarily. Because travel was slow and arduous, serving in the nation's capital required them to spend months away from their families. And because the national government was not the center of power and politics that it is today, many politicians preferred to serve in state capitals.

The modern Congress is very different. Most of its members are professional politicians, and a seat in the U.S. Senate or House is as far as most of them can expect to go in politics. The pay (about $150,000 a year) is reasonably good, and the prestige of their office is substantial, particularly if they serve in the Senate. An extended stay in Congress is what most of its members aspire to attain.[4]

Incumbents have a good chance of being reelected (see Figure 11–1). They are not a sure bet to win again, but the odds are on their side.[5] In the last decade, the reelection rate of House incumbents seeking another term has exceeded 90 percent, as has the reelection rate of Senate incumbents.[6]

These figures overestimate somewhat an incumbent's chances of reelection. Some incumbents retire from Congress when faced with a campaign they fear they will lose. Moreover, incumbents must stand for reelection again and again if they intend to make Congress a career. A single loss will halt or interrupt this goal. Over the period of a few elections, a substantial number of congressional seats can change hands. The 1992 and 1994 congressional elections are an extreme example: the turnover in House membership in these two elections was a combined 188 seats, the highest total of any two consecutive elections since World War II.

Constitutional Qualifications for Serving in Congress

Representatives: "No person shall be a Representative who shall not have attained to the age of twenty-five years, and been seven years a citizen of the United States, and who shall not, when elected, be an inhabitant of that State in which he shall be chosen." (article 1, section 2)

Senators: "No person shall be a Senator who shall not have attained to the age of thirty years, and been nine years a citizen of the United States, and who shall not, when elected, be an inhabitant of the State for which he shall be chosen." (article 1, section 3)

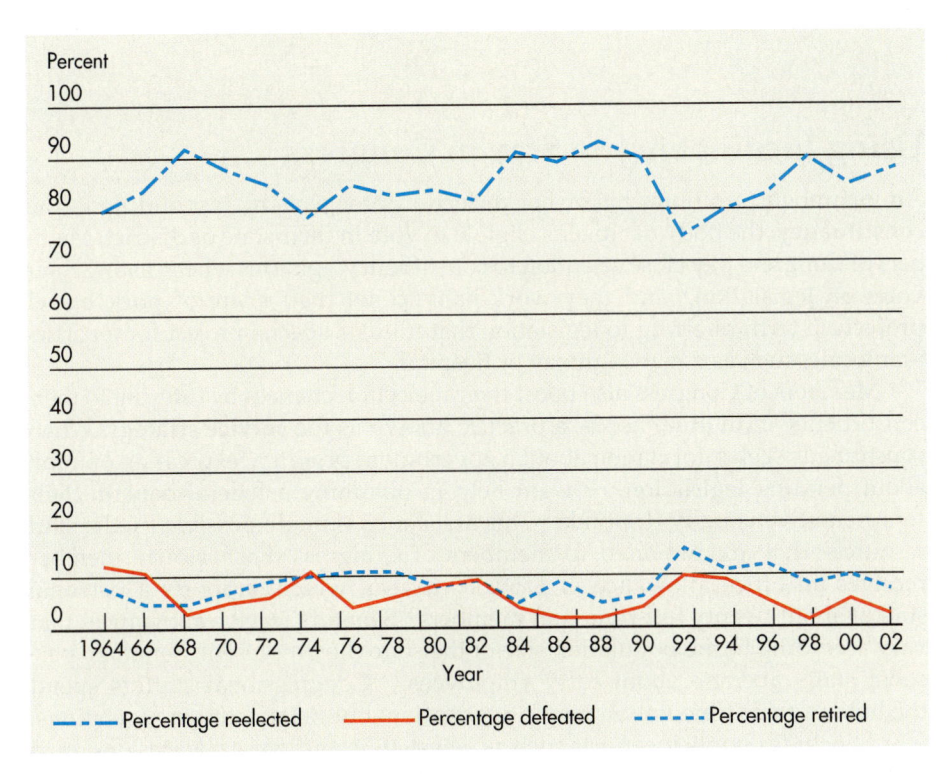

FIGURE 11–1

Reelection Rates of House Incumbents
U.S. House incumbents have a very high rate of reelection, although the percentage declined somewhat in the early 1990s.
Source: *Congressional Quarterly Weekly Report*, various dates; The data for 2002 are based on preliminary estimates.

On balance, however, incumbents have a clear edge over their opponents, as their margin of victory indicates. In recent elections, two-thirds of House incumbents and nearly half of Senate incumbents seeking reelection have received 60 percent or more of the vote. Even when voters are convinced that Congress as an institution is performing badly, they reelect a large majority of its members. One reason is that many congressional districts and a few states are so lopsidedly Democratic or Republican that the candidate of the weaker party has no realistic chance of victory. In recent congressional elections, more than 10 percent of House incumbents have run unopposed for reelection. All incumbents, however, gain important reelection advantages from the office they hold.

FIGURE 11-2

Congressional Campaign Expenditures

The cost of running for congressional office has risen sharply as campaign techniques—television advertising, opinion polling, and so on—have become more elaborate and sophisticated. The increase in spending can be seen from a comparison of the approximate average spending by both candidates per House or Senate seat at ten-year intervals, beginning in 1980.
Source: Federal Election Commission.

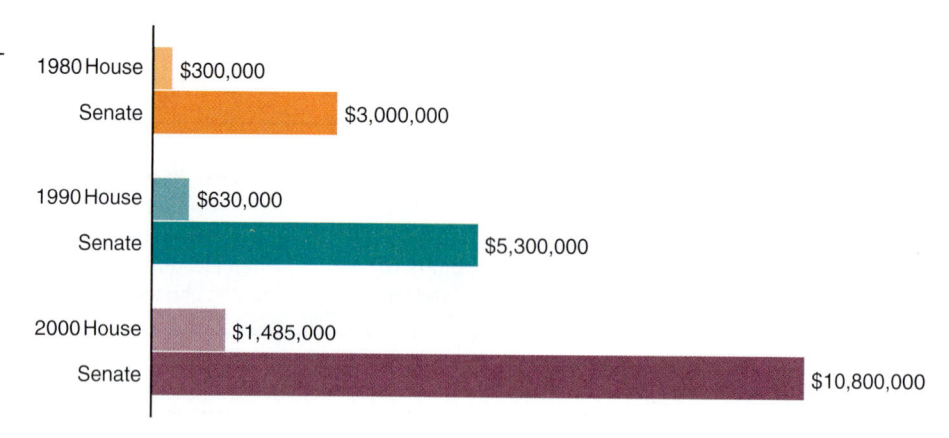

1980	House	$300,000
1980	Senate	$3,000,000
1990	House	$630,000
1990	Senate	$5,300,000
2000	House	$1,485,000
2000	Senate	$10,800,000

constituency The individuals who live within the geographical area represented by an elected official. More narrowly, the body of citizens eligible to vote for a particular representative.

pork barrel projects Laws whose tangible benefits are targeted at a particular legislator's constituency.

service strategy Use of personal staff by members of Congress to perform services for constituents in order to gain their support in future elections.

Using Incumbency to Stay in Congress

An incumbent promotes his or her reelection prospects by responding to the **constituency:** the body of citizens eligible to vote in their state or district. Members of Congress pay close attention to constituency opinions when casting their votes on legislation,[7] and they work hard to get their share of **pork barrel projects** (a term referring to legislation that funds a special project for a particular locale, such as a new highway or hospital).

Members of Congress also boost their reelection chances by catering to their constituents' individual needs, a practice known as the **service strategy.** When constituents seek information about a government program, express an opinion about pending legislation, or want help in obtaining a federal benefit, their representative usually responds.[8] This assistance is made possible by the staff resources that are provided to members of Congress. Each House member receives an office allowance of $750,000 a year, which supports a personal staff of about twenty full-time staff members.[9] Senators receive allowances that vary according to the population size of the state they represent. Senators' personal staffs average about forty employees.[10] Congressional staffers spend the bulk of their time not on legislative matters but on constituency relations, which includes publicity efforts such as newsletters and press releases designed to enhance their legislator's image.[11] Each member of Congress is permitted several free mailings annually to constituent households, a privilege known as the *frank*.

Finally, incumbents have a decided advantage when it comes to raising campaign funds. The cost of running for Congress has risen sharply in recent decades as campaign techniques, such as televised advertising and polling, have become increasingly sophisticated and costly (see Figure 11–2). Today a successful House campaign will often cost a million dollars or more. The price of victory in competitive Senate races is much higher, ranging from several million dollars in small states to $15 million or more in larger states. A study by the *Congressional Quarterly* found that only 10 percent of incumbents said they had trouble raising enough money to conduct an effective campaign, compared with 70 percent of challengers.[12] Many challengers are able to raise only enough money for a token campaign.[13]

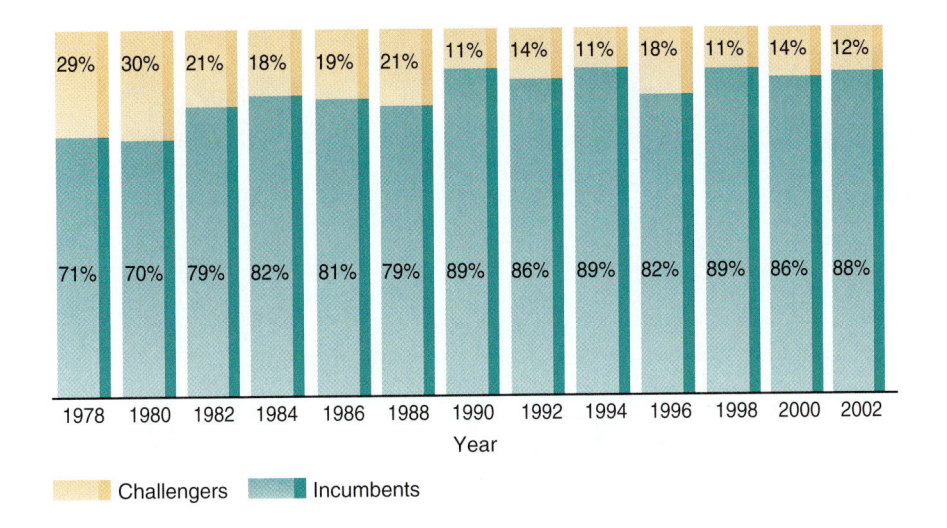

Figure 11-3

Allocation of PAC Contributions Between Incumbents and Challengers in Congressional Races That Included an Incumbent, 1978–2002.

In allocating campaign contributions, PACs favor incumbent member of Congress over their challengers by a wide margin. Figures for 2002 based on preliminary data.

Source: Federal Elections Commission.

Year	Challengers	Incumbents
1978	29%	71%
1980	30%	70%
1982	21%	79%
1984	18%	82%
1986	19%	81%
1988	21%	79%
1990	11%	89%
1992	14%	86%
1994	11%	89%
1996	18%	82%
1998	11%	89%
2000	14%	86%
2002	12%	88%

Incumbents obtain a fund-raising advantage from their past campaigns and constituent service, which enables them to create mailing lists of potential contributors. Individual contributions, most of which are $100 or less, account for about 50 percent of all funds raised by candidates and are obtained mainly through fund-raising events and direct-mail solicitation. Incumbents also have an edge with political action committees, or PACs, which are the fund-raising arm of interest groups (see Chapter 9). More than half the U.S. senators seeking reelection in 2002 received $1 million or more from PACs, and more than a dozen House members received half a million dollars or more. Many PACs are hesitant to oppose an incumbent unless it is clear that the candidate is vulnerable. More than 85 percent of PAC contributions in recent elections have been given to incumbents; their challengers got less than 15 percent (see Figure 11–3).[14] "Anytime you go against an incumbent, you take a minute and think long and hard about what your rationale is," said Desiree Anderson, director of the Realtors PAC.[15]

Though money has been called "the mother's milk of politics," money does not always decide an election; in most elections it is not even the main factor. The political scientist Gary Jacobson has demonstrated that money is no higher than third in importance, ranking behind partisanship and incumbency.[16] Nevertheless, the flow of money in congressional campaigns is significant both in itself and as an indicator of the other crucial factors, particularly the advantages of incumbency. The Federal Election Commission reported that more than half of House incumbents in recent elections outspent their challengers by a ratio of at least five to one.

A race without an incumbent—called an **open-seat election**—usually brings out a strong candidate from each party and involves heavy spending, especially when party competition in the state or district is strong. In 1998, for example, the major-party candidates spent on average more than a million dollars between them in open-seat House races.

Open-seat contests can be critically important to shifts in power in Congress. The Republican party's stunning victory in the 1994 midterm elections, for example, was achieved primarily through its success in open-seat races.

open-seat election An election in which there is no incumbent in the race.

U.S. Representative William (Bill) Clay represents a heavily Democratic district in St. Louis. The biggest reelection obstacles for House members from one-sided districts are redistricting, personal impropriety, scandal, and a well-funded primary election opponent. In the absence of any such factor, as in Clay's case, reelection is nearly a sure thing.

There were fifty-two open House seats and nine open Senate seats in 1994, and the GOP won 80 percent of these races. Without these victories, the Republicans would not have gained control of either the House or Senate.

The Pitfalls of Incumbency

Incumbency is not without its liabilities. The potential pitfalls include troublesome issues, personal misconduct, variation in turnout, strong challengers, and for some House members, redistricting.[17]

Troublesome Issues

Disruptive issues are a potential threat to incumbents. Although most elections are not waged against the backdrop of strong issues, those that are tend to produce the largest turnover in Congress. In the period from 1992 to 1994, when the public was angry over economic and social conditions and believed Congress was performing poorly, the number of incumbents who were defeated exceeded 10 percent. After that, the economy improved and the number dropped to roughly 5 percent.

Personal Misconduct

Members of Congress can also fall prey to scandal. Life in Washington can be fast paced, glamorous, and expensive, and some members of Congress get caught up in influence peddling, sex scandals, and other forms of misconduct. These acts if discovered receive close attention from the news media and are a major threat to the reelection of incumbents. Roughly a fourth of House incumbents who lost their bid for reelection in the past decade were shadowed by ethical questions. "The first thing to being reelected is to stay away from scandal, even minor scandal," says the political scientist John Hibbing.[18] Representative Gary Condit found that out in 2002 when he was defeated in the Democratic primary. A married man, Condit had been romantically linked to Chandra Levy, an intern in his office who was missing and later found dead from foul play.

Even the top leaders are not immune from the effects of scandal, as illustrated by the experience of former House Ways and Means Committee Chairman Dan Rostenkowski. Accused of gross misuse of congressional funds, he lost his House seat in 1994, despite having won by 20 percentage points two years earlier and outspending his 1994 opponent by more than ten to one.

Turnout Variation: The Midterm Election Problem

Historically, the party holding the presidency loses seats in the midterm congressional elections, particularly in the House of Representatives. The 2002 midterm election, when the Republicans had George W. Bush in the White House and picked up several House seats, was only the fourth time in more than a century that the president's party gained seats.

The pattern is attributable to a dropoff in turnout for midterm elections.[19] The voters who go the polls only during presidential election years tend to have weaker party loyalties and are therefore more responsive to the issues of the moment. In any given election, these issues tend to favor one party, which contributes to the success of its congressional candidates as well as its presidential nominee. Most of the party's congressional candidates who win narrowly owe their margin of victory to these voters. However, these voters stay home during midterm elections. Thus, unless these incumbents can make inroads among midterm voters who backed their opponent two years earlier, they stand a good chance of losing. Since many of these voters are strong partisans, they are not easily swayed, and the typical result is the midterm defeat of a significant number of these incumbents.

Strong Challengers: A Problem for Senators

Incumbents are also vulnerable to strong challengers. Senators are particularly likely to face formidable opponents: after the presidency, the Senate is the top rung of the political ladder. Governors and House members are frequent challengers for Senate seats, and they have the electoral base, reputation, and experience to compete effectively. Moreover, the U.S. Senate lures wealthy challengers. Maria Cantwell spent $10 million of her own money to defeat Senator Slade Gorton for the state of Washington's Senate seat in 2000. Cantwell made her fortune as an executive with RealNetworks, a high-tech company.

House incumbents have less reason to fear strong challengers. A House seat is often not attractive enough to induce prominent local politicians, such as mayors or state legislators, to risk their political careers in a challenge to an incumbent.[20] This situation leaves the field open to weak opponents with little or no governmental or political experience.[21]

Redistricting: A Problem for House Members

Every ten years, after each population census, the 435 seats in the House are reallocated among the states in proportion to their population. This process is called **reapportionment.** States that have gained population since the last census may acquire additional House seats, while those that have lost population may lose seats. New York and Illinois are among the states that lost one or more House seats as a result of the 2000 census; Arizona and Washington are

What's Your Opinion?

Minority Redistricting

Congressional representatives tend naturally to favor the opinions of the voters who supported them. Voters who sided with their opponents are unlikely to have their opinions heard.

This tendency can result in the underrepresentation of minority group members because only rarely will they constitute an electoral majority in a congressional district. In 1982, Congress decided that race could be taken into account in congressional redistricting, and after the 1990 census, the boundaries of some House districts were drawn so that black Americans were a voting majority. In a 1996 decision, the Supreme Court held that race cannot be the determining factor in redistricting decisions (because this action violates the Fourteenth Amendment's equal protection clause), although there might be circumstances in which it could be considered along with other factors. Then, in a 2001 decision, the Court held that racial redistricting is permissible if it is the consequence of a reapportionment plan motivated by partisan rather than racial considerations (for example, if the primary purpose was to create a district favorable to Democratic candidates).

What's your view on racial redistricting?

reapportionment The reallocation of House seats among states after each census as a result of population changes.

Fighting Words

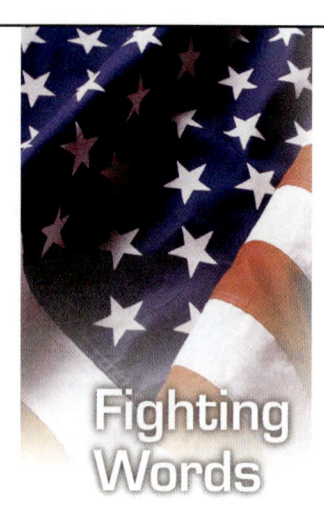

Should Congressional Campaigns Be Publicly Funded?

U.S. congressional campaigns are funded entirely through private sources—individual contributors, political parties, interest groups, and candidates' own money. These campaigns are also extremely expensive. As a result, House and Senate candidates spend an inordinate amount of time on fund-raising. The financing system also raises the question of whether large contributors acquire too much influence over the policy decisions of those who win election to Congress. Some candidates and observers believe that public funding of congressional campaigns is the answer. Others oppose the idea of public funding, either in principle or on pragmatic grounds.

Yes: [America needs] to completely break the dependence of politicians on special interests' campaign cash by creating an alternative source of disinterested "clean" funding for their campaigns. Here in Washington, such a step might induce heart attacks . . . but out across the country, the states are leading the way. [Voters in Maine approved] a sweeping proposal that created a system of "clean election" financing for qualified candidates who agree not to take any private money and abide by spending limits. . . . The concept is pretty simple. In baseball we don't allow the players, the managers, or individual owners to pay the umpires, for obvious reasons. For the same reasons special interests should not be financing politicians' campaigns.
—*Ellen Miller, Executive Director, Public Campaign*

No: To achieve a reduction of special interest influence—if you want to do that, I think that is not a good idea at all, it is blatantly unconstitutional, and the wrong thing to do. . . . For reality ever to square with reformer rhetoric, the Constitution would have to be amended . . . to give the Government the power to restrict all spending, and in support of or in opposition to candidates. . . . [What this] comes down to is an effort to have the Government control all spending.
—*Senator Mitch McConnell (R-Ky.)*

---

among the states that gained one or more seats. (The Senate is not affected by population change, since each state has two senators regardless of its size.)

The responsibility for redrawing House election districts after a reapportionment—a process called **redistricting**—rests with the state governments. States are required by law to make their districts as nearly equal in population as possible. There are many ways, however, to divide a state into districts of nearly equal size, and the party in power in the state legislature will do so in a way that favors candidates of its party. One method is to stack a few districts with overwhelming numbers of voters from the opposing party. This tactic ensures that the opposing party will win easily in these districts, but it also reduces the number of voters from that party in other districts, thus placing it at a disadvantage in most races. The process by which one party draws district boundaries to its advantage is called **gerrymandering**. The courts have placed some limits on gerrymandering (for example, very oddly shaped districts may be ruled unacceptable), but it is a common practice.

---

redistricting The process of altering election districts in order to make them as nearly equal in population as possible. Redistricting takes place every ten years, after each population census.

gerrymandering The process by which the party in power draws election district boundaries in a way that advantages its candidates.

When Massachusetts was redistricted in 1812, Governor Elbridge Gerry had the lines of one district redrawn in order to ensure that a candidate of his party would be elected. The cartoonist Elkanah Tinsdale, noting that the strangely shaped district resembled a salamander, called it a "Gerry-mander."

Reapportionment, redistricting, and gerrymandering are a potential threat to House incumbents. Turnover in House elections is typically higher after a new census than in previous elections. The newly redrawn districts include voters who are unfamiliar with the incumbent, thereby diminishing an advantage that incumbents typically have over their challengers. Moreover, when a state loses congressional seats, there are fewer districts than there are incumbents, who may end up running against each other. Finally, incumbents of the party that does not control the state legislature may find themselves having to compete in redrawn districts that are stacked with opposing voters.

Safe Incumbency and Representation

Although the obstacles to an incumbent's reelection can be substantial, the advantage in most congressional races clearly rests with the incumbent. As a result, Congress is not highly responsive to political change. The Republicans gained a decisive victory in 1994 on the strength of voters' anger at Washington, but a similar public mood in 1980 failed to translate into GOP control of the House of Representatives. In nearly every other Western democracy, the conditions underlying the 1980 election would have produced a change in power. It is worth noting that national legislators in other democracies do not have the large personal staffs and the substantial travel and publicity budgets that members of Congress have. Elsewhere, incumbents tend to win or lose on the popularity of their political party, not on their capacity to generate public support through constituent service.

Safe incumbency weakens the public's influence on Congress. Democracy depends on periodic shifts in power between the parties to bring public policy into closer alignment with public opinion. Research indicates that changes in congressional voting patterns occur primarily around the replacement of defeated or retiring lawmakers with new members. Incumbents tend to hold relatively stable policy positions during their time in office.[22]

Kay Bailey Hutchison was elected to the U.S. Senate from Texas in 1993 to fill the seat vacated by Lloyd Bentsen, who had resigned to become Secretary of the Treasury. Hutchison is among the growing number of women who sit in the U.S. Congress.

Who Are the Winners in Congressional Elections?

Although members of the House and Senate are elected to represent their constituents, the average representative is very different from the average American in virtually every respect.[23] Although only 1 in every 350 Americans is a lawyer, about 1 in 3 members of Congress has studied law. Attorneys are attracted to politics in part by Congress's role in lawmaking and by the public visibility that a campaign for office helps build, which can make a private law practice more successful. Along with lawyers, such professionals as business executives, educators, bankers, and journalists account for more than 90 percent of congressional membership.[24] Blue-collar workers, clerical employees, and homemakers are seldom elected to Congress. Farmers and ranchers are not as rare; a fair number of House members from rural districts have agricultural backgrounds.

Finally, members of Congress are disproportionately white and male. Minority group members and women each account for only about 10 percent of the Congress (see Chapter 5). This proportion, however, is twice that of a decade ago. Safe incumbency is a major obstacle to the election to Congress of more women and minorities. They have been no more successful than other challengers in dislodging congressional incumbents. In elections to state and local office, where incumbency is less important, women and minority candidates have made greater inroads (see "States in the Nation").[25]

CONGRESSIONAL LEADERSHIP

The way in which Congress works is related to the way in which its members win election. Because of their independent power base in their state or district, members of Congress have substantial independence within the institution they serve. The Speaker of the House and the other top leaders in Congress are crucial to its operation, but unlike their counterparts in European legislatures, they

STATES IN THE NATION

Women in the State Legislatures

Men have traditionally dominated elective office, but women are slowly gaining ground, particularly in local and state government. In 1969, fewer than 5 percent of state legislators were women. By 2001, there were 1,663 women state legislators—22.4 percent of the total. Washington state has the highest proportion of women legislators—38.8 percent. Alabama with 7.9 percent has the lowest. The northeastern, plains, and western states tend to have a higher proportion of women in their legislatures than do states in other regions. Of the women in state legislatures, 61 percent are Democrats and 39 percent are Republicans. Women of color account for 16 percent of women legislators.

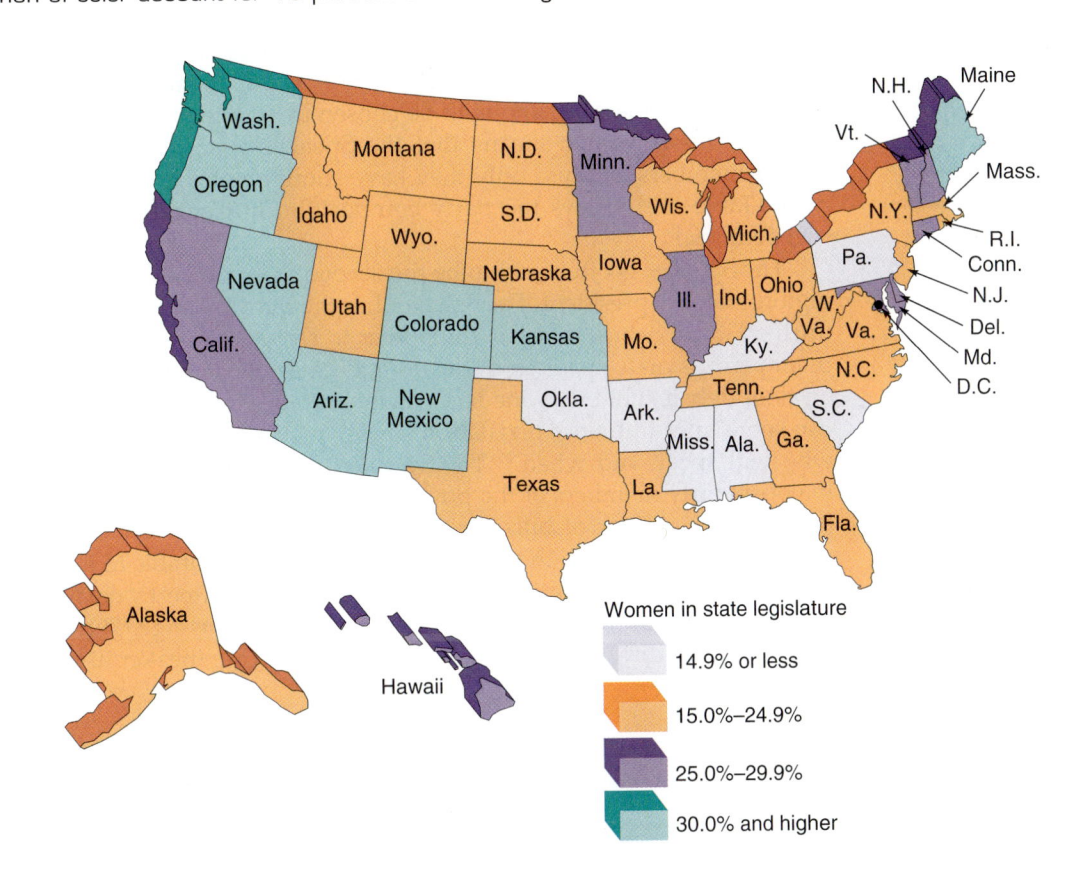

Women in state legislature:
- 14.9% or less
- 15.0%–24.9%
- 25.0%–29.9%
- 30.0% and higher

Source: Created from data gathered by Center for the American Woman and Politics (CAWP), National Information Bank on Women in Public Office, Eagleton Institute of Politics, Rutgers University, 2001.

---

cannot demand the loyalty of the members they lead. There is an inherent tension in Congress between the institution's need for strong leadership at the top and the individual members' need to exercise power on behalf of constituents. The result is an institution where power is dispersed although not evenly: the top party and committee leaders exercise more power than do the other members.

Party Leadership in Congress

The House and Senate are organized along party lines. When members of Congress are sworn in at the start of a new two-year session, they automatically are members of either the Republican or Democratic **party caucus** in their chamber. The caucuses are critical bodies within the Congress. Through them, the Democrats and Republicans in each chamber meet periodically to plan strategy and air their differences in the process of settling on the party's legislative program. The caucuses also select the **party leaders** who represent the party's interests in the chamber and give direction to the party's goals.

The House Leadership

The main party leaders in the House are the Speaker, majority leader, majority whip, minority leader, and minority whip. The Constitution provides only for the post of Speaker, who is to be chosen by a vote of the entire House. In practice, this provision means that the Speaker is selected by the majority party's members, because only they have enough votes to choose one of their own. (Table 11–1 shows the party composition in Congress during the past two decades.)

The Speaker is often said to be the second most powerful official in Washington, after the president. The Speaker has the right to speak first on legislation during House debate and has the power to recognize members—that is, give them permission to speak from the floor. Because the House places a time limit on floor debate, not everyone has a chance to speak on a bill, and the Speaker can sometimes influence legislation simply by exercising the power to decide who will speak and when.[26] The Speaker also chooses the chairperson and majority-party members of the powerful House Rules Committee, which controls the scheduling of bills for debate. Legislation that the Speaker wants passed is likely to reach the floor under conditions favorable to its enactment; for example, the Speaker may ask the Rules Committee to delay sending a bill to the floor until there is enough support for its passage. The Speaker has other ways of directing the work of the House. The Speaker assigns bills to

party caucus A group that consists of a party's members in the House or Senate and that serves to elect the party's leadership, set policy goals, and determine party strategy.

party leaders Members of the House and Senate who are chosen by the Democratic or Republican caucus in each chamber to represent the party's interests in that chamber and who give some central direction to the chamber's deliberations.

TABLE 11-1 Number of Democrats and Republicans in House of Representatives and Senate, 1983–2004

	83-84	85-86	87-88	89-90	91-92	93-94	95-96	97-98	99-00	01-02	02-03
House											
Democrats	269*	253*	258*	262*	268*	259	205*	207*	212*	213	208
Republicans	166	182	177	173	167	176	230	228	223	222	227
Senate											
Democrats	45	47	54*	55*	56*	56	46*	45*	45*	51*	49
Republicans	55	53	46	45	44	44	54	55	55	49	51

*Chamber not controlled by the president's party. Independents are included in the total for the party with which they caucused.

committees, places time limits on the reporting of bills out of committees, and assigns members to conference committees. (The importance of these powers over committee action will become apparent later in this chapter.)

The Speaker is active in developing the party's position on issues and in persuading party members in the House to follow his or her lead.[27] Although the Speaker cannot compel party members to support this program, they look to the Speaker for leadership. The Speaker can draw on shared partisan views and has a few rewards on hand for cooperative party members; the Speaker can, for instance, help them obtain public spending projects for their districts and favorable committee assignments for themselves.

The Speaker is assisted by the House majority leader and the House majority whip, who are elected by the majority party's members. The majority leader acts as the party's floor leader, organizing the debate on bills and working to line up legislative support. The whip has the important job of soliciting votes from party members and of informing them when critical votes are scheduled. As voting is getting under way on the House floor, the whip will sometimes stand at a location that is easily seen by party members and let them know where the leadership stands on the bill by giving them a thumbs-up or thumbs-down signal.

The minority party has its own leaders in the House. The House minority leader heads the party's caucus and policy committee and plays the leading role in developing the party's legislative positions. The minority leader is assisted by a minority whip.

The Senate Leadership

In the Senate, the most important party leadership position is that of the majority leader, who heads the majority-party caucus. The majority leader's role is much like that of the Speaker of the House, in that the majority leader formulates the majority's legislative policies and strategies and seeks to develop influential relationships with colleagues. Like the Speaker, the Senate majority leader chairs the party's policy committee and acts as the party's voice in the chamber.[28] The majority leader is assisted by the majority whip, who sees to it that members know when important votes are scheduled and ensures that the party's strongest advocates on a legislative measure are present for the debate. The Senate also has a minority leader and minority whip, whose roles are comparable to those performed by their counterparts in the House.

Unlike the Speaker of the House, the Senate majority leader is not the chamber's presiding officer. The Constitution assigns this responsibility to the vice president of the United States. However, because the vice president is allowed to vote in the Senate only to break a tie, the vice president seldom presides over Senate debates. The Senate has a president *pro tempore*, who, in the absence of the vice president, has the right to preside over the Senate. President *pro tempore* is largely an honorary position that by tradition is usually held by the majority party's senior member. The presiding official has limited power, since each senator has the right to speak at any length on bills under consideration.

The Senate's tradition of unlimited debate stems mainly from its relatively small size (only 100 members, compared with the House's 435 members). Moreover, senators like to view themselves as the equals of all others in their

The power of Democratic Senate leader Tom Daschle and other party leaders in Congress rests on the trust placed in them by members of their party. Congressional leaders are also in a stronger position when, as in Daschle's case, they represent the party opposite that of the president. In such cases, they become the voice of opposition in the news media.

chamber and are thus reluctant to take orders from their leadership. For such reasons, the Senate majority leader's position is weaker than that of the Speaker of the House.

Party Leaders and Followers

The power of all party leaders, in the Senate and House alike, rests largely on the trust placed in them by the members of their party. They do not have the strong formal powers of parliamentary leaders, but they are expected to lead. If they are adept at promoting ideas and building coalitions, they can exercise considerable power within their chamber.

They also are positioned to influence national debate. They are recognized by the news media as their party's chief spokespersons within the House and Senate, a role that is magnified when their party does not control the White House. In that circumstance, they are the closest thing to an opposition leader (a mainstay of European parliamentary politics) that the U.S. system has. They are pressed by journalists to respond to White House initiatives and to lay out the plans of their own party, as was the case with Democrat Tom Daschle when he became Senate majority leader in 2001. When they are of the same party as the president, however, they are of less interest to the press. It sees the president, not the party's leaders in Congress, as the party's national voice.

Party leaders are in a stronger position today than a few decades ago as a result of changes in the composition of the congressional parties. The GOP once had a substantial progressive faction within it, but this faction has been eclipsed by its conservative wing. At the same time, the Democratic party's conservative wing, represented by its southern lawmakers, has withered away almost entirely. As congressional Republicans have become more alike in their thinking and different from congressional Democrats, each group has found it easier to band together and to stand against the opposing party. Accordingly, the party leaders through the party caucus have found it easier to bring their party's lawmakers together on legislative issues.

At the same time, House and Senate members are less deferential to their leaders than in the past. Until a few decades ago, congressional folkways dictated that newer members, particularly on the House side, would mostly listen

Simulation
www.mhhe.com/patterson6

HOW THE UNITED STATES COMPARES

Legislative Leadership and Authority

The U.S. House and Senate are separate and co-equal chambers, each with its own leadership and rules. This type of legislative structure is not found in most democracies. Although many other democracies have a bicameral legislature like the U.S. Congress, nearly all power is vested in just one of the two chambers. In the British Parliament, for example, the House of Commons is far more powerful than the House of Lords; the latter can delay legislation but cannot kill it. In such a situation, legislative power is more concentrated and easier to exercise. Thus, in Great Britain, the party that controls the House of Commons decides legislative policy. In the United States, a party must control both the House of Representatives and the Senate if it is to exercise such power.

The U.S. Congress is fragmented in other ways as well: it has elected leaders with limited formal powers, a network of relatively independent and powerful committees, and members who are free to follow or ignore other members of their party. Most Democrats and Republicans vote with a majority of their party on major bills, but it is not uncommon for a fourth or more of a party's legislators to vote against their party's position on important legislative issues. In contrast, European legislatures have a centralized power structure: top leaders have substantial authority, the committees are weak, and the parties are unified. European legislators are expected to support their party unless granted permission to vote otherwise on a particular bill. Legislative leadership is much easier to exercise in Europe's hierarchical parliaments than in America's "stratarchical" Congress.

COUNTRY	FORM OF LEGISLATURE
Canada	One house dominant
France	One house dominant
Germany	One house dominant (except on regional issues)
Great Britain	One house dominant
Israel	One house only
Italy	Two equal houses
Japan	One house dominant
Mexico	Two equal houses
United States	Two equal houses

and learn, awaiting the day when through seniority they were positioned to assume a larger role in the institution. There were always a few mavericks who were unwilling to respect this unwritten norm, but most new members willingly took a back seat. Of course, a back seat in the Senate was not the same as one in the House. Because the Senate is a small body and operates on rules that are more egalitarian, a junior senator could rise to prominence more quickly than a junior House member could. Nevertheless, the Senate, too, had a tight inner circle dominated by its more senior members.[29]

Today, junior House and Senate members pursue their own agendas more aggressively. They are elected in a system that rewards self-starters and encourages them to pursue a constant reelection campaign. They seek the visibility that attends a more active legislative role. They also are increasingly likely to have forged close ties with the special interests that support their campaigns, and they are expected by these groups to vigorously pursue legislative goals. Moreover, because the two parties have become more polarized at the activist level, the newer members of Congress have been more ideological and less pragmatic in their beliefs and thus more eager to express their views.[30] Finally, television has provided a path to prominence for junior members who are articulate and engaging. The visibility they obtain outside Congress through the media magnifies their voice within the institution. The old axiom that junior members "should be seen and not heard" is hardly an accurate description of today's Congress.

Committee Chairs: The Seniority Principle

Party leaders are not the only important leaders in Congress. Most of the work of Congress takes place in the meetings of its thirty-five standing (permanent) committees and their numerous subcommittees, each of which is headed by a chairperson. A committee chair schedules committee meetings, determines the order in which committee bills are considered, presides over committee discussions, directs the committee's majority staff, and can choose to lead the debate when a committee bill reaches the floor of the chamber for a vote by the full membership.

Committee chairs are always members of the majority party, and they usually have the most **seniority:** the most consecutive years of service on a particular committee.

Seniority is based strictly on time served on a committee, not on time spent in Congress. If a member switches committees, the years spent on the first committee do not count toward seniority on the second one. The seniority principle was instituted in the Senate in the mid-nineteenth century but was not formally applied in the House until the early twentieth century. The seniority principle remained virtually absolute until the House Democratic majority decided in the early 1970s that committee chairs would henceforth be chosen by secret ballot. Abuses by some committee chairs led to the change. Virginia's Howard Smith, who chaired the House Rules Committee in the 1950s and 1960s and was opposed to racial change, would sometimes leave Washington for his Virginia farm when civil rights legislation reached his committee. Because the Rules Committee could not meet unless he called it into session, Smith's absence was sometimes enough to persuade the full committee to "table" a bill, or set it aside. A committee chair now has less power; for example, a majority of the committee members can vote to convene meetings in the chair's absence.

Although the seniority principle is no longer absolute, the congressional majorities usually abide by it.[31] The 107th Congress (2001–2002) is a recent exception. House Republicans had earlier placed a three-term limit on the committee chairs, and many of these positions came open after the 2000 election. Rather than following a strict seniority rule, the Republicans invited candidates to interview for the posts. Representative Bill Thomas of California was appointed chair of the House Ways and Means Committee even though he had less seniority than Representative Phil Crane of Illinois, who also sought the position.

The seniority system persists because it has several important advantages: it reduces the number of bitter power struggles that would occur if the chair were decided by open competition, it provides experienced and knowledgeable committee leadership, and it enables members to look forward to the reward of a position as chair after years of service on the same committee. A drawback of the seniority system is that it places the committee chairs outside the direct control of the House and Senate's elected leaders.[32]

Congressional organization and leadership extend into subcommittees, which are smaller units within each committee formed to conduct specific aspects of the committee's business. Altogether there are about two hundred

seniority A member of Congress's consecutive years of service on a particular committee.

subcommittees in the House and Senate, each with a chairperson who decides its order of business, presides over its meetings, and coordinates its staff. In both chambers, a subcommittee chair is often the most senior member on the panel, but seniority is not as important in these appointments as it is in the designation of committee chairs.

Oligarchy or Democracy: Which Principle Should Govern?

In 1995, House Republicans gave committee chairs the power to select the chairs of their subcommittees and to appoint all majority-party staff members, including those who work for the subcommittees. The changes were designed to give committee chairs more control over legislation.[33] The changes reversed House reforms of the 1970s that gave subcommittees and their chairs greater authority in order to make the House "more democratic" in its organization.[34]

The opposing forces embedded in the 1970s and 1995 reforms have played themselves out many times in the history of Congress. The institution is at once a place for conducting the nation's business and for promoting constituency interests. At times, the position of top leaders has been strengthened. At other times, the position of rank-and-file members has been enhanced. At all times, there has been an attempt to create a workable balance of the two. The result is an institution very different from European parliaments, where power is thoroughly concentrated at the top (an arrangement reflected even in the name for rank-and-file members: "backbenchers"). The distinguishing feature of congressional power is its dispersion across the membership, with provision for added power at the top.

THE COMMITTEE SYSTEM

As indicated earlier, most of the work in Congress is conducted through **standing committees,** which are permanent committees with responsibility for a particular area of public policy. At present there are twenty standing committees in the House and sixteen in the Senate (see Table 11–2). Both the House and the Senate, for example, have a standing committee that specializes in handling foreign policy issues. Other important standing committees are those that deal with agriculture, commerce, the national budget, the interior (natural resources and public lands), defense, government spending, labor, the judiciary, and taxation. House committees, which average about thirty-five to forty members each, are about twice the size of the Senate committees. Each standing committee has legislative authority in that it can draft and rewrite proposed legislation and can recommend to the full chamber the passage or defeat of the legislation it considers.

Each standing committee in Congress has its own staff, which altogether totals about one thousand employees in the Senate and thirteen hundred employees in the House. Unlike the members' personal staffs, which concentrate on constituency relations, the committee staffs perform an almost entirely legislative function. They help draft legislation, prepare reports, organize hearings, and participate in altering bills within committee.

standing committee A permanent congressional committee with responsibility for a particular area of public policy. An example is the Senate Foreign Relations Committee.

TABLE 11-2 The Standing Committees of Congress

HOUSE OF REPRESENTATIVES	SENATE
Agriculture	Agriculture, Nutrition, and Forestry
Appropriations	Appropriations
Armed Services	Armed Services
Banking and Financial Services	Banking, Housing, and Urban Affairs
Budget	Budget
Education and the Workforce	Commerce, Science, and Transportation
Energy and Commerce	Energy and Natural Resources
Financial Services	Environment and Public Works
Government Reform	Finance
House Administration	Foreign Relations
International Relations	Governmental Affairs
Judiciary	Health, Education, Labor, and Pensions
Resources	Judiciary
Rules	Rules and Administration
Science	Small Business
Small Business	Veterans' Affairs
Standards of Official Conduct	
Transportation and Infrastructure	
Veterans' Affairs	
Ways and Means	

In addition to its standing committees, Congress also has a number of *select committees*, which are created to perform specific tasks and are disbanded after they have done so; *joint committees*, composed of members of both houses, which perform advisory or coordinating functions for the House and the Senate; and *conference committees*, which are joint committees formed temporarily to work out differences in House and Senate versions of a particular bill. The role of conference committees is discussed more fully later in the chapter.

Congress could not possibly handle its workload without the help of its committee system. About ten thousand bills are introduced during each two-year session of Congress. The sheer volume of this legislation would paralyze the institution if it did not have a division of labor. Yet the very existence of committees and subcommittees helps fragment Congress: each of these units is relatively secure in its power, jurisdiction, and membership.[35]

Committee Membership

Each committee includes Republicans and Democrats, but the majority party holds the majority of seats on each committee and subcommittee. The ratio of Democrats to Republicans on each committee is approximately the same as the

U.S. Senator Orrin Hatch (R-Utah) speaks at a Judiciary Committee hearing. Most of the legislative work of Congress is done in committees and their subcommittees.

ratio in the full House or Senate, but there is no fixed rule on this matter, and the majority party sets the proportions as it chooses (mindful that at the next election it could become the chamber's minority). Members of the House typically serve on only two committees. Senators often serve on four, although they can sit on only two major committees, such as Foreign Relations and Finance. There are also limits on subcommittee assignments; no House member, for example, can serve on more than five subcommittees.

Each standing committee has a fixed number of members, and a committee must have a vacancy before a new member can be appointed. These vacancies usually occur at the start of a new congressional session, when the committee positions of members who have retired or been defeated for reelection are reallocated. On nearly all committees, members retain their seats unless they decide to relinquish them or are forced to do so by changes in party ratios or committee size. The biggest change in committee memberships comes when a party loses control of the House or Senate; several Democrats had to relinquish committee assignments when the Republicans took control of the Senate in 2003.

Each party has a special committee in each chamber with responsibility for deciding who will fill vacancies on standing committees. Several factors influence these decisions, including the preferences of the legislators themselves. Most newly elected members of Congress receive a committee assignment that they have requested.[36] New members usually ask for assignment to a committee on which they can serve their constituents' interests and at the same time increase their reelection prospects.[37] For example, when Hillary Clinton was elected to the Senate in 2000 from New York, a state that depends heavily on human services programs, she asked for and received an appointment on the Senate Health, Education, Labor, and Pensions Committee.

Members of Congress also prefer membership on one of the most important committees, such as Foreign Relations or Finance in the Senate and Appropriations or Ways and Means in the House. Such factors as members' intelligence, experience, party loyalty, ideology, region, length of congressional service, and work habits weigh heavily in the determination of appointments to these prestigious committees.[38]

Subcommittee assignments are handled differently. The members of each party on a committee decide who among them will serve on each of its subcommittees. The members' preferences, seniority, and personal backgrounds and the interests of their constituencies are key influences on subcommittee assignments.

Committee Jurisdiction

The 1946 Legislative Reorganization Act requires each bill introduced in Congress to be referred to the proper committee. An agricultural bill introduced in the Senate must be assigned to the Senate Agriculture Committee, a bill dealing with foreign affairs must be sent to the Senate Foreign Relations Committee, and so on. This requirement is a major source of each committee's power. Even if its members are known to oppose certain types of legislation, bills clearly within its **jurisdiction**—the policy area in which it is authorized to act—must be sent to it for deliberation.

However, policy problems are increasingly complex, and jurisdiction has accordingly become an increasingly contentious issue, particularly on major bills. Which House committee, for example, should handle a major bill addressing the role of financial institutions in global trade? Is it the Banking Committee? Or the Commerce Committee? Or the International Relations Committee? Since all committees seek legislative influence and since each is jealous of its jurisdiction, bills that overlap committee boundaries provoke conflict. The political scientist David King describes these conflicts as "turf wars." They also involve the party leaders, who are in charge of assigning bills to committee. The party leaders can take advantage of these situations by shuttling a bill to the committee that is most likely to handle it in the way they would like. But party leaders depend on the committee chairs for support, so they cannot regularly ignore a committee that has a strong claim to a bill. At times, party leaders have responded by dividing up a bill, handing over some of its provisions to one committee and other provisions to a second committee.

House subcommittees have secure jurisdictions like those of the committees: bills must be referred to the appropriate subcommittees within two weeks of their arrival in committee. The Senate has a similar policy. Thus responsibility in Congress is thoroughly divided, with each subcommittee having formal authority over a small area of public policy. The House International Relations Committee, for instance, has five subcommittees: International Economic Policy and Trade, International Operations and Human Rights, Asia and the Pacific, Western Hemisphere, and Africa. Each subcommittee has about a dozen members, and these few individuals do most of the work and have the major voice in the disposition of most bills in their policy domain.

jurisdiction (of a congressional committee) The policy area in which a particular congressional committee is authorized to act.

HOW A BILL BECOMES LAW

Parties, party leaders, and committees are critical actors in the legislative process. Their role and influence, however, vary with the nature of the legislation under consideration.

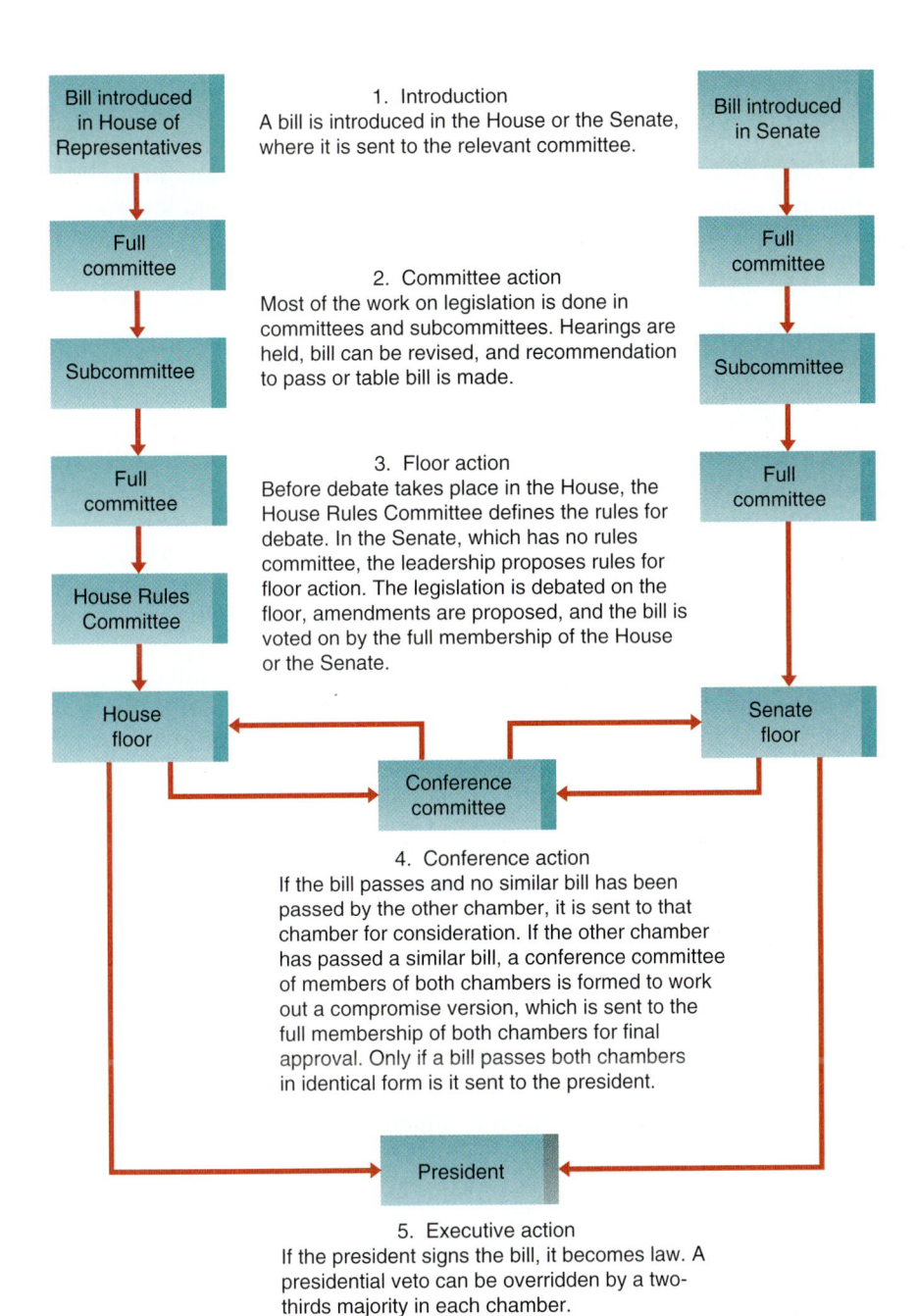

CHAPTER 11   Congress: Balancing National Goals and Local Interests   343

Figure 11–4

How a Bill Becomes a Law
Although the legislative process can be short-circuited in many ways, this diagram describes the most typical way in which a bill becomes a law.

1. Introduction
A bill is introduced in the House or the Senate, where it is sent to the relevant committee.

2. Committee action
Most of the work on legislation is done in committees and subcommittees. Hearings are held, bill can be revised, and recommendation to pass or table bill is made.

3. Floor action
Before debate takes place in the House, the House Rules Committee defines the rules for debate. In the Senate, which has no rules committee, the leadership proposes rules for floor action. The legislation is debated on the floor, amendments are proposed, and the bill is voted on by the full membership of the House or the Senate.

4. Conference action
If the bill passes and no similar bill has been passed by the other chamber, it is sent to that chamber for consideration. If the other chamber has passed a similar bill, a conference committee of members of both chambers is formed to work out a compromise version, which is sent to the full membership of both chambers for final approval. Only if a bill passes both chambers in identical form is it sent to the president.

5. Executive action
If the president signs the bill, it becomes law. A presidential veto can be overridden by a two-thirds majority in each chamber.

Committee Hearings and Decisions

The formal process by which bills become law is shown in Figure 11–4. A **bill** is a proposed legislative act. Many bills are prepared by executive agencies, interest groups, or other outside parties, but members of Congress also draft bills, and only they can formally submit a bill for consideration by their chamber. Once a bill is introduced by a member of the House or Senate, it is given a

bill A proposed law (legislative act) within Congress or another legislature.

number and a title and is then sent to the appropriate committee, which assigns it to one of its subcommittees. Most bills that reach a subcommittee are tabled on the grounds that they are not worthwhile. Only about 10 percent of the bills that committees consider reach the floor for a vote; the others are "killed" when committees decide that they do not warrant further consideration and table them. The full House or Senate can overrule these committee rejections, but this seldom occurs.

The fact that committees kill 90 percent of the bills submitted in Congress does not mean that committees exercise 90 percent of the power in Congress. A committee rarely decides fully the fate of legislation that is important to the majority party or its leadership. Most bills die in committee because they are of little interest to anyone other than a few members of Congress or are so poorly conceived that they lack merit. Some bills are not even supported by the members who introduce them. A member may submit a bill to appease a powerful constituent group and then quietly inform the committee to ignore it.

If a bill seems to have merit, the subcommittee will schedule hearings on it. The subcommittee invites testimony on the proposed legislation by lobbyists, administrators, and experts, who inform members about the suggested policy, provide an indication of the support the bill has, and disclose possible weaknesses in the proposal. After the hearings, if the subcommittee still feels that the legislation is warranted, members recommend the bill to the full committee, which can hold additional hearings. In the House, both the full committee and a subcommittee can "mark up," or revise, a bill; in the Senate, markup is usually reserved for the full committee.

From Committee to the Floor

If a majority of the committee votes to recommend passage of the bill, it is referred to the full chamber for action. In the House, the Rules Committee has the power to determine when the bill will be voted on, how long the debate on the bill will last, and whether the bill will receive a "closed rule" (no amendments will be permitted), an "open rule" (members can propose amendments relevant to any of the bill's sections), or something in between (for example, only certain sections of the bill will be subject to amendment). The Rules Committee has this scheduling power because the House is too large to operate effectively without strict rules for the handling of legislation by the full chamber. The rules are also a means by which the majority party controls legislation. House Democrats employed closed rules to prevent Republicans from proposing amendments to major bills, a tactic House Republicans said they would forgo when they took control in 1995. Once in control, however, the Republicans applied closed rules to a number of major bills. The tactic was too effective to ignore.

The Senate has no Rules Committee, relying instead on the majority leader to schedule bills. All Senate bills are subject to unlimited debate unless a three-fifths majority of the full Senate votes for **cloture,** which limits debate to thirty hours. Cloture is a way of thwarting a Senate **filibuster,** a procedural tactic whereby a minority of senators prevent a bill from coming to a vote by holding the floor and talking until other senators give in and the bill is withdrawn from consideration. The Senate also differs from the House in that its members can propose *any* amendment to *any* bill. Unlike House amendments, those in the

cloture A parliamentary maneuver which, if a three-fifths majority votes for it, limits Senate debate to thirty hours and has the effect of defeating a filibuster.

filibuster A procedural tactic in the U.S. Senate whereby a minority of legislators prevent a bill from coming to a vote by holding the floor and talking until the majority gives in and the bill is withdrawn from consideration.

With their staff members looking on, Senators Edward Kennedy (D-Mass.) and Nancy Kassenbaum (R-Kans.) of the Health, Education, Labor, and Pensions Committee talk during a break in hearings.

Senate do not have to be germane to a bill's content. For example, a senator may propose an antiabortion amendment to a bill dealing with defense expenditures. Such an amendment is called a **rider,** and they are frequently introduced.

rider An amendment to a bill that deals with an issue unrelated to the content of the bill. Riders are permitted in the Senate but not the House.

Leadership and Floor Action

Committee action is usually decisive on bills that address small issues. If a majority of committee members favor such a bill, it normally is passed by the full chamber, often without amendment. In a sense, the full chamber merely votes to confirm or modify decisions made previously by committee and subcommittees. Of course, committees do not operate in a vacuum. In making its decisions, a committee takes into account the fact that its action can be reversed by the full chamber, just as a subcommittee recognizes that the full committee can overrule its decision.[39] Partisanship also serves as a check on committee action. If a committee is nearly unanimous in its support for a bill, other members are likely to conclude that the legislation is acceptable. However, when a committee's vote is sharply divided along party or regional lines, other members may conclude that they need to look more closely at the bill before deciding whether to support it.

On major bills, the party leaders are the critical actors. They will have worked closely with the committee during its deliberations and may assume leadership of the bill when it clears the committee. (In the case of "minor" bills, leadership during floor debate is normally provided by committee members.)

In her book *Unorthodox Lawmaking: New Legislative Processes in the U.S. Congress*, Barbara Sinclair notes that the majority party's leaders (particularly in the House) have increasingly set the legislative agenda and defined the debate on major bills.[40] They shape the bills' broad outlines and set the boundaries of the floor debate. In these efforts, they depend on the support of their party's members. To obtain it, they consult their members informally and through the party

party discipline The willingness of a party's House or Senate members to act together as a cohesive group and thus exert collective control over legislative action.

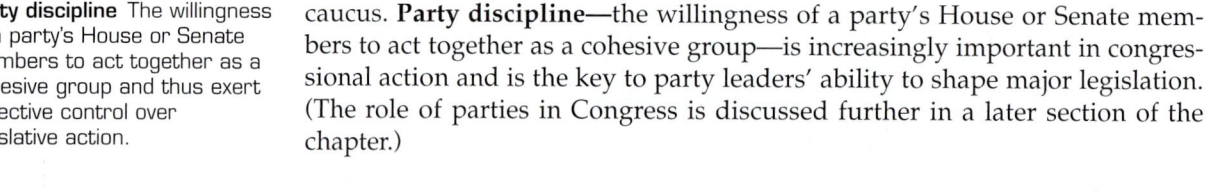

Simulation
www.mhhe.com/patterson6

conference committee A temporary committee that is formed to bargain over the differences in the House and Senate versions of a bill. The committee's members are usually appointed from the House and Senate standing committees that originally worked on the bill.

law (as enacted by Congress) A legislative proposal, or bill, that is passed by both the House and Senate and is either signed or not vetoed by the president.

veto When the president refuses to sign a bill, thereby keeping it from becoming law unless Congress overrides the veto.

caucus. **Party discipline**—the willingness of a party's House or Senate members to act together as a cohesive group—is increasingly important in congressional action and is the key to party leaders' ability to shape major legislation. (The role of parties in Congress is discussed further in a later section of the chapter.)

Conference Committees and the President

For a bill to pass, it must receive the support of a simple majority (50 percent plus one) of the House or Senate members voting on it. To become a law, however, a bill must be passed in identical form by both the House and the Senate. About 10 percent of all proposals that are approved by both chambers—the proportion is larger for major bills—differ in important respects in their House and Senate versions and are referred to conference committees to resolve their differences. Each **conference committee** is formed temporarily to handle a particular bill; its members are usually appointed from the House and Senate standing committees that worked on the bill originally. The conference committee's job is to bargain over the differences in the House and Senate versions and to develop a compromise version. It then goes to the House and Senate floors, where it can be passed, defeated, or returned to conference, but not amended.

Legislation that is passed by the House and the Senate is not assured of becoming a law. The president also has a role. If the president signs the bill it becomes a **law**. If the president exercises the **veto**, a refusal to sign a bill, it is sent back to its originating chamber with the president's reasons for the veto. Congress can override a veto by a two-thirds vote of each chamber; the bill then becomes law. If the president fails to sign a bill within ten days (Sundays excepted) and Congress has remained in session, the bill automatically becomes law anyway. If the president fails to sign a bill within ten days and Congress has adjourned for the term, the bill does not become law. This last situation is called a *pocket veto* and forces Congress in its next session to start from the beginning: the bill must again pass both chambers and is again subject to presidential veto.

CONGRESS'S POLICYMAKING ROLE

The Framers of the Constitution expected Congress to be the leading branch of the national government. It was to the legislature—the embodiment of representative government—that the people were expected to look for policy leadership. During most of the nineteenth century, Congress, not the president, was clearly the dominant national institution. Aside from a few strong leaders such as Jackson and Lincoln, presidents did not play a major legislative role (see Chapter 12). However, as national and international forces combined to place greater leadership and policy demands on the federal government, the president became a vital part of the national legislative process. Today Congress and the president substantially share the legislative effort, although their roles differ greatly.[41]

Congress's policymaking role revolves around its three legislative functions: lawmaking, representation, and oversight. In practice, the three functions overlap, but they are conceptually distinct.

Citizenship

Getting Involved, Making a Difference

Becoming a Legislative Intern

Each year, thousands of college students serve as interns in Congress or state legislatures. Many internships are unpaid, but students can receive college credit for the experience.

Internships provide an opportunity to see the legislative process firsthand. They are not always a great adventure. Many legislative interns envision themselves contributing ideas and research that might influence public policy only to find that they are answering letters, developing mailing lists, or duplicating materials. Nevertheless, few interns conclude that their experience was a waste of time. Most find it rewarding and, ultimately, memorable.

Many executive agencies at the federal and state levels also accept interns, and some have well-organized internship programs. The Department of State has one of the best internship programs, but it is in heavy demand and has an early application decline. The internships offered by executive agencies are typically more challenging than those provided by legislative offices. Legislators dedicate a lot of their staff time to constituency service, whereas agencies concentrate on the administration of policies and programs. On the other hand, legislative offices are usually more spirited, and interns in these offices are more likely to strike up friendships with other interns in the same or nearby offices.

Information about internships can be obtained from the American Political Science Association (www.apsa.org). In addition, there are organizations in Washington that arrange internships in Congress and the executive agencies. These organizations frequently charge a fee for their services, so you might want to contact a legislative office or executive agency directly. It is important to make your request as early as possible in the college year because some internship programs have deadlines and nearly all offices receive more requests than they can accommodate. You could also check with the student services office at your college or university. Some of these offices have information on internship programs and can be of assistance.

The Lawmaking Function of Congress

Under the Constitution, Congress is granted the **lawmaking function:** the authority to make the laws necessary to carry out the powers granted to the national government. However, whether Congress takes the lead in the making of laws depends heavily on the type of policy at issue.

lawmaking function The authority (of a legislature) to make the laws necessary to carry out the government's powers.

Broad Issues: The Limits of Fragmentation on Congress's Role

Congress is structured in a way that makes agreement on large issues difficult to obtain. Congress is not one house, but two, each with its own authority and constituency base. Neither the House nor the Senate can enact legislation without the other's approval, and they are hardly two versions of the same thing. California and North Dakota have exactly the same representation in the Senate, but in the House, which is apportioned by population, California has fifty-two seats compared to North Dakota's one.

Newt Gingrich and three hundred Republican congressional candidates stand in front of the Capitol to dramatize their Contract with America. After their stunning victory in the 1994 elections, they launched an aggressive attempt to reduce the scope of the federal government, illustrating that, in some instances, Congress can take the lead on broad national issues.

Congress also includes a lot of people: 100 members of the Senate and 435 members of the House. They come from different constituencies and represent different and sometimes opposing interests. Since each member has a separate power base, and depends on it for reelection, the members can be expected to take different positions on legislative issues, even when they agree on the general goal. Nearly every member of Congress, for example, supports the principle of global free trade. When it comes to specific trade provisions, however, they often disagree. Foreign competition means different things to manufacturers that produce automobiles, computer chips, and underwear; it means different things to farmers who produce corn, sugar, and grapes; and it means different things to firms that deal in international finance, home insurance, and student loans. And because it means different things to different people in different parts of the country, members of Congress who represent these areas have conflicting views on what the nation's trade policy should be.

For such reasons, Congress often has difficulty taking the lead on broad issues of national policy. A legislative institution can easily lead on such issues only if it assigns this authority to its top leadership. Although the rise in party discipline in Congress has strengthened leaders' role, the fact remains that House and Senate members are relatively free to go their separate ways if they so choose. For this reason, Congress often struggles when faced with the task of developing comprehensive policies that address broad national problems.

The fragmented nature of Congress enables the president to assume leadership of many of these issues. The presidency is better suited to the task. First, whereas Congress's authority is divided, the presidency's authority is not.[42] Executive power is vested constitutionally in the hands of a single individual—the president. As a result, the presidency is capable of a degree of policy planning and coordination that is far beyond the normal capacity of Congress. Second, whereas members of Congress see issues mainly from the perspective of their state or district, the president has a national outlook. The president cannot ignore specific state and local interests, but must concentrate on broad national ones in order to retain power.

Presidential leadership means that Congress will normally pay attention to White House proposals, not that it will adopt them. Congress typically accepts a presidential initiative only as a starting point in its deliberations. It may reject the proposal outright—particularly when the president is from the opposite party—but any such proposal provides Congress a tangible bill on which to focus. If the proposal is at all close to what a congressional majority would regard as acceptable, Congress will modify it in large or small ways to fit the demands of its membership.

The president's leverage is greatest when prompt legislative action is imperative. When Congress must act or face the public's wrath, the presidential veto comes into play. Congress is nearly forced into taking the president's position into account in shaping the legislation, since it is exceedingly difficult to muster the two-thirds majority in each chamber that is required to override a presidential veto. Of course, Congress can dare the president to veto the bill, hoping that public anger will be directed at the White House. But any such showdown is risky, and Congress and the White House normally bargain their way to a bill that accommodates their separate interests. (The legislative roles of Congress and the president are discussed further in Chapter 12.)

In its lawmaking activities, Congress has the support of three congressional agencies. One is the Congressional Budget Office (CBO), which was created as part of the Budget Impoundment and Control Act of 1974. Before this time, the president, through the Office of Management and Budget (OMB), had a significant advantage in budgetary matters. Congress had no independent way to systematically assess the president's budgetary proposals or their projected impact. The CBO gives Congress this capacity. Its two hundred employees provide Congress with general economic projections, overall estimates of government expenditures and revenues, and specific estimates of the costs of proposed programs. Since the CBO's inception, its calculations have often been at odds with those of the OMB. For example, the OMB's estimates of the cost of presidential initiatives are usually optimistic, and the CBO's figures have been a basis by which Congress has trimmed or rejected these proposals. (The budgetary process is described more fully in later chapters.)

A second congressional agency is the General Accounting Office (GAO). With thirty-five hundred employees, the GAO is the largest congressional agency. Formed in 1921, it has primary responsibility for overseeing executive agencies' spending of money that has been appropriated by Congress.[43] The programs that the executive agencies administer are authorized and funded by Congress. The GAO's responsibility is to ensure that executive agencies operate in the manner prescribed by Congress.

The third congressional agency is the Congressional Research Service (CRS). It is the oldest congressional agency, has a staff of one thousand employees, and operates as a nonpartisan reference agency. If a member of Congress needs information, the CRS will conduct the necessary research and provide the information to the member.

Congress in the Lead: Fragmentation as a Policymaking Strength

Congress occasionally does take the lead on large issues. Except during Roosevelt's New Deal, Congress has been a chief source of major labor legislation. Environmental legislation, federal aid to education, and urban development are other areas in which Congress has played an initiating role.[44] The Republicans' Contract with America that was introduced during the 1994 election is yet another example of congressional policy leadership. The contract included broad fiscal, regulatory, and social initiatives. In 1996, for example, the Republican-controlled Congress led the way on legislation that fundamentally changed the nation's welfare system. Nevertheless, Congress does not routinely develop broad policy programs and carry them through to passage. "Congress remains organized," James Sundquist notes, "to deal with narrow problems but not with broad ones."[45]

As it happens, the great majority of the hundreds of bills that Congress considers each session deal with narrow issues. The leading role in the disposition of these bills falls not on the president but on Congress and, in most cases, on a relatively small number of its members. The same fragmentation that makes it difficult for Congress to take the lead on a broad issue makes it easy for Congress to tackle scores of narrow issues simultaneously. Most of the legislation passed by Congress is "distributive"—that is, it distributes benefits to a particular group while spreading the costs among the general public. Veterans' benefits and business tax incentives are examples.[46]

Such legislation, because it directly benefits a constituent group, is the type of policy that members of Congress are most inclined to support. It is also the type of policy that Congress, through its committee system, is organizationally best suited to handle. Most committees parallel a major constituent interest, such as agriculture, commerce, or labor.

The Representation Function of Congress

In the process of making laws, the members of Congress represent various interests within American society, giving them voice and attention in the national legislature. The proper approach to the **representation function** has been debated since the nation's founding. A recurrent issue has been whether the primary concern of a representative should be the interests of the nation as a whole or those of his or her own constituency. These interests overlap to some degree but rarely coincide exactly. Policies that are of benefit to the full society are not always equally advantageous to particular localities and can even cause harm to some constituencies.

representation function The responsibility of a legislature to represent various interests in society.

Representation of States and Districts

The choice between national and local interests is not a simple one, even for a legislator who is inclined toward either orientation. To be fully effective, a member of Congress must be reelected time and again, a necessity that compels him or her to pay attention to local demands. Yet, as part of the nation's legislative body, no member can easily put aside his or her judgment as to the nation's

CHAPTER 11 Congress: Balancing National Goals and Local Interests 351

Members of Congress are keenly sensitive to local opinion on issues of personal interest to their constituents. The representatives from urban areas are more supportive of gun control than are those from rural areas, where sport hunting is widespread.

needs. In making the choice, most members of Congress, it appears, tend toward a local orientation. They are particularly reluctant to oppose local sentiment on issues of intense concern. Support for gun control legislation, for example, has always been much lower among members of Congress from rural areas where sporting guns are part of the fabric of everyday life.

The committee system of Congress also promotes representation of local rather than national interests.[47] Although recent studies of committees indicate that the views of committee members are not radically different from the views of the full House or Senate membership,[48] committee membership is hardly random. Many senators and representatives sit on committees and subcommittees with policy jurisdictions that coincide with state or district interests. For example, farm-state legislators dominate the membership of the House and Senate Agriculture committees, and westerners dominate the Interior committees (which deal with federal lands and natural resources, most of which are concentrated in the West).

Constituency interests are also advanced by **logrolling,** the practice of trading one's vote with another member so that each gets what he or she most wants. The term dates to the early nineteenth century, when a settler would ask neighbors for help in rolling logs off land being cleared for farming, with the understanding that the settler would reciprocate when the neighbors were cutting trees. In Congress, logrolling occurs most often in committees where constituency interests vary. It has not been uncommon, for example, for agriculture committee members from livestock-producing states of the North to trade votes with committee members from the South where crops such as cotton, tobacco, and peanuts are grown.

Nevertheless, representation of constituency interests has its limits. A representative's constituents have little interest in most issues that come before Congress and even less information about them. Whether the government should appropriate a few million dollars in foreign aid for Bolivia or should alter patent requirements for copying machines is not the sort of issue that local

logrolling The trading of votes between legislators so that each gets what he or she most wants.

people are likely to know or care about. Moreover, members of Congress often have no choice but to go against the wishes of a significant portion of their constituency. The interests of small and large farmers in an agricultural state, for example, can differ considerably.

Representation of the Nation Through Parties

When a clear-cut and vital national interest is at stake, members of Congress can be expected to respond to that interest. The difficulty of using the common good as a routine basis for thinking about representation, however, is that Americans often disagree on what constitutes the common good and what government should do to further it.

Most Americans believe, for example, that the nation's education system requires strengthening. The test scores of American schoolchildren on standardized reading, math, and science examinations are significantly below those of children in many industrial democracies. This situation creates pressure for political action. But what action is necessary and desirable? Does more money have to be funneled into public schools, and which level of government—the federal, state, or local—would provide it? Or does the problem rest with teachers? Should they be subject to higher certification and performance standards? Or is the problem a lack of competition for excellence? Should schools be required to compete for students and the tax dollars they represent? Should private schools be part of any such competition, or would their participation wreck the public school system? There is no general agreement on such issues. The quality of America's schools is of vital national interest, and quality schools would serve the common good. But the means to that end are subjects of endless dispute.

In Congress, debates over national goals occur primarily along party lines.[49] Republicans and Democrats have different perspectives on national issues because their parties differ philosophically and politically. In the end-of-the-year budget negotiations in 1998 and 1999, for example, Republicans and Democrats were deadlocked on the issue of new funding to hire thousands of public school teachers. The initiative had come from President Clinton and was supported by congressional Democrats but opposed by congressional Republicans, who objected to spending federal (as opposed to state and local) funds for that purpose, and who also objected to the proposed placement of the new teachers (most would be placed in overcrowded schools, most of which are in Democratic constituencies). Democrats and Republicans alike agreed that more teachers were needed, but they disagreed on how that goal should be reached. In the end, through concessions in other areas, Clinton and the congressional Democrats obtained federal funding for new teachers, but it was obtained through an intensely partisan process.

Partisanship is the main source of division within Congress.[50] There are real and substantial differences between members of the two parties, such that they often vote on the opposite sides of legislative issues (see Figure 11–5). Party-line voting has been relatively high in the past two decades, reflecting the rise of party discipline in Congress and the widening gap between the Democrats and Republicans who serve there. There are now in Congress fewer liberal Republicans and fewer conservative Democrats, as well as fewer moderates of both parties.

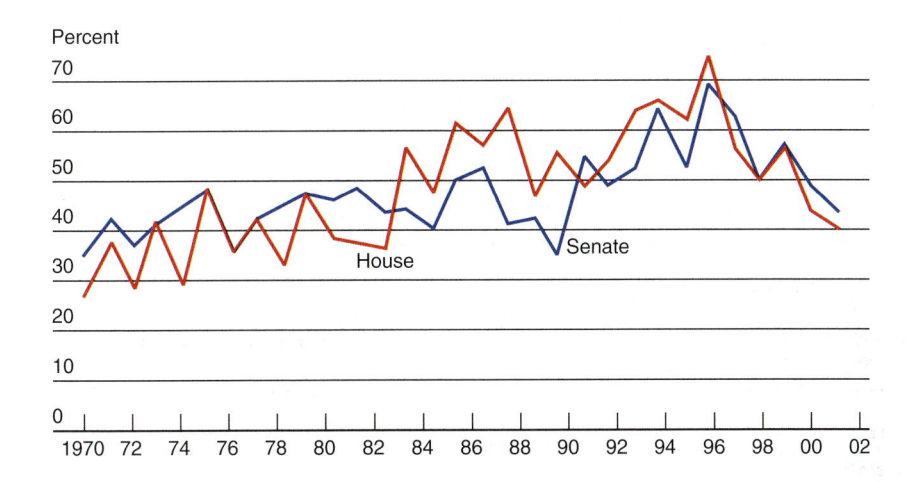

Figure 11-5

Percentage of Roll-Call Votes in House and Senate in Which a Majority of Democrats Voted Against a Majority of Republicans

Democrats and Republicans in Congress are often on opposite sides of issues; party-line voting has been relatively high since the 1980s.

Source: *Congressional Quarterly Weekly*, various dates.

Partisanship also affects the president's relationship with Congress. Presidents serve as legislative leaders not so much for the whole Congress as for members of their own party. More than half the time, opposition and support for presidential initiatives divide along party lines. Accordingly, the president's legislative success can depend on which party controls the Congress. After Republicans took full control of Congress in the 2002 elections, President Bush was in a stronger position to get his policy initiatives enacted into law.

In short, any accounting of representation in Congress that minimizes the influence of party is faulty. If constituency interests drive the thinking of many members of Congress, so do partisan values. In fact, constituent and partisan influences are often difficult to separate in practice. In the case of conflicting interests within their constituencies, members of Congress naturally side with those that align with their party. When local business and labor groups take opposing sides on issues before Congress, for example, Republican members tend to back business's position, while Democratic members tend to line up with labor.

The Oversight Function of Congress

Although Congress enacts the nation's laws and appropriates the money to implement them, the administration of these laws is entrusted to the executive branch. Congress has the responsibility to see that the executive carries out the laws faithfully and spends the money properly, a supervisory activity that is referred to as the **oversight function** of Congress.[51]

Oversight is carried out largely through the committee system of Congress and is facilitated by the parallel structure of the committees and the executive bureaucracy: the House International Relations and Senate Foreign Relations committees oversee the work of the State Department, the House and Senate Agriculture committees look after the Department of Agriculture, and so on. The Legislative Reorganization Act of 1970 spells out each committee's responsibility for overseeing its parallel agency:

> Each standing committee shall review and study, on a continuing basis, the application, administration, and execution of those laws, or parts of laws, the subject matter of which is within the jurisdiction of that committee.

oversight function A supervisory activity of Congress that centers on its constitutional responsibility to see that the executive carries out the laws faithfully and spends appropriations properly.

There are dozens of informal caucuses in Congress that aim to represent the concerns of particular constituencies. Pictured here is U.S. Representative Loretta Sanchez (D-Calif.), a member of the Hispanic caucus.

However, oversight is easier to mandate than to carry out. If congressional committees were to try to monitor all the federal bureaucracy's activities, they would have no time or energy to do anything else. Most members of Congress are more interested in working out new laws and looking after constituents than in laboriously keeping track of the bureaucracy. Although Congress is required by law to maintain "continuous watchfulness" over programs, committees have little incentive to take a hard look at programs that they have enacted or on which their constituent groups depend. Oversight normally is not pursued aggressively unless members of Congress are annoyed with an agency, have discovered that a legislative authorization is being grossly abused, or are reviewing a program for possible major changes.[52]

When an agency is suspected of serious abuses, a committee is likely to hold hearings. Except in cases involving "executive privilege" (the right to withhold confidential information affecting national security), executive-branch officials are compelled to testify at these hearings. If they refuse, they can be cited for contempt of Congress, which is a criminal offense. Congress's investigative power is not listed in the Constitution, but the judiciary has not challenged the power, and Congress has used it extensively.

Most federal programs must have their funding renewed every year, a requirement that gives Congress crucial leverage in its ongoing oversight function. If an agency has acted improperly, Congress may reduce the agency's appropriation or tighten the restrictions on the way its funds can be spent. A major difficulty is that the House and Senate Appropriations committees must review nearly the entire federal budget, a task that limits the amount of attention they can give any particular program.

Oversight conducted after the bureaucracy has acted has an obvious drawback: if a program has been administered improperly, some damage has already been done. For this reason, Congress in recent years has developed ways of limiting the bureaucracy's discretion in advance. One method is to include detailed

Senate Majority Leader Trent Lott of Mississippi (left) addresses the Senate impeachment trial on the day that the Senate voted to acquit President Clinton on two articles of impeachment.

instructions in appropriations bills. Such instructions serve to limit bureaucrats' flexibility when they spend funds on programs and provide a firmer basis for holding them accountable if they disregard the intent of Congress. Another oversight device is the **sunset law,** which fixes a date on which a program will end (or "fade into the sunset") unless it is renewed by Congress. Sunset provisions help to prevent a program from outliving its usefulness, because once its expiration date is reached, Congress can reestablish it only by passing a new law. The "legislative veto" is a more intrusive and controversial oversight tool. It requires that an executive agency have the approval of Congress before it can take a specified action. Legislative vetoes are under challenge as an unconstitutional infringement on executive authority, and their future is unclear.

The biggest obstacle to effective oversight is the sheer magnitude of the task. With its hundreds of agencies and thousands of programs, the bureaucracy is beyond comprehensive scrutiny. Even some of Congress's most publicized oversight activities are relatively trivial when viewed against the sheer scope of the bureaucracy. For example, congressional investigations into the Defense Department's purchase of small hardware items, such as wrenches and hammers, at many times their market value do not begin to address the issue of whether the country is overspending on the military. Overpriced hand tools represent pocket change in a defense budget of billions of dollars. The real oversight question is whether the defense budget as a whole provides cost-effective national security. It is a question that Congress has neither the capacity nor the determination to investigate fully.

Congress's zeal for oversight changes dramatically when allegations of scandal or wrongdoing attract national media attention. Then, members of Congress use the oversight process to hold high-profile hearings. The collapse of the Enron Corporation as a result of financial manipulation is an example. Several congressional committees held hearings in 2002 to grill Enron officials on the practices that led stockholders to lose billions of dollars and Enron employees

sunset law A law containing a provision that fixes a date on which a program will end unless the program's life is extended by Congress.

Why Should I Care?

Electoral Competition: Why It's Important to You

During the past half century, congressional elections have increasingly resulted in the reelection of incumbents. Their advantages are enormous. At taxpayer expense, they have a large staff in Washington and a smaller one in their district or state, and most of these staff resources are used to promote their standing with constituents. When an election year arrives, they also have a substantial fund-raising advantage as a result of their constituency contacts and the support they receive from interest groups that have a stake in gaining favor with members of Congress.

In combination with incumbents' other advantages, the effect of this support is to dampen electoral competition. About 95 percent of House incumbents are reelected. Their margin of reelection is typically very high. In recent House races, about two-thirds of incumbents have won by more than 60 percent of the vote. In fact, about one in six House incumbents have been reelected unopposed—the other major party did not even bother to field a candidate.

This situation weakens the voters' ability to influence government through their votes. When incumbents win almost as a matter of routine and when elections are one-sided, the vote is not a very powerful instrument. People may still vote out of a sense of civic duty, but they have no real reason to think, in most races, that it is going to make all that much difference. And because turnover in Congress is limited in any given election, the likelihood that an election will serve as a basis for major policy change is slim.

Electoral competition is the lifeblood of democracy. It is through their votes that ordinary people have the greatest chance of influencing the course of policy. But if that vote is diminished because of the enormous advantages of incumbency, the public's influence is diminished accordingly.

What do you think might be done to strengthen the competitiveness of congressional elections? Would you favor limits on the number of terms a member of Congress could serve? Would you favor public funding of elections? Would you favor reductions in the size of congressional staffs so that incumbents would have only the staff required for their legislative activities? Would you favor restrictions on PAC contributions?

---

to lose their retirement pensions. The hearings in the Democratic-controlled Senate were the more heated. Enron had close ties to President Bush and Vice President Cheney, and the Enron hearings gave Senate Democrats a chance to embarrass, and pressure the White House. Four years earlier, the parties' roles were reversed. Then, Republicans were in control of the House and Senate, and they held hearings on President Clinton's relationship with Monica Lewinsky, which led to Clinton's impeachment by the House and trial (in which he was acquitted) by the Senate. (Chapter 12 describes the impeachment process and the Lewinsky scandal in greater detail.)

CONGRESS: TOO MUCH PLURALISM?

Congress is an institution divided between service to the nation and service to the separate constituencies within it. Its members have responsibility for the nation's laws. Yet they depend for reelection on the voters of their states and districts and are highly responsive to constituency interests. This focus is facilitated by the committee system, which is organized around particular interests. Agriculture, labor, education, banking, and commerce are among the interests represented through this system. It is hard to conceive of a national legislature structured to respond to special interests more closely than the Congress of the United States. It is even harder to conceive of a national legislature that gives as much real power to these interests through committees as Congress.

Pluralists admire this feature of Congress. They argue that the United States has a majoritarian institution in the presidency and that Congress is a place where a *diversity* of interests are represented. Critics of this view say that Congress is sometimes so responsive to particular interests that the overall national interest is neglected. This criticism is blunted from time to time by a strong majoritarian impulse in Congress. The current period is one of these moments. The high level of party discipline in recent years, coupled with a widening ideological gap between the parties, has placed Congress at the center of many national policy debates, including the issue of the balance of power between Washington and the states.

The fact is, Congress cannot at once be an institution that is highly responsive both to diverse interests and to the national interest. These interests often conflict, as the rise and fall of former Speaker Newt Gingrich illustrates. He sought to make the Republican congressional majority into the driving force in American national politics, but was ousted from his position when the conflicts generated by this goal began to weaken the GOP's support in the states and districts, thereby threatening the reelection chances of Republican incumbents. This inherent tension between Congress's national role and local base has replayed itself many times in U.S. history. In a real sense, the strengths of Congress are also its weaknesses. The features of congressional election and organization that make Congress responsive to separate constituencies are often the very same ones that make it difficult for Congress to act as a strong instrument of a national majority The perennial challenge for members of Congress is to find a workable balance between what Roger Davidson and Walter Oleszek call the "two Congresses": the one embodied by the Capitol in Washington and other embodied by the members' separate districts and states.[53]

Self Quiz
www.mhhe.com/patterson6

SUMMARY

Members of Congress, once elected, are likely to be reelected. Members of Congress can use their office to publicize themselves, pursue a "service strategy" of responding to the needs of individual constituents, and secure pork barrel projects for their states or districts. House members gain a greater advantage from these activities than do senators, whose larger constituencies make it harder for them to build close personal relations with voters and whose office is more likely to attract strong challengers. Incumbency does have some disadvantages.

Members of Congress must take positions on controversial issues, may blunder into political scandal or indiscretion, must deal with changes in the electorate, or may face strong challengers; any of these conditions can reduce their reelection chances. By and large, however, the advantages of incumbency far outweigh the disadvantages. Incumbents' advantages extend into their reelection campaigns. Their influential positions in Congress make it easier for them to raise campaign funds from PACs and individual contributors.

Congress is a fragmented institution. It has no single leader; the House and Senate have separate leaders, neither of whom can presume to speak for the other chamber. The principal party leaders of Congress are the Speaker of the House and the Senate majority leader. They share leadership power with committee and subcommittee chairpersons, who have influence on the policy decisions of their committee or subcommittee.

It is in the committees that most of the day-to-day work of Congress is conducted. Each standing committee of the House or the Senate has jurisdiction over congressional policy in a particular area (such as agriculture or foreign relations), as does each of its subcommittees. In most cases, the full House and Senate accept committee recommendations about passage of bills, although amendments to bills are quite common and committees are careful to take other members of Congress into account when making legislative decisions. Congress is a legislative system in which influence is widely dispersed, an arrangement that suits the power and reelection needs of its individual members. However, partisanship is a strong and binding force in Congress. It is the basis for party leaders' ability to build support for major legislative initiatives. On this type of legislation, party leaders and caucuses rather than committees are the central actors.

The major function of Congress is to enact legislation. Yet the role it plays in developing legislation depends on the type of policy involved. Because of its divided chambers and committee structure, as well as the concern of its members with state and district interests, Congress, through its party leaders and caucuses, occasionally takes the lead on broad national issues. Congress also looks to the president for this leadership; nevertheless, presidential initiatives are passed by Congress only if they meet its members' expectations and usually only after a lengthy process of compromise and negotiation. Congress is more adept at handling legislation dealing with problems of narrow interest. Legislation of this sort is decided mainly in congressional committees, where interested legislators, bureaucrats, and groups concentrate their efforts on issues of mutual concern.

A second function of Congress is the representation of various interests. Members of Congress are highly sensitive to the state or district on which they depend for reelection. Members of Congress do respond to overriding national interests, but for most of them, local concerns generally come first. National and local representation often work through party representation, particularly on issues that divide the Democratic and Republican parties and their constituent groups.

Congress's third function is oversight, the supervision and investigation of the way the bureaucracy is implementing legislatively mandated programs. Although oversight is a difficult process, it is an important means of control over the actions of the executive branch.

KEY TERMS

bill
cloture
conference committee
constituency
filibuster
gerrymandering
jurisdiction
law
lawmaking function
logrolling
oversight function
party caucus
party discipline
party leaders
pork barrel projects
reapportionment
redistricting
representation function
rider
seniority
service strategy
standing committee
sunset law
veto

SUGGESTED READINGS

Galderisi, Peter, Marni Ezra, and Michael Lyons, eds. *Congressional Primaries and the Politics of Representation.* Latham, Md.: Rowman and Littlefield, 2001. A set of readings on the dynamics of congressional primary elections.

Hibbing, John R., and Elizabeth Theiss-Morse. *Congress as Public Enemy: Public Attitudes Toward American Political Institutions.* New York: Cambridge University Press, 1995. An analysis through survey and focus group data of Americans' attitudes toward Congress.

Jacobson, Gary C. *The Politics of Congressional Elections,* 5th ed. New York: Longman, 2001. An overview of the congressional election process and its impact on policy and representation.

King, David C. *Turf Wars: How Congressional Committees Claim Jurisdiction.* Chicago: University of Chicago Press, 1997. An innovative study on how congressional committees claim jurisdiction.

Krasno, Jonathan S. *Challenges, Competition, and Reelection: Comparing Senate and House Elections.* New Haven,

Conn.: Yale University Press, 1995. A comparison of the competitiveness of House and Senate races that uses National Election Study (NES) data as evidence.

Sinclair, Barbara. *Unorthodox Lawmaking: New Legislative Processes in the US. Congress*. Washington, D.C.: Congressional Quarterly Press, 1997. A detailed analysis of the American legislative process.

Witt, Linda, Karen M. Paget, and Glenna Matthews. *Running as a Woman: Gender and Power in American Politics*. New York: Free Press, 1993. A comprehensive study of the problems faced by women candidates.

LIST OF WEBSITES

http://www.rollcall.com
The online version of *Roll Call*, the newspaper of Capitol Hill. The site provides an insider's view of current developments within Congress.

http://thomas.loc.gov
Library of Congress site, named after Thomas Jefferson, that provides information about the congressional process, including the status of pending legislation.

http://www.house.gov
The U.S. House of Representatives' web page; it has information on party leaders, pending legislation, and committee hearing, as well as links to each House member's office and website.

http://www.senate.gov
The U.S. Senate's website, which is similar to that of the House and provides links to each senator's website.

12

[The president's] is the only voice in national affairs. Let him once win the admiration and confidence of the people, and no other single voice will easily overpower him.

Woodrow Wilson[1]

The Presidency:
Leading the Nation

George W. Bush was starting to sink in the polls. His approval rating, which had been slightly more than 60 percent, had dropped below 55 percent. The economy was weakening and the president was being criticized for not doing enough to help the unemployed. Bush had also been at the center of several controversies, most notably the defection of James Jeffords of Vermont, which cost Republicans control of the Senate. The White House had snubbed Jeffords at a ceremonial event marking education, an issue of passionate concern to Jeffords. The press was also starting to turn up the heat on the president. Journalists had accorded him the honeymoon traditionally given to a new president but were now settling into the critical mode that had become their trademark.

All of that changed after September 11, 2001. The terrorist attacks on the World Trade Center and the Pentagon led Americans to rally around their president, particularly after he delivered a stirring speech in which he committed the United States to a war on terrorism. He vowed that America would not rest until the perpetrators of the attack were brought to justice and the international terrorist network of which they were a part had been destroyed. Within a day of his speech, his presidential approval rating had jumped to 90 percent, the highest level ever recorded. It would continue upward, peaking at 96 percent as U.S. forces launched air attacks on the Al Qaeda and Taliban forces in Afghanistan. Not even Franklin Roosevelt and Harry Truman had registered approval ratings that high during the Second World War. The *Washington Post*'s David Broder compared Bush's response to the terrorist attacks to Abraham Lincoln's leadership at the outset of the Civil War.

The Bush story is but one in the saga of the ups and downs of the modern presidency. Lyndon Johnson's and Richard Nixon's dogged pursuit of the Vietnam War led to talk of "the imperial presidency," an office so powerful that constitutional checks and balances were no longer an effective constraint on it. Within a few years, because of the undermining effects of Watergate and of changing international conditions during the Ford and Carter presidencies, the watchword was "the imperiled presidency," an office too weak to meet the nation's demands for executive leadership. Reagan's policy successes before 1986 renewed talk heard in the Roosevelt and Kennedy years of "a heroic presidency," an office that is an inspirational center of American politics. After the Iran-Contra scandal in 1986, Reagan was more often called a lame duck. The first George Bush's handling of the Gulf crisis—leading the nation in 1991 into a major war and emerging from it with a stratospheric public approval rating bolstered the heroic conception of the office. A year later, Bush was on his way to being removed from office by the voters. Bill Clinton overcame a fitful start to his presidency to become the first Democrat since Franklin D. Roosevelt in the 1930s to win reelection. As Clinton was launching an aggressive second-term policy agenda, however, he got entangled in an affair with a White House intern, Monica Lewinsky, that led to his impeachment by the House of Representatives and weakened his claim to national leadership.

President George W. Bush addresses troops of the 101st Airborne Division upon their return to the United States from Afghanistan. Standing next to Bush is General Tommy Franks. The president's constitutional authority as commander in chief of the nation's armed forces is a major source of the office's power.

No other political institution has been subject to such varying characterizations as the modern presidency. One reason is that the formal powers of the office are somewhat limited, and thus presidential power changes with national conditions, political circumstances, and the personal capacity of the office's occupant.[2] The American presidency is always a central office in that its occupant is a focus of national attention. Yet the presidency is not an inherently powerful office in the sense that presidents routinely get what they want. Presidential power is conditional. It depends on the president's own abilities, but even more on the circumstances—on whether the situation demands strong leadership and whether the political support for that leadership exists. When conditions are favorable, the president will seem powerful. When conditions are adverse, the president will seem vulnerable.

This chapter examines the roots of the presidential power, the presidential selection process, the staffing of the presidency, and the factors associated with the success and failure of presidential leadership. The main ideas of this chapter are these:

- *Public expectations, national crises, and changing national and world conditions have required the presidency to become a strong office.* Underlying this development is the public support that the president acquires from being the only nationally elected official.

- *The modern presidential election campaign is a marathon affair in which self-selected candidates must plan for a strong start in the nominating contests and center their general election strategies on media, issues, and a baseline of support.* The lengthy campaign process heightens the public's sense that the presidency is at the center of the U.S. political system.

- *The modern presidency could not operate without a large staff of assistants, experts, and high-level managers, but the sheer size of this staff makes it impossible for the president to exercise complete control over it.*

- *The president's election by national vote and position as sole chief executive ensure that others will listen to the president's ideas; but to lead effectively, the president must have the help of other officials and, to get their help, must respond to their interests as they respond to the president's.*

- *Presidential influence on national policy is highly variable.* Whether presidents succeed or fail in getting their policies enacted depends heavily on the force of circumstance, the stage of their presidency, partisan support in Congress, and the foreign or domestic nature of the policy issue.

FOUNDATIONS OF THE MODERN PRESIDENCY

The writers of the Constitution knew what they wanted from a president—national leadership, statesmanship in foreign affairs, command in time of war or insurgency, enforcement of the laws—but could devise only general phrases to describe the president's constitutional authority. Compared with Article I, which enumerates Congress's specific powers, Article II of the Constitution contains relatively vague statements on the president's powers. This constitutional ambiguity, James W. Davis says, gives presidents "wide latitude in defining their presidential duties."[3]

Over the course of American history, each of the president's constitutional powers has been extended in practice beyond the Framers' intention. For example, the Constitution grants the president command of the nation's military, but only Congress can declare war. In *Federalist* No. 69, Alexander Hamilton wrote that a surprise attack on the United States was the only justification for war by presidential action. Nevertheless, the nation's presidents have sent troops into military action abroad more than two hundred times. Of the more than a dozen wars included in that figure, only five were declared by Congress.[4] All of America's most recent wars—the Korean, Vietnam, Persian Gulf, Balkans, and Afghanistan conflicts—have been undeclared.

The President's Constitutional Authority

Commander in chief. Article II, Section 2: "The President shall be commander in chief of the Army and Navy of the United States, and of the militia of the several states."

Chief executive. Article II, Section 2: "He may require the opinion, in writing, of the principal officer in each of the executive departments, upon any subject relating to the duties of their respective offices, and he shall have power to grant reprieves and pardons for offences against the United States, except in cases of impeachment."

Article II, Section 2: "He shall have power, by and with the advice and consent of the Senate, to make treaties, provided two thirds of the senators present concur; and he shall nominate, and by and with the advice and consent of the Senate, shall appoint ambassadors, other public ministers and consuls, judges of the Supreme Court, and all other officers of the United States, whose appointments are not herein otherwise provided for, and which shall be established by law."

Article II, Section 2: "The President shall have power to fill up all vacancies that may happen during the recess of the Senate, by granting commissions which shall expire at the end of their next session."

Article II, Section 3: "He shall take care that the laws be faithfully executed, and shall commission all the officers of the United States."

Chief diplomat. Article II, Section 2: "He shall have power, and with the advice and consent of the Senate, to make treaties, provided two thirds of the senators present concur."

Article II, Section 3: "He shall receive ambassadors and other public ministers."

Legislative promoter. Article II, Section 3: "He shall from time to time give to the Congress information of the state of the Union, and recommend to their consideration such measures as he shall judge necessary and expedient; he may, on extraordinary occasions, convene both houses, or either of them, and in case of disagreement between them, with respect to the time of adjournment, he may adjourn them to such time as he shall think proper."

The Constitution also empowers the president to act as diplomatic leader with the authority to receive ambassadors and the power to initiate diplomatic relations with other nations. The president is further empowered to appoint U.S. ambassadors and to negotiate treaties with other countries, subject to approval by the Senate. The Framers anticipated that Congress would have responsibility for developing foreign policy, while the president's job would be to oversee its implementation. However, the president has become the principal architect of U.S. foreign policy and has even acquired the power to make treaty-like arrangements with other nations, in the form of executive agreements. In 1937, the Supreme Court ruled that such agreements, signed and approved only by the president, have the same legal status as treaties, which require approval by a two-thirds vote of the Senate.[5] Since World War II, presidents have negotiated more than ten thousand executive agreements, as compared with fewer than one thousand treaties ratified by the Senate.[6]

The Constitution also vests "executive power" in the president. This power includes the responsibility to execute the laws faithfully and to appoint major administrators, such as heads of the various departments of the executive branch. In *Federalist* No. 76, Hamilton indicated that the president's real authority as chief executive was to be found in this appointive capacity. Presidents have indeed exercised substantial power through their appointments, but they have found their administrative authority—the power to execute the laws—to be of even greater value, because it enables them to determine how laws will be interpreted and applied. President Ronald Reagan used his executive power to *prohibit* the use of federal funds by family-planning clinics that offered abortion

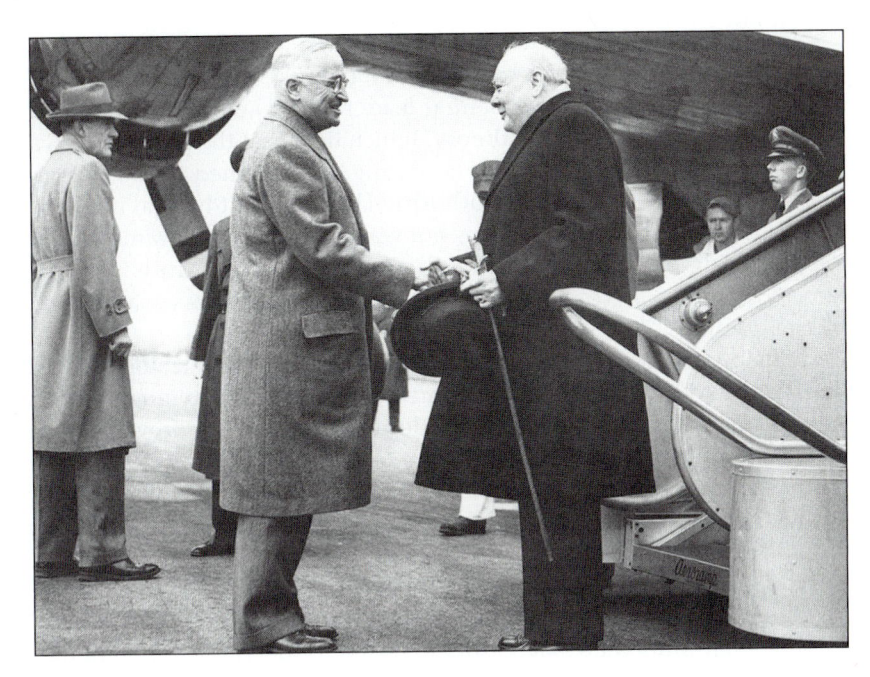

Harry S Truman's presidency was characterized by bold foreign policy initiatives. He authorized the use of nuclear weapons against Japan in 1945, created the Marshall Plan as the basis for the economic reconstruction of postwar Europe, and sent U.S. troops to fight in Korea in 1950. Truman is shown here greeting British Prime Minister Winston Churchill at a Washington airport in early 1952.

counseling. President Bill Clinton exerted the same power to *permit* the use of federal funds for this purpose. The *same* act of Congress was the basis for each of these actions. The act authorizes the use of federal funds for family-planning services, but it neither requires nor prohibits their use for abortion counseling, which enables the president to decide this issue.

Finally, the Constitution provides the president with legislative authority, including use of the veto and the opportunity to recommend proposals to Congress. The Framers expected this authority to be used in a limited and largely negative way. George Washington acted as the Framers anticipated: he proposed only three legislative measures and vetoed only two acts of Congress. Modern presidents have a different, more activist view of their legislative role. They routinely submit legislative proposals to Congress and often veto legislation they find disagreeable.

The presidency is a more powerful office than the Framers envisioned for many reasons, but two features of the office in particular—*national election* and *singular authority*—have enabled presidents to make use of changing demands on government to claim the position of leader of the American people. It is a claim that no other official can routinely make, and it is a key to understanding the role and power of the president.

Asserting a Claim to National Leadership

The first president to forcefully assert a claim to popular leadership was Andrew Jackson, who had been swept into office in 1828 on a tide of public support that broke the hold of the upper classes on the presidency. Jackson used his popular backing to challenge Congress's claim to national policy leadership, contending that he was "the people's tribune."

Historical Background

Whig theory A theory that prevailed in the nineteenth century and held that the presidency was a limited or restrained office whose occupant was confined to expressly granted constitutional authority.

Jackson's view of the presidency, however, was not shared by most of his successors during the nineteenth century, because national conditions did not routinely call for strong presidential leadership. The prevailing conception of the presidency was the **Whig theory**, which held that the presidency was a limited or constrained office whose occupant was confined to the exercise of expressly granted constitutional authority. The president had no implicit powers for dealing with national problems but was primarily an administrator, charged with carrying out the expressed will of Congress. "My duty," said President James Buchanan, a Whig adherent, "is to execute the laws . . . and not my individual opinions."[7]

Theodore Roosevelt rejected the Whig tradition when he took office in 1901; he attacked the business trusts, pursued an aggressive foreign policy, and pressured Congress to adopt progressive domestic policies. Roosevelt embraced the **stewardship theory**, which calls for a strong, assertive presidential role that is confined only at points specifically prohibited by law, not by undefined inherent restrictions. As "steward of the people," Roosevelt said, he was permitted "to do anything that the needs of the Nation demanded unless such action was forbidden by the Constitution or by the laws."[8]

stewardship theory A theory that argues for a strong, assertive presidential role, with presidential authority limited only at points specifically prohibited by law.

Roosevelt's image of a strong presidency was shared by Woodrow Wilson, but his other immediate successors reverted to the Whig notion of the limited presidency.[9] Herbert Hoover's restrained conception of the presidency prevented him from taking decisive action even during the economic devastation that followed the Wall Street crash of 1929. Hoover argued that he lacked the constitutional authority to establish public relief programs for jobless and penniless Americans. However, Hoover's successor, Franklin D. Roosevelt, shared the stewardship theory of his distant cousin Theodore Roosevelt, and FDR's New Deal signaled the end of the limited presidency. As FDR's successor, Harry Truman, wrote in his memoirs: "The power of the President should be used in the interest of the people and in order to do that the President must use whatever power the Constitution does not expressly deny him."[10]

Today the presidency is an inherently strong office.[11] The modern presidency becomes a more substantial office in the hands of a persuasive leader such as Ronald Reagan, but even a less forceful person such as Jimmy Carter is now expected to act assertively. This expectation not only is the legacy of former strong presidents but also stems from changes that have occurred in the federal government's national and international policy responsibilities.

The Need for Presidential Leadership of an Activist Government

During most of the nineteenth century (the Civil War being the notable exception), the United States did not need a strong president. The federal government's policymaking role was small, as was its bureaucracy. Moreover, the nation's major issues were of a sectional nature (especially the North-South split over slavery) and thus suited to action by Congress, which represented state and local interests. The U.S. government's role in world affairs was also small.

Today the situation has greatly changed. The federal government has such broad national and international responsibilities that strong leadership from presidents is essential.

Foreign Policy Leadership

The president has always been the nation's foreign policy leader, but the role was initially a rather undemanding one. The United States avoided getting entangled in the turbulent politics of Europe, and though it was involved in foreign trade, its major preoccupation was its internal development. By the end of the nineteenth century, however, the nation was seeking to expand the world market for its goods, and the size and growing industrial power of the United States was attracting more attention from other nations. President Theodore Roosevelt advocated an American economic empire and looked south toward Latin America and west toward Hawaii, the Philippines, and China (the "Open Door" policy) for new markets. However, the United States' tradition of isolationism remained a powerful influence on national policy. The United States fought in World War I but immediately thereafter demobilized its armed forces. Over President Woodrow Wilson's objections, Congress then voted against the entry of the United States into the League of Nations.

World War II fundamentally changed the nation's international role and the president's role in foreign policy. In 1945 the United States emerged as a global superpower, a giant in world trade, and the recognized leader of the noncommunist world. The United States today has a military presence in nearly every part of the globe and an unprecedented interest in trade balances, energy supplies, and other international issues affecting the nation.[12]

The effects of these developments on America's political institutions have been largely one-sided.[13] Because of the president's constitutional authority as chief diplomat and military commander and the special demands of foreign policy leadership, the president, not Congress, has taken the lead in addressing the United States's increased responsibilities in the world. Foreign policy requires singleness of purpose and, at times, fast action. Congress—a large, divided, and often unwieldy institution—is poorly suited to such a response. In contrast, the president, as sole head of the executive branch, can act quickly and speak authoritatively for the nation as a whole in its relations with other nations.

This capacity was rarely more evident than after the terrorist attacks of September 11, 2001. Nearly the entire initiative in the war on terrorism was centered in the White House. President Bush decided the U.S. response to the attacks and took the lead in obtaining international support for U.S. military, intelligence, and diplomatic initiatives. Congress was united in its support for Bush's actions but, in reality, had little choice but to endorse whatever policies he chose. In other situations, of course, Congress is less compliant. In recent decades, it has contested presidential positions on issues such as global trade and international human rights. Nevertheless, the president remains the dominant force in U.S. foreign policy and the leader to whom many countries turn when global problems surface. (The changing shape of the world and its implications for presidential power and leadership are discussed more fully later in the chapter.)

Liberty & Equality

What's Your Opinion?

The Presidency

When the Constitution was drafted, fear of executive power was widespread. The Framers worried that a too-powerful executive would threaten Americans' hard-won liberty and equality.

Ironically, presidents have been in the vanguard of efforts to expand liberty and equality. Thomas Jefferson, Abraham Lincoln, Franklin Roosevelt, and Lyndon Johnson are among the presidents whose names are nearly synonymous with such efforts.

Can this development be explained by the fact that the president has a nationwide electoral base? Unlike members of Congress, who often see things through the lens of a particular state or district, presidents tend to have a national perspective. Does this broader outlook also create a greater commitment to liberty and equality for all?

Another factor to consider is the nature of executive power. Unlike legislative power, which is widely shared, executive power is vested in a single individual. Have presidents taken the lead on issues of liberty and equality simply because of their greater ability to act assertively?

The White House contains, on the first floor, the president's Oval Office, other offices, and ceremonial rooms. The first family's living quarters are on the second floor.

Historical Background

Domestic Policy Leadership

The change in the president's domestic leadership has also been substantial. Throughout most of the nineteenth century Congress jealously guarded its constitutional powers, making it clear that domestic policy was its business. James Bryce wrote in the 1880s that Congress paid no more attention to the president's views on legislation than it did to the editorial positions of prominent newspaper publishers.[14]

By the early twentieth century, however, the national government was taking on regulatory and policy responsibilities imposed by the nation's transition from an agrarian to an industrial society, and stronger presidential leadership was becoming necessary. In 1921, Congress conceded that it lacked the centralized authority to coordinate the growing national budget and enacted the Budget and Accounting Act, which provided for an executive budget.[15] Federal departments and agencies would no longer submit their annual budget requests directly to Congress. The president would oversee the initiation of the budget by working the various agencies' requests into a comprehensive budgetary proposal, which would then be submitted to Congress as a starting point for its deliberations.

During the Great Depression of the 1930s, Franklin D. Roosevelt's New Deal responded to the public's demand for economic relief with a broad program that involved a level of policy planning and coordination that was beyond the capacity of Congress. In addition to initiating public works projects and social welfare programs aimed at providing immediate relief, the New Deal made the government a partner in nearly every aspect of the nation's economy. If economic regulation was to work, unified and continuous policy leadership was needed, and only the president could routinely provide it.

CHAPTER 12 The Presidency: Leading the Nation 369

Presidential authority has continued to grow since Roosevelt's time. In response to pressures from the public, the national government's role in such areas as education, health, welfare, safety, and protection of the environment has expanded greatly, which in turn has created additional demands for presidential leadership.[16] Big government, with its emphasis on comprehensive planning and program coordination, has favored executive authority at the expense of legislative authority. All democracies have seen a shift in power from their legislature to their executive. In Britain, for example, the prime minister has taken on responsibilities that once belonged to the cabinet or the parliament.

CHOOSING THE PRESIDENT

As the president's policy and leadership responsibilities changed during the nation's history, so did the process of electing presidents. The changes do not parallel each other exactly, but they are related politically and philosophically. As the presidency drew ever closer to the people, their role in selecting the president grew ever more important.[17] The United States in its history has had four systems of presidential selection, each more "democratic" than its predecessor (See Table 12–1). The justification for each new electoral system was **legitimacy**, the idea that the choice of a president should be based on the will of the people as expressed through their votes.

legitimacy (of election) The idea that the selection of officeholders should be based on the will of the people as expressed through their votes.

Toward a More "Democratic" System of Presidential Election

The delegates to the constitutional convention of 1787 were steadfastly opposed to popular election of the president. They feared that popular election would make the office too centralized and too powerful, which would undermine the principles of federalism and separation of powers. The Framers devised a novel system, which came to be called the Electoral College. Under the Constitution, the president is chosen by a vote of electors who are appointed by the states; the candidate who receives the majority of electoral votes is elected president. Each state is entitled to an elector for each member it has in Congress (House and Senate combined).

In choosing the nation's first presidents, electors acted somewhat independently, exercising their own judgment in casting their votes. This pattern changed after the election in 1828 of Andrew Jackson, who believed the people's will had been denied four years earlier when he placed first in the popular voting but failed to gain an electoral majority. Jackson could not persuade Congress to support a constitutional amendment that would have eliminated the Electoral College but did obtain the next-best alternative: he persuaded the states to tie their electoral votes to the popular vote. Under Jackson's reform, which is still in effect today, each party in a state has a separate slate of electors who gain the right to cast a state's electoral votes if their party's candidate places first in the state's popular voting. Thus the popular vote for the candidates directly

TABLE 12-1 The Four Systems of Presidential Selection

SELECTION SYSTEM	PERIOD	FEATURES
1. Original	1788–1828	Party nominees are chosen in congressional caucuses. Electoral College members act somewhat independently in their presidential voting.
2. Party convention	1832–1900	Party nominees are chosen in national party conventions by delegates selected by state and local party organizations. Electoral College members cast their ballots for the popular-vote winner in their respective states.
3. Party convention, primary	1904–1968	As in system 2, except that a *minority* of national convention delegates are chosen through primary elections (the majority still being chosen by party organizations).
4. Party primary, open caucus	1972–present	As in system 2, except that a *majority* of national convention delegates are chosen through primary elections.

Presidential nominating campaigns often attract a large number of contenders. Early in the 2000 presidential race, there were nearly a dozen GOP candidates. By the time of the first contests in Iowa and New Hampshire, six candidates still remained. Pictured here in one of their televised debates are (left to right) activist Gary Bauer, Senator John McCain, Governor George W. Bush, publisher Steve Forbes, former ambassador Alan Keyes, and Senator Orrin Hatch.

affects their electoral vote and one candidate is likely to win both forms of the presidential vote. Since Jackson's time, only Rutherford B. Hayes (in 1876), Benjamin Harrison (in 1888), and George W. Bush (in 2000) have won the presidency after having lost the popular vote.

Fighting Words

Should the Electoral College Be Abolished?

As the votes in the 2000 election were counted, the country was thrown into turmoil by the existence of the electoral vote system. The president is chosen by an indirect system of election. Voters cast ballots for candidates but their votes choose only each state's electors, whose subsequent ballots then result in the actual selection of the president. Electoral votes are apportioned by states based on their representation in Congress, which creates the possibility that the candidate who gets the most popular votes will not get the most electoral votes and thus not be elected president. The 2000 election was of this type, and it renewed calls for the abolition of the electoral vote system.

Yes: Only the President and Vice President of the United States are currently elected indirectly by the Electoral College—and not by the voting citizens of this country. All other elected officials, from the local officeholder up to United States senator, are elected directly by the people. Our bill will replace the complicated electoral college system with the simple method of using the popular vote to decide the winner of a presidential election. By switching to a direct voting system, we can avoid the result of electing a President who failed to win the popular vote.
—U.S. Representative Ray LaHood (R-Ill.)

No: Abolishing the Electoral College would be fine—as long as the American people are also willing to abolish the Senate. They serve a similar purpose in our democracy. When the Founding Fathers laid the foundation for our form of government, they created the Senate as a balance of power in Congress and as a means of equality between the states. When it came time to create a rule of law governing the election of a president, the Founding Fathers continued down this constitutional path of every state's right to a more equal voice, and established the Electoral College.
—U.S. Representative Richard Burr (R-N.C.)

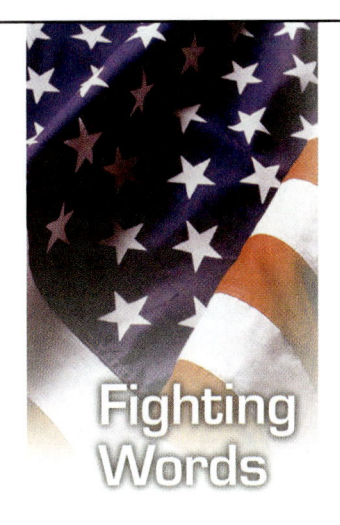

Jackson also championed the national convention as a means of nominating the party's presidential candidate (before this time, nominations were made by party caucuses in Congress and in state legislatures). The parties had their strength at the grass roots, among the people, and Jackson saw the convention process as a means of bringing the citizenry and the presidency closer together. Since Jackson's time, presidential nominees have been formally chosen at national party conventions. Each state party sends delegates to the national convention, and these delegates select the nominee.

Jackson's system of presidential nomination remained fully intact until the early twentieth century, when the Progressives devised the primary election as a means of curbing the power of the party bosses (see Chapter 2). State party leaders had taken control of the nominating process by handpicking their states' delegates. The Progressives sought to shift control to the voters by allowing them to select the delegates. Such a process is called an *indirect primary,* since the voters are not choosing the nominees directly (as they do in House and Senate races) but rather are choosing delegates who in turn select the nominees.

Through 1968, a strong showing in the primaries enabled a candidate to demonstrate popular support but did not guarantee nomination. In 1952, for example, Senator Estes Kefauver beat President Harry Truman in New Hampshire's opening primary and went on to win twelve of the thirteen primaries he entered; however, Kefauver was denied the Democratic nomination because party leaders believed his views were inconsistent with the party's traditions.

In 1968, the Democratic nomination went to Vice President Hubert Humphrey, who had not entered a single primary and was closely identified with the Johnson administration's Vietnam war policy. After Humphrey narrowly lost the 1968 general election to Richard Nixon, reform-minded Democrats forced changes in the nominating process. The new rules gave rank-and-file party voters more control by requiring that states choose their delegates through either primary elections or **open party caucuses** (meetings open to any registered party voter who wants to attend). Although the Democrats initiated the change, the Republicans were also affected by it. Most states that adopted a presidential primary in order to comply with the Democrats' new rules also required Republicans to select their convention delegates through a primary.

Today it is the voters in state primaries and open caucuses who play the decisive role in the selection of the Democratic and Republican presidential nominees.[18] A state's delegates are awarded the candidates in accordance with how well they do in the state's primary or caucus. Thus, to win the majority of national convention delegates necessary for nomination, a candidate must place first in a lot of states and do at least reasonably well in most of the rest. (About forty states choose their delegates through a primary election; the others use a caucus system.)

In sum, the presidential election system has changed from an elite-dominated process to one that is based on popular support. This arrangement has strengthened the presidency by providing the office with the reserve of power that popular election confers on democratic leadership.

The Campaign for Nomination

The modern presidential selection process is a long and grinding process that bears almost no resemblance to the way in which other democratic countries select their chief executives. When Tony Blair gained the office of British prime minister in 2001, the formal campaign lasted just a few weeks. By comparison, a U.S. presidential campaign officially spans nine months and actually starts much earlier. The main reason the U.S. campaign lasts so long is that the voters choose the nominees as well as the final winner. No European democracy uses primary elections as a means of choosing its nominees for public office.

The nominating system is basically open to any politician with the energy and resources to run a major national campaign. Nominating campaigns, except those in which an incumbent president is seeking reelection, often attract a half-dozen or more candidates. The 2000 Republican race, for example, at one time included nearly a dozen contenders, including a governor (Bush), a former governor (Alexander), a former vice president (Quayle), two U.S. senators (McCain and Hatch), a former cabinet member (Dole), a former ambassador (Keyes), a political advocate (Bauer), and a millionaire publisher (Forbes).

---

open party caucuses
Meetings at which a party's candidates for nomination are voted on and that are open to all the party's rank-and-file voters who want to attend.

Why Should I Care?

The Front-Loading of Presidential Primaries

Fifteen states in 2000 held their presidential primaries on March 7. So many contests were held on this day that opponents did not stand a chance against George W. Bush's and Al Gore's superior name recognition, financing, and organization. Bill Bradley quit the Democratic race the next day. John McCain retreated to his Arizona home and, two days later, announced he was dropping out of the Republican contest. Four years earlier, the races were also decided by early March. The 1996 and 2000 races ended before most states had held their primary or caucus. Voters in these states were effectively disenfranchised as a result.

The reason the races end abruptly is *front-loading*—the tendency of states to position their contests toward the front end of the nominating process. Front-loading exists because states gradually came to recognize that the power in the nominating process resides in the early contests. A state that holds back risks the chance of losing its opportunity to influence the outcome. Nevertheless, many states do hold back. Some small and medium-sized states realize their contest will not get much attention from the candidates if it is scheduled at the same time as a dozen contests that include several large-state primaries, including those of California and New York. Other states hold back because they have decided that a March primary is too soon in the year to select nominees for other offices. A statewide primary is expensive to run, and most states are therefore unwilling to conduct an early one for the presidential race and a later one for other races.

Nevertheless, enough states have moved to the front of the process to provide a huge advantage to a candidate with lots of money and high name recognition. In fact, every presidential nominee since 1984 has been the candidate who raised the most money in advance of the first contest. A poorly funded candidate can sometimes win in a single-state contest such as New Hampshire's primary, as McCain did in 2000, but after that, face-to-face campaigning gives way to televised political ads, which cost huge sums.

In *The Vanishing Voter* (2002), Thomas Patterson shows how front-loading has produced two different nominating electorates, one formed by residents of early-contest states and one comprised of residents of late-contest states. The first electorate chooses the nominees and is exposed to an active campaign, which includes televised advertising, candidate visits, and media attention. The second electorate has no meaningful voice in the process and is more or less ignored by the candidates and the media.

Which category is your state in? Does it hold its presidential nominating contest early or late in the process? (The 2000 schedule can be found at www.c-span.org/campaign2000/caucus&primary.asp)

A key to success in the nominating campaign is **momentum**—a solid showing in the early contests that leads to a buildup of public support in subsequent ones. If candidates start off strongly, the press will cover them more heavily, contributors will provide them more funding, and voters will give more thought to supporting them. For these reasons, presidential contenders now give extraordinary attention to the early contests, particularly the first caucuses in Iowa and the first primary in New Hampshire.[19]

Money is a critical factor in the nominating races. Money has long been a key to success in presidential politics, and its importance has grown in the last decade as states have moved their primaries and caucuses to the early weeks of the nominating period in order to increase their influence on the outcome. To compete effectively in so many contests in such a short period, candidates need money—lots of it. A candidate can only be in one place at a time, which requires

momentum A strong showing by a candidate in early presidential nominating contests, which leads to a buildup of public support for the candidate.

that the campaign be carried to other voters through televised political advertising. Ads are expensive to produce and air, and analysts claim that it takes at least $20 million to run a competitive nominating campaign. George W. Bush raised more than $70 million in 2000 for his successful nominating campaign, far more than any of his Republican rivals. In every nominating race of the past two decades, the winner has been the candidate who raised the most money before the start of the primaries.

Candidates in primary elections receive federal funding if they meet the eligibility criteria. The Federal Election Campaign Act of 1974 (as amended in 1979) provides for federal "matching funds" to be given to any candidate who raises at least $5,000 in individual contributions of up to $250 in each of twenty states. Candidates who accept matching funds must agree to limit their expenditures for the nominating phase to a set amount ($40.5 million in 2000), which is adjusted each election year to account for inflation. (Because Bush exceeded the spending limit in 2000, he was ineligible for matching funds.)

After the state primaries and caucuses have been held, the national party conventions occur. These were once tumultuous affairs during which lengthy, heated bargaining took place before a presidential nominee was chosen. An extreme case was the Democratic convention of 1924, at which delegates took 103 ballots and ended up nominating an unknown "dark horse," John W. Davis. Today's conventions are relatively tame; not since 1952 has a nomination gone past the first ballot. The leading candidate has usually acquired enough delegates in the primaries and caucuses to lock up the nomination before the convention even begins. Nevertheless, the party convention is a major event. It brings together the delegates elected in state caucuses and primaries, who then vote to approve a party platform and to nominate the party's presidential and vice presidential candidates.

By tradition, the choice of the vice presidential nominee rests with the presidential nominee. Critics have argued that the vice presidential nomination should be decided in open competition, since the vice president stands a good chance of becoming president someday (see Table 12–2). The chief argument for the existing method is that the president needs a trusted and like-minded vice president.

The Campaign for Election

The winner in the November general election is almost certain to be either the Republican or the Democratic nominee. A minor-party or independent candidate, such as George Wallace in 1968, Ross Perot in 1992 and 1996, or Ralph Nader in 2000, stands almost no chance of victory. A major-party nominee has the critical advantage of support from the party faithful. Although party loyalty has declined in recent decades (see Chapters 6 and 8), two-thirds of the nation's voters still identify themselves as Democrats or Republicans, and a substantial majority of them support the party's presidential candidate. Even Democrat George McGovern, who had the lowest level of party support among recent nominees, was backed in 1972 by 60 percent of his party's voters. To overcome this inherent disadvantage, a minor-party candidate would have to win the support of nearly all independent voters, many of whom have a latent Democratic or Republican preference. It is an impossible task for a candidate even as strong as Ross Perot

Simulation
www.mhhe.com/patterson6

TABLE 12-2 The Path to the White House

PRESIDENT	YEARS IN OFFICE	HIGHEST PREVIOUS OFFICE	SECOND-HIGHEST OFFICE
Theodore Roosevelt	1901–1908	Vice president*	Governor
William Howard Taft	1909–1912	Secretary of war	Federal judge
Woodrow Wilson	1913–1920	Governor	None
Warren G. Harding	1921–1924	U.S. senator	Lieutenant governor
Calvin Coolidge	1925–1928	Vice president*	Governor
Herbert Hoover	1929–1932	Secretary of commerce	War relief administrator
Franklin D. Roosevelt	1933–1945	Governor	Assistant secretary of Navy
Harry S Truman	1945–1952	Vice president*	U.S. senator
Dwight D. Eisenhower	1953–1960	None (Army general)	None
John F. Kennedy	1961–1963	U.S. senator	U.S. representative
Lyndon Johnson	1963–1968	Vice president*	U.S. senator
Richard Nixon	1969–1974	Vice president	U.S. senator
Gerald Ford	1974–1976	Vice president*	U.S. representative
Jimmy Carter	1977–1980	Governor	State senator
Ronald Reagan	1981–1988	Governor	None
George Bush	1989–1992	Vice president	Director, CIA
Bill Clinton	1993–2000	Governor	State attorney general
George W. Bush	2000–	Governor	None

*Became president on death or resignation of incumbent.

was in 1992. He gained just 30 percent of the independent vote—an extraordinary showing for a third-party candidate, but far short of what was required for victory.

On the other hand, a third-party candidate can draw enough votes away from a major-party nominee to tip the balance in a close election. The Green party's presidential nominee Ralph Nader got only 3 percent of the national vote in the 2000 election, but it came primarily at the expense of the Democratic nominee Al Gore (see Figure 12–1). If Nader had not been on the ballot, Gore would have received enough votes in the decisive state of Florida to beat his Republican rival George W. Bush in the presidential race.

Election Strategy

The candidates' strategies in the general election are shaped by many considerations, including the constitutional provision that each state shall have electoral votes equal in number to its representation in Congress. Each state thus gets two electoral votes for its Senate representation and a varying number of electoral votes depending on its House representation. Altogether, there are 538 electoral votes (including 3 for the District of Columbia, even though it has no

Figure 12-1
Support for Ralph Nader's 2000 Presidential Candidacy

Although Ralph Nader drew most of his 3 percent of the presidential vote from independents, he fared better with Democrats than with Republicans, which contributed to the Democratic presidential candidate Al Gore's defeat in 2000.

Source: The Vanishing Voter Project, Joan Shorenstein Center on the Press, Politics, and Public Policy, John F. Kennedy School of Government, Harvard University, 2000. Published by permission of The Vanishing Voter Project.

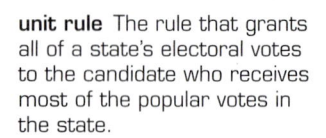

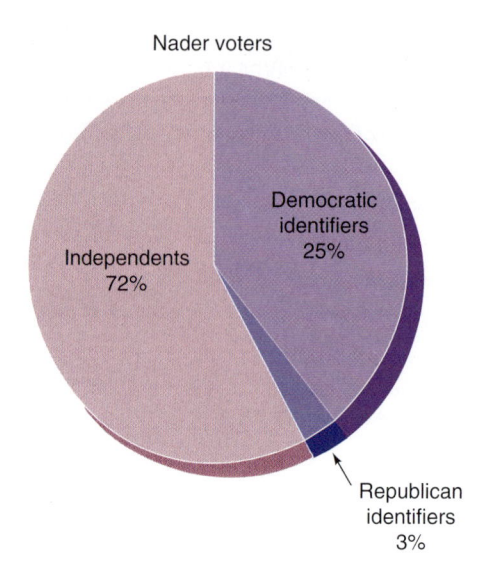

Nader voters
- Democratic identifiers 25%
- Independents 72%
- Republican identifiers 3%

unit rule The rule that grants all of a state's electoral votes to the candidate who receives most of the popular votes in the state.

voting representatives in Congress). To win the presidency, a candidate must receive at least 270 votes, an electoral majority. (If no candidate receives a majority, the election is decided in the House of Representatives. No president since 1824 has been elected in this way. The procedure is defined by the Constitution's Twelfth Amendment, which is reprinted in this book's appendix.)

The importance of the electoral votes is magnified by the existence of the **unit rule**; all the states except Maine and Nebraska grant all their electoral votes as a unit to the candidate who wins the state's popular vote. For this reason, candidates are particularly concerned with winning the most populous states, such as California (with 55 electoral votes), Texas (34), New York (31), Florida (27), Pennsylvania (21), Illinois (21), and Ohio (20). Victory in the eleven largest states alone would provide an electoral majority, and presidential candidates therefore spend most of their time campaigning in those states.[20]

In 2000, Bush was elected with 271 electoral votes, one more than required (see "States in the Nation"). Bush finished second in the popular voting, receiving 50.5 million popular votes to Gore's 51.0 million. Bush is the first president since Harrison in 1888 to win the presidency despite losing the popular vote. The 2000 election was decided by the Florida vote. Bush received Florida's 25 electoral votes by a virtue of 537-vote margin that excluded ballots that could not be read by voting machines. The U.S. Supreme Court blocked a count of these ballots (see Chapter 14).

Media and Money

The modern presidential campaign is a media campaign. At one time, candidates relied heavily on party organization and rallies to carry their messages to the voters, but now they rely on the media, particularly television.[21] Candidates strive to produce the pithy ten-second sound bites that the television networks prefer to highlight on the evening newscasts. They also rely on the power of the "new media," making frequent appearances on such programs as *Larry King Live* and creating their own Internet websites.

CHAPTER 12   The Presidency: Leading the Nation

STATES IN THE NATION

Electoral Votes and the 2000 Election

There are a total of 538 electoral votes, and a candidate must receive a majority to win the presidency. In 2000, George W. Bush was elected with 271 electoral votes—one more than required. Bush finished second in the popular voting, receiving 50.5 million popular votes to Al Gore's 51.0 million. Electoral votes are linked to popular votes—the winner of the popular vote in a state gets its electoral votes. (Exceptions are Maine and Nebraska where the statewide winner gets two votes and congressional district winners get one vote for each district they win.) Because electoral votes are allocated on a state-by-state basis, the loser of the national popular vote can gain an electoral-vote majority. Bush is the first president since Benjamin Harrison in 1888 to win the presidency in this way. The 2000 election was decided by the Florida vote. Bush received Florida's 25 electoral votes by virtue of a 537-vote popular margin that excluded ballots that could not be read by voting machines. The U.S. Supreme Court blocked a count of these ballots (see Chapter 14).

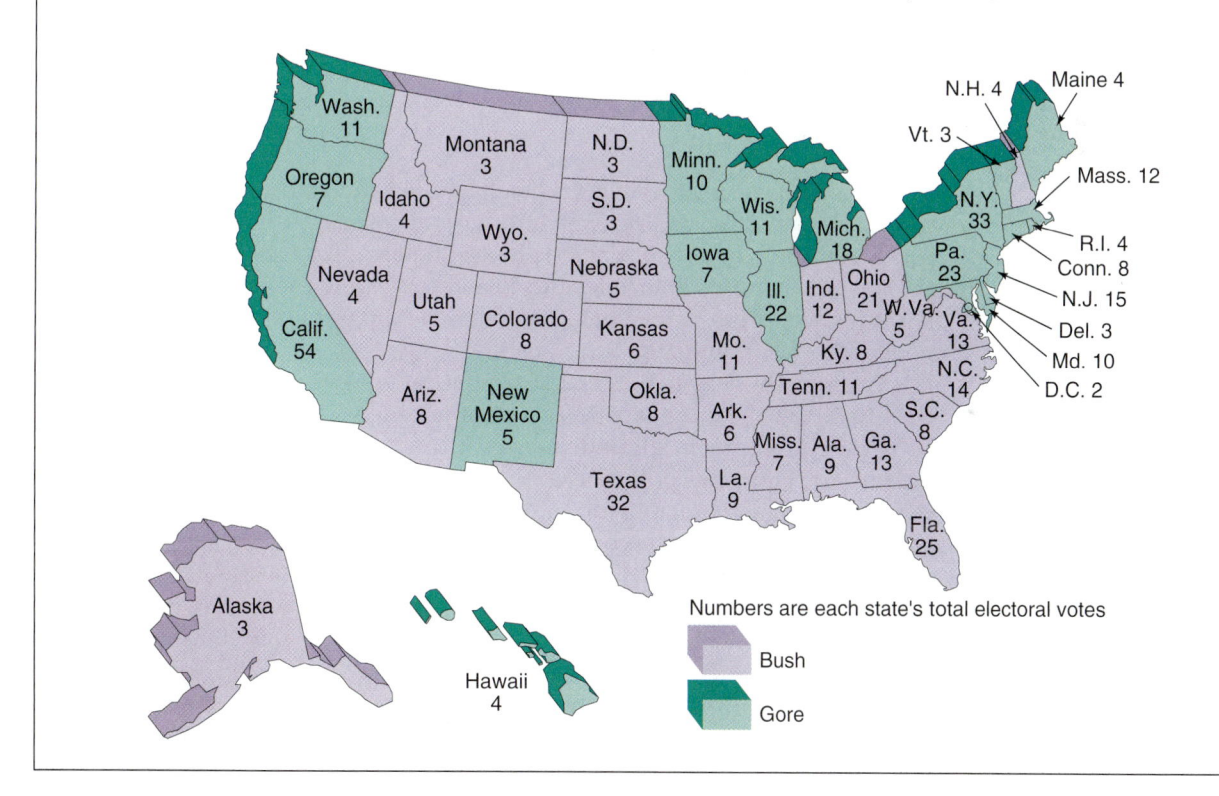

Numbers are each state's total electoral votes

- Bush
- Gore

State	EV	State	EV	State	EV
Wash.	11	Iowa	7	N.H.	4
Oregon	7	Ill.	22	Maine	4
Idaho	4	Ind.	12	Vt.	3
Montana	3	Ohio	21	Mass.	12
N.D.	3	Mich.	18	N.Y.	33
Minn.	10	Wis.	11	Pa.	23
S.D.	3	Mo.	11	R.I.	4
Wyo.	3	Ky.	8	Conn.	8
Nebraska	5	Tenn.	11	N.J.	15
Nevada	4	Ark.	6	W.Va.	5
Utah	5	Miss.	7	Va.	13
Colorado	8	Ala.	9	Del.	3
Kansas	6	Ga.	13	Md.	10
Calif.	54	La.	9	N.C.	14
Ariz.	8	Texas	32	S.C.	8
New Mexico	5	Okla.	8	D.C.	2
Alaska	3	Hawaii	4	Fla.	25

   Television is the forum for the major confrontation of the fall campaign: the presidential debates. The first televised debate took place in 1960 between Kennedy and Nixon, and an estimated one hundred million people saw at least one of their four debates.[22] Televised debates resumed in 1976 and have become an apparently permanent fixture of presidential campaigns. Elections are sometimes decided by a small margin, and the debates can make a difference. In 2000, Gore had an edge in the polls before the first debate. He was also the more experienced debater and had a firmer grasp of policy issues. But Gore drew a

> ## Formal and Informal Requirements for Becoming President
>
> *Formal requirements.* Article II of the U.S. Constitution requires a president to be:
>
> - At least thirty-five years old
> - A natural-born U.S. citizen
> - A resident in the United States for at least fourteen years
>
> *Informal Requirements.* In the nation's history, presidents have been:
>
> - Male, without exception
> - White, without exception
> - Protestant, with the exception of John F. Kennedy
> - Married, with the exceptions of James Buchanan and Grover Cleveland (who married in the White House)
> - Career public servants—four were army generals, thirteen were vice presidents (seven succeeded upon a president's death, one upon a president's resignation), eight were federal administrators, and the remainder were U.S. senators, U.S. representatives (only one), or state governors.

negative response from viewers when he huffed and grimaced while Bush was talking. Meanwhile, Bush gave a stronger performance than pundits had expected, which led them to conclude he had helped his candidacy. Gore was unable in the second and third debates to overcome fully the image created by his performance in the first debate, which some analysts believe was a turning point in the 2000 campaign.

The television campaign includes political advertising. Televised commercials are by far the most expensive part of presidential campaign politics. Since 1976, political commercials on television have accounted for about half the candidates' expenditures in the general election campaign. Although candidates typically emphasize their own candidacies in their ads, they do not shrink from attacking their foes. Media consultants have perfected what is called the "attack ad," a blistering assault on the opponent. A classic example is a 1988 Bush campaign ad that showed a revolving door that was meant to represent the Massachusetts prison furlough program. The ad implied that Dukakis, Bush's opponent and the governor of Massachusetts, was personally responsible for the actions of furloughed prisoners. One such prisoner was the notorious Willie Horton, who raped a Maryland woman and brutalized her husband after escaping during a prison furlough. The "revolving door" ad has been credited with helping Bush defeat Dukakis, who at one point in the race led by as many as fifteen percentage points.

The Republican and Democratic nominees are each eligible for federal funding of their general election campaigns even if, as in Bush's case in 2000, they did not accept it during the primaries. The amount for the general election was set at $20 million in 1975 and has been adjusted for inflation in succeeding elections. The major-party nominees in the 2000 presidential election each received $67.5 million. The only string attached to this money is that candidates who accept it can spend no additional funds on their campaigns (although the party can spend additional money on their behalf; see Chapter 8).

Candidates can choose not to accept public funding, in which case the amount they spend is limited only by their ability to raise money privately. However, all major-party nominees since 1976 have accepted public funding. Other candidates for the presidency qualify for federal funding if they receive at least 5 percent of the vote and do not spend more than $50,000 of their own money on the campaign. Such candidates receive an amount of funds equal to the proportion of their vote to the average of that of the two major-party nominees. In 1992, Perot spent over $60 million of his own money and thus was ineligible for federal funding. He accepted federal funding in 1996, receiving about half as much as the major-party nominees, since in 1992 his vote total was roughly half that averaged by the two major-party candidates. In 2000, Perot's party, the Reform party, received more than $10 million in federal funding by virtue of Perot's 8 percent of the vote in 1996.

The Winners

The Constitution specifies only that the president must be at least thirty-five years old, a natural-born U.S. citizen, and a U.S. resident for at least fourteen years. Yet the holding of high public office is nearly a prerequisite for gaining the presidency. Except for four army generals, all presidents had previously served as vice presidents, members of Congress, state governors, or top federal executives. The vice presidency in particular has been the inside track to the presidency (see Table 12–2); roughly a third of the nation's presidents first served as vice president.

The presidency has been monopolized by white males, but it is likely only a matter of time before the nation has its first minority-group president or its first woman president. Until the early 1950s, a majority of Americans in polls said they would not vote for a woman for president. By the 1990s, however, fewer than 10 percent held this view. A similar change of opinion preceded John Kennedy's election to the presidency in 1960. Kennedy was the nation's first Catholic president and only the second Catholic to have received a major party's nomination. Anti-Catholic sentiment was once a barrier to presidential election but no longer is.

Graphics
www.mhhe.com/patterson6

STAFFING THE PRESIDENCY

When Americans go to the polls on election day, they have in mind the choice between two individuals, the Democratic and the Republican presidential nominees. In effect, however, they are choosing a lot more than a single executive leader. They are also picking a secretary of state, the director of the FBI, the chair of the Federal Reserve Board, and a host of other executives, all of whom are presidential appointees.

Presidential Appointees

Newly elected presidents gain important advantages from their appointment powers. First, their appointees are a source of policy information. Modern policymaking requires a detailed understanding of policy issues, and this

Figure 12-2

Executive Office of the President (EOP)

The EOP helps the president manage the rest of the executive branch and promotes the president's policy and political goals.
Source: U.S. Government Manual.

Offices surrounding THE PRESIDENT:
- Council on Environmental Quality
- Council of Economic Advisers
- Office of Science and Technology Policy
- National Security Council
- Office of the United States Trade Representative
- Office of Administration
- Office of the Vice President
- Office of Management and Budget
- Office of Policy Development
- White House Office
- Office of National Drug Control Policy

knowledge is a source of considerable power in Washington. Second, these appointees extend the president's reach into the huge federal bureaucracy, exerting influence on the day-to-day workings of the agencies they head.

Not surprisingly, presidents have tended to appoint individuals who are members of their political party. They have also appointed individuals who can further their policy goals. In his initial appointments, President George W. Bush sought to create a team of experienced officials who could help to offset his lack of Washington experience. His appointees included General Colin Powell and Donald Rumsfeld, both of whom had held top positions in earlier Republican administrations. Powell and Rumsfeld played key roles in developing Bush's response to the terrorist attacks of September 11, 2001, on the World Trade Center and the Pentagon.

The Executive Office of the President

The key staff organization is the Executive Office of the President (EOP), which Congress created in 1939 to provide the president with the staff necessary to coordinate the activities of the executive branch.[23] The EOP has since become the command center of the presidency.[24] It currently consists of the Office of the Vice President and ten other organizations (see Figure 12–2). They include the White House Office (WHO), which consists of the president's closest personal advisers; the Office of Management and Budget (OMB), which consists of experts who formulate and then administer the federal budget; the National Security Council (NSC), which advises the president on foreign and military affairs; and the Council of Economic Advisers (CEA), which advises the president on the national economy.[25]

The Constitution assigns no policy authority to the vice president, whose role is determined by the president. Recent vice presidents, including Dick Cheney, pictured here with President Bush, have been assigned major policy responsibilities. Earlier vice presidents played smaller roles.

The Vice President Although the vice president works in the White House, no constitutional executive authority comes along with this office. Accordingly, the president decides the role the vice president will play. Earlier presidents often refused to assign any significant duties to their vice presidents, which diminished the office's appeal. Nomination to the vice presidency was refused by many leading politicians, including Daniel Webster and Henry Clay. Said Webster, "I do not propose to be buried until I am really dead."[26] Recent presidents, however, have assigned important duties to their vice presidents. George W. Bush, for example, chose Dick Cheney as his running mate in part because Cheney had been White House chief of staff and secretary of defense during previous Republican administrations. Once in office, Bush relied heavily on Cheney for policy and management advice.

The White House Office Of the EOP's ten other organizations, the White House Office serves the president most directly and personally. The WHO consists of the president's personal assistants, including close personal advisers, press agents, legislative and group liaison aides, and special assistants for domestic and international policy. They work in the White House, and the president can hire and fire them at will. The personal assistants do much of the legwork for the president and serve as a main source of advice. Most of them are skilled at developing political strategy, recognizing political opportunities, and communicating with the public, Congress, key groups, and the news media. Because of their closeness and loyalty to the president, they are among the most powerful individuals in Washington.

Policy Experts The president is also served by the policy experts in the EOP's other organizations, who include economists, legal analysts, national security specialists, and others. The president is advised on economic issues, for

Presidents rely heavily on their top-ranking cabinet officers and personal assistants in making major policy decisions. During the Cuban missile crisis in 1962, this group of advisers to President John F. Kennedy met regularly to help him decide on a naval blockade as a means of forcing the Soviet Union to withdraw its missiles from Cuba.

cabinet A group consisting of the heads of the (cabinet) executive departments, who are appointed by the president, subject to confirmation by the Senate. The cabinet was once the main advisory body to the president but no longer plays this role.

example, by the National Economic Council (NEC). The NEC gathers information to develop indicators of the economy's strength and applies economic theories to various policy alternatives. Modern policymaking cannot be conducted in the absence of such expert advice and knowledge.

The President's Cabinet

The heads of the fourteen executive departments, such as the Department of Defense and the Department of Agriculture, constitute the president's **cabinet**. They are appointed by the president, subject to confirmation by the Senate. Although the cabinet once served as the president's main advisory group, it has not played this role since Herbert Hoover's administration. As national issues have become increasingly complex, the cabinet has become outmoded as a policymaking forum: department heads are likely to understand issues only in their respective policy areas.[27] Cabinet meetings have been largely reduced to gatherings at which only the most general matters are discussed.

Although the cabinet as a collective decision-making body is a thing of the past, the cabinet members, as individuals who head major departments, are important figures in any administration. The president chooses them for their prominence in politics, business, government, or the professions. Many of them, like Powell and Rumsfeld, also bring to their office a high level of experience in public affairs.[28]

Other Presidential Appointees

In addition to cabinet secretaries, the president appoints the directors and top deputies of federal agencies, members of federal commissions, and heads of regulatory agencies. Altogether, the president appoints more than five thousand executive officials. However, most of these appointees are selected at the agency level or are part-time workers. This still leaves nearly seven hundred appointees who serve the president more or less directly, a much larger number than is appointed by the chief executive of any other democracy.[29]

The Problem of Control

Although the president's appointees are a valuable asset, they also pose a problem: because they are so numerous, the president has difficulty controlling them. Most appointees are not under the president's direct supervision and have considerable freedom to act on their own initiative—not necessarily in accord with the president's wishes. President Truman had a wall chart in the Oval Office listing more than one hundred officials who reported directly to him and often told visitors, "I cannot even see all of these men, let alone actually study what they are doing."[30] Since Truman's time, the number of bureaucratic agencies has more than doubled, compounding the problem of presidential control over subordinates.[31]

The nature of the control problem varies with the type of appointee. The advantages of having the advice of policy experts, for example, are offset somewhat by the fact that these experts often have little political experience and tend to exaggerate the importance of their particular policy interests. As a result, their proposals are sometimes impractical or politically unacceptable. On the other hand, top political appointees, while adept at politics, have a tendency to act too independently. WHO assistants tend naturally to skew information in a direction that supports the course of action they favor.[32] At times they even presume to undertake important actions without first obtaining clearance from the president or a chief assistant, leading others to question the president's authority or performance.[33] In 1996, for example, President Clinton found himself embroiled in controversy when it became known that a low-ranking White House assistant, Craig Livinstone, had unlawfully requested hundreds of personnel files from the FBI, many of them on top Republicans who had served in the Reagan and Bush administrations. "Filegate," as the incident came to be called, resulted in congressional hearings and news stories that were highly critical of Clinton's administrative oversight.

The problem of presidential control is even more severe in the case of appointees who work outside the White House, in the departments and agencies. The loyalty of agency heads and cabinet secretaries is often split between a desire to promote the president's goals and an interest in boosting themselves or the agencies they lead.[34] Lower-level appointees within the departments and agencies pose a different type of problem. The president rarely, if ever, sees them, and they are typically political novices (most have fewer than two years of government experience) and not very knowledgeable about policy. These appointees are often "captured" by the agency in which they work because they depend for advice on the agency's career bureaucrats. (Chapter 13 examines further the relationship between presidential appointees and career bureaucrats.)

In sum, the modern presidency is a double-edged sword. Presidents today have grater responsibilities than their predecessors, and the increase in responsibilities expands their opportunities to exert power. At the same time, the range of these responsibilities is so broad that presidents must rely on staffers who

HOW THE UNITED STATES COMPARES

Systems of Executive Policy Leadership

The United States instituted a presidential system in 1789 as part of its constitutional checks and balances. This form of executive leadership was copied in Latin America but not in Europe. European democracies adopted parliamentary systems, in which executive leadership is provided by a prime minister, who is a member of the legislature. In recent years, some European prime ministers have campaigned and governed as if they were a singular authority rather than the head of a collective institution. France in the 1960s created a separate chief executive office but retained its parliamentary form of legislature.

The policy leadership of a president can differ substantially from that of a prime minister. As a singular head of an independent branch of government, a president does not have to share executive authority but nevertheless depends on the legislative branch for support. By comparison, a prime minister shares executive leadership with a cabinet, but once agreement within the cabinet is reached, he or she is almost assured of the legislative support necessary to carry out policy initiatives.

PRESIDENTIAL SYSTEM	PRESIDENTIAL/ PARLIAMENTARY SYSTEM	PARLIAMENTARY SYSTEM
Mexico	Finland	Australia
United States	France	Belgium
Venezuela		Canada
		Germany
		Great Britain
		Israel
		Italy
		Japan
		Netherlands
		Sweden

may or may not act in the president's best interests. The modern president's recurring problem is to find some way of making sure that aides serve the interests of the presidency above all others. (The subject of presidential control of the executive branch will be discussed further in Chapter 13.)

FACTORS IN PRESIDENTIAL LEADERSHIP

The president operates within a system of separate institutions that share power (see "How the United States Compares"). Significant presidential action normally depends on the approval of Congress, the cooperation of the bureaucracy, and sometimes the acceptance of the judiciary. Since other officials have their own priorities, presidents do not always get their way. Congress in particular—more than the courts or the bureaucracy—holds the key to presidential success. Without congressional authorization and funding, most presidential proposals are nothing but ideas, empty of action.

Given that presidents must elicit support from others if they are to succeed, what is the record of presidential success? One way to judge is to measure the extent to which Congress backs legislative initiatives developed by the White House. No president has come close to getting enactment of all the programs that he has placed before Congress. The average success rate is just below

President Lyndon Johnson addresses a joint session of Congress in 1965. Johnson had an extraordinary record of success with Congress, which adopted the great majority of his legislative proposals.

50 percent, but there has been wide variation.[35] Johnson saw 69 percent of his 1965 initiatives enacted, whereas Nixon attained only 20 percent in 1973. Moreover, presidents have had markedly less success on their more ambitious proposals than on lesser ones.[36]

Whether a president's initiatives are likely to succeed or fail depends on several factors, including the force of circumstance, the stage of the president's term, the nature of the issue, the president's support in Congress, and the level of public support for the president's leadership. The remainder of this chapter examines each of these factors.

The Force of Circumstance

During his first months in office and in the midst of the Great Depression, Franklin D. Roosevelt accomplished the most sweeping changes in domestic policy in the nation's history. Congress moved quickly to pass nearly every New Deal initiative he proposed. In 1964 and 1965, Lyndon Johnson pushed landmark civil rights and social welfare legislation through Congress on the strength of the civil rights movement, the legacy of the assassinated President Kennedy, and large Democratic majorities in the House and Senate. When Reagan assumed the presidency in 1981, high unemployment and inflation had greatly weakened the national economy and created a mood for significant change, which enabled Reagan to persuade Congress to support some of the most notable taxing and spending changes in history.

From presidencies such as these has come the popular impression that presidents single-handedly decide national policy. However, each of these periods of presidential dominance was marked by a special set of circumstances: a decisive election victory that gave added force to the president's leadership, a compelling national problem that convinced Congress and the public that bold presidential action was needed, and a president who was mindful of what was expected and who vigorously advocated policies consistent with those expectations.

When conditions are favorable, the power of the presidency appears awesome. The problem for most presidents is that conditions are not normally conducive to strong leadership. The political scientist Erwin Hargrove suggests that presidential influence depends largely on circumstance.[37] Some presidents serve in periods when resources are scarce or when important problems are surfacing in American society but have not yet become critical. Such a situation, Hargrove contends, works against the president's efforts to accomplish significant policy change. In 1994, reflecting on the constraints of budget deficits and other factors beyond his control, Bill Clinton said he had no choice but "to play the hand that history had dealt him."

The Stage of the President's Term

If conditions conducive to great accomplishments occur infrequently, it is nonetheless the case that nearly every president has favorable moments. Such moments tend to come during the first months in office. Most newly elected presidents enjoy a **honeymoon period** during which Congress, the press, and the public anticipate initiatives from the Oval Office and are more predisposed than usual to support these initiatives.

honeymoon period The president's first months in office, a time when Congress, the press, and the public are more inclined than usual to support presidential initiatives.

Not surprisingly, presidents have put forth more new programs in their first year in office than in any subsequent year. James Pfiffner uses the term *strategic presidency* to refer to a president's need to move quickly on priority items to take advantage of the policy momentum that is gained from the election.[38] Later in their terms, presidents tend to do less well in presenting initiatives and getting them enacted. They may run out of good ideas or, more likely, deplete their political resources: the momentum of their election is gone and sources of opposition have emerged. Furthermore, if they blunder or if conditions turn sour—and it is hard for any president to serve for any length of time without a serious setback of one kind or another—they will lose some of their credibility and public support. Even highly successful presidents like Johnson and Reagan tend to have weak records in their final years. Franklin Roosevelt began his presidency with a remarkable period of achievement—the celebrated "Hundred Days"—but during his last six years in office, few of his major domestic proposals were enacted.

An irony of the presidency, then, is that presidents are usually most powerful when they are least knowledgeable—during their first months in office. These months can, as a result, be times of risk as well as times of opportunity. An example is the Bay of Pigs fiasco during the first year of John Kennedy's presidency, in which a U.S.-backed invasion force of anticommunist Cubans was easily defeated by Fidel Castro's army.

The Nature of the Issue: Foreign or Domestic

In the 1960s, the political scientist Aaron Wildavsky wrote that although the nation has only one president, it has two presidencies: one domestic and one foreign.[39] Wildavsky was referring to Congress's greater tendency to defer to

Secretary of State Colin Powell shakes hands with Israeli Prime Minister Ariel Sharon. The secretary of state is always a prominent member of the administration, a reflection of the president's constitutional authority in the realm of foreign affairs.

presidential leadership on foreign policy issues than on domestic policy issues. He had in mind the broad leeway Congress had granted Truman, Eisenhower, Kennedy, and Johnson in their foreign policies. Wildavsky's thesis is now regarded as a somewhat time-bound conception of presidential influence. He wrote before the Vietnam War had weakened congressional support for presidential leadership in foreign affairs. Today, many of the same factors that affect a president's success on domestic policy, such as the partisan composition of Congress, also affect success on foreign policy.[40]

Nevertheless, presidents are still somewhat more likely to get what they want when the issue is foreign policy, because they have more authority to act on their own and are more likely to get support from the opposite party in Congress.[41] The clash between powerful interest groups that occurs on many domestic issues is less prevalent in the foreign policy area. Moreover, foreign policy often springs from negotiations between nations. The president is recognized by other nations as America's voice in world affairs, and even when members of Congress disagree with the president's position, they sometimes accept it out of a concern for America's credibility abroad. In some cases, Congress effectively has no choice but to accept presidential leadership. When President Bush in his 2002 State of the Union address declared that Iraq, Iran, and North Korea were an "axis of evil," even members of Congress who might have questioned his choice of words or whether all three countries belonged on the list had little option but to express their support for Bush's leadership in the war on terrorism.

Presidents also gain some leverage in foreign and defense policy because of their commanding position with the defense, diplomatic, and intelligence agencies. These are sometimes labeled "presidential agencies." As chief executive, the president is in charge of all federal agencies, but in practice the president's influence is strongest in those agencies that connect with his constitutional

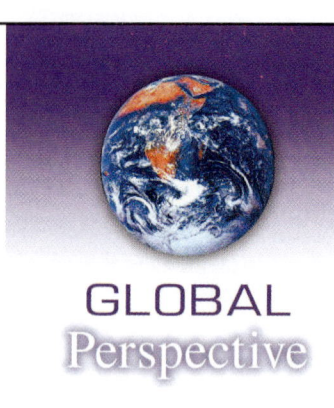

Americans in an Interdependent World

Fast-Track Authority on Trade

The president has always been the nation's foreign policy leader. Negotiations with other countries require that the nation speak with one voice so that these countries know where the United States stands on the issue under discussion.

Nevertheless, Congress is ordinarily unwilling to grant presidents a free hand in the area of foreign policy negotiations. In particular, it is not surprising that Congress has taken a keen interest in issues of international trade, because such trade has direct implications for U.S. firms and workers. An example is congressional ambivalence to granting the president fast-track authority on global trade. With this authority, the president can negotiate a trade agreement, which Congress then must accept or reject in its entirety. Without this authority, Congress retains the power to reject or accept specific provisions of an agreement.

Presidents naturally prefer fast-track authority. It allows a president to guarantee another nation that any trade agreement negotiated with the United States will, if accepted, be accepted in its entirety. Because trade negotiations involve concessions on both sides, other nations at least know that the concessions they gained in the negotiations will not be selectively deleted from the agreement.

Presidents at times have had fast-track authority. At other times, Congress has withheld it. Support in Congress for fast-track authority is strongest among advocates of unrestricted free trade and weakest among members who believe that, too often, labor and environmental issues are not given enough weight in trade negotiations and members who believe that important industries in their state or district are disadvantaged by global free trade.

Where do you stand on this issue? Should the president have fast-track authority, or does this grant of power unreasonably restrict Congress's ability to oversee presidential action in the area of international trade?

---

authority as chief diplomat and commander in chief, such as the departments of State and Defense and the CIA. These agencies have a tradition of deference to presidential authority that is not found in agencies that deal primarily with domestic policy. The Department of Agriculture, for example, responds to presidential direction but is also responsive (perhaps even more responsive) to farm-state senators and representatives. As Chapter 13 describes, bureaucratic support is important to a president's success with Congress, and that support is more likely to be forthcoming when the agency in question is part of the defense, diplomatic, or intelligence bureaucracy.

Relations with Congress

Although the presidency is not nearly as powerful as most Americans assume, the capacity of presidents to influence the agenda of national debate is unrivaled, reflecting their unique claim to represent the whole country. Whenever the president directs attention to a particular issue or program, the attention of others usually follows. But will those others follow the president's lead? The answer is sometimes yes and sometimes no, depending in part on whether the president takes their concerns into account.

Seeking Cooperation from Congress

As the center of national attention, presidents can easily start to believe that their ideas should prevail over those of Congress. This line of reasoning invariably gets any president into trouble. Jimmy Carter had not held national office before he was elected in 1976, so he had no clear understanding of how Washington operates.[42] Soon after taking office, Carter deleted from his budget nineteen public works projects that he believed were a waste of taxpayers' money, ignoring the importance that members of Congress attach to obtaining federally funded projects for their constituents. Carter's action set the tone for a conflict-ridden relationship with Congress.

In order to get the help of members of Congress, the president must respond to their interests as they respond to the president's. The political scientist Fred Greenstein concludes that "whatever else his qualities, the president needs to be a working politician who can work with or otherwise win over the Washington community."[43]

The use of the presidential veto illustrates the point. Presidents can sometimes force Congress to accommodate their views through the use or threatened use of the veto. Congress can seldom muster the two-thirds majority in each chamber required to override a presidential veto and so the threat of a veto can make Congress more responsive to the president's demands.[44] When a major civil rights bill was being debated in Congress in 1991, George Bush said flatly that he would veto any bill that imposed hiring "quotas" on employers; his ultimatum forced Congress to alter provisions of the bill. Yet the veto is more effective as a presidential restraint on Congress than as a device by which Congress can be forced to take positive action on the president's proposals. The presidential scholar Richard Neustadt argues that the veto is more a sign of presidential weakness than of strength, because it usually comes into play when Congress has refused to go along with the president's ideas.[45]

According to Neustadt, the most basic fact about presidential leadership is that it takes place in the context of a system of divided powers. Although the president gets most of the attention, Congress has most of the constitutional authority in the American system. The powers of the presidential office are insufficient by themselves to keep the president in a strong position. Congress is a constituency that all presidents must serve if they expect to get its support.[46] Neustadt concludes that presidential power, at base, is "the power to persuade."[47] Like any singular notion of presidential power, Neustadt's has limitations. Presidents at times have the power to command and to threaten. But Congress can never be taken for granted. Theodore Roosevelt expressed the wish that he could "be the president and Congress, too," if only for a day, so that he would have the power to enact as well as propose laws.

Partisan Support in Congress

For most presidents, the next-best-thing to being "Congress, too" is to have a Congress filled with members of their own party. The sources of division within Congress are many. Legislators from urban and rural areas, wealthier and poorer constituencies, and different regions of the country often have very different views of the national interest. To obtain majority support in Congress, the president must find ways to overcome these differences.

Figure 12-3

Percentage of Bills Passed by Congress on Which the President Announced a Position, 1953–2001

In most years, presidents have been supported by Congress on a majority of policy issues on which they have taken a stand. Presidents fare better when their party controls Congress.

Source: *Congressional Quarterly Weekly Report*, various dates. Used by permission.

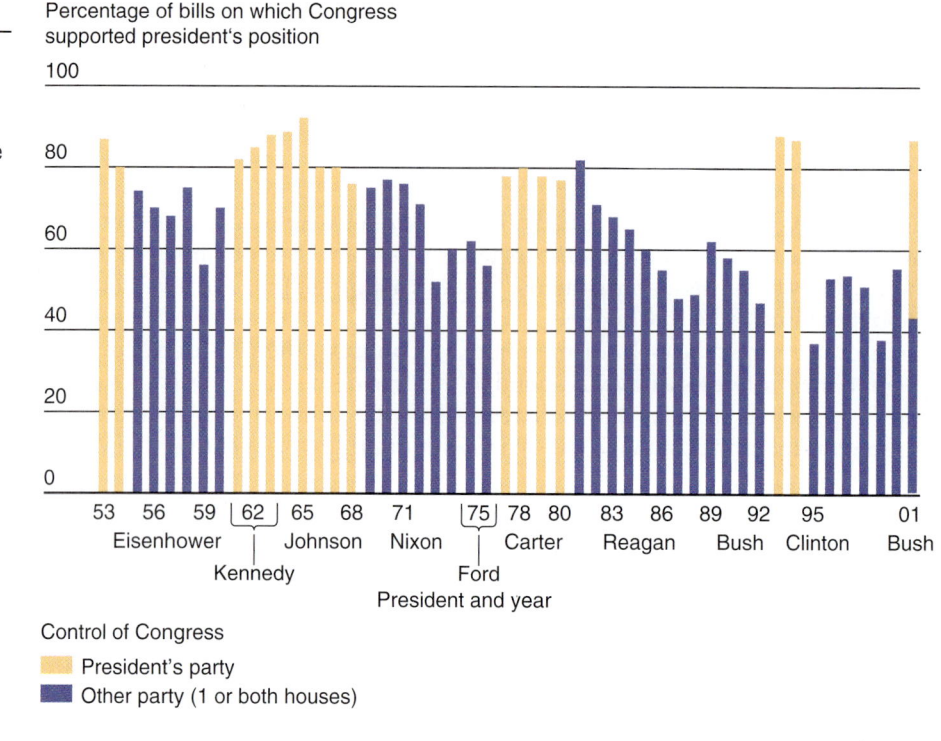

Control of Congress
- President's party
- Other party (1 or both houses)

No source of unity is more important to presidential success than partisanship. Presidents are more likely to succeed when their own party controls Congress (see Figure 12-3). Between 1954 and 1992, each Republican president—Eisenhower, Nixon, Ford, Reagan, and Bush—had to contend with a Democratic majority in one or both houses of Congress. Congress passed a smaller percentage of the initiatives supported by each of these presidents than by any Democratic president of the period: Kennedy, Johnson, or Carter.[48] In his first two years in office, backed by Democratic majorities in the House and Senate, Clinton had a high proportion of his initiatives enacted into law. After Republicans took control of Congress in 1995, Clinton's legislative success rate sank to the lowest of any recent Democratic president, a dramatic illustration of the way presidential power is affected by whether the president's party controls Congress.

In 2001, George W. Bush had an 87 percent success rate, the highest since Lyndon Johnson's 93 percent in 1965. Bush's extraordinary success in winning congressional support was achieved in a way never before seen. When he took office, his Republican party controlled both the House and the Senate, which virtually ensured a responsive Congress. In mid-summer, however, Senator James Jeffords of Vermont bolted the GOP, leaving the Democrats in control of the Senate. This shift occurred shortly before Congress's summer recess, which meant few bills were considered in the first weeks after Jeffords's defection. Then, shortly after Congress resumed its work, terrorist attacks on the World Trade Center and the Pentagon led congressional members of both parties to rally behind the president. After September 11, Bush won eleven of twelve House votes and thirty of thirty-one Senate votes, contributing to the highest presidential success rate in more than three decades.

Colliding with Congress

On rare occasions, presidents have pursued their goals so zealously that Congress has been compelled to take steps to curb their use of power.

The ultimate sanction of Congress is its constitutional power to impeach and remove the president from office. The House of Representatives decides whether the president should be impeached (placed on trial), and the Senate conducts the trial and then votes on the president's guilt, with a two-thirds vote required for removal from office. In 1868, Andrew Johnson was impeached and came within one Senate vote of being removed from office for his opposition to Congress's harsh Reconstruction policies after the Civil War. In 1974, Richard Nixon's resignation halted congressional proceedings on the Watergate affair that would almost certainly have ended in his impeachment and removal from office.

The prospect of impeachment was raised again in 1998 when the House of Representatives by a vote of 258 to 176 authorized an investigation of President Clinton's conduct. He was accused of lying under oath about his relationship with Monica Lewinsky and of obstructing justice by trying to conceal the affair. The gravity of the allegations was leavened by the circumstances. The charges had grown out of an extramarital affair rather than a gross abuse of executive power and were tied to a controversial five-year $40-million investigation by independent counsel Kenneth Starr. For their part, the American people were ambivalent about the whole issue. Most people approved of Clinton's handling of the presidency and did not believe his actions warranted removal from office, but they were also critical of his relationship with Lewinsky. Not surprisingly, congressional Republicans and Democrats differed sharply on the impeachment issue. At all formal stages of the process—the House vote to authorize an inquiry, the House vote on the articles of impeachment, and the Senate vote on whether to convict the president—the vote divided largely along party lines. In the end, Clinton was acquitted by the Senate, but his legacy will forever be tarnished by his impeachment by the House.

The gravity of impeachment action makes it an unsuitable basis for curbing presidential power except in rare instances. More often, Congress has responded legislatively to executive abuses. An example is the Budget Impoundment and Control Act of 1974, which prohibits a president from refusing to release funds that have been appropriated by Congress. The legislation was enacted in response to the Nixon administration's practice of withholding funds from programs it disliked.

Congress's most significant effort in history to curb presidential power, however, is the War Powers Act. During the Vietnam War, presidents Johnson and Nixon repeatedly misled Congress, supplying it with intelligence estimates that painted a falsely optimistic picture of the military situation. This information contributed to the willingness of Congress to appropriate the funds necessary for continuation of the war. However, congressional support changed abruptly in 1971 with *The New York Times's* publication of classified documents (the so-called Pentagon Papers) that revealed the Vietnam situation to be much worse than portrayed by Johnson and Nixon.

To prevent future presidential wars, Congress in 1973 passed the War Powers Act. Nixon vetoed the measure, but Congress overrode his veto. The act requires the president to notify Congress of the reason for committing combat troops within forty-eight hours of their deployment; requires that hostilities

Simulation
www.mhhe.com/patterson6

Richard M. Nixon
(1913–1994)

Richard Nixon is one of the most controversial presidents in the nation's history. His presidency saw major triumphs, including the reestablishment of relations with China and the reduction of tensions with the Soviet Union. However, his presidency also included major reversals. He was forced to resign his office because of the Watergate scandal, and his high-handed actions led Congress to enact the War Powers Act and the Budget Impoundment Act, which restricted presidential authority. Before gaining the presidency, Nixon served as a U.S. representative, U.S. senator, and vice president. He narrowly lost to John F. Kennedy in the 1960 presidential election. He gained the presidency by narrowly defeating Hubert Humphrey in 1968.

---

must end within sixty days unless Congress extends the period; gives the president an additional thirty days to withdraw the troops from hostile territory, although Congress can shorten the period; and requires the president to consult with Congress whenever feasible before dispatching troops into a hostile situation.

Every president since Nixon has claimed that the act infringes on his constitutional power as commander in chief, and each has refused to accept it fully. Nevertheless, the War Powers Act is a potentially significant constraint on the president's warmaking power.

Thus the effect of executive efforts to circumvent congressional authority is heightened congressional opposition. Even if presidents gain in the short run by acting on their own, they undermine their capacity to lead in the long run by failing to keep in mind that Congress is a coequal branch of the American governing system.

Nurturing Public Support

Public support has a powerful effect on presidents' ability to achieve their policy goals.[49] Much of their power rests on a claim to national leadership, and the legitimacy of that claim is roughly proportional to public support of the president's performance. With public backing, the president's leadership cannot easily be dismissed by other Washington officials. If public support sinks, they are less inclined to accept presidential leadership.[50]

Every recent president has had the public's confidence at the very start of the term of office. When asked in polls whether they "approve or disapprove of how the president is doing his job," a majority have expressed approval during the first months of the term. Sooner or later, however, all **presidential approval ratings** have slipped below this high point, and fewer than half of recent presidents have left office with a final-year average higher than 50 percent (see Table 12–3).

presidential approval rating
A measure of the degree to which the public approves or disapproves of the president's performance in office.

Events and Issues

The public's support for the president is affected by national and international conditions. Threats from abroad tend to produce a patriotic "rally 'round the flag" reaction that initially creates widespread support for the president. Every foreign policy crisis in the past four decades has fitted this pattern. The preeminent example, of course, is Americans' response to the terrorist attacks on the World Trade Center and the Pentagon. Not only did Americans rise in support of President Bush's leadership, pushing his approval rating to the highest in history, they rose in support of the flag itself. Four of every five Americans flew the flag in one form or another, whether on their home, their vehicle, or their lapel.

Ongoing crises, however, can eventually erode a president's support if they are not resolved or pursued successfully. Public support for Franklin D.

Impeaching, Convicting, and Removing the President

In October 1998, for only the third time in American history, Congress authorized an official impeachment investigation of the president of the United States. Bill Clinton joined Andrew Johnson and Richard Nixon as presidents whose legacy will be forever linked with the word *impeachment*.

Although *impeachment* technically applies only to the indictment stage of congressional action, it is commonly used to refer also to the conviction stage. But these are separate stages, and the Constitution divides the responsibility for them. The House is granted under Article I, Section 2 of the Constitution the power to impeach (indict) the president. The Senate under Article I, Section 3 has the power to try, convict, and remove the president.

The Constitution is not overly specific on the presidential acts that would justify the removal from office. Article II, Section 4 states that impeachable acts are "Treason, Bribery, or Other High Crimes and Misdemeanors" but does not spell out what these other high crimes and misdemeanors shall include. Any such definition in the context of the presidential office would necessarily be somewhat subjective. As a result, the impeachment process is inevitably a political as well as a constitutional one. Nevertheless, it can be assumed that the contemporary use of the term *misdemeanors* includes lesser crimes (such as a speeding ticket) than the writers of the Constitution would have had in mind. It is also clear from the historical record that the Framers deliberately created a process that would make it difficult to remove the president from office in order to discourage Congress from seeking to get rid of a president for purely political reasons.

The steps that Congress would take in removing the president from office are the following:

1. The House of Representatives by simple majority vote would authorize an investigation of the president.
2. The House Judiciary Committee would conduct the inquiry and submit its findings to the full House.
3. The House through simple majority vote would indict the president on one or more charges (thus "impeaching" the president).
4. The Senate would hold a trial on the charges. The chief justice of the Supreme Court would preside over the trial, and the senators would be under oath to express themselves truthfully.
5. The Senate through a two-thirds majority would convict, causing the president's removal from office. The Senate would be prohibited from imposing any additional penalty (although subsequent action against the president in a court of law would not be precluded).

The Clinton impeachment process ended with step 4; the Senate did not vote to convict. The course of Andrew Johnson's impeachment was the same, although the Senate, in his case, came within one vote of conviction. Nixon resigned shortly before the House vote on impeachment (step 3).

Roosevelt stayed high throughout World War II as U.S. forces fought their way through Europe and the Pacific. On the other hand, Jimmy Carter's public support slipped away during the year-long Iranian hostage crisis. Within a month after Iranian extremists invaded the U.S. embassy in Teheran in November 1979 and took fifty-nine Americans hostage, Carter's public approval rating jumped by twenty points.[51] As months passed without a resolution of the hostage situation, however, Carter's popularity began to sink and his hold on the presidency began to slip. He lost the 1980 election, partly because the hostage crisis remained unresolved.

Economic downswings tend to sharply reduce the public's confidence in the president.[52] Ford, Carter, and the first President Bush experienced precipitous declines in popularity in conjunction with deepening economic problems. A poor economy probably cost Ford a second term and was clearly the key factor in the failed bids for reelection of both presidents Carter and Bush. In contrast, Clinton's popularity rose in 1995 and 1996 as the economy strengthened,

TABLE 12–3 — Percentage of Public Expressing Approval of President's Performance

Presidential approval ratings are generally higher at the beginning of the term than at the end.

PRESIDENT	YEARS IN OFFICE	AVERAGE DURING PRESIDENCY	FIRST-YEAR AVERAGE	FINAL-YEAR AVERAGE
Harry Truman	1945–1952	41%	63%	35%
Dwight Eisenhower	1953–1960	64	74	62
John Kennedy	1961–1963	70	76	62
Lyndon Johnson	1963–1968	55	78	40
Richard Nixon	1969–1974	49	63	24
Gerald Ford	1974–1976	46	75	48
Jimmy Carter	1977–1980	47	68	46
Ronald Reagan	1981–1989	53	58	57
George Bush	1989–1992	61	65	40
Bill Clinton	1993–2000	57	50	60
George W. Bush	2001–	—	68	—

Source: Averages compiled from Gallup polls.

contributing to his reelection in 1996. In 2002, a slumping economy cost George W. Bush some of the support generated by his pursuit of the war on terrrorism. Apparently the best thing in most cases that a president can do to ensure long-term political success is to preside over a healthy economy.

The irony, of course, is that presidents do not actually have all that much control over the economy. If they did, it would always be strong. Nevertheless, their popularity moves up and down with the economy, and so does the strength of their claim to national leadership.

The Televised Presidency

A major advantage that presidents enjoy in their efforts to nurture public support is their guaranteed access to the media, particularly television.[53] The television medium exalts personality, and the president is ordinarily the most compelling and familiar figure in the American political system. Only the president can expect the television networks to provide free air time on occasion, and in terms of the amount of news coverage, the president and his top advisors receive half again as much coverage as all members of Congress combined.

The political scientist Samuel Kernell calls it "going public" when the president bypasses inside bargaining with Congress and promotes "himself and his policies by appealing to the American public for support."[54] Such appeals are at least as old as Theodore Roosevelt's use of the presidency as a "bully pulpit" but have increased substantially in recent years.[55] As the president has moved from the role of administrative leader to that of policy advocate and agenda setter, public support has become increasingly important to presidential success.[56] Television has made it easier for presidents to go public with their programs. Ronald Reagan was called the "Great Communicator" in part because of his ability to use television to generate public support for his initiatives.

Bush press secretary Ari Fleischer briefs reporters in the cramped space of the White House briefing room. Effective communication is an essential part of the modern presidency.

However, the press is also adept at putting its own spin on events, and this spin is typically a negative one. The press is often very critical of politicians and of the process within which they operate. During Clinton's first year, for example, the press roundly criticized him for reneging on his campaign promises. This for a president who according to a Knight-Ridder summary had kept or was actively pursuing in Congress 75 percent of the promises he had made during his election campaign; included were major legislative battles already won, such as a tax increase on upper incomes, gun control, an end to the ban on abortion counseling in federally funded clinics, and budget-deficit reduction. The press's version of reality was based on broken promises on a couple of problems that would not go away. Clinton had backed away from a pledge to open the nation's shores to the Haitian boat people, and each tide of immigrants produced additional stories on his broken promise. In contrast, the promises he kept were in the news only a day or two and then not mentioned again. Kept promises are not nearly so newsworthy as broken ones. The media's interpretation of Clinton's presidency had a substantial impact. Every rise in the press criticism of Clinton was followed soon thereafter by a drop in his public approval rating.

Scandal is the biggest threat to the president's ability to control the news agenda. When scandal strikes, a media "feeding frenzy" ensues, and power shifts from the White House to the press and the president's political opponents. The Clinton-Lewinsky scandal is a prime example. Throughout 1998, it was at the top of the news. Clinton's efforts to direct the nation's attention to other issues, such as the financial crisis spreading across Asia, were unsuccessful. In less dramatic fashion, the flurry of accounting scandals that came to light in 2002 enabled the press to disrupt the Bush administration's efforts to control the policy agenda. The press played up the contributions that Enron, Worldcom, and other errant corporations had made to Bush's 2000 campaign and also dug up embarrassing facts about the business dealings of Bush and Vice President Cheney. For example, when Bush announced his support of legislation that would prohibit business firms from giving low-interest personal loans to their officers, the press was quick to point out that Bush himself had been the beneficiary of two such loans when he was on the board of Harken Energy Corporation in the 1980s.

The Illusion of Presidential Government

Presidents have no choice but to try to counter this type of press coverage with their own version of their accomplishments. A public relations effort can carry a president only so far, however. National conditions ultimately determine the level of public confidence in the president. Indeed, presidents run a risk by trying to build up their images through public relations. Through their frequent television appearances and claims of success, presidents contribute to the public's belief that the president is in charge of the national government, a perception that the political scientist Hugh Heclo calls "the illusion of presidential government."[57]

Because the public expects so much from its presidents, they get too much credit when things go well and too much blame when things go badly. Therein lies an irony of the presidential office. More than from any constitutional grant, more than from any statute, and more than from any crisis, presidential power derives from the president's position as the sole official who can claim to represent the whole American public. Yet because presidential power rests on a popular base, it erodes when public support declines. The irony is that the presidential office typically grows weaker as problems mount: just when the country could most use effective leadership, that leadership is often hardest to achieve.[58]

Self Quiz
www.mhhe.com/patterson6

SUMMARY

The presidency has become a much stronger office than the Framers envisioned. The Constitution grants the president substantial military, diplomatic, legislative, and executive powers, and in each case the president's authority has increased measurably. Underlying this change is the president's position as the one leader chosen by the whole nation and as the sole head of the executive branch. These features of the office have enabled presidents to claim broad authority in response to the increased demands placed on the federal government by changing world and national conditions.

During the course of American history, the presidential selection process has been altered in ways that were intended to make it more responsive to the preferences of ordinary people. Today, they have a vote not only in the general election, but also in the selection of nominees. To gain nomination, a presidential hopeful must gain the support of the electorate in state primaries and open caucuses. Once nominated, the candidates receive federal funds for their general election campaigns, which are based on televised appeals.

Although the campaign tends to personalize the presidency, the responsibilities of the modern presidency far exceed any president's personal capacities. To meet their obligations, presidents have surrounded themselves with large staffs of advisers, policy experts, and managers. These staff members enable the president to extend control over the executive branch while providing the information necessary for policymaking. All recent presidents have discovered, however, that their control of staff resources is incomplete and that some things that others do on their behalf actually work against what they are trying to accomplish.

As sole chief executive and the nation's top elected leader, presidents can always expect that their policy and leadership efforts will receive attention. However, other institutions, particularly Congress, have the authority to make this leadership effective. No president has come close to winning approval of all the programs he has placed before Congress, but the presidents' records of success have varied considerably. The factors in a president's success include the presence or absence of national conditions that require strong leadership from the White House and whether the president's party has a majority in Congress.

To retain an effective leadership position, the president depends on the backing of the American people. Recent presidents have made extensive use of the media to build support for their programs. Yet they have had difficulty maintaining that support throughout their terms of office. A major reason is that the public expects far more from its presidents than they can deliver.

KEY TERMS

cabinet
honeymoon period
legitimacy (of election)
momentum
open party caucuses
presidential approval rating
stewardship theory
unit rule
Whig theory

SUGGESTED READINGS

Cohen, Jeffrey E. *Presidential Responsiveness and Public Policymaking: The Publics and the Policies That Presidents Choose*. Ann Arbor: University of Michigan Press, 1997. An accounting of presidential responsiveness and public policymaking.

Jackson, John S., and William J. Crotty. *The Politics of Presidential Selection*. New York: Longman, 2001. A careful look at the presidential election process by two of its finest analysts.

Jones, Charles. *Separate But Equal Branches*. New York: Chatham House, 1999. An insightful analysis of presidential power in a system of divided powers.

Kernell, Samuel. *Going Public: New Strategies of Presidential Leadership*, 3d ed. Washington, D.C.: Congressional Quarterly Press, 1997. An examination of presidential use of going public to gain support.

Kessel, John H. *Presidents, the Presidency, and the Political Environment*. Washington, D.C.: Congressional Quarterly Press, 2001. An insightful assessment of the politics of the presidency.

Neustadt, Richard E. *Presidential Power and the Modern Presidents: The Politics of Leadership from Roosevelt to Reagan*. New York: Free Press, 1990. The classic analysis of the limitations on presidential power.

Pfiffner, James P. *The Strategic Presidency: Hitting the Ground Running*, 2d ed. Chicago: Dorsey Press, 1996. A study of the way a newly elected president can convert electoral support into power in office.

Relyea, Harold C. and Charles V. Arja. *Vice Presidency of the United States: Evolution of the Modern Office*. Huntington, N.Y.: Nova Science Publishers, 2002. An assessment of how the vice presidency has changed into the office that it is today.

Walcott, Charles E., and Karen M. Hult. *Governing the White House: From Hoover through LBJ*. Lawrence: University Press of Kansas, 1995. An innovative study of how the organization of the White House affects presidential performance.

LIST OF WEBSITES

http://sunsite.unc.edu:80/lia/president
A site with general information on specific presidents and links to the presidential libraries.

http://www.ipl.org/ref/POTUS
Profiles of the nation's presidents, their cabinet officers, and key events during their time in office.

http://www.vote-smart.org/executive
Information on the presidency and the Executive Office of the President as well as links to key executive agencies and organizations.

http://www.whitehouse.gov
The White House's home page; it has an e-mail guest book and includes information on the president, the vice president, and current White House activities.

13

[No] industrial society could manage the daily operations of its public affairs without bureaucratic organizations in which officials play a major policymaking role.

—Norman Thomas[1]

The Federal Bureaucracy:
Administering the Government

Early on the morning of September 7, 1993, a truck pulled up to the south lawn of the White House and unloaded pallets stacked with federal rules and regulations. The display was the backdrop for a presidential speech announcing the completion of the National Performance Review or, as it is commonly called, NPR. The federal regulations piled atop the pallets symbolized bureaucratic red tape, and NPR was a statement of the Clinton administration's effort to make government more responsive. "Our goal," said Clinton, "is to make the entire federal government both less expensive and more efficient, and to change the culture of our national bureaucracy away from complacency and entitlement toward initiative and empowerment. We intend to redesign, to reinvent, to reinvigorate the entire national government."[2]

The origins of the National Performance Review were plain enough. For years, the federal bureaucracy had been derided as too big, too expensive, and too intrusive. These charges gained weight as federal budget deficits increased and the public became increasingly dissatisfied with the performance of the government in Washington. Reform attempts in the 1970s and 1980s had some success but did not stem the tide of federal deficits or markedly improve the bureaucracy's performance. Clinton campaigned on the issue of "reinventing government" and acted swiftly on the promise. During the transition phase, Vice President–elect Al Gore was placed in charge of the National Performance Review. Once in office, Gore assembled more than two hundred career bureaucrats who knew firsthand how the bureaucracy operated and organized them into "reinventing teams" that would recommend ways of improving government administration. The NPR's report included 384 specific recommendations, which were grouped into four broad imperatives: reducing red tape, putting customers first, empowering administrators, and cutting government back to basic services.[3]

NPR is the latest in a lengthy list of major twentieth-century efforts to remake the federal bureaucracy. NPR was different in its particulars, but its claim to improve administration while saving money was consistent with the claims of earlier reform panels, including the Brownlow, Hoover, and Volcker commissions.[4] Like those efforts, NPR addressed an enduring issue of American politics: the bureaucracy's efficiency, responsiveness, and accountability.

Modern government would be impossible without a bureaucracy. It is the government's enormous administrative capacity that makes it possible for the United States to have such ambitious programs as space exploration, social security, environmental protection, interstate highways, and universal postal service. Yet the bureaucracy is also a problem. Even those who work in federal agencies agree that current bureaucratic systems are not working all that well. Both these elements—the need for bureaucracy and the problems associated with it—must be taken into account in any effort to understand the bureaucracy's place in modern American politics.

The bureaucracy's responsibilities include the space exploration program. The National Aeronautics and Space Administration is the federal agency in charge of the program.

This chapter describes the nature of the federal bureaucracy and the politics that surrounds it. The discussion initially aims to clarify the bureaucracy's responsibilities, organizational structure, and management practices. But the chapter also shows that the bureaucracy is very much a part of the play of politics. Bureaucrats necessarily and naturally take an "agency point of view," seeking to promote their agency's objectives. The three constitutional branches of government impose a degree of accountability on the bureaucracy, but the sheer size and fragmented nature of the U.S. government confound the problem of control and make efforts to reform the bureaucracy a high priority. The main points discussed in this chapter are the following:

- *Bureaucracy is an inevitable consequence of complexity and scale.* Modern government could not function without a large bureaucracy. Through authority, specialization, and rules, bureaucracy provides a means of managing thousands of tasks and employees.

- *The bureaucracy is expected simultaneously to respond to the direction of partisan officials and to administer programs fairly and competently.* These conflicting demands are addressed through a combination of personnel management systems—the patronage, merit, and executive leadership systems.

- *Bureaucrats naturally take an "agency point of view," which they promote through their expert knowledge, support from clientele groups, and backing by Congress or the president.*

- *Although agencies are subject to scrutiny by the president, Congress, and the judiciary, bureaucrats are able to achieve power in their own right.* The issue of bureaucratic power and responsiveness is a basis of current efforts at "reinventing" government.

FEDERAL ADMINISTRATION: FORM, PERSONNEL, AND ACTIVITIES

For many Americans, the word *bureaucracy* brings to mind waste, mindless rules, and rigidity. This image is not unfounded, but it is one-sided. Bureaucracy is also an efficient and effective method of organization. Although Americans tend to equate bureaucracy with the federal government, bureaucracy is found wherever there is a need to manage large numbers of people and tasks. Bureaucracy alone facilitates the coordination of a large work force. All large-scale, task-oriented organizations—public and private—are bureaucratic in form.[5] General Motors is a bureaucracy, and so is the Catholic church and every large medical complex and educational institution. The state governments are every bit as "bureaucratic" as the federal government (see "States in the Nation").

In formal terms, **bureaucracy** is a system of organization and control that is based on three principles: hierarchical authority, job specialization, and formalized rules. **Hierarchical authority** refers to a chain of command whereby the officials and units at the top of a bureaucracy have authority over those in the middle, who in turn control those at the bottom. In a system of **job specialization**, the responsibilities of each job position are explicitly defined, and there is a precise division of labor within the organization. **Formalized rules** are the standardized procedures and established regulations by which a bureaucracy conducts its operations.

These features are the reason that bureaucracy, as a form of organization, is the most efficient means of getting people to work together on tasks of great magnitude and complexity. Hierarchy speeds action by reducing conflict over the power to make decisions: the higher an individual's position in the organization, the more decision-making power he or she has. Specialization yields efficiency because each individual is required to concentrate on a particular job: workers acquire specialized skills and knowledge. Formalized rules enable workers to make quick and consistent judgments because decisions are made on the basis of preestablished guidelines rather than by deliberation and personal inclination.

These organizational characteristics are also the cause of bureaucracy's pathologies. Administrators perform not as whole persons but as parts of an organizational entity. Their behavior is governed by position, specialty, and rule. At its worst, bureaucracy grinds on, heedless of the feelings and needs of its members or their clients. Fixed rules come to dominate everything.[6]

If bureaucracy is an indispensable condition of large-scale organization, gross bureaucratic inefficiency and unresponsiveness are not, or at least that is the assumption underlying current efforts to reform the administration of government, a topic that is examined later in this chapter.

bureaucracy A system of organization and control based on the principles of hierarchical authority, job specialization, and formalized rules.

hierarchical authority A basic principle of bureaucracy that refers to the chain of command within an organization whereby officials and units have control over those below them.

job specialization A basic principle of bureaucracy that holds that the responsibilities of each job position should be explicitly defined and that a precise division of labor within the organization should be maintained.

formalized rules A basic principle of bureaucracy that refers to the standardized procedures and established regulations by which a bureaucracy conducts its operations.

The Federal Bureaucracy in Americans' Daily Lives

The U.S. federal bureaucracy has more than 2.5 million employees, who have responsibility for administering thousands of programs. The president and Congress may get far more attention in the news, but it is the bureaucracy that

STATES IN THE NATION

The Size of State Bureaucracies

Although the federal bureaucracy is often criticized as being "too big," it is actually smaller on a per capita basis than even the smallest of the state bureaucracies. There are 1.0 federal employees for every 100 Americans. California, with 1.2 state employees for every 100 residents, has the smallest state bureaucracy on a per capita basis. Hawaii, with 5.0 state employees per 100 residents, has the largest. In general, the least populous states, and especially those that are larger geographically, have the largest bureaucracies on a per capita basis. This pattern reflects the fact that a state, whatever its population, has basic functions (such as highway maintenance and policing) that it must perform.

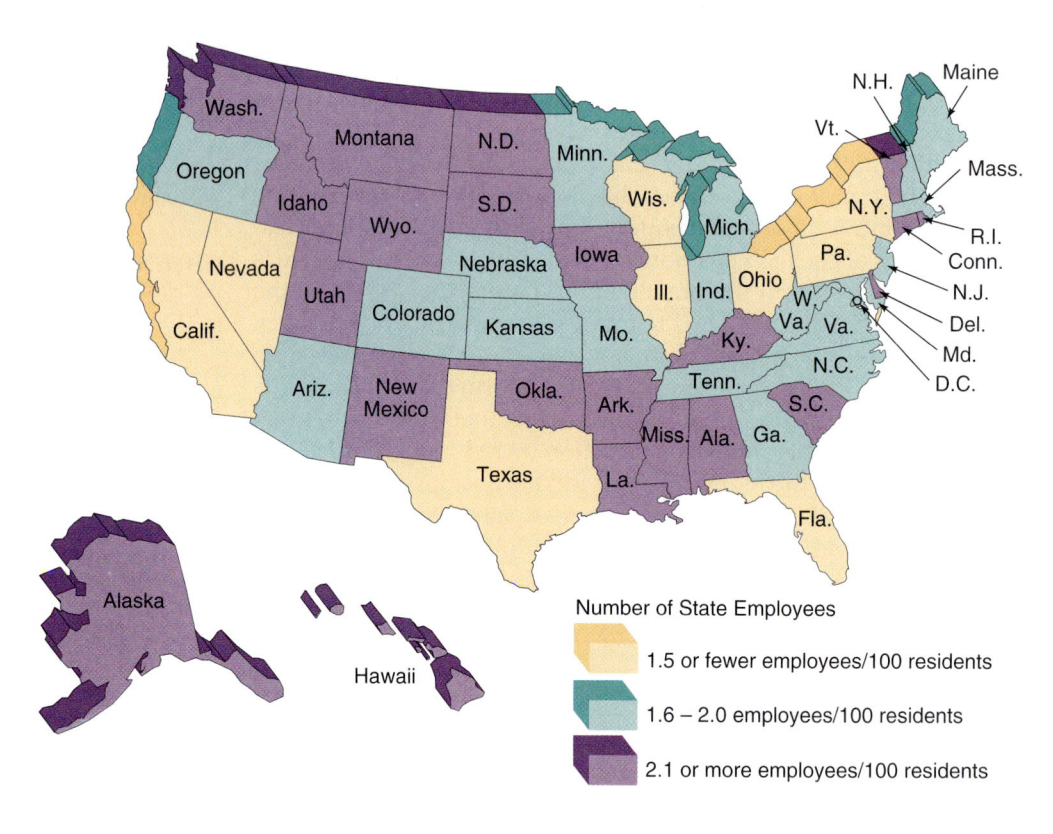

Number of State Employees
- 1.5 or fewer employees/100 residents
- 1.6 – 2.0 employees/100 residents
- 2.1 or more employees/100 residents

Source: U.S. Bureau of the Census, 1999.

has the more immediate impact on the daily lives of Americans. The federal bureaucracy performs a wide range of functions: for example, it delivers the daily mail, maintains the national forests and parks, administers social security, builds dams and generates hydroelectric power, enforces environmental protection laws, develops the country's defense systems, provides foodstuffs for school lunch programs, and regulates the stock markets.

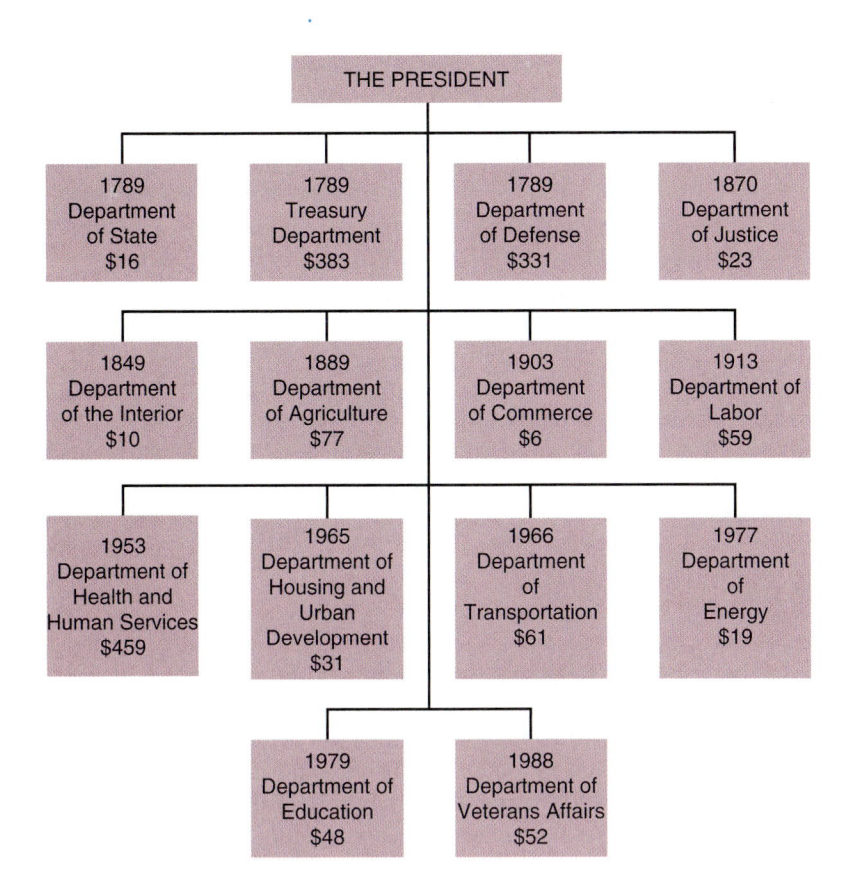

Figure 13-1

Cabinet (Executive) Departments

```
                            THE PRESIDENT
    ┌───────────────────┬───────────┬───────────────┬──────────────┐
    1789                1789        1789            1870
    Department          Treasury    Department      Department
    of State            Department  of Defense      of Justice
    $16                 $383        $331            $23

    1849                1889        1903            1913
    Department          Department  Department      Department of
    of the Interior     of Agriculture of Commerce  Labor
    $10                 $77         $6              $59

    1953                1965        1966            1977
    Department of       Department of Department    Department
    Health and          Housing and of              of
    Human Services      Urban       Transportation  Energy
    $459                Development $61             $19
                        $31

                        1979        1988
                        Department of Department of
                        Education   Veterans Affairs
                        $48         $52
```

Each executive department is responsible for a general policy area and is headed by a secretary or, in the case of Justice, the attorney general, who serves as a member of the president's cabinet. Shown are each department's year of origin (above the title) and annual budget in billions of dollars (below the title). (The Attorney General's office was created in 1789 and became the Justice Department in 1870.)

Source: White House Office of Management and Budget, FY2003.

Types of Administrative Organizations

The chief organizational feature of the U.S. federal bureaucracy is its division into areas of specialization. One agency handles veterans' affairs, another specializes in education, a third is responsible for agriculture, and so on. No two units are exactly alike. Nevertheless, most of them take one of five general forms: cabinet department, independent agency, regulatory agency, government corporation, or presidential commission.

Cabinet Departments

The major administrative units are the fourteen **cabinet** (or **executive**) **departments** (see Figure 13–1). Except for the Department of Justice, which is headed by the attorney general, the top official in each department is its secretary (for example, the secretary of defense), who serves as a member of the president's cabinet and is responsible for establishing the department's general policy and overseeing its operations.

Cabinet departments vary greatly in their visibility, size, and importance. The Department of State is one of the oldest and most prestigious departments, but it is also one of the smallest, with approximately twenty-five thousand employees. The Department of Defense has the largest work force, with more than

cabinet (executive) departments The major administrative organizations within the federal executive bureaucracy, each of which is headed by a secretary or, in the case of Justice, the attorney general. Each department has responsibility for a major function of the federal government, such as defense, agriculture, or justice.

six hundred and fifty thousand civilian employees (apart from the more than 2.3 million uniformed active and reserve members of the armed services). The Treasury Department has the second largest budget, primarily because it pays the interest on the national debt. The Department of Health and Human Services has the largest budget; its activities account for more than a fourth of all federal spending, much of it for social security benefits. The Department of Veterans Affairs is one of the newest departments, dating from 1988.

Each cabinet department has responsibility for a general policy area. But executive departments are not monoliths: each department has a number of semiautonomous operating units that typically carry the label of "bureau," "agency," "division," or "service." The Department of Justice, for example, has thirteen such operating units, including the Federal Bureau of Investigation (FBI), Immigration and Naturalization Service (INS), and Drug Enforcement Administration (DEA). In short, the Department of Justice is itself a large, complex bureaucracy.

Independent Agencies

Independent agencies resemble the cabinet departments, but most of them have a narrower area of responsibility. They include such organizations as the Central Intelligence Agency (CIA) and the National Aeronautics and Space Administration (NASA). The heads of these agencies are appointed by and report to the president but are not members of the cabinet. Like the executive departments, each of the independent agencies is divided into smaller operating units. In general, the independent agencies exist apart from cabinet departments because their placement within a department would pose symbolic or practical policy problems. NASA, for example, could conceivably be located in the Department of Defense, but this positioning would suggest that the space program is intended for military purposes and not also for civilian purposes such as space exploration and satellite communication.

Regulatory Agencies

Regulatory agencies are created when Congress recognizes the importance of close and continuous regulation of an economic activity. Because such regulation requires more time and expertise than Congress can provide, the responsibility is delegated to a regulatory agency. The Securities and Exchange Commission (SEC), which oversees the stock and bond markets, is a regulatory agency. So is the Environmental Protection Agency (EPA), which monitors and prevents industrial pollution. Table 13–1 lists some of the regulatory agencies and other noncabinet units of the federal bureaucracy.

Beyond their executive functions, regulatory agencies have legislative and judicial functions. They issue regulations, implement them, and then judge whether individuals or organizations have complied. Some regulatory agencies, particularly the older ones (such as the SEC), are "independent" by virtue of their relative freedom from ongoing political control. They are headed by a commission of several members who are appointed by the president and confirmed by Congress but who are not subject to removal by the president.

Graphic
www.mhhe.com/patterson6

independent agencies
Bureaucratic agencies that are similar to cabinet departments but usually have a narrower area of responsibility. Each such agency is headed by a presidential appointee who is not a cabinet member. An example is the National Aeronautics and Space Administration.

regulatory agencies
Administrative units, such as the Federal Communications Commission and the Environmental Protection Agency, that have responsibility for the monitoring and regulation of ongoing economic activities.

TABLE 13-1 Selected U.S. Regulatory Agencies, Independent Agencies, Government Corporations, and Presidential Commissions

Central Intelligence Agency	National Labor Relations Board
Commission on Civil Rights	National Railroad Passenger Corporation (Amtrak)
Consumer Product Safety Commission	National Science Foundation
Environmental Protection Agency	National Transportation Safety Board
Equal Employment Opportunity Commission	Nuclear Regulatory Commission
Export-Import Bank of the United States	Occupational Safety and Health Review Commission
Farm Credit Administration	Office of Personnel Management
Federal Communications Commission	Peace Corps
Federal Deposit Insurance Corporation	Securities and Exchange Commission
Federal Election Commission	Selective Service System
Federal Emergency Management Agency	Small Business Administration
Federal Maritime Commission	U.S. Arms Control and Disarmament Agency
Federal Reserve System, Board of Governors	U.S. Information Agency
Federal Trade Commission	U.S. International Development Cooperation Agency
General Services Administration	U.S. International Trade Commission
National Aeronautics and Space Administration	U.S. Postal Service
National Archives and Records Administration	
National Foundation on the Arts and the Humanities	

Source: *The U.S. Government Manual.*

Commissioners serve a fixed term, a legal stipulation intended to free their agencies from political interference. The newer regulatory agencies (such as the EPA) lack such autonomy. They are headed by a presidential appointee who can be removed at the president's discretion.

Government Corporations

Government corporations are similar to private corporations in that they charge clients for their services and are governed by a board of directors. However, government corporations receive federal funding to help defray operating expenses, and their directors are appointed by the president with Senate approval. The largest government corporation is the U.S. Postal Service, with roughly 800,000 employees. Other government corporations include the Federal Deposit Insurance Corporation (FDIC), which insures savings accounts against bank failures, and the National Railroad Passenger Corporation (Amtrak), which provides passenger rail service.

government corporations Bodies, such as the U.S. Postal Service and Amtrak, that are similar to private corporations in that they charge for their services, but different in that they receive federal funding to help defray expenses. Their directors are appointed by the president with Senate approval.

The U.S. Postal Service is one of the most efficient in the world, delivering hundreds of millions of pieces of mail each day inexpensively and without undue delay. Yet, like many other government agencies, it is often criticized for its inefficiency and ineptness.

Presidential Commissions

presidential commissions
Organizations within the bureaucracy that are headed by commissioners appointed by the president. An example of such a commission is the Commission on Civil Rights.

Some **presidential commissions** are permanent commissions that provide ongoing recommendations to the president in particular areas of responsibility. Two such commissions are the Commission on Civil Rights and the Commission on Fine Arts. Other presidential commissions are temporary and disband after making recommendations on specific issues. An example is the commission on racial reconciliation that was appointed by President Clinton in 1997; it concluded its work in 1998.

Federal Employment

The roughly 2.5 million civilian employees of the federal government include professionals who bring their expertise to the problems of governing a large and complex society, service workers who perform such tasks as the typing of correspondence and the delivery of mail, and middle and top managers who supervise the work of the various federal agencies.

More than 90 percent of federal employees are hired by merit criteria, which include educational attainment, employment experience, and performance on competitive tests (such as the civil service and foreign service examinations). The merit system is intended to protect the public from the inept or discriminatory administrative practices that can result if partisanship is the employment criterion. A 1990 Supreme Court ruling prohibits patronage in all personnel operations (hiring, firing, transfers, promotions, training, and so on) unless the

As one of thousands of services provided by the federal bureaucracy, the National Hurricane Service monitors hurricane activity and provides early warning to affected coastal areas.

government can convincingly show that party affiliation is *positively* related to effective performance in a particular position.[7] This beneficial relationship can be demonstrated in some cases, but not in the large majority of personnel operations, which are thereby off limits to partisan politics.

Federal employees are underpaid in comparison with their counterparts in the private sector. The large majority of federal employees have a GS (Graded Service) job ranking. The rankings range from GS-1 (the lowest rank) to GS-18 (the highest). College graduates who enter the federal service usually start at the GS-5 level, which provides a salary of about $22,000 for a beginning employee. With a master's degree, the level is GS-9 at a $33,000 salary. Federal employees' salaries increase with rank and length of service. Public employees receive substantial fringe benefits, including full health insurance, secure retirement plans, and generous vacation time and sick leave.

Public service has its drawbacks. Federal employees have few rights of collective action. They can join labor unions, but their unions by law have limited authority: the government maintains full control of job assignments, compensation, and promotion. Moreover, the Taft-Hartley Act of 1947 prohibits strikes by federal employees and permits the firing of workers who do go on strike. When federal air traffic controllers went on strike anyway in 1981, they were fired by President Reagan. There are also some limits on the partisan activities of civil servants. The Hatch Act of 1939 prohibited them from holding key positions in election campaigns. In 1993, Congress relaxed this prohibition but retained it for certain high-ranking career bureaucrats.

The Federal Bureaucracy's Policy Responsibilities

The Constitution mentions executive departments but does not grant them any powers. Their authority derives from grants of power to the three constitutional branches: Congress, the president, and the courts. Nevertheless, the bureaucracy is far more than an administrative extension of the three branches. It never merely follows orders. The primary function of administrative agencies is **policy implementation**, which is to say that they carry out the authoritative decisions of Congress, the president, and the courts.

policy implementation
The primary function of the bureaucracy—it refers to the process of carrying out the authoritative decisions of Congress, the president, and the courts.

The U.S. Coast Guard is the federal agency with the mission of safeguarding the nation's ports, waterways, and coastlines. Lifesaving is one of the Cost Guard's missions. About 4,000 mariners a year are estimated to owe their lives to Coast Guard assistance.

Although implementation is sometimes described as "mere administration," it is a highly significant and creative function. Many ideas for legislative programs are initiated by the bureaucracy. In the course of their work, administrators come up with policy ideas that are then brought to the attention of the president or members of Congress. Administrative agencies also develop public policy in the process of implementing it. The decisions of Congress, the president, and the courts typically need to be fleshed out by the bureaucracy.[8] Most legislative acts identify general goals, which bureaucrats must then translate into specific programs. The Telecommunications Act of 1996, for example, had the stated goal "to promote competition and reduce regulation in order to secure lower prices and higher quality services for American telecommunication consumers and encourage the rapid deployment of new telecommunications technologies." Although the act included specific provisions, its implementation was left in large part for the Federal Communications Commission (FCC) to decide. The FCC decided, for example, that regional telephone companies (the Bell companies) had to open their networks to AT&T and other competitors at wholesale rates that were far below what they were charging their retail customers. The purpose was to enable AT&T and other carriers to compete with the Bell companies for local phone customers; in other words, the FCC was responding to its legislative mandate to promote "competition." But it was the FCC, not Congress, that determined the wholesale rates and many of the interconnection rules. This development of policy—often through *rule making*—is perhaps the chief way that administrative agencies exercise real power. To an important degree, they decide how the law will operate in practice.

Agencies are also charged with the delivery of services—carrying the mail, processing welfare applications, approving government loans, and the like. Such activities are governed by rules, and in most instances the rules decide what gets done. But some services allow agency employees enough discretion that laws end up being applied arbitrarily, a situation that Michael Lipsky describes as "street-level bureaucracy."[9] For example, FBI agents are more diligent in their pursuit of organized crime than of white-collar crime, even though the law does not designate white-collar criminals as somehow more deserving of more lenient treatment.

In sum, administrators necessarily exercise discretion in carrying out their policy responsibilities. They initiate policy, develop it, evaluate it, apply it, and determine whether others are complying with it. The bureaucracy does not simply administer policy, it also *makes policy*.

DEVELOPMENT OF THE FEDERAL BUREAUCRACY: POLITICS AND ADMINISTRATION

The organization and the staffing of the bureaucracy have been administrative and political issues throughout the country's history. Agencies are responsible for carrying out programs that serve the society, and yet each agency was created and is maintained in response to partisan interests. Each agency thus confronts two simultaneous but incompatible demands: that it administer programs fairly and competently and that it respond to partisan claims.

Historically, this conflict has worked itself out in ways that have made the organization of the modern bureaucracy a blend of the political and the administrative. This dual line of development is clearly reflected in the mix of management systems that characterizes the bureaucracy today—the *patronage, merit*, and *executive leadership* systems.

Small Government and the Patronage System

The federal bureaucracy was originally small (three thousand employees in 1800, for instance). Under the U.S. Constitution, the states retained responsibility for nearly all domestic policy areas. The federal government's role was confined mainly to defense and foreign affairs, currency and interstate commerce, and the delivery of the mail. The nation's first six presidents, from George Washington through John Quincy Adams, believed that only distinguished men should be entrusted with the management of the national government. Nearly all top presidential appointees were men of education and political experience, and many of them were members of socially prominent families. They often remained in their jobs year after year.

The nation's seventh president, Andrew Jackson, did not share his predecessors' admiration for the wellborn. In Jackson's view, government would be more responsive to the people if it were administered by common men of good sense.[10] Jackson also believed that top administrators should remain in office for short periods, so that there would be a steady influx of fresh ideas.

Jackson's version of the **patronage system** was popular with the public, but critics labeled it a **spoils system**—a device for placing political cronies in government office as a reward for partisan service. Although Jackson was motivated as much by a concern for democratic government as by his desire to reward partisan supporters, later presidents were often more interested in distributing the spoils of victory. Jackson's successors extended patronage to all levels of administration.[11]

Historical Background

patronage system An approach to managing the bureaucracy whereby people are appointed to important government positions as a reward for political services they have rendered and because of their partisan loyalty.

spoils system The practice of granting public office to individuals in return for political favors they have rendered.

Fighting Words

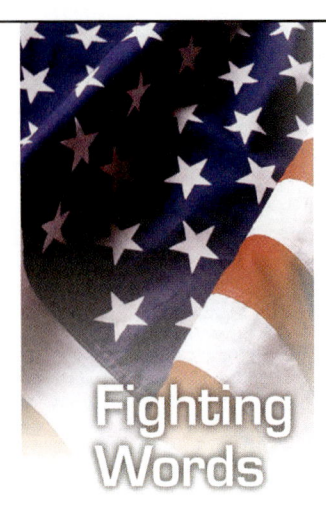

Do Bureaucrats Have Too Much Discretion? The Case of the FDA and Tobacco

The bureaucracy is more than an administrative body. It is also a policymaking body. In implementing and interpreting the policy decisions of Congress, the president, and the courts, bureaucrats necessarily make choices that affect the everyday lives of Americans. Even if this responsibility is an inevitable consequence of bureaucracy, there are differences of opinion on just how much latitude bureaucrats should have. These disputes are never simply the clash of opposing philosophies of government. More often, they are the result of a particular bureaucratic decision and whether it works to one side's political advantage. One such conflict took place regarding whether the Food and Drug Administration (FDA) had authority to regulate tobacco products. The Supreme Court ruled in *FDA v. Brown & Williamson Tobacco Co.* (2000) that the FDA did not have the authority. The majority and dissenting opinions in the case illustrate the conflict.

Yes: Regardless of how serious the problem an administrative agency seeks to address, . . . it may not exercise its authority "in a manner that is inconsistent with the administrative structure that Congress enacted into law." And although agencies are generally entitled to deference in the interpretation of statutes that they administer, a reviewing "court, as well as the agency, must give effect to the unambiguously expressed intent of Congress." In this case, we believe that Congress has clearly precluded the FDA from asserting jurisdiction to regulate tobacco products. Such authority is inconsistent with the intent that Congress has expressed in the . . . overall regulatory scheme and in the tobacco-specific legislation that it has enacted. . . . In light of this clear intent, the FDA's assertion of jurisdiction is impermissible.
—Justice Sandra Day O'Connor, for the majority

No: The Food and Drug Administration (FDA) has the authority to regulate "articles (other than food) intended to affect the structure or any function of the body . . ." Unlike the majority, I believe that tobacco products fit within this statutory language. . . . [T]he statute's basic purpose—the protection of public health—supports the inclusion of cigarettes within its scope. . . . I believe that the most important indicia of statutory meaning—language and purpose—along with the . . . legislative history are sufficient to establish that the FDA has authority to regulate tobacco. . . . [T]he Court today holds that a regulatory statute aimed at unsafe drugs and devices does not authorize regulation of a drug (nicotine) and a device (a cigarette) that the Court itself finds unsafe . . . [T]his particular drug and device risks the life-threatening harms that administrative regulation seeks to rectify.
—Justice Stephen G. Breyer, in dissent

Growth in Government and the Merit System

Because the government of the early nineteenth century was relatively small and limited in scope, it could be managed by employees who had little or no administrative training or experience. As the century advanced, however, the nature of the bureaucracy changed rapidly, as did the bureaucracy's personnel needs.

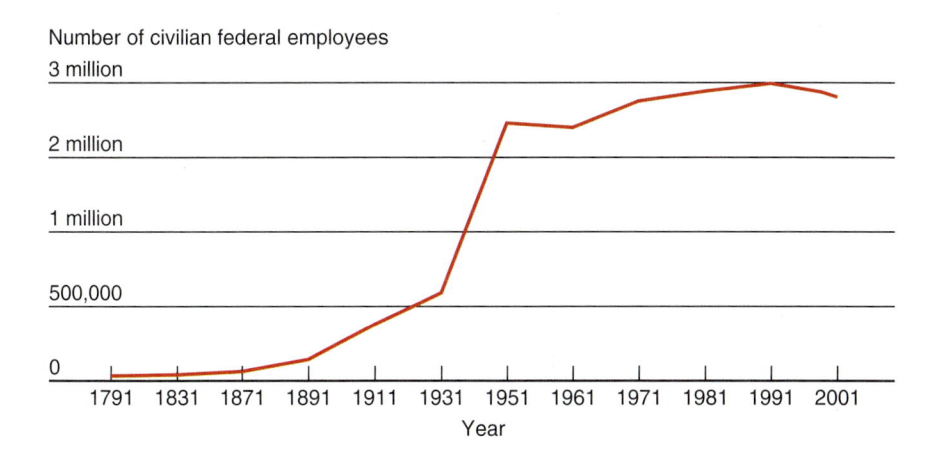

Figure 13–2

Number of Persons Employed by the Federal Government

The federal bureaucracy grew slowly until the 1930s, when an explosive growth began in the number of programs that required ongoing administration by the federal government.

Source: Historical Statistics of the United States and Statistical Abstract of the United States, 1986, 322; recent figures from U.S. Office of Personnel Management.

An impetus for change was the Industrial Revolution, which was creating a truly national economy and was prompting economic groups to pressure Congress to protect and promote their interests. Farmers were one of the groups that looked to the federal government for market and price assistance. In response, Congress created the Department of Agriculture in 1889. Business and labor interests also pressed their claims, and in 1903 Congress established the Department of Commerce and Labor to "promote the mutual interest" of the nation's firms and workers. (The separate interests of business and labor proved stronger than their shared concerns, and so in 1913 Labor became a separate department.)[12]

Because of the increased need for continuous administration of government, an ever-larger bureaucracy was required (see Figure 13–2). By 1930, federal employment had reached six hundred thousand, a sixfold increase over the level of the 1880s.[13] During the 1930s, as a result of President Franklin Roosevelt's New Deal, the federal work force increased enormously, to 1.2 million. Roosevelt's programs were generated in response to public demands for relief from the economic hardship and uncertainty of the Great Depression. Administration of these programs necessitated the formation of economic and social welfare agencies such as the Securities and Exchange Commission and the Social Security Board. The effect was to give the federal government an ongoing role in promoting Americans' economic well-being.

A large and active government requires skilled and experienced personnel. In 1883, Congress passed the Pendleton Act, which established a **merit system** (or **civil service system**) whereby certain federal employees were hired through competitive examinations or by virtue of having special qualifications, such as an advanced degree in a particular field. The transition to a career civil service was gradual. Only 10 percent of federal positions in 1885 were filled on the basis of merit. But the pace accelerated when the Progressives (see Chapter 2) promoted the merit system as a way of eliminating partisan graft and corruption in the administration of government. By 1920, as the Progressive era was concluding, more than 70 percent of federal employees were merit appointees. Since 1950, the proportion of merit employees has not dipped below 80 percent.[14]

merit (civil service) system
An approach to managing the bureaucracy whereby people are appointed to government positions on the basis of either competitive examinations or special qualifications, such as professional training.

The assassination of President James A. Garfield in 1881 by Charles Guiteau, a disappointed officeseeker, did much to end the spoils system of distributing government jobs.

The Pendleton Act created the Civil Service Commission to establish job classifications, administer competitive examinations, and oversee merit employees. The commission was replaced by two independent agencies in 1978. The Merit Service Protection Board handles appeals of personnel actions, and the Office of Personnel Management (OPM) supervises the hiring and classification of federal employees.

The administrative objective of the merit system is **neutral competence**.[15] A merit-based bureaucracy is "competent" in the sense that employees are hired and retained on the basis of their skills, and it is "neutral" in the sense that employees are not partisan appointees and thus are expected to do their work on behalf of everyone, not just those who support the incumbent administration.

Although the merit system contributes to the impartial and proficient administration of government programs, it has its own sources of bias and inefficiency. Career bureaucrats tend to place their agency's interests ahead of those of other agencies and typically oppose substantial efforts to trim their agency's activities. They are not partisans in the sense of Democratic or Republican politics, but they are partisans when it comes to protecting their own positions and agencies, as will be explained more fully later in the chapter.

neutral competence The administrative objective of merit-based bureaucracy. Such a bureaucracy should be "competent" in the sense that its employees are hired and retained on the basis of their expertise and "neutral" in the sense that it operates by objective standards rather than partisan ones.

Big Government and the Executive Leadership System

As problems with the merit system surfaced after the early years of the twentieth century, reformers looked to a strengthened presidency—an **executive leadership system**—as a means of coordinating the bureaucracy's activities to increase its efficiency and responsiveness.[16] The president was to provide the general leadership that would overcome agency fragmentation and provide a common direction. As Chapter 11 described, Congress in 1939 provided the president with some of the tools needed for improved coordination of the bureaucracy. The Office of Management and Budget (OMB) was created to give

executive leadership system An approach to managing the bureaucracy that is based on presidential leadership and presidential management tools, such as the president's annual budget proposal.

the president the authority to coordinate the annual budgetary process. Agencies would be required to prepare their budget proposals under the direction of the president, who would then submit the overall budget to Congress for its approval and modification. The president was also empowered to reorganize the bureaucracy, subject to congressional approval, in order to reduce duplication of activities and strengthen the chain of command from the president to the agencies. Finally, the president was authorized to develop the Executive Office of the President, which oversees the agencies' activities on the president's behalf, assisting in the development and implementation of policy programs.

Like the merit and patronage systems, the executive leadership system has brought problems as well as improvements to the administration of government. The executive leadership concept, if carried too far, can threaten the balance between executive power and legislative power on which the U.S. constitutional system is based, and it can make the president's priorities, not fairness, the criterion by which provision of services is determined. Richard Nixon abused the system, for example, by ordering the OMB to impound (that is, fail to spend) more than $40 billion in appropriated funds of programs he disliked. (The courts ruled that Nixon's action was an unlawful infringement on Congress's constitutional authority over spending. To prevent a recurrence of the problem, Congress in 1974 passed legislation that gives the president the authority to withhold funds for only forty-five days unless Congress passes legislation to rescind the appropriation.)

The executive leadership system is not a panacea but, along with the patronage and merit systems, is a necessary component of any effective strategy for managing the modern federal bureaucracy.[17] The federal bureaucracy today embodies aspects of all three systems, a situation that reflects the tensions inherent in governmental administration. The bureaucracy is expected to carry out programs fairly, but it is also expected to respond to political forces and to principles of effective management. The first of these requirements is addressed primarily through the merit system, the second through the patronage system, and the third through the executive leadership system (see Table 13–2).

THE BUREAUCRACY'S POWER IMPERATIVE

A common misperception is that the president, as the chief executive, has the sole claim on the bureaucracy's loyalty. In fact, each of the elected institutions has reason to claim proprietorship: the president as chief executive and Congress as the source of the authorization and funding of the bureaucracy's programs. Faced with a threat from either Congress or the presidency, agencies often find an ally in the other institution. One presidential appointee asked a congressional committee whether it had any problem with his plans to reduce one of his agency's programs. The committee chairman replied, "No, you have the problem, because if you touch that bureau I'll cut your job out of the budget."[18]

The U.S. system of separate institutions sharing power results in a natural tendency for each institution to guard its turf. In addition, the president and members of Congress differ in their constituencies and thus in the interests to which they are most responsive. For example, although the agricultural sector

TABLE 13–2 Strengths and Weaknesses of Major Systems for Managing the Bureaucracy

SYSTEM	STRENGTHS	WEAKNESSES
Patronage	Makes the bureaucracy more responsive to election outcomes by allowing the president to appoint some executive officials.	Gives executive authority to individuals chosen for their partisan loyalty rather than administrative or policy expertise; can favor interests that supported the president's election.
Merit	Provides for *competent* administration in that employees are hired on the basis of ability and allowed to remain on the job and thereby become proficient, and provides for *neutral* administration in that civil servants are not partisan appointees and are expected to work in an evenhanded way.	Can result in fragmented, unresponsive administration since career bureaucrats are secure in their jobs and tend to place the interests of their particular agency ahead of those of other agencies or the nation's interests as a whole.
Executive leadership	Provides for presidential leadership of the bureaucracy in order to make it more responsive and to coordinate and direct it (left alone, the bureaucracy tends toward fragmentation).	Can upset the balance between executive and legislative power and can make the president's priorities, not fairness or effective management, the basis for administrative action.

is just one of many concerns of the president, it is of vital interest to senators and representatives from farm states. Finally, because the president and Congress are elected separately, the White House and one or both houses of Congress may be in the hands of opposing parties. Since 1968, this source of executive-legislative conflict has been more often the rule than the exception.

If agencies are to operate successfully in this system, they must seek support where they can find it—if not from the president, then from Congress; if not today, then tomorrow. In other words, agencies must play politics.[19] Any agency that is content to sit idly by while new priorities for money and policy are determined is virtually certain to lose out to other agencies that are willing to fight for power.

The Agency Point of View

agency point of view The tendency of bureaucrats to place the interests of their agency ahead of other interests and ahead of the priorities sought by the president or Congress.

Administrators have little choice but to look out for their agency's interests, a perspective that is called the **agency point of view**.[20] This perspective comes naturally to most high-ranking civil servants. Their careers within the bureaucracy have taught them to do their part in making the organization effective. Many bureaucrats are also personally committed to their agency's objectives as a result of having spent years working on its programs. More than 80 percent of all top careerists reach their high-level positions by rising through the ranks of the same agency.[21] As one top administrator said when testifying before the House Appropriations Committee, "Mr. Chairman, you would not think it proper for me to be in charge of this work and not be enthusiastic about it . . . would you? I have been in it for thirty years, and I believe in it."[22]

Professionalism also cements agency loyalties. As public policy making has become more complex, high-level administrative positions have increasingly been filled by scientists, engineers, lawyers, educators, physicians, and other professionals. Most of them take jobs in an agency whose programs are consistent with their professional values.

Studies confirm that bureaucrats believe in the importance of their agency's work. One study found that social welfare administrators are three times as likely as other civil servants to believe that social welfare programs should be given a high budget priority.[23]

Sources of Bureaucratic Power

In promoting their agency's interests, bureaucrats rely on their specialized knowledge, the support of interests that benefit from the programs they run, and the backing of the president and Congress.

The Power of Expertise

Most of the policy problems that the federal government confronts do not lend themselves to simple solutions. Whether the issue is space travel or hunger in America, expert knowledge is essential to the development of effective public policy. Much of this expertise is held by bureaucrats. They spend their careers working in a particular policy area, and many of them have had scientific, technical, or other specialized training.[24]

By comparison, elected officials are generalists. To some degree, members of Congress do specialize through their committee work, but they rarely have the time or inclination to acquire a commanding knowledge of a particular issue. The president's understanding of policy issues is even more general. Not surprisingly, the president and members of Congress regularly depend on the bureaucracy for policy advice and guidance.

Not all agencies acquire a great amount of leverage from their staffs' expert knowledge. Those that have an edge have highly specialized, professional staffs. For example, the expert judgments of the health scientists and physicians in the National Institutes of Health (NIH) are rarely challenged by elected officials. They may question the political assessments of these health professionals but are unlikely to question their scientific evaluations, which are sometimes decisive. For example, as much as some elected officials may have wanted to avoid the issues surrounding the emerging AIDS epidemic during the 1980s, they were eventually forced into action by the warnings of health scientists about the dire consequences of a do-nothing policy.

The power of expertise is conditioned by the extent to which an agency's employees share the same goals. In many agencies, such as the NIH, careerists with different professional backgrounds have similar values. In other agencies, professional infighting breaks down this cohesiveness and gives outsiders an opportunity to support the faction whose aims agree with their own. An example is the Federal Trade Commission (FTC), which is divided between its lawyers, who tend to emphasize issues that can be quickly and successfully litigated, and its economists, who tend to stress larger and more complicated issues that have broad implications for national commerce.[25]

Nevertheless, all agencies acquire some power through their careerists' expertise. No matter how simple a policy issue may appear at first, it invariably

HOW THE UNITED STATES COMPARES

Educational Backgrounds of Bureaucrats

To staff its bureaucracy, the U.S. government tends to hire persons with specialized educations to hold specialized jobs. This approach heightens the tendency of bureaucrats to take the agency point of view. By comparison, Great Britain tends to recruit its bureaucrats from the arts and humanities, on the assumption that general aptitude is the best qualification for detached professionalism. The continental European democracies also emphasize detached professionalism, but in the context of the supposedly impartial application of rules. As a consequence, high-ranking civil servants in Europe tend to have legal educations. The college majors of senior civil servants in the United States and other democracies reflect these various tendencies.

COLLEGE MAJOR OF SENIOR CIVIL SERVANTS	DENMARK	GERMANY	GREAT BRITAIN	ITALY	NETHERLANDS	UNITED STATES
Natural science/engineering	16%	8%	26%	10%	25%	32%
Social science/humanities/business	20	18	52	37	28	50
Law	60	63	3	53	45	18
Other	4	11	19	—	2	—
	100%	100%	100%	100%	100%	100%

From THE POLITICS OF BUREAUCRACY 4th ed. by B. Guy Peters. Copyright 1995 by Longman Publishers USA. Reprinted by permission of Addison-Wesley Educational Publishers Inc.

involves more than meets the eye. A recognition that the United States has a trade deficit with Japan, for example, can be the premise for policy change, but this recognition does not begin to address such basic issues as the form that the new policy might take, its probable cost and effectiveness, and its connection to other trade issues. Among the officials most likely to understand these issues are the bureaucrats in the Commerce Department and the Federal Trade Commission.

The Power of Clientele Groups

clientele groups Special-interest groups that benefit directly from the activities of a particular bureaucratic agency and are therefore strong advocates of the agency.

Most agencies have **clientele groups**, which are special interests that benefit directly from an agency's programs. Clientele groups place pressure on Congress and the president to retain the programs from which they benefit.[26] A result is that agency programs, once started, are difficult to terminate. "Government activities," as public administration expert Herbert Kaufman says, "tend to go on indefinitely."[27]

The importance of clientele groups was evident in 1995 when House Speaker Newt Gingrich threatened to "zero out" funding for the Corporation for Public Broadcasting. The threat produced an immediate response (some of

The popular children's program *Sesame Street* is produced through the Corporation for Public Broadcasting, a government agency that gains leverage in budgetary deliberations from its public support. The singer Garth Brooks is shown here with two muppets during his appearance on *Sesame Street*.

it orchestrated by public broadcasting stations) from audience members and from groups such as the Childrens Television Workshop. They wrote, called, faxed, and cajoled members of Congress, saying that programs like *Sesame Street* and *All Things Considered* were irreplaceable by anything available from commercial broadcasting. Within a few weeks, Gingrich had relented somewhat, saying that a phase-out plan for ending the funding would be preferable to an abrupt cessation and that it might be prudent to retain funding for some activities, such as support of stations in rural areas not adequately served by commercial broadcasters.

In general, agencies lead and are led by the clientele groups that depend on the programs they administer.[28] Many agencies were created for the purpose of promoting particular interests in society. For example, the Department of Agriculture's career bureaucrats are dependable allies of farm interests year after year. The same cannot be said of the president, Congress as a whole, or either political party; they must balance farmers' demands against those of other interests.

The Power of Friends in High Places

Although members of Congress and the president sometimes appear to be at war with the bureaucracy, they need it as much as it needs them. An agency's resources—its programs, expertise, and group support—can assist elected officials in their efforts to achieve their goals. When President George W. Bush announced plans in 2001 for a war on terrorism, he needed the help of careerists in the Central Intelligence Agency, the Department of Defense, and the Justice Department to make his efforts successful. At a time when other agencies were feeling the pinch of a tight federal budget, these agencies received substantial new funding.

Bureaucrats also seek favorable relations with members of Congress. Congressional support is vital because agencies' funding and programs are established through legislation. Agencies that offer benefits to major constituency interests are particularly likely to have close ties to Congress. In some policy areas, more or less permanent alliances—iron triangles—form among agencies,

Figure 13–3
Rating Federal Agencies, Selected Examples

The Federal Performance Project evaluates federal agencies and gives them a "report card" based on the quality of their management of finances, human resources, programs, information, and physical assets. The Social Security Administration is one of the top-rated agencies. The Bureau of Indian Affairs is one of the lowest rated agencies.

Source: Created from data in Anne Laurent, "Managing for Results," *Government Executive*, April 2001, pp. 8–12.

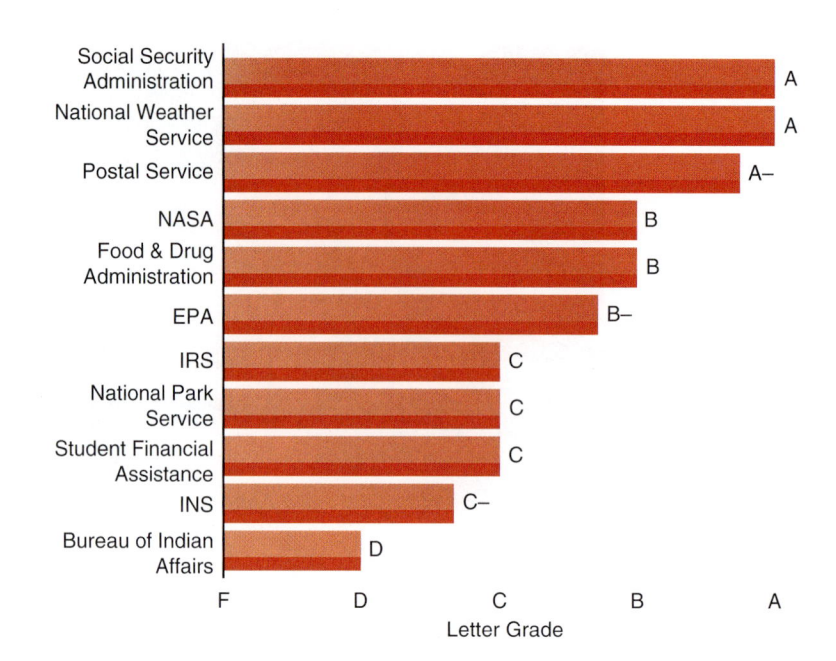

Agency	Grade
Social Security Administration	A
National Weather Service	A
Postal Service	A–
NASA	B
Food & Drug Administration	B
EPA	B–
IRS	C
National Park Service	C
Student Financial Assistance	C
INS	C–
Bureau of Indian Affairs	D

clientele groups, and congressional subcommittees. In other policy areas, temporary issue networks form among bureaucrats, lobbyists, and members of Congress. As seen in Chapters 9 and 11, these alliances enable agencies and interest groups to promote the programs they want and provide members of Congress with electoral support.

BUREAUCRATIC ACCOUNTABILITY

Bureaucratic politics raises the specter of a huge, permanent, and uncontrollable organization run by entrenched unelected officials. This image certainly characterizes the way that many Americans perceive the federal bureaucracy. Even though most Americans say that they have a favorable impression of their most recent personal experience with the bureaucracy (as, say, when a senior citizen applies for social security), they have an unfavorable impression of the bureaucracy as a whole. This view is somewhat unfair—the effectiveness of the U.S. federal bureaucracy has been found in studies to compare favorably with that of other governmental bureaucracies at home and abroad[29] Agencies differ substantially in their effectiveness (see Figure 13–3), but management experts rate the federal bureaucracy as one of the world's best.

Nevertheless, it is easy to understand why Americans believe otherwise. For one thing, the news media do not cover the bureaucracy heavily except when it makes a colossal mistake, fostering the impression that bureaucratic incompetence is widespread. In addition, the bureaucracy is a faceless institution that is largely beyond the citizens' direct control. When combined with Americans' traditional mistrust of concentrated political power, it is no surprise that they have qualms about the federal bureaucracy and want it more closely controlled.

Adapting the requirements of the bureaucracy to those of democracy has been a persistent challenge for public administration.[30] The issue is **accountability**: the capacity of the public to hold officials responsible for their actions. In the case of the bureaucracy, accountability works primarily through other institutions: the presidency, Congress, and the courts.

accountability The ability of the public to hold government officials responsible for their actions.

Accountability Through the Presidency

The president can only broadly influence, not directly control, the bureaucracy. "We can outlast any president" is a maxim of bureaucratic politics. Each agency has its clientele and its congressional supporters, as well as statutory authority for its existence and activities. No president can unilaterally eliminate an agency or its funding and programs. Nor can the president be indifferent to the opinions of career civil servants—not without losing their support and expertise in developing and implementing presidential policy objectives.

To encourage the bureaucracy to cooperate, the president has important management tools that have developed out of the "executive leadership" concept discussed previously. These tools include reorganization, presidential appointees, and the executive budget.

Reorganization

The bureaucracy's extreme fragmentation—its hundreds of separate agencies—makes presidential coordination of its activities difficult. Agencies pursue independent, even contradictory paths, resulting in an undetermined amount of waste and duplication of effort. For example, more than one hundred units are responsible for different pieces of education policy.

All recent presidents have tried to streamline the bureaucracy and make it more accountable.[31] For George W. Bush, the challenge came after the terrorist attacks on the World Trade Center and the Pentagon. Breakdowns in the FBI and CIA had undermined whatever chance there might have been to prevent the attacks. These agencies had not shared or vigorously pursued the intelligence information they had gathered. Bush concluded, and Congress agreed, that a reorganization of the FBI and CIA, as well as the creation of a new homeland security agency, was necessary. Nevertheless, neither the White House nor Congress was under the illusion that this reorganization would fully correct the coordination problems plaguing the agencies charged with stopping terrorist attacks on American soil.

Presidents have frequently been able to make less sweeping changes in the bureaucracy's organization, such as reducing the autonomy or number of employees of particular agencies. These changes serve to upgrade or downgrade programs but ordinarily have not greatly improved presidential control of the bureaucracy.[32]

Presidential Appointments

Although there is almost no direct confrontation with a bureaucrat that a president cannot win, the president does not have time to deal personally with every troublesome careerist or make sure that the bureaucracy has complied with

Why Should I Care?

Quality of the Federal Bureaucracy

Most American do not think highly of the federal bureaucracy. When questioned in polls, people say the bureaucracy is wasteful of taxpayers' money and is staffed by people who are not particularly talented and who do not work all that hard.

These stereotypes have some basis. There is waste in federal programs, and some civil servants do take advantage of the job security provided by a civil service appointment. However, these problems are not as large as many people think. As former New York governor Mario Cuomo pointed out, fairness rather than efficiency is the goal of many federal programs. Loans to college students, for example, are awarded on the basis of need, which means they simply cannot be handed out in equal amounts to anyone who applies. That approach would be much less expensive to administer, but a need-based program requires a detailed application process and a case-by-case assessment of the applicants.

Some deadbeats work in the federal bureaucracy, which is not surprising in view of the fact that it has more than two million federal employees. Interestingly, when people are asked about their direct experiences with federal employees, they usually express satisfaction with the service they personally have received from postal workers, social security administrators, National Park Service rangers, and other civil servants.

However, the federal bureaucracy has had difficulty attracting top-notch employees. As the gap has widened between the pay and benefits in the public sector relative to the private sector, college graduates have shown less interest in careers in government. A 2001 survey found that only one in ten graduates were considering such a career path.

A government career is not without its frustrations. A 2002 study by Harvard's Kennedy School of Government found that management-level public-sector employees have less opportunity than comparable private-sector employees to pursue initiatives. Their work is more constrained because the operating rules and budget allocations are less flexible than in the private sector. However, the Kennedy School's study also found that public-sector managers get more intrinsic satisfaction from their work, which focuses on improving public life, than do private-sector managers.

The quality of the nation's public servants affects the quality of governance. Ultimately, an organization is no better than the people who staff it. What would it take for you to consider a career in government? What agency could you envision working in? For people who want to pursue a government career, a first step is often a master's degree program in public administration or public policy. Many of these programs require only a year of study after the bachelor's degree. For an entry-level employee with a master's degree rather than a bachelor's degree, the initial salary is nearly 50 percent higher. Appointees with master's degrees enter the civil service at a higher rank (GS-9 rather than GS-5) and are placed in positions that entail greater responsibility than those assigned to newly hired appointees with bachelor's degrees.

---

every presidential order. The president relies on political appointees in the agencies to ensure that directives are followed.

The power of presidential appointees is greater in those agencies where wide latitude exists in the making of decisions. Although the Social Security Administration has a huge budget and gives monthly payments to more than forty million Americans, the eligibility of recipients is determined by relatively fixed rules. In contrast, most regulatory agencies have broad discretion over regulatory policy, and a change in leadership can have a substantial impact. For example, President Reagan's appointee to head the Federal Trade Commission, James Miller III, was a strong-willed economist who shared Reagan's belief that consumer protection policy had gone too far and was adversely affecting business interests. In Miller's first year as head of the FTC, the commission dropped one-fourth of its pending cases against business firms.[33] Overall, enforcement actions declined by about 50 percent during Miller's tenure compared with the previous period.

However, as was noted in Chapter 12, there are limits to what a president can accomplish through appointments. High-level presidential appointees number in the hundreds, and their turnover rate is high: the average appointee remains in the administration for less than two years before moving on to other employment.[34] No president can keep track of all appointees, much less instruct them in detail on all intended policies. In addition, some presidential appointees will have a vested interest in the agencies they head. In choosing political appointees, the president is lobbied by groups that depend on agency programs. Rather than antagonize these groups, the president will accept their recommendations in some cases.

The Executive Budget

Faced with the difficulty of controlling the bureaucracy, presidents have come to rely heavily on their personal bureaucracy, the Executive Office of the President (EOP).

In terms of presidential management, the key unit within the EOP is the Office of Management and Budget (OMB). Funding, programs, and regulations are the mainstays of every agency, and the OMB has substantial influence on each of these areas. No agency can issue a major regulation without the OMB's verification that the regulation's benefits outweigh its costs, and no agency can propose legislation to Congress without the OMB's approval. However, the OMB's greatest influence over agencies derives from its budgetary role. At the start of the annual budget cycle, the OMB assigns each agency a budget limit in accord with the president's directives. The agency's tentative allocation requests are sent back to the OMB, which then conducts a final review of all requests before sending the full budget to Congress in the president's name.

In most cases, an agency's overall budget does not change much from year to year. This fact indicates that a significant portion of the bureaucracy's activities persist regardless of who sits in the White House or Congress.[35] It must be noted, however, that the bulk of federal spending is for programs such as social security that, although enacted in the past, have the continuing support of the president, Congress, and the public.

Accountability Through Congress

Congress has powerful means of influencing the bureaucracy. All agencies depend on Congress for their existence, authority, programs, and funding.

The most substantial control that Congress exerts on the bureaucracy is through its power to authorize and fund programs. Without authorization or funding, a program simply does not exist, regardless of the priority an agency claims it deserves. Congress can also void an administrative decision through legislation that prohibits it or mandates an alternative course of action. However, Congress lacks the institutional capacity to work out complex policies

The Budgetary Process: Funding The Agencies

The annual federal budget allocates the hundreds of billions of dollars that support federal agencies and programs. As the last three chapters have indicated, Congress, the president, and the bureaucracy all play substantial roles in shaping the budget. The following is a simplified step-by-step summary of the process:

1. In the calendar year preceding enactment of the budget, the Office of Management and Budget (OMB) instructs each agency to prepare its budget request within guidelines established by the White House.

2. Agencies work out their budget proposals in line with White House guidelines and their own goals. Once completed, agency proposals are sent to OMB for review and adjustment to fit the president's goals.

3. In January, the president submits the budget to Congress.

4. The president's budget is reviewed by the Congressional Budget Office (CBO) and is referred to the House and Senate budget and appropriations committees. The budget committees in each chamber then set expenditure ceilings in particular areas, which are voted upon by the members of Congress. Once established (usually in April), the budget ceilings establish temporary limits within which the appropriations committees must act.

5. Through subcommittee hearings, the House and Senate appropriations committees meet with agency heads and adjust the president's budgetary recommendations to fit congressional goals. Once the appropriations committees have completed their work, the proposals are submitted to the full House and Senate for a vote. Differences in the House and Senate versions are reconciled in conference committee.

6. The legislation is sent to the president for approval or veto. Before this point, the White House and Congress will have engaged in intense negotiations to resolve differences in their priorities. If the White House is satisfied with the outcome of the bargaining, the president can be expected to sign the legislation.

7. The new budget takes effect October 1, unless Congress has not completed its work by then or if the president vetoes the legislation. If agreement has not been reached by this date, temporary funding (authorized by Congress and approved by the president) is required to keep the government in operation until a permanent budget can be enacted. If temporary funding is not provided, a shutdown of nonessential government services occurs.

down to the last detail.[36] The bureaucracy would grind to a halt if it had to get congressional approval for all its policy decisions. Congress has no option in most cases but to give the bureaucracy leeway in its decisions.

Correcting Administrative Error: Legislative Oversight

Congress also exerts some control through its oversight function, which involves monitoring the bureaucracy's work to ensure compliance with legislative intent.[37] As was noted in Chapter 11, however, oversight is a difficult and relatively unrewarding task, and members of Congress ordinarily place less emphasis on oversight than on their other major duties. Only when an agency has clearly stepped out of line is Congress likely to take decisive corrective action by holding hearings to ask tough questions and to warn of legislative punishment.[38]

Congress has sometimes legislated its own authority to void bureaucratic decisions—a device called the *legislative veto*. When Congress authorized the Alaska oil pipeline, for example, it retained the authority to veto bureaucratic decisions about the pipeline's route. In 1983, however, the Supreme Court voided the use of a legislative veto as interference with the president's constitutional authority to execute the laws but limited its ruling to the law in question. During the same year, the Court affirmed two lower-court rulings that the legislative veto was unconstitutional. Whether the Supreme Court in some situations will rule differently remains to be tested by future cases, but Congress has from time to time continued to include the legislative veto in bills that presidents have signed into law.[39]

Because oversight is so difficult and unrewarding, Congress has shifted much of its oversight responsibility to the General Accounting Office (GAO). The GAO's primary function once was to keep track of the funds spent within the bureaucracy; now it also monitors the implementation of policies. The Congressional Budget Office (CBO) also does oversight studies. When the GAO or CBO uncovers a major problem with an agency's handling of a program, it notifies Congress, which can then take remedial action. In 2002, the GAO made headlines when it sued the executive branch in an attempt to obtain records of meetings between Vice President Cheney and Enron Corporation officials in the aftermath of Enron's collapse. At issue was whether Enron officials, who had made large contributions to the Bush-Cheney campaign, had exercised undue influence over the Bush administration's energy policies.

Restricting the Bureaucracy in Advance

Of course, an awareness by bureaucrats that misbehavior can trigger a response from Congress helps to keep them in line. Nevertheless, oversight cannot correct mistakes or abuses that have already occurred. Recognizing this limit on oversight, Congress has devised ways to constrain the bureaucracy *before* it acts. The simplest method is to draft laws that contain very specific provisions that limit bureaucrats' options when they implement policy. Another restrictive device is the sunset law, which establishes a specific date when a law will expire unless it is reenacted by Congress. Advocates of sunset laws see them as a means to counter the bureaucracy's reluctance to give up programs that have outlived their usefulness. Since members of Congress usually want their policies to last far into the future, however, most legislation does not include a sunset provision.

Accountability Through the Courts

The judiciary's influence on agencies is less direct than that of the elected branches, but the courts, too, can and do act to ensure the bureaucracy's compliance with Congress's requirements. Legally, the bureaucracy derives its authority from acts of Congress, and an injured party can bring suit against an agency on the grounds that it has failed to carry out the law properly. Judges can then order an agency to change its application of the law.[40]

However, the courts have tended to support administrators if their actions seem at all consistent with the laws they are administering. The Supreme Court

Liberty & Equality

What's Your Opinion?

Democracy and Bureaucracy

The power of the bureaucracy is both undeniable and difficult to reconcile with the concept of democracy. Bureaucracy entails hierarchy, command, permanence of office, appointment to office, and fixed rules, whereas democracy involves equality, consent, rotation of office, election to office, and open decisions. At base, the conflict between bureaucracy and democracy centers on the degree of power held by unelected officials.

Eliminating the bureaucracy is not an answer to the problem. American society would collapse without the defense establishment, the education and welfare programs, the regulation of business, the transportation systems, and the hundreds of other activities of the federal bureaucracy.

Oversight by Congress, the president, and the judiciary has been America's answer to the problem. Can you think of ways this oversight might be made more effective? Can you also think of ways of reorganizing the bureaucracy that would enhance accountability? For example, do you think the bureaucracy would be more accountable if civil servants rotated from one agency to another every few years, much as military personnel rotate in their assignments? What would be the disadvantages of a personnel system of this kind?

Whistle-blowers Diane Klipfel and Mike Caseli of the Bureau of Alcohol, Tobacco, and Firearms (ATF) alleged that police officers assigned to ATF had stolen money from drug dealers. Soon thereafter, Klipfel and Caseli and their family were subject to threats, and action to fire the two was initiated. Although the Klipfel and Caseli case is an extreme one, whistle-blowers are frequently the target of retaliation from within their organization.

has held that agencies can choose rule-making procedures that meet the minimal threshold set down by Congress, that agencies can apply any reasonable interpretation of statutes unless Congress has specifically stated something to the contrary, and that agencies in many instances have wide discretion in deciding whether to enforce statutes.[41] These positions reflect the need for flexibility in administration. The bureaucracy and the courts would both grind to a halt if judges routinely chose to substitute their interpretations of the law for those of administrators. The judiciary cannot conduct a decision-by-decision oversight of the bureaucracy. Judges recognize that constraints on the bureaucracy must work mainly through the Congress and the president. The judiciary has promoted bureaucratic accountability primarily by encouraging administrators to act responsibly in their dealings with the public and by protecting individuals and groups from the bureaucracy's worst abuses.

Accountability Within the Bureaucracy Itself

A recognition of the difficulty of ensuring adequate accountability of the bureaucracy through the presidency, Congress, and the courts has led to the development of mechanisms of accountability within the bureaucracy itself. Two measures, whistle-blowing and demographic representativeness, are particularly noteworthy.

Whistle-Blowing

whistle-blowing An internal check on the bureaucracy whereby employees report instances of mismanagement that they observe.

Although the bureaucratic corruption that is rampant in some countries is relatively uncommon in the United States, a certain amount of waste, fraud, and abuse is inevitable in a bureaucracy as big as that of the federal government.

TABLE 13-3 Federal Job Rankings (GS) of Various Demographic Groups

Women and minority group members are underrepresented in the top jobs of the federal bureaucracy but their representation has been increasing.

GRADE LEVEL*	WOMEN'S SHARE 1976	WOMEN'S SHARE 2000	BLACKS' SHARE 1982	BLACKS' SHARE 2000	HISPANICS' SHARE 1982	HISPANICS' SHARE 2000
GS 1–4 (lowest ranks)	78%	68%	23%	27%	5%	9%
GS 5–8	60	68	19	25	4	8
GS 9–12	20	45	10	15	4	7
GS 13–15 (highest ranks)	5	31	5	10	2	4

*In general, the higher-numbered grades are managerial and professional positions, and the lower-numbered grades are clerical and manual labor positions.

Source: Office of Workforce Information, 2002.

Whistle-blowing, the act of reporting instances of corruption or mismanagement by one's fellow bureaucrats, is a potentially effective internal check.[42] A case in point is Coleen Rowley, a Minneapolis-based FBI agent, who accused top FBI officials of blocking an investigation that might have prevented the September 11, 2001, terrorist attacks. Agents in Minneapolis had wanted to investigate Zacarias Moussaaoui, who was being held in Minnesota on immigration charges. Moussaaoui had been enrolled in flight school, and the agents suspected he might be part of a terrorist plot. Rowley's revelation that FBI headquarters had blocked the investigation led to Senate hearings in which Rowley was the star witness.[43]

However, whistle-blowing has not been a highly successful policy. Many federal employees will not report instances of mismanagement because they fear reprisals from their superiors. To encourage them to come forward with their information, Congress enacted the Whistle Blower Protection Act to protect them from retaliation.

Demographic Representativeness

Although the bureaucracy is an unrepresentative institution in the sense that its officials are not elected by the people, it can be representative in the demographic sense. If bureaucrats were a demographic microcosm of the general public, they presumably would treat the various groups and interests in society more fairly.[44]

At present, the bureaucracy is not demographically representative at its top levels (see Table 13–3). More than 60 percent of managerial and professional positions are held by white males. However, the employment status of women and, to a lesser extent, minorities has improved somewhat in recent years, and top officials in the bureaucracy include a greater proportion of women and

demographic representativeness The idea that the bureaucracy will be more responsive to the public if its employees at all levels are demographically representative of the population as a whole.

minorities than is found in Congress or the judiciary. Moreover, if all levels of the federal bureaucracy are considered, it comes reasonably close to being representative of the nation's population.[45]

Demographic representativeness is only a partial answer to the problem of bureaucratic accountability. A fully representative civil service would still be required to play agency politics. The careerists in, say, defense agencies and welfare agencies are not very different in their demographic backgrounds, but they differ markedly in their opinions about policy. Each group believes that the goals of its agency should take priority. The inevitability of agency politics is the most significant of all political facts about the U.S. federal bureaucracy.[46]

REINVENTING GOVERNMENT

There have been numerous attempts during the twentieth century to enhance the bureaucracy's efficiency, responsiveness, and accountability. Another wave of this reform effort began in the 1990s, and it seeks to improve the administration of government by the reduction of its size, cost, and lines of authority.

In *Reinventing Government*, David Osborne and Ted Gaebler argue that the bureaucracy of today was created in response to earlier problems, particularly those spawned by the Industrial Revolution and a rampant spoils system. They claim that the information age requires a different kind of administrative structure, one that is more flexible and less hierarchical. Instead of the provision of goods and services, the bureaucracy ought to be in the business of creating incentives that will encourage individuals to make their own way and ought to foster competition among and between agencies and private firms. This approach requires a more decentralized form of administration that is oriented toward consumers and results. Osborne and Gaebler would empower lower-level employees to make decisions that previously were made at the top of the bureaucracy.[47]

This concept informed the Clinton administration's National Performance Review and is now embedded in some laws and administrative practices. An example is a law that requires agencies to monitor their performance by standards such as efficiency, responsiveness, and outcomes. These standards have long been considered gauges of administrative effectiveness but have often been overlooked as bureaucrats went about their customary ways of doing business. The law seeks to overcome this inertia by *requiring* agencies to actively monitor their performance.

Some analysts question the logic and presumed consequences of the new philosophy of administration. They have asked, for example, whether the principles of decentralized management and market-oriented programs are as sound as their advocates claim. The delegation of control to lower-level administrators weakens the hierarchical connection between elected and administrative officials. A reason for hierarchy was to ensure that decisions made at the bottom of the bureaucracy were faithful to the laws made by Congress. Free to act on their own, lower-level administrators, as they did under the spoils system, might favor certain people and interests over others.[48] There is also the issue of the identity of the "customers" in a market-oriented administration.[49] Who are the Security and Exchange Commission's customers—firms, brokerage houses, or shareholders? Will not some agencies inevitably favor their more powerful customers at the expense of the less powerful ones?

Americans in an Interdependent World

Bureaucracy Around the World

In polls, only about one in four Americans express confidence in the performance of the federal bureaucracy. Comparisons with other national bureaucracies, however, suggest that the U.S. bureaucracy is relatively effective. In fact, Charles Goodsell, a public administration expert, concludes that America's bureaucracy is among the best in the world. "Some national bureaucracies," he writes in *The Case for Bureaucracy*, "may be roughly the same [as the U.S. bureaucracy] in quality of overall performance, but they are few in number."

In many countries, the bureaucracy is thoroughly inefficient and corrupt. Tasks are completed slowly and sometimes not at all unless a bribe has been paid. In other countries, the bureaucracy is overly rigid, centralized, and remote. The rules are more important than the policy goals that these rules are designed to achieve.

Neither of these extreme tendencies is characteristic of the U.S. federal bureaucracy. Comparisons of national postal services, for example, confirm that the U.S. postal bureaucracy is one of the best worldwide. The U.S. mail usually arrives on time, at the right destination, and with the proper postage. In many countries, the mail is chronically late, often misrouted, frequently lost, and sometimes posted at the wrong rate.

Such comparisons suggest that Americans' complaints are grounded less in how their particular bureaucracy performs than in how bureaucracies generally perform. An encounter with a bureaucracy may require the completion of a lengthy form and then a considerable wait before action is taken. If such steps are necessary to ensure that people in the same situation receive the same treatment, the process is a source of frustration. Americans at least have the satisfaction of knowing that their applications are likely to be acted upon and that the action will be fair. In many parts of the world, applicants have no such guarantee.

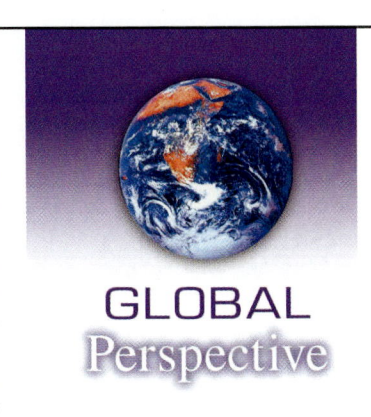

GLOBAL Perspective

Furthermore, there are practical limits on how much the federal bureaucracy can be trimmed. Some activities can be delegated to states and localities, and others can be privatized, but most of Washington's programs cannot be reassigned. National defense, social security, and Medicare are but three examples, and they alone account for more than half of all federal spending. National problems require national solutions, which is why national crises inevitably bring about an expansion of federal activity and authority. The war on terrorism that began in 2001, for example, has resulted in increased federal spending on military defense, intelligence gathering, law enforcement, and homeland security. Another example is the Enron scandal. In response to the collapse in 2002 of the nation's seventh largest firm from financial improprieties, new federal laws and regulations were developed to protect financiers, stockholders, and employees from unscrupulous business practices.

Thus, although the current wave of administrative reform is unique in its specific elements, it involves long-standing issues about the bureaucracy and about America's national needs. How can the federal government be made more efficient and yet accomplish all that Americans expect of it? How can it be made more responsive and yet act fairly? How can it be made more creative and yet be held accountable? There are, as history makes clear, no easy or final answers to these questions.

Self-Quiz
www.mhhe.com/patterson6

SUMMARY

Bureaucracy is a method of organizing people and work. It is based on the principles of hierarchical authority, job specialization, and formalized rules. As a form of organization, bureaucracy is the most efficient means of getting people to work together on tasks of great magnitude and complexity. It is also a form of organization that is prone to waste and rigidity, which is why efforts are being made to "reinvent" it.

The United States could not be governed without a large federal bureaucracy. The day-to-day work of the federal government, from mail delivery to provision of social security to international diplomacy, is done by the bureaucracy. Federal employees work in roughly four hundred major agencies, including cabinet departments, independent agencies, regulatory agencies, government corporations, and presidential commissions. Yet the bureaucracy is more than simply an administrative giant. Administrators exercise considerable discretion in their policy decisions. In the process of implementing policy, they make important policy and political choices.

Each agency of the federal government was created in response to political demands on national officials. Because of its origins in political demands, the administration of government is necessarily political. An inherent conflict results from two simultaneous but incompatible demands on the bureaucracy: that it respond to the preferences of partisan officials but also that it administer programs fairly and competently. These tensions are evident in the three concurrent personnel management systems under which the bureaucracy operates: patronage, merit, and executive leadership.

Administrators are actively engaged in politics and policymaking. The fragmentation of power and the pluralism of the American political system result in a policy process that is continually subject to conflict and contention. There is no clear policy or leadership mandate in the American system, and hence government agencies must compete for the power required to administer their programs effectively. Accordingly, civil servants tend to have an agency point of view: they seek to advance their agency's programs and to repel attempts by others to weaken their position. In promoting their agency, civil servants rely on their policy expertise, the backing of their clientele groups, and support from the president and Congress.

Administrators are not elected by the people they serve, yet they wield substantial independent power. Because of this, the bureaucracy's accountability is a central issue. The major checks on the bureaucracy are provided by the president, Congress, and the courts. The president has some power to reorganize the bureaucracy and the authority to appoint the political head of each agency. The president also has management tools (such as the executive budget) that can be used to limit administrators' discretion. Congress has influence on bureaucratic agencies through its authorization and funding powers and through various devices (including sunset laws and oversight hearings) that hold administrators accountable for their actions. The judiciary's role in ensuring the bureaucracy's accountability is smaller than that of the elected branches, but the courts do have the authority to force agencies to act in accordance with legislative intent, established procedures, and constitutionally guaranteed rights. Nevertheless, administrators are not fully accountable. They exercise substantial independent power, a situation that is not easily reconciled with democratic values.

Efforts are currently under way to scale down the federal bureaucracy. This reduction includes cuts in budgets, staff, and organizational units and also involves changes in the way the bureaucracy does its work. This process is a response to political forces and also to new management theories.

KEY TERMS

accountability
agency point of view
bureaucracy
cabinet (executive) departments
clientele groups
demographic representativeness
executive leadership system
formalized rules
government corporations
hierarchical authority
independent agencies
job specialization

merit (civil service) system
neutral competence
patronage system
policy implementation
presidential commissions
regulatory agencies
spoils system
whistle-blowing

SUGGESTED READINGS

Aberbach, Joel D., and Bert A. Rockman. *In the Web of Politics: Two Decades of the U.S. Federal Executive*. Washington, D.C.: Brookings Institution, 2000. An evaluation of the federal bureaucracy and its evolving nature.

Brehm, John, and Scott Gates. *Working, Shirking, and Sabotage: Bureaucratic Response to a Democratic Public*. Ann Arbor: University of Michigan Press, 1996. A generally favorable assessment of the bureaucracy's responsiveness to the public it serves.

Cook, Brian J. *Bureaucracy and Self-Government: Reconsidering the Role of Public Administration in American Politics*. Baltimore, Md.: Johns Hopkins University Press, 1996. A thorough history of public administration in American politics.

Kettl, Donald F., Patricia W. Ingraham, Ronald P. Sanders, and Constance Horner. *Civil Service Reform: Building a Government That Works*. Washington, D.C.: Brookings Institution Press, 1996. A careful analysis of government management.

Osborne, David, and Ted Gaebler. *Reinventing Government: How the Entrepreneurial Spirit Is Transforming the Public Sector*. New York: Addison-Wesley, 1992. The book that Washington policymakers in the 1990s regarded as the guide to transforming the bureaucracy.

Sagini, Meshack M. *Organizational Behavior: The Challenges of the New Millennium*. Lanham, Md.: University Press of America, 2001. A comprehensive assessment of bureaucratic structures and behaviors.

Wood, B. Dan, and Richard W. Waterman. *Bureaucratic Dynamics: The Role of Bureaucracy in a Democracy*. Boulder, Colo.: Westview Press, 1994. A penetrating analysis of bureaucratic agencies and their power relationships with the president, Congress, and constituent groups.

LIST OF WEBSITES

http://iccweb.com/federal
A site for those interested in finding employment with the federal government. The site provides job applications and other information for the various federal agencies.

http://www.census.gov
Website of the Census Bureau; the bureau is the best source of statistical information on Americans and the government agencies that administer programs affecting them.

http://www.whistleblower.org
The Government Accountability Project's website; this project is designed to protect and encourage whistle-blowers by providing information and support to federal employees.

http://www.whitehouse.gov/WH/Cabinet
Lists the cabinet secretaries and provides links to each cabinet-level department.

14

It is emphatically the province and duty of the judicial department to say what the law is. Those who apply the rule to particular cases, must of necessity expound and interpret that rule. If two laws conflict with each other, the courts must decide on the operation of each.

—John Marshall[1]

The Federal Judicial System:
Applying the Law

Through its ruling in *Bush v. Gore*, the U.S. Supreme Court effectively ended the 2000 presidential election.[2] At issue was whether the "undervotes" in Florida—ballots on which counting machines had detected no vote for president—would be tabulated by hand. Florida's top court had ordered a statewide manual recount, but the U.S. Supreme Court by a narrow 5-4 margin had issued a rare emergency order halting the action. Three days later, the Supreme Court's majority delivered its ruling, saying that the manual recount violated the constitution's equal protection clause. Florida's high court had said that officials should base the hand count on the "intent of the voter." The Supreme Court held that this standard gave county officials in Florida too much leeway and violated the right of citizens to have their votes counted fairly and equally.

The ruling brought charges that the Supreme Court had acted politically rather than on any strict interpretation of the law. In issuing a halt to the recount, the Court had divided sharply along ideological lines. The majority consisted of its most conservative members, all of whom were Republican appointees: Chief Justice William Rehnquist and associate justices Sandra Day O'Connor, Anthony Kennedy, Antonin Scalia, and Clarence Thomas. In a dissenting opinion, Justice John Paul Stevens said: "Preventing the recount from being completed will inevitably cast a doubt upon the legitimacy of the election." Stevens argued that the Florida high court's decision had properly reflected "the basic principle, inherent in our Constitution and our democracy, that every legal vote should be counted."

Bush v. Gore was hardly the first time that the Supreme Court has been a center of controversy.[3] If liberals were angered by its 2000 election decision, conservatives were outraged, for example, by a series of abortion rulings that began with *Roe v. Wade* in 1973.[4] The *Roe* decision touched off a heated debate within the legal community. Some legalists supported the decision, arguing that the judiciary must act to protect basic rights, even ones, including abortion, that are not explicitly provided by the Constitution.[5] Other legalists claimed that the Court had overstepped its authority. From their perspective, the problem with the *Roe* decision was that a right of abortion is not supported by any specific constitutional guarantee and therefore should not be established by judicial fiat.[6]

These examples illustrate three key points about court decisions. First, the judiciary is an extremely important policymaking body. Some of its rulings are as consequential as nearly any law passed by Congress or executive action taken by the president. Second, the judiciary has considerable discretion in its rulings. The *Bush v. Gore* and *Roe v. Wade* decisions were not based on any literal reading of the law: the justices in each case invoked *their* interpretation of the Constitution's provisions for individual rights.

Third, the judiciary is a political as well as legal institution, as illustrated by the conflict surrounding recent Supreme Court nominations. Once a law is established, it is expected to be administered in an evenhanded way. But the law itself is a product of contending political forces, is developed through a political process, has political content, and is applied by political appointees.

This chapter describes the federal judiciary and the work of its judges and justices. Like the executive and legislative branches, the judiciary is an independent branch of the U.S. government, but unlike the two other branches, its top officials are not elected by the people. The judiciary is not a democratic institution, and its role is different from and, in some areas, more controversial than those of the executive and legislative branches. This chapter explores this issue in the process of discussing several main points:

- *The federal judiciary includes the Supreme Court of the United States, which functions mainly as an appellate court; courts of appeals, which hear appeals; and district courts, which hold trials.* Each state has a court system of its own, which for the most part is independent of supervision by the federal courts.

- *Judicial decisions are constrained by applicable constitutional law, statutory law, and precedent.* Nevertheless, political factors have a major influence on judicial appointments and decisions; judges are political officials as well as legal ones.

- *The judiciary has become an increasingly powerful policymaking body in recent decades, which has raised the question of the judiciary's proper role in a democracy.* The philosophies of judicial restraint and judicial activism provide different answers to this question.

THE FEDERAL JUDICIAL SYSTEM

The writers of the Constitution were determined that the judiciary would be a separate branch of the federal government but, for practical reasons, did not spell out the full structure of the federal court system. The Constitution provides for the Supreme Court of the United States but grants to Congress the power to determine the number and structure of lower federal courts.

Federal judges are nominated by the president, and if confirmed by the U.S. Senate, they are appointed by the president to the office. The Constitution states that judges "shall hold their offices during good behavior." However, the Constitution does not contain a precise definition of "good behavior," and no Supreme Court justice and only a very small number of lower-court judges have been removed from office through impeachment and conviction by Congress. In practice, federal judges and justices serve until they retire or die.

Unlike the offices of president, senator, and representative, the Constitution places no age, residency, or citizenship qualifications on federal judicial office. Nor does the Constitution require a judge to have legal training. Tradition alone dictates that federal judges have an educational or professional background in the law.

Demonstrators rally outside the U.S. Supreme Court building during hearings on the *Bush v. Gore* case that effectively brought the 2000 presidential election to an end. At times, the policy rulings of the judiciary are as significant as the decisions of the president or Congress.

The Supreme Court of the United States

The Supreme Court of the United States is the nation's highest court. The chief justice of the United States presides over the Supreme Court and, like the eight associate justices, is selected by the president and is subject to Senate confirmation. The chief justice has the same voting power as the other justices but has usually exercised additional influence because of the position's leadership role.

The Constitution grants the Supreme Court both original and appellate jurisdiction. A court's **jurisdiction** is its authority to hear cases of a particular type. **Original jurisdiction** is the authority to be the first court to hear a case. The Supreme Court's original jurisdiction embraces legal disputes involving foreign diplomats and those in which the opposing parties are state governments. The Court in its entire history has convened as a court of original jurisdiction only a few hundred times and has rarely done so in recent years.

The Supreme Court does its most significant work as an appellate court. **Appellate jurisdiction** is the authority to review cases that have already been heard in lower courts and are appealed to the higher court by the losing party; such courts are called appeals courts or appellate courts. The Supreme Court's appellate jurisdiction extends to cases arising under the Constitution, federal law and regulations, and treaties. The Court also hears appeals involving admiralty or maritime issues and legal controversies that cross state or national boundaries. Appellate courts, including the Supreme Court, do not retry cases; rather, they determine whether a trial court acted in accord with applicable law.

jurisdiction (of a court) A given court's authority to hear cases of a particular kind. Jurisdiction may be original or appellate.

original jurisdiction The authority of a given court to be the first court to hear a case.

appellate jurisdiction The authority of a given court to review cases that have already been tried in lower courts and are appealed to it by the losing party; such a court is called an appeals court or appellate court.

Selecting Cases

The primary function of the judiciary is to interpret the law in such a way that rules made in the past (for example, the Constitution or legislation) can be applied reasonably in the present. This function gives the courts—all courts—a

Figure 14–1

Supreme Court Opinions, 1950–2000

The number of signed Supreme Court opinions each term is relatively small. The Court has considerable control over the cases it selects. The cases that are heard by the Supreme Court tend to be ones that have legal significance beyond the particular case itself.

Source: Supreme Court of the United States. The Court's term runs from October 1 to June 30; the year indicated is the closing year of the term.

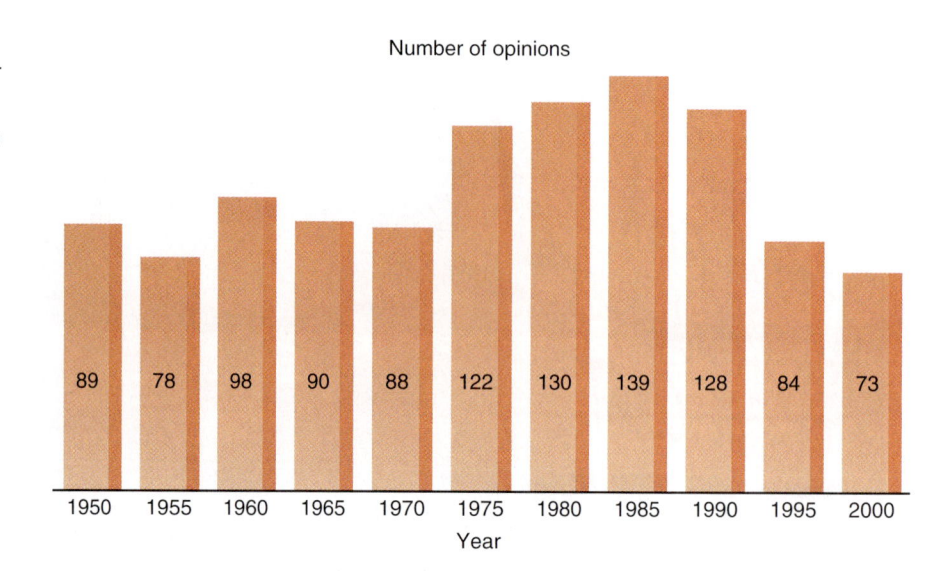

Year	Number of opinions
1950	89
1955	78
1960	98
1965	90
1970	88
1975	122
1980	130
1985	139
1990	128
1995	84
2000	73

writ of certiorari Permission granted by a higher court to allow a losing party in a legal case to bring the case before it for a ruling; when such a writ is requested of the U.S. Supreme Court, four of the Court's nine justices must agree to accept the case before it is granted certiorari.

role in policymaking. Antitrust legislation, for example, is designed to prevent uncompetitive business practices, but like all such legislation, it is not self-enforcing. It is up to the courts to decide whether and how these laws apply to the case at hand.

As the nation's highest court, the Supreme Court is particularly important in establishing legal precedents that guide lower courts. A *precedent* is a judicial decision that serves as a rule for settling subsequent cases of a similar nature. Lower courts are expected to follow precedent—that is, to resolve cases of a like nature in ways consistent with upper-court rulings. However, for reasons that will be explained later, they do not always do so.

The Supreme Court's ability to set legal precedent is strengthened by its nearly complete discretion in choosing the cases it will hear. The large majority of cases reach the Supreme Court through a **writ of certiorari** in which the losing party in a lower-court case explains in writing why its case should be ruled on by the Court. Four of the nine justices must agree to accept a particular case before it is granted a writ. Each year roughly seven thousand parties apply for certiorari, but the Court accepts only about a hundred cases for a full hearing and signed ruling (see Figure 14–1). The Court issues another one hundred to two hundred *per curiam* (unsigned) decisions, which are made summarily without a hearing and simply state the facts of the case and the Court's decision. The Court is most likely to grant certiorari when the U.S. government through the solicitor general (the high-ranking Justice Department official who serves as the government's lawyer in Supreme Court cases) requests it.[7]

Case selection is a vital part of the Supreme Court's work. Through its review of applications for certiorari, the Court keeps abreast of legal controversies. Justice William Brennan noted that the certiorari process enables the Court to acquire a general idea of the compelling legal issues arising in lower courts and to address those that are most in need of immediate attention.[8] When the Court does accept a case, chances are that most of the justices disagree with the lower court's ruling. In recent years about three-fourths of the Supreme Court's decisions have reversed the judgments of lower courts.[9]

The Supreme Court building is located across from the Capitol in Washington, D.C. The courtroom, the justices' offices, and the conference room are on the first floor. Administrative staff offices and the Court's records and reference materials occupy the other floors.

The Court seldom accepts a routine case, even if the justices believe that a lower court has erred. The Supreme Court's job is not to correct every mistake of other courts, but to resolve broad legal questions. As a result, the justices usually choose cases that involve substantial legal issues. This criterion is vague but essentially means that a case must center on an issue of significance not merely to the parties involved but to the nation. As a result, most of the cases heard by the Court raise major constitutional issues, or affect the lives of many Americans, or address issues that are being decided inconsistently by the lower courts, or are in conflict with a previous Supreme Court ruling.[10] The last of these situations is particularly likely to propel a case to the Supreme Court, which naturally takes a keen interest in lower-court judgments that depart from its rulings.

Deciding Cases

Once the Supreme Court accepts a case, it sets a date on which the attorneys for the two sides will present their oral arguments. Strict time limits, usually thirty minutes per side, are placed on these arguments, because each side has already submitted written arguments to the justices.

The open hearing is far less important than the **judicial conference** that follows, which is attended only by the nine justices. The conference's proceedings are kept strictly confidential. This secrecy allows the justices to speak freely and tentatively about a case. The chief justice presides over the conference and ordinarily speaks first.[11] The other justices then speak in order of their seniority (length of service on the Court). This arrangement enhances the senior members' ability to influence the discussion. After the discussion, the justices vote on the case; the least senior justice usually votes first and the chief justice votes last.

judicial conference A closed meeting of the justices of the U.S. Supreme Court to discuss and vote on the cases before them; the justices are not supposed to discuss conference proceedings with outsiders.

Simulation
www.mhhe.com/patterson6

decision A vote of the Supreme Court in a particular case that indicates which party the justices side with and by how large a margin.

opinion (of a court) A court's written explanation of its decision, which serves to inform others of the legal basis for the decision. Supreme Court opinions are expected to guide the decisions of other courts.

majority opinion A Supreme Court opinion that results when a majority of the justices are in agreement on the legal basis of the decision.

plurality opinion A court opinion that results when a majority of justices agree on a decision in a case but do not agree on the legal basis for the decision. In this instance, the legal position held by most of the justices on the winning side is called a plurality opinion.

concurring opinion A separate opinion written by a Supreme Court justice who votes with the majority in the decision on a case but who disagrees with their reasoning.

dissenting opinion The opinion of a justice in a Supreme Court case that explains his or her reasons for disagreeing with the majority's decision.

The chief justice is expected to provide leadership but has no power to compel the other justices to respond. Consequently, the chief justice's intellectual capacities, knowledge of the law, political awareness, and persuasiveness are significant aspects of the chief justice's leadership. Charles Evans Hughes is reputed to have been the most effective leader in the Court's history, although John Marshall is generally regarded as the greatest chief justice. The current chief justice, William Rehnquist, is widely viewed as a personally aloof but intellectually assertive leader.

Issuing Decisions and Opinions

After a case has been discussed and decided on in conference, the Court prepares and issues its ruling, which consists of a decision and one or more opinions. The **decision** indicates which party the Court supports and by how large a margin. The **opinion** explains the reasons behind the decision. The opinion is the most important part of a Supreme Court ruling because it informs others of the justices' interpretations of laws. For example, in the landmark *Brown v. Board of Education of Topeka* (1954) opinion, the Court held that government-sponsored school segregation was unconstitutional because it violated the Fourteenth Amendment's guarantee that all Americans are entitled to equal protection under the laws. Enforced segregation of the public schools was therefore constitutionally impermissible. This opinion became the legal basis by which communities throughout the southern states were ordered by lower courts to end their policy of segregating students in their public schools by race.[12]

When a majority of the justices agree on the legal basis of a decision, the result is a **majority opinion**. In some cases there is no majority opinion because a majority of the justices agree on the decision but cannot agree on the legal basis for it. The result is a **plurality opinion**, which presents the view held by most of the justices who side with the winning party. Another type of opinion is a **concurring opinion**, which is a separate view written by a justice who votes with the majority but disagrees with its reasoning.

Justices on the losing side can write a **dissenting opinion** to explain their reasons for disagreeing with the majority position. Sometimes these dissenting views become a later Court's majority position. In a 1942 dissenting opinion, Justice Hugo Black wrote that defendants in state felony trials should have legal counsel, even if they could not afford to pay for it. Two decades later, in *Gideon v. Wainwright* (1963), the Court adopted this position.[13]

When part of the majority, the chief justice decides which of the justices will write the majority opinion. Otherwise, the senior justice in the majority determines the author. Chief justices have often given themselves the influential task of writing the majority opinion in important cases. John Marshall did so often: *Marbury v. Madison* (1802) and *McCulloch v. Maryland* (1819) were among the opinions he wrote.

The justice who writes the Court's majority opinion has an important and difficult job, since the other justices who voted with the majority must agree with the written opinion. Because the vote on a case is not considered final until the decision is made public, plenty of compromising and old-fashioned horse trading can take place during the writing stage. The majority opinion often goes through a series of drafts and is circulated among all nine justices. In *Brown v.*

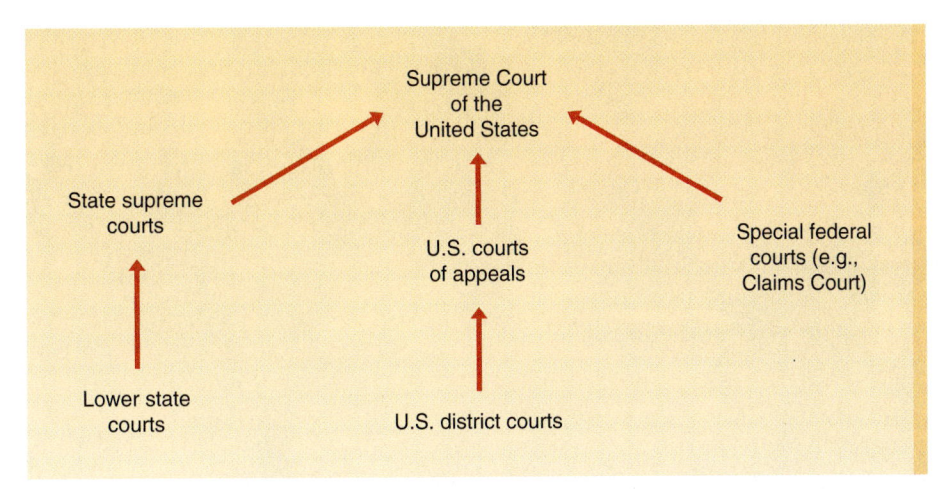

Figure 14-2

The Federal Judicial System
The simplified diagram shows the relationships among the various levels of federal courts and between state and federal courts. The losing party in a case can appeal a lower-court decision to the court at the next-highest level, as the arrows indicate. Decisions can normally be removed from state courts to federal courts only if they raise a constitutional question.

Board of Education, Justice Felix Frankfurter, the lone initial holdout, was persuaded to make the decision unanimous by the continued urgings of his colleagues and by their willingness to incorporate some of his concerns into the majority opinion.

Other Federal Courts

There are more than one hundred federal courts but there is only one Supreme Court, and its position at the top of the country's judicial system gives the Supreme Court unparalleled importance. It is a mistake, however, to conclude that the Supreme Court is the only court of consequence. Judge Jerome Frank once wrote of the "upper-court myth," which is the view that appellate courts and in particular the Supreme Court make up the only truly significant judicial arena and that lower courts just dutifully follow the rulings handed down by the appellate level.[14] The reality is very different, as the following discussion will explain.

U.S. District Courts

The lowest federal courts are the district courts (see Figure 14-2). There are more than ninety federal district courts altogether—at least one in every state and as many as four in some states. District court judges, who number about eight hundred in all, are appointed by the president with the consent of the Senate. Federal cases usually originate in district courts, which are trial courts where the parties argue their sides. District courts are the only courts in the federal system in which juries hear testimony. Most cases at this level are presented before a single judge.

Lower federal courts unquestionably rely on and follow Supreme Court decisions in their own rulings. The Supreme Court reiterated this requirement in a 1982 case, *Hutto v. Davis*: "Unless we wish anarchy to prevail within the federal judicial system, a precedent of this Court must be followed by the lower federal courts no matter how misguided the judges of those courts may think it to be."[15]

The Supreme Court is not the only federal court that "matters" in the American judicial system. Most federal cases originate in U.S. district courts, and most appealed cases are settled in U.S. courts of appeals, never reaching the Supreme Court. Shown here is testimony at a trial in district court, the only level in the federal system in which juries decide the outcome of cases.

However, the idea that lower courts are guided strictly by Supreme Court rulings is part of the upper-court myth. District court judges may misunderstand the Supreme Court's position and deviate from it for that reason. In addition, the facts of a case before a district court are seldom identical to those of a case settled by the Supreme Court. The lower-court judge must decide whether a different legal principle must be invoked. In some cases, district court judges have willfully disregarded Supreme Court precedent, finding a basis for decision that allows them to reach a judgment they prefer. For example, after the Supreme Court declared in *Brown v. Board of Education* that racial segregation of public schools violated the Fourteenth Amendment's guarantee of equal protection under the law, many southern district court judges who opposed the principle of racial equality concluded that the issue in the school desegregation cases before them was not equal protection but the maintenance of public order and that school desegregation could not be allowed because it would disrupt public order. Finally, it is not unusual for the Supreme Court to take a very broad legal position that is general and ambiguous enough to allow lower courts to decide its exact meaning in practice. Trial-court judges then have a creative role in judicial decision making that rivals that of appellate court judges.

Most federal cases end with the district court's decision; the losing party does not appeal the decision to a higher court. This fact is another indication of the highly significant role of district court judges.

U.S. Courts of Appeals

When cases are appealed from district courts, they go to a federal court of appeals. These appellate courts make up the second level of the federal court system. Courts of appeals do not use juries. No new evidence is submitted in an appealed case; appellate courts base their decisions on a review of lower-court records. Appellate judges act as supervisors in the legal system, reviewing trial-court decisions and correcting what they consider to be legal errors. Facts (i.e., the circumstances of a case) found by district courts are presumed to be correct.

Americans in an Interdependent World

The International Criminal Court

After World War II, the United States led the way in establishing the temporary Nuremberg and Tokyo tribunals to try German and Japanese leaders accused of war crimes. The third such temporary tribunal in modern history is now underway at The Hague, Netherlands. The International Criminal Tribunal was established several years ago to assess the guilt and innocence of the people accused of war crimes in the Balkan wars of the 1990s. Slobodan Milosevic, the president of the former Yugoslavia, is the most prominent defendant.

In 1998, 120 member countries of the United Nations endorsed a plan to create, for the first time in world history, a permanent international court to handle atrocities committed under the guise of war. Although such atrocities in an earlier time might not have attracted worldwide attention, the globalization of the media and the widening role of international bodies such as the United Nations now ensure that they will be noticed. The permanent court—which is called the International Criminal Court (ICC)—will handle such cases. At the 1998 conference, it was decided that the ICC would begin its work after sixty nations had ratified the treaty that authorized it. This threshold was reached in 2002.

Not every nation supports the ICC. The United States is among the holdouts. The Bush administration has refused to endorse the treaty, and a majority in Congress opposes its ratification. Many U.S. policymakers fear that an American might someday be brought before the ICC, which provides fewer legal protections than Americans enjoy under the Constitution. For example, the ICC offers no right to a trial by jury, and a majority vote of the judges is sufficient for conviction.

A larger concern of U.S. policymakers is that the ICC will become a means by which other countries would put American soldiers on trial. During the war in Vietnam, for example, U.S. air and ground forces killed thousands of noncombatants and defoliated vast areas of land. Were such actions the unfortunate consequence of a deadly war, or were they, in some instances, crimes of war? Many U.S. leaders would prefer to leave that judgment to U.S. courts rather than entrusting it to the international court.

Some analysts believe the United States has more to lose than to gain by refusing to support the International Criminal Court. They argue that the United States has enough clout in international circles to prevent the court from becoming a weapon in the hands of the nation's enemies. They say the only countries that need to fear the international court are autocratic regimes that use wanton murder and terrorism as instruments of national policy.

Where do you stand on the question of whether the world needs the International Criminal Court and whether the United States should participate in it?

GLOBAL Perspective

The United States has twelve general appeals courts, each of which serves a "circuit" that is comprised of between three and nine states, except the one that serves the District of Columbia only. There is also the U.S. Court of Appeals for the Federal Circuit, which specializes in appeals of cases involving patents and international trade. Between four and twenty-six judges sit on each court of appeals, but each case is usually heard by a panel of three judges. On rare occasions, all the judges of a court of appeals sit as a body (*en banc*) in order to resolve difficult controversies, typically ones that have resulted in conflicting decisions within the same circuit.

Courts of appeals offer the only real hope of reversal for many appellants, since the Supreme Court hears so few cases. Fewer than 1 percent of the cases heard by federal appeals courts are later reviewed by the Supreme Court.

Special U.S. Courts

In addition to the Supreme Court, the courts of appeals, and the district courts, the federal judiciary includes a few specialty courts. Among them are the U.S. Claims Court, which hears cases in which the U.S. government is being sued for damages; the U.S. Court of International Trade, which handles cases involving appeals of U.S. Customs Office rulings; and the U.S. Court of Military Appeals, which hears appeals of military courts-martial. Some federal agencies and commissions also have adjudicative powers, and their decisions can be appealed to a federal court of appeals.

The State Courts

The American states are separate governments within the United State's federal system. Each state is protected in its sovereignty by the Tenth Amendment, and each state has its own court system. Like the federal courts, state court systems have trial courts at the bottom level and appellate courts at the top.

Each state decides for itself the structure of its courts and the method of judicial appointment. In some states, judges are appointed by the governor, but judgeships are *elective offices* in most states. The common form involves competitive elections of either a partisan or nonpartisan nature, although some states use a system called the *merit plan* (also called the "Missouri Plan" because Missouri was the first state to use it) under which the governor selects a judge from a short list of acceptable candidates provided by a judicial selection commission. After a year or more on the bench, the judge selected must be approved by the voters in order to serve a longer term. Thereafter, the judge must face a periodic (usually every six years) "retention election" in which voters decide whether he or she will continue in the office (see "States in the Nation").

Besides the upper-court myth, there exists a "federal court myth," which holds that the federal judiciary is the most significant part of the judicial system and that state courts play a subordinate role. This view is inaccurate as well. More than 95 percent of the nation's legal cases are decided in state courts. Most crimes (from shoplifting to murder) and most civil controversies (such as divorces and corporate disputes) are defined by state or local law. Moreover, nearly all cases that originate in state courts also end there. The federal courts never come into the picture because the case does not involve a federal issue.

In state criminal cases, after a person has been convicted and after all avenues of appeal in the state court system have been exhausted, the defendant can seek a writ of habeas corpus from a federal district court (see Chapter 4). The federal court often confines itself to the federal aspects of the matter, such as whether the defendant in a criminal case received the protections guaranteed by the U.S. Constitution. In addition, the federal court must accept the facts determined by the state court unless such findings are clearly in error. In short, legal and factual determinations of state courts can bind the federal courts—a clear contradiction of the federal court myth.

STATES IN THE NATION

Principal Methods of Selecting Judges for States' Highest Court

The states rely on a variety of methods for selecting the judicial officers of their highest court, including the merit plan, partisan election, nonpartisan election, and political appointment. Only a fourth of the states appoint their top judges, which, of course, is the method for choosing federal judges and justices. Most of the states that appoint their judges wrote their original constitutions in the same era that the U.S. Constitution was written. The states that appoint judges grant this power to the governor except in Virginia, Connecticut, and South Carolina, where the legislature makes the choice.

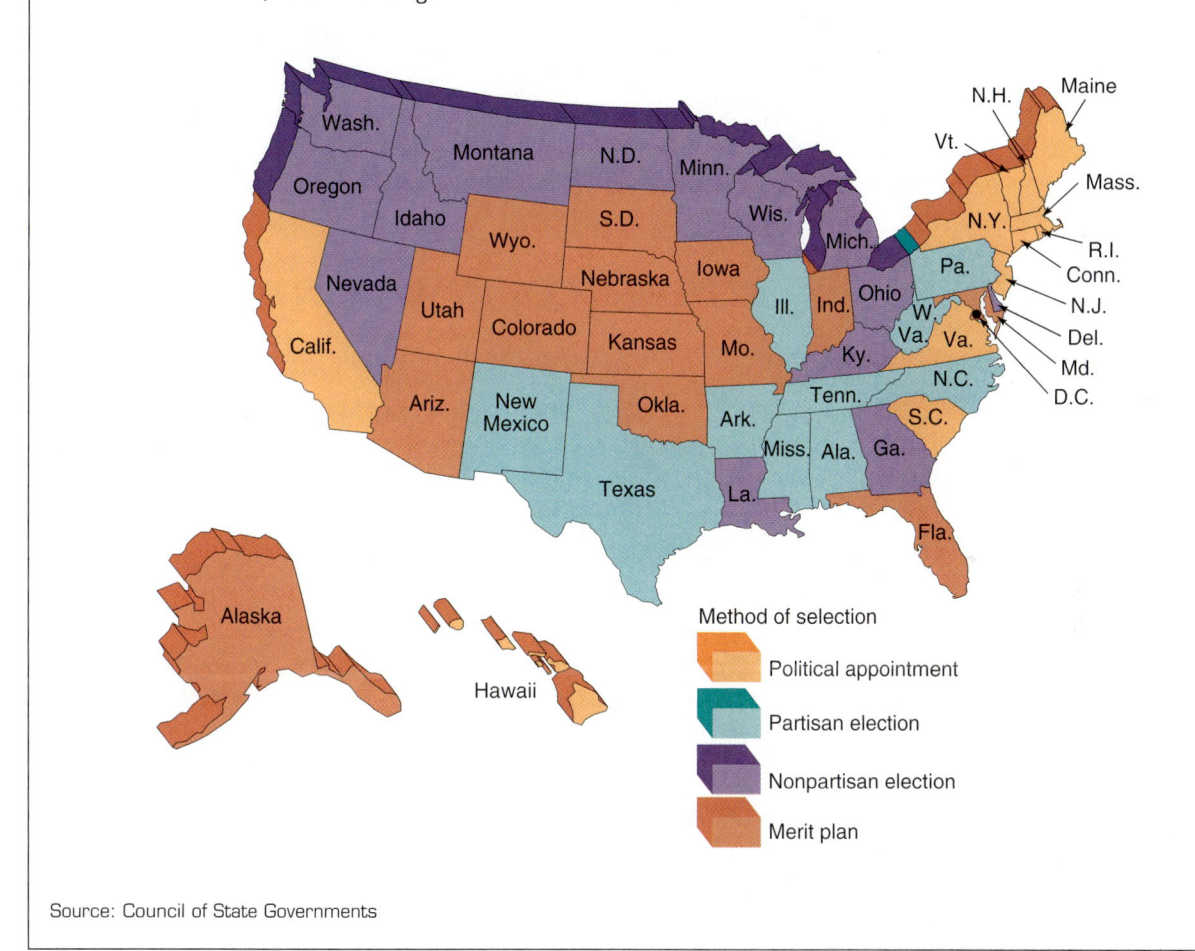

Method of selection:
- Political appointment
- Partisan election
- Nonpartisan election
- Merit plan

Source: Council of State Governments

However, cases traditionally within the jurisdiction of the states can become federal cases through rulings of federal courts. In *Roe v. Wade* (1973), for example, the Supreme Court concluded that women had the right under the Constitution to choose an abortion, thus making abortion rights, which had been a state issue, also a federal one.[16] (This situation is called "diversity of citizenship" jurisdiction, meaning that both state and federal courts have some jurisdiction over the issue.)

The Florida Supreme Court hears the arguments that led it to order a statewide canvass of uncounted ballots in the Bush-Gore presidential contest. Less than a day after it was rendered, the court's order was blocked by the U.S. Supreme Court. It was a rare intervention. Upwards of 95 percent of the nation's legal cases are decided entirely within the state court system, an indication of the federal court myth.

FEDERAL COURT APPOINTEES

The quiet setting of the courtroom, the dignity of its proceedings, and the lack of fanfare with which a court delivers its decisions give the impression that the judiciary is about as far removed from the world of politics as a governmental institution can possibly be. The reality is different. Federal judges and justices are political officials who exercise the authority of a separate and powerful branch of government. All federal jurists bring their political views with them to the courtroom and have regular opportunities to promote their political beliefs through the cases they decide. Accordingly, the process by which federal judges are appointed is a partisan one.

Selecting Supreme Court Justices and Federal Judges

The formal mechanism for appointments to the Supreme Court and the lower federal courts is the same: the president nominates and the Senate confirms or rejects. Beyond that basic similarity, however, there are significant differences.

Supreme Court Nominees

A Supreme Court appointment is a critical choice for a president.[17] The cases that come before the Court tend to be controversial and have far-reaching implications. And since the Court is a small body, each justice's vote can be crucial to the decisions it makes. Because most justices retain their positions for many years, presidents can influence judicial policy through their appointments long after they have left office. The careers of some Supreme Court justices provide dramatic testimony to the enduring effects of judicial appointments. Franklin D. Roosevelt appointed William O. Douglas to the Supreme Court in 1939, and for thirty years after Roosevelt's death in 1945, Douglas remained a strong liberal influence on the Court.

The Justices of the U.S. Supreme Court pose for a photo. From left, they are: Clarence Thomas, Antonin Scalia, Sandra Day O'Connor, Anthony Kennedy, David Souter, Stephen Breyer, John Paul Stevens, Chief Justice William Rehnquist, and Ruth Bader Ginsburg.

Presidents have employed a variety of approaches in their efforts to select a Supreme Court nominee who will reflect their political philosophy. Presidents may choose to depend chiefly on their own counsel, ask the Justice Department for advice, or seek the views of interested parties who share the president's general philosophy. Nominees must also be acceptable to many other people. Every nominee is closely scrutinized by the legal community, interested groups, and the media; must undergo an extensive background check by the FBI; and then must gain the approval of a Senate majority.

Within the Senate, a key body is the Judiciary Committee, whose members have responsibility for conducting hearings on judicial nominees and recommending their confirmation or rejection by the full Senate. Nearly 20 percent of presidential nominees have been rejected by the Senate on grounds of judicial qualification, political views, personal ethics, or partisanship. Most of these rejections in the country's history occurred before 1900, and partisan politics was the main reason. Today a nominee with strong professional and ethical credentials is less likely to be blocked for partisan reasons alone. An exception was Robert Bork, whose 1987 nomination by President Reagan was rejected primarily because of strong opposition from Senate Democrats who disagreed with his judicial philosophy. Middle-of-the-road, noncontroversial nominees almost always are approved by the Senate. One such nominee, Ruth Bader Ginsburg, was confirmed by a 96-3 Senate vote in 1993.

Lower-Court Nominees

The president normally gives the deputy attorney general the task of screening potential nominees for lower-court judgeships.[18] **Senatorial courtesy** is also a consideration in these appointments: this tradition, which dates back to the 1840s, holds that a senator from the state in which a vacancy has arisen should

senatorial courtesy The tradition that a U.S. senator from the state in which a federal judicial vacancy has arisen should have a say in the president's nomination of the new judge if the senator is of the same party as the president.

President Dwight D. Eisenhower shakes hands with William Brennan in the Oval Office after selecting Brennan to be an associate justice of the Supreme Court. Eisenhower would later say that he made a mistake in appointing Brennan to the Court. Brennan's decisions were more liberal than Eisenhower had expected.

be given a say in the nomination if the senator is of the same party as the president.[19] If not consulted, the senator involved can request that confirmation be denied, and other senators will normally grant the request as a "courtesy" to a fellow senator.[20] Not surprisingly, presidents have preferred to give senators a voice in judicial appointments.

Although the president does not become as personally involved in selecting lower-court nominees as in naming potential Supreme Court justices, lower-court appointments are collectively a significant factor in the impact of a president's administration. Recent presidents have appointed about two hundred judges each term.

Justices and Judges as Political Officials

Presidents generally manage to appoint jurists who have a similar political philosophy. Although Supreme Court justices are free to make their own decisions, their legal positions can usually be inferred from their prior activities. A study by the judicial scholar Robert Scigliano found that about three of every four appointees have behaved on the Supreme Court approximately as presidents could have expected.[21] Of course, a president has no guarantee that a nominee will fulfill his hopes. Justices Earl Warren and William Brennan proved more liberal than President Dwight D. Eisenhower would have liked. When he was asked whether he had made any mistakes as president, Eisenhower replied, "Yes, two, and they are both sitting on the Supreme Court."[22]

The Role of Partisanship

In nearly every instance, presidents have chosen members of their own party as Supreme Court nominees. Partisanship is also decisive in nominations to lower-court judgeships. More than 90 percent of recent district and appeals court nominees have been members of the president's own party.[23]

Why Should I Care?

Judicial Appointments

As a presidential campaign draws to a close, supporters of both candidates urge people to consider that, in choosing a president, they are also deciding who will be appointed to positions on the federal courts. Judging from opinion polls, not many voters are swayed one way or the other by this argument.

Nevertheless, the argument has some basis. For one thing, judicial appointments are essentially lifetime appointments, which means that a judicial nominee is likely to hold office long after the president leaves office. The most renowned jurist in American history, John Marshall, was appointed chief justice in 1801 by the second president, John Adams, and served until 1835, when the seventh president, Andrew Jackson, was nearing the end of his second term.

Second, the judiciary is a powerful and independent branch of the federal government. Because the United States has a federal system and a separation of powers, the judiciary is thrust into the middle of many controversies. The French theorist Alexis de Tocqueville observed that there is barely a political controversy in America that sooner or later does not become also a judicial controversy. Abortion, age-related discrimination, and Internet content are but a few recent examples. Moreover, unlike some national courts, U.S. federal courts have the power of judicial review. They are not simply empowered to hear cases arising under statutory and administrative law. They can invalidate state and national law if they conclude it violates the U.S. Constitution.

Third, partisanship affects the decisions that judges and justices make. Although the law is supposedly neutral, the partisan leanings of a judicial officer can affect the outcome of a case, particularly when the facts are murky or the applicable laws are vague. On civil rights cases, for example, there is a small but measurable tendency for Democratic appointees to side more often with the party alleging discrimination and for Republican appointees to side more often with the party alleged to have engaged in discrimination.

In sum, a president's judicial appointments are consequential. Whether you should weigh this fact heavily when you choose a presidential candidate is debatable, but you should not doubt that a president's nominees will leave their imprint on the law for years to come.

The fact that judges and justices are chosen through a partisan political process should not be interpreted to mean that they engage in blatant partisanship while on the bench. Judges and justices are officers of a separate branch and prize their judicial independence. All Republican appointees do not vote the same way on cases, nor do all Democrats. Nevertheless, the partisan backgrounds of judges are a significant influence on their decisions. A study of the voting records of appellate court judges, for example, found that Republican appointees tend to be more conservative than Democratic appointees in their civil rights and civil liberties decisions.[24] In Supreme Court cases, Democratic and Republican appointees have often been on opposite sides, although other divisions also occur.

Other Characteristics of Judicial Appointees

In recent years, increasing numbers of federal justices and judges have had prior judicial experience; the assumption is that such individuals are best qualified for appointment to the federal bench. Most recent appellate court appointees have been district or state judges or have worked in the office of the attorney general.[25] Elective office (particularly a seat in the U.S. Senate) was

TABLE 14-1 Justices of the Supreme Court, 2002
Most recent appointees held an appellate court position before being nominated to the Supreme Court.

JUSTICE	YEAR OF APPOINTMENT	NOMINATING PRESIDENT	POSITION BEFORE APPOINTMENT
William Rehnquist*	1971	Nixon	Assistant attorney general
John Paul Stevens	1975	Ford	Judge, U.S. Court of Appeals
Sandra Day O'Connor	1981	Reagan	Judge, Arizona Court of Appeals
Antonin Scalia	1986	Reagan	Judge, U.S. Court of Appeals
Anthony Kennedy	1988	Reagan	Judge, U.S. Court of Appeals
David Souter	1990	Bush	Judge, U.S. Court of Appeals
Clarence Thomas	1991	Bush	Judge, U.S. Court of Appeals
Ruth Bader Ginsburg	1993	Clinton	Judge, U.S. Court of Appeals
Stephen Breyer	1994	Clinton	Judge, U.S. Court of Appeals

*Appointed chief justice in 1986.

once a common route to the Supreme Court,[26] but now justices have typically held an appellate court judgeship before their appointment (see Table 14–1).

White males are greatly overrepresented on the federal bench, just as they dominate in Congress and at the top levels of the executive branch.[27] However, the number of women and minority-group judges increased substantially as a result of the appointments of President Clinton. About a third of Clinton's appointees were women compared with a seventh of the appointees of the two previous presidents (Reagan and Bush).

The Supreme Court itself is also demographically unrepresentative. Until 1916, when Louis D. Brandeis was appointed to the Court, no Jewish justice had ever served. At least one Catholic, but at most times only one, has been on the Court almost continuously for nearly a century. Thurgood Marshall in 1967 became the first black justice, and Sandra Day O'Connor in 1981 became the first woman. Antonin Scalia in 1986 became the Court's first justice of Italian descent. No person of Hispanic or Asian descent has ever been a member of the Court.

Judicial scholars disagree on the importance of the Court's demographic makeup. Henry J. Abraham dismisses concerns about it, claiming that the Court was never meant to be a representative body. In contrast, Sheldon Goldman asserts that the judiciary's sensitivity to society's diverse interests depends to a degree on the social backgrounds that the justices bring with them to the Court.[28]

THE NATURE OF JUDICIAL DECISION MAKING

Federal judges and justices are political officials: they constitute one of three coequal branches of the national government. Yet, unlike members of Congress or the president, judges serve in a legal institution and make their decisions in a legal context. As a consequence, their discretionary power is less than that of elected officials. Article 3 of the Constitution bars the federal judiciary from issuing decisions except on actual cases before it. This restriction prevents the courts from developing legal positions outside the context of the judicial process. As federal judge David Bazelon noted, a judge "can't wake up one morning and simply decide to give a helpful little push to a school system, a mental hospital, or the local housing agency."[29]

The most substantial restriction on the courts is the law itself. Although a president or Congress can make almost any decision that is politically acceptable, the judiciary must justify its decision in terms of existing provisions of the law.[30] When asked by a friend to "do justice," Oliver Wendell Holmes Jr. replied, "That is not my job. My job is to play the game according to the rules."[31] In playing according to the rules, judges engage in a creative legal process that requires them to identify the facts of the case, determine and sometimes formulate the relevant legal principles or rules, and then apply them to the case at hand.

The Constraints of the Facts

A basic distinction in any legal case is between "the facts" and "the laws." The **facts** of a case, as determined by trial courts, are the relevant circumstances of a legal dispute or offense. In the case of a person accused of murder, for example, key facts would include evidence about the murder and whether the rights of the accused were respected by police in the course of their investigation. The facts of a case are crucial because they determine which law or laws are applicable to the case. The courts must respond to the facts of a dispute. This restriction is a very substantial one. A murder case cannot be used as an occasion to pronounce judgment on freedom of religion.

facts (of a court case) The relevant circumstances of a legal dispute or offense as determined by a trial court. The facts of a case are crucial because they help determine which law or laws are applicable in the case.

The Constraints of the Law

In deciding cases, the judiciary is also constrained by existing laws. As distinct from the facts of a case, the **laws** of a case are the constitutional provisions, legislative statutes, or judicial precedents that apply to the situation. To use an obvious comparison, the laws governing a case of alleged murder differ from the laws that apply to a traffic violation. Very different laws govern these two cases, and the judge must apply the law or laws that fit the particular case. A judge must treat a murder case as a murder case, applying to it the laws that define murder and the penalties that can be imposed when someone is found guilty of murder.

laws (of a court case) The constitutional provisions, legislative statutes, or judicial precedents that apply to a court case.

The Constitution and Its Interpretation

The Constitution of the United States is the nation's highest law, and the judges and justices are sworn to uphold it. When a case raises a constitutional issue, a court has the duty to apply the Constitution to the case. For example, the Constitution prohibits the states from printing their own currency. If a state decided that it would do so anyway, a federal judge would be obligated to rule against the practice.

Nevertheless, some constitutional provisions are open to interpretation in some cases. For example, the Fourth Amendment of the Constitution protects individuals against "unreasonable searches and seizures," but the meaning of

Sources of Law that Constrain the Decisions of the Federal Judiciary

U.S. Constitution: The federal courts are bound by the provisions of the U.S. Constitution. The sparseness of its wording, however, requires the Constitution to be applied in the light of present circumstances. Thus, judges are accorded some degree of discretion in their constitutional judgments.

Statutory law: The federal courts are constrained by statutes and by administrative regulations derived from the provisions of statutes. Most laws, however, are somewhat vague in their provisions and often have unanticipated applications. As a result, judges have some freedom in deciding cases based on statutes.

Precedent: Federal courts tend to follow precedent (or stare decisis), which is a legal principle developed through earlier court decisions. Because times change and not all cases have a clear precedent, judges have some discretion in their evaluation of the way earlier cases apply to a current case.

"unreasonable" is not spelled out. Nevertheless, judges respect the Constitution's purpose and intent. A judge must determine what the Framers had in mind when they wrote a particular provision. For example, in a decision as to whether wiretapping and other electronic means of surveillance are covered by the prohibition against unreasonable searches and seizures, the issue is what rights the Fourth Amendment was designed to protect. Electronic surveillance was not invented until 150 years after the Fourth Amendment was ratified. But the Fourth Amendment was intended to protect individuals against the government's intrusion into their private lives. For this reason, the courts have concluded that government cannot indiscriminately tap a person's telephone.

Statutes and Their Interpretation

The vast majority of cases that arise in courts involve issues of statutory law rather than constitutional law. Most criminal acts (such as murder and assault) and civil actions (such as divorce and contract disputes) are covered by laws (statutes) created by legislative action or by regulations that have been developed by administrators on the basis of statutory law. There are thousands upon thousands of such laws and regulations, and they are usually what is at issue in a court case. No constitutional provision is ordinarily at issue, for example, when a worker sues a company over a job-related injury or when a person is charged with burglary.

All federal courts are bound by federal statutes (laws passed by Congress) and by federal administrative regulations as well as by treaties. When hearing a case involving statutory law or administrative regulation, judges must work within the limits of the applicable law or regulation. A company that is charged with violating federal environmental law will be judged within the context of that law—what it permits and what it prohibits, and the penalties that would apply if the company is found to have broken the law.

When hearing such a case, judges will often try to determine whether the meaning of the statute or regulation can be determined by common sense (the "plain meaning rule"). The question for the judge is what the law or regulation was intended to safeguard (such as a particular issue of environmental protection). In most instances the law or regulation is clear enough that when the facts of the case are judged against it, a reasonable decision can be reached. Not all cases, however, are clear-cut in their facts or in the applicable law or laws. In these instances, courts have no choice but to exercise their judgment.

Legal Precedents (Previous Rulings) and Their Interpretation

The U.S. legal system developed from the English common-law tradition, which includes the principle that a court's decision on a case should be consistent with previous judicial rulings. This principle is known as **precedent** and reflects the philosophy of stare decisis (Latin for "to stand by things that have been settled"): the doctrine that principles of law, once established, should be accepted as authoritative in all subsequent similar cases. Judges and justices often cite past rulings as a justification for their decisions in the cases before them.

Precedent is important because it gives predictability to the application of law. If courts routinely ignored how similar cases had been decided in the past, they would create confusion and uncertainty among those who must make choices on the basis of their understanding of how the law has been applied in previous situations.[32] A business firm that is seeking to comply with environmental protection laws, for example, can develop company policies that will keep the company safely within the law if court decisions in this area are predictable. But if courts routinely ignore precedent, a firm might unintentionally engage in activity that a court could arbitrarily conclude was unlawful.

Government has an obligation to citizens and firms alike to make clear what its laws are and how they are being applied. Precedent is one of the means by which greater consistency in the application of the law can be achieved.

precedent A judicial decision in a given case that serves as a rule of thumb for settling subsequent cases of a similar nature; courts are generally expected to follow precedent.

POLITICAL INFLUENCES ON JUDICIAL DECISIONS

Although judicial rulings are justified by reference to laws, judges nearly always have some degree of discretion in their decisions.[33] The Constitution is a sparsely worded document and must be adapted to new and changing situations. As a result, federal judges must interpret the Constitution in the context of the issue at hand. The judiciary also has no choice at times but to apply its own judgment to statutory law. Congress often cannot anticipate or reach agreement on all the specific applications of a legislative act and therefore uses general language to state the act's purpose. The judiciary must decide what this language means in the context of a specific case arising under the act. Precedent is even less precise as a guide to decision. Precedent is more a rule of thumb than a strict command; it must constantly be weighed against what Justice Oliver Wendell Holmes Jr. described as the "felt necessities of the time."

The Supreme Court's rulings in a 1998 case (*Faragher v. Boca Raton*) involving sexual harassment in the workplace illustrates the ambiguity that can exist in the written law. The Court developed its ruling in the context of the antidiscrimination provisions of the Civil Rights Act of 1964. The act itself, however, contains no description of, or even reference to, job-related sexual harassment.

The judicial branch is increasingly an arena in which interest groups contend for influence. Many of these disputes have pitted environmental groups against economic interest. Shown here are demonstrators on the issue of whether the Maine Atlantic Salmon should be declared an endangered species and placed off limits to commercial fishing.

Nevertheless, the act does prohibit workplace discrimination, and the Court was unwilling to dismiss sexual harassment as an irrelevant form of job-related discrimination. In judging the case, however, the Court had no choice except to determine for itself which actions in the workplace are instances of harassment and which are not. In this sense, the Court was "making" law; it was deciding how legislation enacted by Congress applied to actions that Congress had not addressed when it wrote the legislation.[34]

In sum, judges have leeway in their decisions. As a consequence, their rulings reflect not only legal influences but political ones, which come from both outside and inside the judicial system.

Outside Influences on Court Decisions

The courts can make unpopular choices, but in the long run, judicial decisions must be seen as fair if they are to be obeyed. In other words, the judiciary cannot ignore the expectations of the general public, interest groups, and elected representatives.

Judges are responsive to public opinion, although much less so than are elected officials. In some cases, for example, the Supreme Court has tailored its rulings in an effort to gain public support or dampen public resistance. In the *Brown* case, the justices, recognizing that school desegregation would be an explosive issue in the South, required only that desegregation take place "with all deliberate speed" rather than immediately or on a fixed timetable. The Supreme Court's apparent strategy has been to stay close enough to popular opinion to avoid seriously eroding public support for its decisions.[35]

Organized groups make their opinions known to the judiciary through the lawsuits they file. The range of interests that use lawsuits as a policy tactic includes traditional advocacy groups such as the American Civil Liberties Union (ACLU) and newer ones such as the Christian Legal Society's Center for Law and Religious Freedom. Groups also participate in cases brought by others through amicus curiae ("friend of the court") briefs, which they file in support of one of the parties to a case.[36]

The influence of groups and the general public on the judiciary also takes place indirectly, through the elected branches of government. In response to public and group pressure, elected officials try to persuade the judiciary to hand down rulings favored by their constituents. Both Congress and the president have powerful means of influencing the federal judiciary.

Congress is constitutionally empowered to establish the Supreme Court's size and appellate jurisdiction, and Congress can rewrite legislation that it feels the judiciary has misinterpreted. Although Congress seldom punishes the judiciary directly, its members have often expressed displeasure with judicial action. In a 1998 Senate speech, the chair of the Judiciary Committee, Orrin Hatch (R-Utah), lashed out at judges who he claimed were "making laws instead of interpreting the law." Such judges, Hatch asserted, "should resign to run for public office—at least they would be accountable for their actions."[37] Other Republicans on the Judiciary Committee shared Hatch's view, and they delayed confirmation of a number of President Clinton's judicial nominees on the grounds that they were unlikely to be "strict constructionists." (*Strict constructionism* holds that a judicial officer should apply a narrow interpretation of the laws, whereas *loose constructionism* holds that a judicial officer can apply an expansive interpretation.)

The president also has ways to influence the judiciary. The president is responsible for enforcing court decisions and has some influence on the types of cases that come before the courts. Under President Ronald Reagan, for instance, the Justice Department vigorously backed several suits challenging affirmative action programs and made no great attempt to push cases that would have expanded the application of such programs.

Presidents can also influence the federal courts through their judicial appointments.[38] When Democrat Bill Clinton took office in 1993, more than a hundred federal judgeships were vacant. President Bush had expected to win reelection and had not moved quickly to fill vacancies as they arose. By the time it was apparent that Bush might lose the election, the Democrat-controlled Congress was able to delay action on the appointments. This enabled Clinton to fill the positions with loyal Democrats who could be expected to partially offset the influence of the Republican judges appointed during the previous twelve years by presidents Reagan and Bush. The tables were turned in 2001 when George W. Bush took office. Senate Republicans had slowed action on Clinton nominees, enabling Bush to appoint Republicans to existing vacancies.

Although the judiciary is subject to the influence of elected institutions, judges and justices tend to see certain positions as basic to individual rights rather than as matters of majority opinion. In such instances, the judiciary seldom lets the public or elected officials dictate its course of action. Despite continuing public support for school prayer (see Figure 14–3), for instance, the Supreme Court has not backed down from its basic position that prayer in the schools

Figure 14–3
Opinons on Prayer in Public Schools
Despite public support for allowing daily prayer in schools, the Supreme Court has held that such prayer violates the First Amendment.
Source: Gallup poll, September 2000.

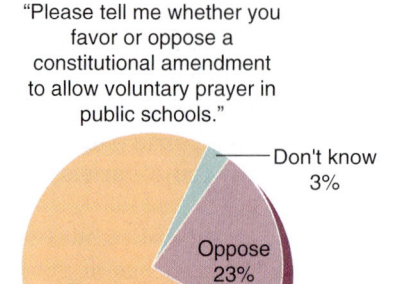

"Please tell me whether you favor or oppose a constitutional amendment to allow voluntary prayer in public schools."

- Favor 74%
- Oppose 23%
- Don't know 3%

violates the First Amendment's establishment clause. The Court prizes its independence and its position as a coequal branch of government. The fact that judges are not popularly elected and that they hold their appointments indefinitely makes it possible for them to resist pressures from Congress and the president.

Inside Influences: The Justices' Own Political Beliefs

The judiciary symbolizes John Adams's characterization of the U.S. political system as "a government of laws, and not of men." The characterization has value as myth, but as the judicial scholar John Schmidhauser noted, "laws are made, enforced, and interpreted by men."[39] As an inevitable result, the decisions of the courts bear the indelible imprint of judges' political beliefs.[40]

This influence is most evident in the case of the Supreme Court. The justices are frequently divided in their opinions, and the divisions often reflect the justices' political backgrounds. During the 2001 Supreme Court term, for example, twenty-six cases were decided by a 5-4 decision. In most of those cases, Chief Justice William Rehnquist and justices Antonin Scalia and Clarence Thomas, all of whom are Republican appointees, were opposed by justices Stephen Breyer and Ruth Bader Ginsburg, the two Democratic appointees on the Court.[41]

Most Supreme Court justices hold relatively stable political views during their tenure. As a result, major shifts in the Supreme Court's position usually occur in conjunction with changes in its membership. When the Court in the 1980s moved away from the criminal justice rulings of the 1960s, it was largely because the more recently appointed justices believed that government should have more leeway in its efforts to fight crime. Such shifts are related to political trends. Justices are political appointees who are nominated in part because their legal positions seem compatible with those of the president.

JUDICIAL POWER AND DEMOCRATIC GOVERNMENT

The issue of judicial power is heightened by the fact that federal judges are not elected. The principle of self-government asserts that lawmaking majorities have the power to decide society's policies. Because the United States has a

TABLE 14–2 Significant Supreme Court Cases
Included are some of the most influential cases decided by the U.S. Supreme Court.

CASE	RULING
Marbury v. Madison (1803)	Established principle of judicial review (Chapter 2)
McCullough v. Maryland (1819)	Strengthened national power over states (Chapter 3)
Dred Scott v. Sanford (1857)	Decided that slaves were property and not citizens (Chapter 3)
Plessy v. Ferguson (1896)	Established the "separate but equal" doctrine (Chapter 5)
Gitlow v. New York (1925)	Protected free expression from state action by Fourteenth Amendment (Chapter 4)
Brown v. Topeka Board of Education (1954)	Abolished the "separate but equal" doctrine and banned segregation in public schools (Chapter 5)
Gideon v. Wainwright (1963)	Decided that states must provide an attorney for poor defendants accused of committing felonies (Chapter 4)
Miranda v. Arizona (1966)	Decided that the police must inform suspects of their rights when they are arrested (Chapter 4)
Roe v. Wade (1973)	Decided that women have full freedom to choose abortion during the first three months of pregnancy under the right of privacy (Chapter 4)

constitutional system that places checks on the will of the majority, there is obviously an important role in the system for a counter-majoritarian institution such as the judiciary (see Table 14–2). Yet court decisions often reflect the political philosophy of the judges, who constitute a tiny political elite that wields significant power.[42] A critical question is how far unelected judges ought to go in substituting their policy judgments for those of legislative and executive officials who are elected by the people.

The judiciary's power is most evident when it declares executive or legislative action to be unconstitutional. The power of the courts to make such determinations is called **judicial review** and was first asserted in the landmark *Marbury v. Madison* case of 1803, when the Supreme Court rebuked both the president and Congress (See Chapter 2). Without judicial review, the federal courts would be unable to restrain an elected official or institution that had gone out of control.

Yet judicial review places the judgment of the courts above that of elected officials when interpretation of the Constitution is at issue, creating the possibility of conflict between the courts and the elected branches. The imposing nature of judicial review has led the judiciary to apply judicial review somewhat sparingly, although the Supreme Court alone has invoked it in more than one

judicial review The power of courts to decide whether a governmental institution has acted within its constitutional powers and, if not, to declare its action null and void.

The Supreme Court resists pressure from the public and from elected officials on some issues, such as school prayer, that it considers to be questions of individual rights rather than of majority opinion.

thousand cases—the large majority of which have involved action by state and local officials rather than the president or Congress. Many of these cases, as seen in Chapters 4 and 5, involved issues of civil liberties (e.g., free expression) and civil rights (e.g., racial discrimination).

Even in the area of statutory law, however, there is plenty of room for the exercise of judicial power. Most statutes (legislative acts) specify general goals, which judges then have to apply in particular situations. Often, a case reaches the courts precisely because the law in question is vague as to how it might apply to the case, which enables courts to make the determination.

The Debate over the Proper Role of the Judiciary

legitimacy (of judicial power)
The issue of the proper limits of judicial authority in a political system based in part on the principle of majority rule.

The question of judicial power centers on the basic issue of **legitimacy:** the proper authority of the judiciary in a political system based in part on the principle of majority rule. The judiciary's policymaking significance and discretion have been sources of controversy throughout the country's history, but the controversies have seldom been livelier than during recent decades.

The judiciary at times has acted almost legislatively by defining broad social policies, such as abortion, busing, affirmative action, church-state relations, and prison reform. In a recent year, for example, the prison systems in forty-two states were operating under court orders that mandated improvements in health care or overcrowding. School prayer is an older example. Until the Supreme Court in 1962 prohibited the reciting of prayer in public schools, the practice was governed by state legislatures and, in some cases, by local school districts. Through such actions the judiciary has restricted the policymaking authority of the states, has narrowed legislative discretion, and has made judicial action an effective alternative to election victory for certain interests.[43]

The judiciary has become more extensively involved in policymaking for many of the same reasons that Congress and the president have been thrust into new policy areas and become more deeply involved in old ones. Social and economic changes have required government to play a larger role in society, and this development has generated a seemingly endless series of new legal controversies.

Judicial action raises an important question. How far should the judiciary go in asserting its authority when that authority collides with or goes beyond the action of elected institutions? There are two general schools of thought on this question: one advocates judicial restraint and the other supports judicial activism. Although these terms are somewhat imprecise and often misused, they are helpful in efforts to clarify opposing philosophical positions on the Court's proper role.[44]

The Doctrine of Judicial Restraint

The doctrine of **judicial restraint** holds that the judiciary should be highly respectful of precedent and should defer to the judgment of legislatures. The restraint doctrine emphasizes the consistency of law and rule through elected institutions. It holds that broad issues of the public good should be decided in nearly all cases by the majority through legislation enacted by elected officials. The judges' role is to discover the application of legislation and precedent to specific cases rather than to search for new principles that essentially change the meaning of the law.

Advocates of judicial restraint support their position with two major arguments. First, they contend that when the judiciary assumes policy functions that traditionally belong to elected institutions, it undermines the fundamental premise of self-government: the right of the majority to choose society's policies.[45] Second, judicial self-restraint is admired because it preserves the public support that is essential to the long-term authority of the courts.[46] The judiciary must be concerned with **compliance**—with whether its decisions will be respected and obeyed. If the judiciary thwarts the majority's desires, public confidence in its legitimacy can be endangered, and other officials may act to undermine judicial decisions.[47]

Advocates of judicial restraint acknowledge that established law is never so precise as to provide exact answers to every question raised by every case and requires some degree of judicial discretion. And in rare circumstances, decisive judicial action may be both appropriate and necessary, as in the historic *Brown v. Board of Education* decision (1954). Although the Constitution does not provide an explicit basis for school desegregation, government-supported racial discrimination violates the principle of equal justice under the law.[48] Louis Lusky is among the advocates of judicial restraint who argue that the broad moral language of the Fourteenth Amendment, which says that no state shall deny to any person the equal protection of its laws, was adequate justification for the Supreme Court to require state governments to end their policy of segregated public schools.[49]

Yet many advocates of judicial restraint see no constitutional justification for many of the Supreme Court's civil rights decisions. In *Romer v. Evans* (1996), for example, the Court struck down an amendment to the Colorado constitution that was adopted by majority vote in a statewide referendum. The amendment had nullified existing civil rights protections for homosexuals in the state and had also barred the passage of new ones. In a blistering dissent, Justice Antonin Scalia said the Court's decision to invalidate the Colorado amendment was "an act not of judicial judgment but of political will." Scalia said that the statewide referendum was "the most democratic of procedures" and that the decision of Colorado voters should have been upheld.[50]

Liberty & Equality

What's Your Opinion?

Judicial Review

Judicial review is the process by which a court invalidates legislative or executive action because it violates the Constitution. Judicial review is most dramatic in cases where the Supreme Court strikes down action taken by Congress or the president. However, most applications of judicial review take place in the context of action taken by state or local governments. The Supreme Court has struck down well over a thousand state laws and local ordinances, most of which involved issues of liberty and equality. Examples include *Near v. Minnesota* (freedom of the press), *Brown v. Board of Education* (racial segregation in the schools), and *Gideon v. Wainwright* (legal counsel for the poor).

Why have encroachments on people's rights occurred more frequently at the hands of state and local governments? Is it simply because there are so many of them that, by chance alone, most constitutional cases will arise at these levels? Or do you accept James Madison's claim (*Federalist* No. 10) that the smaller the sphere of government, the more likely it is that a dominant faction will disregard the interests of a weaker one?

The Supreme Court in 1996 struck down an amendment to the Colorado constitution that would have barred civil rights protections for homosexuals. The ruling was criticized by some advocates of judicial restraint.

judicial restraint The doctrine that the judiciary should be highly respectful of precedent and should defer to the judgment of legislatures. The doctrine claims that the job of judges is to work within the confines of laws set down by tradition and lawmaking majorities.

compliance The issue of whether judicial decisions will be respected and obeyed.

judicial activism The doctrine that the courts should develop new legal principles when judges see a compelling need, even if this action places them in conflict with the policy decisions of elected officials.

The Doctrine of Judicial Activism

In contrast to the judicial restraint position is the idea that the courts should take a generous view of judicial power and involve themselves extensively in interpreting and enlarging upon the law. Although advocates of this doctrine, which is known as **judicial activism,** acknowledge the principles of precedent and majority rule, they claim that the courts should not be overly deferential to existing legal principles or to the judgments of elected officials.

Until recently, the doctrine of judicial activism was associated almost entirely with liberal activists who contend that courts should resort to general principles of fairness when existing law is insufficient. Liberal judicial activists argue, for example, that fairness for African-American children requires that in some circumstances children should be bused to achieve school integration. In areas where social justice depends substantially on protection of the rights of the individual, the judiciary is said to have a responsibility to act positively and decisively.[51]

Activists who emphasize the Court's obligation to protect civil rights and liberties find justification for their position in the U.S. Constitution's strong moral language and several of its provisions.[52] They view the Constitution as designed chiefly to protect people from unreasonable governmental interference in their lives—a goal that can be accomplished only by a judiciary that is willing to stand up to the lawmaking majority whenever the latter tries to restrict individual choice. They see the Constitution as a charter for liberties, not as a set of narrow rules. An activist interprets the Sixth Amendment's right to counsel, for example, not just as the right of a defendant to hire counsel but as the right to have a competent lawyer even if the defendant cannot afford one. When the Sixth Amendment was enacted in the late eighteenth century, criminal trials were short and straightforward, and it was at least possible in some instances for poor people to defend themselves competently. But criminal law and procedures today are so complex that a defendant without legal counsel would

HOW THE UNITED STATES COMPARES

Judicial power

U.S. courts are highly political by comparison with the courts of most other democracies. First, U.S. courts operate within a common-law tradition, which makes judge-made law (through precedent) a part of the legal code. Many democracies have a civil-law tradition, in which nearly all law is defined by legislative statutes. Second, because U.S. courts operate in a constitutional system of divided power, they are required to rule on conflicts between state and nation or between the executive and legislative branches, which thrusts the judiciary into the middle of political conflicts. It should not be surprising, then, that federal judges and justices are appointed through an overtly political process in which partisan views and activities are major considerations. Many federal judges, particularly at the district level, have no significant prior judicial experience. In fact, the United States is one of the few countries that does not mandate formal training for judges.

The pattern is different in most European democracies. Judgeships there tend to be career positions. Individuals are appointed to the judiciary at an early age and then work their way up the judicial ladder largely on the basis of seniority. Partisan politics does not play a large role in appointment and promotion. By tradition, European judges see their job as the strict interpretation of statutes, not the creative application of them.

The power of U.S. courts is nowhere more evident than in the exercise of judicial review—the voiding of a legislative or executive action on the grounds that it violates the Constitution. Judicial review had its origins in European experience and thought, but it was first formally applied in the United States when, in *Marbury v. Madison* (1803), the Supreme Court declared an act of Congress unconstitutional. Some democracies, including Great Britain, still do not allow broadscale judicial review, but most democracies now provide for it.

In the so-called American system of judicial review, all judges can evaluate the applicability of constitutional law to particular cases and can declare ordinary law invalid when it conflicts with constitutional law. By comparison, the so-called Austrian system restricts judicial review to a special constitutional court. Judges in other courts cannot declare a law void on the grounds that it is unconstitutional: they must apply ordinary law as it is written. In the Austrian system, moreover, constitutional decisions are often made in response to requests for judicial review by political officials (such as the chief executive).

---

be at a serious disadvantage. Moreover, society today can afford to provide poor defendants with legal assistance. By such reasoning, the judicial activist school would argue that the Supreme Court was acting properly when it ruled in *Gideon v. Wainwright* (1963) that state governments had to provide indigent defendants with counsel at public expense.[53]

Judicial activism is not, however, confined to liberals. In the period from the 1860s to the 1930s, conservative activists on the Supreme Court struck down most legislative efforts to regulate economic activity (see Chapter 3). Judicial activism from the right recently became an issue again when the Court overturned several precedents in the area of the rights of the accused. In 1990, Chief Justice William Rehnquist, in a rare action, asked Congress to restrict the right of those convicted in state courts to file habeas corpus appeals in federal courts. Congress rejected the proposal, and in 1991 a majority on the Rehnquist Court took action on its own to achieve the goal. In one ruling, the Court held that an inmate could not obtain a federal appeal simply because his or her lawyer had made a procedural mistake during the trial in a state court. Chief Justice Rehnquist wrote that precedent is not "an inexorable command."[54]

The handwritten letter that Clarence Gideon (insert) sent to the Supreme Court in 1962. The letter led eventually to the *Gideon* decision in which the Court held that states must provide poor defendants with legal counsel (see Chapter 4). Seen by many people at the time as judicial activism, the ruling is now fully accepted.

Conservative activism is also evident in recent Supreme Court cases on the issue of federalism. Since the late 1930s, the Court had deferred to Congress on commerce policy, but it has recently struck down several commerce-related statutes (see Chapter 3). The Court's four most conservative justices (Rehnquist, Scalia, Thomas, and Kennedy), joined by Justice O'Connor, supported the major decisions, each of which was decided by a 5-4 margin. In one of these cases, *Kimel v. Florida Board of Regents* (2000), the Court ruled that Congress did not have the power to require states to comply with the federal age-discrimination law because age is not among the forms of discrimination expressly prohibited by the Fourteenth Amendment's equal protection clause. The various rulings reflected Chief Justice William Rehnquist's long-held goal of limiting Congress's authority over the states.[55] "[The Rehnquist Court] doesn't defer to government at any level," said Walter Dellinger, a former solicitor general. "The Court is confident it can come up with the right decisions, and it believes it is constitutionally charged with doing so."[56]

Arguably, conservative activism was never more evident than in the Supreme Court's *Bush v. Gore* (2000) decision. The five justices in the majority were the same justices who in previous decisions had upheld states' rights and had opposed expansive applications of the Fourteenth Amendment's equal protection clause. Yet they invoked the equal protection clause to block the statewide manual recount that had been ordered by Florida's high court because no uniform standard for counting the ballots existed. When the Court issued a rare stay order to stop the recount, Justice Antonin Scalia claimed that it was justified because the recount could cast doubt on the legitimacy of Bush's election. The fact was, Bush had not yet been officially elected. Some observers suggested that if Bush had been trailing in the Florida vote, the Court's majority would have

Should All the Florida Ballots Have Been Counted?

In *Colegrove v. Green* (1946), Justice Felix Frankfurter warned the Supreme Court about getting involved in election politics, saying that it "ought not to enter this political thicket." In 2000, the Court thrust itself into the thorniest political thicket of all—a presidential campaign. In *Bush v. Gore*, the Court by a narrow majority blocked a statewide manual recount of uncounted ballots in Florida, thereby settling the election in favor of Republican George W. Bush. His Democratic opponent, Al Gore, had argued that all the Florida votes—not just those that could be read by machine—should count. Bush supporters retorted that a manual recount would be inherently subjective and open to mischief. These opposing views also existed within the Supreme Court, as the following opinions show.

Yes: [The Florida Supreme Court's] decisions were rooted in long established precedent. . . . [I]t relied on the sufficiency of the general "intent of the voter" standard articulated by the state legislature. . . . What must underlie . . . [the] assault on this procedure is an unstated lack of confidence in the impartiality and capacity of the state judges who would make the critical decisions if the vote count were to proceed. Otherwise, their position is wholly without merit.
—Justice John Paul Stevens's dissenting opinion

No: [T]he standards for accepting or rejecting contested ballots might vary not only from county to county but indeed within a single county from one recount team to the next. . . . [I]t is obvious that the recount cannot be conducted in compliance with the requirements of equal protection and due process without substantial additional work. It would require not only the adoption (after opportunity for argument) of adequate statewide standards for determining what is a legal vote, and practicable procedures to implement them, but also orderly judicial review of any disputed matters that might arise.
—Supreme Court majority's opinion

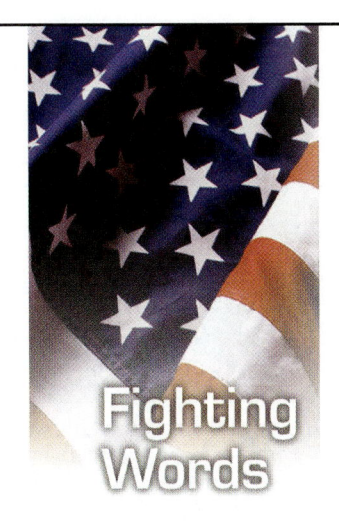

Fighting Words

allowed the recount to continue. Justice John Paul Stevens, who thought the Florida high court had acted properly in ordering a manual count, basically accused his colleagues on the Supreme Court of devising a ruling based on their partisan desires rather than on the law. Stevens noted that different standards for casting and counting ballots were found throughout the United States. The Court's ruling in *Bush v. Gore*, said Stevens, "can only lend credence to the most cynical appraisal of the work of judges throughout the land."[57]

Whether from the right or the left, judicial activism is characterized by a willingness to pit the judgment and power of the courts against the judgment and power of elected representatives or their administrative agents. To a degree, all judges are activists in the sense that their decisions are necessarily creative ones. The law as expressed through the Constitution, statutes, and precedent is not precise enough to provide an automatic answer to every court case. Judges and justices have no choice but to exercise judgment when the text of the law is inexact. And, to a degree, all judges are restrained in the sense that their decisions must have roots in the law. Judges cannot simply make any decision they might choose; they are confined by the facts of a case and the laws that might reasonably be applied to it. But judges and justices vary in the degree to which

Is the Supreme Court Suited to the Making of Broad Social Policy?

As the Supreme Court has extended its reach into areas that were once dominated by Congress and the president, some analysts have questioned whether the Court has the capacity (as distinct from the right) to devise workable policies in all these areas. The structure and procedures of the judiciary obviously differ greatly from those of elected institutions. The way in which the Supreme Court gathers information and formulates decisions bears little resemblance to the way in which Congress or the White House carries out its tasks. These differences, Donald Horowitz argues in *The Courts and Social Policy* (1977), prevent the Supreme Court from being a fully effective policymaking body when it comes to such issues as school integration.

Horowitz notes that, unlike members of Congress or executive officials, who usually start their policy deliberations from a general perspective, justices of the Supreme Court start with a particular case, which often involves unusual or extreme circumstances. The Court's initial busing decision in the 1971 *Swann* case, for example, involved Mecklenburg County, North Carolina, which had a long history of government-sponsored racial segregation. Yet the *Swann* decision became binding on a great number of communities, many of which had nothing approaching the level of institutionalized racism in Mecklenburg County.

Horowitz also notes that the Court acts on the basis of less complete information than Congress, which often holds hearings, conducts research, and by other means considers a wide range of facts before deciding on policy. The basic function of courts is to resolve specific disputes, and admissible evidence is generally limited to material directly relevant to the case at hand. Research studies on social conditions, for example, cannot ordinarily be introduced in a court of law, because pieces of paper cannot be cross-examined on the witness stand. To be sure, the Supreme Court is more likely than lower courts to look for information beyond an immediate case. The justices can, for example, invite interested groups to submit *amicus curiae* ("friend of the court") briefs in the hope that the advice thus obtained will broaden their understanding of a case's implications. The Court has a heavy schedule, however, and time and procedural tradition usually permit only a cursory assessment of information beyond what is contained in the trial record of a lower court.

Finally, the Court has no oversight mechanism of its own, which makes compliance a somewhat different issue than it is in the context of legislative or executive action. Although the Court has, for example, banned school prayer, it continues to be said daily in some public schools. There is not much that the Court can do to compel teachers to stop the practice. On the other hand, Congress through its spending power and the executive through its administrative power are more readily able to get others to comply with their authoritative orders. The judiciary at times has resorted to direct action to achieve compliance. In some communities, for example, judges took on the role of overseeing busing plans for the purpose of achieving racial integration in public schools. However, courts are normally wary of getting directly involved in the implementation of their decisions, leaving this task to elected and administrative officers who, for their own reasons, may be less than zealous in forcing people and organizations to comply with Court rulings in sensitive areas of social policy.

Nevertheless, limits on the Court's policymaking capacity need to be kept in perspective. If the criterion for deciding whether an institution should establish broad policies were the likelihood of complete success, no institution would qualify. Every problem associated with judicial policymaking is also a problem confronted by legislative and executive institutions. Congress and the president also must act on the basis of imperfect information. In view of their resources, organization, and incentives, the elected institutions are better at fact finding and are more representative than the Court, but they are not without flaws of their own. The difference is one of degree, not of kind.

they are willing to contest the judgment of other political institutions and the degree to which they are willing to depart from the wording of the law. These differences separate the judicial activists from the practitioners of judicial restraint.

The Judiciary's Proper Role: A Question of Competing Values

The dispute between advocates of judicial activism and advocates of judicial restraint is a philosophical one that involves opposing values. The debate is important because it addresses the normative question of what role the judiciary ought to play in American democracy. Should unelected judges involve themselves deeply in policy by adopting a broad conception of their power, or should they give wide discretion to elective institutions? Should judges defer to precedent, or should they be willing to change course, even at the risk of sending the law down uncharted paths? These questions cannot be answered simply on the basis of whether one personally agrees or disagrees with a particular judicial decision. The answer necessarily depends on a value judgment about the role of the judiciary in a governing system based on the often-conflicting concepts of majority rule and individual rights.

The United States is a constitutional democracy that recognizes both the power of the majority to rule and the claim of the minority to protection of its rights. The judiciary was not established as the nation's moral conscience and does not have a monopoly on the issue of minority interests and rights. Yet the judiciary was established as a coequal branch of government and was charged with the responsibility for protecting individual rights and minority interests. In short, the constitutional question of how far the courts should be allowed to go in substituting their judgment for that of elected institutions and established law is open to interpretation. The trade-off is significant on all issues: minority rights versus majority rule, states' rights versus federal power, legislative authority versus judicial authority. The question of whether judicial restraint or judicial activism is more desirable is one that every student of American government should ponder.

Self-Quiz
www.mhhe.com/patterson6

SUMMARY

At the lowest level of the federal judicial system are the district courts, where most federal cases begin. Above them are the federal courts of appeals, which review cases appealed from the lower courts. The U.S. Supreme Court is the nation's highest court. Each state has its own court system, consisting of trial courts at the bottom and one or two appellate levels at the top. Cases originating in state courts ordinarily cannot be appealed to the federal courts unless a federal issue is involved, and then the federal courts can choose to rule only on the federal aspects of the case. Federal judges at all levels are nominated by the president, and if confirmed by the Senate, they are appointed by the president to the office. Once on the federal bench, they serve until they die, retire, or are removed by impeachment and conviction.

The Supreme Court is unquestionably the most important court in the country. The legal principles it establishes are binding on lower courts, and its capacity to define the law is enhanced by the control it exercises over the cases it hears. However, it is inaccurate to assume that lower courts are inconsequential (the upper-court myth). Lower courts have considerable discretion, and the great majority of their decisions are not reviewed by a higher court. It is also inaccurate to assume that federal courts are far more significant than state courts (the federal court myth).

The courts have less discretionary authority than elected institutions do. The judiciary's positions are constrained by the facts of a case and by the laws as defined through the Constitution, statutes and government regulations, and legal precedent. Yet existing legal guidelines are seldom so precise that judges have no choice in their decisions. As a result, political influences have a strong impact on the judiciary. It responds to national conditions, public opinion, interest groups, and elected officials, particularly the president and members of Congress. Another political influence on the judiciary is the personal beliefs of judges, who have individual preferences that are evident in the way they decide on issues that come before the courts. Not surprisingly, partisan politics plays a significant role in judicial appointments.

In recent decades, the Supreme Court has issued broad rulings on individual rights, some of which have required governments to take positive action on behalf of minority interests. As the Court has crossed into areas traditionally left to lawmaking majorities, the legitimacy of its policies has been questioned. Advocates of judicial restraint claim that the justices' personal values are inadequate justification for exceeding the proper judicial role. They argue that the Constitution entrusts broad issues of the public good to elective institutions and that judicial activism ultimately undermines public respect for the judiciary. Judicial activists counter that the courts were established as an independent branch and should not hesitate to promote new principles when they see a need, even if this action puts them into conflict with elected officials.

KEY TERMS

appellate jurisdiction
compliance
concurring opinion
decision
dissenting opinion
facts (of a court case)
judicial activism
judicial conference
judicial restraint
judicial review
jurisdiction (of a court)
laws (of a court case)
legitimacy (of judicial power)
majority opinion
opinion (of a court)
original jurisdiction
plurality opinion
precedent
senatorial courtesy
writ of certiorari

SUGGESTED READINGS

Carp, Robert A. *The Federal Courts*, 3d ed. Washington, D.C.: Congressional Quarterly Press, 1998. An overview of the federal judiciary system.

Gillman, Howard. *Votes That Counted: How the Court Decided the 2000 Presidential Election*. Chicago: University of Chicago Press, 2001. An accounting of the *Bush v. Gore* ruling.

McGuire, Kevin T. *Understanding the Supreme Court: Cases and Controversies*. New York: McGraw-Hill, 2002. An overview of Supreme Court decisions and approaches to legal disputes.

O'Brien, David M. *Storm Center*, 5th ed. New York: Norton, 2000. An analysis of the Supreme Court in the context of the controversy surrounding the role of the judiciary in the U.S. political system.

Salokar, Rebecca Mae. *The Solicitor General: The Politics of Law*. Philadelphia, Pa.: Temple University Press, 1992. A study of the important and increasingly political role of the nation's top trial lawyer.

Scalia, Antonin. *A Matter of Interpretation: Federal Courts and the Law*. Princeton, N.J.: Princeton University Press, 1997. A critical assessment of how the Supreme Court interprets law.

Schwartz, Bernard. *Decision: How the Supreme Court Decides Cases*. New York: Oxford University Press, 1996. A behind-the-scenes look at Supreme Court justices' decisions.

Watson, George L., and John Alan Stookey. *Shaping America: The Politics of Supreme Court Appointments*. New York: Longman, 1995. An examination of the process by which Supreme Court justices are nominated and confirmed.

LIST OF WEBSITES

http://www.courttv.com/cases
A website that allows you to take the facts of actual court cases, examine the law and the arguments, and then decide each case for yourself.

http://www.fjc.gov
The home page of the Federal Judicial Center, an agency created by Congress to conduct research and provide education on the federal judicial system.

http://www.lib.umich.edu/libhome/Documents.center/fedjudi.html
A University of Michigan web page that provides detailed information on the federal judicial system.

http://www.rominger.com/supreme.htm
A vast site that provides links to the Supreme Court, pending cases, the state court systems, and other subjects.

PART FOUR

State and Local Governments

"All politics is local," said Tip O'Neill, the legendary Speaker of the U.S. House of Representatives. O'Neill was referring to the powerful influence that local interests have on Washington policymakers, but he could have been talking about the American experience more broadly. From the earliest days of the Republic, Americans have embraced the notion of local control of government. To be sure, Americans have periodically looked to Washington for answers to their policy problems and have gradually entrusted federal officials with a larger share of governing responsibility. But states and localities remain vital centers of policy and politics, and they continue to offer citizens the most direct forms of popular political participation.

The chapter in this section examines state and local governments. It explores their constitutional foundation, their governing institutions, their provisions for popular participation, their politics, and their programs and policies.

Every society makes provisions for forms of local and regional government, but few countries do so more thoroughly than the United States. It has about 80,000 different local and regional governments. The chapter that follows will describe what they are, what they do, and how they impact on American life.

CHAPTER OUTLINE

15 State and Local Politics: Maintaining Our Differences 466

15

The powers not delegated to the United States by the Constitution, nor prohibited by it to the States, are reserved for the States . . .
—Tenth Amendment

State and Local Politics:
Maintaining Our Differences

The Supreme Court in *Reno v. Condon* (2000) upheld a federal law that prohibited states from selling their computer files of information acquired from drivers' license applicants. Some states had been making millions of dollars from the sale of the databases to mass marketing and other firms. When citizens objected to the practice, Congress responded with the 1994 Drivers Privacy Protection Act. The state of South Carolina brought suit, claiming that Congress lacked the authority to tell the states what they could do with their databases. The Supreme Court ruled against South Carolina, saying that the law simply "regulates the states as owners of databases," an action permissible under Congress's constitutional power to regulate commerce. "[The] sale or release [of databases] into the interstate stream of business is sufficient to support Congressional regulation."[1]

One day earlier, however, the Supreme Court in *Kimel v. Florida Board of Regents* (2000) ruled that the states were not bound by the Federal Age Discrimination Act. The legislation was passed in 1967 and later amended to include state government employees, who were granted the power to sue in federal courts in cases of alleged age discrimination in the workplace. In 1995, a group of faculty members and librarians at Florida State University brought suit, charging that the state's wage policy violated the federal act. The State of Florida, in turn, claimed that the law infringed in its authority as a sovereign government. The Supreme Court ruled in Florida's favor, saying that the law "is not 'appropriate legislation' under . . . the Fourteenth Amendment." The Court said that age discrimination is not inherently unconstitutional and thus Congress lacked the authority to require state governments to apply a federal age-discrimination law.[2]

These cases reflect both the dynamic and contentious nature of American federalism. The U.S. political system, as was described in detail in Chapter 3 and discussed elsewhere in this text, divides power between a national government and the separate states.

During the more than two centuries that the United States has existed, there has been a gradual expansion of national power and a corresponding reduction in state-to-state differences. Yet the states and their creations, the local governments, continue to be vitally important centers of politics and policies. In terms of their day-to-day impact on Americans' lives, they are far more significant than the government in Washington. The roads that Americans drive on, the schools they attend, the laws they obey, and much more, are defined principally by state and local action rather than by federal action. In fact, contrary to what many Americans might believe, states and localities have nearly six times as many employees as the federal government does (see Figure 15–1).

The purpose of this chapter is to describe more fully the American states and the localities within them. The great number of state and local governments, and the variety they exhibit, hinder any easy summary of what they are all about. Yet there are some general patterns, and it is these patterns on which this chapter concentrates. It

Figure 15–1

Employees of the Federal, State, and Local Governments

Levels of employment in state and local governments have increased in recent years, whereas the number of federal government employees has remained fairly constant.

Source: U.S. Bureau of the Census, 2000.

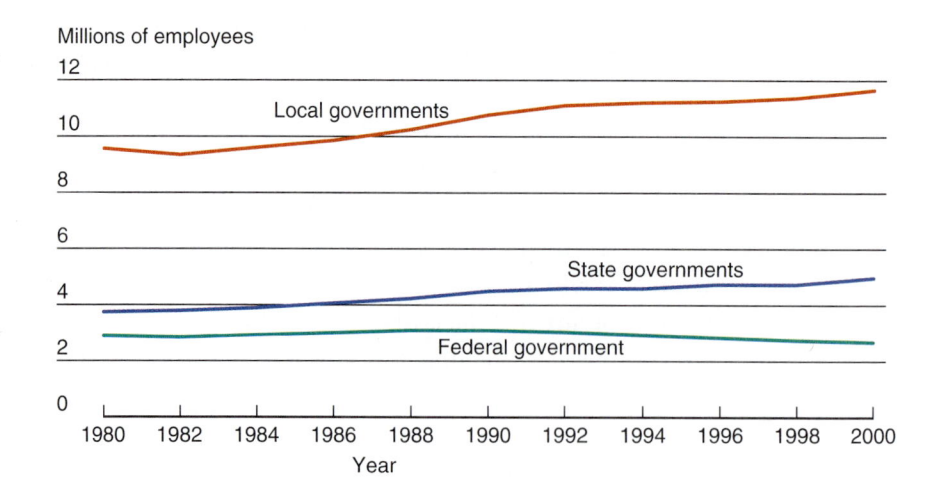

includes a comparison of the states, which will indicate major factors behind some of the differences in their politics and policies. The main points of discussion in this chapter are the following:

- *All states apply the constitutional principle of separation of powers, but the states otherwise differ from one another, and from the federal government, in the way in which they structure their governments.* The use of elections as a means of choosing officials of all types, including judges and lesser executives (for example, state treasurer), is widespread.

- *Local governments are not sovereign; they are chartered by their state government, which sets the limits of their power.* Of the units of local government (county, municipality, township, school district, and special district), the basic unit is the municipality. A municipality may be governed in one of four ways—the strong mayor–council, weak mayor–council, commission, or city manager system.

- *States and localities have primary responsibility for most of the policies, such as public education, that directly touch Americans' daily lives.* The nature of these policies is affected by the wealth of the state or locality and also by its political culture, party system, and group system.

THE STRUCTURE OF THE STATE GOVERNMENT

The Constitution of the United States contains provisions that forbid the states from interfering with the lawful exercise of national authority, and the states are required by the Constitution to provide their residents with a "republican" (that is, representative) form of government. In addition, the "supremacy clause" of the Constitution requires the states to comply with legitimate national laws while the "full faith and credit" provision requires them to respect the laws of

The U.S. Constitution in its emphasis on a separation of executive, legislative, and judicial power has been a model for state constitutions. The U.S. Capitol Building has also served as a model for the states. Shown here is the capitol building of the state of Texas. It is located in Austin.

other states (for example, a contract issued by one state is legally binding in other states).

Nevertheless, the Constitution was intended primarily to define national power and national institutions and does not say very much about the states or their powers. In fact, the Framers of the Constitution did not believe it was necessary to define the powers of the states. They held that the Constitution implied that the states held all legitimate governing powers not granted to the national government. This situation was unsettling to states'-rights advocates, who insisted on a constitutional amendment—the Tenth—which reserves for the states those powers not delegated to the national government (see Chapter 3).

The Tenth Amendment is part of the Bill of Rights, whose provisions for individual rights initially applied only to action by the federal government. It was not until the twentieth century that the Bill of Rights was extended to include action by state and local governments (see Chapters 4 and 5). The Fourteenth Amendment was the basis for the change. It prohibits a state from depriving any person of "life, liberty, or property, without due process of law" or from denying any person within its jurisdiction the "equal protection of the laws."

The State Constitutions

Each state's constitution is its supreme law, except where valid national law applies. In each state, the constitution establishes executive, legislative, and judicial branches and defines the lawful powers of each one. The concept of checks and balances—the notion that each branch will act as a curb on the power of the others—is embedded in all state constitutions. All of them also include a bill of rights.

Although the state constitutions in these respects resemble the Constitution of the United States, they have distinctive features. On average they are roughly four times the length of the U.S. Constitution. Vermont is the only state whose constitution is shorter than the nation's. Until it was replaced in 1974, Louisiana's constitution was by far the longest and most detailed. At 250,000 words, it was nearly thirty times the length of the U.S. Constitution. The longest state constitution still in effect today is Alabama's, which has approximately 175,000 words and has been amended more than five hundred times (compared with twenty-seven times for the U.S. Constitution).

HOW THE UNITED STATES COMPARES

State Power in a Federal System

Federalism involves the division of sovereign authority between a national government and area (state) governments. As was discussed in Chapter 3, the first federal system of government in world history was established in the United States in 1787. The American states already existed, and the only realistic alternative for the writers of the Constitution was a form of government that protected the states' integrity and authority.

Other nations of the period had unitary systems (sovereignty invested solely in the national government), and most nations today still have that system. However, the federal system has been adopted in some countries, including Canada and Germany.

Federal systems, however, are not the same everywhere. They differ primarily in the degree of autonomy granted to the subnational (state) governments. The United States allocates an extraordinary level of authority to the state governments. They have more discretionary authority and more far-reaching power than is typically the case in a federal system, a reflection of the American tradition of local control and of Americans' long-standing suspicion of centralized power.

The American states and their local units, for example, have a degree of control over education policy that is nearly unmatched. The federal government provides some of the funding for public schools and has imposed anti-discrimination requirements on these institutions. It has also established a national testing program that affects the amount of federal assistance a school is entitled to receive. However, the states and localities decide nearly all aspects of education policy. They set the school calendar, course requirements, achievement standards, teacher qualifications, and so on.

The length of state constitutions reflects the significant issues they address, such as the lawful powers and forms of local governments, the tax authority of both the state and local governments, and the executive agencies of the state government. However, the state constitutions contain many provisions that more properly belong in statutes than in a constitution. Enterprising state legislators have often preferred to embed their favorite policies in constitutional amendments, which are harder to change than ordinary laws are. For example, many of the state constitutions include benefits for special-interest groups, such as veterans, farmers, and businesses. Minnesota's constitution was amended in the early 1970s to permit the state to give each Vietnam veteran from the state a $600 bonus. California's constitution is filled with all sorts of tax provisions, which, among other things, limit the types and amount of taxation.

Most constitutional scholars would agree that the length of state constitutions is a drawback. The U.S. Constitution is a sparsely worded document, which, as was indicated in Chapter 2, has enabled succeeding generations to adapt it to their changing needs. Not so with many of the state constitutions. They are often so loaded down with narrow and detailed provisions that they deny policymakers the flexibility to respond effectively to change.

The length of state constitutions reflects in part the relative ease with which they can be amended. Unlike amendments to the U.S. Constitution, which require a two-thirds majority in the House and Senate and then ratification by three-fourths of the state legislatures, a state constitution can be amended by legislative action combined with voter ratification. The typical process is a two-thirds vote of approval in each chamber of the state legislature and ratification by a simple majority of voters in the next election. Delaware is the only state where voter ratification is not required; however, two consecutive sessions of the Delaware legislature must approve an amendment for it to be ratified. More than forty states also provide for amendment by a **state constitutional convention,** and more than two hundred such conventions have been held. Finally, a third of the states permit amendment through a **constitutional initiative.** By obtaining the signatures of a certain number of registered voters, a citizen or group can petition to place a proposed amendment on the ballot at the next election. If it gets majority support, it becomes part of the constitution. In 1996, for example, California voters approved Proposition 209, which bans in the state any public employment, education, or contracting program that is based on race, ethnicity, or sex. California leads the nation in terms of the number of constitutional initiatives proposed and enacted. California's constitution has roughly five hundred amendments, many of which were added through the initiative process.

state constitutional convention A state convention convened to amend the state constitution or draft a new one.

constitutional initiative The process by which a citizen or group can petition to place a proposed amendment on the ballot at the next election by obtaining the signatures of a certain number of registered voters, and if the amendment gets majority support, it becomes part of the constitution.

Branches of Government

All states make use of the principle of checks and balances that underpins the national government (see Chapter 2). There is nothing in the Constitution of the United States that would prohibit a state from adopting a parliamentary form of government, but no state has tried it. The executive, legislative, and judiciary in each state are separate branches that share power. Each branch thus serves as a check on the power of the others.

The Executive Branch

Most states wrote their first constitutions during periods when mistrust of executive authority was high. Consequently, they provided for relatively weak governors. The model still applies in some states, especially in the South and in New England. Texas's governor, for example, has only modest formal powers. The governor can propose legislation, but by tradition, the Texas House and Senate leaders set the legislative agenda without including the governor in their deliberations. In 1999, Texas governor George W. Bush did persuade the Texas legislature to cut taxes, but House and Senate leaders responded only after forcing him to accept many provisions that he opposed.[3]

Roughly half the states impose a two-term limit on their governors. Virginia, Mississippi, and Kentucky restrict the governor to a single term. In nearly all states, the governor's term of office is four years, but New Hampshire and Vermont confine it to two years.

Although the governorship is not a very powerful office in most states, governors have gained power in recent decades as a result of an increase in the size and complexity of government. The initiation of the state budget now resides with the governor rather than the legislature in nearly every state. And every state now grants the governor the power to veto legislative acts. There was a time when a number of states denied their governors this power. North Carolina was the last to change; it amended its constitution in 1996 to give the governor veto power. In forty-three states, the governor also has a line-item veto, which enables the governor to reject a part of an appropriations bill without voiding the whole act.

Governors have the power to appoint the heads of agencies and commissions. This power has become increasingly important as state agencies have assumed broader policy responsibilities. In most states, governors also have the power to reorganize the executive branch (for example, the merging of two agencies), subject to the legislature's veto. The extent of such powers, however, varies from state to state. The political scientist Thad Boyle has systematically evaluated the institutional powers of the states' governors and concluded that the office is "very strong" in nine states (including Ohio, Pennsylvania, and Tennessee), "strong" in twenty-one states (including Arizona, Kentucky, and Michigan), "moderate" in seventeen states (including California, Florida, and Texas), and "weak" in three states (Vermont, North Carolina, and South Carolina).[4]

Regardless of formal powers, however, the governor is often the most visible and widely known politician in the state. This position provides a bully pulpit that allows the governor to assume a leadership role on policy issues. This role has increased in importance as policy control has "devolved" from Washington to the states in recent years (see Chapter 3).

In 1998, Jesse "The Body" Ventura, a former professional wrestler who had not previously held a prominent public office, was elected Minnesota's governor. He was an exception. Most governors have previously held other public office, such as state lieutenant governor, state attorney general, big-city mayor, or state legislator. To gain the governor's post, they have typically had first to win their party's primary. However, there are a few states where nomination is gained through a party convention.

Campaigns for governor, like those for the U.S. Senate, have become increasingly expensive. In a large state like New York or Texas, spending in the governor's campaign can easily top $20 million. Spending in California's 1998 race exceeded $50 million; Gray Davis, the winner, spent $34 million.

The governor is the state's chief executive but, in nearly every state, is not the sole elected executive official (see "States in the Nation"). In all but three states, the voters also directly choose one or more of the following executives: lieutenant governor, attorney general, secretary of state, state treasurer, education commissioner, agriculture commissioner, and public utilities commissioner. The governor is the chief executive but shares executive power with other officials, who are separately elected and who may be of the opposite party. Only in Maine, New Hampshire, and New Jersey is the governor the sole elected executive official.

The direct election of multiple executive officials has roots in early Americans' distrust of executive power and also in the Jacksonian and Progressive eras, when accountability to the people through the vote was a prevailing philosophy. The multiple executive system weakens the governor's control of the executive branch. At times, even the governor's control of his own office can be at risk. In California, the lieutenant governor is elected separately from the governor and becomes acting governor when the governor travels outside the state's borders. When Jerry Brown was California's governor, the state's lieutenant governor, Mike Curb, was from the opposite party, and Brown would sometimes cancel, delay, or shorten a trip outside the state in order to prevent the lieutenant governor from taking action while he was away. On one of Brown's trips, Curb lifted the state's pollution control regulations. Upon his return, Brown issued an executive order reinstating them.[5]

CHAPTER 15 State and Local Politics: Maintaining Our Differences 473

STATES IN THE NATION

Divided Power in the Executive

The president operates in a system of divided power where joint action by Congress is often required for the president's programs to be adopted. The chief executives in the American states are the governors, and nearly all of them must contend with a further division—a separation of power within the executive branch itself. Maine and New Jersey are the only states where executive power is vested solely in a governor. Five other states have separately elected and (unlike the vice president) constitutionally empowered lieutenant governors. In most of the other states, other major executive officials, such as the attorney general and secretary of state, are also elected. Finally, there are twelve states in which even minor executive officials, such as the commissioner of education, are chosen by the voters. In the federal government, these other major and minor officials are appointed by the president.

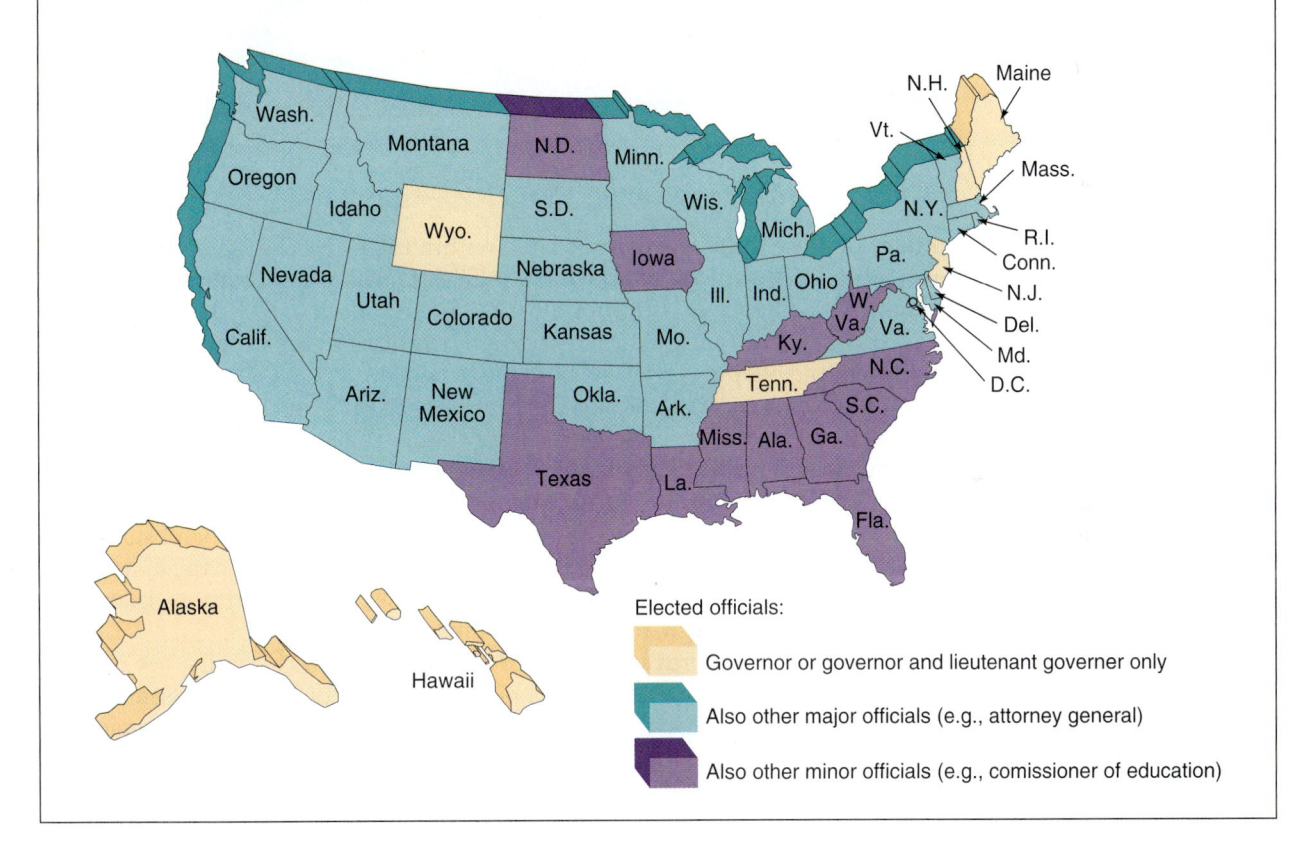

Elected officials:
- Governor or governor and lieutenant governer only
- Also other major officials (e.g., attorney general)
- Also other minor officials (e.g., comissioner of education)

Of the executive officials other than governor, the most powerful is the attorney general, who is elected to the post in forty-three states. The attorney general is the state's chief legal officer and sets priorities for legal action. An attorney general might decide, for example, to concentrate the state's legal resources on environmental protection or investigations of alleged political corruption. The office of attorney general has often been a stepping stone to a governorship or a seat in the U.S. Senate.

Shown here is the senate chamber of the New York legislature. Except for Nebraska, all states have a two-chamber legislature.

The Legislature

Like Congress, state legislatures have within their authority the most impressive array of constitutional powers that a democracy can bestow. The legislatures make the laws, appropriate the money, define the structure of the executive and the judiciary, oversee the operations of the other branches, and represent the people.

bicameral legislatures A legislature having two chambers.

With one exception, the state legislatures are **bicameral**—that is, they have two chambers. The upper house in every state is called the senate. State senates average about forty members, who serve four-year terms in most states. The lower house is always the larger one. Lower houses average about 100 members, who are elected to two-year terms in most states. In nearly all states, the lower chamber is called either the house of representatives or the general assembly. Nebraska is the only state with a unicameral (one-house) legislature. It is called, simply enough, the Nebraska Unicameral Legislature.

The state legislatures are organized and operate in ways similar to Congress (see Chapter 11). Their leadership is provided by party leaders chosen by each chamber's members, but most of the legislative work and executive oversight is carried out in committees. Unlike Congress, however, there are some states where legislative bills can be submitted for consideration directly by executive officials. In Congress, only the members themselves have the power to submit bills, although the bills are sometimes drafted in the executive branch.

Like Congress, the state legislatures could not manage their workload if they lacked committees to which tasks were delegated. More than fifty thousand bills are enacted into law each year by state legislatures—an average of more than one thousand bills for each state.

The distribution of power within state legislatures varies widely. Some legislatures are extraordinarily democratic in the sense that power is widely disbursed, and the job of the leaders is primarily to organize the members' work. In other states, power is concentrated in the top leadership, and other members, especially relative newcomers, are expected to follow their lead. In New York State, the annual budget is determined through bargaining among three top officials—the senate majority leader, the speaker of the assembly, and the governor. They negotiate until a final "deal" is reached, which the legislature as a whole is then expected to enact in its entirety.

For a long period, state legislatures were synonymous with malapportionment. Cities were grossly underrepresented because rural legislators, who had controlled the state legislatures since the days when the United States was a farming nation, refused to reapportion them. Vermont was the extreme case. From 1793 to the 1960s, its legislative distribution did not change. In the state's lower house, each village, town, or city had one representative, regardless of population. Thus, the city of Burlington had exactly the same voting power as the smallest village in the state. Not surprisingly, the policy needs of America's cities were neglected by state legislatures, while the interests of farmers and rural communities were quite well served.

Malapportionment ended in the early 1960s when the U.S. Supreme Court declared that state legislatures must represent people rather than communities or areas. The "one person, one vote" method of apportioning state legislatures immediately gave a larger share of legislative seats to populated urban areas—although, ironically, the cities never got their full due. By the time the Supreme Court outlawed malapportionment in the 1960s, so many people had moved out of the central cities that the suburbs gained the most advantage from reapportionment. The suburbs, like the rural areas, are more conservative and more Republican than the cities; thus, there has never been a time when the concerns of cities have dominated the actions of state legislatures.

Until the past few decades, most of the state legislatures were relatively unimposing institutions. They were in session only for short periods each year, were deficient in staff and information resources, and were vulnerable to powerful lobbying groups. Beginning in the 1960s, however, they began to meet for longer periods and to expand their staffs. Legislators' pay also increased significantly at this time. The increase was substantial enough in a few states, such as New York and California, to create professional legislators—individuals whose chief occupation is an elective position within a state legislature. New York's legislators are paid more than $75,000 a year in salary. Many of them also hold party or committee leadership positions, for which they receive supplementary allowances.

Most analysts have welcomed the change toward more professional state legislatures. The Advisory Commission on Intergovernmental Relations, an agency established by Congress, noted in one of its reports: "Today's state legislatures are more functional, accountable, independent, and representative, and are equipped with greater information handling capacity than their predecessors."[6]

Some states have resisted the tendency toward longer sessions, larger staffs, and higher salaries. New Hampshire, Alabama, Texas, and Wyoming are among the states that pay their legislators $10,000 a year or less. A recent development that could partly restore the "citizen legislature" is *term limitations,* or legal restrictions on the number of years that elected officials can remain in office. The term-limit movement has been based on the public's dissatisfaction with government, a belief that "professional" politicians are part of the problem, and a

Why Should I Care?

Your State Government

Most Americans know less about their state government than about their national or local government. The main reason is simple enough: the news media cover Washington and city hall more closely than they cover the state capital.

The news media are in the audience delivery business. That is, they must attract and hold an audience in order to get advertisers to buy ads, which are their principal source of revenue. As a result, they concentrate on the concerns of people within their "media market." For network television and newspapers such as *USA Today*, the *Wall Street Journal*, and *The New York Times*, the media market is the nation as a whole. As a result, their news coverage concentrates on national government—the one government in which Americans have a common interest. All major news organizations have bureaus in Washington, D.C., and have reporters stationed at the White House and on Capitol Hill. For local newspapers and local television affiliates, the media market is the local community.

State governments are the odd entity. In most cases, state boundaries do not coincide with media markets. Media markets may even cut across state lines, as in the case of the St. Louis and Kansas City markets. Accordingly, state governments tend to get substantial coverage only from media that are physically located in capital cities. New York state government, for example, gets a lot more attention from the Albany media than from the Buffalo, Rochester, Syracuse, or New York City media.

Not surprisingly, citizens are more likely to contact their representatives in Washington and local government than their representatives in state government. Out of sight and out of mind is a fairly apt description of many people's awareness of state officials, except for the governor. The irony is that the policies of state governments have more impact on people's daily lives than do those of either the national government or local governments. Schools, roadways, and hospitals are among the areas governed largely through state policies. State governments are deserving of your attention, even if news coverage in many locations makes that a difficult task.

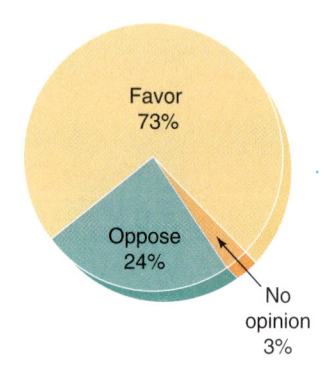

Figure 15–2
The Public's View of Term Limitations
Most Americans favor term limits for elected officials.
Source: Gallup Poll, March 1999.

- Favor 73%
- Oppose 24%
- No opinion 3%

sense that an answer to the problem is to replace them with "amateurs" who are more closely connected to the people they serve (see Figure 15–2). Voters in Oklahoma were the first to act on this belief, deciding by a two-to-one margin in 1990 to limit state legislators to twelve years of service. California and Colorado voters followed suit in the same year, and nearly half the states now have term limits for at least some offices.

The Courts

As a consequence of America's federal system, each state has its separate court system. Like the federal system, the state systems have trial courts at the bottom level and appellate courts at the top. About two-thirds of the states have two appellate levels, and the other third have only a single appellate court (the state's supreme court). Most of the less-populated states have determined that they do not need a second appellate level. Those with a second appellate level have created it primarily to relieve the heavy caseload that would otherwise fall on the top court.

The states vary in the way they organize and label their courts. Most of the states have district courts and a supreme court, but the states tend also to give some lower courts specialized titles and jurisdictions. Family courts, for example, settle such issues as divorce and child custody disputes, and probate courts handle the disposition of the estates of people who have died. Below such specialized trial courts are less-formal trial courts, such as magistrate courts and justice of the peace courts. They handle a variety of minor cases, such as traffic infractions, and usually do not use a jury. Jury trial is not a constitutional requirement of the states, nor do they have to follow the federal tradition of a twelve-member jury or of a unanimous verdict when a jury is used.

States also vary in their methods of selecting judges. In about a fourth of the states, judges are appointed by the governor, but in most states, judgeships are elective offices. Several states use the Missouri Plan (so called because Missouri was the first state to use it), under which a judicial selection commission provides a short list of acceptable candidates from which the governor selects one. After a trial period of a year or more, the judge selected must be approved by the electorate in a yes-no vote in order to serve a longer term.

State courts are undeniably important. As was indicated in Chapter 14, there is a federal court myth that holds that the federal courts are the more significant component of the American judicial system. In fact, the state judiciary is the locus of most court action. Upward of 95 percent of the nation's legal cases are decided in state courts (or local courts, which are agents of the states). Moreover, nearly all cases that originate in state courts also end there; the federal courts never enter the picture. Of course, one federal court—the U.S. Supreme Court—is a silent partner of the state and local courts, requiring them to act within minimum standards of justice (for example, the prohibition of forced confessions).

The workload on the state court system is enormous. State courts handle more than 100 million cases annually, and though many of these cases involve minor infractions, more than ten million have potentially serious consequences for at least one party in the case, including imprisonment, financial deprivation, or personal loss, as in the case of a parent who loses a child custody dispute.

The application of justice in the state court systems is relatively uneven. To say that the state courts are riddled with incompetence and favoritism would be unfair to the many skilled and conscientious jurists who work within them. But it is accurate to say that the state courts do not have enough resources to handle adequately the staggering load of cases thrust on them. Long delays are commonplace, which places pressure on these systems to reduce the caseload through plea bargains and other mechanisms that increase the likelihood of arbitrary outcomes. Many judges, particularly those who operate in the lower courts, are poorly informed about the laws they are asked to apply. And a few are downright incompetent, having acquired their positions simply because they had political connections or the name recognition to win a judicial election.

Most states have made efforts in recent decades to raise the performance level of their court systems. Administrative and legal procedures have been changed, for example, to expedite the handling of cases. In the past, the pursuit of justice in many state courts was slow and procedurally arbitrary. There are still delays and procedural injustices, but they are less prevalent today as a result of federally imposed standards and state-initiated reforms, such as those that require law enforcement officials to dismiss a case unless it is presented to a judge or grand jury within a specified period of time. States have also established disciplinary boards to identify and remove or reprimand incompetent or biased judges.

Elections are a hallmark of American government at all levels. Over the course of an average year, citizens in many locations could easily vote in three or four different elections. In most states, citizens can also vote directly on issues of public policy through the referendum or initiative.

Citizens, Parties, and Elections

When the Framers wrote the U.S. Constitution, they allowed for only minimal popular participation. The House of Representatives was the only popularly elected institution and the only one with a short term of office, two years. The democratic spirit of the Revolution of 1776 was more apparent at the state level. Every state but South Carolina held an annual legislative election, and several states chose their governors through annual election by the people.

Today, the states hold elections less frequently, but they have stayed ahead of the federal government in their emphasis on elections as a means of popular influence and control. As was noted previously, most states elect their treasurer, attorney general, and secretary of state by popular ballot. Many states also choose their judges by direct election. No federal judges are chosen by this means.

Citizens as Legislators

State voters also get the opportunity to vote directly on issues of policy. In all states except Delaware, amendments to the state constitution require the approval of the electorate. In addition, more than a third of the states give popular majorities the power of the **initiative,** which allows citizens through signature petitions to place legislative measures on the ballot. If such a measure receives a majority vote, it becomes law, just as if it had been enacted by the state's legislature. A related measure is the **referendum,** which permits the legislature to submit proposals to the voters for approval or rejection. The initiative and referendum were introduced around 1900 as Progressive reforms. The Progressives also sought to protect the public from wayward state and local officials through the **recall,** in which citizens can petition for the removal from office of an elected official before the scheduled completion of his or her term. The state of Arizona would probably have recalled its governor, Evan Mecham, in 1987 had he not been impeached by the state legislature before the recall process could be completed.

Of these mechanisms, the initiative has been the most important. Increasingly, it has become an instrument of group politics.[7] The average citizen does not have the time or money to organize a statewide petition drive. Many groups

initiative The process by which citizens can place legislative measures on the ballot through signature petitions, and if the measure receives a majority vote, it becomes law.

referendum The process through which the legislature may submit proposals to the voters for approval or rejection.

recall The process by which citizens can petition for the removal from office of an elected official before the scheduled completion of his or her term.

do, and they have increasingly recognized that the initiative is an alternative to the traditional method of lobbying the state legislature. Not only are their chances of success often greater, but they also get the opportunity to decide exactly how the measure will be worded. Once the initiative is placed on the ballot, a group can use its resources to mount a statewide advertising campaign to urge its passage. An irony is that the initiative was devised by the Progressives to protect citizens against the hold that powerful interests had acquired over state legislatures. The initiative was to be a means by which citizens could bypass the legislature and thus overcome the power of entrenched interests. Oregon is among the states where restrictions on the use of the initiative by organized interests is under debate. It is even conceivable that some states may choose in the future to abolish the initiative.

Voter Registration and Turnout

Although the states have been electoral innovators, their history also includes attempts to restrict access to the ballot. The clearest example is that of southern states after the Civil War. The Fifteenth Amendment was ratified in 1870, prohibiting states from using race as the basis for denial of suffrage. Southern states responded with a number of devices that were designed to keep African Americans from voting. Through poll taxes, the grandfather clause, whites-only primary elections, and rigged literacy tests as a qualification for registration to vote, blacks in many areas of the South were effectively disenfranchised.[8]

Action by the national government was necessary to bring a halt to state efforts to disenfranchise large groups of voters (see Chapter 5). Major steps included a Supreme Court decision outlawing whites-only primaries, a constitutional amendment barring poll taxes, and the Voting Rights Act of 1965, which forbids discrimination in voting and registration. However, the legacy of a century of state-supported efforts to keep blacks and poor whites from voting in the South is still evident. The region has the lowest voter turnout rate in the nation. By comparison, states like Minnesota, Wisconsin, and Idaho, which have pioneered methods such as election-day registration that are designed to encourage voting, are among the leaders in voter turnout.

The decline in voter turnout in presidential and congressional elections in recent decades (see Chapter 7) has also been characteristic of state elections. The average turnout in gubernatorial elections that do not coincide with a presidential election, for example, is less than 40 percent—a drop of several percentage points since the early 1960s.

THE STRUCTURE OF LOCAL GOVERNMENT

If the significance of a level of government was determined strictly on the basis of numbers, the local level would win handily. The United States has one national government and fifty state governments, but it has more than eighty thousand local governments, which include counties, municipalities, school districts, and special districts, such as water, sewage, and conservation districts.

Historical Background

Dillon's rule The term used to describe relations between state and local government; it holds that local governments are creatures of the state, which in theory even has the power to abolish them.

Local governments, however, do not have sovereignty—that is, they do not have final authority within their governing spheres. Their authority drives from that of the state within which they are located. The general principle that describes the relationship between state power and localities is called **Dillon's rule**. It holds that local governments are creatures of their states, which in theory even have the power to abolish them. The rule derives its name from the judge, John F. Dillon, who propounded it in a nineteenth-century treatise on municipal governments. These governments, he wrote, possess only those powers that are "expressly granted" them by their state or are "necessarily . . . implied in or incident to" these powers.[9]

The most important aspect of Dillon's rule is that local governments must act within constraints placed on them by the state. The state's reach extends even to the issue of whether a local unit of government will provide a particular service. The state of Wisconsin, for example, requires each of its cities to have a solid-waste disposal facility.

States differ markedly in the degree of freedom they grant their local units. The states that grant the highest degree of autonomy to local units, and those that grant the least, are found in all regions of the country. For example, Oregon, North Carolina, and Connecticut rank high on local autonomy, while Idaho, Mississippi, and Massachusetts rank low.

charter The chief instrument by which a state governs its local units; it spells out in detail what a local government can and cannot do.

The chief instrument by which a state governs its local units is the **charter**. No local government can exist without a charter, which is issued by the state and defines the limits within which a local unit must operate. By tradition, local charters are restrictive. They spell out in considerable detail what a local government can and cannot do. A typical charter, for example, specifies the types and limits of taxation that a local government may impose on its residents. The charters of some types of local government include a grant of lawmaking power. These governments can issue **ordinances,** which are local laws. A locality might, for example, pass an ordinance requiring dog owners to leash their pet or an ordinance specifying a curfew for teenagers.

ordinance A law issued by a local government under authority granted by the state government.

There are limits to a state's ability to control its local units. A state government does not have the time, the money, or the staff to make all the decisions concerning its many local units. Nor can a state expect the same restrictions to work equally well for all local units. A charter that is suited to a city of a million inhabitants would probably not be suited to a village of several hundred people. Accordingly, all states give their local units some discretionary authority and make allowance for differences among them. In most cases, the charters for cities are different from those for towns, which in turn differ from those for villages.

home rule A device designed to give local governments more leeway in their policies; it allows a local government to design and amend its own charter, subject to the laws and constitution of the state and also subject to veto by the state.

Home rule is a device that is designed to give local governments more leeway in their policies. It developed out of a protest movement that sought to free local government from meddlesome interference by the states. Its guiding principle was the so-called **Cooley's rule,** articulated in an 1871 ruling by Michigan judge Thomas Cooley who boldly declared that cities should be self-governing.[10] Home rule was first tried in 1875 in Missouri, and it allows a local government to design and amend its own charter, subject to the laws and constitution of the state and also subject to veto by the state.

Cooley's rule The term used to describe the idea that cities should be self-governing, articulated in an 1871 ruling by Michigan judge Thomas Cooley.

The long-term trend in the states has been toward home rule and other means of granting localities a larger measure of independence. It is partly a

Flanked by firefighters, New York City Mayor Rudolph Guiliani pays tribute to the people who lost their lives in the terrorist attacks on the World Trade Center. Guiliani's inspirational response at the time of the attacks demonstrated the importance of strong leadership in local government. Guiliani was named "Person of the Year" by *Time* magazine for his part in helping New Yorkers and Americans elsewhere cope with the tragedy.

philosophical issue: Americans are accustomed to a substantial degree of local autonomy and expect their state governments to refrain from interfering too deeply in local affairs. It is also a practical issue: states lack the capacity to make the everyday decisions of their local governments.

Local government is the source of most public employment. Compared with fewer than three million federal workers and four million state employees, more than ten million people work in local government. They are one of the most heavily unionized groups in the country. Schoolteachers are represented through the American Federation of Teachers (AFT) and the National Education Association (NEA), and other local public employees are represented through such unions as the International Association of Fire Fighters (IAFF) and the American Federation of State, County, and Municipal Employees (AFSCME). These unions have more than three million members, and they have been quite successful in obtaining better working conditions and job benefits for their members.

Types of Local Government

There is wide variation within and among states in the structure and responsibilities of local government. A full description of the various types could fill several books. The purpose of the following sections is to highlight some of the major types.

County Government

The oldest form of local government in the United States is the county, and it remains a top local governing unit in rural areas and in those few states, such as New York, where the county has broad responsibility for providing government services. The county is governed through an elected county commission (which, in some states, is called a county legislature or board of supervisors). In most states, there are also elected county sheriffs and county attorneys, and a few states have elected chief county executives.

Counties are subdivisions of a state. They blanket the state in the sense that it is divided completely into county units. The shape and number of these county units, however, varies markedly. Texas is divided into 254 counties. Alaska is larger in area but has only 16 county units. In most states, the county functions as an administrative subdivision of the state. The county's responsibility is to carry out programs, such as highway maintenance or welfare services, that are established by the state. Some analysts believe that the county will increase in importance in upcoming years because of the prominence of issues such as waste disposal that cannot be addressed adequately at the municipal level but require a regional response.

County government illustrates the variation that exists in local governmental structures. Two states, Louisiana and Alaska, call their counties by another name (parishes in Louisiana, boroughs in Alaska). Moreover, the role of the county is not always the same even within a particular state. The county is typically a more visible unit of government in rural areas (where, for example, the county sheriff is often the most widely known public official) than in urban areas (where, for example, residents may not even know where their county officials are located). Also, counties vary greatly in population. They range from some urban counties with more than a million inhabitants to some rural counties with only a few thousand residents. The largest is Los Angeles County in California, which has a population of roughly eight million.

Municipal Government

In most parts of the United States, the major unit of local government is the municipality, which can be a city, town, or village. Municipalities exist partly to carry out activities of the state government, but they exist primarily to serve the self-governing needs of their residents. Most Americans depend on their municipal governments for law enforcement, water, and sanitation services.

Municipalities are legal entities that operate under a charter granted by the state. As indicated previously, a charter defines the limits within which a local governing unit must operate. Over the years, and consistent with the philosophy of local autonomy, municipal charters have become less restrictive. Moreover, rather than drafting separate charters for each municipality, states have developed more general charters that apply to all municipalities within a category (such as "small city" or "medium-sized city," as defined by population). Of course, some municipalities are in a class by themselves and require a specific charter. New York City, for example, has taxing and other powers not granted to other municipalities in New York State.

The traditional and most common form of municipal government is the mayor-council system, which includes the mayor as the chief executive and the local council as the legislative body (see Table 15-1). The mayor-council system takes two forms. The more common form is the **strong mayor–council system,** in which the mayor has veto power and a prescribed responsibility for budgetary and other policy actions. The mayor, rather than the council, is the more powerful policymaker. The alternative is the **weak mayor–council system,** in

---

strong mayor–council system Most common form of municipal government, consisting of the mayor as chief executive and the local council as the legislative body, in which the mayor has veto power and a prescribed responsibility for budgetary and other policy actions.

weak mayor–council system Form of municipal government in which the mayor's policymaking powers are less substantial than the council's; the mayor has no power to veto the council's actions and often has no formal role in such activities as budget making.

TABLE 15-1 Common Forms of Municipal Government

Strong Mayor–Council System

An elected mayor has veto power over an elected council and has substantial authority over the budget and other policies

Weak Mayor–Council System

An elected mayor does not have veto power and is generally weak relative to the elected council.

Commission System

Executive and legislative power is vested in an elected commission whose members each have a specified policy role, such as police commissioner.

City Manager System

An appointed chief executive administers programs and can be fired by the elected council.

---

which the mayor's policymaking powers are less substantial than the council's. The mayor has no power to veto the council's actions and often has no formal role in such activities as budget making.

A different type of municipal government entirely is the **commission system.** This form invests executive and legislative authority in a commission, with each commissioner serving as a member of the local council but also having a specified executive role, such as police commissioner or public works commissioner. The commission system has lost considerable favor in recent decades. Its major weakness is that it has no chief executive with the power and responsibility to set the local government's overall direction. There are now only about 100 U.S. communities that employ this governing system. Fargo, North Dakota, is one of the cities in this group.

A final type of municipal government is the **city manager system,** which was pioneered in Ohio during the Progressive era as a reaction against inefficiency and partisan corruption in many of the nation's cities. The system entrusts the executive role to a professionally trained manager, who is chosen, and can be fired, by the city council. This arrangement ensures that the manager will be at least somewhat responsive to political and popular pressures. Most city managers have specialized university training in the operation of municipal government. The typical form of this education is the master of public administration (MPA), which includes courses in areas such as public finance, budgeting, and organization. However, city managers are usually "outsiders" who did not grow up in the community they administer and who typically lack the political support that is necessary to exert strong leadership. Most of the larger cities that installed the city manager system have since reverted to the mayor-council system, but the city manager form is the most common type of government in smaller cities. California is one of the states where the city manager system has been widely adopted. San Jose is among the California cities with this form of local government.

A local chief executive, whether a mayor or city manager, is, above all, an administrator whose main responsibility is to oversee the work of the component units of local government—the police, fire, sanitation, and other departments.

commission system Form of municipal government that invests executive and legislative authority in a commission, with each commissioner serving as a member of the local council but also having a specified executive role, such as police commissioner or public works commissioner.

city manager system Form of municipal government that entrusts the executive role to a professionally trained manager, who is chosen, and can be fired, by the city council.

Increasingly, local chief executives are also expected to provide economic leadership by fostering a business climate that will keep old firms in the community and attract new ones. In many cities, including Baltimore, San Antonio, and Minneapolis, mayors have played key roles in the revitalization of downtown areas. Of course, not all chief executives accomplish much, or even get the opportunity. In smaller towns and villages particularly, the position of mayor is often more honorary than active; it is a part-time position held by a trusted member of the community.

Towns and Townships

The word *town* is used in reference to a municipality that is smaller than a city and larger than a village. In most areas of New England, however, a town more often refers to a governing unit that functions as both a municipality and a county. In these areas, the county is often nothing more than a geographical entity, since the town encompasses both one or more communities and their contiguous rural areas. The town has responsibility for both community streets and rural roads as well as other local services. The fabled town meetings that once governed New England towns still exist, but they now seldom attract many people, and the towns are effectively governed by a town council of elected officials, who, in the larger towns, usually entrust day-to-day operations to a full-time town manager.

In several Midwestern states, and a few states elsewhere, townships are an important governing unit. They are subunits of counties and, in rural areas particularly, have key policy responsibilities, including roadways and other public services. They resemble New England towns in that they were created as geographic units and vary widely in their population density. Thus, they are unlike municipalities where, for the most part, residents live closely together. Townships also differ from municipalities in that, as subunits of the county, they are not empowered to enact local ordinances. They carry out county policy; they do not make policy of their own.

School Districts

The tradition of local public schools is deeply embedded in the American political experience. Unlike Europe, where private schools and national educational standards have historically been more important, the United States has emphasized public education and local control. This control is exercised through local school boards. In a few places, the school board is subordinate to the municipal government, but elsewhere it is an independent body. School policy is established by the local board rather than by the local mayor or council. The chief executive of the local public school system is a specially trained professional, the superintendent of schools. The superintendent is hired, and can be fired, by the local board.

Some states have recently authorized charter schools as an alternative to traditional public schools. Such schools are granted a charter (much as local governments have a charter) within which they must operate. Charter schools have greater freedom than do other public schools in selecting their admission, curriculum, and other policies.

Members of the Metro Dade police departments say the Pledge of Allegiance during a public ceremony. Miami and surrounding communities in south Florida have a metropolitan government. It provides police, sanitation, and other services to the area's residents. In most U.S. metropolitan areas, such services are provided by each community separately.

Special Districts and Metropolitan Government

Another form of municipal government, and one of increasing importance, is the special district. As society has become more complex and interdependent, a need has arisen for local governing institutions that are responsive to the resulting policy needs. Special districts that deal with such policy areas as water supply, soil conservation, and waste disposal are an answer. These districts also provide an answer to the problem of coordinating the efforts of independent municipal governments. Issues such as pollution control are not easily addressed within a single community. Special districts bring municipalities together; the typical form of governance of these districts is a board that includes a member from each municipality within the district's boundaries. The day-to-day operations of these districts, however, are typically entrusted to trained administrators, who often have specialized educations, such as the waste-management engineers who oversee municipal sewage systems.

Special districts ordinarily have responsibility for a specific policy activity, such as solid-waste management or soil conservation. In some urban areas, however, local governments have joined to create a **metropolitan government** that is given responsibility for a broader range of activities. An example is the Dade County (Florida) Metropolitan Government, which includes Miami and surrounding communities. Each community is represented on the Dade County Commission, which has responsibility for providing most of the local services. A metropolitan government is designed to reduce the waste and duplication that results when every locality in a densely populated area has its own police force, its own sanitation department, its own planning board, and so on. Although a metropolitan government is more efficient, the tradition of strong local autonomy makes it an unappealing option to many Americans.

metropolitan government Form of local government created when local governments join together and assign it responsibility for a range of activities, such as police and sanitation, so as to reduce the waste and duplication that results when every locality in a densely populated area provides its own services.

Local Elections and Participation

The principle of elective office dominates local government. In addition to an elected mayor, most communities have an elected town or city council. The office of county commissioner is also an elective office throughout the country. Except in a few eastern states, local officials are chosen in nonpartisan elections. No party labels appear on the ballot.

Perhaps no local institution symbolizes the nature of American democracy better than the public schools. School board members are elected, and in many communities, the voters even have the opportunity to approve or reject school budgets and bonding proposals. In contrast, school officials in European countries are typically appointed to their positions, and school budgets are set primarily by national governments.

Voting in local elections is subject to state registration laws. However, as noted in Chapter 7, many local governments have tried to weaken the link between their level of government and the state and national levels by scheduling local elections for odd-numbered years rather than the even-numbered ones during which all federal and most state elections are held. A predictable effect of this scheduling is that voter turnout is somewhat lower at each level than would be the case if national, state, and local elections were held simultaneously. The average turnout in local elections in most states is very low—30 percent or less. Turnout figures can be deceptive. There are countless instances of extraordinary turnout in local elections when a contentious issue is on the ballot. School bonding issues, for example, often produce a high turnout, and increasingly have pitted families with children in the public schools against the growing number of elderly Americans who, on the whole, are less supportive of school spending proposals.[11]

Local elections embody many of the conflicts that are found, in one form or another, throughout U.S. politics. Many communities, for example, use at-large (community-wide) districts to elect members of the local council. The justification for the approach is the notion that at-large council members will act on behalf of the whole community and not sections of it, as might be the case if they were elected from separate districts within the community. However, at-large districts tend to result in the election of council members who are demographically similar to the majority of voters. Black and Hispanic candidates have fared poorly in these systems, which has created pressures to change at-large districts to separate-district systems.

Elections, however, are only one form of citizen influence on local government. Although the opportunities for ordinary citizens to direct state and national officials are confined mostly to periodic elections, there are additional opportunities available in local settings. As seen in Chapter 7, group participation is relatively high in the United States, and many groups are involved in community-oriented activities. A few cities, including St. Paul, Minnesota, have even delegated authority to neighborhood councils that may have responsibility, for example, for creating and operating community centers or playgrounds.

The news media are also influential in local politics. Local newspapers and television stations sometimes take the lead in highlighting local issues and exposing inept or unethical officials. In any case, most local officials are wary of antagonizing the local media. On the state level, the media are less powerful since a state's boundaries rarely coincide with a news organization's market. Thus, state officials and policy actions receive less scrutiny from the press.

It would be a mistake to conclude, however, that local officials are highly responsive to local residents as a whole. Studies have found that in some locations officials are primarily attentive to the community's economic and social elite. They constitute a local power structure that, even more than public officials themselves, decides community policies.[12]

STATE AND LOCAL FINANCE

The federal government raises more tax revenues than do all fifty states and the thousands of local governments combined. Although states and localities have a substantial tax base, they are in an inherently competitive situation. People and businesses faced with state or local tax increases can move to another state or locality where taxes are lower. Between the 1960s and 1980s, there was a substantial movement of business firms from the northeast and midwest to the south and southwest. These firms were lured by the cheaper labor and lower energy costs of the sunbelt and also by the lower tax rates of southern states.

Local governments are also in a relatively weak tax position. They compete with one another for the jobs and income that business firms represent. Every sizable city in the United States offers tax breaks or other incentives to companies that might relocate there. The predatory nature of the competition makes it difficult for any locality to raise its tax rate substantially and virtually forces them to give tax breaks to firms that could well afford to pay.

A community may even find that it has to pay a business to remain in the community. An obvious example, but not the only one, is the sports franchise that threatens to move its team unless the host city builds an expensive new stadium or arena. San Francisco, Houston, and Miami are among the cities that decided it was in the community's interest to comply with such a demand. Los Angeles is among those that refused the demand and lost a professional sports team as a result.

States and localities are denied a form of taxation available to the federal government—tariffs. Congress has the power to levy taxes on goods shipped to the United States from abroad. The U.S. Constitution prohibits states from placing a duty on goods that cross their borders since such action would disrupt interstate commerce.

Sources of Revenue

The major sources of state revenue are sales taxes, personal income taxes, corporate income taxes, and user fees, such as motor vehicle licenses (see Figure 15–3). There are, however, substantial variations in the taxing policies of the states. A few states have no personal income tax. South Dakota is one of these states. It also has no corporate income tax. Not surprisingly, South Dakota has one of the lowest levels of public services in the nation. Its neighboring state of Minnesota, for example, spends substantially more per capita on public education than does South Dakota.

Income Taxes

Although a few states do not levy an income tax, it is still a major revenue source, accounting for roughly 40 percent of all state tax revenue. The competitive nature of state tax policy, however, serves to hold down income tax rates. The highest marginal rate on personal income on federal tax returns is 39.5 percent. The highest ordinary rate at the state level is less than 10 percent and, in most states, is roughly 5 percent. A few localities—New York City, among

Figure 15–3

Sources of State and Local Government Revenue
States rely on sales and personal income taxes for most of their revenues. Localities depend heavily on property taxes.
Source: U.S. Bureau of Census, 2002.

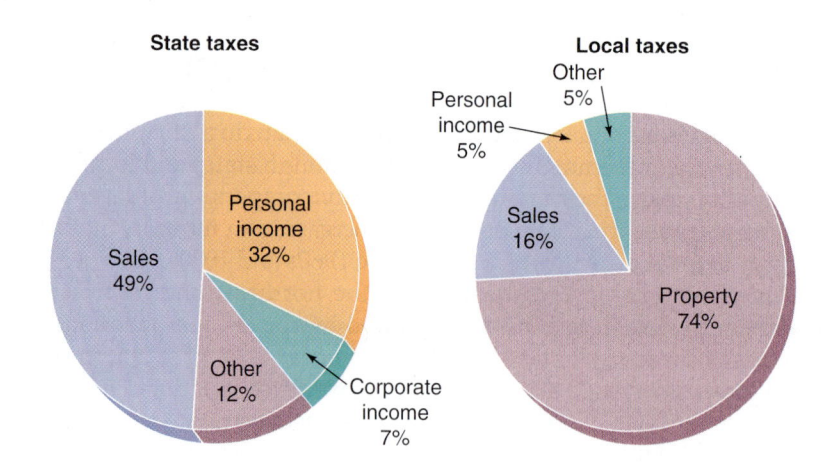

State taxes
- Sales 49%
- Personal income 32%
- Other 12%
- Corporate income 7%

Local taxes
- Property 74%
- Sales 16%
- Personal income 5%
- Other 5%

them—raise revenue through income taxes. These taxes enable a local government to collect revenue from individuals who work in the community and use its services in the process, but who live elsewhere, usually a nearby suburb.

Sales Tax

The *general sales tax* is the chief source of revenue for the states, accounting for about half of all taxes they raise. The sales tax is a flat-rate tax on consumer goods and thereby places a relatively heavy burden on lower-income persons, who spend a higher proportion of their income on such goods than do upper-income persons. The regressive nature of the sales tax has been a source of criticism, and some states exempt food and medicine from the sales tax in order to relieve somewhat the burden it places on lower-income people. Nevertheless, the sales tax is a reliable method of raising large sums of money, and the states have increasingly used it to obtain their revenues.

In many states, local governments also obtain revenue from the sales tax, and in some states, the local share varies by location. In New York, for example, the state's sales tax is four cents on the dollar while the local tax varies from two cents to four cents. Another form of sales tax is the *excise tax*, which is applied only to selected items, such as gasoline and jewelry. It is sometimes called the "sin tax" because liquor and cigarettes are among the items included.

Lotteries and Fees

Although sales and income taxes account for a very large share of state revenues, they are not the only significant revenue sources. Lotteries, for example, account for a small but rising percentage of revenue. They were banned by Congress as a form of illegal gambling until a few decades ago, but today, more than two-thirds of the states run a lottery. The major complaint today about state lotteries is that many of the regular players are low-income Americans who cannot afford to play but who dream of striking it rich. In their lottery advertising, states play up this dream but rarely mention that the odds of winning the biggest jackpots are roughly those of being hit, not once but twice, by lightning. States also do not publicize the fact that they retain more than half the money spent to purchase lottery tickets.

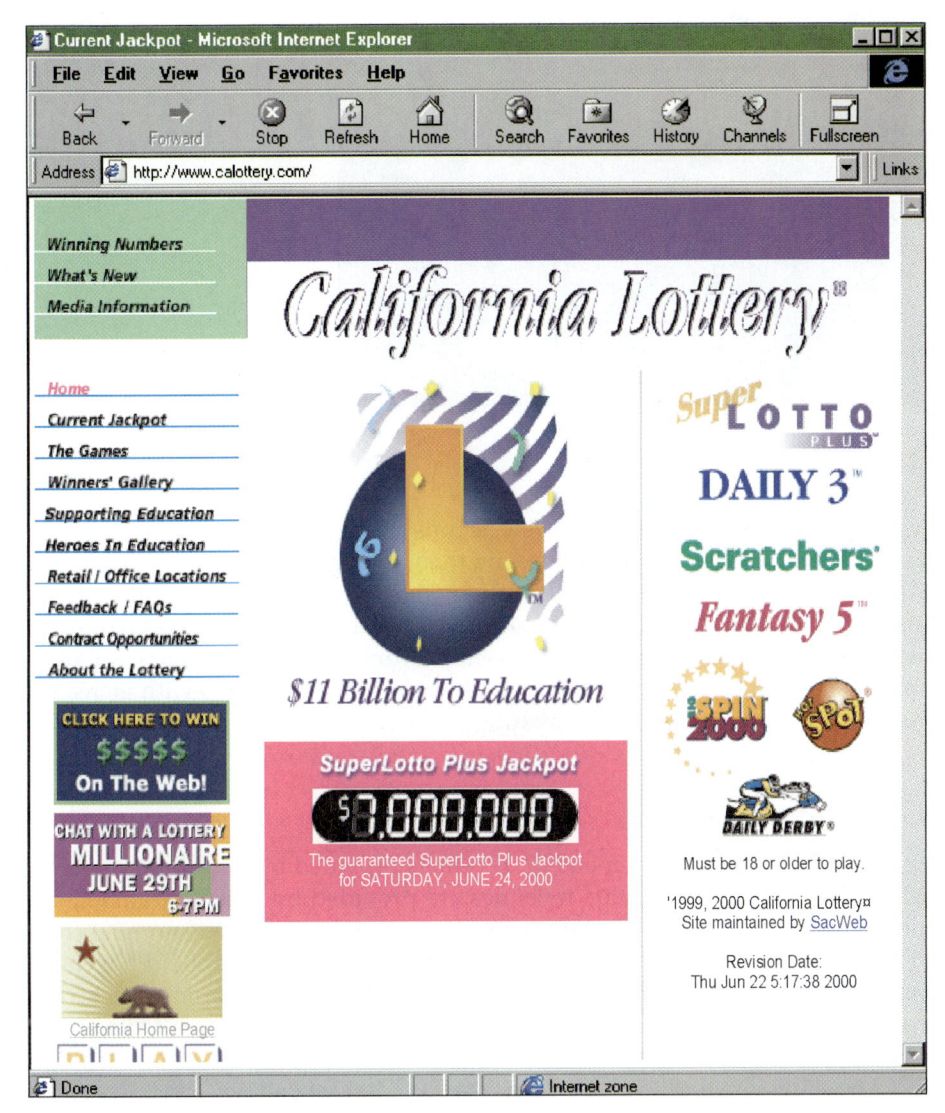

CHAPTER 15　　State and Local Politics: Maintaining Our Differences　　489

States are in an inherently competitive situation with regard to taxation. A state cannot raise taxes very high without losing firms and residents to a state where taxes are lower. This situation has led states to develop alternative sources of revenue. One of the most common is a state lottery. The payout to lottery winners and vendors is typically about half the amount taken in; the rest goes to the state government.

License and user fees are a fourth source of state revenue. The most important are the license fees that states charge for vehicle registration and drivers' licenses. But there are also, for example, license fees charged to doctors and lawyers that allow them to practice in a state and liquor license fees charged to stores and restaurants that sell or dispense liquor. A few states also derive substantial revenue from severance taxes that are imposed on those who extract natural resources, such as oil, coal, or bauxite, from the state's soil.

Property Taxes

As Figure 15–3 indicates, local governments rely primarily on the property tax for their revenues. This form of taxation accounts for three-fourths of all revenues raised directly by local government, but it has drawbacks. It is paid, for example, in a lump sum, which heightens taxpayers' awareness of its cost and

The state of Hawaii is one of many states that depend heavily on federal spending for their economic vitality. Shown here is a scene from the naval base at Pearl Harbor.

leads them to resist any increase. Few actions are more likely to result in the defeat of a local official in the next election than a steep increase in property taxes. Accordingly, localities have turned increasingly to sales taxes (shared with the state and collected with the state's permission) and local income taxes (collected with the state's permission). The revenues from these sources increase automatically when the economy expands, thus providing localities with increased revenues without a raise in the tax rate.

Government Grants

States and localities also depend on revenues provided by other governments. More than 15 percent of state revenues are provided by federal grants-in-aid programs, while local governments get about 30 percent of their revenues from the state and 5 percent from Washington. States and localities could not easily manage without these grants, but the money has a drawback not attached to their other revenues—it comes with strings attached. As Chapter 3 explained, grants are provided for specific uses only.

The states and localities also benefit from federal spending. The states of the south and west, particularly, owe many of their jobs to federal programs. In Hawaii, for example, thirty thousand active U.S. military personnel are stationed at bases that include Pearl Harbor (Navy), Schofield Barracks (Army), and Hickam Field (Air Force).

Federal grants-in-aid and other federal policies tend to reduce the importance of state-to-state differences in wealth as a factor in state and local policies. Federal assistance is targeted disproportionately for less affluent states and communities. In addition, many federal programs require matching grants and uniform standards of participating states. However, the leveling effect of this federal policy is not very great, and states differ enormously in their economic wealth. The level of public services in all areas—education, welfare, health, and so on—is higher in wealthier states. In comparison with the five poorest states (Mississippi, West Virginia, Utah, Arkansas, and South Carolina), the five wealthiest states (Connecticut, New Jersey, Alaska, Massachusetts, and New York) spend over $1,000 per pupil more on public education each year.

Fighting Words

Should Congress Exempt the Internet from Sales Taxes?

The Internet Tax Freedom Act was passed in 1998 by Congress and placed a three-year moratorium on state and local taxes on e-commerce. It also barred the federal government from levying taxes on Internet commerce, declaring that the Internet should be a tariff-free zone. When Congress reconsidered the issue in 2000, there was a substantial division of opinion both within the institution and outside. Advocates of the exemption claimed that a sales tax would inhibit the growth of the Internet and of e-commerce. Opponents claimed that a tax-free Internet was unfair to the mail-order and walk-in retailers whose goods and services were subject to taxation. Critics also said that state and local government services would be adversely affected by the loss of sales tax revenues. In 2001, Congress voted to extend the moratorium for five years.

Yes: The benefits which we, as a nation, have obtained as a result . . . of being the incubator, the developer, and now the provider in expertise in the area of the Internet, and the use of the Internet for commerce . . . are basically incalculable; the amount of new jobs which have been created; the number of people whose standard of living has been increased; the number of people who have been able to purchase goods at less of a price. . . . These benefits dramatically exceed a large number of different states or municipalities to start taxing the Internet for the purposes of expanding their local governments.
—Senator Judd Gregg (R-N.H.)

No: Requiring online merchants to collect an existing sales tax does not create a new tax. Brick-and-mortar retailers are required—by law—to collect sales tax on all consumer goods purchased in their stores. [We favor] equal application of the sales tax on all commercial transactions. . . . Commerce on the Internet is growing at a phenomenal rate, increasing the potential for loss of major tax revenues. . . . According to the U.S. Census Bureau, more than 47.9 percent of state revenues come from sales tax. These revenues fund essential community needs such as schools, police, and transportation services. If sales tax is not collected on e-commerce transactions, state and local governments stand to lose more than $10 billion per year by the year 2003.
—E-Fairness

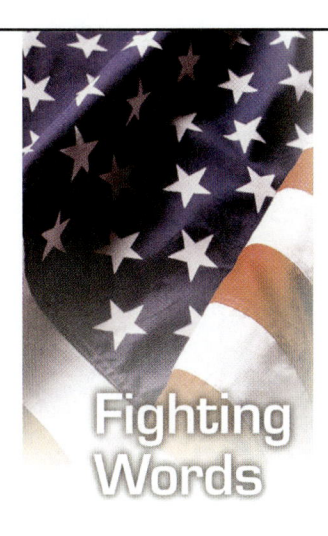

Borrowing

A final source of revenue is borrowing. States and localities issue bonds for purchase by investors. Although borrowing is sometimes necessary, state and local governments try to hold it to a minimum since the funds at some point will have to be repaid, with interest.

The Ups and Downs of State and Local Finance

Some analysts have concluded that economics, not politics, is the chief determinant of a state's public policies. Whether that observation is literally true, there is no question that the wealth of a state has a great influence on its policies. In the mid-1980s, the states were beneficiaries of a sharp upturn in the national

With passage of the 1996 Welfare Reform Act, the states assumed the primary responsibility for welfare and employment policy.

economy. As corporate and personal incomes rose, so did the tax revenues flowing into the state treasuries. Policy initiatives flowed from the states, which seemed especially adept at combining programs designed to stimulate economic development with programs designed to tighten fiscal responsibility.

Innovative governors were leaders of the change. Their experimental economic and social programs, from technological development to welfare reform, were widely publicized.[13] An example was the so-called Massachusetts Miracle. In Boston and the surrounding area, dozens of high-technology firms sprang up almost overnight, creating unprecedented prosperity for the state. Its governor, Michael Dukakis, was given much of the credit for the economic boom. He was voted the nation's most effective governor by the other governors, which contributed to the political reputation that helped him gain the Democratic party's 1988 presidential nomination.

By 1990, however, many of the states were in trouble. More than half had budget deficits and faced the prospect of service cuts and tax increases. Many states faced serious long-term economic problems in the form of declining industries and strong foreign competitors. All the states had no choice but to cut back on either their plans or their programs; they had no money for significant new initiatives.

This situation also encouraged states to develop new approaches in areas such as health and welfare policy. Led by innovative governors, such as Wisconsin's Tommy Thompson, the states devised programs that were more efficient and in many instances more effective than the previous ones.[14] By 1995, the state capitals had clearly eclipsed Washington as a source of policy ideas. This realization encouraged Congress to shift additional policy responsibilities to the states through, for example, the expanded use of block grants (see Chapter 3).

As the national economy grew rapidly after 1995, the states once again were in a strong financial position. An increase in tax revenues from heightened business activity and personal income enabled them to spend more in areas such as education and highway construction. States also used their surplus revenues to cut taxes, reduce outstanding debt, and build up cash reserves as a hedge against the next economic downswing. By 2002, however, the states were once again in financial trouble. A downturn in the economy had sharply reduced their tax revenues. Nearly every state was forced to reduce programs in order to balance its budget.

This pattern of boom and bust results because the states and localities, unlike the federal government, have only a limited capacity to borrow money. The U.S. Constitution denies them the authority to print their own currency, which means, in hard times, that they have little choice but to cut back their services.

STATE AND LOCAL POLICY

Through the Tenth Amendment, the states possess what is sometimes called the **police power,** a term that refers to the broad power of government to regulate the health, safety, and morals of the citizenry. Possession of this power has meant that the American states carry out many of the policy responsibilities that in other countries are dealt with at the national level. Law enforcement, public education, public health, and roads are among the policy areas that in America are defined largely by the state and local governments.

Although the policies enacted by Congress get more attention from the press, the acts of state legislatures have more influence on the day-to-day lives of most Americans. For example, most crimes are defined by state law, most criminal acts are investigated by authorities operating under state law, most trials take place under state law, and most prisoners are held in penitentiaries and jails that operate under laws enacted by state legislatures.

police power A term that refers to the broad power of government to regulate the health, safety, and morals of the citizenry.

Policy Priorities

One way to see how the states use their power is to rank policy areas by level of spending (see Figure 15–4). The top spending category for the states is public education, followed by public welfare, health and hospitals, and highways.

State spending
- Education 32%
- Welfare 22%
- Highways 7%
- Health and hospitals 7%
- Other 32%

Local spending
- Education 39%
- Public safety 16%
- Health and hospitals 10%
- Welfare 5%
- Other 30%

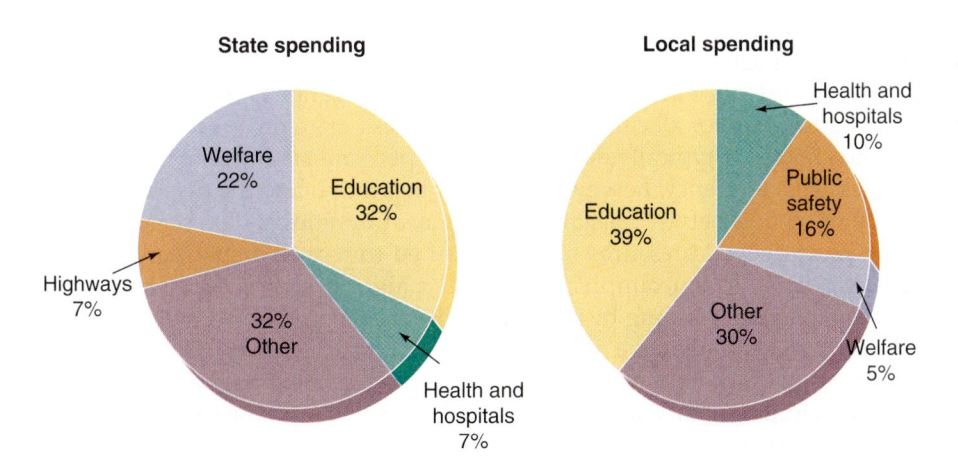

Figure 15–4

Spending Priorities of State and Local Governments
Education is the major spending category for both state and local governments.
Source: U.S. Bureau of Census, 2000 (state), 1999 (local).

These four areas are by far the most significant components of state spending. There is a large dropoff in spending between the fourth category, highways, and the fifth one, police.

The policy priorities of local governments are less easily described (see Figure 15–4). Some local units, such as school boards, operate in only one policy area. Municipalities vary in size from the largest cities to the smallest villages, and their policies differ accordingly. Despite such differences, a few patterns to local spending are discernible. Far and away the biggest expense for local governments is public education; it accounts for about 40 percent of all spending at the local level. Public safety (police, fire, corrections) ranks second at roughly 15 percent, with health and hospitals in third place with about 10 percent. Welfare and roads are the leading areas among the other spending categories.

Public Policy Patterns

A brief description of some of the policy activities of state and local governments, and where they get the money to pay for these activities, will provide a broader perspective on the role of states and localities in the American system.

Education

Public education, including primary schools, secondary schools, and colleges and universities, accounts for the largest share of combined state and local spending, about a third of the total. Education spending by state and local governments dwarfs that of the federal government—more than 90 percent to less than 10 percent. Even higher education is mainly a state and local responsibility, which means that the greatest share of the country's investment in the technical research and personnel that underpin the economy is provided by subnational governments. They also make the key substantive policy decisions in the education area, from curriculum to performance standards to length of schooling.

Of the many issues affecting public education in the states, two stand out in recent years. One is the disparity in spending among school districts, which, in most instances, reflects differences in communities' wealth. Suburban schools, for example, are typically better funded and have better facilities than the inner-city schools in the same metropolitan area. Should such differences be allowed? In a 1973 Texas case, the Supreme Court concluded that a state has no obligation to provide students with an equal education: its obligation is "to provide an 'adequate' education for all children."[15] Nevertheless, state financial contributions to local schools are typically designed to help poorer districts more than wealthier ones. This tendency, however, does not begin to offset the disparity in the quality of schools between a state's poorest communities and its richest ones.

In recent years, pressures have intensified to reduce disparities in school spending. In 1998, for example, New Jersey's highest court settled a years-long battle over school funding by ordering Governor Christine Todd Whitman to develop a plan to equalize spending in the state's public schools. Courts in about twenty states have ruled against inequitable school financing systems, although they have not gone as far as New Jersey's top court in ordering an equalization plan.[16]

Liberty & Equality

What's Your Opinion?

The Fourteenth Amendment

As originally formulated, the Bill of Rights had a limitation. It applied only to actions of the national government. Thus, for example, the First Amendment prohibited Congress from abridging freedom of speech but did not restrict the state governments from doing so. Ratification of the Fourteenth Amendment in 1868 provided a basis for protecting the liberties in the Bill of Rights from actions by the state and local governments. The Fourteenth Amendment says that no state shall "deprive any person of life, liberty, or property, without due process of law." Although a significant period of time elapsed before the Supreme Court interpreted the Fourteenth Amendment as a substantial limitation on state and local governments, it eventually did so (see Chapter 4).

Do you think that Americans today, regardless of the state or community in which they live, would have roughly the same rights that they have now even if the Supreme Court had not acted? How, if at all, does your answer relate to your view about the proper balance of national and state power in America's federal system of government?

CHAPTER 15   State and Local Politics: Maintaining Our Differences   495

Police and firefighters are among the most visible symbols of local government. Their courageous actions in New York City on September 11, 2001, cost hundreds of them their lives and serve as a tragic reminder of the indispensable role they play in the America's communities.

Another major education issue is the quality of America's public schools. U.S. students do poorly on standardized tests in comparison with students of other advanced industrialized nations. Twelfth-grade American students are not even among the top ten in physics, chemistry, math, or any other subject where cross-national comparisons can reliably be made. This situation has contributed to debates over merit pay for teachers, national tests for all U.S. students, and parent-student choice of schools. Some analysts claim that American public schools are simply not providing the quality of education found in other Western democracies and that alternative approaches must be found. Other analysts say the schools are not the problem, or at least not the major problem. They say that both the diversity of American society and the absence of a strong intellectual tradition limit the schools' ability to educate students at the highest level.

Welfare Assistance

The most expensive social welfare program in the United States is entirely a national one—social security for retirees. However, the states are vitally involved in the provision of most welfare services, particularly public assistance programs for the needy (see Chapter 3). Programs such as TANF, Medicaid, and food stamps operate within federal guidelines, but the states have discretionary authority over benefit and eligibility levels. These programs are funded jointly by the state and national governments and are administered primarily by the state governments. They have the local offices that are necessary for administering need-based welfare programs, which, as was noted in Chapter 16, require regular contacts between caseworkers and welfare recipients.

Welfare programs account for about 15 percent of all state and local spending. This spending and the American tradition of self-reliance make welfare a contentious political issue. The states have devised various ways of holding down spending. In response to the rapid increase in Medicaid costs, for example, the state of Oregon conducted a systematic study of medical procedures in order to identify, and make ineligible for Medicaid reimbursement, those procedures that physicians apply electively. Medicaid, however, is sure to remain a central issue. It is a joint federal-state program, but the high costs of medical care have made Medicaid the single largest item in state budgets. Health care costs are certain to rise in the future. Just as certain is the continuing need of poorer Americans for medical care. At some point, these fiscal and medical realities are sure to collide.

Health and Hospitals

Nearly 10 percent of state and local expenditures are in the health and hospitals policy area. All states and many localities operate public hospitals, and most of the laws and regulations affecting medical practices are established by state governments. In addition, states and localities have public health programs such as immunization campaigns, mobile x-ray units, and health inspections of motels and restaurants.

Highways

Until the 1950s, the roadways of America were built almost entirely with state and local funds. The interstate highway system was begun in the 1950s and was funded largely by the national government. Today, Washington provides about a third of the total spending on highways, and states and localities contribute the rest. State and local governments set most policies governing use of highways, including traffic infractions and shipping methods. Highway spending accounts for about 5 percent of state and local expenditures.

Police and Prisons

Some democracies have a large national police force, but the United States does not. Its law enforcement is entrusted almost entirely to local and state police forces. They enforce state laws and local ordinances, which collectively govern most aspects of crime and punishment. The state police include the highway patrol, game wardens, prison guards, and liquor control officers, and they are generally well trained and highly professional. Local police are less specialized, are more uneven in their training and professionalism, and are required to do most of the "dirty" work of law enforcement—crime control and the maintenance of public order. Roughly 8 percent of state and local spending is for police-related activities.

States and localities in recent years have invested heavily in prisons and other correctional facilities. As was indicated in Chapter 4, the United States on a per capita basis is rivaled only by Russia in the number of its people who are imprisoned. The large prison population in the United States reflects a policy of lengthened and mandatory sentencing that developed in the past decade

The environment has become an important issue of state and local politics as a result of the public's growing awareness of the damage caused by pollution. Here, a bucket of oysters was dumped into New York harbor as part of an effort to restock oyster beds destroyed by contaminated wastes.

largely because of escalating drug-related crime. Many prisoners are in jail for possession or purchase of relatively small quantities of illegal drugs. As the fiscal and human costs of this policy have increased, some state and local officials have questioned its wisdom and have sought alternatives, including giving judges more discretion in the sentencing of nonviolent first offenders.

The Environment

The environment is a relatively small part of state and local budgets, but money alone is not a reliable indicator of policy effort in the environmental area, since much of it works through regulatory activities that impose costs on firms and consumers.

Most states and localities were complacent about environmental protection until the federal government in the 1960s and 1970s greatly broadened the scope of its activities. Today, states and localities are active participants in the effort to protect the environment. For example, they routinely require environmental impact statements for major development projects and have acted to protect their land and water resources from pollutants. In addition, conservation through the preservation of parks, natural resources, and wildlife has increasingly been a focus of state policy. New York, for example, has taken steps to purchase and otherwise protect tens of thousands of acres of undeveloped land in its Adirondack Mountains.

Sewage and garbage disposal is a special problem for local governments. As environmental standards have increased, it has become an increasingly costly activity, ranking only behind schools, roadways, and public safety as an expenditure category for cities. It has also become increasingly contentious because neighborhoods nearly always resist the nearby placement of a new sewage treatment place, garbage incinerator, or landfill. Public resistance has forced many communities into costly solutions such as the shipping of garbage to distant landfills, which, because of the cost, also displeases residents.

The Politics of State and Local Policy

The general economic conditions of a state, as was mentioned previously, has a substantial impact on its policies. Richer states are simply in a stronger position to provide more and better services than poorer states are. West Virginia with its per capita income of $19,362 can hardly be expected to have schools, hospitals, roadways, and other facilities that match those of Washington state with a per capita income of $27,961.

Wealth alone, however, cannot fully explain state-to-state differences. Public policies also reflect variations in state politics, as the following discussion indicates.

Party Competition

The fifty states vary significantly in their support for one major party or the other. Where the Republicans are stronger, as in the mountain states, taxes and the level of public services tend to be lower. Where Democrats are stronger, as in the northeast, the reverse situation tends to hold.

The intensity of party competition has a somewhat less obvious, but no less important, relationship to public policy. In states where party competition is weak, politics tends to be somewhat exclusive: a sizable share of the population, usually the poorest groups, will be more or less ignored by government. The dominant party has gained control without the help of these groups, and the minority party could not gain control even with their help. In other words, neither party has a strong incentive to seek their vote. The classic case of a neglected public was the black community in the south in the period before the modern civil rights movement of the 1950s and 1960s. African Americans were politically powerless. Neither the white Democrats who ran the south nor the white Republicans who offered token opposition had a real interest in bringing black people into their coalition.

Where party competition is more intense, any sizable group in a state is likely to receive the attention of one party or the other and thus to be in a position to influence public policy. In the modern south, which is increasingly competitive between the parties, black voters are a growing force and have tipped the balance in some elections. They are also more likely than at any time in the past to have policy influence.

The state party systems have become more competitive by some indicators and less competitive by others. Compared with the 1960s, there are fewer states today in which one party controls the governor's seat and both chambers of the

Political Culture

One People Out of Many

America's Political Subcultures

Although Americans share a common political heritage that is built around principles such as liberty, equality, and self-government, distinctive regional subcultures persist. These subcultures, as the political scientist Daniel Elazar noted in *American Federalism*, reflect differences in ethnic settlement patterns, historical episodes, economic conditions, and other influences.

The states in the northern tier of the nation have what Elazar describes as a *moralistic subculture*. It is characterized by an emphasis on "good government" (the public interest) and "clean government" (honesty). The states that share this subculture were populated primarily by northern Europeans, including the English, Germans, and Scandinavians. Minnesota is an example of a moralistic state. Minnesota has one of the highest rates of voter turnout in the country and one of the lowest rates of political corruption. Political competition in this subculture tends to focus on issues rather than personalities, and activist government is accepted. Taxes are relatively high, but so is the level of public services. States in this region spend more heavily than other states in areas such as public education, and their students tend to score higher on standardized tests than do students in other regions.

The middle part of the United States—from Massachusetts to Maryland and then westward through Illinois and Missouri to southwestern states such as Arizona—is described by Elazar as having an *individualistic subculture*. This subculture is oriented toward private life and economic gain, and politics is largely an extension of this perspective. Political conflict is rough-and-tumble, political power is closely guarded, and public policy is often narrowly applied. Compared with states that have a moralistic subculture, those with an individualistic subculture tend to spend less per capita on public services. They place greater emphasis on self-sufficiency.

A *traditionalistic subculture*, in Elazar's terms, typifies the states of the old Confederacy and a few states bordering on it, such as West Virginia. This subculture reflects the stratified, plantation society out of which it grew: it is conservative in its focus and elitist in its leadership. Government is likely to be a topic of considerable interest in a traditionalistic state, but not because government is activist. In fact, traditionalists prefer a government that reinforces the existing economic, social, and political structure.

These subcultures do not coincide exactly with state borders, and elements of each subculture are found in every region of the country. Other subcultures also exist. The South, for example, has a populist heritage that runs counter to its dominant traditionalist subculture. Several of the South's best-known politicians, including Alabama's George Wallace and Louisiana's Huey Long, rose to prominence by attacking entrenched power structures in their own states. Nevertheless, Elazar's typology illustrates the important point that the American states are politically diverse. They operate within the framework of a common federal government and a larger political culture, but they have distinctive features that make and mold their politics and policies.

---

state legislature (see "States in the Nation"). However, the number of state legislative races in which the incumbent has no or only token opposition has increased.[17] Faced with a well-funded and popular incumbent, the opposing party has increasingly conceded the election. The professionalization of state legislatures has had an effect similar to the professionalization of Congress: legislators have used their positions to solidify public support and dominate campaign contributions, which in turn have discouraged election challengers.

STATES IN THE NATION

Party Control of State Government

The strength of the major parties varies substantially among states. An indicator of party dominance is whether one party controls all elected institutions: the governor's seat and the two legislative chambers (except in Nebraska, which has a unicameral, nonpartisan legislature). As of 2002, the Republican party had a slight edge on the Democrats.

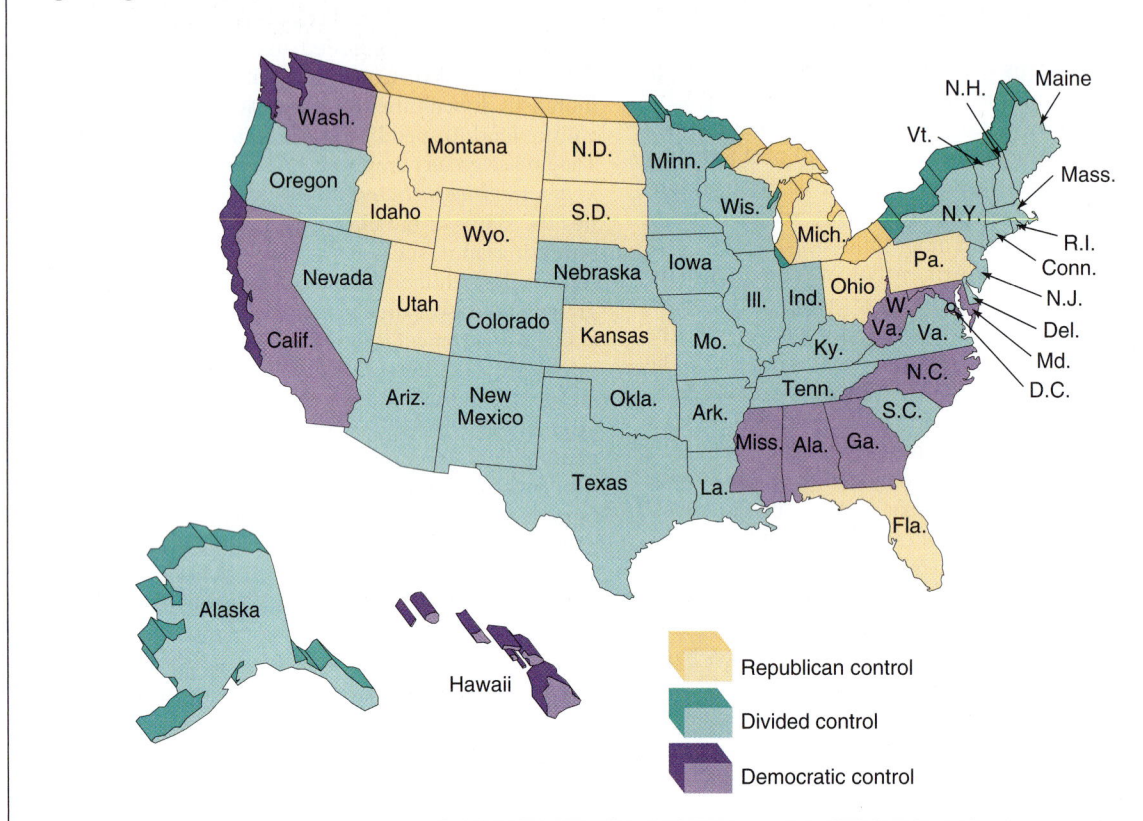

- Republican control
- Divided control
- Democratic control

Group Competition

Interest-group systems can be looked at in a similar way. In those states where interest groups are many in number and somewhat evenly balanced in their political resources, public policy tends to serve a broad range of interests. An example is the state of New York, which has many competing factions, including, for example, business and labor, the upstate and downstate areas, and environmentalists and developers. Almost any legislation that makes it through the New York state legislature requires negotiation among numerous groups.

In states where a particular group or interest is dominant, however, government tends to serve that group or interest above all others. A classic example was the Anaconda Copper Company in Montana, which, during the period

Utah is a state where political alternatives are substantially shaped by a dominant interest. Policy proposals that are actively opposed by the Church of Jesus Christ of Latter-day Saints have almost no chance of becoming law. Shown here is a winter picture with holiday lights of the Mormon Temple in Salt Lake City. In 2002, Salt Lake City was host to the Winter Olympics.

that it accounted for nearly all the state's mining and manufacturing, nearly ran the state. A more recent example is the influence of the Church of Jesus Christ of Latter-day Saints in Utah. The large share of the state's residents are Mormons, and a policy alternative that is actively opposed by the church has almost no chance of becoming law. Thus, the church for years opposed the sale of hard liquor in Utah, and such sales were prohibited by law. The law was changed recently, but only after Mormon leaders agreed not to oppose the change, which was prompted by the state's desire to improve its ability to attract tourists and conventions. Utah succeeded even in winning the bid to host the 2002 Winter Olympics.

Utah with its Mormon population is one of the most distinctive states in the union, but every state has its special characteristics. California is no more like Mississippi than Mississippi is like Rhode Island. Yet, as this chapter has shown, the American states also have many aspects in common. The differences and similarities among the states are testimony to the enduring nature of the American governing experiment. The states are different enough to provide their residents with a special identity and a special political experience; yet they are alike enough to allow the triumph of the national union that the Framers so keenly envisioned two hundred years ago.

THE GREAT BALANCING ACT: LOCALISM IN A LARGE NATION

The structure of U.S. government—federalism and localism—was established when the nation was founded two centuries ago. The seven million Americans of the time lived closer together, and yet farther apart, than Americans of today. They were crowded along the eastern seaboard, but travel from Savannah in the south to Boston in the north could take weeks. Communication was equally slow: news traveled no faster than people and ships could carry it. The United States today has 275 million people spread across a continent, reaching even into Alaska and Hawaii. Yet communication is instantaneous, and an airplane can span the distance between Boston to Los Angeles in a few hours.

Is the constitutional structure that was created two hundred years ago suited to modern needs? It is a question that scholars and policymakers sometimes ask. Yet none have concluded that the nation would be better off without its three relatively distinctive levels of government. They accept the essential wisdom of James Madison's argument on the strength of "a compound republic."[18]

The arguments today are confined to issues of the relative balance of power among the three levels. And if conservatives are more inclined than liberals to stress localism, each side embraces the alternative position when doing so furthers its policy goals.

Accordingly, the relative balance among the levels has shifted from time to time. Throughout most of the twentieth century, power shifted upward toward the federal government as society became ever more complex and interdependent. The demand for greater efficiency and equality could only be met through a stronger national response. The U.S. economy had to be transformed into a national economy, and demands for equal treatment by disadvantaged Americans had to be addressed nationally if they were to be met.

In more recent years, there has been a flow of power back to the states and localities. The trend can be explained in part by the discovery that national solutions to certain policy problems are less effective than their original advocates envisioned. It is also attributable to Americans' respect for local differences and their willingness to experiment with new approaches. The federal social welfare programs that were established in the 1960s were not failures—they did succeed in lifting millions of Americans out of poverty. But they were also not unbridled successes—they fostered welfare dependency and fueled taxpayer resentment. The welfare reform legislation enacted in 1996 sought a new balance, one that would preserve a safety net for low-income Americans yet encourage the able-bodied among them to enter the work force. Few analysts believe that the act is the final answer to Americans' welfare needs. But it is the current answer and will remain so until an emerging problem generates political pressure for something different. Whether that "something" will enlarge or diminish the federal, state, or local role cannot be predicted. The response will depend on the nature of the problem and the political outlook of the moment. As the historian Daniel Boorstin observed, pragmatism rather than orthodoxy is the defining characteristic of American politics.[19]

If anything, this pragmatism will be even more evident in the years to come. Americans will become more, not less, interdependent as a result of expected changes in communication, computer technology, and the global economy. An effect of interdependency, as noted in Chapter 3, is an increase in the demands on government at all levels. The examples are countless. Homeland security, for instance, was barely an issue until the terrorist attacks on the World Trade Center and the Pentagon in 2001 forced Americans to take notice. Once they did, they turned to all levels of government for answers. As the national, state, and local governments responded, it became apparent to officials at each level that effective solutions would require cooperation among them. The federal government took the lead, particularly on overseas terrorist threats, but state and local officials in law enforcement and other areas were deeply involved in the effort to heighten Americans' security.

The writers of the U.S. Constitution could not possibly have envisioned life in twenty-first-century America. Theirs was a world of horse-drawn carriages and candlelight, not a world of jet airplanes and computers.[20] But they did envision a governing system flexible enough to respond to changing needs during changing times. The persistence of this system across more than two centuries is testimony to their vision and to the willingness of succeeding generations of Americans to find a combination of national, state, and local authority that could meet their governing needs.

Self-Quiz
www.mhhe.com/patterson6

SUMMARY

Although developments in the twentieth century have narrowed the differences among the American states, they, and the localities that govern under their authority, remain distinctive and vital systems of government.

All states apply the constitutional principle of separate branches sharing power, but the structure of the state governments differs in some respects from that of the federal government. An example is the more widespread use of elections at the state level. Most states elect by popular vote their judges and a number of executives, including an attorney general and treasurer in addition to a governor. Through the initiative or the referendum, nearly all states also allow their residents to vote directly on issues of policy.

Local governments are chartered by the state. They are not sovereign governments, but most states have chosen to grant local units a considerable level of policymaking discretion. Local governments include counties, municipalities, school districts, and special districts. Of these, the independent school district is the most distinctively American institution, but the municipality is the primary governing unit. Municipalities are governed by one of four types of systems: the strong mayor–council system, the weak mayor–council system, the commission system, or the city manager system.

The states and localities have primary responsibility for most of the public policies that directly touch Americans' daily lives. For example, the major share of legislation devoted to public education and about 90 percent of the funding for it are provided by the states and localities. Public welfare, public health, roads, and police are other policy areas dominated by these subnational governments. They do not, however, have the amount of revenue that is available to the federal government. Competition between them holds down their taxing capacity. Their policies are also conditioned by the wealth of the state or locality and by the structure of its party and interest group systems.

KEY TERMS

bicameral legislature
charter
city manager system
commission system
constitutional initiative
Cooley's rule
Dillon's rule
home rule
initiative
metropolitan government
ordinance
police power
recall
referendum
state constitutional convention
strong mayor–council system
weak mayor–council system

SUGGESTED READINGS

Broder, David. *Democracy Derailed.* San Diego: Harcourt, 2000. An analysis of how powerful groups have captured the initiative process.

Ehrenhalt, Alan. *Democracy in the Mirror.* Washington, D.C.: Congressional Quarterly, 1998. A look at grassroots politics in America.

Hero, Rodney. *Faces of Inequality*. New York: Oxford University Press, 2000. An assessment of how states' politics and policies are shaped by their racial and ethnic composition.

Hunter, Kenneth G. *Interest Groups and State Economic Development Policies*. Westport, Conn.: Praeger, 1999. A look at the influence of groups in state policy decisions.

Morehouse, Sarah McCally. *The Governor as Party Leader*. Ann Arbor: University of Michigan Press, 1998. An examination of how governors campaign and govern.

Tarr, G. Alan. *Understanding State Constitutions*. Princeton, N.J.: Princeton University Press, 1998. A thorough assessment of state constitutions and how they differ from the U.S. Constitution.

LIST OF WEBSITES

http://www.nga.org
The website of the National Governors Association.

http://www.nyc.gov
The website for New York City's government. Most cities and towns have their own website.

http://www.state.tx.us
The website for the state of Texas. Every state government has a website.

http://www.usmayors.org
The website for the U.S. Conference of Mayors.

APPENDIXES

The Declaration of Independence

The Constitution of the United States of America

Federalist No. 10

Federalist No. 51

THE DECLARATION OF INDEPENDENCE

IN CONGRESS, JULY 4, 1776

The Unanimous Declaration of the Thirteen United States of America

When, in the course of human events, it becomes necessary for one people to dissolve the political bands which have connected them with another, and to assume, among the powers of the earth, the separate and equal station to which the laws of nature and of nature's God entitle them, a decent respect to the opinions of mankind requires that they should declare the causes which impel them to the separation.

We hold these truths to be self-evident, that all men are created equal; that they are endowed by their Creator with certain unalienable rights; that among these, are life, liberty, and the pursuit of happiness. That, to secure these rights, governments are instituted among men, deriving their just powers from the consent of the governed; that, whenever any form of government becomes destructive of these ends, it is the right of the people to alter or to abolish it, and to institute a new government, laying its foundation on such principles, and organizing its powers in such form, as to them shall seem most likely to effect their safety and happiness. Prudence, indeed, will dictate that governments long established, should not be changed for light and transient causes; and, accordingly, all experience hath shown, that mankind are more disposed to suffer, while evils are sufferable, than to right themselves by abolishing the forms to which they are accustomed. But, when a long train of abuses and usurpations, pursuing invariably the same object, evinces a design to reduce them under absolute despotism, it is their right, it is their duty, to throw off such government and to provide new guards for their future security. Such has been the patient sufferance of these colonies, and such is now the necessity which constrains them to alter their former systems of government. The history of the present King of Great Britain is a history of repeated injuries and usurpations, all having, in direct object, the establishment of an absolute tyranny over these States. To prove this, let facts be submitted to a candid world:

He has refused his assent to laws the most wholesome and necessary for the public good.

He has forbidden his governors to pass laws of immediate and pressing importance, unless suspended in their operation till his assent should be obtained; and, when so suspended, he has utterly neglected to attend to them.

He has refused to pass other laws for the accommodation of large districts of people, unless those people would relinquish the right of representation in the legislature; a right inestimable to them, and formidable to tyrants only.

He has called together legislative bodies at places unusual, uncomfortable, and distant from the depository of their public records, for the sole purpose of fatiguing them into compliance with his measures.

He has dissolved representative houses repeatedly for opposing, with manly firmness, his invasions on the rights of the people.

He has refused, for a long time after such dissolutions, to cause others to be elected; whereby the legislative powers, incapable of annihilation, have returned to the people at large for their exercise; the state remaining, in the meantime, exposed to all the danger of invasion from without, and convulsions within.

He has endeavored to prevent the population of these States; for that purpose, obstructing the laws for naturalization of foreigners, refusing to pass others to encourage their migration hither, and raising the conditions of new appropriations of lands.

He has obstructed the administration of justice, by refusing his assent to laws for establishing judiciary powers.

He has made judges dependent on his will alone, for the tenure of their offices, and the amount and payment of their salaries.

He has erected a multitude of new offices, and sent hither swarms of officers to harass our people, and eat out their substance.

He has kept among us, in time of peace, standing armies, without the consent of our legislatures.

He has affected to render the military independent of, and superior to, the civil power.

He has combined, with others, to subject us to a jurisdiction foreign to our Constitution, and unacknowledged by our laws; giving his assent to their acts of pretended legislation:

For quartering large bodies of armed troops among us:

For protecting them by a mock trial, from punishment, for any murders which they should commit on the inhabitants of these States:

For cutting off our trade with all parts of the world:

For imposing taxes on us without our consent:

For depriving us, in many cases, of the benefit of trial by jury:

For transporting us beyond seas to be tried for pretended offences:

For abolishing the free system of English laws in a neighboring province, establishing therein an arbitrary government, and enlarging its boundaries, so as to render it at once an example and fit instrument for introducing the same absolute rule into these colonies:

For taking away our charters, abolishing our most valuable laws, and altering, fundamentally, the powers of our governments:

For suspending our own legislatures, and declaring themselves invested with power to legislate for us in all cases whatsoever.

He has abdicated government here, by declaring us out of his protection, and waging war against us.

He has plundered our seas, ravaged our coasts, burnt our towns, and destroyed the lives of our people.

He is, at this time, transporting large armies of foreign mercenaries to complete the works of death, desolation, and tyranny, already begun, with circumstances of cruelty and perfidy scarcely paralleled in the most barbarous ages, and totally unworthy of the head of a civilized nation.

He has constrained our fellow citizens, taken captive on the high seas, to bear arms against their country, to become the executioners of their friends, and brethren, or to fall themselves by their hands.

He has excited domestic insurrections amongst us, and has endeavored to bring on the inhabitants of our frontiers, the merciless Indian savages, whose known rule of warfare is an undistinguished destruction of all ages, sexes, and conditions.

In every stage of these oppressions, we have petitioned for redress, in the most humble terms; our repeated petitions have been answered only by repeated injury. A prince, whose character is thus marked by every act which may define a tyrant, is unfit to be the ruler of a free people.

Nor have we been wanting in attention to our British brethren. We have warned them, from time to time, of attempts made by their legislature to extend an unwarrantable jurisdiction over us. We have reminded them of the circumstances of our emigration and settlement here. We have appealed to their native justice and magnanimity, and we have conjured them, by the ties of our common kindred, to disavow these usurpations, which would inevitably interrupt our connections and correspondence. They, too, have been deaf to the voice of justice and of consanguinity. We must, therefore, acquiesce in the necessity which denounces our separation, and hold them as we hold the rest of mankind, enemies in war, in peace, friends.

We, therefore, the representatives of the United States of America, in general Congress assembled, appealing to the Supreme Judge of the world for the rectitude of our intentions, do, in the name, and by the authority of the good people of these colonies, solemnly publish and declare, that these united colonies are, and of right ought to be, free and independent states: that they are absolved from all allegiance to the British Crown, and that all political connection between them and the state of Great Britain is, and ought to be, totally dissolved; and that, as free and independent states, they have full power to levy war, conclude peace, contract alliances, establish commerce, and to do all other acts and things which independent states may of right do. And, for the support of this declaration, with a firm reliance on the protection of Divine Providence, we mutually pledge to each other our lives, our fortunes, and our sacred honor.

The foregoing Declaration was, by order of Congress, engrossed, and signed by the following members:

JOHN HANCOCK

New Hampshire
Josiah Bartlett
William Whipple
Matthew Thornton

Massachusetts Bay
Samuel Adams
John Adams
Robert Treat Paine
Elbridge Gerry

Rhode Island
Stephen Hopkins
William Ellery

Connecticut
Roger Sherman
Samuel Huntington
William Williams
Oliver Wolcott

New York
William Floyd
Philip Livingston
Francis Lewis
Lewis Morris

New Jersey
Richard Stockton
John Witherspoon
Francis Hopkinson
John Hart
Abraham Clark

Pennsylvania
Robert Morris
Benjamin Rush
Benjamin Franklin
John Morton
George Clymer
James Smith
George Taylor
James Wilson
George Ross

Delaware
Caesar Rodney
George Reed
Thomas M'Kean

Maryland
Samuel Chase
William Paca
Thomas Stone
Charles Carroll, of Carrollton

Virginia
George Wythe
Richard Henry Lee
Thomas Jefferson
Benjamin Harrison
Thomas Nelson, Jr.
Francis Lightfoot Lee
Carter Braxton

North Carolina
William Hooper
Joseph Hewes
John Penn

South Carolina
Edward Rutledge
Thomas Heyward, Jr.
Thomas Lynch, Jr.
Arthur Middleton

Georgia
Button Gwinnett
Lyman Hall
George Walton

Resolved, That copies of the Declaration be sent to the several assemblies, conventions, and committees, or councils of safety, and to the several commanding officers of the continental troops; that it be proclaimed in each of the United States, at the head of the army.

THE CONSTITUTION OF THE UNITED STATES OF AMERICA[1]

We the People of the United States, in Order to form a more perfect Union, establish Justice, insure domestic Tranquility, provide for the common defence, promote the general Welfare, and secure the Blessings of Liberty to ourselves and our Posterity, do ordain and establish this CONSTITUTION for the United States of America.

ARTICLE I

SECTION 1

All legislative Powers herein granted shall be vested in a Congress of the United States, which shall consist of a Senate and House of Representatives.

SECTION 2

The House of Representatives shall be composed of Members chosen every second Year by the People of the several States, and the Electors in each State shall have the Qualifications requisite for Electors of the most numerous Branch of the State Legislature.

No Person shall be a Representative who shall not have attained to the Age of twenty-five Years, and been seven Years a Citizen of the United States, and who shall not, when elected, be an Inhabitant of that State in which he shall be chosen.

[Representatives and direct Taxes[2] shall be apportioned among the several States which may be included within this Union, according to their respective Numbers, which shall be determined by adding to the whole Number of free Persons, including those bound to Service for a Term of Years, and excluding Indians not taxed, three fifths of all other Persons.][3] The actual Enumeration shall be made within three Years after the first Meeting of the Congress of the United States, and within every subsequent Term of ten Years, in such Manner as they shall by Law direct. The Number of Representatives shall not exceed one for every thirty Thousand, but each State shall have at Least one Representative; and until such enumeration shall be made, the State of New Hampshire shall be entitled to chuse three, Massachusetts eight, Rhode-Island and Providence Plantations one, Connecticut five, New York six, New Jersey four, Pennsylvania eight, Delaware one, Maryland six, Virginia ten, North Carolina five, South Carolina five, and Georgia three.

When vacancies happen in the Representation from any State, the Executive Authority thereof shall issue Writs of Election to fill such Vacancies.

The House of Representatives shall chuse their Speaker and other Officers; and shall have the sole Power of Impeachment.

SECTION 3

The Senate of the United States shall be composed of two Senators from each State, chosen by the Legislature thereof, for six Years; and each Senator shall have one Vote.

Immediately after they shall be assembled in Consequence of the first Election, they shall be divided as equally as may be into three Classes. The Seats of the Senators of the first Class shall be vacated at the Expiration of the second Year, of the second Class at the Expiration of the fourth Year, and of the third Class at the Expiration of the sixth Year, so that one-third may be chosen every second Year;

---

1. This version, which follows the original Constitution in capitalization and spelling, was published by the United States Department of the Interior, Office of Education, in 1935.
2. Altered by the Sixteenth Amendment.
3. Negated by the Fourteenth Amendment.

and if Vacancies happen by Resignation, or otherwise, during the Recess of the Legislature of any State, the Executive thereof may make temporary Appointments until the next Meeting of the Legislature, which shall then fill such Vacancies.

No Person shall be a Senator who shall not have attained to the Age of thirty Years, and been nine Years a Citizen of the United States, and who shall not, when elected, be an Inhabitant of that State for which he shall be chosen.

The Vice President of the United States shall be President of the Senate, but shall have no vote, unless they be equally divided.

The Senate shall chuse their other Officers, and also a President pro tempore, in the absence of the Vice President, or when he shall exercise the Office of President of the United States.

The Senate shall have the sole Power to try all Impeachments. When sitting for that purpose they shall be on Oath or Affirmation. When the President of the United States is tried, the Chief Justice shall preside: And no person shall be convicted without the Concurrence of two thirds of the Members present.

Judgment in Cases of Impeachment shall not extend further than to removal from Office, and disqualification to hold and enjoy any Office of honor, Trust, or Profit under the United States: but the Party convicted shall nevertheless be liable and subject to Indictment, Trial, Judgment and Punishment, according to Law.

SECTION 4

The Times, Place and Manner of holding Elections for Senators and Representatives, shall be prescribed in each State by the Legislature thereof; but the Congress may at any time by Law make or alter such Regulations, except as to the Places of Chusing Senators.

The Congress shall assemble at least once in every Year, and such Meeting shall be on the first Monday in December, unless they shall by Law appoint a different Day.

SECTION 5

Each House shall be the Judge of the Elections, Returns and Qualifications of its own Members, and a Majority of each shall constitute a Quorum to do Business; but a smaller number may adjourn from day to day, and may be authorized to compel the Attendance of absent Members, in such Manner, and under such Penalties, as each House may provide.

Each House may determine the Rules of its Proceedings, punish its Members for disorderly Behaviour, and, with the Concurrence of two thirds, expel a Member.

Each House shall keep a Journal of its Proceedings, and from time to time publish the same, excepting such Parts as may in their Judgment require Secrecy; and the Yeas and Nays of the Members of either House on any question shall, at the Desire of one fifth of those Present, be entered on the Journal.

Neither House, during the Session of Congress, shall, without the Consent of the other, adjourn for more than three days, nor to any other Place than that in which the two Houses shall be sitting.

SECTION 6

The Senators and Representatives shall receive a Compensation for their Services, to be ascertained by Law, and paid out of the Treasury of the United States. They shall in all Cases, except Treason, Felony, and Breach of the Peace, be privileged from Arrest during their Attendance at the Session of their respective Houses, and in going to and returning from the same; and for any Speech or Debate in either House, they shall not be questioned in any other Place.

No Senator or Representative shall, during the Time for which he was elected, be appointed to any civil Office under the Authority of the United States, which shall have been created, or the Emoluments whereof shall have been increased, during such time; and no Person holding any Office under the United States shall be a Member of either House during his continuance in Office.

SECTION 7

All Bills for raising Revenue shall originate in the House of Representatives; but the Senate may propose or concur with Amendments as on other bills.

Every Bill which shall have passed the House of Representatives and the Senate, shall, before it becomes a Law, be presented to the President of the United States; if he approve he shall sign it, but if not he shall return it, with his Objections, to that

House in which it shall have originated, who shall enter the Objections at large on their Journal, and proceed to reconsider it. If after such Reconsideration two thirds of that House shall agree to pass the bill, it shall be sent, together with the objections, to the other House, by which it shall likewise be reconsidered, and if approved by two thirds of that House, it shall become a Law. But in all such Cases the Votes of both Houses shall be determined by Yeas and Nays, and the Names of the Persons voting for and against the Bill shall be entered on the Journal of each House respectively. If any Bill shall not be returned by the President within ten Days (Sundays excepted) after it shall have been presented to him, the Same shall be a Law, in like Manner as if he had signed it, unless the Congress by their Adjournment prevent its Return, in which Case it shall not be a Law.

Every Order, Resolution, or Vote to which the Concurrence of the Senate and House of Representatives may be necessary (except on a question of Adjournment) shall be presented to the President of the United States; and before the Same shall take Effect, shall be approved by him, or being disapproved by him, shall be repassed by two thirds of the Senate and House of Representatives, according to the Rules and Limitations prescribed in the Case of a Bill.

SECTION 8

The Congress shall have Power To lay and collect Taxes, Duties, Imposts and Excises, to pay the Debts and provide for the common Defence and general Welfare of the United States; but all Duties, Imposts and Excises shall be uniform throughout the United States;

To borrow money on the credit of the United States;

To regulate Commerce with foreign Nations, and among the several States, and with the Indian Tribes;

To establish a uniform rule of Naturalization, and uniform Laws on the subject of Bankruptcies throughout the United States;

To coin Money, regulate the Value thereof, and of foreign Coin, and fix the Standard of Weights and Measures;

To provide for the Punishment of counterfeiting the Securities and current Coin of the United States;

To establish Post Offices and post Roads;

To promote the Progress of Science and useful Arts, by securing for limited Times to Authors and Inventors the exclusive Right to their respective Writings and Discoveries;

To constitute Tribunals inferior to the Supreme Court;

To define and punish Piracies and Felonies committed on the high Seas, and Offenses against the Law of Nations;

To declare War, grant Letters of Marque and Reprisal, and make Rules concerning Captures on Land and Water;

To raise and support Armies, but no Appropriation of Money to that Use shall be for a longer Term than two Years;

To provide and maintain a Navy;

To make Rules for the Government and Regulation of the land and naval forces;

To provide for calling forth the Militia to execute the Laws of the Union, suppress Insurrections and repel Invasions;

To provide for organizing, arming, and disciplining the Militia, and for governing such Part of them as may be employed in the Service of the United States, reserving to the States respectively, the Appointment of the Officers, and the Authority of training the Militia according to the discipline prescribed by Congress;

To exercise exclusive Legislation in all Cases whatsoever, over such District (not exceeding ten Miles square) as may, by Cession of particular States, and the acceptance of Congress, become the Seat of the Government of the United States, and to exercise like Authority over all Places purchased by the Consent of the Legislature of the State in which the Same shall be, for the Erection of Forts, Magazines, Arsenals, Dock-yards, and other needful Buildings;—And

To make all Laws which shall be necessary and proper for carrying into Execution the foregoing Powers, and all other Powers vested by this Constitution in the Government of the United States, or in any Department or Officer thereof.

SECTION 9

The Migration or Importation of such Persons as any of the States now existing shall think proper to admit, shall not be prohibited by the Congress prior to the Year one thousand eight hundred and eight, but a tax or duty may be imposed on such Importation, not exceeding ten dollars for each Person.

The privilege of the Writ of Habeas Corpus shall not be suspended, unless when in Cases of Rebellion or Invasion the public Safety may require it.

No bill of Attainder or ex post facto Law shall be passed.

No capitation, or other direct, Tax shall be laid unless in Proportion to the Census or Enumeration herein before directed to be taken.

No Tax or Duty shall be laid on Articles exported from any State.

No Preference shall be given by any Regulation of Commerce or Revenue to the Ports of one State over those of another: nor shall Vessels bound to, or from, one State, be obliged to enter, clear, or pay Duties in another.

No Money shall be drawn from the Treasury, but in Consequence of Appropriations made by Law; and a regular Statement and Account of the Receipts and Expenditures of all public Money shall be published from time to time.

No Title of Nobility shall be granted by the United States: And no Person holding any Office of Profit or Trust under them, shall, without the Consent of the Congress, accept of any present, Emolument, Office, or Title, of any kind whatever, from any King, Prince, or foreign State.

SECTION 10

No State shall enter into any Treaty, Alliance, or Confederation; grant Letters of Marque and Reprisal; coin Money; emit Bills of Credit; make any Thing but gold and silver Coin a Tender in Payment of Debts; pass any Bill of Attainder, ex post facto Law, or Law impairing the Obligation of Contracts, or grant any Title of Nobility.

No State shall, without the Consent of the Congress, lay any Imposts or Duties on Imports or Exports, except what may be absolutely necessary for executing its inspection Laws; and the net Produce of all Duties and Imposts, laid by any State on Imports or Exports, shall be for the use of the Treasury of the United States; and all such Laws shall be subject to the Revision and Control of the Congress.

No state shall, without the Consent of Congress, lay any duty of Tonnage, keep Troops, or Ships of War in time of Peace, enter into any Agreement or Compact with another State, or with a foreign Power, or engage in War, unless actually invaded, or in such imminent Danger as will not admit of delay.

ARTICLE II

SECTION 1

The executive Power shall be vested in a President of the United States of America. He shall hold his Office during the Term of four years, and, together with the Vice President, chosen for the same Term, be elected, as follows:

Each State shall appoint, in such Manner as the Legislature thereof may direct, a Number of Electors, equal to the whole Number of Senators and Representatives to which the State may be entitled in the Congress: but no Senator or Representative, or Person holding an Office of Trust or Profit under the United States, shall be appointed an Elector.

[The Electors shall meet in their respective States, and vote by Ballot for two persons, of whom one at least shall not be an Inhabitant of the same State with themselves. And they shall make a List of all the Persons voted for, and of the Number of Votes for each; which List they shall sign and certify, and transmit sealed to the Seat of the Government of the United States, directed to the President of the Senate. The President of the Senate shall, in the Presence of the Senate and House of Representatives, open all the Certificates, and the Votes shall then be counted. The Person having the greatest Number of Votes shall be the President, if such Number be a Majority of the whole Number of Electors appointed; and if there be more than one who have such Majority, and have an equal Number of Votes, then the House of Representatives shall immediately chuse by Ballot one of them for President; and if no Person have a Majority, then from the five highest on the List the said House shall in like Manner chuse the President. But in chusing the President, the Votes shall be taken by States, the Representation from each State having one Vote; a quorum for this Purpose shall consist of a Member or Members from two-thirds of the States, and a Majority of all the States shall be necessary to a Choice. In every Case, after the Choice of the President, the Person having the greatest Number of Votes of the Electors shall be the Vice President. But if there should remain two or more who have equal votes, the Senate shall chuse from them by Ballot the Vice President.]4

The Congress may determine the Time of chusing the Electors, and the Day on which they shall give their Votes; which Day shall be the same throughout the United States.

No person except a natural-born Citizen, or a Citizen of the United States, at the time of the Adoption of this Constitution, shall be eligible to the Office of President; neither shall any Person be eligible to that Office who shall not have attained to the Age of thirty-five years, and been fourteen Years a Resident within the United States.

In Case of the Removal of the President from Office, or of his Death, Resignation, or Inability to discharge the Powers and Duties of the said Office, the same shall devolve on the Vice President, and the Congress may by Law provide for the Case of Removal, Death, Resignation, or Inability, both of the President and Vice President, declaring what Officer shall then act as President, and such Officer shall act accordingly, until the disability be removed, or a President shall be elected.

The President shall, at stated Times, receive for his Services a Compensation, which shall neither be increased nor diminished during the Period for which he shall have been elected, and he shall not receive within that Period any other Emolument from the United States, or any of them.

Before he enter on the execution of his Office, he shall take the following Oath or Affirmation:—"I do solemnly swear (or affirm) that I will faithfully execute the Office of President of the United States, and will, to the best of my Ability, preserve, protect, and defend the Constitution of the United States."

SECTION 2

The President shall be Commander in Chief of the Army and Navy of the United States, and of the Militia of the several States, when called into the actual Service of the United States; he may require the Opinion, in writing, of the principal Officer in each of the executive Departments, upon any subject relating to the Duties of their respective Offices, and he shall have Power to Grant Reprieves and Pardons for Offenses against the United States, except in Cases of Impeachment.

He shall have Power, by and with the Advice and Consent of the Senate, to make Treaties, provided two-thirds of the Senators present concur; and he shall nominate, and by and with the Advice and Consent of the Senate, shall appoint Ambassadors, other public Ministers and Consuls, Judges of the supreme Court, and all other Officers of the United States, whose Appointments are not herein otherwise provided for, and which shall be established by Law: but the Congress may by Law vest the Appointment of such inferior Officers, as they think proper, in the President alone, in the Courts of Law, or in the Heads of Departments.

The President shall have Power to fill up all Vacancies that may happen during the Recess of the Senate, by granting Commissions which shall expire at the End of their next Session.

SECTION 3

He shall from time to time give to the Congress Information of the State of the Union, and recommend to their Consideration such Measures as he shall judge necessary and expedient; he may, on extraordinary occasions, convene both Houses, or either of them, and in Case of Disagreement between them, with respect to the Time of Adjournment, he may adjourn them to such Time as he shall think proper; he shall receive Ambassadors and other public Ministers; he shall take care that the Laws be faithfully executed, and shall Commission all the Officers of the United States.

SECTION 4

The President, Vice President and all civil Officers of the United States, shall be removed from Office on Impeachment for, and Conviction of, Treason, Bribery, or other high Crimes and Misdemeanors.

ARTICLE III

SECTION 1

The judicial Power of the United States, shall be vested in one supreme Court, and in such inferior Courts as the Congress may from time to time ordain

---

4. Revised by the Twelfth Amendment.

and establish. The Judges, both of the supreme and inferior Courts, shall hold their Offices during good Behaviour, and shall, at stated Times, receive for their Services, a Compensation, which shall not be diminished during their Continuance in Office.

SECTION 2

The judicial Power shall extend to all Cases, in Law and Equity, arising under this Constitution, the Laws of the United States, and Treaties made, or which shall be made, under their Authority;—to all Cases affecting ambassadors, other public ministers and consuls;—to all cases of admiralty and maritime Jurisdiction;—to Controversies to which the United States shall be a Party;—to Controversies between two or more states;—between a State and Citizens of another State;[5]—between Citizens of different States—between Citizens of the same State claiming Lands under Grants of different States, and between a State, or the Citizens thereof, and foreign States, Citizens, or Subjects.

In all Cases affecting Ambassadors, other public Ministers and Consuls, and those in which a State shall be Party, the supreme Court shall have original Jurisdiction. In all the other Cases before mentioned, the supreme Court shall have appellate Jurisdiction, both as to Law and Fact, with such Exceptions, and under such Regulations as the Congress shall make.

The trial of all Crimes, except in Cases of Impeachment, shall be by Jury; and such Trial shall be held in the State where the said Crimes shall have been committed; but when not committed within any State, the Trial shall be at such Place or Places as the Congress may by Law have directed.

SECTION 3

Treason against the United States, shall consist only in levying War against them, or in adhering to their Enemies, giving them Aid and Comfort. No Person shall be convicted of Treason unless on the Testimony of two Witnesses to the same overt Act, or on Confession in open Court.

The Congress shall have power to declare the Punishment of Treason, but no Attainder of Treason shall work Corruption of Blood, or Forfeiture except during the Life of the Person attainted.

ARTICLE IV

SECTION 1

Full Faith and Credit shall be given in each State to the public Acts, Records, and judicial Proceedings of every other State. And the Congress may by general Laws prescribe the Manner in which such Acts, Records and Proceedings shall be proved, and the Effect thereof.

SECTION 2

The Citizens of each State shall be entitled to all Privileges and Immunities of Citizens in the several States.

A Person charged in any State with Treason, Felony, or other Crime, who shall flee from Justice, and be found in another State, shall on demand of the executive Authority of the State from which he fled, be delivered up, to be removed to the State having Jurisdiction of the crime.

No Person held to Service or Labour in one State, under the Laws thereof, escaping into another, shall, in Consequence of any Law or Regulation therein, be discharged from such Service or Labour, but shall be delivered up on Claim of the Party to whom such Service or Labour may be due.

SECTION 3

New States may be admitted by the Congress into this Union; but no new State shall be formed or erected within the Jurisdiction of any other State; nor any State be formed by the Junction of two or more States, or parts of States, without the Consent of the Legislatures of the States concerned as well as of the Congress.

The Congress shall have Power to dispose of and make all needful Rules and Regulations respecting the Territory or other Property belonging to the United States; and nothing in this Constitution shall be so construed as to Prejudice any Claims of the United States, or of any particular State.

---

5. Qualified by the Eleventh Amendment.

SECTION 4

The United States shall guarantee to every State in this Union a Republican Form of Government, and shall protect each of them against Invasion; and on Application of the Legislature, or of the Executive (when the Legislature cannot be convened) against domestic Violence.

ARTICLE V

The Congress, whenever two-thirds of both Houses shall deem it necessary, shall propose Amendments to this Constitution, or, on the Application of the Legislatures of two-thirds of the several States, shall call a Convention for proposing Amendments, which, in either Case, shall be valid to all Intents and Purposes, as part of this Constitution, when ratified by the Legislatures of three-fourths of the several States, or by Conventions in three-fourths thereof, as the one or the other Mode of Ratification may be proposed by the Congress; Provided that no Amendment which may be made prior to the Year One thousand eight hundred and eight shall in any Manner affect the first and fourth Clauses in the Ninth Section of the first Article; and that no State, without its Consent, shall be deprived of its equal Suffrage in the Senate.

ARTICLE VI

All Debts contracted and Engagements entered into, before the Adoption of this Constitution, shall be as valid against the United States under this Constitution, as under the Confederation.

This Constitution, and the Laws of the United States which shall be made in Pursuance thereof; and all Treaties made, or which shall be made, under the Authority of the United States, shall be the supreme Law of the Land; and the Judges in every State shall be bound thereby, any Thing in the Constitution or Laws of any State to the Contrary notwithstanding.

The Senators and Representatives before mentioned, and the Members of the several State Legislatures, and all executive and judicial Officers, both of the United States and of the several States, shall be bound by Oath or Affirmation to support this Constitution; but no religious Tests shall ever be required as a qualification to any Office or public Trust under the United States.

ARTICLE VII

The Ratification of the Conventions of nine States shall be sufficient for the Establishment of this Constitution between the States so ratifying the same.

Done in Convention by the Unanimous Consent of the States present the Seventeenth Day of September in the Year of our Lord one thousand seven hundred and Eighty seven, and of the Independence of the United States of America the Twelfth. In Witness whereof We have hereunto subscribed our Names.[6]

George Washington
President and deputy from Virginia

New Hampshire
John Langdon
Nicholas Gilman

Massachusetts
Nathaniel Gorham
Rufus King

Connecticut
William Samuel Johnson
Roger Sherman

New York
Alexander Hamilton

New Jersey
William Livingston
David Brearley
William Paterson
Jonathan Dayton

Pennsylvania
Benjamin Franklin
Thomas Mifflin
Robert Morris
George Clymer
Thomas FitzSimmons
Jared Ingersoll
James Wilson
Gouverneur Morris

Delaware
George Read
Gunning Bedford, Jr.
John Dickinson
Richard Bassett
Jacob Broom

Maryland
James McHenry
Daniel of St. Thomas Jenifer
Daniel Carroll

---

6. These are the full names of the signers, which in some cases are not the signatures on the document.

Virginia
John Blair
James Madison, Jr.

North Carolina
William Blount
Richard Dobbs Spaight
Hugh Williamson

South Carolina
John Rutledge
Charles Cotesworth
　Pinckney
Charles Pinckney
Pierce Butler

Georgia
William Few
Abraham Baldwin

Articles in Addition to, and Amendment of, the Constitution of the United States of America, Proposed by Congress, and Ratified by the Legislatures of the Several States, Pursuant to the Fifth Article of the Original Constitution[7]

AMENDMENT I

Congress shall make no law respecting an establishment of religion, or prohibiting the free exercise thereof; or abridging the freedom of speech, or of the press; or the right of the people peaceably to assemble, and to petition the Government for a redress of grievances.

AMENDMENT II

A well regulated Militia, being necessary to the security of a free State, the right of the people to keep and bear Arms shall not be infringed.

AMENDMENT III

No Soldier shall, in time of peace, be quartered in any house, without the consent of the Owner, nor in time of war, but in a manner to be prescribed by law.

AMENDMENT IV

The right of the people to be secure in their persons, houses, papers, and effects, against unreasonable searches and seizures, shall not be violated, and no Warrants shall issue, but upon probable cause, supported by Oath or affirmation, and particularly describing the place to be searched, and the persons or things to be seized.

AMENDMENT V

No person shall be held to answer for a capital or otherwise infamous crime, unless on a presentment or indictment of a Grand Jury, except in cases arising in the land or naval forces, or in the Militia, when in actual service in time of War or public danger; nor shall any person be subject for the same offence to be twice put in jeopardy of life or limb; nor shall be compelled in any criminal case to be a witness against himself, nor be deprived of life, liberty, or property, without due process of law; nor shall private property be taken for public use, without just compensation.

AMENDMENT VI

In all criminal prosecutions, the accused shall enjoy the right to a speedy and public trial, by an impartial jury of the State and district wherein the crime shall have been committed, which district shall have been previously ascertained by law, and to be informed of the nature and cause of the accusation; to be confronted with the witnesses against him; to have compulsory process for obtaining witnesses in his favour, and to have the Assistance of Counsel for his defence.

AMENDMENT VII

In suits at common law, where the value in controversy shall exceed twenty dollars, the right of trial by jury shall be preserved, and no fact tried by a jury, shall be otherwise reexamined in any Court of the United States, than according to the rules of the common law.

AMENDMENT VIII

Excessive bail shall not be required, nor excessive fines imposed, nor cruel and unusual punishments inflicted.

---

7. This heading appears only in the joint resolution submitting the first ten amendments, which are collectively known as the Bill of Rights. They were ratified on December 15, 1791.

AMENDMENT IX

The enumeration of the Constitution, of certain rights, shall not be construed to deny or disparage others retained by the people.

AMENDMENT X

The powers not delegated to the United States by the Constitution, nor prohibited by it to the States, are reserved to the States respectively, or to the people.

AMENDMENT XI [1798]

The Judicial power of the United States shall not be construed to extend to any suit in law or equity, commenced or prosecuted against one of the United States by Citizens of another State, or by Citizens or Subjects of any Foreign State.

AMENDMENT XII [1804]

The Electors shall meet in their respective States and vote by ballot for President and Vice-President, one of whom, at least, shall not be an inhabitant of the same State with themselves; they shall name in their ballots the person voted for as President, and in distinct ballots the person voted for as Vice-President, and they shall make distinct lists of all persons voted for as President, and of all persons voted for as Vice-President, and of the number of votes for each, which lists they shall sign and certify, and transmit sealed to the seat of the government of the United States, directed to the President of the Senate;—The President of the Senate shall, in the presence of the Senate and House of Representatives, open all the certificates and the votes shall then be counted;—The person having the greatest number of votes for President, shall be the President, if such number be a majority of the whole number of Electors appointed; and if no person have such majority, then from the persons having the highest numbers not exceeding three on the list of those voted for as President, the House of Representatives shall choose immediately, by ballot, the President. But in choosing the President, the votes shall be taken by states, the representation from each state having one vote; a quorum for this purpose shall consist of a member or members from two-thirds of the states, and a majority of all the states shall be necessary to a choice. And if the House of Representatives shall not choose a President whenever the right of choice shall devolve upon them, before the fourth day of March next following, then the Vice-President shall act as President, as in the case of the death or other constitutional disability of the President.—The person having the greatest number of votes as Vice-President, shall be the Vice-President, if such number be a majority of the whole number of Electors appointed, and if no person have a majority, then from the two highest numbers on the list, the Senate shall choose the Vice-President; a quorum for the purpose shall consist of two-thirds of the whole number of Senators, and majority of the whole number shall be necessary to a choice. But no person constitutionally ineligible to the office of President shall be eligible to that of Vice-President of the United States.

AMENDMENT XIII [1865]

SECTION 1

Neither slavery nor involuntary servitude, except as a punishment for crime whereof the party shall have been duly convicted, shall exist within the United States, or any place subject to their jurisdiction.

SECTION 2

Congress shall have power to enforce this article by appropriate legislation.

AMENDMENT XIV [1868]

SECTION 1

All persons born or naturalized in the United States, and subject to the jurisdiction thereof, are citizens of the United States and of the State wherein they reside. No State shall abridge the privileges or immunities of citizens of the United States; nor shall any State deprive any person of life, liberty, or property, without due process of law; nor deny to any person within its jurisdiction the equal protection of the laws.

SECTION 2

Representatives shall be apportioned among the several States according to their respective numbers, counting the whole number of persons in each State, excluding Indians not taxed. But when the right to vote at any election for the choice of electors for President and Vice-President of the United States, Representatives in Congress, the Executive and Judicial officers of a State, or the members of the Legislature thereof, is denied to any of the male inhabitants of such State, being twenty-one years of age, and citizens of the United States, or in any way abridged, except for participation in rebellion, or other crime, the basis of representation therein shall be reduced in the proportion which the number of such male citizens shall bear to the whole number of male citizens twenty-one years of age in such State.

SECTION 3

No person shall be a Senator or Representative in Congress, or elector of President and Vice-President, or hold any office, civil or military, under the United States, or under any State, who, having previously taken an oath, as a member of Congress, or as an officer of the United States, or as a member of any State legislature, or as an executive or judicial officer of any State, to support the Constitution of the United States, shall have engaged in insurrection or rebellion against the same, or given aid or comfort to the enemies thereof. But Congress may by a vote of two-thirds of each House, remove such disability.

SECTION 4

The validity of the public debt of the United States, authorized by law, including debts incurred for payment of pensions and bounties for services in suppressing insurrection or rebellion, shall not be questioned. But neither the United States nor any State shall assume or pay any debts or obligation incurred in aid of insurrection or rebellion against the United States, or any claim for the loss or emancipation of any slave; but all such debts, obligations, and claims shall be held illegal and void.

SECTION 5

The Congress shall have the power to enforce, by appropriate legislation, the provisions of this article.

AMENDMENT XV [1870]

SECTION 1

The right of citizens of the United States to vote shall not be denied or abridged by the United States or by any State on account of race, color, or previous condition of servitude—

SECTION 2

The Congress shall have power to enforce this article by appropriate legislation.

AMENDMENT XVI [1913]

The Congress shall have power to lay and collect taxes on incomes, from whatever source derived, without apportionment among the several States, and without regard to any census or enumeration.

AMENDMENT XVII [1913]

The Senate of the United States shall be composed of two Senators from each State, elected by the people thereof, for six years; and each Senator shall have one vote. The electors in each State shall have the qualifications requisite for electors of the most numerous branch of the State legislatures.

When vacancies happen in the representation of any State in the Senate, the executive authority of such State shall issue writs of election to fill such vacancies: *Provided*, That the legislature of any State may empower the executive thereof to make temporary appointments until the people fill the vacancies by election as the legislature may direct.

This amendment shall not be so construed as to affect the election or term of any Senator chosen before it becomes valid as part of the Constitution.

AMENDMENT XVIII [1919]

SECTION 1

After one year from the ratification of this article the manufacture, sale, or transportation of intoxicating liquors within, the importation thereof into, or the exportation thereof from the United States and all territory subject to the jurisdiction thereof for beverage purposes is hereby prohibited.

SECTION 2

The Congress and the several States shall have concurrent power to enforce this article by appropriate legislation.

SECTION 3

This article shall be inoperative unless it shall have been ratified as an amendment to the Constitution by the legislatures of the several States, as provided in the Constitution, within seven years from the date of the submission hereof to the States by the Congress.

AMENDMENT XIX [1920]

The right of citizens of the United States to vote shall not be denied or abridged by the United States or by any State on account of sex.

Congress shall have power to enforce this article by appropriate legislation.

AMENDMENT XX [1933]

SECTION 1

The terms of the President and Vice-President shall end at noon on the 20th day of January, and the terms of Senators and Representatives at noon on the 3d day of January, of the years in which such terms would have ended if this article had not been ratified; and the terms of their successors shall then begin.

SECTION 2

The Congress shall assemble at least once in every year, and such meeting shall begin at noon on the 3d day of January, unless they shall by law appoint a different day.

SECTION 3

If, at the time fixed for the beginning of the term of the President, the President elect shall have died, the Vice-President elect shall become President. If a President shall not have been chosen before the time fixed for the beginning of his term or if the President elect shall have failed to qualify, then the Vice-President elect shall act as President until a President shall have qualified; and the Congress may by law provide for the case wherein neither a President elect nor a Vice-President elect shall have qualified, declaring who shall then act as President, or the manner in which one who is to act shall be selected, and such person shall act accordingly until a President or Vice-President shall have qualified.

SECTION 4

The Congress may by law provide for the case of the death of any of the persons from whom the House of Representatives may choose a President whenever the right of choice shall have devolved upon them, and for the case of the death of any of the persons from whom the Senate may choose a Vice-President whenever the right of choice shall have devolved upon them.

SECTION 5

Sections 1 and 2 shall take effect on the 15th day of October following the ratification of this article.

SECTION 6

This article shall be inoperative unless it shall have been ratified as an amendment to the Constitution by the legislatures of three-fourths of the several States within seven years from the date of its submission.

AMENDMENT XXI [1933]

SECTION 1

The eighteenth article of amendment to the Constitution of the United States is hereby repealed.

SECTION 2

The transportation or importation into any State, Territory, or possession of the United States for delivery or use therein of intoxicating liquors, in violation of the laws thereof, is hereby prohibited.

SECTION 3

This article shall be inoperative unless it shall have been ratified as an amendment to the Constitution by conventions in the several States, as provided in the Constitution, within seven years from the date of the submission hereof to the States by the Congress.

AMENDMENT XXII [1951]

No person shall be elected to the office of the President more than twice, and no person who has held the office of President, or acted as President, for more than two years of a term to which some other person was elected President shall be elected to the office of the President more than once.

But this Article shall not apply to any person holding the office of President when this Article was proposed by the Congress, and shall not prevent any person who may be holding the office of President, or acting as President, during the term within which this Article becomes operative from holding the office of President or acting as President during the remainder of such term.

This article shall be inoperative unless it shall have been ratified as an amendment to the Constitution by the legislatures of three-fourths of the several states within seven years from the date of its submission to the states by the Congress.

AMENDMENT XXIII [1961]

SECTION 1

The District constituting the seat of Government of the United States shall appoint in such manner as the Congress may direct:

A number of electors of President and Vice-President equal to the whole number of Senators and Representatives in Congress to which the District would be entitled if it were a State, but in no event more than the least populous State; they shall be in addition to those appointed by the States, but they shall be considered, for the purposes of the election of President and Vice-President, to be electors appointed by a State; and they shall meet in the District and perform such duties as provided by the twelfth article of amendment.

SECTION 2

The Congress shall have power to enforce this article by appropriate legislation.

AMENDMENT XXIV [1964]

SECTION 1

The right of citizens of the United States to vote in any primary or other election for President or Vice President, for electors for President or Vice President, or for Senator or Representative in Congress, shall not be denied or abridged by the United States or any state by reason of failure to pay any poll tax or other tax.

SECTION 2

The Congress shall have the power to enforce this article by appropriate legislation.

AMENDMENT XXV [1967]

SECTION 1

In case of the removal of the President from office or of his death or resignation, the Vice President shall become President.

SECTION 2

Whenever there is a vacancy in the office of the Vice President, the President shall nominate a Vice President who shall take office upon confirmation by a majority vote of both Houses of Congress.

SECTION 3

Whenever the President transmits to the President Pro Tempore of the Senate and the Speaker of the House of Representatives his written declaration that he is unable to discharge the powers and duties of his office, and until he transmits to them a written declaration to the contrary, such powers and duties shall be discharged by the Vice President as Acting President.

SECTION 4

Whenever the Vice President and a majority of either the principal officers of the executive departments or of such other body as Congress may by law provide, transmit to the President Pro Tempore of the Senate and the Speaker of the House of Representatives their written declaration that the President is unable to discharge the powers and duties of his office, the Vice President shall immediately assume the powers and duties of the office as Acting President.

Thereafter, when the President transmits to the President Pro Tempore of the Senate and the Speaker of the House of Representatives his written declaration that no inability exists, he shall resume the powers and duties of his office unless the Vice President and a majority of either the principal officers of the executive departments or of such other body as Congress may by law provide, transmit within four days to the President Pro Tempore of the Senate and the Speaker of the House of Representatives their written declaration that the President is unable to discharge the powers and duties of his office. Thereupon Congress shall decide the issue, assembling within forty-eight hours for that purpose if not in session. If the Congress, within twenty-one days after receipt of the latter written declaration, or, if Congress is not in session, within twenty-one days after Congress is required to assemble, determines by two-thirds vote of both Houses that the President is unable to discharge the powers and duties of his office, the Vice President shall continue to discharge the same as Acting President; otherwise, the President shall resume the powers and duties of his office.

AMENDMENT XXVI [1971]

SECTION 1

The right of citizens of the United States, who are eighteen years of age or older, to vote shall not be denied or abridged by the United States or by any State on account of age.

SECTION 2

The Congress shall have the power to enforce this article by appropriate legislation.

AMENDMENT XXVII [1992]

No law varying the compensation for the service of Senators and Representatives shall take effect until an election of Representatives shall have intervened.

FEDERALIST NO. 10 (JAMES MADISON)

Among the numerous advantages promised by a well-constructed union, none deserves to be more accurately developed than its tendency to break and control the violence of faction. The friend of popular governments never finds himself so much alarmed for their character and fate as when he contemplates their propensity to this dangerous vice. He will not fail, therefore, to set a due value on any plan which, without violating the principles to which he is attached, provides a proper cure for it. The instability, injustice, and confusion introduced into the public councils have, in truth, been the mortal diseases under which popular governments have everywhere perished, as they continue to be the favorite and fruitful topics from which the adversaries to liberty derive their most specious declamations. The valuable improvements made by the American constitutions on the popular models, both ancient and modern, cannot certainly be too much admired; but it would be an unwarrantable partiality to contend that they have as effectually obviated the danger on this side, as was wished and expected. Complaints are everywhere heard from our most considerate and virtuous citizens, equally the friends of public and private faith and of public and personal liberty, that our governments are too unstable, that the public good is disregarded in the conflicts of rival parties, and that measures are too often decided, not according to the rules of justice and the rights of the minor party, but by the superior force of an interested and overbearing majority. However anxiously we may wish that these complaints had no foundation, the evidence of known facts will not permit us to deny that they are in some degree true. It will be found, indeed, on a candid review of our situation, that some of the distresses under which we labor have been erroneously charged on the operation of our governments; but it will be found, at the same time, that other causes will not alone account for many of our heaviest misfortunes; and, particularly, for that prevailing and increasing distrust of public engagements and alarm for private rights which are echoed from one end of the continent to the other. There must be chiefly, if not wholly, effects of the unsteadiness and injustice with which a factious spirit has tainted our public administration.

By a faction I understand a number of citizens, whether amounting to a majority or minority of the whole, who are united and actuated by some common impulse of passion, or of interest, adverse to the rights of other citizens, or to the permanent and aggregate interests of the community.

There are two methods of curing the mischiefs of faction: the one, by removing its causes; the other, by controlling its effects.

There are again two methods of removing the causes of faction: the one, by destroying the liberty which is essential to its existence; the other, by giving to every citizen the same opinions, the same passions, and the same interests.

It could never be more truly said than of the first remedy that it was worse than the disease. Liberty is to faction what air is to fire, an ailment without which it instantly expires. But it could not be a less folly to abolish liberty, which is essential to political life, because it nourishes faction than it would be to wish the annihilation of air, which is essential to animal life, because it imparts to fire its destructive agency.

The second expedient is as impracticable as the first would be unwise. As long as the reason of man continues fallible, and he is at liberty to exercise it, different opinions will be formed. As long as the connection subsists between his reason and his self-love, his opinions and his passions will have a reciprocal influence on each other; and the former will be objects to which the latter will attach themselves. The diversity in the faculties of men, from which the rights of property originate, is not less an insuperable obstacle to a uniformity of interest. The protection of these faculties is the first object of government. From the protection of different and unequal faculties of acquiring property, the possession of different degrees and kinds of property immediately results; and from the influence of these on the sentiments and views of the respective proprietors ensues a division of the society into different interests and parties.

The latent causes of faction are thus sown in the nature of man; and we see them everywhere brought into different degrees of activity, according to the different circumstances of civil society. A zeal for different opinions concerning religion, concerning government, and many other points, as well of speculation as of practice; an attachment to different leaders ambitiously contending for pre-eminence and power; or to persons of other descriptions whose fortunes have been interesting to the human passions, have, in turn, divided mankind into parties, inflamed them with mutual animosity, and rendered them much more disposed to vex and oppress each other than to co-operate for their common good. So strong is this propensity of mankind to fall into mutual animosities that where no substantial occasion presents itself the most frivolous and fanciful distinctions have been sufficient to kindle their unfriendly passions and excite their most violent conflicts. But the most common and durable source of factions has been the various and unequal distribution of property. Those who hold and those who are without property have ever formed distinct interests in society. Those who are creditors, and those who are debtors, fall under a like discrimination. A landed interest, a manufacturing interest, a mercantile interest, a moneyed interest, with many lesser interests, grow up of necessity in civilized nations, and divide them into different classes, actuated by different sentiments and views. The regulation of these various and interfering interests forms the principal task of modern legislation and involves the spirit of party and faction in the necessary and ordinary operations of government.

No man is allowed to be a judge in his own cause, because his interest would certainly bias his judgment, and, not improbably, corrupt his integrity. With equal, nay with greater reason, a body of men are unfit to be both judges and parties at the same time; yet what are many of the most important acts of legislation but so many judicial determinations, not indeed concerning the rights of single persons, but concerning the rights of large bodies of citizens? And what are the different classes of legislators but advocates and parties to the causes which they determine? Is a law proposed concerning private debts? It is a question to which the creditors are parties on one side and the debtors on the other. Justice ought to hold the balance between them. Yet the parties are, and must be, themselves the judges; and the most numerous party, or in other words, the most powerful faction must be expected to prevail. Shall domestic manufacturers be encouraged, and in what degree, by restrictions on foreign manufacturers? [These] are questions which would be differently decided by the landed and the manufacturing classes, and probably by neither with a sole regard to justice and the public good. The apportionment of taxes on the various descriptions of property is an act which seems to require the most exact impartiality; yet there is, perhaps, no legislative act in which greater opportunity and temptation are given to a predominant party to trample on the rules of justice. Every shilling with which they overburden the inferior number is a shilling saved to their own pockets.

It is in vain to say that enlightened statesmen will be able to adjust these clashing interests and render them all subservient to the public good. Enlightened statesmen will not always be at the helm. Nor, in many cases, can such an adjustment be made at all without taking into view indirect and remote considerations, which will rarely prevail over the immediate interest which one party may find in disregarding the rights of another or the good of the whole.

The inference to which we are brought is that the *causes* of faction cannot be removed and that relief is only to be sought in the means of controlling its *effects*.

If a faction consists of less than a majority, relief is supplied by the republican principle, which enables the majority to defeat its sinister views by regular vote. It may clog the administration, it may convulse the society; but it will be unable to execute and mask its violence under the forms of the Constitution. When a majority is included in a faction, the form of popular government, on the other hand, enables it to sacrifice to its ruling passion or interest both the public good and the rights of other citizens. To secure the public good and private rights against the danger of such a faction, and at the same time to preserve the spirit and the form of popular government, is then the great object to which our inquiries are directed. Let me add that it is the great desideratum by which alone this form of government can be rescued from the opprobrium under which it has so long labored and be recommended to the esteem and adoption of mankind.

By what means is this object attainable? Evidently by one of two only. Either the existence of the same passion or interest in a majority at the same time must be prevented, or the majority, having such coexistent passion or interest, must be rendered, by their number and local situation, unable to concert and carry into effect schemes of oppression. If the impulse and the opportunity be suffered to coincide, we well know that neither moral nor religious motives can be relied on as an adequate control. They are not found to be such on the injustice and violence of individuals, and lose their efficacy in proportion to the number combined together, that is, in proportion as their efficacy becomes needful.

From this view of the subject it may be concluded that a pure democracy, by which I mean a society consisting of a small number of citizens, who assemble and administer the government in person, can admit of no cure for the mischiefs of faction. A common passion or interest will, in almost every case, be felt by a majority of the whole, a communication and concert results from the form of government itself; and there is nothing to check the inducements to sacrifice the weaker party or an obnoxious individual. Hence it is that such democracies have ever been spectacles of turbulence and contention; have ever been found incompatible with personal security or the rights of property; and have in general been as short in their lives as they have been violent in their deaths. Theoretic politicians, who have patronized this species of government, have erroneously supposed that by reducing mankind to a perfect equality in their political rights, they would at the same time be perfectly equalized and assimilated in their possessions, their opinions, and their passions.

A republic, by which I mean a government in which the scheme of representation takes place, opens a different prospect and promises the cure for which we are seeking. Let us examine the points in which it varies from pure democracy, and we shall comprehend both the nature of the cure and the efficacy which it must derive from the Union.

The two great points of difference between a democracy and a republic are: first, the delegation of the government, in the latter, to a small number of citizens elected by the rest; secondly, the greater number of citizens and greater sphere of country over which the latter may be extended.

The effect of the first difference is, on the one hand, to refine and enlarge the public views by passing them through the medium of a chosen body of citizens, whose wisdom may best discern the true interest of their country and whose patriotism and love of justice will be least likely to sacrifice it to temporary or partial considerations. Under such a regulation it may well happen that the public voice, pronounced by the representatives of the people, will be more consonant to the public good than if pronounced by the people themselves, convened for the purpose. On the other hand, the effect may be inverted. Men of factious tempers, of local prejudices, or of sinister designs, may, by intrigue, by corruption, or by other means, first obtain the suffrages, and then betray the interests of the people. The question resulting is, whether small or extensive republics are most favorable to the election of proper guardians of the public weal; and it is clearly decided in favor of the latter by two obvious considerations.

In the first place it is to be remarked that however small the republic may be the representatives must be raised to a certain number in order to guard against the cabals of a few; and that however large it may be they must be limited to a certain number in order to guard against the confusion of a multitude. Hence, the number of representatives in the two cases not being in proportion to that of the constituents, and being proportionally greatest in the small republic, it follows that if the proportion of fit characters be not less in the large than in the small republic, the former will present a greater option, and consequently a greater probability of a fit choice.

In the next place, as each representative will be chosen by a greater number of citizens in the large than in the small republic, it will be more difficult for unworthy candidates to practice with success the vicious arts by which elections are too often carried; and the suffrages of the people being more free, will be more likely to center on men who possess the most attractive merit and the most diffusive and established characters.

It must be confessed that in this, as in most other cases, there is a mean, on both sides of which inconveniencies will be found to lie. By enlarging too much the number of electors, you render the representative too little acquainted with all their local circumstances and lesser interests; as by reducing it too much, you render him unduly attached to these, and too little fit to comprehend and pursue great and national objects. The federal Constitution forms a happy combination in this respect; the great and aggregate interests being referred to the national, the local and particular to the State legislatures.

The other point of difference is the greater number of citizens and extent of territory which may be brought within the compass of republican than of democratic government; and it is this circumstance principally which renders factious combinations less to be dreaded in the former than in the latter. The smaller the society, the fewer probably will be the distinct parties and interests composing it; the fewer the distinct parties and interests, the more frequently will a majority be found of the same party; and the smaller the number of individuals composing a majority, and the smaller the compass within which they are placed, the more easily will they concert and execute their plans of oppression. Extend the sphere and you take in a greater variety of parties and interests; you make it less probable that a majority of the whole will have a common motive to invade the rights of other citizens; or if such a common motive exists, it will be more difficult for all who feel it to discover their own strength and to act in unison with each other. Besides other impediments, it may be remarked that, where there is a consciousness of unjust or dishonorable purposes, communication is always checked by distrust in proportion to the number whose concurrence is necessary.

Hence, it clearly appears that the same advantage which a republic has over a democracy in controlling the effects of faction is enjoyed by a large over a small republic—is enjoyed by the Union over the States composing it. Does this advantage consist in the substitution of representatives whose enlightened views and virtuous sentiments render them superior to local prejudices and to schemes of injustice? It will not be denied that the representation of the Union will be most likely to possess these requisite endowments. Does it consist in the greater security afforded by a greater variety of parties, against the event of any one party being able to outnumber and oppress the rest? In an equal degree does the increased variety of parties comprised within the Union increase this security. Does it, in fine, consist in the greater obstacles opposed to the concert and accomplishment of the secret wishes of an unjust and interested majority? Here again the extent of the Union gives it the most palpable advantage.

The influence of factious leaders may kindle a flame within their particular States but will be unable to spread a general conflagration through the other States. A religious sect may degenerate into a political faction in a part of the Confederacy; but the variety of sects dispersed over the entire face of it must secure the national councils against any danger from that source. A rage for paper money, for an abolition of debts, for an equal division of property, or for any other improper or wicked project, will be less apt to pervade the whole body of the Union than a particular member of it, in the same proportion as such a malady is more likely to taint a particular county or district than an entire State.

In the extent and proper structure of the Union, therefore, we behold a republican remedy for the diseases most incident to republican government. And according to the degree of pleasure and pride we feel in being republicans ought to be our zeal in cherishing the spirit and supporting the character of federalists.

FEDERALIST NO. 51 (JAMES MADISON)

To what expedient, then, shall we finally resort, for maintaining in practice the necessary partition of power among the several departments as laid down in the constitution? The only answer that can be given is that as all these exterior provisions are found to be inadequate, the defect must be supplied, by so contriving the interior structure of the government as that its several constituent parts may, by their mutual relations, be the means of keeping each other in their proper places. Without presuming to undertake a full development of this important idea i will hazard few general observations which may perhaps place it in a clearer light, and enable us to form a more correct judgment of the principles and structure of the government planned by the convention.

In order to lay a due foundation for that separate and distinct exercise of the different powers of government, which to a certain extent is admitted on all hands to be essential to the preservation of liberty, it is evident that each department should have a will of its own; and consequently should be so constituted that the members of each should have as little agency as possible in the appointment of the members of the others. Were this principle rigorously adhered to, it would require that all the appointments for the supreme executive, legislative, and judiciary magistracies should be drawn from the same fountain of authority, the people, through channels having no communication whatever with one another. Perhaps such a plan of constructing the several departments would be less difficult in practice than it may be in contemplation appear. Some difficulties, however, and some additional expense would attend the execution of it. Some deviations, therefore, from the principle must be admitted. In the constitution of the judiciary department in particular, it might be inexpedient to insist rigorously on the principle; first, because peculiar qualifications being essential in the members, the primary consideration ought to be to select that mode of choice which best secures these qualifications; second, because the permanent tenure by which the appointments are held in that department must soon destroy all sense of dependence on the authority conferring them.

It is equally evident that the members of each department should be as little dependent as possible on those of the others for the emoluments annexed to their offices. Were the executive magistrate, or the judges, not independent of the legislature in this particular, their independence in every other would be merely nominal.

But the great security against a gradual concentration of the several powers in the same department consists in giving to those who administer each department the necessary constitutional means and personal motives to resist encroachments of the others. The provision for defense must in this, as in all other cases, be made commensurate to the danger of attack. Ambition must be made to counteract ambition. The interest of the man must be connected with the constitutional rights of the place. It may be a reflection on human nature that such devices should be necessary to control the abuses of government. But what is government itself but the greatest of all reflections on human nature? If men were angels no government would be necessary. If angels were to govern men, neither external nor internal controls on government would be necessary. In framing a government which is to be administered by men over men, the great difficulty lies in this: you must first enable the government to control the governed; and in the next place oblige it to control itself. A dependence on the people is, no doubt, the primary control on the government; but experience has taught mankind the necessity of auxiliary precautions.

This policy of supplying, by opposite and rival interests, the defect of better motives, might be traced through the whole system of human affairs, private as well as public. We see it particularly displayed in all the subordinate distributions of power, where the constant aim is to divide and arrange the several offices in such a manner as that each may be a check on the other—that the private interest of every individual may be a sentinel over the public rights. These inventions of prudence cannot be less requisite in the distribution of the supreme powers of the State.

But it is not possible to give to each department an equal power of self-defense. In republican government, the legislative authority necessarily predominates. The remedy for this inconveniency is to divide the legislature into different branches; and to render them, by different modes of election and different principles of action, as little connected with each other as the nature of their common functions and their common dependence on the society will admit. It may even be necessary to guard against dangerous encroachments by still further precautions. As the weight of the legislative authority requires that it should be thus divided, the weakness of the executive may require, on the other hand, that it should be fortified. An absolute negative on the legislature appears, at first view, to be the natural defense with which the executive magistrate should be armed. But perhaps it would be neither altogether safe nor alone sufficient. On ordinary occasions it might not be exerted with the requisite firmness, and on extraordinary occasions it might be perfidiously abused. May not this defect of an absolute negative be supplied by some qualified connection between this weaker department and the weaker branch of the stronger department, by which the latter may be led to support the constitutional rights of the former, without being too much detached from the rights of its own department?

If the principles on which these observations are founded be just, as I persuade myself they are, and they be applied as a criterion to the several State constitutions, and to the federal Constitution, it will be found that if the latter does not perfectly correspond with them, the former are infinitely less able to bear such a test.

There are, moreover, two considerations particularly applicable to the federal system of America, which place that system in a very interesting point of view.

First. In a single republic, all the power surrendered by the people is submitted to the administration of a single government; and the usurpations are guarded against by a division of the government into distinct and separate departments. In the compound republic of America, the power surrendered by the people is first divided between two distinct governments, and then the portion allotted to each subdivided among distinct and separate departments. Hence a double security arises to the rights of the people. The different governments will control each other, at the same time that each will be controlled by itself.

Second. It is of great importance in a republic not only to guard the society against the oppression of its rulers, but to guard one part of the society against the injustice of the other part. Different interests necessarily exist in different classes of citizens. If a majority be united by a common interest, the rights of the minority will be insecure. There are but two methods of providing against this evil: the one by creating a will in the community independent of the majority—that is, of the society itself; the other, by comprehending in the society so many separate descriptions of citizens as will render an unjust combination of a majority of the whole very improbable, if not impracticable. The first method prevails in all governments possessing an hereditary or self-appointed authority. This, at best, is but a precarious security; because a power independent of the society may as well espouse the unjust views of the major as the rightful interests of the minor party, and may possibly be turned against both parties. The second method will be exemplified in the federal republic of the United States. Whilst all authority in it will be derived from and dependent on the society, the society itself will be broken into so many parts, interests and classes of citizens, that the rights of individuals, or of the minority, will be in little danger from interested combinations of the majority. In a free government the security for civil rights must be the same as that for religious rights. It consists in the one case in the multiplicity of interests, and in the other in the multiplicity of sects. The degree of security in both cases will depend on the number of interests and sects; and this may be presumed to depend on the extent of country and number of people comprehended under the same government. This view of the subject must particularly recommend a proper federal system to all the sincere and considerate friends of republican government, since it shows that in exact proportion as the territory of the Union may be formed into more circumscribed Confederacies, or States, oppressive combinations of a majority will be facilitated; the best security, under the republican forms, for the rights of every class of citizen, will be diminished; and consequently the stability and independence of some member of the government, the only other security, must be proportionately increased. Justice is the end of government. It is the end of civil society. It ever has been and ever will be pursued until it be obtained, or until liberty be lost in the pursuit. In a society under the forms of which the stronger faction can readily unite and oppress the weaker, anarchy may as truly be said to reign as in a state of nature, where the weaker individual is not secured against the violence of the stronger; and as, in the latter state, even the stronger individuals are prompted, by the uncertainty of their condition, to submit to a government which may protect the weak as well as themselves; so, in the former state, will the more powerful factions or parties be gradually induced, by a like motive, to wish for a government which will protect all parties, the weaker as well as the more powerful. It can be little doubted that if the State of Rhode Island was separated from the Confederacy and left to itself, the insecurity of rights under the popular form of government within such narrow limits would be displayed by such reiterated oppressions of factious majorities that some power altogether independent of the people would soon be called for by the voice of the very factions whose misrule had proved the necessity of it. In the extended republic of the United States, and among the great variety of interests, parties, and sects which it embraces, a coalition of a majority of the whole society could seldom take place on any other principles than those of justice and the general good; whilst there being thus less danger to a minor from the will of a major party, there must be less pretext, also, to provide for the security of the former, by introducing into the government a will not dependent on the latter, or, in other words, a will independent of the society itself. It is no less certain than it is important, notwithstanding the contrary opinions which have been entertained, that the larger the society, provided it lie within a practicable sphere, the more duly capable it will be of self-government. And happily for the *republican cause,* the practicable sphere may be carried to a very great extent by a judicious modification and mixture of the federal principle.

GLOSSARY

accountability The ability of the public to hold government officials responsible for their actions.

affirmative action A term that refers to programs designed to ensure that women, minorities, and other traditionally disadvantaged groups have full and equal opportunities in employment, education, and other areas of life.

age-cohort tendency The tendency for a significant break in the pattern of political socialization to occur among younger citizens, usually as the result of a major event or development that disrupts preexisting beliefs.

agency point of view The tendency of bureaucrats to place the interests of their agency ahead of other interests and ahead of the priorities sought by the president or Congress.

agenda setting The power of the media through news coverage to focus the public's attention and concern on particular events, problems, issues, personalities, and so on.

agents of socialization Those agents, such as the family and the media, that have significant impact on citizens' political socialization.

air wars A term that refers to the fact that modern campaigns are often a battle of opposing televised advertising campaigns.

alienation A feeling of personal powerlessness that includes the notion that government does not care about the opinions of people like oneself.

Anti-Federalists A term used to describe opponents of the Constitution during the debate over ratification.

apathy A feeling of personal noninterest or unconcern with politics.

appellate jurisdiction The authority of a given court to review cases that have already been tried in lower courts and are appealed to it by the losing party; such a court is called an appeals court or appellate court. (See also **original jurisdiction**.)

authority The recognized right of an individual or institution to exercise power. (See also **power**.)

balanced budget When the government's tax revenues for the year are roughly equal to its expenditures.

bicameral legislature A legislature having two chambers.

bill A proposed law (legislative act) within Congress or another legislature. (See also **law**.)

Bill of Rights The first ten amendments to the Constitution. They include such rights as freedom of speech and trial by jury.

block grants Federal grants-in-aid that permit state and local officials to decide how the money will be spent within a general area, such as education or health. (See also **categorical grants**.)

budget deficit When the government's expenditures exceed its tax revenues.

budget surplus When the government's tax and other revenues exceed its expenditures.

bureaucracy A system of organization and control based on the principles of hierarchical authority, job specialization, and formalized rules. (See also **formalized rules; hierarchical authority; job specialization**.)

bureaucratic rule The tendency of large-scale organizations to develop into the bureaucratic form, with the effect that administrators make key policy decisions.

cabinet A group consisting of the heads of the (cabinet) executive departments, who are appointed by the president, subject to confirmation by the Senate. The cabinet was once the main advisory body to the president but no longer plays this role. (See also **cabinet departments**.)

cabinet (executive) departments The major administrative organizations within the federal executive bureaucracy, each of which is headed by a secretary (cabinet officer) and has responsibility for a major function of the federal government, such as defense, agriculture, or justice. (See also **cabinet; independent agencies**.)

candidate-centered politics Election campaigns and other political processes in which candidates, not political parties, have most of the initiative and influence. (See also **party-centered politics**.)

capital-gains tax Tax that individuals pay on money gained from the sale of a capital asset, such as property or stocks.

capitalism An economic system based on the idea that government should interfere with economic transactions as little as possible. Free enterprise and self-reliance are the collective and individual principles that underpin capitalism.

categorical grants Federal grants-in-aid to states and localities that can be used only for designated projects. (See also **block grants**.)

charter The chief instrument by which a state governs its local units;

G-1

it spells out in detail what a local government can and cannot do.

checks and balances The elaborate system of divided spheres of authority provided by the U.S. Constitution as a means of controlling the power of government. The separation of powers among the branches of the national government, federalism, and the different methods of selecting national officers are all part of this system.

citizens' (noneconomic) groups Organized interests formed by individuals drawn together by opportunities to promote a cause in which they believe but that does not provide them significant individual economic benefits. (See also **economic groups; interest group.**)

city manager system Form of municipal government that entrusts the executive role to a professionally trained manager, who is chosen, and can be fired, by the city council.

civic duty The belief of an individual that civic and political participation is a responsibility of citizenship.

civil liberties The fundamental individual rights of a free society, such as freedom of speech and the right to a jury trial, which in the United States are protected by the Bill of Rights.

civil rights (equal rights) The right of every person to equal protection under the laws and equal access to society's opportunities and public facilities.

civil service system See **merit system.**

clear-and-present-danger test A test devised by the Supreme Court in 1919 to define the limits of free speech in the context of national security. According to the test, government cannot abridge political expression unless it presents a clear and present danger to the nation's security.

clientele groups Special-interest groups that benefit directly from the activities of a particular bureaucratic agency and are therefore strong advocates of the agency.

cloture A parliamentary maneuver that, if a three-fifths majority votes for it, limits Senate debate to thirty hours and has the effect of defeating a filibuster. (See also **filibuster.**)

cold war The lengthy period after World War II when the United States and the USSR were not engaged in actual combat (a "hot war") but were nonetheless locked in a state of deep-seated hostility.

collective (public) goods Benefits that are offered by groups (usually citizens' groups) as an incentive for membership but that are nondivisible (e.g., a clean environment) and therefore are available to nonmembers as well as members of the particular group. (See also **free-rider problem; private goods.**)

commerce clause The clause of the Constitution (Article I, Section 8) that empowers the federal government to regulate commerce among the states and with other nations.

commission system Form of municipal government that invests executive and legislative authority in a commission, with each commissioner serving as a member of the local council but also having a specified executive role, such as police commissioner or public works commissioner.

common-carrier role The media's function as an open channel through which political leaders can communicate with the public. (See also **public representative role; signaler role; watchdog role.**)

comparable worth The idea that women should get pay equal to men for work that is of similar difficulty and responsibility and that requires similar levels of education and training.

compliance The issue of whether a court's decisions will be respected and obeyed.

concurring opinion A separate opinion written by a Supreme Court justice who votes with the majority in the decision on a case but who disagrees with their reasoning. (See also **dissenting opinion; majority opinion; plurality opinion.**)

confederacy A governmental system in which sovereignty is vested entirely in subnational (state) governments. (See also **federalism; unitary system.**)

conference committee A temporary committee that is formed to bargain over the differences in the House and Senate versions of a bill. The committee's members are usually appointed from the House and Senate standing committees that originally worked on the bill.

conservatives Those who emphasize the marketplace as the means of distributing economic benefits but look to government to uphold traditional social values. (See also **liberals; libertarians; populists.**)

constituency The individuals who live within the geographical area represented by an elected official. More narrowly, the body of citizens eligible to vote for a particular representative.

constitution The fundamental law that defines how a government will legitimately operate.

constitutional democracy A government that is democratic in its provisions for majority influence through elections and constitutional in its provisions for minority rights and rule by law.

constitutional initiative The process by which a citizen or group can petition to place a proposed amendment on the ballot at the next election by obtaining the signatures of a certain number of registered voters, and if the amendment gets majority support, it becomes part of the constitution.

constitutionalism The idea that there are definable limits on the rightful power of a government over its citizens.

containment A doctrine, developed after World War II, based on the assumptions that the Soviet Union was an aggressor nation and that only a determined United States could block Soviet territorial ambitions.

Cooley's rule The term used to describe the idea that cities should be self-governing, articulated in an 1871 ruling by Michigan judge Thomas Cooley.

cooperative federalism The situation in which the national, state, and local levels work together to solve problems.

de facto discrimination Discrimination on the basis of race, sex, religion, ethnicity, and the like that results from social, economic, and cultural biases and conditions. (See also **de jure discrimination**.)

de jure discrimination Discrimination on the basis of race, sex, religion, ethnicity, and the like that results from a law. (See also **de facto discrimination**.)

dealignment A situation in which voters' partisan loyalties have been substantially and permanently weakened. (See also **party identification; party realignment**.)

decision A vote of the Supreme Court in a particular case that indicates which party the justices side with and by how large a margin.

deficit spending When the government spends more than it collects in taxes and other revenues.

delegates Elected representatives whose obligation is to act in accordance with the expressed wishes of the people whom they represent. (See also **trustees**.)

demand-side economics A form of fiscal policy that emphasizes "demand" (consumer spending). Government can use increased spending or tax cuts to place more money in consumers' hands and thereby increase demand. (See also **fiscal policy; supply-side economics**.)

democracy A form of government in which the people govern, either directly or through elected representatives.

demographic representativeness The idea that the bureaucracy will be more responsive to the public if its employees at all levels are demographically representative of the population as a whole.

denials of power A constitutional means of limiting governmental action by listing those powers that government is expressly prohibited from using.

deregulation The rescinding of excessive government regulations for the purpose of improving economic efficiency.

descriptive reporting The style of reporting that aims to describe *what* is taking place or has occurred.

détente A French word meaning "a relaxing" and used to refer to an era of improved relations between the United States and the Soviet Union that began in the early 1970s.

deterrence The idea that nuclear war can be discouraged if each side in a conflict has the capacity to destroy the other with nuclear weapons.

devolution The passing down of authority from the national government to states and localities.

Dillon's rule The term used to describe relations between state and local government; it holds that local governments are creatures of the state, which in theory even has the power to abolish them.

direct primary See **primary election**.

dissenting opinion The opinion of a justice in a Supreme Court case that explains his or her reasons for disagreeing with the majority's decision. (See also **concurring opinion; majority opinion; plurality opinion**.)

diversity The principle that individual and group differences should be respected and are a source of national strength.

dual federalism A doctrine based on the idea that a precise separation of national power and state power is both possible and desirable.

due process clause (of the Fourteenth Amendment) The clause of the Constitution that has been used by the judiciary to apply the Bill of Rights to the actions of state governments.

economic depression A very severe and sustained economic downturn. Depressions are rare in the United States: the last one was in the 1930s.

economic globalization The increased interdependence of nations' economies. The change is a result of technological, transportation, and communication advances that have enabled firms to deploy their resources across the globe.

economic groups Interest groups that are organized primarily for economic reasons but that engage in political activity in order to seek favorable policies from government. (See also **citizens' groups; interest group**.)

economic recession A moderate but sustained downturn in the economy. Recessions are part of the economy's normal cycle of ups and downs.

economy A system of production and consumption of goods and services that are allocated through exchange among producers and consumers.

efficiency An economic principle that holds that firms should fulfill as many of society's needs as possible while using as few of its resources as possible. The greater the output (production) for a given input (for example, an hour of labor), the more efficient the process.

elastic clause See **"necessary and proper" clause**.

electoral college An unofficial term that refers to the electors who cast the states' electoral votes.

electoral votes The method of voting that is used to choose the U.S. president. Each state has the same number of electoral votes as it has members in Congress (House and Senate combined). By tradition, electoral voting is tied to a state's popular voting; thus, the presidential candidate with the most popular votes overall has usually also had the most electoral votes.

elitism The view that the United States is essentially run by a tiny elite (composed of wealthy or well-connected individuals) who control public policy through both direct and indirect means.

entitlement program Any of a number of individual benefit programs, such as social security, that require government to provide a designated benefit to any person who meets the legally defined criteria for eligibility.

enumerated (expressed) powers The seventeen powers granted to the national government under Article I, Section 8 of the Constitution. These powers include taxation and the regulation of commerce as well as the authority to provide for the national defense.

equal protection clause A clause of the Fourteenth Amendment that forbids any state to deny equal protection of the laws to any individual within its jurisdiction.

equal rights See **civil rights**.

equality The notion that all individuals are equal in their moral worth, in their treatment under the law, and in their political voice.

equality of opportunity The idea that all individuals should be given an equal chance to succeed on their own.

equality of result The objective of policies intended to reduce or eliminate the effects of discrimination so that members of traditionally disadvantaged groups will have the same benefits of society as do members of advantaged groups.

equity (in relation to economic policy) The situation in which the outcome of an economic transaction is fair to each party. An outcome can usually be considered fair if each party enters into a transaction freely and is not knowingly at a disadvantage.

establishment clause The First Amendment provision that government may not favor one religion over another or favor religion over no religion, and that prohibits Congress from passing laws respecting the establishment of religion.

exclusionary rule The legal principle that government is prohibited from using in trials evidence that was obtained by unconstitutional means (for example, illegal search and seizure).

executive departments See **cabinet departments**.

executive leadership system An approach to managing the bureaucracy that is based on presidential leadership and presidential management tools, such as the president's annual budget proposal. (See also **merit system; patronage system**.)

expressed powers See **enumerated powers**.

externalities Burdens that society incurs when firms fail to pay the full cost of resources used in production. An example of an externality is the pollution that results when corporations dump industrial wastes into lakes and rivers.

facts (of a court case) The relevant circumstances of a legal dispute or offense as determined by a trial court. The facts of a case are crucial because they help determine which law or laws are applicable in the case.

federalism A governmental system in which authority is divided between two sovereign levels of government: national and regional. (See also **confederacy; unitary system**.)

Federalists A term used to describe supporters of the Constitution during the debate over ratification.

filibuster A procedural tactic in the U.S. Senate whereby a minority of legislators prevents a bill from coming to a vote by holding the floor and talking until the majority gives in and the bill is withdrawn from consideration. (See also **cloture**.)

fiscal federalism A term that refers to the expenditure of federal funds on programs run in part through states and localities.

fiscal policy A tool of economic management by which government attempts to maintain a stable economy through its taxing and spending decisions. (See also **demand-side economics; monetary policy; supply-side economics**.)

formalized rules A basic principle of bureaucracy that refers to the standardized procedures and established regulations by which a bureaucracy conducts its operations. (See also **bureaucracy**.)

free-exercise clause A First Amendment provision that prohibits the government from interfering with the practice of religion or prohibiting the free exercise of religion.

free-rider problem The situation in which the benefits offered by a group to its members are also available to nonmembers. The incentive to join the group and to promote its cause is reduced because nonmembers (free riders) receive the benefits (e.g., a cleaner environment) without having to pay any of the group's costs. (See also **collective goods**.)

free trade The view that the long-term economic interests of all countries are advanced when tariffs and other trade barriers are kept to a minimum. (See also **protectionism**.)

freedom of expression Americans' freedom to communicate their views, the foundation of which is the First Amendment rights of freedom of conscience, speech, press, assembly, and petition.

gender gap The tendency of women and men to differ in their political attitudes and voting preferences.

gerrymandering The process by which the party in power draws election district boundaries in a way that advantages its candidates.

government The institutions, processes, and rules that facilitate control of a particular area and its inhabitants.

government corporations Bodies, such as the U.S. Postal Service and Amtrak, that are similar to private corporations in that they charge for their services, but different in that they receive federal funding to help defray expenses. Their directors are appointed by the president with Senate approval.

graduated personal income tax A tax on personal income in which the tax rate increases as income increases; in other words, the tax rate is higher for higher income levels.

grants-in-aid Federal cash payments to states and localities for programs they administer.

grants of power The method of limiting the U.S. government by confining its scope of authority to those powers expressly granted in the Constitution.

grassroots lobbying A form of lobbying designed to persuade officials that a group's policy position has strong constituent support.

grassroots party A political party organized at the level of the voters and dependent on their support for its strength.

Great Compromise The agreement of the constitutional convention to create a two-chamber Congress with the House apportioned by population and the Senate apportioned equally by state.

hard money Campaign funds given directly to candidates to spend as they choose.

hierarchical authority A basic principle of bureaucracy that refers to the chain of command within an organization whereby officials and units have control over those below them. (See also **bureaucracy**.)

hired guns The professional consultants who run campaigns for high office.

home rule A device designed to give local governments more leeway in their policies; it allows a local government to design and amend its own charter, subject to the laws and constitution of the state and also subject to veto by the state.

honeymoon period The president's first months in office, a time when Congress, the press, and the public are more inclined than usual to support presidential initiatives.

ideology A consistent pattern of opinion on particular issues that stems from a core belief or set of beliefs.

imminent lawless action test A legal test that says government cannot lawfully suppress advocacy that promotes lawless action unless such advocacy is aimed at producing, and is likely to produce, imminent lawless action.

implied powers The federal government's constitutional authority (through the "necessary and proper" clause) to take action that is not expressly authorized by the Constitution but that supports actions that are so authorized. (See also **"necessary and proper" clause**.)

in-kind benefits Government benefits that are cash equivalents, such as food stamps or rent vouchers. This form of benefit ensures that recipients will use public assistance in a specified way.

inalienable (natural) rights Those rights that persons theoretically possessed in the state of nature, prior to the formation of governments. These rights, including those of life, liberty, and property, are considered inherent and as such are inalienable. Since government is established by people, government has the responsibility to preserve these rights.

independent agencies Bureaucratic agencies that are similar to cabinet departments but usually have a narrower area of responsibility. Each such agency is headed by a presidential appointee who is not a cabinet member. An example is the National Aeronautics and Space Administration. (See also **cabinet departments**.)

individual goods See **private goods**.

individualism The idea that people should take the initiative, be self-sufficient, and accumulate the material advantages necessary for their well-being.

inflation A general increase in the average level of prices of goods and services.

initiative The process by which citizens can place legislative measures on the ballot through signature petitions, and if the measure receives a majority vote, it becomes law.

inside lobbying Direct communication between organized interests and policymakers, which is based on the assumed value of close ("inside") contacts with policymakers.

insurgency A type of military conflict in which irregular soldiers rise up against an established regime.

interest group A set of individuals who are organized to promote a shared political interest. (See also **citizens' groups; economic groups**.)

interest-group liberalism The tendency of public officials to support the policy demands of self-interested groups (as opposed to judging policy demands according to whether they serve a larger conception of "the public interest").

intermediate scrutiny test A test applied by courts to laws that attempt a gender classification. In effect, the test eliminates gender as a legal classification unless it serves an important objective and is substantially related to the objective's achievement.

internationalism The view that the country should involve itself deeply in world affairs. (See also **isolationism**.)

interpretive reporting The style of reporting that aims to explain *why* something is taking place or has occurred.

iron triangle A small and informal but relatively stable group of well-positioned legislators, executives, and lobbyists who seek to promote policies beneficial to a particular interest. (See also **issue network**.)

isolationism The view that the country should deliberately avoid a large role in world affairs and, instead, concentrate on domestic concerns. (See also **internationalism**.)

issue network An informal network of public officials and lobbyists who have a common interest and expertise in a given area and who are brought together temporarily by a proposed policy in that area. (See also **iron triangle**.)

job specialization A basic principle of bureaucracy that holds that the responsibilities of each job position should be explicitly defined and that a precise division of labor within the organization should be maintained. (See also **bureaucracy**.)

judicial activism The doctrine that the courts should develop new legal principles when judges see a compelling need, even if this action places them in conflict with the policy decisions of elected officials. (See also **judicial restraint**.)

judicial conference A closed meeting of the justices of the U.S. Supreme Court to discuss and vote on the cases before them; the justices are not supposed to discuss conference proceedings with outsiders.

judicial restraint The doctrine that the judiciary should be highly respectful of precedent and should defer to the judgment of legislatures. The doctrine claims that the job of judges is to work within the confines of laws set down by tradition and lawmaking majorities. (See also **judicial activism**.)

judicial review The power of courts to decide whether a governmental institution has acted within its constitutional powers and, if not, to declare its action null and void.

jurisdiction (of a congressional committee) The policy area in which a particular congressional committee is authorized to act.

jurisdiction (of a court) A given court's authority to hear cases of a particular kind. Jurisdiction may be original or appellate.

laissez-faire doctrine A classic economic philosophy that holds that owners of businesses should be allowed to make their own production and distribution decisions without government regulation or control.

law (as enacted by Congress) A legislative proposal, or bill, that is passed by both the House and Senate and is either signed or not vetoed by the president. (See also **bill**.)

lawmaking function The authority (of a legislature) to make the laws necessary to carry out the government's powers. (See also **oversight function; representation function**.)

laws (of a court case) The constitutional provisions, legislative statutes, or judicial precedents that apply to a court case.

legitimacy (of election) The idea that the selection of officeholders should be based on the will of the people as reflected through their votes.

legitimacy (of judicial power) The issue of the proper limits of judicial authority in a political system based in part on the principle of majority rule.

libel Publication of material that falsely damages a person's reputation.

liberals Those who favor activist government as an instrument of economic security and redistribution but reject the notion that government should favor a particular set of social values. (See also **conservatives; libertarians; populists**.)

libertarians Those who oppose government as an instrument of traditional values and of economic security. (See also **conservatives; liberals; populists**.)

liberty The principle that individuals should be free to act and think as they choose, provided they do not infringe unreasonably on the rights and freedoms of others.

limited government A government that is subject to strict limits on its lawful uses of powers and hence on its ability to deprive people of their liberty.

lobbying The process by which interest-group members or lobbyists attempt to influence public policy through contacts with public officials.

logrolling The trading of votes between legislators so that each gets what he or she most wants.

majoritarianism The idea that the majority prevails not only in elections but also in determining policy.

majority opinion A Supreme Court opinion that results when a majority of the justices is in agreement on the legal basis of the decision. (See also **concurring opinion; dissenting opinion; plurality opinion**.)

material incentive An economic or other tangible benefit that is used to attract group members.

means test The requirement that applicants for public assistance must demonstrate they are poor in order to be eligible for the assistance. (See also **public assistance**.)

merit (civil service) system An approach to managing the bureaucracy whereby people are appointed to government positions on the basis of either competitive examinations or special qualifications, such as professional training. (See also **executive leadership system; patronage system**.)

metropolitan government Form of local government created when local governments join together and assign it responsibility for a range of activities, such as police and sanitation, so as to reduce the waste and duplication that results when every locality in a densely populated area provides its own services.

military-industrial complex The three components (the military establishment, the industries that manufacture weapons, and the members of Congress from states and districts that depend heavily on the arms industry) that mutually benefit from a high level of defense spending.

momentum A strong showing by a candidate in early presidential nominating contests, which leads to a buildup of public support for the candidate.

monetary policy A tool of economic management, available to government, based on manipulation of the amount of money in circulation. (See also **fiscal policy**.)

money chase A term used to describe the fact that U.S. campaigns are very expensive and that candidates must spend a great amount of time raising funds in order to compete successfully.

multilateralism The situation in which nations act together in response to problems and crises.

multinational corporations Business firms with major operations in more than one country.

multiparty system A system in which three or more political parties have the capacity to gain control of government separately or in coalition.

national debt The total cumulative amount that the U.S. government owes to creditors.

natural rights See **inalienable rights.**

"necessary and proper" clause (elastic clause) The authority granted Congress in Article I, Section 8 of the Constitution "to make all laws which shall be necessary and proper" for the implementation of its enumerated powers. (See also **implied powers.**)

negative government The philosophical belief that government governs best by staying out of people's lives, thus giving individuals as much freedom as possible to determine their own pursuits. (See also **positive government.**)

neutral competence The administrative objective of a merit-based bureaucracy. Such a bureaucracy should be "competent" in the sense that its employees are hired and retained on the basis of their expertise and "neutral" in the sense that it operates by objective standards rather than partisan ones.

New Jersey (small-state) Plan A constitutional proposal for a strengthened Congress but one in which each state would have a single vote, thus granting a small state the same legislative power as a larger state.

news The news media's version of reality, usually with an emphasis on timely, dramatic, and compelling events and developments.

news media See **press.**

nomination The designation of a particular individual to run as a political party's candidate (its "nominee") in the general election.

noneconomic groups See **citizens' groups.**

North-South Compromise The agreement over economic and slavery issues that enabled northern and southern states to settle differences that threatened to defeat the effort to draft a new constitution.

objective journalism A model of news reporting that is based on the communication of "facts" rather than opinions and that is "fair" in that it presents all sides of partisan debate. (See also **partisan press.**)

open party caucuses Meetings at which a party's candidates for nomination are voted on and that are open to all the party's rank-and-file voters who want to attend.

open-seat election An election in which there is no incumbent in the race.

opinion (of a court) A court's written explanation of its decision, which serves to inform others of the legal basis for the decision. Supreme Court opinions are expected to guide the decisions of other courts. (See also **concurring opinion; dissenting opinion; majority opinion; plurality opinion.**)

ordinance A law issued by a local government under authority granted by the state government.

original jurisdiction The authority of a given court to be the first court to hear a case. (See also **appellate jurisdiction.**)

outside lobbying A form of lobbying in which an interest group seeks to use public pressure as a means of influencing officials.

oversight function A supervisory activity of Congress that centers on its constitutional responsibility to see that the executive carries out the laws faithfully and spends appropriations properly. (See also **lawmaking function; representation function.**)

packaging (of a candidate) A term of modern campaigning that refers to the process of recasting a candidate's record into an appealing image.

partisan press Newspapers and other communication media that openly support a political party and whose news in significant part follows the party line. (See also **objective journalism.**)

party caucus A group that consists of a party's members in the House or Senate and that serves to elect the party's leadership, set policy goals, and determine party strategy.

party-centered politics Election campaigns and other political processes in which political parties, not individual candidates, hold most of the initiative and influence. (See also **candidate-centered politics.**)

party coalition The groups and interests that support a political party.

party competition A process in which conflict over society's goals is transformed by political parties into electoral competition in which the winner gains the power to govern.

party discipline The willingness of a party's House or Senate members to act together as a cohesive group and thus exert collective control over legislative action.

party identification The personal sense of loyalty that an individual may feel toward a particular political party. (See also **dealignment; party realignment.**)

party leaders Members of the House and Senate who are chosen by the Democratic or Republican caucus in each chamber to represent the party's interests in that chamber and who give some central direction to the chamber's deliberations.

party organizations The party organizational units at national, state, and local levels; their influence has decreased over time because of many factors. (See also **candidate-centered politics; party-centered politics; primary election.**)

party realignment An election or set of elections in which the electorate responds strongly to an extraordinarily powerful issue that has disrupted the established political order. A realignment has a lasting impact on public policy, popular support for the parties, and the composition of the party coalitions. (See also **dealignment; party identification.**)

patronage system An approach to managing the bureaucracy whereby people are appointed to important government positions as a reward for political services they have rendered and because of their partisan loyalty. (See also **executive**

leadership system; merit system; spoils system.)

pluralism A theory of American politics that holds that society's interests are substantially represented through the activities of groups.

plurality opinion A court opinion that results when a majority of justices agree on a decision in a case but do not agree on the legal basis for the decision. In this instance, the legal position held by most of the justices on the winning side is called a plurality opinion. (See also **concurring opinion; dissenting opinion; majority opinion**.)

police power A term that refers to the broad power of government to regulate the health, safety, and morals of the citizenry.

policy Generally, any broad course of governmental action; more narrowly, a specific government program or initiative.

policy implementation The primary function of the bureaucracy; it refers to the process of carrying out the authoritative decisions of Congress, the president, and the courts.

political action committee (PAC) The organization through which an interest group raises and distributes funds for election purposes. By law, the funds must be raised through voluntary contributions.

political culture The characteristic and deep-seated beliefs of a particular people.

political movements See **social movements**.

political participation A sharing in activities designed to influence public policy and leadership, such as voting, joining political parties and interest groups, writing to elected officials, demonstrating for political causes, and giving money to political candidates.

political party An ongoing coalition of interests joined together to try to get their candidates for public office elected under a common label.

political socialization The learning process by which people acquire their political opinions, beliefs, and values.

political system The various components of American government. The parts are separate, but they connect with each other, affecting how each performs.

politics The process through which society makes its governing decisions.

popular consent The principle that the people are the ultimate source of governing authority.

population In a public opinion poll, the people (for example, the citizens of a nation) whose opinions are being estimated through interviews with a sample of these people.

populists Those who favor activist government as a means of promoting both economic security and traditional values. (See also **conservatives; liberals; libertarians**.)

pork barrel projects Legislative acts whose tangible benefits are targeted at a particular legislator's constituency.

positive government The philosophical belief that government intervention is necessary in order to enhance personal liberty when individuals are buffeted by economic and social forces beyond their control. (See also **negative government**.)

poverty line As defined by the federal government, the annual cost of a thrifty food budget for an urban family of four, multiplied by three to allow also for the cost of housing, clothes, and other expenses. Families below the poverty line are considered poor and are eligible for certain forms of public assistance.

power The ability of persons or institutions to control policy. (See also **authority**.)

precedent A judicial decision in a given case that serves as a rule of thumb for settling subsequent cases of a similar nature; courts are generally expected to follow precedent.

presidential approval rating A measure of the degree to which the public approves or disapproves of the president's performance in office.

presidential commissions Organizations within the bureaucracy that are headed by commissioners appointed by the president. An example is the Commission on Civil Rights.

press (news media) Those print and broadcast organizations that are in the news-reporting business.

primacy tendency The tendency for early learning to become deeply embedded in one's mind.

primary election A form of election in which voters choose a party's nominees for public office. In most states, eligibility to vote in a primary election is limited to voters who designated themselves as party members when they registered to vote. A primary is direct when it results directly in the choice of a nominee; it is indirect (as in the case of presidential primaries) when it results in the selection of delegates who then choose the nominee.

prior restraint Government prohibition of speech or publication before the fact, which is presumed by the courts to be unconstitutional unless the justification for it is overwhelming.

private (individual) goods Benefits that a group (most often an economic group) can grant directly and exclusively to the individual members of the group. (See also **collective goods**.)

probability sample A sample for a poll in which each individual in the population has a known probability of being selected randomly for inclusion in the sample. (See also **public opinion poll**.)

procedural due process The constitutional requirement that government must follow proper legal procedures before a person can be legitimately punished for an alleged offense.

proportional representation A form of representation in which seats in the legislature are allocated proportionally according to each political party's share of the popular vote. This system enables smaller parties

Glossary

to compete successfully for seats. (See also **single-member districts**.)

prospective voting A form of electoral judgment in which voters choose the candidate whose policy promises most closely match their own preferences. (See also **retrospective voting**.)

protectionism The view that the immediate interests of domestic producers should have a higher priority (through, for example, protective tariffs) than should free trade between nations. (See also **free trade**.)

public assistance A term that refers to social welfare programs funded through general tax revenues and available only to the financially needy. Eligibility for such a program is established by a means test. (See also **means test; social insurance**.)

public goods See **collective goods**.

public opinion Those opinions held by ordinary citizens that they express openly.

public opinion poll A device for measuring public opinion whereby a relatively small number of individuals (the sample) is interviewed for the purpose of estimating the opinions of a whole community (the population). (See also **probability sample**.)

public policy A decision of government to pursue a course of action designed to produce an intended outcome.

public representative role A role whereby the media attempt to act as the public's representatives. (See also **common-carrier role; signaler role; watchdog role**.)

purposive incentive An incentive to group participation based on the cause (purpose) that the group seeks to promote.

realignment See **party realignment**.

reapportionment The reallocation of House seats among states after each census as a result of population changes.

reasonable basis test A test applied by courts to laws that treat individuals unequally. Such a law may be deemed constitutional if its purpose is held to be "reasonably" related to a legitimate government interest.

recall The process by which citizens can petition for the removal from office of an elected official before the scheduled completion of his or her term.

redistricting The process of altering election districts in order to make them as nearly equal in population as possible. Redistricting takes place every ten years, after each population census.

referendum The process through which the legislature may submit proposals to the voters for approval or rejection.

registration The practice of placing citizens' names on an official list of voters before they are eligible to exercise their right to vote.

regulation Government restrictions on the economic practices of private firms.

regulatory agencies Administrative units, such as the Federal Communications Commission and the Environmental Protection Agency, that have responsibility for the monitoring and regulation of ongoing economic activities.

representation function The responsibility of a legislature to represent various interests in society. (See also **lawmaking function; oversight function**.)

representative democracy A system in which the people participate in the decision-making process of government not directly but indirectly, through the election of officials to represent their interests.

republic Historically, the form of government in which representative officials met to decide on policy issues. These representatives were expected to serve the public interest but were not subject to the people's immediate control. Today, the term *republic* is used interchangeably with *democracy*.

reserved powers The powers granted to the states under the Tenth Amendment to the Constitution.

retrospective voting A form of electoral judgment in which voters support the incumbent candidate or party when their policies are judged to have succeeded and oppose the candidate or party when their policies are judged to have failed. (See also **prospective voting**.)

rider An amendment to a bill that deals with an issue unrelated to the content of the bill. Riders are permitted in the Senate but not in the House.

sample In a public opinion poll, the relatively small number of individuals interviewed for the purpose of estimating the opinions of an entire population. (See also **public opinion poll**.)

sampling error A measure of the accuracy of a public opinion poll. It is mainly a function of sample size and is usually expressed in percentage terms. (See also **probability sample**.)

selective incorporation The absorption of certain provisions of the Bill of Rights (for example, freedom of speech) into the Fourteenth Amendment so that these rights are protected from infringement by the states.

self-government The principle that the people are the ultimate source and proper beneficiary of governing authority; in practice, a government based on majority rule.

senatorial courtesy The tradition that a U.S. senator from the state in which a federal judicial vacancy has arisen should have a say in the president's nomination of the new judge if the senator is of the same party as the president.

seniority A member of Congress's consecutive years of service on a particular committee.

separated institutions sharing power The principle that, as a way to limit government, its powers should be divided among separate branches, each of which also shares in the power of the others as a means of checking and balancing them. The result is that no one branch can exercise power decisively without the support or acquiescence of the others.

separation of powers The division of the powers of government among separate institutions or branches.

service relationship The situation where party organizations assist candidates for office but have no power to require them to accept or campaign on the party's main policy positions.

service strategy Use of personal staff by members of Congress to perform services for constituents in order to gain their support in future elections.

signaler role The accepted responsibility of the media to alert the public to important developments as soon as possible after they happen or are discovered. (See also **common-carrier role; public representative role; watchdog role**.)

single-issue politics The situation in which separate groups are organized around nearly every conceivable policy issue and press their demands and influence to the utmost.

single-member districts The form of representation in which only the candidate who gets the most votes in a district wins office. (See also **proportional representation**.)

slander Spoken words that falsely damage a person's reputation.

social capital The sum of face-to-face interactions among citizens in a society.

social insurance Social welfare programs based on the "insurance" concept, so that individuals must pay into the program in order to be eligible to receive funds from it. An example is social security for retired people. (See also **public assistance**.)

social (political) movements Active and sustained efforts to achieve social and political change by groups of people who feel that government has not been properly responsive to their concerns.

soft money Campaign contributions that are not subject to legal limits and are given to parties rather than directly to candidates.

sovereignty The ultimate authority to govern within a certain geographical area.

split-ticket voting The pattern of voting in which the individual voter in a given election casts a ballot for one or more candidates of each major party. (See also **straight-ticket voting**.)

spoils system The practice of granting public office to individuals in return for political favors they have rendered. (See also **patronage system**.)

standing committee A permanent congressional committee with responsibility for a particular area of public policy. An example is the Senate Foreign Relations Committee.

state constitutional convention A state convention convened to amend the state constitution or draft a new one.

stewardship theory A theory that argues for a strong, assertive presidential role, with presidential authority limited only at points specifically prohibited by law. (See also **Whig theory**.)

straight-ticket voting The pattern of voting in which the individual voter in a given election supports only candidates of one party. (See also **split-ticket voting**.)

strict scrutiny test A test applied by courts to laws that attempt a racial or ethnic classification. In effect, the strict scrutiny test eliminates race or ethnicity as legal classification when it places minority group members at a disadvantage. (See also **suspect classifications**.)

strong mayor–council system Most common form of municipal government, consisting of the mayor as chief executive and the local council as the legislative body, in which the mayor has veto power and a prescribed responsibility for budgetary and other policy actions.

structuring tendency The tendency of earlier political learning to structure (influence) later learning.

suffrage The right to vote.

sunset law A law containing a provision that fixes a date on which a program will end unless the program's life is extended by Congress.

supply-side economics A form of fiscal policy that emphasizes "supply" (production). An example of supply-side economics would be a tax cut for business. (See also **demand-side economics; fiscal policy**.)

supremacy clause Article VI of the Constitution, which makes national law supreme over state law when the national government is acting within its constitutional limits.

suspect classifications Legal classifications, such as race and national origin, that have invidious discrimination as their purpose and are therefore unconstitutional. (See also **strict scrutiny test**.)

symbolic speech Action (for example, the waving or burning of a flag) for the purpose of expressing a political opinion.

transfer payment A government benefit that is given directly to an individual, as in the case of social security payments to a retiree.

trustees Elected representatives whose obligation is to act in accordance with their own consciences as to what policies are in the best interests of the public. (See also **delegates**.)

two-party system A system in which only two political parties have a real chance of acquiring control of the government.

tyranny of the majority The potential of a majority to monopolize power for its own gain and to the detriment of minority rights and interests.

unitary system A governmental system in which the national government alone has sovereign (ultimate) authority. (See also **confederacy; federalism.**)

unit rule The rule that grants all of a state's electoral votes to the candidate who receives most of the popular votes in the state.

unity The principle that Americans are one people and form an indivisible union.

veto When the president refuses to sign a bill, thereby keeping it from becoming law unless Congress overrides the veto.

Virginia (large-state) Plan A constitutional proposal for a strong Congress with two chambers, both of which would be based on numerical representation, thus granting more power to the larger states.

voter turnout The proportion of persons of voting age who actually vote in a given election.

watchdog role The accepted responsibility of the media to protect the public from deceitful, careless, incompetent, and corrupt officials by standing ready to expose any official who violates accepted legal, ethical, or performance standards. (See also **common-carrier role; public representative role; signaler role.**)

weak mayor–council system Form of municipal government in which the mayor's policymaking powers are less substantial than the council's; the mayor has no power to veto the council's actions and often has no formal role in such activities as budget making.

Whig theory A theory that prevailed in the nineteenth century and held that the presidency was a limited or restrained office whose occupant was confined to expressly granted constitutional authority. (See also **stewardship theory.**)

whistle-blowing An internal check on the bureaucracy whereby individual bureaucrats report instances of mismanagement that they observe.

writ of certiorari Permission granted by a higher court to allow a losing party in a legal case to bring the case before it for a ruling; when such a writ is requested of the U.S. Supreme Court, four of the Court's nine justices must agree to accept the case before it is granted certiorari.

NOTES

CHAPTER 1

1. Alexis de Tocqueville, *Democracy in America (1835–1840)*, ed. J. P. Mayer and A. P. Kerr (Garden City, N.Y.: Doubleday/Anchor, 1969), 640.
2. John Harmon McElroy, *American Beliefs: What Keeps a Big Country and a Diverse People United* (Chicago: I. R. Dec, 1999).
3. Clinton Rossiter, *Conservatism in America* (New York: Vintage, 1962), 67.
4. Tocqueville, *Democracy in America*, 310.
5. James Bryce, *The American Commonwealth*, vol. 2 (New York: Macmillan, 1960), 247–54. First published in 1900.
6. Ralph Barton Perry, *Puritanism and Democracy* (New York: Vanguard, 1944), 124–25; see also Peter D. Salins, *Assimilation, American Style* (New York: Basic Books, 1996); Philip L. Fetzer, *The Ethnic Moment* (Armonk, N.Y.: M. E. Sharpe, 1996).
7. See Gabriel Almond and Sidney Verba, *The Civic Culture* (Boston: Little, Brown, 1965); Richard Merelman, *Making Something of Ourselves: On Culture and Politics in the United States* (Berkeley: University of California Press, 1984).
8. Paul Gagnon, "Why Study History?" *Atlantic Monthly*, November 1988, 47.
9. Louis Hartz, *The Liberal Tradition in America* (New York: Harcourt, Brace, 1953), 12.
10. James Bryce, *The American Commonwealth*, vol. 2 (Indianapolis, Ind.: Liberty Fund, 1995), 1419.
11. Times Mirror Center for the People and the Press survey, 1990–1991.
12. See Douglas Muzzio and Richard Behn, "Thinking About Welfare," *The Public Perspective*, February/March 1995, 35–38; Stanley Feldman and John Zaller, "The Political Culture of Ambivalence: Ideological Responses to the Welfare State," *American Journal of Political Science*, 36 (1992): 268–307.
13. See Seymour Martin Lipset, *American Exceptionalism: A Double-Edged Sword* (New York: Norton, 1996); Claude Levi-Strauss, *Structural Anthropology* (Chicago: University of Chicago Press, 1983); Clifford Geertz, *Myth, Symbol, and Culture* (New York: Norton, 1974).
14. U.S. Census Bureau figures.
15. Quoted in Ralph Volney Harlow, *The Growth of the United States*, vol. 2 (New York: Henry Holt, 1943), 497.
16. Survey of American Political Culture, James Davison Hunter and Carol Bowman, directors, University of Virginia, 1996; Debra L. DeLaet, *U.S. Immigration Policy in an Age of Rights* (Westport, Conn.: Praeger Publishers, 2000).
17. Harold D. Lasswell, *Politics: Who Gets What, When, How* (New York: McGraw-Hill, 1938).
18. Theodore Lowi and Benjamin Ginsberg, *American Government: Freedom and Power* (New York: Norton, 1990), 8.
19. Harold D. Lasswell and Abraham Kaplan, *Power and Society* (New Haven, Conn.: Yale University Press, 1950), 75–77.
20. See Charles H. McIlwain, *Constitutionalism: Ancient and Modern* (Ithaca, N.Y.: Cornell University Press, 1983).
21. Alan S. Rosenbaum, ed., *Constitutionalism: The Philosophical Dimension* (Westport, Conn.: Greenwood, 1988), 4.
22. Tocqueville, *Democracy in America*, ch. 6.
23. Benjamin I. Page and Robert Shapiro, "Effects of Public Opinion on Policy," *American Political Science Review* 77 (March, 1983): 178; see also Urie Bronfenbrenner, Peter McClelland, Stephen Leci, Phyllis Moen, and Elaine Wethington, *The State of Americans* (New York: Free Press, 1996).
24. See Robert Dahl, *Democracy and Its Critics* (New Haven, Conn.: Yale University Press, 1989).
25. C. Wright Mills, *The Power Elite* (New York: Oxford University Press, 1965).
26. G. William Domhoff, *Who Rules America?* (Mountain View, Calif.: Mayfield Publishing, 1998).
27. See, for example, Robert Dahl, *On Democracy* (New Haven, Conn.: Yale University Press, 1998).
28. See H. H. Gerth and C. Wright Mills, eds., *From Max Weber: Essays in Sociology* (New York: Oxford University Press, 1958).
29. Roberto Michels, *Political Parties* (New York: Collier Books, 1962). First published in 1911.
30. David Easton, *The Political System* (New York: Knopf, 1965), 97.
31. E. E. Schattschneider, *Two Hundred Million Americans in Search of a Government* (New York: Holt, Rinehart & Winston, 1969), 42.

CHAPTER 2

1. Quoted in Charles S. Hyneman, "Republican Government in America," in George J. Graham Jr. and Scarlett G. Graham, eds., *Founding Principles of American Government*, rev. ed. (Chatham, N.J.: Chatham House, 1984), 19.
2. Tape of White House Conversation, March 22, 1973.
3. John Locke, *The Two Treatises of Government*, ed. Thomas I. Cook (New York: Hafner, 1947), 159–86, 228–47; see also A. John Simmons, *The Lockean Theory of Rights* (Princeton, N.J.: Princeton University Press, 1994).
4. See Russell Hardin, *Liberalism, Constitutionalism, and Democracy* (New York: Oxford University Press, 1999).
5. George Bancroft, *History of the Formation of the Constitution of the United States of America*, 3d ed., vol. 1 (New York: D. Appleton, 1883), 166.
6. Catherine Drinker Bowen, *Miracle at Philadelphia* (Boston: Little, Brown, 1986), 10.
7. Alfred H. Kelly, Winifred A. Harbison, and Herman Belz, *The American Constitution*, 7th ed. (New York: Norton, 1991), 122.
8. Max Weber, "Politics as a Vocation," in Hans H. Gerth and C. Wright Mills, eds., *From Max Weber: Essays in Sociology* (New York: Oxford University Press, 1958), 78.
9. Gaillard Hunt, ed., *The Writings of James Madison* (New York: Putnam, 1904), 274; Garret Ward Sheldon, *The Political Philosophy of James Madison* (Baltimore: Johns Hopkins University Press, 2000).
10. *Federalist* No. 47.
11. See *Federalist* Nos. 47 and 48.
12. Richard Neustadt, *Presidential Power* (New York: Macmillan, 1986), 33.
13. Henry J. Abraham, *The Judicial Process*, 6th ed. (New York: Oxford University Press, 1993), 320–22.
14. *Marbury v. Madison*, 1 Cranch 137 (1803).
15. Martin Diamond, *The Founding of the Democratic Republic* (Itasca, Ill.: Peacock, 1981), 62–71.
16. *Federalist* No. 10.
17. Leslie F. Goldstein, "Judicial Review and Democratic Theory: Guardian Democracy vs. Representative Democracy," *Western Political Quarterly* 40 (1987): 391–412.
18. Benjamin Ginsberg, *The Consequences of Consent* (New York: Random House, 1982), 22.
19. Robert Dahl, *Pluralist Democracy in the United States* (Chicago: Rand McNally, 1967), 92.
20. This interpretation is taken from Walter Lippmann, *Public Opinion* (New York: Free Press, 1965), 178–79; for a general discussion of the uncertain meaning of the Constitution, see Lawrence H. Tribe and Michael C. Dorf, *On Reading the Constitution* (Cambridge, Mass.: Harvard University Press, 1991).
21. Charles S. Beard, *An Economic Interpretation of the Constitution* (New York, Macmillan, 1941). First published in 1913.

CHAPTER 3

1. Woodrow Wilson, *Constitutional Government in the United States* (New York: Columbia University Press, 1908), 173.
2. Thomas E. Patterson, *The 1996 Election and Other Recent Developments* (New York: McGraw-Hill, 1997), 29.
3. See Samuel Beer, *To Make a Nation: The Rediscovery of American Federalism* (Cambridge, Mass.: The Belknap Press of Harvard University, 1993).
4. *Federalist* No. 2; for the anti-federalist view, see Saul Cornell, *The Other Founders* (Chapel Hill: University of North Carolina Press, 1999).
5. *Federalist* No. 45.
6. *McCulloch v. Maryland*, 4 Wheaton 316 (1819).
7. *Gibbons v. Ogden*, 22 Wheaton 1 (1824).
8. Oliver Wendell Holmes Jr., *Collected Legal Papers* (New York: Harcourt, Brace, 1920), 295–96.
9. John C. Calhoun, *The Works of John C. Calhoun* (New York: Russell & Russell, 1968).
10. See *Cooley v. Board of Wardens of the Port of Philadelphia*, 53 Howard 299 (1851).
11. *Dred Scott v. Sanford*, 19 Howard 393 (1857).
12. *U.S. v. Cruikshank*, 92 U.S. 452 (1876).
13. Edward S. Corwin, *The Constitution and What It Means Today*, 12th ed. (Princeton, N.J.: Princeton University Press, 1958), 248.
14. *Slaughter-House Cases*, 16 Wallace 36 (1873).
15. *Civil Rights Cases*, 109 U.S. 3 (1883).
16. *Plessy v. Ferguson*, 163 U.S. 537 (1896).
17. *Santa Clara County v. Southern Pacific Railroad Co.*, 118 U.S. 394 (1886).
18. *U.S. v. E. C. Knight Co.*, 156 U.S. 1 (1895).
19. *Hammer v. Dagenhart*, 247 U.S. 251 (1918).
20. *Lochner v. New York*, 198 U.S. 25 (1905).
21. Alfred H. Kelly, Winifred A. Harbison, and Herman Belz, *The American Constitution*, 7th ed. (New York: Norton, 1991), 529.
22. James E. Anderson, *The Emergence of the Modern Regulatory State* (Washington, D.C.: Public Affairs Press, 1962), 2–3.
23. *Schechter Poultry Co. v. United States*, 295 U.S. 495 (1935).
24. *NLRB v. Jones and Laughlin Steel*, 301 U.S. 1 (1937).
25. *American Power and Light v. Securities and Exchange Commission*, 329 U.S. 90 (1946); see also Richard A. Maidment, *The Judicial Response to the New Deal: The U.S. Supreme Court and Economic Regulation* (New York: Manchester University Press, 1992).
26. Louis Fisher, *American Constitutional Law* (New York: McGraw-Hill, 1990), 384.

27. Maidment, *Judicial Response to the New Deal.*
28. *Heart of Atlanta Motel v. United States,* 379 U.S. 241 (1964).
29. *Brown v. Board of Education,* 347 U.S. 483 (1954).
30. *Miranda v. Arizona,* 384 U.S. 436 (1966).
31. *Garcia v. San Antonio Transit Authority,* 469 U.S. 528 (1985).
32. See Thomas Anton, *American Federalism and Public Policy* (Philadelphia: Temple University Press, 1989).
33. Morton Grodzins, *The American System: A New View of Government in the United States* (Chicago: Rand McNally, 1966).
34. See Paul A. Peterson, *The Price of Federalism* (Washington, D.C.: The Brookings Institution, 1995).
35. Rosella Levaggi, *Fiscal Federalism and Grants-in-Aid* (Brookfield, Vt.: Avebury, 1991).
36. See David L. Shapiro, *Federalism: A Dialogue* (Evanston, Ill.: Northwestern University Press, 1995). See also Douglas D. Rose, "National and Local Forces in State Politics," *American Political Science Review* 67 (December 1973): 1162–63.
37. Charles Schultze, "Federal Spending: Past, Present and Future," in Henry Owen and Charles Schultze, eds., *Setting National Priorities: The Next Ten Years* (Washington, D.C.: Brookings Institution, 1976), 323–69.
38. Richard Nathan and Fred Doolittle, *Reagan and the States* (Princeton, N.J.: Princeton University Press, 1987); Timothy J. Conlan, *From New Federalism to Devolution* (Washington, D.C.: Brookings Institution, 1998).
39. *Garcia v. San Antonio Authority,* 469 U.S. 528 (1985).
40. *United States v. Lopez,* 514 U.S. 549 (1995).
41. *Printz v. United States,* 117 S. Ct. 2157 (1997).
42. *Kimel v. Florida Board of Regents,* No. 98-791 (2000).
43. *Board of Trustees of the University of Alabama v. Garrett,* No. 99-1240 (2002).
44. *Reno v. Condon,* No. 98-1464 (2000).
45. Andrew W. Dobelstein, *Politics, Economics, and Public Welfare* (Englewood Cliffs, N.J.: Prentice-Hall, 1980), 5.
46. Lloyd A. Free and Hadley Cantril, *The Political Beliefs of Americans* (New York: Simon & Schuster, 1968), 21; see also William Lunch, *The Nationalization of American Politics* (Berkeley: University of California Press, 1987).
47. Survey for the Times Mirror Center for the People and the Press by Princeton Survey Research Associates, July 12–27, 1994; see also Tommy Thompson, *Power to the People* (New York: HarperCollins, 1996).
48. Daniel J. Boorstin, *The Americans: The Democratic Experience* (New York: Vintage Books, 1974).

CHAPTER 4

1. Julian P. Boyd, ed., *The Papers of Thomas Jefferson,* vol. 12 (Princeton, N.J.: Princeton University Press, 1955), 440.
2. *Anderson v. Creighton,* 483 U.S. 635 (1987).
3. *Bose Corp. v. Consumers Union of the United States,* 466 U.S. 485 (1984).
4. *Schenck v. Pro-Choice Network,* No. 95-106 (1997).
5. *Schenck v. United States,* 249 U.S. 47 (1919).
6. *Dennis v. United States,* 341 U.S. 494 (1951).
7. See, for example, *Yates v. United States,* 354 U.S. 298 (1957); *Noto v. United States,* 367 U.S. 290 (1961); *Scales v. United States,* 367 U.S. 203 (1961).
8. *United States v. Carolene Products Co.,* 304 U.S. 144 (1938).
9. *United States v. O'Brien,* 391 U.S. 367 (1968).
10. *United States v. Eichman,* 496 U.S. 310 (1990).
11. *Texas v. Johnson,* 109 S. Ct. 2544 (1989).
12. *Buckley v. Valeo,* 424 U.S. 1 (1976).
13. *New York Times Co. v. United States,* 403 U.S. 713 (1971).
14. *Nebraska Press Assn. v. Stuart,* 427 U.S. 539 (1976).
15. *Barron v. Baltimore,* 7 Peters 243 (1833).
16. *Gitlow v. New York,* 268 U.S. 652 (1925).
17. *Fiske v. Kansas,* 274 U.S. 30 (1927); *Near v. Minnesota,* 283 U.S. 697 (1931); *DeFonge v. Oregon,* 299 U.S. 253 (1937); and *Hamilton v. Regents, U. of California,* 293 U.S. 245 (1934).
18. *Near v. Minnesota,* 283 U.S. 697 (1931).
19. *Brandenburg v. Ohio,* 395 U.S. 444 (1969).
20. *R.A.V. v. St. Paul,* No. 90-7675 (1992).
21. *Wisconsin v. Mitchell,* No. 92-515 (1993).
22. *National Socialist Party v. Skokie,* 432 U.S. 43 (1977).
23. *Forsyth County v. Nationalist Movement,* No. 91-538 (1992).
24. *New York Times Co. v. Sullivan,* 376 U.S. 254 (1964).
25. *Milkovich v. Lorain Journal,* 497 U.S. 1 (1990); see also *Masson v. The New Yorker,* No. 89-1799 (1991).
26. *National Endowment for the Arts v. Finley,* No. 97-371 (1998).
27. *Roth v. U.S.,* 354 U.S. 476 (1957).
28. *Miller v. California,* 413 U.S. 15 (1973).
29. *Barnes v. Glen Theatre,* No. 90-26 (1991).
30. *Stanley v. Georgia,* 394 U.S. 557 (1969).
31. *Osborne v. Ohio,* 495 U.S. 103 (1990).
32. *Denver Area Consortium v. Federal Communications Commission,* No. 95-124 (1996).
33. *Reno v. American Civil Liberties Union,* No. 96-511 (1997).
34. See Michael J. Perry, *Religion in Politics* (New York: Oxford University Press, 1997).
35. *Board of Regents v. Allen,* 392 U.S. 236 (1968).
36. *Lemon v. Kurtzman,* 403 U.S. 602 (1971).
37. Ibid.
38. *Mitchell v. Helms,* No. 98-1648 (2000).
39. *Zelman v. Simmons-Harris,* No. 00-1751 (2002).
40. *Engel v. Vitale,* 370 U.S. 421 (1962).
41. *Abington School District v. Schempp,* 374 U.S. 203 (1963).
42. *Wallace v. Jaffree,* 472 U.S. 38 (1985).

43. *Santa Fe Independent School District v. Does*, No. 99-62 (2000).
44. *Goldman v. Weinberger*, 475 U.S. 503 (1986).
45. *City of Boerne v. Flores*, No. 95-2074 (1997).
46. *Wisconsin v. Yoder*, 406 U.S. 295 (1972); see also *Church of the Lukumi Babalu Aye v. City of Hialeah*, No. 91-948 (1993).
47. *Edwards v. Aguillard*, 487 U.S. 578 (1987).
48. *Griswold v. Connecticut*, 381 U.S. 479 (1965).
49. *Roe v. Wade*, 401 U.S. 113 (1973).
50. *Webster v. Reproductive Health Services*, 492 U.S. 490 (1989); see also *Rust v. Sullivan*, No. 89-1391 (1991).
51. *Planned Parenthood v. Casey*, No. 91-744 (1992).
52. *Stenberg v. Carhart*, No. 99-830 (2000).
53. *Bowers v. Hardwick*, 478 U.S. 186 (1986).
54. *Vacco v. Quill*, 117 S.C. 36 (1996); *Washington v. Glucksberg*, No. 96-110 (1997).
55. *Powell v. Alabama*, 287 U.S. 45 (1932).
56. *Palko v. Connecticut*, 302 U.S. 319 (1937).
57. *Mapp v. Ohio*, 367 U.S. 643 (1961).
58. *Gideon v. Wainwright*, 372 U.S. 335 (1963).
59. *Malloy v. Hogan*, 378 U.S. 1 (1964).
60. *Miranda v. Arizona*, 384 U.S. 436 (1966); see also *Escobedo v. Illinois*, 378 U.S. 478 (1964).
61. *Pointer v. Texas*, 380 U.S. 400 (1965).
62. *Klopfer v. North Carolina*, 386 U.S. 213 (1967).
63. *Duncan v. Louisiana*, 391 U.S. 145 (1968).
64. *Benton v. Maryland*, 395 U.S. 784 (1969).
65. *Dickerson v. United States*, No. 99-5525 (2000).
66. *Michigan v. Sitz*, No. 88-1897 (1990).
67. *Indianapolis v. Edmund*, No. 99-1030 (2001).
68. *Kyllo v. United States*, No. 99-8508 (2001).
69. *Richards v. Wisconsin*, No. 96-5955 (1997).
70. *Ferguson v. Charleston*, No. 99-936 (2001).
71. *Weeks v. United States*, 232 U.S. 383 (1914).
72. *Nix v. Williams*, 467 U.S. 431 (1984); see also *United States v. Leon*, 468 U.S. 897 (1984).
73. *Whren v. United States*, 517 U.S. 806 (1996).
74. *U.S. v. Drayton et al.*, No. 01-631 (2002).
75. *Townsend v. Sain*, 372 U.S. 293 (1963).
76. *Keeney v. Tamaya-Reyes*, No. 90-1859 (1992); see also *Coleman v. Thompson*, No. 89-7662 (1991).
77. *Brecht v. Abrahamson*, No. 91-7358 (1993); see also *McCleskey v. Zant*, No. 89-7024 (1991).
78. *Felker v. Turpin*, No. 95-8836 (1996); but see *Stewart v. Martinez-Villareal*, No. 97-300 (1998).
79. *Williams v. Taylor*, No. 99-6615 (2000).
80. Kurt Heine, "Philadelphia Cops Beat One of Their Own," *Syracuse Herald-American*, January 15, 1995, A13.
81. Richard Sobel, "Anti-Terror Campaign Has Wide Support, Even at Expense of Cherished Rights," *Chicago Tribune*, November 4, 2001, Internet copy.
82. *Wilson v. Seiter*, No. 89-7376 (1991).
83. *Harmelin v. Michigan*, No. 89-7272 (1991).
84. *Atkins v. Virginia*, No. 01-8452 (2002).
85. Sobel, "Anti-Terror Campaign."
86. See Alpheus T. Mason, *The Supreme Court: Palladium of Freedom* (Ann Arbor: University of Michigan Press, 1962); see also Henry J. Abraham, *Freedom and the Court* (New York: Oxford University Press, 1998).

CHAPTER 5

1. Speech of Martin Luther King Jr. in Washington, D.C., August 2, 1963.
2. *Washington Post* wire story, May 14, 1991.
3. Reported on *CBS Evening News*, January 16, 1989.
4. Robert Nisbet, "Public Opinion Versus Popular Opinion," *Public Interest* 41 (1975): 171.
5. See, for example, John R. Howard, *The Shifting Wind* (Albany: State University of New York Press, 1999).
6. The classic analysis of this system of legalized segregation is C. Vann Woodward, *The Strange Career of Jim Crow*, 3d rev. ed. (New York: Oxford University Press, 1974).
7. *Plessy v. Ferguson*, 163 U.S. 537 (1896).
8. See, for example, *Missouri ex rel. Gaines v. Canada*, 305 U.S. 57 (1938).
9. *Brown v. Board of Education of Topeka*, 347 U.S. 483 (1954).
10. See Francis M. Wilhoit, *The Politics of Massive Resistance* (New York: Braziller, 1973).
11. See David J. Garrow, *Protest at Selma: Martin Luther King and the Voting Rights Act of 1965* (New Haven, Conn.: Yale University Press, 1978).
12. See Steven A. Shull, *The President and Civil Rights Policy: Leadership and Change* (Westport, Conn.: Greenwood, 1989).
13. See Sar Levitan, William Johnson, and Robert Taggert, *Still a Dream* (Cambridge, Mass.: Harvard University Press, 1975).
14. See Derrick Bell, *And We Are Not Saved: The Elusive Quest for Racial Justice* (New York: Basic Books, 1987); Robert C. Smith and Richard S. Hzer, *Race, Class, and Culture* (Albany: State University of New York Press, 1992).
15. See Keith Reeves, *Voting Hopes or Fears?* (New York: Oxford University Press, 1997).
16. See Glenna Matthews, *The Rise of Public Women* (New York: Oxford University Press, 1994).
17. *Tinker v. Colwell*, 193 U.S. 473 (1904).
18. For a history of the women's voting rights movement, see Eleanor Flexner, *Century of Struggle*, rev. ed. (Cambridge, Mass.: Harvard University Press, 1975).
19. See Ellen Carol DuBois, *Feminism and Suffrage: The Emergence of an Independent Women's Movement in America, 1848–1869* (Ithaca, N.Y.: Cornell University Press, 1978).
20. See Jane Mansbridge, *Why We Lost the ERA* (Chicago: University of Chicago Press, 1986).
21. See Kathleen Hall Jamieson, *Beyond the Double Bind* (New York: Oxford University Press, 1995).

22. Linda Witt, Karen M. Paget, and Glenna Matthews, *Running as a Woman* (New York: Free Press, 1994).
23. Mary Lou Kendrigan, *Political Equality in a Democratic Society: Women in the United States* (Westport, Conn.: Greenwood, 1984); Timothy Bledsoe and Mary Herring, "Victims of Circumstance: Women in Pursuit of Political Office," *American Political Science Review* 84 (1990): 213–24.
24. *County of Washington v. Gunther*, No. 80-429 (1981).
25. See, however, Sara M. Evans and Barbara Nelson, *Wage Justice* (Chicago: University of Chicago Press, 1989).
26. *Faragher v. City of Boca Raton*, No. 97-282 (1998); *Burlington Industries v. Ellerth*, No. 97-569 (1998).
27. See Joane Nagel, *American Indian Ethnic Renewal* (New York: Oxford University Press, 1996).
28. See Rudulfo O. de la Garza, Louis DeSipio, F. Chris Garcia, John Garcia, and Angelo Falcon, *Latino Voices* (Boulder, Colo.: Westview Press, 1992).
29. *De Canas v. Bica*, 424 U.S. 351 (1976).
30. Nancy Gibbs, "Keep Out, You Tired, You Poor...," *Time*, October 3, 1994, 46–47.
31. James Truslow Adams, *The March of Democracy*, vol. 4 (New York: Scribner's, 1933), 284–85; see also Charles McClain, *In Search of Equality* (Berkeley: University of California Press, 1994).
32. *Lau v. Nichols*, 414 U.S. 563 (1974).
33. *Cedar Rapids v. Garrett F.*, No. 96-1793 (1999).
34. *Sutton v. United Air Lines*, No. 97-1943 (1999); *Murphy v. United Parcel Service*, No. 97-1992 (1999).
35. *Bowers v. Hardwick*, 478 U.S. 186 (1986).
36. *Boy Scouts of America v. Dale*, No. 99-699 (2000).
37. *Romer v. Evans*, 517 U.S. 620 (1996).
38. *Craig v. Boren*, 429 U.S. 190 (1976).
39. *Rostker v. Goldberg*, 453 U.S. 57 (1980).
40. *United States v. Virginia*, No. 94-1941 (1996).
41. Survey by Federal Financial Institutions Examination Council, 1998.
42. U.S. Conference of Mayors Report, 1998.
43. See J. Morgan Kousser, *The Shaping of Southern Politics: Suffrage Restriction and the Establishment of the One-Party South, 1880–1910* (New Haven, Conn.: Yale University Press, 1974).
44. V. O. Key Jr., *Southern Politics* (New York: Knopf, 1949), 495.
45. *Smith v. Allwright*, 321 U.S. 649 (1944).
46. See Bernard Grofman, Lisa Handley, and Richard Niemi, *Minority Representation and the Quest for Voting Equality* (New York: Cambridge University Press, 1992); David Lublin, *The Paradox of Representation* (Princeton, N.J.: Princeton University Press, 1997).
47. *Bush v. Verg*, No. 94-805 (1996); *Shaw v. Hunt*, No. 94-923 (1996); *Muller v. Johnson*, No. 94-631 (1995).
48. *Easley v. Cromartie*, No. 99-1864 (2001).
49. See Terry Eastland, *Ending Affirmative Action* (New York: Basic Books, 1997); but see also Barbara A. Bergmann, *In Defense of Affirmative Action* (New York: Basic Books, 1997).
50. *University of California Regents v. Bakke*, 438 U.S. 265 (1978).
51. *Steelworkers v. Weber*, 443 U.S. 193 (1979); *Fullilove v. Klutnick*, 448 U.S. 448 (1980).
52. *Local No. 28, Sheet Metal Workers v. Equal Employment Opportunity Commission*, 478 U.S. 421 (1986); see also *Local No. 93, International Association of Firefighters v. Cleveland*, 478 U.S. 501 (1986); *Firefighters v. Stotts*, 459 U.S. 969 (1984); *Wygant v. Jackson*, 476 U.S. 238 (1986).
53. See *Wards Cove Packing v. Antonio*, 490 U.S. 642 (1989).
54. *Adarand v. Pena*, No. 94-310 (1995).
55. Jodi Wilgoren, "New Law in Texas Preserves Racial Mix in State's Colleges," *The New York Times*, November 24, 1999, A1.
56. *Swann v. Charlotte-Mecklenburg County Board of Education*, 402 U.S. 1 (1971).
57. See Jennifer Hochschild, *The New American Dilemma* (New Haven, Conn.: Yale University Press, 1984); Michael W. Giles and Thomas G. Walker, "Judicial Policy-Making and Southern School Segregation," *Journal of Politics* 37 (1975): 936.
58. *Milliken v. Bradley*, 418 U.S. 717 (1974).
59. Christopher Jencks and Meredith Phillips, eds., *The Black-White Test Score Gap* (Washington, D.C.: Brookings Institution Press, 1998).
60. Quoted in Megan Twohey, "Desegregation Is Dead," *National Journal* 31, no. 38 (September 18, 1999), 2614.
61. *Board of Education of Oklahoma City v. Dowell*, 498 U.S. 237 (1991).
62. *Missouri v. Jenkins*, 515 U.S. 70 (1995).
63. *Sheff v. O'Neill*, No. 95-2071 (1996).
64. Quoted in Twohey, "Desegregation Is Dead." See also David J. Armor, *Forced Justice: School Desegregation and the Law* (New York: Oxford University Press, 1995).
65. Linda Darling-Hammond, "Black America: Progress and Prospects," Brookings Institution, 1998.
66. Gunnar Myrdal, *An American Dilemma: The Negro Problem and Modern Democracy* (New York: Harper, 1944).

CHAPTER 6

1. V. O. Key Jr., *Public Opinion and American Democracy* (New York: Knopf, 1961), 8.
2. See Benjamin I. Page and Robert Shapiro, *The Rational Public* (Chicago: University of Chicago Press, 1992), 285–88.
3. Jerry L. Yeric and John R. Todd, *Public Opinion*, 3rd ed. (Itasca, Ill.: Peacock, 1996), 3.
4. Elisabeth Noelle-Neumann, *The Spiral of Silence*, 2d ed. (Chicago: University of Chicago Press, 1993), ch. 1.
5. Survey of students of the eight Ivy League schools by Luntz & Weber Research and Strategic Services, for the University of Pennsylvania's Ivy League Study, November 13–December 1, 1992.

6. Sidney Verba and Norman H. Nie, *Participation in America: Political Democracy and Social Equality* (New York: Harper & Row, 1972), 281–84.
7. Steven A. Peterson, *Political Behavior: Patterns in Everyday Life* (Newbury Park, Calif.: Sage Publications, 1990), 28–29.
8. Ibid.
9. M. Kent Jennings and Richard G. Niemi, *Generations and Politics* (Princeton, N.J.: Princeton University Press, 1981); David Easton and Jack Dennis, *Children in the Political System* (New York: McGraw-Hill, 1969).
10. See Robert D. Hess and Judith V. Torney, *The Development of Political Attitudes in Children* (Chicago: Aldine, 1967), 219; Orit Ichilov, *Political Socialization, Citizenship Education, and Democracy* (New York: Teachers College Press, 1990).
11. Thomas E. Patterson, *Out of Order* (New York: Vintage, 1994), ch. 2.
12. Noelle-Neumann, *Spiral of Silence*.
13. See E. J. Dionne, *Why Americans Hate Politics* (New York: Simon & Schuster, 1992); E. J. Dionne, *They Only Look Dead* (New York: Simon & Schuster, 1996); David Frum, *What's Right?* (New York: Basic Books, 1996).
14. John L. Sullivan, James E. Pierson, and George E. Marcus, "Ideological Constraint in the Mass Public," *American Journal of Political Science* 22 (May 1978): 233–49.
15. CNN/USA Today poll conducted by the Gallup Organization, 1997.
16. Philip Converse, "The Nature of Belief Systems in Mass Publics," in David Apter, ed., *Ideology and Discontent* (New York: Free Press, 1965), 206.
17. "The Gender Story," *The Public Perspective,* August/September 1996, 1–33; Sue Tolleson Rinehart, *Gender Consciousness and Politics* (New York: Routledge, 1992).
18. Susan A. MacManus, *Young v. Old: Generational Combat in the Twenty-first Century* (Boulder, Colo.: Westview Press, 1996).
19. See Angus Campbell, Philip Converse, Warren Miller, and Donald Stokes, *The American Voter* (New York: Wiley, 1960), chs. 3 and 4.
20. Martin P. Wattenberg, *The Decline of American Political Parties, 1952–1996* (Cambridge, Mass.: Harvard University Press, 1998).
21. See E. E. Schattschneider, *The Semisovereign People* (New York: Holt, Rinehart & Winston, 1980), ch. 8.
22. See William Domhoff, *The Power Elite and the State* (New York: Aldine de Gruyter, 1990).
23. Benjamin I. Page and Robert Y. Shapiro, "Effects of Public Opinion on Policy," *American Political Science Review* 77 (March 1983): 178; see also Richard Sobel, *The Impact of Public Opinion on U.S. Foreign Policy* (New York: Oxford University Press, 2001).
24. See Benjamin Ginsberg, *The Consequences of Consent* (New York: Random House, 1982); but also see Samuel L. Popkin, *The Reasoning Voter: Communication and Persuasion in Presidential Campaigns* (Chicago: University of Chicago Press, 1991).
25. See Paul Brace and Barbara Hinckley, *Follow the Leader: Opinion Polls and Modern Presidents* (New York: Basic Books, 1992).

CHAPTER 7

1. Walter Lippmann, *Public Opinion* (New York: Free Press, 1965), 36.
2. Sidney Verba, Kay Schlozman, and Henry Brady, *Voice and Equality* (Cambridge, Mass.: Harvard University Press, 1995); see also Steven J. Rosenstone and John Mark Hansen, *Mobilization, Participation, and Democracy in America* (New York: Macmillan, 1993).
3. Quoted in Ralph Volney Harlow, *The Growth of the United States* (New York: Henry Holt, 1943), 312.
4. See William H. Flanigan and Nancy Zingale, *The Political Behavior of the American Electorate,* 10th ed. (Washington, D.C.: Congressional Quarterly Press, 2002), 24–26.
5. Example from Gus Tyler, "One Cheer for the Democrats," *New Leader,* November 3, 1986, 6.
6. Turnout figures provided by Washington, D.C., embassies of the respective countries, 2000.
7. See Stanley Kelley Jr., Richard E. Ayres, and William G. Bowen, "Registration and Voting: Putting First Things First," *American Political Science Review* 61 (June 1967): 359–79.
8. Ivor Crewe, "Electoral Participation," in David Butler, Howard R. Penniman, and Austin Ranney, eds., *Democracy at the Polls* (Washington, D.C.: American Enterprise Institute, 1981), 249.
9. Vanishing Voter Project, Joan Shorenstein Center on Press, Politics, and Public Policy, Harvard University, May 2000.
10. Crewe, "Electoral Participation," 251–53.
11. Malcom Jewell and David Olson, *American State Politics and Elections* (Homewood, Ill.: Irwin Press, 1978), 50.
12. A. Karnig and B. Walter, "Municipal Elections," in *Municipal Yearbook, 1977* (Washington, D.C.: International City Management Assn., 1977).
13. Richard Boyd, "Decline of U.S. Voter Turnout," *American Politics Quarterly* 9 (April 1981): 142.
14. Austin Ranney, "Candidate Selection," in Butler, Penniman, and Ranney, *Democracy at the Polls,* 88.
15. Ruy A. Teixeira, *The Disappearing American Voter* (Washington, D.C.: Brookings Institution, 1992).
16. Crewe, "Electoral Participation," 251–53.
17. G. Bingham Powell, "Voting Turnout in Thirty Democracies," in Richard Rose, ed., *Electoral Participation: A Comparative Analysis* (Beverly Hills, Calif.: Sage, 1980), 6.
18. M. Margaret Conway, Gertrude A. Steuernagel, and David Ahern, *Women and Political Participation:*

Cultural Change in the Political Arena (Washington, D.C.: Congressional Quarterly Press, 1997); see also Nancy Burns, Kay Lehman Schlozman, and Sidney Verba, *The Private Roots of Public Action* (Cambridge, Mass.: Harvard University Press, 2001).
19. See, for example, Norman H. Nie, G. Bingham Powell, and Kenneth Prewitt, "Social Structure and Political Participation," *American Political Science Review* 63 (September 1969).
20. See Joseph Nye, David King, and Philip Zelikow, *Why People Don't Trust Government* (Cambridge, Mass.: Harvard University Press, 1997).
21. Ibid.
22. John M. Strate, Charles J. Parrish, Charles D. Elder, and Coit Ford III, "Life Span Civic Development and Voting Participation," *American Political Science Review* 83 (June 1989): 443–65.
23. M. Margaret Conway, *Political Participation in the United States*, 3d ed. (Washington, D.C.: Congressional Quarterly Press, 2000), 23–25.
24. Verba, Schlozman, and Brady, *Voice and Equality;* Jan Leighley, *Strength in Numbers* (Princeton, N.J.: Princeton University Press, 2001).
25. Vanishing Voter Project.
26. Sidney Verba and Norman Nie, *Participation in America* (New York: Harper & Row, 1972), 340.
27. But see Jeffrey Stonecash, *Class and Party in American Politics* (Boulder, Colo.: Westview Press, 2000).
28. Vanishing Voter Survey, 2000.
29. Michael Delli Carpini and Scott Keeter, *What Americans Know About Politics* (New Haven, Conn.: Yale University Press, 1996).
30. Thomas E. Patterson, *The Mass Media Election* (New York: Praeger, 1980), chs. 7–10.
31. Thomas E. Patterson, *The Vanishing Voter* (New York: Knopf, 2002), ch. 4.
32. Gallup Reports, 1936–2000.
33. V. O. Key Jr., *The Responsible Electorate* (Cambridge, Mass.: Belknap Press of Harvard University Press, 1966), ch. 1.
34. Verba, Schlozman, and Brady, *Voice and Equality.*
35. Joseph Schumpeter, *Capitalism, Socialism, and Democracy* (New York: Harper Torchbooks, 1950), 269.
36. W. Russell Neuman, *The Paradox of Mass Politics* (Cambridge, Mass.: Harvard University Press, 1986), 176.
37. Samuel H. Barnes et al., eds., *Political Action* (Beverly Hills, Calif.: Sage, 1979), 541–42.
38. Russell J. Dalton, *Citizen Politics in Western Democracies*, 3d ed. (Chatham, N.J.: Chatham House, 1996), 43.
39. Robert Putnam, *Bowling Alone* (New York: Simon & Schuster, 2000).
40. For example, interest group membership has risen.
41. Patterson, *Vanishing Voter,* chs. 1, 4.
42. Survey of Pew Center for People and the Press, 1990.
43. See Benjamin Ginsberg, *The Consequences of Consent* (New York: Random House, 1982), ch. 2.
44. See Laura R. Woliver, *From Outrage to Action* (Urbana: University of Illinois Press, 1993).
45. Lee Bruce Stokes, "New Players in the Trade Game," *National Journal,* December 18, 1999, 3630.
46. Dalton, *Citizen Politics in Western Democracies,* 38.
47. Ibid., 68.
48. Ronald Inglehart, "Post-Materialism in an Environment of Insecurity," *American Political Science Review* 75 (1981): 880–900; Edward N. Mueller and Mitchell A. Seligson, "Inequality and Insurgency," *American Political Science Review* 81 (1987): 425–51.
49. William Watts and Lloyd A. Free, eds., *The State of the Nation* (New York: University Books, Potomac Associates, 1967), 97.
50. Harry Holloway with John George, *Public Opinion,* 2d ed. (New York: St. Martin's Press, 1986), 157.
51. Robert E. Lane, "Market Justice, Political Justice," *American Political Science Review* 80 (1986): 383; see also Jennifer Nedelsky, *Private Property and the Limits of American Constitutionalism* (New York: Oxford University Press, 1990).
52. Verba and Nie, *Participation in America,* 131.
53. See Verba and Nie, *Participation in America,* 332; V. O. Key Jr., *Southern Politics* (New York: Vintage Books, 1949), 527; Lawrence Jacobs and Robert Shapiro, *Politicians Don't Pander* (Chicago: University of Chicago Press, 2000).

CHAPTER 8

1. E. E. Schattschneider, *Party Government* (New York: Rinehart, 1942), 1.
2. E. E. Schattschneider, *The Semisovereign People: A Realist's View of Democracy in America* (New York: Holt, Rinehart & Winston, 1961), 140.
3. See John Aldrich, *Why Parties? The Origin and Transformation of Political Parties in America* (Chicago: University of Chicago Press, 1995).
4. L. Sandy Maisel, *Parties and Elections in America,* 3d ed. (Latham, Md.: Rowman and Littlefield, 1999), 27.
5. Thomas E. Patterson, *The Vanishing Voter* (New York: Knopf, 2002), ch. 2.
6. Aldrich, *Why Parties?*
7. See Richard P. McCormick, *The Second American Party System: Party Formation in the Jacksonian Era* (Chapel Hill: University of North Carolina Press, 1966).
8. Alexis de Tocqueville, *Democracy in America (1835–1840),* ed. J. P. Mayer and A. P. Kerr (Garden City, N.Y.: Doubleday/Anchor, 1969), 60.
9. Aldrich, *Why Parties?* 151.
10. See Kristi Andersen, *The Creation of a Democratic Majority, 1928–1936* (Chicago: University of Chicago Press, 1979).

11. See Kevin Phillips, *The Emerging Republican Majority* (New Rochelle, N.Y.: Arlington House, 1969).
12. See Harold W. Stanley, "Southern Partisan Changes: Dealignment, Realignment or Both?" *Journal of Politics* 50 (1988): 64–88; Earl Black and Merle Black, *Politics and Society in the South* (Cambridge, Mass.: Harvard University Press, 1987); Robert H. Swansbrough and David M. Brodsky, eds., *The South's New Politics: Realignment and Dealignment* (Columbia: University of South Carolina Press, 1988); Dewey L. Grantham, *The Life and Death of the Solid South* (Lexington: University of Kentucky Press, 1988).
13. William H. Flanigan and Nancy Zingale, *Political Behavior of the American Electorate*, 9th ed. (Washington, D.C.: Congressional Quarterly Press, 1998), 58–63.
14. Frederick G. Dutton, *Changing Sources of Power* (New York: McGraw-Hill, 1971), ch. 6.
15. See E. J. Dionne Jr., *Why Americans Hate Politics* (New York: Simon & Schuster, 1992).
16. The classic account of the relationship of electoral and party systems is Maurice Duverger, *Political Parties* (New York: Wiley, 1954), bk. 2, ch. 1; see also Arend Lijphardt, *Electoral Systems and Party Systems* (New York: Oxford University Press, 1994).
17. Clinton Rossiter, *Parties and Politics in America* (Ithaca, N.Y.: Cornell University Press, 1960), 11.
18. Nancy Gibbs and Michael Duffy, "Fall of the House of Newt," *Time*, November 16, 1998, 47.
19. Gerald M. Pomper, *Passions and Interests: Political Party Concepts of American Democracy* (Lawrence: University of Kansas Press, 1992), ch. 1.
20. Ibid.
21. John F. Bibby, *Politics, Parties, and Elections in America*, 5th ed. (Belmont, Calif.: Wadsworth, 2002), 275–83.
22. Steven J. Rosenstone, Roy L. Behr, and Edward H. Lazarus, *Third Parties in America*, 2d ed. (Princeton, N.J.: Princeton University Press, 1996).
23. Daniel A. Mazmanian, *Third Parties in Presidential Elections* (Washington, D.C.: Brookings Institution, 1984), 143–44.
24. See Lawrence Goodwyn, *The Populist Movement* (New York: Oxford University Press, 1978).
25. Anthony King, *Running Scared* (New York: Free Press, 1997).
26. See Alan Ehrenhalt, *The United States of Ambition* (New York: Times Books, 1991).
27. See Paul S. Herrnson and John C. Green, eds., *Responsible Partisanship* (Lawrence: University Press of Kansas, 2003).
28. See James L. Gibson, John P. Frendreis, and Laura L. Vertz, "Party Dynamics in the 1980s: Change in County Party Organizational Strength, 1980–1984" *American Journal of Political Science* 33 (1989): 67–90.
29. James L. Gibson, Cornelius Cotter, John Bibby, and Robert Huckshorn, "Assessing Party Organizational Strength," *American Journal of Political Science* 27 (May 1983): 200.
30. See Sarah McCally Morehouse, "Money Versus Party Effort," *American Journal of Political Science* 34 (1990): 706–24.
31. David Adamany, "Political Parties in the 1980s," in Michael J. Malbin, ed., *Money and Politics in the United States* (Chatham, N.J.: Chatham House, 1984), 114.
32. Joseph Napolitan, *The Election Game and How to Win It* (New York: Doubleday, 1972).
33. David B. Magleby and Candice J. Nelson, *The Money Chase: Congressional Campaign Finance Reform* (Washington, D.C.: Brookings Institution, 1990).
34. John F. Bibby, *Politics, Parties, and Elections in America*, 3d ed. (Chicago: Nelson-Hall, 1996), 205.
35. Federal Elections Commission data, 2002.
36. David Chagall, *The New King-Makers* (New York: Harcourt Brace Jovanovich, 1981).
37. Michael W. Traugott and Paul J. Lavrakas, *The Voters' Guide to Election Polls* (Chatham, N.J.: Chatham House, 1996).
38. Kiku Adatto, "Sound Bite Democracy," Joan Shorenstein Center on the Press, Politics, and Public Policy, Research Paper R-2, Harvard University, Cambridge, Mass., June 1990.
39. Darrell M. West, *Air Wars: Television Advertising in Election Campaigns, 1952–2000* (Washington, D.C.: Congressional Quarterly Press, 2001), 140–46.
40. Ibid.
41. Stephen Ansolabehere and Shanto Iyengar, *Going Negative* (New York: Free Press, 1995), ch. 5.
42. West, *Air Wars*, 12.
43. Ibid., 143.
44. Thomas E. Patterson, *Out of Order* (New York: Vintage, 1994), ch. 2.
45. Associated Press Wire, "Candidates Try E-mail Route to Election: Presidential Hopefuls All Using Web Sites," November 26, 1999.
46. David E. Price, *Bringing Back the Parties* (Washington, D.C.: Congressional Quarterly Press, 1984), 116.
47. See James P. Pfiffner, *The Modern Presidency* (New York: St. Martin's Press, 1994), ch. 6.

CHAPTER 9

1. E. E. Schattschneider, *The Semisovereign People: A Realist's View of Democracy in America* (New York: Holt, Rinehart & Winston, 1960), 35.
2. Quoted in Norman J. Ornstein and Shirley Elder, *Interest Groups, Lobbying, and Policymaking* (Washington, D.C.: Congressional Quarterly Press, 1978), 11.
3. Alexis de Tocqueville, *Democracy in America (1835–1840)*, ed. J. P. Mayer and A. P. Kerr (Garden City, N.Y.: Doubleday/Anchor, 1969), bk. 2, ch. 4.

4. Mancur Olson, *The Logic of Collective Action*, rev. ed. (Cambridge, Mass.: Harvard University Press, 1971), 147.
5. See Jack L. Walker, *Mobilizing Interest Groups in America* (Ann Arbor: University of Michigan Press, 1991).
6. See Lawrence Rothenberg, *Linking Citizens to Government: Interest Group Politics at Common Cause* (New York: Cambridge University Press, 1992); Jeffrey M. Berry, *The New Liberalism: The Rising Power of Citizen Groups* (Washington, D.C.: Brookings Institution Press, 1999).
7. Olson, *Logic of Collective Action*, 64.
8. Christopher J. Bosso, "The Color of Money: Environmental Groups and the Pathologies of Fund Raising," in Allan J. Cigler and Burdett Loomis, *Interest Group Politics*, 4th ed. (Washington, D.C.: Congressional Quarterly Press, 1995), 101–3.
9. Kay Lehman Schlozman and John T. Tierney, *Organized Interests and American Democracy* (New York: Harper & Row, 1986), 54; see also Ronald J. Hrebenar and Ruth K. Scott, *Interest Group Politics in America* (Englewood Cliffs, N.J.: Prentice-Hall, 1990), 167.
10. See Beverly A. Cigler, "Not Just Another Special Interest: Intergovernmental Representation," in Cigler and Loomis, *Interest Group Politics*, 4th ed., 131–53.
11. Ornstein and Elder, *Interest Groups, Lobbying, and Policymaking*, 82–86.
12. See John Mark Hansen, *Gaining Access* (Chicago: Chicago University Press, 1991).
13. Robert H. Salisbury and Paul Johnson, "Who You Know Versus What You Know," *American Journal of Political Science* 33 (February 1989): 175–95; see also William P. Browne, *Cultivating Congress* (Lawrence: University Press of Kansas, 1995).
14. Ornstein and Elder, *Interest Groups, Lobbying, and Policymaking*, 70.
15. Quoted in ibid., 77.
16. See Marver Bernstein, *Regulating Business by Independent Commission* (Princeton, N.J.: Princeton University Press, 1955).
17. Paul J. Quirk, *Industry Influence in Federal Regulatory Agencies* (Princeton, N.J.: Princeton University Press, 1981).
18. John E. Chubb, *Interest Groups and the Bureaucracy: The Politics of Energy* (Stanford, Calif.: Stanford University Press, 1983), 200–201.
19. Charles T. Goodsell, *The Case for Bureaucracy*, 3rd ed. (Chatham, N.J.: Chatham House, 1994), 55–60.
20. Lee Epstein and C. K. Rowland, "Interest Groups in the Courts," *American Political Science Review* 85 (1991): 205–17.
21. See Hansen, *Gaining Access*; but, see Browne, *Cultivating Congress*.
22. Hugh Heclo, "Issue Networks and the Executive Establishment," in Anthony King, ed., *The New American Political System* (Washington, D.C.: American Enterprise Institute, 1978), 87–124.
23. Ornstein and Elder, *Interest Groups, Lobbying, and Policymaking*, 88–93.
24. Ernest Wittenberg and Elisabeth Wittenberg, *How to Win in Washington* (Cambridge, Mass.: Blackwell, 1989), 81.
25. Quoted in Mark Green, "Political PAC-Man," *The New Republic*, December 13, 1982, 20; see also Frank J. Sorauf, *Inside Campaign Finance* (New Haven, Conn.: Yale University Press, 1992).
26. Quoted in Larry Sabato, *PAC Power: Inside the World of Political Action Committees* (New York: Norton, 1984), 72.
27. Federal Elections Commission, 2002.
28. See Michael J. Malbin, "Of Mountains and Molehills," in Michael J. Malbin, *Parties, Interest Groups, and Campaign Finance Laws* (Washington, D.C.: American Enterprise Institute, 1981), 157–77.
29. See Dan Clawson, Alan Neustadtl, and Denise Scott, *Money Talks* (New York: Basic Books, 1992); Thomas L. Gatz, *Improper Influence* (Ann Arbor: University of Michigan Press, 1996).
30. V. O. Key Jr., *Public Opinion and American Democracy* (New York: Knopf, 1961), 428; Gene M. Grossman and Elhanan Helpman, *Interest Groups and Trade Policy* (Princeton, N.J.: Princeton University Press, 2002).
31. See Robert Dahl, *Who Governs?* (New Haven, Conn.: Yale University Press, 1961).
32. Walker, *Mobilizing Interest Groups in America*, 112.
33. Theodore J. Lowi, *The End of Liberalism: The Second Republic of the United States* (New York: Norton, 1979).
34. See William Domhoff, *The Power Elite and the State* (New York: Aldine de Gruyter, 1990).
35. See Rothenberg, *Linking Citizens to Government*.
36. Benjamin Ginsberg, *The Consequences of Consent* (New York: Random House, 1982), 214.
37. Jonathan Rauch, *Demosclerosis: The Silent Killer of American Government* (New York: Times Books, 1994).

CHAPTER 10

1. Theodore H. White, *The Making of the President, 1972* (New York: Bantam Books, 1973), 327.
2. See Richard Davis, *The Press and American Politics*, 2d ed. (Upper Saddle River, N.J.: Prentice Hall, 1996), 24–27.
3. Comment at the annual meeting of the American Association of Political Consultants, Washington, D.C., 1977.
4. Thomas Jefferson to Colonel Edward Carrington, January 16, 1787.
5. Frank Luther Mott, *American Journalism, a History: 1690–1960* (New York: Macmillan, 1962), 114–15.
6. Culver H. Smith, *The Press, Politics, and Patronage* (Athens: University of Georgia Press, 1977), 163–68.

7. Doris A. Graber, *Mass Media and American Politics*, 5th ed. (Washington, D.C.: Congressional Quarterly Press, 1997), 36; Mark Wahlgren Summers, *The Press Gang* (Chapel Hill: University of North Carolina Press, 1994).
8. See Michael Schudson, *Discovering the News* (New York: Basic Books, 1978).
9. Mott, *American Journalism*, 122–23, 220–27.
10. Commission on Freedom of the Press, *A Free and Responsible Press* (Chicago: University of Chicago Press, 1974), 62–63.
11. Mott, *American Journalism*, 220–27, 241, 243.
12. Edwin Emery, *The Press and America: An Interpretive History of the Mass Media* (Englewood Cliffs, N.J.: Prentice-Hall, 1977), 350.
13. Quoted in Mott, *American Journalism*, 529.
14. See Dean Alger, *The Media and Politics*, 2d ed. (Belmont, Calif.: Wadsworth, 1996), 122–23.
15. Quoted in David Halberstam, *The Powers That Be* (New York: Knopf, 1979), 208–9.
16. Leo Bogart, *The Age of Television* (New York: Unger, 1956), 213.
17. Theodore H. White, *America in Search of Itself: The Making of the President, 1956–1980* (New York: Harper & Row, 1982), 172–73.
18. Quoted in Michael Robinson and Margaret Sheehan, *Over the Wire and on TV* (New York: Russell Sage Foundation, 1983), 226.
19. William Cole, ed. *The Most of A. J. Liebling* (New York: Simon, 1963), 7.
20. Figures from *Standard Rate and Data Service and Electronic Media*, various dates.
21. Ibid.
22. Graber, *Mass Media and American Politics*, 36.
23. See Ben Bagdikian, *The Media Monopoly*, 6th ed. (Boston: Beacon, 2000).
24. Edward J. Epstein, *News from Nowhere: Television and the News* (New York: Random House, 1973), 37.
25. White, *The Making of the President, 1972*, 346–48.
26. See John Chancellor and Walter R. Mears, *The News Business* (New York: Harper & Row, 1983).
27. David L. Paletz and Robert M. Entman, *Media Power Politics* (New York: Free Press, 1981), 16.
28. James David Barber, "Characters in the Campaign: The Literary Problem," in James David Barber, ed., *Race for the Presidency* (Englewood Cliffs, N.J.: Prentice-Hall, 1978), 114–15.
29. See Timothy E. Cook, *Governing with the News* (Chicago: University of Chicago Press, 1997); Bartholomew Sparrow, *Uncertain Guardians* (Baltimore: Johns Hopkins University Press, 1999).
30. Dean Alger, *Megamedia* (Lanham, Md.: Rowman & Littlefield, 1998).
31. Ibid., 13–14; see also Leonard Downie Jr. and Robert G. Kaiser, *The News About the News: American Journalism in Peril* (New York: Knopf, 2002).
32. Study for Committee of Concerned Journalists, 2000.
33. Walter Lippmann, *Public Opinion* (New York: Free Press, 1965), 214. First published in 1922.
34. See Kenneth T. Walsh, *Feeding the Beast* (New York: Free Press, 1996).
35. Donald Shaw and Maxwell McCombs, *The Emergence of American Political Issues: The Agenda-Setting Function of the Press* (St. Paul, Minn.: West Publishing, 1977).
36. See, for example, F. Cook, T. Tyler, E. Goetz, M. Gordon, D. Protess, D. Leff, and H. Molotch, "Media and Agenda Setting: Effects on the Public, Interest Group Leaders, Policy Makers, and Policy," *Public Opinion Quarterly* 47 (1983): 16–35.
37. Bernard C. Cohen, *The Press and Foreign Policy* (Princeton, N.J.: Princeton University Press, 1963), 13.
38. See John Anthony Maltese, *Spin Control* (Chapel Hill: University of North Carolina Press, 1994); Howard Kurtz, *Spin Cycle* (New York: Free Press, 1998).
39. Kiku Adatto, "Sound Bite Democracy," Joan Shorenstein Center on the Press, Politics, and Public Policy, Research Paper R-2, Harvard University, Cambridge, Mass., June 1990.
40. See James Fallows, *Breaking the News* (New York: Pantheon, 1996).
41. Thomas E. Patterson, *Out of Order* (New York: Vintage, 1994), ch. 3.
42. Thomas E. Patterson, "Bad News, Bad Governance," *ANNALS* 546 (July 1996): 97–108; Larry J. Sabato, Mark Stencel, and S. Robert Lichter, *Peep Show: Media and Politics in the Age of Scandal* (Latham, Md.: Rowman and Littlefield, 2000).
43. Data from Center for Media and Public Affairs, Washington, D.C., 1996.
44. Quoted in Doreen Carvajal, "For News Media, Some Introspection," *The New York Times*, April 5, 1998, 28.
45. Quoted in Max Kampelman, "The Power of the Press," *Policy Review* 6 (1978): 19.
46. Ibid.
47. James Reston, "End of the Tunnel," *The New York Times*, April 30, 1975, 41.
48. Quoted in Epstein, *News from Nowhere*, ix.
49. "Internal Affairs: TV News Coverage of the White House Sex Scandals." *Media Monitor*, Center for Media and Public Affairs, Washington, D.C., March/April 1998.
50. Lippmann, *Public Opinion*, 221.
51. Bill Kovach and Tom Rosenstiel, *Warp Speed* (New York: The Century Foundation Press, 1999).

CHAPTER 11

1. Roger H. Davidson and Walter J. Oleszek, *Congress and Its Members*, 2d ed. (Washington, D.C.: Congressional Quarterly Press, 1985), 7.

2. See Paul S. Herrnson, *Congressional Elections: Campaigning at Home and in Washington* (Washington, D.C.: Congressional Quarterly Press, 1995).
3. See Gary C. Jacobson, *The Politics of Congressional Elections*, 5th ed. (New York: Longman, 2001).
4. See Jonathan S. Krasno, *Challenges, Competition, and Reelection* (New Haven, Conn.: Yale University Press, 1995).
5. David R. Mayhew, *Congress: The Electoral Connection* (New Haven, Conn.: Yale University Press, 1974), 16; Richard F. Fenno Jr., *Home Style: House Members in Their Districts* (Boston: Little, Brown, 1978), 167.
6. *Congressional Quarterly Weekly Report*, various dates.
7. Lawrence C. Dodd, "A Theory of Congressional Cycles," in Gerald Wright, Leroy Rieselbach, and Lawrence C. Dodd, *Congress and Policy Change* (New York: Agathon, 1986).
8. Bruce Cain, John Ferejohn, and Morris P. Fiorina, *The Personal Vote* (Cambridge, Mass.: Harvard University Press, 1987).
9. Information provided by Clerk of the House.
10. Harold W. Stanley and Richard G. Niemi, *Vital Statistics on American Politics*, 5th ed. (Washington, D.C.: Congressional Quarterly Press, 1995), 217.
11. See Diana Evans Yiannakis, "House Members' Communication Styles," *Journal of Politics* 44 (November 1982): 1049–73.
12. *Congressional Quarterly Guide to Congress*, 3d ed. (Washington, D.C.: Congressional Quarterly Press, 1982), 666; see also Frank J. Sorauf, *Inside Campaign Finance* (New Haven, Conn.: Yale University Press, 1992), 67, 86.
13. Federal Elections Commission data, 2002.
14. Federal Elections Commission, 2002.
15. Jennifer Babson and Kelly St. John, "Momentum Helps GOP Collect Record Amounts from PACs," *Congressional Quarterly Weekly Report*, December 3, 1994, 3456.
16. See Jacobson, *Politics of Congressional Elections*.
17. Gary C. Jacobson, *The Electoral Origins of Divided Government* (Boulder, Colo.: Westview Press, 1990).
18. Quoted in "A Tale of Myths and Measures: Who Is Truly Vulnerable?" *Congressional Quarterly Weekly Report*, December 4, 1993, 7; see also Dennis F. Thompson, *Ethics in Congress* (Washington, D.C.: Brookings Institution Press, 1995).
19. James E. Campbell, *The Presidential Pulse of Congressional Elections* (Lexington: University Press of Kentucky, 1993).
20. Linda L. Fowler and Robert D. McClure, *Political Ambition* (New Haven, Conn.: Yale University Press, 1989); see also Jonathan S. Krasno and Donald Philip Green, "Preempting Quality Challengers in House Elections," *Journal of Politics* 50 (November 1988): 878.
21. Thomas Kazee, "Recruiting Challengers in U.S. House Elections," *Legislative Studies Quarterly* (August 1983): 469–80.
22. Keith R. Poole and Howard Rosenthal, "Patterns of Congressional Voting," *American Journal of Political Science*, 35 (February 1991): 228.
23. See Linda L. Fowler, *Candidates, Congress, and the American Democracy* (Ann Arbor: University of Michigan Press, 1994).
24. *Congressional Quarterly Weekly Report*, various dates.
25. Linda Witt, Karen M. Paget, and Glenna Matthews, *Running as a Woman: Gender and Power in American Politics* (New York: Free Press, 1993); see also Sue Thomas, *How Women Legislate* (New York: Oxford University Press, 1994).
26. Ronald M. Peters Jr., *The American Speakership* (Baltimore: Johns Hopkins University Press, 1990).
27. See Barbara Sinclair, *Legislators, Leaders, and Lawmaking* (Baltimore, Md.: Johns Hopkins University Press, 1995).
28. Fred R. Harris, *Deadlock or Decision: The U.S. Senate and the Rise of National Politics* (New York: Oxford University Press, 1993), 182.
29. See, for example, Donald Matthews, *U.S. Senators and Their World* (Chapel Hill: University of North Carolina Press, 1960).
30. See Barbara Sinclair, *Transformation of the U.S. Senate* (Baltimore, Md.: Johns Hopkins University Press, 1989).
31. See Sinclair, *Legislators, Leaders, and Lawmaking*.
32. See David W. Rohde, *Parties and Leaders in the Postreform House* (Chicago: University of Chicago Press, 1991).
33. Jonathan D. Salant, "New Chairman Swing to Right: Freshmen Get Choice Posts," *Congressional Quarterly Weekly Report*, December 10, 1994, 3493.
34. See Steven H. Haeberle, "The Institutionalization of the Subcommittee in the United States House of Representatives," *Journal of Politics* 40 (November 1978): 1054–65.
35. Ibid.
36. David W. Rhode and Kenneth A. Shepsle, "Domestic Committee Assignments in the House of Representatives," *American Political Science Review*, September 1973, 889–905.
37. Steven S. Smith, *The American Congress* (Boston: Houghton Mifflin, 1995), 189–98.
38. See Stephen E. Frantzich and Steven E. Schier, *Congress: Games and Strategies* (Dubuque, Iowa: Brown & Benchmark, 1995), 127.
39. See Gerald S. Strom, *The Logic of Lawmaking* (Baltimore: Johns Hopkins University Press, 1990).
40. See Barbara Sinclair, *Unorthodox Lawmaking: New Legislative Processes in the U.S. Congress* (Washington, D.C.: Congressional Quarterly Press, 1997).
41. See Robert Spitzer, *President and Congress* (New York: McGraw-Hill, 1993).
42. See Paul C. Light, *The President's Agenda*, rev. ed. (Baltimore: Johns Hopkins University Press, 1991).

43. Walter J. Oleszek, *Congressional Procedures and the Policy Process*, 4th ed. (Washington, D.C.: Congressional Quarterly Press, 1995), ch. 10.
44. See Gary Orfield, *Congressional Power: Congress and Social Change* (New York: Harcourt Brace Jovanovich, 1975).
45. James L. Sundquist, "Congress and the President: Enemies or Partners?" in Lawrence C. Dodd and Bruce I. Oppenheimer, eds., *Congress Reconsidered* (New York: Praeger, 1977), 240.
46. See Paul C. Light, *Forging Legislation* (New York: Norton, 1992).
47. Steven S. Smith and Christopher J. Deering, *Committees in Congress*, 3d ed. (Washington, D.C.: Congressional Quarterly Press, 1997), 74.
48. Keith Krehbiel, "Are Congressional Committees Composed of Preference Outliers?" *American Political Science Review* 84 (1990): 149–64; Richard L. Hall and Bernard Grofman, "The Committee Assignment Process and the Conditional Nature of Committee Bias," *American Political Science Review* 84 (1990): 1149–66.
49. See Gary W. Cox and Mathew D. McCubbins, *Legislative Leviathan* (Berkeley: University of California Press, 1993).
50. Eric M. Uslaner, *The Decline of Comity in Congress* (Ann Arbor: University of Michigan Press, 1994).
51. Joel A. Aberbach, *Keeping a Watchful Eye* (Washington, D.C.: Brookings Institution, 1990); William T. Gormley, *Taming the Bureaucracy* (Princeton, N.J.: Princeton University Press, 1989).
52. Mathew D. McCubbins and Thomas Schwartz, "Congressional Oversight Overlooked," *American Journal of Political Science* 2 (February 1984): 165–79.
53. Davidson and Oleszek, *Congress and Its Members*, 2d ed., 7.

CHAPTER 12

1. Woodrow Wilson, *Constitutional Government in the United States* (New York: Columbia University Press, 1908), 67.
2. Charles O. Jones, *Separate But Equal Branches* (New York: Chatham House, 1999).
3. James W. Davis, *The American Presidency* (New York: Harper & Row, 1987), 13.
4. See Barry M. Blechman and Stephen S. Kaplan, *Force Without War* (Washington, D.C.: Brookings Institution, 1978).
5. *United States v. Belmont*, 57 U.S. 758 (1937).
6. Robert DiClerico, *The American President*, 4th ed. (Englewood Cliffs, N.J.: Prentice-Hall, 1995), 47.
7. Quoted in Wilfred E. Binkley, *President and Congress*, 3d ed. (New York: Vintage, 1962), 142.
8. Theodore Roosevelt, *An Autobiography* (New York: Scribner's, 1931), 383.
9. See Richard M. Pious, *The American Presidency* (New York: Basic Books, 1979), 83.
10. Harry S Truman, *1946–1952: Years of Trial and Hope* (New York: Signet, 1956), 535.
11. Robert J. Spitzer, *President and Congress* (New York: McGraw-Hill, 1993), 35–37; Raymond Tatalovich and Byron W. Daynes, *Presidential Power in the United States* (Monterey, Calif.: Brooks/Cole, 1984), 322–23.
12. Kenneth A. Oye, Robert J. Lieber, and Donald Rothchild, *Eagle in a New World* (New York: HarperCollins, 1992).
13. Spitzer, *President and Congress*, 137–232.
14. James Bryce, *The American Commonwealth* (New York: Commonwealth Edition, 1908), 230.
15. Davis, *The American Presidency*, 20.
16. Hugh Heclo, "Introduction: The Presidential Illusion," in Hugh Heclo and Lester M. Salamon, eds., *The Illusion of Presidential Government* (Boulder, Colo.: Westview Press, 1981), 6.
17. Thomas R. Marshall, *Presidential Nominations in a Reform Age* (New York: Praeger, 1981); James W. Ceaser, *Presidential Selection: Theory and Development* (Princeton, N.J.: Princeton University Press, 1979).
18. Thomas E. Patterson, *Out of Order* (New York: Vintage, 1994); John S. Jackson and William J. Crotty, *The Politics of Presidential Selection* (New York: Longman, 2001).
19. See Hugh Winebrenner, *The Iowa Precinct Caucuses* (Ames: Iowa State University Press, 1987); Gary R. Orren and Nelson W. Polsby, eds., *Media and Momentum: The New Hampshire Primary and Nomination Politics* (Chatham, N.J.: Chatham House, 1987).
20. Myron A. Levine, *Presidential Campaigns and Elections* (Itasca, Ill.: Peacock, 1995), 30.
21. Kiku Adatto, "Sound Bite Democracy," Joan Shorenstein Center on the Press, Politics, and Public Policy, Research Paper R-2, Harvard University, Cambridge, Mass., June 1990.
22. Sidney Kraus, ed., *The Great Debates* (Bloomington: Indiana University Press, 1962), 190.
23. John P. Burke, *The Institutionalized Presidency* (Baltimore: Johns Hopkins University Press, 1992); Charles E. Walcott and Karen M. Hult, *Governing the White House* (Lawrence: University Press of Kansas, 1995).
24. Davis, *The American Presidency*, 240; see also Bradley Patterson, *The Ring of Power* (New York: Basic Books, 1988), 90–91.
25. James Pfiffner, *The Modern Presidency* (New York: St. Martin's Press, 1994), 91–96.
26. Quoted in Stephen J. Wayne, *Road to the White House, 1992* (New York: St. Martin's Press, 1992), 143; see also Timothy Welch, ed., *At the President's Side* (Columbia: University of Missouri Press, 1997).
27. See Shirley Anne Warshaw, *Powersharing: White House–Cabinet Relations in the Modern Presidency* (Albany: State University of New York Press, 1995).

28. See Jeffrey E. Cohen, *The Politics of the United States Cabinet* (Pittsburgh: University of Pittsburgh Press, 1988).
29. Pfiffner, *The Modern Presidency*, 123.
30. Quoted in James MacGregor Burns, "Our Super-Government—Can We Control It?" *The New York Times*, April 24, 1949, 32.
31. See Paul C. Light, *Thickening Government: Federal Hierarchy and the Diffusion of Accountability* (Washington, D.C.: Brookings Institution, 1995).
32. James Pfiffner, "The President's Chief of Staff: Lessons Learned," *Presidential Studies Quarterly* 22 (Winter 1993): 77–102.
33. See Richard Rose, *The Postmodern President*, 2d ed. (Chatham, N.J.: Chatham House, 1991).
34. Pfiffner, *The Modern Presidency*, 117–22.
35. Michael Mezey, *Congress, the President, and Public Policy* (Boulder, Colo.: Westview Press, 1989), 110–15.
36. George Edwards III, *At the Margins* (New Haven, Conn.: Yale University Press, 1989), 39–46.
37. Erwin Hargrove, *The Power of the Modern Presidency* (New York: Knopf, 1974); see also John H. Kessel, *Presidents, the Presidency, and the Political Environment* (Washington, D.C.: Congressional Quarterly Press, 2001).
38. James P. Pfiffner, *The Strategic Presidency: Hitting the Ground Running*, 2d ed. (Chicago: Dorsey Press, 1996).
39. Aaron Wildavsky, "The Two Presidencies," *Trans-Action*, December 1966, 7.
40. See Lance T. LeLoup and Steven A. Shull, "Congress Versus the Executive: The Two Presidencies Reconsidered," *Social Science Quarterly*, March 1979, 707.
41. Pfiffner, *The Modern Presidency*, ch. 6.
42. Thomas P. (Tip) O'Neill, with William Novak, *Man of the House: The Life and Political Memoirs of Speaker Tip O'Neill* (New York: Random House, 1987), 297.
43. Fred I. Greenstein, ed., *Leadership in the Modern Presidency* (Cambridge, Mass.: Harvard University Press, 1988), ch. 10.
44. Robert J. Spitzer, *The Presidential Veto: Touchstone of the American Presidency* (Albany: State University of New York Press, 1988).
45. Richard E. Neustadt, *Presidential Power and the Modern Presidents* (New York: Free Press, 1990), 71–72.
46. Ibid., 33.
47. Ibid.
48. *Congressional Quarterly Weekly Report*, December 11, 1999.
49. Mary E. Stuckey, *The President as Interpreter-in-Chief* (Chatham, N.J.: Chatham House, 1991).
50. Harvey G. Zeidenstein, "Presidents' Popularity and Their Wins and Losses on Major Issues: Does One Have a Greater Influence over the Other?" *Presidential Studies Quarterly*, Spring 1985, 287–300; see also Richard Brody, *Assessing the President* (Stanford, Calif.: Stanford University Press, 1991).
51. Gallup Polls, November 2–5, 1979, and November 30–December 3, 1979.
52. John E. Mueller, "Presidential Popularity from Truman to Johnson," *American Political Science Review* 64 (March 1970): 18–34; Kathleen Frankovic, "Public Opinion in the 1992 Campaign," in Gerald M. Pomper, ed., *The Election of 1992* (Chatham, N.J.: Chatham House, 1993).
53. See John Anthony Maltese, *Spin Control* (Chapel Hill: University of North Carolina Press, 1994); Howard Kurtz, *Spin Cycle* (New York: Basic Books, 1998).
54. Samuel Kernell, *Going Public: New Strategies of Presidential Leadership*, 3d ed. (Washington, D.C.: Congressional Quarterly Press, 1997), 1.
55. Jeffrey Tulis, *The Rhetorical Presidency* (Princeton, N.J.: Princeton University Press, 1987); Craig Allen Smith, *The White House Speaks* (Westport, Conn.: Greenwood, 1994); but also see Kenneth Walsh, *Feeding the Beast* (New York: Random House, 1996).
56. Stuckey, *The President as Interpreter-in-Chief*.
57. Heclo, "Introduction: The Presidential Illusion," 2.
58. Theodore J. Lowi, *The "Personal" Presidency: Power Invested, Promise Unfulfilled* (Ithaca, N.Y.: Cornell University Press, 1985); see also Jeffrey E. Cohen, *Presidential Responsiveness and Public Policymaking* (Ann Arbor: University of Michigan Press, 1997).

CHAPTER 13

1. Norman Thomas, *Rule 9: Politics, Administration, and Civil Rights* (New York: Random House, 1966), 6.
2. Quoted in Albert Gore Jr., *From Red Tape to Results: Creating a Government That Works Better and Costs Less* (Washington, D.C.: U.S. Superintendent of Documents, 1993), 1.
3. James P. Pfiffner, "The National Performance Review in Perspective," working paper 94-4, Institute of Public Policy, George Mason University, 1994, 2.
4. Ibid., 12.
5. Max Weber, *Economy and Society*, trans. Guenther Roth and Claus Wittich (New York: Bedminster Press, 1968), 23.
6. See John J. DiIulio, ed., *Deregulating the Public Service* (Washington, D.C.: Brookings Institution, 1994).
7. *Rutan v. Republican Party of Illinois*, 497 U.S. 62 (1990).
8. See Cornelius M. Kerwin, *Rulemaking* (Washington, D.C.: Congressional Quarterly Press, 1994).
9. Michael Lipsky, *Street-Level Bureaucracy* (New York: Russell Sage Foundation, 1980); see also George Serra, "Citizen-Initiated Contact and Satisfaction with Bureaucracy," *Journal of Public Administration* 5 (April 1995): 175–88.
10. Paul Van Riper, *History of the United States Civil Service* (Evanston, Ill.: Peterson, 1958), 36.
11. Jay M. Shafritz, *Personnel Management in Government* (New York: Marcel Dekker, 1981), 9–13; Herbert

Kaufman, "Emerging Conflicts in the Doctrine of Public Administration," *American Political Science Review* 50 (December 1956): 1060.
12. James Q. Wilson, "The Rise of the Bureaucratic State," *Public Interest* 41 (Fall 1975): 77–103.
13. U.S. Bureau of the Census, *Historical Statistics of the United States: Colonial Times to 1970,* pt. 2 (Washington, D.C.: U.S. Government Printing Office, 1975), 1102.
14. David H. Rosenbloom, *Federal Service and the Constitution* (Ithaca, N.Y.: Cornell University Press, 1971), 83.
15. Kaufman, "Emerging Conflicts in the Doctrine of Public Administration," 1060.
16. Ibid., 1062.
17. See Richard W. Waterman, *Presidential Influence and the Administrative State* (Knoxville: University of Tennessee Press, 1989).
18. Quoted in Hugh Heclo, *A Government of Strangers* (Washington, D.C.: Brookings Institution, 1977), 225.
19. Norton E. Long, "Power and Administration," *Public Administration Review* 10 (Autumn 1949): 269; Joel D. Aberbach and Bert A. Rockman, *In the Web of Politics* (Washington, D.C.: Brookings Institution Press, 2000).
20. See Herbert Kaufman, *The Administrative Behavior of Federal Bureaucrats* (Washington, D.C.: Brookings Institution, 1981), 4.
21. See Heclo, *A Government of Strangers,* 117–18.
22. Quoted in Aaron Wildavsky, *The Politics of the Budgetary Process,* 4th ed. (Boston: Little, Brown, 1984), 19.
23. Joel D. Aberbach and Bert A. Rockman, "Clashing Beliefs Within the Executive Branch," *American Political Science Review* 70 (June 1976): 461.
24. See B. Dan Wood and Richard W. Waterman, *Bureaucratic Dynamics* (Boulder, Colo.: Westview Press, 1994).
25. Kenneth J. Meier, *Regulation* (New York: St. Martin's Press, 1985), 164.
26. See John Brehm and Scott Gates, *Working, Shirking, and Sabotage* (Ann Arbor: University of Michigan Press, 1996).
27. Herbert Kaufman, *Are Government Organizations Immortal?* (Washington, D.C.: Brookings Institution, 1976), 76.
28. Long, "Power and Administration," 269; see also John Mark Hansen, *Gaining Access* (Chicago: University of Chicago Press, 1991).
29. See B. Guy Peters, *The Politics of Bureaucracy,* 4th ed. (New York: Longman, 1995).
30. See Martin Laffin, "Reinventing the Federal Government," in Christopher Peele, Christopher J. Bailey, Bruce Cain, and B. Guy Peters, eds., *Developments in American Politics 2* (Chatham, N.J.: Chatham House, 1995), 172–76.
31. See Paul Light, *Thickening Government* (Washington, D.C.: Brookings Institution, 1995).
32. James G. March and Johan P. Olson, "Organizing Political Life: What Administrative Reorganization Tells Us About Government," *American Political Science Review* 77 (June 1983): 281–96.
33. Meier, *Regulation,* 110–11.
34. See Heclo, *A Government of Strangers.*
35. See William F. West, *Controlling the Bureaucracy* (Armonk, N.Y.: Sharp, 1995).
36. See Donald Kettl, *Deficit Politics* (New York: Macmillan, 1992).
37. See Joel D. Aberbach, *Keeping a Watchful Eye* (Washington, D.C.: Brookings Institution, 1990).
38. B. Dan Wood and Richard W. Waterman, "Political Control of the Bureaucracy," *American Political Science Review* 85 (September 1991): 820–21; see also Cathy Marie Johnson, *The Dynamics of Conflict Between Bureaucrats and Legislators* (Armonk, N.Y.: Sharpe, 1992).
39. Louis Fisher, *American Constitutional Law* (New York: McGraw-Hill, 1990), 280–81.
40. David Rosenbloom, "The Evolution of the Administrative State, and Transformations of Administrative Law," in David Rosenbloom and Richard Schwartz, eds., *Handbook of Regulation and Administrative Law* (New York: Marcel Dekker, 1994), 3–36.
41. See *Vermont Yankee Nuclear Power Corp. v. National Resources Defense Council, Inc.,* 435 U.S. 519 (1978); *Chevron v. National Resources Defense Council,* 467 U.S. 837 (1984); *Heckler v. Chaney,* 470 U.S. 821 (1985); but see *FDA v. Brown & Williamson Tobacco Co.* (2000).
42. Roberta Ann Johnson and Michael E. Kraft, "Bureaucratic Whistleblowing and Policy Change," *Western Political Quarterly* 43 (December 1990): 849–74.
43. "FBI Whistleblower to Speak," *CNN.com,* June 6, 2002.
44. See Brian J. Cook, *Bureaucracy and Self-Government* (Baltimore, Md.: Johns Hopkins University Press, 1996).
45. Ibid.
46. See Wood and Waterman, *Bureaucratic Dynamics.*
47. David Osborne and Ted Gaebler, *Reinventing Government: How the Entrepreneurial Spirit Is Transforming the Public Sector* (New York: Addison-Wesley, 1992); see also Michael Barzelay and Babak J. Armajani, *Breaking Through Bureaucracy* (Berkeley: University of California Press, 1992); Robert D. Behn, *Leadership Counts* (Cambridge, Mass.: Harvard University Press, 1991).
48. Pfiffner, "The National Performance Review in Perspective," 7.
49. Ronald C. Moe, "The 'Reinventing Government' Exercise: Misinterpreting the Problem, Misjudging the Results," *Public Administration Review* (March/April 1994): 125–36.

CHAPTER 14

1. *Marbury v. Madison,* 1 Cranch 137 (1803).

2. *Bush v. Gore*, No. 00-949 (2000).
3. *Planned Parenthood v. Casey*, No. 91-744 (1992).
4. *Roe v. Wade*, 401 U.S. 113 (1973).
5. See Michael J. Perry, *The Constitution and the Courts* (New York: Oxford University Press, 1994).
6. Raoul Berger, *Government by Judiciary: The Transformation of the Fourteenth Amendment* (Cambridge, Mass.: Harvard University Press, 1977).
7. Rebecca Mae Salokar, *The Solicitor General: The Politics of Law* (Philadelphia: Temple University Press, 1992); see also Cornell W. Clayton, *The Politics of Justice: The Attorney General and the Making of Legal Policy* (Armonk, N.Y.: Sharpe, 1992).
8. D. Marie Provine, *Case Selection in the United States Supreme Court* (Chicago: University of Chicago Press, 1980), 62–63; see also H. W. Perry, *Deciding to Decide* (Cambridge, Mass.: Harvard University Press, 1991).
9. Henry Glick, *Courts, Politics, and Justice*, 3d ed. (New York: McGraw-Hill, 1993), 214.
10. See Bernard Schwartz, *Decision: How the Supreme Court Decides Cases* (New York: Oxford University Press, 1996).
11. Lawrence Baum, *The Supreme Court*, 4th ed. (Washington, D.C.: Congressional Quarterly Press, 1996), 117.
12. *Brown v. Board of Education of Topeka*, 347 U.S. 483 (1954).
13. *Gideon v. Wainwright*, 372 U.S. 335 (1963).
14. From a letter to the author by Frank Schwartz of Beaver College. This section reflects substantially Professor Schwartz's recommendations to the author, as does the later section that addresses the federal court myth. See also Robert A. Carp, *The Federal Courts*, 3d ed. (Washington, D.C.: Congressional Quarterly Press, 1998).
15. *Hutto v. Davis*, 370 U.S. 256 (1982).
16. *Roe v. Wade*, 401 U.S. 113 (1973).
17. See George L. Watson and John Alan Stookey, *Shaping America: The Politics of Supreme Court Appointments* (New York: Longman, 1995).
18. See Carp, *The Federal Courts*.
19. Stephen L. Wasby, *The Supreme Court in the Federal Judicial System*, 4th ed. (Chicago: Nelson-Hall, 1993), 75.
20. Henry J. Abraham, *The Judicial Process*, 7th ed. (New York: Oxford University Press, 1998), 24–26.
21. Robert Scigliano, *The Supreme Court and the Presidency* (New York: Free Press, 1971), 146; see also David Savage, *Turning Right: The Making of the Rehnquist Supreme Court* (New York: Wiley, 1992).
22. Quoted in Baum, *The Supreme Court*, 37.
23. See John C. Hughes, *The Federal Courts, Politics, and the Rule of Law* (New York: Longman, 1995).
24. John Gottschall, "Reagan's Appointments to the U.S. Courts of Appeals," 70 *Judicature* 48 (1986): 54.
25. Carp, *The Federal Courts*.
26. Joseph B. Harris, *The Advice and Consent of the Senate* (Berkeley: University of California Press, 1953), 313.
27. People for the American Way data, 1998.
28. Henry J. Abraham, "The Judicial Function Under the Constitution," *News for Teachers of Political Science* 41 (Spring 1984): 14; Sheldon Goldman, "Should There Be Affirmative Action for the Judiciary?" *Judicature* 62 (May 1979): 494.
29. Quoted in Louis Fisher, *American Constitutional Law* (New York: McGraw-Hill, 1990), 5.
30. Baum, *The Supreme Court*, 117.
31. Quoted in Charles P. Curtis, *Law and Large as Life* (New York: Simon & Schuster, 1959), 156–57.
32. See Joan Biskupic and Elder Witt, *The Supreme Court and the Powers of the American Government* (Washington, D.C.: Congressional Quarterly Press, 1996), ch. 1.
33. See Lee Epstein and Jack Knight, *The Choices Justices Make* (New York: Longman, 1995).
34. *Faragher v. City of Boca Raton*, No. 97-282 (1998).
35. Wasby, *The Supreme Court in the Federal Judicial System*, 53.
36. See Lee Epstein, *Conservatives in Court* (Knoxville: University of Tennessee Press, 1985), 80–88.
37. Linda Greenhouse, "Sure Justices Legislate. They Have To," *The New York Times*, July 5, 1998, sect. 4, p. 1.
38. See Watson and Stookey, *Shaping America*.
39. John Schmidhauser, *The Supreme Court* (New York: Holt, Rinehart & Winston, 1964), 6.
40. Jeffrey A. Segal and Harold J. Spaeth, *The Supreme Court and the Attitudinal Model* (New York: Cambridge University Press, 1993).
41. Linda Greenhouse, "In Year of Florida Vote, Supreme Court Also Did Much Other Work," *The New York Times*, July 2, 2001, p. A12.
42. David M. O'Brien, *Storm Center: The Supreme Court in American Politics*, 5th ed. (New York: Norton, 2000), 14–15.
43. Ibid., 59–61.
44. Some of the references cited in the following sections are taken from Abraham, "The Judicial Function," 12–14; see also Harry H. Wellington, *Interpreting the Constitution* (New Haven, Conn.: Yale University Press, 1990).
45. Abraham, "The Judicial Function," 14.
46. Alexander M. Bickel, *The Supreme Court and the Idea of Progress* (New Haven, Conn.: Yale University Press, 1978), 173–81.
47. See Antonin Scalia, *A Matter of Interpretation* (Princeton, N.J.: Princeton University Press, 1997).
48. Louis Lusky, *By What Right? A Commentary on the Supreme Court's Power to Revise the Constitution* (Charlottesville, Va.: Michie, 1975), 214–16.
49. Ibid.
50. *Romer v. Evans*, No. 94-1039 (1996).
51. Abraham, "The Judicial Function," 13.

52. See Larry W. Yackle, *Reclaiming the Federal Courts* (Cambridge, Mass.: Harvard University Press, 1994).
53. *Gideon v. Wainwright*, 372 U.S. 335 (1963). Case example and argument are from Richard A. Posner, "What Am I? A Potted Plant?" *The New Republic*, September 28, 1987, 25.
54. "Good for the Left, Now Good for the Right," *Newsweek*, July 8, 1991, 22.
55. Linda Greenhouse, "The Justices Decide Who's in Charge," *The New York Times*, June 27, 1999, sect. 4, p. 1.
56. Quoted in ibid.
57. *Bush v. Gore*, No. 00-949 (2000).

CHAPTER 15

1. *Reno v. Condon*, No. 98-1464 (2000).
2. *Kimel v. Florida Board of Regents*, No. 98-791 (2000).
3. Paul Burka, "What a Texas Record Can't Tell," *The New York Times*, April 28, 2000, A23.
4. Thad Beyle, "Governors: The Middlemen and Women in Our Political System," in Virginia Gray and Herbert Jacobs, *Politics in the American States: A Comparative Analysis* (Washington, D.C.: Congressional Quarterly Press, 1996), 237.
5. Amy Pyle, "California and the West," *Los Angeles Times*, October 24, 1999, A30.
6. Advisory Commission on Intergovernmental Relations (ACIR), *The Question of State Government Capability* (Washington, D.C.: ACIR, 1985), 123.
7. David Broder, *Democracy Derailed* (San Diego: Harcourt, 2000).
8. V. O. Key Jr., *Southern Politics* (New York: Knopf, 1949), 495.
9. John F. Dillon, *Commentaries on the Law of Municipal Corporations*, 5th ed. (Boston: Little, Brown, 1911), vol. 1, sec. 237.
10. *People v. Hurlbut*, 24 Michigan 44 (1871).
11. Susan MacManus, *Young v. Old: Generational Combat in the Twenty-first Century* (Boulder, Colo.: Westview Press, 1996).
12. See, for example, Robert Dahl, *Pluralist Democracy in the United States* (Chicago: Rand McNally, 1967).
13. David Osborne, *Laboratories of Democracy: A New Breed of Governor Creates Models for National Growth* (Cambridge, Mass.: Harvard Business School, 1988).
14. Tommy Thompson, *Power to the People: An American State at Work* (New York: HarperCollins, 1996).
15. *San Antonio Independent School District v. Rodriquez*, 411 U.S. 1 (1973).
16. Abby Goodnough, "Major Court Challenge on How State Allocates School Funds," *The New York Times*, October 12, 1999, B1.
17. Thomas R. Dye, *Politics in States and Communities*, 8th ed. (Englewood Cliffs, N.J.: Prentice-Hall, 1994), 162.
18. *Federalist* No. 10.
19. Daniel J. Boorstin, *The Americans: The Democratic Experience* (New York: Vintage Books, 1974).
20. Lawrence Grossman, *The Electronic Republic* (New York: Viking, 1995).

CREDITS

LINE ART AND TEXT

Chapter 1
Table 1–1: From the Survey of American Political Culture, James Davison Hunter and Carl Bowman, Directors, Institute for Advanced Studies in Culture, University of Virginia. Used by permission.
Box—How the US Compares: Americans as a Political People: From *The World Values Survey*. Used by permission of the World Values Survey Association, Stockholm, Sweden.

Chapter 4
Figure 4–2: Data from Fox News/Opinion Dynamics Poll, Nov. 28–29, 2001. Used with permission.

Chapter 5
Table 5–1: From *Latino National Political Survey*, reported in Rudolfo O. de la Garza, Angelo Falcon, F. Chris Garcia, and John A. Garcia, "Hispanic Americans in the Mainstream of U.S. Politics," *The Public Perspective*, July/August 1992, p. 19. Copyright © 1992 Public Perspective, a publication of the Roper Center for Public Opinion Research, University of CT, Storrs. Reprinted by permission.

Chapter 6
Figure 6–1: Used by permission of National Opinion Research Center, University of Chicago.
Figure 6–3: Copyright © 2001 The Gallup Organization, Princeton, NJ. Reprinted with permission.
Figure 6–5: Copyright © 2001 The Gallup Organization, Princeton, NJ. Reprinted with permission.

Chapter 7
Table 7–1: From the *1996 Survey of American Political Culture*, James Davison Hunter and Carl Bowman, Directors, Institute for Advanced Studies in Culture, University of Virginia. Used with permission.

Figure 7–2: Used by permission of the Shorenstein Center Poll for the Vanishing Voter Project.
Figure 7–4: From Helmut I. Anheier, Lester M. Aalamon, and Edith Archambault, "Participating Citizens" U.S.-Europe Comparisons in Volunteer Action," *The Public Perspective*, March/April 1994, p. 17. Copyright © 1994 Public Perspective, a publication of the Roper Center for Public Opinion Research, University of CT, Storrs. Reprinted by permission.

Chapter 10
Figure 10–2: Adapted in part from Daniel C. Hallin, "Sound Bite News: Television Coverage of Elections 1968–1988," *Journal of Communication*, 42 (Spring 1992), p. 6; and in part from Center for Media and Public Affairs. Reprinted with permission.
Figure 10–3: *Out of Order* by Thomas E. Patterson, p. 20, Copyright ©1993 by Thomas E. Patterson. Used by permission of Alfred A. Knopf, a division of Random House, Inc. For 1960–1992 coverage, Center for Media and Public Affairs, 1996, 2000.

Chapter 12
Figure 12–1: Used by permission of the Shorenstein Center Poll for the Vanishing Voter Project.
Figure 12–3: Republished with permission of CQ Press, from *Congressional Quarterly Weekly Report*, December 11, 1999; permission conveyed through Copyright Clearance Center, Inc.

Chapter 13
Box—How the US Compares. From *The Politics of Bureaucracy*, 4th ed. by B. Guy Peters. Copyright © 1995 by Longman Publishers USA. Reprinted by permission of Pearson Education, Inc.

Chapter 14
Figure 14–3: Copyright © 2001 The Gallup Organization, Princeton, NJ. Reprinted with permission.

Credits

PHOTOS

Table of Contents
p. viii: © Corbis-Bettmann; p. xi: © Bob Daemmrich/Image Works; p. xiii: © Dennis Brack/Black Star; p. xvi: © AP/Wide World Photos

Chapter 1
p. 6: © AP/Wide World Photos; p. 9: © Joseph Sohm/Stock Boston; p. 10: Library of Congress, Prints & Photographs Division, [LC-USZC4-2474]; p. 15: © Bob Daemmrich/Image Works; p. 17: © Newhouse News Service; p. 19: © Walter Hodges/Stone; p. 22: © Bob Daemmrich/Image Works; p. 23: © Bob Daemmrich/Image Works; p. 24: © Najlah Feanny/Saba; p. 29: © John Neubauer/PhotoEdit

Chapter 2
p. 36: © Jim Wells/Archive Photos/Getty Images; p. 38: © Corbis-Bettmann; p. 40: © Corbis-Bettmann; p. 41: Library of Congress; p. 43: © Corbis-Bettmann; p. 45: © The Granger Collection; p. 47: Library of Congress, Prints & Photographs Division, [LC-USZ62-13004]; p. 50: © The Granger Collection; p. 56: Library of Congress, Prints & Photographs Division, [LC-USZ62-54940]; p. 57: © The Granger Collection; p. 60: Architect of the Capitol

Chapter 3
p. 68: © The Granger Collection; p. 71: Library of Congress, Prints & Photographs Division, [LC-USZ62-48272]; p. 72: © Archive Photos/Getty Images; p. 76: © The Granger Collection; p. 77: Library of Congress; p. 78: © Bettmann/CORBIS; p. 80: © Corbis-Bettmann; p. 81: Library of Congress; p. 82: © AP/Wide World Photos; p. 86: © David Adame/AP/Wide World Photos; p. 91: © AP/Wide World Photos; p. 92: Collection, The Supreme Court Historical Society, Photographed by Dane Penland, Smithsonian Institution

Chapter 4
p. 99: © Paul Conklin/PhotoEdit; p. 100: Library of Congress, Prints & Photographs Division, [LC-USZ62-47817]; p. 103: © AP/Wide World Photos; p. 108: © Clark Jones/Impact Visuals; p. 109: Bonnie Kamin/PhotoEdit; p. 111: © Donna Binder/Impact Visuals; p. 114: © Greg Gibson/Wide World Photos; p. 116: © Marilyn K. Yee/New York Times Pictures; p. 120: © Alan Klehr/Stone/Getty Images; p. 125: Stephen Ferry/Liaison Agency/Getty Images; p. 127: © Paul Conklin/PhotoEdit

Chapter 5
p. 133: Charles Moore/Black Star; p. 134: Library of Congress, Prints & Photographs Division, U.S. News & World Report Magazine Collection, [LC-U9-11696-frame #9A]; p. 137: Library of Congress, Prints and Photographs Division [LC-USZ62-46713]; p. 139: © Chip Henderson/Stone/Getty Images; p. 141: © Corbis Images; p. 143: AP/Wide World Photos; p. 144: Tony Freeman/PhotoEdit; p. 145: © Frank Siteman/Stock Boston/PictureQuest; p. 150: U.S. Air Force photo by Staff Sgt. Pamela Farlin (VIRIN: 01116-F-9186F-006); p. 155: © Jay Mallin/Impact Visuals; p. 158: © Kim Kulish/Saba; p. 162: © Karim-Shamsi-Basha/Saba

Chapter 6
p. 170: Department of Defense photo by Petty Officer 1st Class Greg Messier, U.S. Navy; p. 171: © Joel Stettenheim/Saba; p. 176: © Corbis-Bettmann; p. 179: © Charles Gupton/Corbis Stock Market; p. 183: © Paul Conklin/PhotoEdit; p. 187: © Charles E. Rotkin/Corbis Images; p. 191: © Reuters NewMedia Inc./CORBIS

Chapter 7
p. 198: Culver Pictures; p. 204: © Robert King/Liaison Agency/Getty Images; p. 206: © Jonathon Nourok/Stone/Getty Images; p. 208: Reuters NewMedia Inc./CORBIS; p. 211: © Paul Warner/AP/Wide World Photos; p. 213: Michael Newman/PhotoEdit; p. 217: © Lara Jo Regan/Gamma Liaison/Getty Images; p. 218: © Corbis Images; p. 221: Loren Callahan/Liaison Agency/Getty Images

Chapter 8
p. 226: © AFP/CORBIS; p. 229: Library of Congress, Prints and Photographs Division [LC-USZ62-117120]; p. 230: Library of Congress, Prints and Photographs Division [LC-USZ62-13016]; p. 231: Bettmann/CORBIS; p. 234: © I.P.O.L., NYC; p. 235: © AFP/CORBIS; p. 241: © Eric Miller/Liaison Agency/Getty Images; p. 245: © AP/Wide World Photos. 246 left: Democratic National Committee; p. 246 right: Republican National Committee; p. 250: Allen Tannenbaum; p. 256: © Porter Gifford/Liaison Agency/Getty Images

Chapter 9
p. 263: Courtesy AARP; p. 266 top left: Used by permission from Ford Motor Company; p. 266 bottom left: Used by permission from DaimlerChrysler Corporation; p. 266 right: Used by permission from General Motors.; p. 268: Library of Congress; p. 269: AP/Wide World Photos; p. 270: © Fred Chartrand/AP/Wide World Photos; p. 271: © Terry Ashe/Gamma Liaison/Getty Images; p. 276: © Tom McCarthy/PhotoEdit; p. 280: Frederic Neema/Corbis Sygma; p. 281: © AP/Wide World Photos; p. 287: Davis Barber/PhotoEdit; p. 289: © Dennis Cook/AP/Wide World Photos

Chapter 10
p. 294: AP/Wide World Photos; p. 297: © Stock Montage; p. 299: © Brown Brothers; p. 310 left: U.S. House of Representatives; p. 301 right: U.S. Senate; p. 305: © AFP/CORBIS; p. 307: © Jeff Greenberg/PhotoEdit;

Chapter 11

p. 310: AP Photo/Gino Domenico; p. 313: © Allan Tannenbaum; p. 316: Reuters NewMedia Inc./CORBIS

Chapter 11

p. 324: Vanessa Vick/Photo Researchers; p. 328: © Wide World Photos; p. 331: © Corbis-Bettmann; p. 332: © Bob Daemmrich/Corbis/ Sygma; p. 336: Courtesy of Senator Tom Daschle; p. 341: © F. Lee Corkran/Corbis/Sygma; p. 345: © AP/Wide World Photos; p. 348: Bettmann/CORBIS; p. 349: U.S. General Accounting Office; p. 351: © John Van Hasselt/Cors/ Sygma; p. 354: © Jonathan Nourok/PhotoEdit; p. 355: © US Senate/AP/Wide World Photos

Chapter 12

p. 362: © AP/Wide World Photos; p. 365: © UPI/Corbis-Bettmann; p. 368: © Bruce Hoertel/Gamma Liaison/ Getty Images; p. 370: © AFP/Corbis; p. 381: © AP/Wide World Photos; p. 382: © UPI/Corbis-Bettmann; p. 385: © Rene Burri/Magnum Photos; p. 387: © Corbis/SABA; p. 392: Library of Congress, Prints & Photographs Division, [LC-USZ62-13037]; p. 395: © AP/Wide World Photos

Chapter 13

p. 400: © NASA/Liaison Agency/Getty Images; p. 406: © Bob Daemmrich/Stock Boston; p. 407: © Paul Chesley/Stone/Getty Images; p. 408: © Mark Mackowiak/U. S. Coast Guard; p. 412: © Corbis-Bettmann; p. 417: © Don Perdue/Gamma Liaison/Getty Images; p. 424: © Steve Liss/Gamma Liaison/ Getty Images

Chapter 14

p. 433: AP/Wide World Photos; p. 435: © Dennis Brack/Black Star; p. 438: © Billy Barnes/Stock Boston; p. 442: © AP/Wide World Photos; p. 443: © Ken Heinen/AP/Wide World Photos; p. 444: © AP/Wide World Photos; p. 450: © Michael C. York/AP/Wide World Photos; p. 454: © Byrce Flynn; p. 456: © Karl Gehring/Gamma Liaison/Getty Images; p. 458: © AP/Wide World Photos

Chapter 15

p. 469: © Larry Kolvoord/Image Works; p. 474: © Sandra Baker/Liaison Agency/Getty Images; p. 478: © John Elderfield/Gamma Liaison; p. 481: © AP/Wide World Photos; p. 485: © Lunne Sladky/AP/Wide World Photos; p. 489: Reprinted with permission of the California State Lottery; p. 490: © Gerd Ludwig/Woodfin Camp & Assoc.; p. 492: © Andy Sacks/Stone/Getty Images; p. 495: © Matthew McDermott/Corbis Sygma; p. 497: © Mike Derer/AP/Wide World Photos; p. 501: © Craig J. Brown/Gamma Liaison/Getty Images.

INDEX

Note: Bold words indicate glossary terms. Bold numbers indicate the page on which the definition of each term can be found.

Aberbach, Joel D., 429
Abortion,
    opinions on, 186, 277
    woman's right of, 114–115
Abraham, Henry J., 129, 446
Accountability, 419
    within bureaucracy, 424–426
    bureaucratic, 418–426
    through Congress, 421–423
    through presidency, 418–421
    through Supreme Court, 423–424
Acts of Toleration, 110
Adamany, David, 247
Adams, John, 40, 55, 59, 100, 452
Adams, Sam, 39
Adarand v. Pena, 155
Administrative organizations, types of, 403–406
Affirmative action, 154–159
    defined, **154**
    differing views of, 154
    key decisions on, 156–157
Afghanistan, 19, 169, 170, 192, 303, 305, 308, 316, 361, 362
AFL-CIO, 266, 275
African Americans, 132–135, 486. *See also* Affirmative action; Civil rights movement; National Association for the Advancement of Colored People (NAACP); Segregation; Slavery
    affirmative action and, 154–159
    in bureaucracy, 425
    busing, 159–162
    civil rights movement, 134–135, 145, 218
    criminal justice and, 135
    discrimination against, 131
    economic status of, 154
    elections and, 135
    historical discrimination, 14–15, 498
    and judicial appointees, 446
    laws and, 148–153

African Americans—*Continued*
    leaders of, 135
    opinions and, 188
    public accommodations and, 132–134
    public schools and, 161
    representation of, 136
    rights of, 148–1153
    suffrage and, 198–199
    voter turnout of, 204, 205
Age, voting and, 207–208
Age-cohort tendency, 179
Age discrimination, 147
Age Discrimination Act, 74, 147
Age Discrimination in Employment Act, 147
Age gap, 189
Agency point of view, 414–415
Agenda setting, 308
Agents of political socialization, 179–182
Agricultural groups, 267
Air wars, 254
Alabama, 469
Aldrich, John, 259
Alger, Dean, 305
Alienation, 207
Al Qaeda, 169, 170, 192, 305, 316, 361
Amendments. *See* Bill of Rights; *individual amendments*
America. *See* United States
American Association of Retired Persons (AARP), 263, 281
American Creed, 12
American Farm Bureau Federation, 267
American flag, burning, 102, 106–107
American Independent party, 240
American Indians. *See* Native Americans
American Medical Association (AMA), 267
American Petroleum Institute, 265, 274
American Revolution, 37–38, 50
Americans for Democratic Action (ADA), 272
Americans as political people, 20
Americans with Disabilities Act, 79, 146
Ames, Fisher, 34
Amicus curiae briefs, 277
Anderson, Desiree, 327
Annapolis Convention, 43

Anthony, Susan B., 137, 198
Anti-Federalists, 46, 71
Apathy, 194
Appellate courts, 438
Appellate jurisdiction, 433
Arab Americans, 125, 127, 163
Arizona, 576
Armor, David, 162, 164
Articles of Confederation, 41–42, 43, 69, 71, 72
Ashcroft, John, 24, 101
Ashcroft v. ACLU, 109
Ashcroft v. Free Speech Coalition, 109
Asian Americans. *See also* Affirmative action; Civil rights movement
    affirmative action and, 154–159
    demographic pattern of, 8, 15–16, 145
    discrimination against, 131, 145
    economic status of, 146
    education and, 146
    immigration of, 8, 15–16, 145
Atkin v. Virginia, 119, 125
Authority, 19
Axis of Evil, 387

"Bad News," 312–313
Bagdikian, Ben H., 318
Bakke, Alan, 155–156
Barron v. Baltimore, 104
Bay of Pigs, 386
Bazelon, David, 447
Beard, Charles S., 61, 65
Beard's economic theory of Constitution, 61
Beer, Samuel H., 95
Behr, Roy L., 259
Beliefs, cultural, 9–12
Belz, Herman, 81
Bentley, Arthur F., 261
Benton v. Maryland, 118
Bergmann, Barbara, 164
Bernstein, Carl, 311
Berry, Jeffrey M., 290
Bicameral legislatures, 474
"Big Three," 266

Bill. *Also see* Law
   committee hearings to floor debate on, 343–344
   defined, **342**
   from floor debate into law, 344–345
   into law, 343–346
Bill of Rights, 53, 54, 64, **98,** 118, 126. *See also individual amendments*
   applied to states, 117
   Indian, 142
bin Laden, Osama, 104, 169, 315
Black, Hugo, 436
Blacks. *See* African Americans
Block grants, 88
Board of Education of Independent School District No. 92 of Potlawatomie County v. Earls, 121
Board of Trustees of the University of Alabama v. Garrett, 92
Boorstin, Daniel J., 94, 502
Bork, Robert, 443
Borrowing, 491
Boston Tea Party, 38
Bowers v. Hardwick, 116, 148
Boxer, Barbara, 137
Boyle, Thad, 472
Bradley, Bill, 373
Brady, Henry, 223
Brandenburg v. Ohio, 105
Breckinridge, John C., 229
Brehm, John, 429
Brennan, William, 434, 444
Breyer, Stephen, 410
British Labour Party, 256
Broadcast media development, 297–298
Broadcasting, Scarcity Principle, 307
Broder, David S., 361, 504
Brown, Jerry, 472
Brown v. Board of Education of Topeka, 133–134, 436, 438, 450, 455
Browne, William P., 290
Bryan, William Jennings, 230, 240
Bryce, James, 7, 10, 44, 48
Buchanan, James, 366
Buchanan, Pat, 241
Buckley v. Valeo, 103
Budget and Accounting Act, 368
Budgetary process, 422
Budget Impoundment and Control Act, 349, 391
Bull Moose party, 239
Bureaucracy, 401
   accountability within, 418–426
   federal. *See* Federal bureaucracy
   representativeness of, 425–426
Bureaucratic accountability, 418–426
Bureaucratic rule, 27, **29**
Bureaucrats, educational backgrounds of, 416

Burke, Edmund, 57, 321
Burns, Nancy, 223
Burr, Richard, 371
Bush, George, 211, 255
Bush, George W., 113, 457
   and election 2000, 21, 176, 210, 216, 225, 238, 240, 251, 252, 370, 374, 375, 376, 377, 378, 394
   and Florida vote (in 2000), 22, 190–191, 204
   presidential appointees of, 380
   public opinion and, 392
   and scandal, 356, 395
   and success with Congress, 390
   and terrorism, 5, 169, 170, 367, 387, 394, 417, 419
Bush, Jeb, 157
Bush v. Gore, 431, 433, 458, 459
Business groups, 265–266
Busing, 159–162

Cabinet, 382
Cabinet departments, 403
Cable News Network (CNN), 298
Calhoun, John C., 77
California, 470, 472, 483
Campaign
   for election, 374–376
   for nomination, 372–374
Campaign activities, 212
   participation in, 212–213
Campaign contributions, 327
Campaign finance, 248, 374, 376–379
Campaign funds, 247
Campaign media, 376–379
Campaign spending for Congress, 326
Candidate-centered campaigns, 256–257
Candidate-centered politics, 225, 226
Cantwell, Maria, 329
Capitalism, 25
Capture theory, 276–277
Carp, Robert A., 462
Carter, Jimmy, 389, 393
Castro, Fidel, 293
Categorical grants, 88
Catholics, 186, 237
Caucus, 334
Center for Responsible Journalism, 316
Central Intelligence Agency (CIA), 101, 419
Certiorari, writ of, 434
Chagall, David, 252
Challenger, 326
Chavez, Cesar, 143
Checks and balances, 50
   system of, 53
   United States and, 49–52
Cheney, Dick, 225, 356, 381, 395, 423

Child Online Protection Act (COPA), 109
Child pornography, 109
Chinese Americans. *See* Asian Americans
Christian Moral Government Fund, 272
Christians, fundamentalist, 237
Churches, as agents of socialization, 182
Church burnings, 162
Church of Jesus Christ of Latter-day Saints, 501
Cigler, Allan J., 290
Citadel, 150
Citizens' groups, 267–268, 270
   defined, **267**
Citizens party, 240
Citizenship, 83
   opinions on obligations of, 199
City manager system, 483
Civic duty, 206–207
Civil liberties, 53, 96–129
Civil rights, 131, 132
Civil Rights Act of 1964, 83, 124, 136, 137, 142, 143, 146, 150, 151
Civil Rights Act of 1968, 151
Civil Rights Act of 1991, 137, 156
Civil rights movement, 134–135, 145, 218
Civil Service system, 411–412
Civil War, 77, 78
   realignment after, 229–230
Claims Court, U.S., 440
Class, as a frame of reference, 187
Clear-and-present-danger test, 100
Clientele groups, 416–417
Clinton, Hillary Rodham, 250, 341
Clinton, William, 211, 236, 255
   appointees of, 446
   Congress and, 365, 390, 451
   "Filegate" and, 383
   health care plan and, 221
   immigration and, 395
   Lewinsky scandal and, 302, 313, 314, 315, 356
Closed rule, 344
Cloture, 344
Colan, Timothy J., 95
Colegrove v. Green, 459
Collective goods, 268
Collective interest, 285
College enrollment, 14
Colonial America, 37–43
Commerce clause, 80
Commission system, 483
Committee chairpersons, 338–339
Committee hearings to floor debate on bill, 343–344
Committee membership, 340–342
Committee jurisdiction, 342
Common-carrier role, 308–310
Common Cause, 271
Common Good, 285

Index

Common law, 449
Common Sense, 38
Communications Act, 299
Communications Decency Act, 109, 110
Communism, 24
Community activities, participation in, 213–214
Comparable worth, 140
Competition for power, 18
Compliance, 455, 456
Concurrent powers, 69
Concurring opinion, 436
Condit, Gary, 315, 328
Confederacy, 69
Conference committees, 340
Congress, U.S. *See also* House of Representatives, U.S.; Senate, U.S., 322–359
   accountability through, 421–423
   bicameral, 474
   bills in, 343–346
   bureaucracy and, 421–423
   campaign spending for, 326
   committees, 338, 339–342
   committee action, 343–344
   committee chairpersons in, 338–339
   committee jurisdiction, 342
   committee membership, 340–342
   committee power in, 343
   committee system in, 339–342
   conference committees, 340
   constituency influence on, 350–352
   constitutional qualifications for serving in, 325
   election to, 324–332
   fragmentation in policymaking, 347–348
   incumbents in, 324–332
   Joint Committees of, 340
   lawmaking function of, 347
   leadership in, 332–339
   minorities in, 332
   oversight function of, 353–356
   partisanship in, 345–346
   party composition, 334
   party influence on, 352–353
   party leaders in, 334–338
   pluralism in, 356–357
   policymaking role of, 346–350
   presidency and, 348–350
   reelection, 325, 326
   representation function of, 350–353
   select committees, 340
   seniority principle in, 338
   standing committees of, 339–340
   subcommittees, 338
   winners in elections to, 332
   women in, 332
Congressional Budget Office (CBO), 349

Congressional election 1994, 236, 348, 350
Congressional election 2002, 197
Congressional Research Service (CRS), 340
Conservatives, 183, 184
   by state, 186
Constituency, 326
Constitution, defined, 48
Constitution, U.S., 5, 9, 43–54, 68–74. *See also* Bill of Rights; *individual amendments*
Constitutional convention of 1787, 43–47, 72
Constitutional democracy, 34, 63
Constitutional interpretation, 447–448
Constitutional initiative, 471
Constitutional Revolution, 60
Constitutionalism, 22, 48
Constitutional restraints on political power, 48–56
Contemporary community standards, 108
Contract with America, 236, 348, 350
Converse, Philip E., 185
Cook, Brian J., 429
Cook, Timothy E., 318
Cooley's rule, 480
Coolidge, Calvin, 15
Cooperative federalism, 85
Cornell, Samuel, 95
Cornya, John, 86
Corporations, 80
Corporation for Public Broadcasting, 416–417
County government, 481–482
Court of Military Appeals, U.S., 440
Courts. *See also* Supreme Court, U.S.
   federal, 437–440
   state, 440–441
Courts of appeal, U.S., 438
Craig v. Boren, 149
Creationism, 113
Creighton, Robert and Sarisse, 97
Cross-cutting cleavages, 189
Cruel and unusual punishment, 119, 124
Cuban Americans. *See* Hispanic Americans
Cultural beliefs, 9–12
Cultural thinking guiding public opinion, 183
Culture
   as a frame of reference, 183
   political, 5–12
Curb, Mike, 472
Cureton, Adrienne, 123
Customs Office, U.S., 440

Dahl, Robert A., 27, 32
Dahmer, Jeffrey, 304

Daley, Richard, 245
Daschle, Tom, 336
Davidson, Roger H., 322
Davis, John W., 374
Dealignment, 232–233
Death penalty, 119, 125
De Canas v. Bica, 193
Decision, 436
Declaration of Independence, 5, 9, 12, 39–41
De facto discrimination, 153
De jure discrimination, 153
DeJonge v. Oregon, 105
DeLaet, Debra L., 32
Delegates, 61
Delli Carpini, Michael X., 194
Dellinger, Walker, 458
Democracy, **21–22,** 57
Democratic National Committee (DNC), 246
Democratic party, 190, 228, 229–233
Demographic groups, federal job rankings in, 426–427
Demographic representativeness, 426
Demosclerosis, 289
Denials of power, 99
Department of Defense (DOD), 403
Department of Health and Human Services, 404
Department of Justice, 404
Department of State, 403
Department of the Treasury, 404
Department of Veterans Affairs, 404
Descriptive reporting, 298
Devolution, 85, **90**–93
Dewey, Thomas E., 176
Dickerson v. United States, 120
Dillon's rule, 480
Direct election, 61
Direct primary, 242
Disabled, 146
Disabled Americans, rights of, 146
Discrimination
   in accommodations, 150–151
   de facto, 153
   de jure, 153
   in housing, 151
   in jobs, 150–151
   in voting, 151–153
   against women in workplace, 139–140
Dissenting opinion, 436
District courts, U.S., 437–438
Diversity, **12,** 189
Doctrine of nullification, 77
Dole, Robert, 211
Domhoff, G. William, 29, 32
Donald, Keith, 429
Double jeopardy, 118

Douglas, Stephen A., 229
Douglas, William O., 442
Downie, Leonard, Jr., 318
Dred Scott decision, 77
Driver's Privacy Act, 467
Drudge, Matt, 302
"Drudge Report", 302
Drug tests, 121
Dual federalism, 78–83
Due process, 98
Due process clause (of Fourteenth Amendment), **104**
Dukakis, Michael, 378, 492
Duncan, John J., Jr., 63
Duncan v. Louisiana, 118
Dunn, Charles, 194

Easley v. Cromartie, 153
Easton, David, 30
Eck, Diana, 32
Economic class, voting and, 208–209
Economic groups, 264–267
 advantages and, 270
 defined, **265**
 disadvantages and, 270
Economic interests, government promoting, 287–288
Economic interpretation of the constitution, 61
Education, 13–14, 86
Education for All Handicapped Children Act, 146
Ehrenhalt, Alan, 504
Eighteenth Amendment, 49
Eighth Amendment, 117, 119, 124, 125
Eisenhower, Dwight, 134, 444
Elastic clause, 73
Elazar, Daniel, 499
Elderly, 236–237
Elderly Americans, rights of, 147
Election funding (federal), 378–379
Election polls, 252
Elections, 217. *See also* Voting
 African Americans and, 135
 Congress and, 326–332
 contesting, 250–256
 decline of party control and, 242–249
 federal funding of, 378–379
 frequency of, 204–205
 Internet and, 255–256
 local, 478-479
 media and, 253–255
 midterm, House of Representatives and, 329
 open-seat, 327
 political advertising and, 378
 presidential. *See* Presidential elections

Elections—*Continued*
 primary. *See* Primary elections
 state, 251
Electoral College, 21, 58, 60, 369, 371, 375–376
Electoral competition, 356
Electoral majority, 226
Electoral votes, 58, 277, 369, 371, 375–376
Elitism, 27, **28,** 171
Elkins, Stanley, 95
Emily's List, 252
Employees, federal, 406–407, 410–411
Employees, government, 86, 468
Employees of Federal, State, and Local Governments, 86, 468
Employment, federal, 406–407, 410–411
Engel v. Vitale, 112
England's Glorious or Bloodless Revolution of 1689, 110
English, as America's official language, 11
Enlightenment period, 7
Enron Corporation, 249, 282, 310, 315, 355, 356, 395, 423, 427
Enumerated powers, 72–73
Environmental groups, 271
Epstein, Lee, 129
Equality, 10–11, 16
 under the law, 148–153
 struggle for, 132–148
Equality of result, 153
Equal Pay Act, 137
Equal protection clause, 148–149
Equal rights, 130–165
 defined, 132
Equal Rights Amendment (ERA), 137
Era of Good Feeling, 228
Eriksson, Erik McKinley, 219
Espionage Act, 100
Establishment clause, 111
Ethics in Government Act, 275
Ethnic profiling, 127
Ethnicity, 188
European democracies, 234
Exclusionary rule, 120, **121**–122
Executive. *See* Presidency
Executive agencies, lobbying, 276–277
Executive agreements, 364
Executive branch, checks and balances and, 51
Executive budget, 421
Executive departments, 403
Executive leadership system, 412–413
Executive Office of the President (EOP), 380–382
Executive power, 363–369
 shared, 51
Executive privilege, 354
Exigent circumstances, 97
Exon, James, 110

Expertise, power of, 415–416
Ex post facto laws, 49
Expressed powers, 72–73
Expression, freedom of, 99–104
Ezra, Marni, 358

Factional parties, 239–240
Factions, 262
Facts (of a court case), **447**
Families
 as agents of political socialization, 180–181
Family and Medical Leave Act, 137, 139
Farm Bureau, 267
Farmers Union, 267
Farrand, Max, 65
Fast track authority on trade, 388
FDA v. Brown & Williamson Tobacco Co., 410
Federal Age Discrimination Act, 467
Federal Bureau of Investigation, 419
Federal bureaucracy, 398–429
 accountability of, 418–426
 agency point of view in, 414–415
 in Americans' daily lives, 401–402
 democratic values, 423
 development of, 409–413
 effectiveness of, 426
 employees, 406–407
 management systems of, 409–413
 policy responsibilities of, 407–409
 power imperative of, 413–414
 representativeness, 426–428
 sources of power, 415–418
 types of agencies, 403–406
Federal Communications Commission (FCC), 276, 299, 408
Federal court appointees, 444–445
Federal courts, 437
Federal court myth, 440
Federal Deposit Insurance Corporation (FDIC), 83
Federal Election Campaign Act, 374
Federal employees, number of, 406
 pay of, 407
 union activity by, 407
Federal employment, 406–407, 410–411
Federal government, employees of, 406–407
Federal grants-in-aid, 89
Federalism, 48, 66–95
 argument for, 70–72
 contemporary, 83–94
 cooperative, 85
 defined, **69**
 dual, 78–83
 fiscal, 87
 in historical perspective, 74–84
 new, 90

Index

Federalism—*Continued*
    public influence on, 93–94
    system of, 470
Federalist No. 10, 50, 57, 71, 265
Federalist No. 28, 71
Federalist No. 51, 35
Federalist No. 69, 363
Federalist No. 76, 364
Federalist Papers, 47
Federalists, 47, 228
Federal judicial system, 430–461
    appointment of judges and justices, 432, 442–444
    partisan influences on, 444–445
    power of, 452–463
    democracy and, 452–463
Federal Reserve Board, 29
Federal system, 67
Federal Trade Commission (FTC), 415, 420–421
Feinstein, Dianne, 137
Felker v. Turpin, 123
Female. *See* Women
Fenno, John, 295
Ferguson v. Charlestown, 121
Ferraro, Geraldine, 137
Ferris, J. F., 40
Fifteenth Amendment, 137, 151, 481
Fifth Amendment, 117
Filegate, 383
Filibuster, 344
First Amendment, 9, 23, 99, 106, 111
First Bank of the United States, 75
First Continental Congress, 38
Fiscal Federalism, 87
Fiske v. Kansas, 105
Flag, burning American, 102, 106–107
Flanigan, William H., 259
Fleischer, Ari, 395
Florida, and 2000 election, 190, 221, 376–377, 431, 442
Food and Drug Administration (FDA), 410
Forbes, Steve, 255
Formalized rules, 401
Fourteenth Amendment, 79, 104, 148, 150, 455, 458, 494
    selective incorporation and, 105, 117–120
Fourth Amendment, 97, 117, 121, 447–448
Fragmentation, 21
Frames of Reference, 182–192
Frank, Reuven, 299
Franks, Tommy, 362
Franked mail, 326
Franklin, Benjamin, 40, 43
Free, Lloyd A., 220
Freedom
    of assembly, 102, 106

Freedom—*Continued*
    of expression, 98, **99**–114
    of the press, 103–104
    of religion, 110–113
Free enterprise system, 25
Free-exercise clause, 112
Free expression, state governments and, 104–107
Free-rider problem, 268–270
Free speech, 102
French and Indian War, 37
Freneau, Philip, 295
Frontloading
    of presidential primaries, 373
Fullilove v. Klutnik, 156
Fundamentalist Christians, 186, 237
Furman v. Georgia, 119

Gaebler, Ted, 426
Gagnon, Paul, 8
Galderisi, Peter, 358
Gallup, George, 177
Garcia v. San Antonio Transit Authority, 92
Garfield, James A., 412
Gates, Bill, 24, 202
Gates, Scott, 429
Gatz, Thomas L., 290
Gay rights, 116, 148, 455
Gazette of the United States, 295
Gender, guiding public opinion, 188
Gender gap, 137, 139, 237
General Accounting Office (GAO), 349, 423
Georgia, 69
Gerry, Elbridge, 330
Gerrymandering, **330**
Gettysburg Address, 163
Gibbons v. Ogden, 76
Gideon v. Wainwright, 118, 120, 436, 455, 458
Gillman, Howard, 462
Gingrich, Newt, 90, 235, 357, 416–417
Ginsberg, Ruth Bader, 443
Gitlow v. New York, 104, 105
Giuliani, Rudy, 481, 499
Gladstone, William, 3
Goldwater, Barry, 235
Gonzalez, Elian, 293
GOP. *See* Republican party
Gore, Al, 21, 176, 204, 210, 225, 238, 240, 375, 376, 377, 378, 399
Government, 19
    authority of, 19
    constitutional, 22–23
    dividing authority of, 49–52
    employees, 86, 468
    federal, 69
    as interest group, 273
    limited. *See* Limited government

Government—*Continued*
    moderating the power of, 48–56
    popular, 56
    reinventing, 426–427
    unitary, 70
Government corporations, 404
Government grants, 87
Government licensing, news media and, 307
Government tax revenue, shares of, 87
Governors, 471–472
Graded (federal) service, 407
Grants
    block, 88
    categorical, 88
Grants-in-aid, federal, 87
Grants of power, 49
Grassroots lobbying, 281, 289
Grassroots party, 228
Great Compromise, 44
Great Depression, 81, 82, 94
Great Society, 84, 82, 94
Green party, 240, 375
Gregg, Judd, 491
Gregg v. Georgia, 119
Griswold v. Connecticut, 114
Grossman, Gene, 290
Groups, as a frame of reference, 185
Group competition, 500–501
Groupthink, 303
Group thinking, guiding public opinion, 185
GS (Graded Service) job ranking, 407
Gulf war. *See* Persian Gulf war

Habeas corpus, 49, 122–123
Hamilton, Alexander, 47, 71, 75, 101, 227, 295, 363, 364
Hamilton v. Regents U. of California, 105
Hammer v. Dagenhart, 80
Hanson, Mark, 210
Harassment, sexual, in workplace, 140
Harbison, Winifred A., 81
Hard money, 248
Hardin, Russell, 65
Harken Energy Corporation, 395
Harlan, John Marshall, 79
Harrison, Benjamin, 61, 370
Hartz, Louis, 9
Haskell, John, 65
Hastert, Dennis, 235
Hatch, Orrin, 451
Hatch Act, 407
Hate speech, 106
Hawaii, 490
Hayes, Rutherford B., 61, 370
Health care reform, 221
Hearst, William Randolph, 297

Helpman, Elhanan, 290
Henry, Patrick, 39, 68
Hero, Rodney, 504
Hierarchical authority, 401
Highways, 496
Hired guns (political consultants), **252**
Hispanic Americans. *See also* Affirmative action; Civil rights movement, 142–145, 486
   affirmative action and, 158
   in bureaucracy, 425
   demographic pattern of, 28
   differences among, 142
   discrimination against, 131
   economic status of, 154
   growing political power of, 144–145
   as illegal aliens, 143–144
   individual appointment of, 446
   party identification by national origin, 143
   political action of, 144–145
   in public office, 145
   representation of, 136
   rights of, 142–143
   voting pattern of, 144–145
Hoffer, Peter Charles, 129
Holmes, Oliver Wendell, Jr., 76, 100, 447
Holocaust
   public opinion on, 177
Homeland Security, 427, 502
Homeland Security Agency, 419
Home Rule, 480
Homosexuals and their rights, 116, 148, 455
   discrimination against, 131, 151
Honeymoon period, 386
Hoover, Herbert, 230, 366
Horner, Constance, 429
Horowitz, Donald, 460
House of Representatives, U.S., 58, 324. *See also* Congress, U.S.
   committee chairpersons in, 338
   committee system in, 339–342
   constitutional qualifications for serving in, 325
   impeachment of President and, 391
   incumbents in, 324–331
   midterm elections and, 329
   party control of, 334
   party leaders in, 334–335
   redistricting and, 329–330
   Speaker of, 324–335
   standing committees of, 340
House Rules Committee, 338
Housing
   discrimination in, 151
   subsidized, 477
Howard, John R., 164
Hull, N. E. H., 129
Humphrey, Hubert, 372

Hunter, Kenneth, G., 504
Hutchinson, Kay Bailey, 332
Hutto v. Davis, 437

Ideals, 9–17
   limits of, 13–14
   power of, 12–13
Ideological groups, 271–272
Ideological identification, 183–185
Ideological parties, 240–241
Ideological thinking, guiding public opinion, 183–185
Ideology, 184
Immigration, 7–8, 15, 16, 293
Immigration Reform and Control Act, 143
Imminent lawless action test, 106
Impeachment, 391, 392
Implied powers, 72, **73**, 76
Inalienable rights, 40
Incarceration rates
   U.S. and other nations, 124
Income, 154
Income taxes, 487-488
Incumbency
   pitfalls of, 328–333
   using, 325–328, 333–334
Independent agencies, 404
Independent candidates, 242
Indian Bill of Rights, 142
Indianapolis v. Edmund, 121
Indians, American. *See* Native Americans
Indirect primary, 371
Individual goods, 265
Individualism, **12**, 159, 201
   public opinion and, 13
Individualistic subculture, 499
Individual rights, 23, 99, 131
Information, public opinion without, 172–174
Infotainment, 307
Ingraham, Patricia W., 429
Initiative, 286, **478**
   in states, 62
Inputs to political system, 31
Inside lobbying, 273–279
   defined, **274**
Integration, 159, 161
Interdependency, 85
Interest-group liberalism, 287
Interest groups, 260–291
   agricultural, 267
   bias of, 285–289
   business, 266–267
   categories of, 265–268
   citizens', 271–272
   defined, **262**
   economic, 266–267
   government as, 273

Interest groups—*Continued*
   ideological, 271–272
   influence of, 273–285
   and initiatives, 286
   labor, 267
   professional, 267
   public, 271
   and self-government, 285–289
   single-issue, 271
   system, 263–273
Intergovernmental relations, 85
Intermediate-scrutiny test, 150
International criminal courts, 439
Internet, 217, 301–302
   citizens' interest groups and, 269
   news media and, 301, 302
   obscenity and, 109–110
   in political campaigns, 255–256
   political participation and, 216
   sales tax and, 491
Interpretive reporting, 298
Interstate commerce, 75, 80
Intrastate commerce, 75, 80
Iron triangles, 278, 279, 417
Islam, 192
Islamic militants, 316
Israeli-Palestinian conflict, 300
Issue networks, 278–279, 418

Jackson, Andrew, 60, 228, 229, 365, 369, 408, 409
Jacksonian democracy, 60–61, 228
Jackson State College, 219
Jacobs, Lawrence, 194
Jacobson, Gary C., 327, 358
Japanese Americans. *See* Asian Americans
Jefferson, Thomas, 10, 40, 42, 48, 53, 55, 59, 75, 96, 100, 132, 227, 395
Jeffersonian democracy, 59–60
Jeffersonian Republicans, 228
Jeffords, James, 390
Jews, 237
Jim Crow era, 15
Jobs, discrimination in, 155
Job specialization, 401
Johnson, Andrew, 391
Johnson, Gregory Lee, 102
Johnson, Lyndon, 135, 385
Joint committees, 340
Journalism,
   objective, 297–298
   "yellow," 297
Judges as political officials, 58
Judicial activism, 456–458
Judicial appointees,
   characteristics of, 445–446
   partisan factors, 444–445
   selection of, 442–444

Index

Judicial conference, 435
Judicial decisions, 446–449
    "inside" influences on, 452
    interest groups and, 450–451
    "outside" influences on, 450–452
    political influences on, 449–452
    public officials and, 451–452
    public opinion and, 450–451
Judicial power, 452–461
    democratic government and, 452–454, 461
    shared, 52
Judicial protection of business, 80–81
Judicial restraint, 455, **456**
Judicial review, 54–56, **453,** 456
Judicial style, 92–93
Judicial supremacy, 81
Judicial system, federal, 458–464
Judiciary. *See also* Courts; Supreme Court, U.S.
    checks and balances and, 52
    debate over proper role of, 454–461
Judiciary Act of 1789, 55
Jurisdiction (of a congressional committee), 342–343
Jurisdiction (of a court), **433**

Kaiser, Robert G., 318
Kaplan, Robert, 210
Kaufman, Herbert, 416
Keeter, Scott, 194
Kefauver, Estes, 397
Kelly, Alfred H., 81
Kennan, George, 531
Kennedy, John, 314, 379, 382
Kennedy, Robert F., 225
Kent State University, 219
Key, V. O., Jr., 168
Kimel v. Florida Board of Regents, 92, 458, 467
King, Anthony, 259
King, David, 342, 358
King, Martin Luther, Jr., 130, 134, 147, 218
King George III, 38
Klopfer v. North Carolina, 118
Know nothing party, 15
Krasno, Jonathan, S., 358
Kyno v. United States, 121
Kyoto Accord, 84

Labor
    child, 81
Labor groups, 266–267
Labor unions, 267
Laden, Osama bin, 104, 169, 315
LaHood, Ray, 371
Laissez-faire capitalism, 80

Lasswell, Harold D., 18
Latin Americans. *See* Hispanic Americans
Lau v. Nichols, 146
Lavrakas, Paul J., 194
Law, 342, **346**
    bill from floor debate into, 344–345
    bill into, 342–346
Lawmaking function (of Congress), **347**
Laws (of a court case), 447
Lazarus, Edward H., 259
Lazio, Rick, 250
League of Women Voters, 271
Legislative leadership, 337
Legislative oversight, 422–423
Legislative powers, shared, 51
Legislative Reorganization Act, 342, 353
Legislative veto, 353, 423
Legislatures. *See* Congress, U.S.; House of Representatives, U.S.; Senate.
Legitimacy (of election), **369**
Legitimacy (of judicial power), **459**
Leighley, Jan, 223
Letter to the Sheriffs of Boston, 57
Levy, Chandra, 315, 328
Lewinsky, Monica, 391
Lewis, Anthony, 129
Lexington and Concord, 38
Libel, 107, 302
Liberals, 183, 184
    by state, 186
Libertarian party, 240
Libertarians, 184
Liberty, 9–10, 16, 56, 71, 303
License fees, 489
Lieberman, Joseph, 225
Lijphardt, Arend, 259
Limbaugh, Rush, 299
Limited government, 35, **36**
    providing for, 48–56
Lincoln, Abraham, 77, 163, 229, 230
Lippmann, Walter, 194, 317
Lipset, Seymour Martin, 32
Literacy tests, 151
Little Rock schools, desegregation of, 134
Lobbying
    Congress, 274–276
    courts, 277–278
    defined, 274
    executive agencies, 276–277
    grassroots. *See* Grassroots lobbying
    inside. *See* Inside lobbying
    outside. *See* Outside lobbying
Lobbying group, participation in, 214
Local elections, 485–486
Local finance, 487-488
Local governments
    employees of, 481
    finances of, 487–493
    participation in, 485–486

Local governments—*Continued*
    policies of, 493-498
    structure of, 479–486
    types of, 481–485
Local party organizations, 244–245
Local political structures, 481
    county government, 481–482
    local elections, 485–486
    metropolitan government, 485
    municipal government, 482–483
    school districts, 484
    special districts, 485
    towns and townships, 484
Lochner v. New York, 81
Locke, John, 39, 40, 71, 111
Logrolling, 351
Loose constructionism, 451
Lott, Trent, Sen., 67, 355
Lotteries, 488
Louisiana, 469
Lowi, Theodore, 286, 287, 290
Lyons, Michael, 358

McCain, John, 248, 249, 255, 373
McClain, Charles J., 164
McConnell, Mitch, 330
McCulloch, Edwin, 75
McCulloch v. Maryland, 75, 76
McElroy, John Harmon, 32
McGovern, George, 235
McGuire, Kevin T., 462
MacManus, Susan A., 189, 194
Madison, James, 35, 43, 48, 50, 71, 227, 265, 288
Madisonian Dilemma, 288–289
Majoritarianism, 26–27, 171
Majority, tyranny of the, 56
Majority leader of the House, 335
Majority leader of the Senate, 335–336
Majority opinion, 436
Majority rule, 26–27
Malapportionment, 73
Mallory v. Hogan, 118
Maltese, John A., 318
Mandamus, writ of, 55
Mapplethorpe, Robert, 107
Mapp v. Ohio, 118, 120, 121
Marbury, William, 55
Marbury v. Madison, 55, 453
March on Washington for Jobs and Freedom 1963, 134
Marijuana, medical use of, 93
Marshall, John, 55, 56, 75, 76, 77, 430, 436
Marshall, Thurgood, 446
Massachusetts, 42, 492
Mass media. *See* News media
Material incentive, 265
Matthews, Glenna, 359

Means test, 512
Mecham, Evan, 478
Media concentration, 303
Megamedia, 305
Merit plan (for judges), 440, 477
Merit Service Protection Board, 412
Merit system, 411–414
Metropolitan government, 485
Mexico, 17, 49, 63
Mfume, Kwesi, 157
Michels, Roberto, 29
Middle-class bias in politics, 221
Middle Eastern immigrants, 123, 126
Midterm elections, House of Representatives and, 329
Miller v. California, 108
Miller, Ellen, 330
Miller, James, III, 420–421
Millionaire's Club, 61
Mills, C. Wright, 28
Minnesota, 470
Minor parties, 239–242
Minority redistricting, 329
Minority set-asides (quotas), 156–157
Miranda v. Arizona, 83, 118, 120
Missouri Compromise of 1820, 77
Missouri Plan, 440, 477
Momentum, 373
Money chase, 250
Monroe, James, 228
Montana, 500
Montesquieu, 50, 71
Moral Action, 147
Moralistic subculture, 499
Morehouse, Sarah McCally, 504
Mormons, 501
"Motor voter" registration law, 202–203
Mott, Lucretia, 136
Moynihan, Daniel Patrick, 67
MTV, 208
Multiparty system, 234
Municipal government, 482-484
Myrdal, Gunnar, 162

Nader, Ralph, 240, 395, 376
Nager, Joane, 164
Napolitan, Joseph, 250
National Aeronautics and Space Administration (NASA), 404
National Association for the Advancement of Colored People (NAACP), 272, 277
National Association of Auto Dealers, 287
National Gazette, 295
National Governors Conference, 273
National identity, 4–5
National Industry Recovery Act (NIRA), 82

National Institutes of Health (NIH), 415
National Labor Relations Act, 83
National Organization for Women (NOW), 272
National party conventions, 374
National party organizations, 246–247
National Performance Review (NPR), 399, 426
National pride in United States, 180
National Public Radio (NPR), 269
National Railroad Passenger Corporation (Amtrak), 405
National Republican Congressional Committee (NRCC), 247
National Republican Senatorial Committee (NRSC), 247
National Rifle Association (NRA), 281
Native Americans, 141–142
   casinos and, 142
   discrimination against, 141
   militant, 141–142
   reservations, 141
Natural rights, 40
Nazi party, American, 108
NBC News, 296
Near, Jay, 105
Near v. Minnesota, 105
Nebraska Unicameral Legislature, 474
"Necessary and proper" clause, 73
Neuman, W. Russell, 223
Neustadt, Richard, 51, 389
Neutral competence, 412
New Deal, 81, 238, 368
New federalism, 90
New Hampshire, 42
New Hampshire Primary, 373
New Jersey, 494
New Jersey (small-state) Plan, 44
News, 293, 294
   as compelling, 293
   as dramatic, 293
   as timely, 293
News exposure, 214
News media, 292–319
   as agents of political socialization, 181
   audience of, 214–216
   "bad news" focus of, 311–312
   broadcast development, 299–301
   common carrier role of, 310–311
   defined, **293**, 294
   development of, 295–302
   elections and
   following politics in, 214–216
   freedom and conformity in, 302–307
   government licensing and, 299–301
   history of, 295–302
   homogeneity of, 303–304
   Internet and, 301–302

News media—*Continued*
   journalistic values and, 304–305
   lack of accountability of, 314
   as link, 307–316
   mergers in, 305–306
   neutrality of, 309
   public and, 318–319
   public representative role of, 313–317
   roles of, 307–316
   signaler role of, 308–309
   size of, 302–303
   watchdog role of, 311–313
News values, 304–305
New York, 47, 475,495,497
   2000 senate election, 250
New York Times, The, 298, 304
New York Times Co. v. Sullivan, 107
New York Times Co. v. United States, 103
Niebuhr, Reinhold, 147
Nineteenth Amendment, 137, 151, 198
Ninth Amendment, 114
Nisbet, Robert, 177
Nixon, Richard, 35, 391–392, 413
Noelle-Neumann, Elisabeth, 194
Nofziger, Lyn, 93
Nominations, 242
Noneconomic groups, 267
North Carolina, 69, 471
North-South Compromise, 44–45

O'Brien, David M., 462
Objective journalism, 297–298
Obscenity, 107–110
Ochs, Adolph, 298
O'Connor, Sandra Day, 137, 410
Office of Management and Budget (OMB), 349, 412–413, 421
Office of Personnel Management (OPM), 412
Ogden, Aaron, 76
Oklahoma, 476
Oleszek, Walter J., 322
Olson, Mancur, Jr., 269, 290
One Florida, 157
"Open Door" policy, 367
Open party caucuses, 372
Open rule, 344
Open-seat elections, 327
Opinion (of a court), **436**
Opinion-poll respondents, sampling error by number of, 175
Opinion sampling, 175
Ordinance, 480
Oregon, 496
Original jurisdiction, 433
Osborne, David, 426
Otis, James, 38

Index

Outputs from political system, 31
Outside lobbying, 280–285
    defined, **280**
Oversight function, of Congress, 353–356

Pack journalism, 303
Packaging (of candidates), 254
PACs. *See* Political action committees
Page, Benjamin I., 27, 192
Paget, Karen M., 359
Paine, Thomas, 38
Pakistan, 307, 316
Palko v. Connecticut, 118
Participation, and the public's influence, 220–222
Partisan press, 295–297
Partisanship, 190, 345–346, 352
Partisan support in Congress, 345–346
Partisan thinking, 190–191
Party caucuses, 334
Party-centered politics, 225, **226**
Party coalition, 236
Party competition, **227**, 498–499
Party control, 500
Party differences, 205
Party discipline, 346
Party identification, **190**, 230
Party leaders (in Congress), 334
Party-line voting, 232
Party organizations, 242–249
    structure of, 243–244
    money and, 247–249
Party platforms, 234–236
Party realignment, 229–231
Paterson, William, 44
Patriotism, U.S. and other nations, 20
Patronage system, **409**
Patterson, Kelly D., 259
Patterson, Thomas E., 223, 318
Peace demonstrations, opinions about, 219–220
Peers as agents of political socialization, 181
Pendleton Act, 411
Pennsylvania, 50
Pentagon, The, 5, 20, 21, 25, 39, 54, 102, 169, 188, 207, 210, 307, 314, 315, 316, 361, 380, 390, 392, 419, 502
Pentagon Papers, 103
Per curiam decisions, 434
Perry, Michael, 129
Perot, Ross, 240, 374–375, 379
Philadelphia constitutional convention, 43–47, 72
Phillips, Wendell, 198
Physician-assisted suicide, 116
"Plain meaning rule", 448
Planned Parenthood v. Casey, 115
Platforms, party. *See* Party platforms

"Pledge of Allegiance," 20
Plessy, Adolph, 79
Plessy v. Ferguson, 79, 133
Pluralism, 27–28, 285–286
Pluralist theory, 27–28, 285–286
Plurality opinion, 436
Pointer v. Texas, 118
Police, 496-497
Police power, 493
Police practices, 123–125
Policy, 21
Policy implementation, 407
Policymaking
    congressional, 346–350
    presidential, 385–394
Policy responsibilities of federal bureaucracy, 407–409
Political action committees (PACs), **282**–283, 327
    business related, 283
    defined, **283**
    growth in number of, 282–283
    and incumbents, 283
    limits on spending of, 284
Political advertising, 252–253
Political competition, 226
Political conflict, 18–19
Political consultants, 252
Political culture, 7–18, 219
Political images, communicating, 252–253
Political leaders and institutions as agents of political socialization, 31, 182
Political machines, big-city, decline of, 244–245
Political movements, 217
Political officials, justices and judges as, 444–445
Political participation, 196–223
    defined, 198
Political parties, 225–257. *See also individual parties*
    advantages of, 225, 227
    American, origins of, 227–233
    candidate-centered campaigns in, 250–257
    coalition formation in, 236–238
    competition and collective action in, 226–227
    controlling nominations, 242–243
    dealignment of, 231–233
    decline of control by, elections and, 250
    defined, 226
    expenditures, 247–249
    factional, 239–246
    first, 227–228
    history of U.S. parties, 227–233, 239–241
    ideological parties, 240–241
    leaders in Congress, 334–338
    local organizations, 244–245

Political parties—*Continued*
    minor, 239–242
    money and media and, 247
    national chairpersons of, 246
    national conventions, 374
    national organizations, 246–247
    platforms of, 234–236
    policy formulation in, 234–236
    public's influence and, 256–257
    realignments and, 229–231
    single-issue parties, 239
    state organizations, 245–246
    strong, primary elections and, 243
    structure and role of, 243–244
    systems of, 233–242
    third parties, prospects for, 241–242
Political power, constitutional restraints on, 49–52
Political socialization, 17, 178–192
    agents of, 179–182
    defined, **178**
    process of, 178–179
Political strategy, 253
Political subcultures, 499
Political structures, state. *See* State political structures
Political system, 30–31
    inputs of, 31
    outputs of, 31
Politics, 18–30
Polk, James K., 295
Polling error, sources of, 175–176
Poll results, describing, 175–176
Poll taxes, 151, 198
Pomper, Gerald M., 259
Popular consent, 11
Popular rule, limited, 57–58
Population (in polling), 174
Populist party, 240
Populists, 184
Pork barrel projects, 326
Pornography, 107–110
Powell, Colin, 380, 387
Power, 19
    bureaucratic, sources of, 415–418
    of clientele groups, 416–417
    denials of, 49
    executive. *See* Executive power
    of expertise, 415–416
    fragmentation of, 21
    grants of, 49
    judicial. *See* Judicial power
    political. *See* Political power, constitutional restraints on
    separated institutions sharing, 51–52
    theories of, 26–30
    using power to offset, 51–52
    wealth and, 25
Power elite, 27, 28

Power imperative of federal bureaucracy, 413–414
Prayer, school, 112, 451–452, 454
Precedent, 434, 438, 449
Presidency, 360–397. *See also individual presidents*
    accountability through, 418–421
    bureaucracy and, 418–421
    campaign for election, 374–379
    campaign for nomination, 372–374
    checks and balances and, 51–52
    colliding with Congress, 391–392
    Congress and, 348–350, 388–392
    Constitution and, 363–365
    crises and, 392–393
    domestic policy and, 368–369
    election of, 369–379
    fast track authority and, 288
    force of circumstance in, 385–386
    foreign policy and, 367
    foundations of, 363–369
    increase in power of, 365–369
    leadership and, 365–369, 384–395
    news media and, 394–395
    organizing of, 379–385
    path to, 375
    problem of control of, 383–384
    public response to crises and, 392–393
    public support of, 392–396
    requirements in Constitution, 378
    staffing, 379–383
    stages of term, 386
    strong, emerging tradition of, 365–369
    televised, 394–395
Presidential appointees, 382–383, 419–421
Presidential approval, 392–393
Presidential approval rating, 392
Presidential cabinet, 382, 403
Presidential commissions, 406
Presidential debates, 215–216
Presidential election 1892, 240
Presidential election 1896, 240
Presidential election 1912, 239
Presidential election 1964, 235
Presidential election 1972, 235
Presidential election 2000, 190, 193, 204, 235, 240, 252, 431
Presidential elections, 369–379
    money and, 373–374, 376–377
    strategy, 375–378, 391–392
Presidential impeachment, 391
Presidential leadership, 384–396
Presidential policymaking, 385–394
Presidential primary, 371–374
Presidential selection system, development of, 58
Presidential success,
    and circumstance, 385–386
    and Congress, 388–392

Presidential success—*Continued*
    and nature of issue, 386–388
    and public support, 392–394
    and stage of term, 386
    and television, 394–395
Presidential support,
    in Congress, 389–391
    among public, 392–394
Presidential vetoes, 346, 389
President *pro tempore* of Senate, 335
Press, 294. *See also* News media
    Censorship, 303
    freedom of the, 302–303
    partisan, 295–297
Pressure groups. *See* Interest groups
Primacy tendency, 178
Primary elections, 61, 205, **242–243**
Prime Time Live, 131
Prince George County, 161
Print media. *See* News media
Printz v. United States, 92
Prior restraint, 103
Prisons, 496-497
Prison population, 124
Privacy, right of, 114–116
Private discrimination, 151
Private (individual) goods, 265
Private parties, discrimination by, 151
Probability sample, 176
Probable cause, 97, 122
Procedural due process, 117, 118
Procedural rights, selective incorporation of, 105, 117–120
Professional groups, 267
Progressive era, 61
Progressive movement, 239
Progressive reforms, 61, 478
Progressives, 61
Prohibition party, 239
Property taxes, 489
Proportional representation, 234
Proposition 187, 144
Proposition 209, 158
Proposition 227, 146
Prospective voting, 211
Protestants, 186, 237
Public broadcasting, 277
Public education, 13–14, 86
Public funding of congressional campaigns, 330
Public goods, 268
Public information, 172–173
Public interest groups, 271
Public opinion,
    characteristics, 168–195
    defined, **171**
    frames of reference guiding, 182–191
    government by, 192–193
    influence of, on policy, 192–193

Public opinion—*Continued*
    information and, 192–193
    measurement of, 174–178
    nature of, 170–174
    role of, 177, 192–193
Public opinion poll, 174–176
Public policy, 21
Public representative role, 313–316
Puerto Ricans. *See* Hispanic Americans
Pulitzer, Joseph, 297
Purposive incentive, 268
Putnam, Robert, 223, 272

Race, guiding public opinion, 188
Racial bias in justice system, opinions on, 135
Racial profiling, 123
Racial redistricting, 152–153
Radio, 300–301
Rapid Response, 255
Ratification of Constitution, 45–47
Rauch, Jonathan, 289
Reagan, Ronald, 364, 394, 451
Realignments, 229–231
Reapportionment, 329
Reasonable-basis test, 149
Recall, 478
Reconstruction, 133
Redistricting, 330
Redlining, 151
Reeves, Keith, 164
Referendum, 62, **478**
Reform Party, 240, 241
Regents of the University of California v. Bakke, 277
Region, as a frame of reference, 187–188
Registration, 200, 207
Regulatory agencies, 404–405
Rehnquist, William, 92, 457
Reinventing government, 426–427
Religion
    as agent of political socialization, 182
    as a frame of reference, 185–186
    freedom of, 110–113
    "free exercise" of, 112–113
    guiding public opinion, 182, 183, 185–187
Religious Freedom Restoration Act, 112
Religious freedom, 112
    Amish and, 112
    medical treatment and, 112
    Yarmulkes and, 112
Religious right, 187
Remington, Frederic, 297
Reno v. ACLU, 109, 110
Reno v. Condon, 92, 467
Reorganization, 419

Index

I-11

Reporting
   descriptive, 298
   interpretive, 298
Representation function (of Congress), **350**–353
Representative democracy, 57
Republic, 57, 71
Republican National Committee (RNC), 246
Republican party, 225, 228, 229–233
Reserved powers, 72, 74
Reston, James, 314
Result, equality of. *See* Equality
Retrospective voting, 211–212
Revenues, government, 485, 487-493
Reverse discrimination, 155
Revolutionary War, 37–38, 50
Revolution of 1800, 59
Rhode Island, 45, 56
Rider (to Senate bill), **345**
Rights of Englishmen, 37–38
Rights of persons accused of crimes, 117–123
Right-to-Life party, 239
Right of privacy, 114–116
Rimmerman, Craig, 223
Ring v. Arizona, 119
Robinson v. California, 118
Rockman, Bert A., 429
"Rock the Vote," 208
Roe v. Wade, 74, 114, 115, 431, 441
Roll-call votes, 353
Roman Catholics, 186, 237
Romer v. Evans, 148, 455
Roosevelt, Franklin, 10, 81, 82, 230, 299, 366, 411
Roosevelt, Theodore, 239, 366, 367
Rosenstone, Steven J., 210, 259
Ross, William, 95
Rostenkowski, Dan, 329
Rostker v. Goldberg, 149–150
Roth v. United States, 108
Rowley, Coleen, 425
Rules Committee, House, 344
Rumsfeld, Donald, 380
Rutledge, John, 45

Sabato, Larry J., 318
Safe Drinking Water Act, 471
Salant, Richard, 314
Sales tax, 488
Salokar, Rebecca Mae, 462
Same-sex unions, 148
Sample, 194
Sampling error, 175
Sanchez, Loretta, 144, 354
Sanders, Ronald P., 429
San Francisco Call, 307

Scalia, Antonin, 446, 455, 458, 462
Scandal, 328–329
Scarcity, 18
Schattschneider, E. E., 31, 224, 225, 260, 288
Schechter v. United States, 82
Schenck v. United States, 100
Schlozman, Kay Lehman, 223
Schmidhauser, John, 452
Schmidt, Ronald, 32
School districts, 582
School prayer, 112, 451–452, 454
School vouchers, 111
Schools
   as agents of political socialization, 181
   church-affiliated, 110
Schudson, Michael, 223
Schwartz, Bernard, 462
Scigliano, Robert, 444
Scott, Dred, 77
Search and seizure, 121
Second Bank of the United States, 75
Sedition Act of 1798, 100
Segregation, 18, 133–135, 159–161
   racial, 133–134, 150–151, 161
   schools, 133–134, 159–161
Select committees, 340
Selective incorporation, 105, 117–120
   Fourteenth Amendment and, 105
   of procedural rights, 117–120
Self-government, 36, 56, 64, 119
Self-incrimination, 117
Senate, U.S., 32, 45. *See also* Congress, U.S.
   committee chairpersons in, 338
   committee system in, 339–342
   constitutional qualifications for serving in, 325
   incumbents in, 324–331
   majority leader of, 335
   party control of, 334
   party leaders in, 335–336
   president *pro tempore*, 335
   special problem of strong challengers in, 329
   standing committees of, 340
Senators, U.S., 58, 329
Senatorial courtesy, 443–444
Seneca Falls, 136
Seniority, 338
Seniority principle in Congress, 338
Separate and unequal, 133
Separated institutions sharing power, 51–52
Separation of church and state, 111
Separation of powers, 50
September 11, 2001, 5, 16, 20, 21, 23, 25, 39, 54, 102, 104, 125, 127, 169, 180, 188, 189, 192, 207, 210, 307, 314, 315, 316, 361, 367, 380, 390, 494
Service relationship, 247

Service strategy, 326
Sessenbrenner, James, 25
Seventeenth Amendment, 61
Sexual harassment in workplace, 140
Shaiko, Ronald G., 290
Shapiro, Robert, 27, 192, 194
Sharon, Ariel, 387
Shays, Daniel, 42
Shays' Rebellion, 42–43
Sheldon, Garret Ward, 65
Sherman Antitrust Act, 80
Sierra Club, 271
Signaler role, 308
Silent prayer, 112
Simpson, O. J., 314
Simpson-Mizzoli Act, 143
Sinclair, Barbara, 354, 359
Single-issue groups, 271
Single-issue parties, 239
Single-issue politics, 261, 262
Single-member districts, 234
Sixth Amendment, 117, 119, 456
Skrentny, John David, 164
Slander, 107
Slavery, 5, 14, 15, 46
Smith, Bob, 468
Smith, Howard, 338
Sobel, Richard, 194
Social capital, 213, 272
Socialism, 24
Social movements, 217–220
Soft money, 249
Solicitor general, 434
Solid South, 230
Somalia, 300
Sound Bites, 311
Southern Manifesto, 134
South Carolina, 77
South Dakota, 487
South-North constitutional compromise, 44–45
Sovereignty, 69
Spanish American War, 297
Spanish speakers. *See* Hispanic Americans
Sparrow, Bartholomew H., 318
Speaker of House of Representatives, 333, 334–335
Special Courts, U.S., 440
Special interest, 262
Speech
   free, 102
   hate, 106
Split-ticket voting, 232
Spoils system, 409
Stamp Act, 38
Stamp tax, 38
Standing committees, 339–340
Stanton, Elizabeth Cady, 136
Stare decisis, philosophy of, 449

Starr, Kenneth, 391
State and local finance, 487–493
State and local policy, 466–504
State and local politics, 498–501
State bureaucracies, size of, 402
State constitutional convention, 470–471
State constitutions, 469–471
State courts in federal system, 440–441, 476–477
　selection of judges, 441
State elections
　public funding of, 281
State governments, 468–478
　branches of, 471–478
　citizens' role in, 468–479
　constitutions of, 469–471
　courts, 476–477
　executive officials, 471–474
　finances of, 487–493
　legislatures, 475–476
　media coverage of, 476
　policies of, 493–498
　politics of, 498–501
　structure of, 468–477
State judges, methods of selecting, 477
State party organizations, 245–246
State political structures, 471–477
　executive branch, 471–477
　judicial branch, 476–477
　legislative branch, 474–475
State politics, 498–501
State powers, national powers and, 73–74
States
　Bill of Rights applied to, 104–105, 117–120
　in constitutional system, 73–74, 468–469
States' Rights party, 240
Statutes, interpretation of, 448–449
Stavans, Hans, 164
Stenberg v. Carhart, 115
Stevens, John Paul, 431, 459
Stewardship theory, 366
Stone, Harlan Fiske, 102
Stookey, John Alan, 462
Straight-ticket voting, 232
Strategic Presidency, 386
Strict constructionism, 451
Strict-scrutiny test, 149
Strong mayor-council system, 482
Structuring tendency, 198
Student testing, 495
Suffrage, 198
Sundquist, James, 350
Sunset law, **355,** 423
Supremacy clause, 73
Supreme Court, U.S., 433–437. *See also individual cases*

Supreme Court—*Continued*
　accountability through, 452
　appointment to, 442, 445
　case selection and, 433–434
　checks and balances and, 51–53
　Chief Justice of, 433
　current justices, 443, 446
　deciding cases, 435–437, 453
　free society and, 125–127
　issuing decisions and opinions, 433–437
　nominees, 442–443
　number of opinions, 434
　partisan influences on, 444–445
　public confidence in, 455
　selecting cases, 433–435
Supreme Court justices
　political beliefs of, 444–445, 452
　selecting, 442–443
Suspect classifications, 149
Swann v. Charlotte-Mecklenburg County Board of Education, 159, 160
Symbolic speech, 102

Taft, William Howard, 239
Taft-Hartley Act, 407
Taliban, 169, 170, 305, 316, 361
Tarr, G. Alan, 504
Taxes
　colonial, 38–39
　income, 487–488
　property, 489
　rates, 26
　sales, 488
　U.S. and other nations, 26
Taxing and spending, 487–493
Tax revenue, government, shares of, 87
Telecommunications Act of 1996, 408
Televised debates, 377–378
Televised political advertising, 378
Televised presidency, 394–395
Television, 298
Television Campaign Practices, 254
Temporary Assistance for Needy Families (TANF), 91
Tenet, George, 315
Tenth Amendment, 74, 466, 469, 493
Term limitations, 475–476
　public opinion on, 63
Terrorism, 316. *See also* Homeland security; Osama bin Laden; Pentagon; September 11, 2001; War on terrorism; World Trade Center
Texas, 159, 469, 471
Theiss-Morse, Elizabeth, 358
Thomas, Norman, 398
Thompson, Tommy, 95, 492
Third parties, 241–242

Three-fifths compromise, 44
Time-Warner, 470
Title IX of the Education Amendment of 1972, 137
Tocqueville, Alexis de, 4, 5, 23, 228, 263, 264, 272
Townshend Act, 38
Township, 484
Trade
　fast trade authority on, 388
Traditionalistic subculture, 499
Transportation Bill, 323
Traugott, Michael W., 194
Truman, Harry, 176, 366, 383
Trustees, **57**
Turf Wars, 342
Turnout, voter, 219
Twenty-first Amendment, 49
Twenty-fourth Amendment, 198
Twenty-sixth Amendment, 199
Two-party system, 233–238
Two-presidencies thesis, 386–387
Two treaties of government, 39
Tyranny of the majority, 56

Unconventional activism, 217–220
Unfunded Mandates Reform Act of 1995, 91
Unions, labor. *See* Labor unions
Unitary governments, 70
Unitary system, 70
United Auto Workers (UAW), 265
United States
　awareness of public affairs in, 172–174
　checks and balances and, 53
　democracy in, 21–22, **57**
　frequency of elections in, 204–205
　government of, 21–26
　group activity in, 263
　immigration to, 7–8, 15, 16, 293
　incarceration rate of, 124
　politics in, 18–30
　two-party system in, 233–238
Unit rule, 376
Unity, **12**
Universal Declaration of Human Rights, 113
University of California Regents v. Bakke, 155
Upper court myth, 437–438, 440
Urban Institute, 131
U.S.A. Patriot Act of 2001, 24, 25, 101
U.S. Chamber of Commerce, 265
U.S. Coast Guard, 408
U.S. Court of Appeals, 438
U.S. District Courts, 437–438
Use of force, attitudes on, 188
U.S. Postal Service, 406

Index

U.S. v. Drayton et al, 122
U.S. v. Lopez, 92
U.S. v. Oakland Cannabis Buyers Cooperative, 93
U.S. v. Virginia, 150
Utah, 501

Ventura, Jesse, 240, 472
Verba, Sidney, 223
Vermont, 469, 475
Veto, 346, 387
Vice-president, 374, 379, 381
Vietnam war, 391
Virginia, 47, 53
Virginia (large-state) Plan, 44
Virginia Military Institute, 150
Virtual Participation, 216–217
Voter participation, 210
Voter registration, 479
Voter turnout, 152, 197, **199**–209, 479
Voting, 198–212. *See also* Elections
   age and, 207–208
   economic class and, 208–209
   education and, 208
   in elections, 198–199
   fraudulent, 200
   impact of, 209
   income level and, 208–209
   Internet, 202
   party differences and, 205
   prospective, 211
   retrospective, 211–212
   trust in government and, 207
Voting Rights Act, 136, 151–153, 199, 479
Voucher system. *See* School vouchers.

Walker, David B., 95
Walker, Jack L., 286
Walker, Thomas G., 129
Wallace, George, 240
War on Terrorism, 126, 169, 188, 189, 192, 417, 427

War Powers Act, 391–392
Warren, Earl, 134
Washington, George, 42, 43, 45, 47, 227, 365
Washington Post, 311
Watchdog role, 311–313
Watergate affair, 35, 311
Watson, George L., 462
Watts, William, 220
Weak mayor-council system, 482
Weaver, James B., 240
Weber, Max, 29
Webster v. Reproductive Health Services, 114
Welfare Reform Act of 1996, 67, 91
West, Darrell M., 254, 259
Wherry, Kenneth, Sen., 31
Whig party, 229
Whig theory, 366
Whistle Blower Protection Act, 425
Whistle-blowing, 424–425
White House Office (WHO), 381
   of communication, 310
   press office, 310
White, Theodore H., 292
Whites-only primaries, 151
Whitman, Christine Todd, 494
Whren v. United States, 122
Wilcox, Clyde, 290
Will, George, 293
Williams, Jody, 59, 270
Wilson, Woodrow, 20, 66, 239, 360
Wirenius, John F., 129
Witt, Linda, 359
Women. *See also* Affirmative action; Civil rights movement; National Organization for Women (NOW).
   affirmative action and, 154–159
   in bureaucracy, 425
   Civil Rights Act of 1991 and, 137, 156
   comparable worth issue and, 140
   in Congress, 332
   discrimination against, 131
   economic status of, 154
   election to public office, 137

   Equal Rights Amendment and, 137
   family leave issue and, 137, 139
   as federal judges, 446
   "gender gap" in voting, 137, 139, 237
   glass ceiling and, 140
   historical inequality, 135–137
   income of, 140
   jobs and, 138
   judicial appointments, 446
   legal and political gains, 137
   legal status of, 135–140
   party coalitions and, 237
   party identification, 237
   political action and, 137–139
   political gains, 137
   representation of, 138, 332–333
   reproductive rights of, 114–115
   sexual harassment of, 140
   in state legislatures, 332–333
   suffrage, 198
   as Supreme Court justices, 137
   turnout, 219
Woodard, J. David, 194
Woodward, Bob, 311
Workers' party, 240
Workplace
   discrimination against women in, 140
   sexual harassment in, 140
WorldCom, 395
World Trade Center, 5, 6, 20, 21, 25, 39, 54, 102, 169, 188, 207, 210, 307, 314, 315, 316, 361, 380, 390, 419
World Trade Organization (WTO), 84, 221
   protests in Seattle, 218–219
Wounded Knee, 141
***Writ of certiorari*, 434**
Writ of mandamus, 55

Yellow journalism, 297

Zaller, John, 194
Zingale, Nancy, 259